THE LEGAL PROTECTION OF RIGHTS IN AUSTRALIA

How do you protect rights without a Bill of Rights? Australia does not have a national bill or charter of rights and looks further away than ever from adopting one. But it does have a range of individual elements sourced from common law, statute and the Constitution which, though unsystematic, do provide Australians with some meaningful rights protection. This book outlines and explains the unique human rights journey of Australia. It moves beyond the criticisms long made of the Australian position – that its 'formalism', 'legalism' and 'exceptionalism' compromise its capacity for rights protection – to consider how the many elements of its novel legal structure operate. This book analyses the interlocking legal framework for the protection of rights in Australia. A key theme of the book is that the many different elements of a fragmented scheme can add up to something significant, albeit with significant gaps and flaws like any other legal rights protection framework. It shows how the jumbled influences of a common law heritage, a written constitution, differing paths taken by jurisdictions within a single federal state, statutory and common law innovations and a strong dose of comparative legal influences have led to the unique patchwork of rights protection in Australia. It will provide valuable reading for all those researching in human rights, constitutional and comparative law.

The Legal Protection of Rights in Australia

Edited by
Matthew Groves
Janina Boughey
and
Dan Meagher

•HART•
OXFORD • LONDON • NEW YORK • NEW DELHI • SYDNEY

HART PUBLISHING

Bloomsbury Publishing Plc

Kemp House, Chawley Park, Cumnor Hill, Oxford, OX2 9PH, UK

HART PUBLISHING, the Hart/Stag logo, BLOOMSBURY and the Diana logo are trademarks of Bloomsbury Publishing Plc

First published in Great Britain 2019

A catalogue record for this book is available from the British Library.

A catalogue record for this book is available from the Library of Congress.

ISBN: HB: 978-1-50991-983-3
ePDF: 978-1-50991-982-6
ePub: 978-1-50991-984-0

Typeset by Compuscript Ltd, Shannon
Printed and bound in Great Britain by CPI Group (UK) Ltd, Croydon CR0 4YY

FSC www.fsc.org MIX Paper from responsible sources FSC® C013604

To find out more about our authors and books visit www.hartpublishing.co.uk. Here you will find extracts, author information, details of forthcoming events and the option to sign up for our newsletters.

FOREWORD

Australian Exceptionalism?

THE HON. MICHAEL KIRBY AC CMG

The New World Legal Order

In January 1941 President F D Roosevelt, in an address to the United States Congress, declared four goals to guide America's global policies on the brink of war. Specifically, he identified 'four freedoms' which people everywhere had a right to enjoy. They were: freedom of speech; freedom of worship; freedom from want; and freedom from fear.

These objectives were later to become a centrepiece of the Allied war aims, agreed to by Winston Churchill. In turn, they became foundational ideas in the creation of the United Nations Organisation. The Charter of the United Nations declared that the new body would be based on the reaffirmation of 'faith in fundamental human rights, in the dignity and worth of the human person, in the equal rights of men and women and of nations large and small'. Those asserted rights were not granted by the United Nations. They preceded it. They inhered in the 'Peoples' of the United Nations whose resolution gave rise to the new body. The revealed sufferings of the War, the departures from 'justice and respect for the obligations arising from treaties and other sources of international law' as well as the great crimes revealed in the conflict and the genocide required a new foundation for a new world order.

It was originally contemplated that the Charter would include a Bill of Rights for the international community. However, as in the drafting of the United States Constitution, the delegates ran out of time. In the result, work continued in a high-level committee chaired by the President's widow, Eleanor Roosevelt. Her late husband's 'four freedoms' found their way into the second preamble of the *Universal Declaration of Human Rights* (UDHR).[1] It was adopted without dissent in the third session of the General Assembly of the United Nations with Dr H V Evatt, Australia's delegate, in the chair as third President of the Assembly. Directly or indirectly, all subsequent United Nations treaty law for universal human rights can be traced to the Charter and the UDHR.

These were not mere aspirations, like President Woodrow Wilson's *Fourteen Points* of 1918. These declarations of rights became part of the growing body of international law on human rights. Australia was a foundation member of the United Nations. It has ratified all of its important human rights treaties. It has played an active part of the governance

[1] Adopted 10 December 1948 GA Res 217A(III) 1948.

of the United Nations. It is presently an elected member of the UN Human Rights Council which monitors global compliance with human rights law. It has served on many of the treaty bodies and provided many mandate-holders to be guardians and rapporteurs on global compliance. It openly judges other countries by reference to the emerging standards of universal human rights. And it is judged itself by such standards.

Resistance to Universal Rights

Against this well-known background, the chronicle recorded in this book tells us about the Australian response to these developments. In the nineteenth century, Australia's political leaders, judges, officials and practicing lawyers could, for the most part, leave all such international concerns to the 'Mother Country' and to British officials in Whitehall. Substantially, they could do so up to and even after Federation was achieved in 1901.[2] However, war, technology, transport, trade and ceaseless global problems meant that, certainly by 1945, indifference towards, and ignorance of, the international law of human rights could not continue unchanged for a country like Australia. In their own domains other professions realised this. But many Australian politicians, judges, officials and practicing lawyers resisted acceptance and adaptation. Many still do.

This book is a study of the imperfect adaptation of the Australian legal system to the world post-1945. It is a chronicle of the failure of many influential Australians to see the need for change and the default of Australia's institutions to adapt accordingly. If Australia's continuing exceptionalism did not have immediately adverse consequences for the nation and its people, the phenomenon could be ignored or attributed to misguided self-satisfaction that would eventually be forced to face reality. But times kept changing.

The Australian national Constitution is one of the oldest such documents still operating as such. Only the written Constitutions of the United States of America, Sweden, Canada and the Swiss Confederation are older. It is therefore not altogether surprising that the Australian text should reflect the thinking of the elite group of men (there were no women) who drafted it: reflecting common racial, religious and social experiences of their class and times.

Looking back, it is certainly unsurprising that in the 1890s, our founders should have rejected notions of 'universal rights' that needed to be included in their text. It is also unsurprising that the chief proponent for borrowing that American invention was Andrew Inglis Clark of Tasmania. He was a visitor to, and friend of, America. But his colleagues in the constitutional conventions saw themselves as 'British subjects' hostile to such ideas. Theirs was the way of evolution not revolution. At the time all of the significant dominions of the British Crown were in the same boat. They looked to a local legislature, untroubled by charters of rights, to provide for the governance of the 'white' dominions: the United Kingdom, Canada, Australia, New Zealand and Union of South Africa. This book explains how each of the foregoing, in their different ways, and later Ireland, India, post-apartheid South Africa, but not Australia, embraced special constitutional protections for fundamental rights. Putting it bluntly, they did so in order to provide better government for those

[2] See Adam Fletcher (ch 5) citing Justin Gleeson, 'The Increasing Internationalisation of Australian Law' (2017) 28 *Public Law Review* 25, 28.

who might otherwise be left behind by untrammelled majoritarian rule. Later, they did so in order to adapt local arrangements to the international and regional charters of rights that grew out of the Charter and UDHR of the United Nations.

This was not the poppy or honeydew of dream-inducing addiction to charters of rights, as Justice Heydon asserted.[3] It was the hard-nosed assessments of those who hammered out the modern constitutions of just about every country on Planet Earth. Everywhere, that is, except Australia where the sun-induced drug of lethargy produces blindness to injustice to minorities regarded as of 'no priority' to elected governments.

The Chapters of this Book

The successive chapters in this book describe the now virtually unique feature of Australian governance, when it comes to protecting the rights of its people where those rights could be described as 'fundamental', 'universal', or 'basic'. Unlike all the other nations (variously described as 'liberal democratic', 'Anglophone', 'parliamentary democracies' or 'modern') Australia does not have a significant overarching protection for such rights, neither in our national or State constitutions. We do, of course, have many specific and particular laws that protect identified rights. However, unusually, this is done by a legal framework that is 'odd' because it is so nonconceptual, multitudinous and 'messy'.

In the first chapter, the editors, Matthew Groves, Dan Meagher and Janina Boughey, draw an analogy to the Australian platypus, with its rare duck-like feet, soft bear-like fur, with a tail like a beaver, and the bill of an exotic bird. This was an 'odd' creature indeed. At first it was thought to be a hoax told by travellers who returned from a far away place. Later, based on scientific reports and actual inspection, it was accepted as truthful. But it was 'odd' nonetheless. So is the semi-chaotic collection of hundreds of laws and rules provided in Australia to do the work that, just about everywhere else, is performed by a constitutional Bill or Charter of Rights.

The majority of the chapters collected here proceed to analyse the 'odd' collection of laws that Australians need to rely on. George Williams (Chapter 2) describes the imperfect collection of protective provisions in the *Australian Constitution* itself, both express and implied. Anthony Gray (Chapter 3) focuses on the implied rights that have been spelt out of the words in Chapter III of the *Australian Constitution* to defend some but not all due process rights. It is a search that, he declares, delivers 'small potatoes' including several varieties that he finds positively unpalatable. Tony Blackshield (Chapter 4) digs deeper for other implications derived from reading between the lines of the *Australian Constitution*. Yet he declares that the High Court's experiment with implied constitutional rights has generally been met with 'outright hostility' or, more typically 'awkward timidity'. It has been a small and disappointing response.

Adam Fletcher (Chapter 5) examines another line of argument, raised in the High Court for default of a modern Bill of Rights with a frank collection of fundamental matters available to the judges as worthy of judicial protection. The several ways that the dissenting Justices in *Al-Kateb v Godwin*[4] explained their conclusion that indefinite detention of

[3] See G. Williams (ch 5) citing *Momcilovic v The Queen* (2011) 245 CLR 1 at 183; [2011] HCA 34 at [243].
[4] (2004) 219 CLR 562; [2004] HCA 37. See 589–595 [62]–[73] per McHugh J, 617–630 [152]–[193] per Kirby J.

undesired aliens in unpleasant facilities was beyond federal constitutional power are set out. Included is my own resort to a suggested interpretive principle drawing on the new context of international human rights law. In just about every other jurisdiction of the world such a suggestion would have been regarded as trite, uncontroversial, with the contrary being virtually unarguable. However, the majority in the High Court of Australia in *Al-Kateb* concluded that it was impermissible reasoning; even possibly a damnable 'heresy'. Adam Fletcher seemed as surprised as I was at the time by all the fuss that this comparatively modest suggestion attracted. This, it seemed, was the ultimate price Australians had to pay for their physical isolation in the far Antipodes. They were cut off from intellectual links that were taken for granted just about everywhere else.

Matthew Groves (Chapter 6) looks back at the *Teoh*[5] case on the use of international treaty law. At least where Australia had ratified the treaty concerned this could be considered in bringing enacted laws into harmony, so far as was possible. But after further exegesis in the High Court,[6] even this modest statutory aid to interpretation was abandoned or certainly cast into doubt.

Leaving the courts in the spiritual siding where their train had been parked, Edward Santow (Chapter 7) examines the functions of the Australian Human Rights Commission, an independent body of the Executive Government, to persuade that Government to match its rhetoric on international human rights law with local reality. But the recent history of the savage attacks on that Commission's highest officers, who dared to disagree with opinionated ministers, is a woeful tale that brings feelings of shame and despair in circles that know something about universal human rights. Much the same can be said of the chapter by Lisa Burton Crawford (Chapter 8). She describes the parliamentary mechanism for identifying any proposed federal laws that appear inconsistent with the nation's accepted international obligations. Overwhelmingly, the parliamentary advice on this score has simply been ignored. Colin Campbell (Chapter 9) comes to similarly disappointing conclusions about the role of federal anti-discrimination law in upholding universal principles for equal treatment for vulnerable minorities, such as international law requires.

The book then turns to Simon Rice's chapter (Chapter 10) on the protective role of the local human rights statute in the Australian Capital Territory. However, he too concludes that it has had relatively little impact, reflecting its comparatively modest aspirations. Janina Boughey's study (Chapter 11) on the Victorian Charter is likewise very cautious, noting the reluctance of lawyers and judges to embrace this newfound tool for scrutinising alleged human rights infractions. Madeline Chiam (Chapter 12) chronicles Australia's general international attitude of superiority and rejection that has, she concludes, often marked its response in recent years to the critical conclusions about Australia's domestic record. She insists that this attitude does not appear to change much with changing politics in Canberra. This is amongst the most disturbing chapters in this book.

One could probably expect the chapter on the recognition and protection of indigenous rights (Chapter 13) by Edward Synot and Dylan Lino to be upsetting. And so it is. The immediate denial of land rights; the dispossession; the record rates of indigenous incarceration in Australian prisons; and the summary dismissal of the *Uluru Statement from the*

[5] *Minister for Immigration and Ethnic Affairs v Teoh* (1995) 183 CLR 273.
[6] *Re Minister for Immigration and Multicultural and Indigenous Affairs; Exp. Lam* (2003) 214 CLR 1; [2003] HCA 6.

Heart expressing the wishes of our Indigenous peoples add melancholy illustrations to the failures of our political and legal systems to respond adequately to Indigenous disadvantage. Those who attack universal human rights and criticise 'activist judges' who could uphold justiciable rights if they existed in Australia need to be reminded that it was the High Court and not a local Parliament that abolished *terra nullius* in the Australian legal system. It did so after that error had endured for 150 years, causing an economic catastrophe to some of the oldest continuous human communities on Earth.

The two chapters that follow are by Gabrielle Appleby and Adam Webster (Chapter 14) on marriage equality for LGBTIQ Australians and the chapter on freedom of religion (Chapter 15) by Benjamin Saunders and Nicholas Aroney. These are chapters somewhat different in kind from the others in the book. They recount what the authors contend 'should be'. They do not confine themselves to 'what it is'. Because of this, those chapters would, no doubt, attract strong feelings amongst different readers. At the moment, those feelings have to run the gauntlet of power and influence in the political system. In Australia, such conflicts are not resolved by evaluations based on the reconciliation of the entitlements laid down in the law on fundamental rights. Clearly, there is an irony in the fact that many of those who have been most vocal in their opposition to the legal protection of fundamental human rights are now most insistent on the enactment of new laws to uphold their 'religious freedoms'. These include, apparently, the potential right to insult, humiliate, dismiss, isolate and exclude LGBTIQ Australians from taxpayer-funded religious institutions that are amongst the largest schools and employers in the nation.

The remaining chapters by Rebecca Ananian-Welsh (Chapter 16) on fair trial for accused terrorists; by Emma Dunlop, Jane McAdam and Greg Weeks (Chapter 17) on migration and refugee cases; and on the principle of proportionality (Chapter 18) by Shipra Chordia include many troubling cases that presently have to be addressed without the conceptual analysis and proportionate balances that are such a feature of human rights reasoning where a national constitution or general law allows for such reasoning. Decisions in the legislature or in the bureaucracy are typically projects of political intuition and ultimately brute legislative power. Decisions in courts and tribunals, exercising a human rights jurisdiction, must give reasons. They must afford consistency that can be scrutinised. They must be subject to appeal and review. People, including minorities, are more likely to accept such outcomes, hurtful to their interests though they may sometimes be, where they derive from a rational reasoning process. Less so where they are no more than assertion.

The Three Remedial Models

The last section in this book collects three remedial models for human rights protection and analyses them in turn. Dan Meagher (Chapter 19) examines the utility of relying on a kind of 'common law bill of rights', defended by interpretive presumptions protective of such rights. Alas, such presumptions frequently end in the wind and disappear where clear legislation abolishes the common law rule, as has happened more than once when Australia's refugee decisions in the courts are quickly reversed by parliamentary majorities.

Jeffrey Goldsworthy provides his familiar and typically thoughtful case against a constitutional bill of rights (Chapter 20). He acknowledges the arguments both ways and correctly concludes that the choice Australians face is whether the present chaos of our legal protections is to be preferred over the suggested dangers that might come with non-elected judicial resolution of complex and sensitive problems. It is here, of course, that advocates of change can invoke the fact that the rest of the world, including in the United States, Ireland, India, South Africa, Canada and New Zealand, not to mention Belize, Taiwan, Botswana and many others work within the universal human rights protection paradigm. These other states, great and small, can call on, and share, the jurisprudence that is now substantially transnational. That jurisprudence largely deals with similar provisions worldwide. It derives significantly from the United Nations treaties and their regional counterparts. If those nations are not complaining about this useful supplement to parliamentary lawmaking, it seems likely that we in Australia might similarly find such tools to be at least no more imperfect than the 'odd' and semi-chaotic collection of legal remedies we are currently obliged to live with.

The last chapter (Chapter 21) by Scott Stephenson explores how one would go about re-designing an Australian bill of rights. He is nothing if not bold. He insists that any such reform must be part of a wider refurbishment of the legal system. It must be constitutional and not merely a resort to an ordinary statute that can be repealed or changed in anger. And it must wholeheartedly engage the population and all minorities as well as the majority still living in the community that earlier wrote the text of the present *Australian Constitution*. Given the discouraging record of over 120 years in referendums, necessary to secure a formal change to the text of the *Australian Constitution*, many a heart would sink on reading this proposed agenda. Recent political events have shown that decisions that engage the Australian electors tend to be more successful if the targets are minimalised and if the controversies they present are simplified. Brave spirits of boldness are not much in vogue in Australia just now.

The Prospects of Change?

Nevertheless, change in response to the basic problem presented by this book is possible and it has happened. In the United Kingdom, Australia and New Zealand, Labour Governments were long opponents of charters of rights. Their leaders believed that conservative judges should not be allowed to hold back the firm government needed by an agenda that seeks to change society. Yet it was Tony Blair and Gordon Brown of the British Labour Party who introduced, and supported, the Bill of Rights Act 1998 (UK). And it was great liberal judges, like Lord Scarman, who pointed to their reforming potential. And to the fact it had been Anglo-American lawyers who had largely drafted the UDHR and the human rights treaties in the United Nations, based mostly on ancient principles of the common law.[7]

In Australia, E G Whitlam, at first an opponent of a charter of rights as Jeffrey Goldsworthy points out (Chapter 20), came around to the advocacy of the idea by his reforming Attorney-General, Lionel Murphy. Likewise, Bob Hawke eventually accepted the arguments of his minister Gareth Evans. Kevin Rudd, whilst postponing action on the report of Fr Frank Brennan, promised that he would return to it if re-elected. But the

[7] M D Kirby, 'Law Reform, Human Rights and Modern Governance: Australia's Debt to Lord Scarman' (2006) 60 ALJ 299 at 310–311, citing Lord Scarman's Hamlyn Lectures (1974) *English Law – The New Dimension* (Stevens & Sons, London, 1974) 16–18.

moment had passed. Isolation on a big picture question issue can be an uncomfortable posture, at least in the long run.

Whilst David Cameron, as Prime Minister of the United Kingdom, was critical of the decisions of the European Court of Human Rights on prisoners' rights,[8] he was reminded that the *European Convention on Human Rights* was part of the most important legacy of Winston Churchill. This was adopted deliberately to defend European citizens against any revival of autocratic rule in Europe. Yet again, on a matter of long-term strategy, Churchill has been vindicated as citizens in contemporary Poland, Hungary and the Russian Federation (with their access to the European Court of Human Rights) will loudly affirm. This story is told in a new book by an Australian lawyer, Marco Duranti, who had access to the British and European archives of the 1940s. He shows how the European project was defensive of individual rights.[9] But are we in contemporary Australia immune from such concerns?

The challenges to the survival of individual rights in the context of an ever-enlarging bureaucracy were addressed in Australia by the Government of Malcolm Fraser in the 'new administrative law', of the 1970s and 80s. Fraser regarded those reforms as amongst his chief achievements. As disclosed in these pages, the challenges to individual rights and the rule of law today, in the age of mass surveillance, enlarged security powers and enhanced governmental intrusions are legitimate concerns of politicians on all sides in Australian politics. Struggling on with a hotchpotch of imperfect legal remedies, cut off from the thinking of those operating in similar communities, is not a sensible long-term position for the survival of a liberal democratic order in Australia. All of our politicians give at least lip service to that idea. Bringing our rhetoric into harmony with reality and providing systemic protections is an objective that, eventually, all sides of Australian politics have a stake in.

So this is the ultimate significance of this book. It constitutes a challenge to Australians concerned, as they should be, by the oddity and inadequacy of our current legal arrangements to defend universal human rights in our country. The platypus survived in isolated Australia over millennia despite a slowly changing environment. The rule of law, liberal democracy, and universal human rights are somewhat more fragile in Australia today. The habitat's change is large and remorseless. New and additional protections are needed. From the perspective of Australian exceptionalism, this book shows why.

Michael Kirby
22 June 2019

[8] See *Roach v Electoral Commissioner* (2007) 233 CLR 162 at 178–179, [2007] HCA 43 [16]–[17] per Gleeson CJ; 203–204; [2007] HCA 43 at [100]–[101] per Gummow, Kirby and Crennan JJ.

[9] Marco Duranti, *The Conservative Human Rights Revolution: European Identity, Transnational Politics and the Origins of the European Convention* (OUP, Oxford, 2017); A W Bryan Simpson, *Human Rights and the End of Empire – Britain and the Genesis of the European Convention* (OUP, Oxford, 2004).

TABLE OF CONTENTS

LIST OF CONTRIBUTORS

Rebecca Ananian-Welsh is a Senior Lecturer in Law at the University of Queensland where she teaches in the areas of public law, national security and human rights.

Gabrielle Appleby is a Professor at UNSW Law who researches and teaches in public law, with expertise in constitutional recognition of First Nations, the role, powers and accountability of the Executive; the role of government lawyers; and the integrity of the judicial branch. She is the Director of the Judiciary Project at the Gilbert + Tobin Centre of Public Law.

Nicholas Aroney is Professor of Constitutional Law at the University of Queensland. He holds a PhD from Monash University and has published widely in constitutional law, federalism, rights, and law and religion.

Tony Blackshield AO is an Emeritus Professor of Law at Macquarie University, where he taught from 1988 to 1999, having previously taught at the University of Sydney (1961–1970), the University of New South Wales (1971–1978) and La Trobe University (1979–1988, as Professor of Legal Studies).

Colin Campbell is a Senior Lecturer in the Law Faculty of Monash University. He holds a LLM and PhD in law from the University of Cambridge. Colin researches and teaches in public law and has published articles in many journals including the *Cambridge Law Journal* and the *Law Quarterly Review*.

Madelaine Chiam is a lecturer at La Trobe Law School. Her research focusses on the histories of international law, the relationships between the global and the local, and the role of international law in Australian life. Her monograph, International Law in Public Debate, will be published by Cambridge University Press in 2020.

Shipra Chordia is a barrister at the NSW Bar and a Teaching Fellow at the University of NSW. She holds a Bachelor of Laws (with first class honours) from the University of Sydney and a PhD in Constitutional Law from the University of NSW. Shipra is a Centre Fellow of the Gilbert + Tobin Centre of Public Law, and has published on constitutional law in leading academic journals.

Lisa Burton Crawford is a Senior Lecturer and Deputy Director of the Gilbert + Tobin Centre of Public Law at the University of New South Wales. She teaches and researches in the fields of constitutional law, administrative law, statutory interpretation and legal theory.

Emma Dunlop is a PhD candidate at UNSW Sydney. She holds a Bachelor of Laws and a Bachelor of Arts (Hons) from the University of Sydney, an LL.M in International Legal Studies from New York University, where she studied as a Hugo Grotius Scholar, and an MSt from the University of Oxford.

Adam Fletcher is a lecturer in the Graduate School of Business and Law at RMIT University, teaching Human Rights and Administrative Law. He previously worked as a legal adviser to the Australian Government and international organisations, as well as a Research Fellow at the Castan Centre for Human Rights Law.

Jeffrey Goldsworthy worked for 33 years at Monash University Law School, where he is now an Emeritus Professor of Law. He is also a Professorial Fellow at The University of Melbourne, and an Adjunct Professor of Law at The University of Adelaide.

Anthony Gray is a Professor of Law at the University of Southern Queensland. Anthony has published extensively in refereed journals in Australia and internationally in the area of constitutional law and human rights, and is the author of three books to date. His monograph *Vicarious Liability: Critique and Reform* was published with Hart in 2018.

Dylan Lino is a Lecturer at the University of Western Australia Law School. His main research interests are in Indigenous peoples' rights, constitutional law and theory, imperialism and legal history.

Jane McAdam is Scientia Professor of Law and Director of the Kaldor Centre for International Refugee Law at UNSW Sydney. She publishes widely in international refugee law and forced migration, with a particular focus on climate change and mobility. She is Editor-in-Chief of the *International Journal of Refugee Law*, and has served as an expert advisor to a number of international bodies, including the United Nations High Commissioner for Refugees.

Simon Rice is a Professor of Law at the University of Sydney. He is a co-author of *The International Law of Human Rights*, and a former legal adviser to the Australian Parliamentary Joint Committee on Human Rights.

Edward Santow is Australia's Human Rights Commissioner and a Senior Visiting Fellow at the University of New South Wales (UNSW) Law Faculty. He has previously served as chief executive of the Public Interest Advocacy Centre and was a Senior Lecturer at UNSW.

Benjamin B Saunders is a Senior Lecturer and Alfred Deakin Postdoctoral Research Fellow at Deakin Law School, Deakin University. He holds a PhD from the University of Queensland and researches principally in constitutional law, corporate law and public governance.

Scott Stephenson is a Senior Lecturer at Melbourne Law School, The University of Melbourne. His research focuses on topics of Australian and comparative constitutional law and theory, including federalism, the migration of constitutional ideas, models of rights protection, political backlash against courts, and quasi-constitutional law.

Edward Synot is a Wamba Wamba First Nations person and a Lecturer at the Griffith Law School at Griffith University. Edward's research focuses on Indigenous Australian experiences and understandings of the law.

Adam Webster is a Departmental Lecturer in Law and Public Policy at the Blavatnik School of Government, University of Oxford who researches and teaches in public law. Adam is the Co-Director of the Master of Public Policy programme.

Greg Weeks is an Associate Professor and Deputy Head of School in the ANU College of Law at the Australian National University. He is a co-author of *Judicial Review of Administrative Action and Government Liability* (Thomson Reuters, 6th edn, 2017), Australia's leading administrative law text, and is the General Editor of the Australian Journal of Administrative Law.

George Williams AO is the Dean, the Anthony Mason Professor, and a Scientia Professor at UNSW Law.

1

Rights, Rhetoric and Reality: An Overview of Rights Protection in Australia

MATTHEW GROVES, JANINA BOUGHEY AND DAN MEAGHER

In his description of the arrival of the first Europeans to Australia, the famed art critic and some-time historian Robert Hughes recounted many natural features that astounded European eyes, such as trees that shed their bark instead of their leaves.[1] The natural environment of Australia, and perhaps more than a few of its people, remain an object of curiosity to the rest of the world but one in particular provides an apt metaphor for this book. That is the platypus. When the first specimens of this shy and still largely unknown mammal were sent to Britain, they were widely suspected to be a hoax. How else could such a strange creature be explained? It had the webbed feet of a duck, the soft fur of a young bear, the tail of a beaver and the bill of an exotic bird. The female laid eggs. The male had a venomous spur. The platypus was eventually accepted to be genuine,[2] but the fact of its existence makes it no less odd. The same might be said of the legal framework for the protection of rights in Australia.

Australia has become an outlier in the common law world because it lacks a national bill or charter of rights, either within its written constitution or as a freestanding instrument. The Australian Constitution does expressly protect a handful of 'rights'; but they are an odd mix, are very limited, and are often couched as limits on Commonwealth power rather than personal or individual rights. For instance, section 117 protects the right to equal treatment between residents of different states,[3] and section 51(xxxi) provides that the Commonwealth Parliament's power to compulsorily acquire property is limited by a requirement that it provide compensation 'on just terms'.[4] Section 80 provides people charged upon indictment

[1] Robert Hughes, *The Fatal Shore – The Epic of Australia's Founding* (New York, Penguin Random House, 1988).

[2] The platypus was first catalogued in England, and accepted as genuine, by George Shaw, *Naturalist's Miscellany – Volume 10* (Nodder & Co, 1799) 227–32.

[3] But the apparent role of that section as a right is apparent more from its heading rather than its content. The heading of s 117 is 'Rights of Residents in States'. The right to equal treatment is essentially a negative one arising from the substantive restriction on legislative power in s 117, which provides that any resident of a state 'shall not be subject in any disability or discrimination which would not be equally applicable to him if he were a subject of the Queen resident in such other State.'

[4] The scope of this limit on federal legislative power has beed held to be amplified by the inclusion of 'property' and 'acquisition'. Both words embody concepts that may be interpreted broadly. The clause was described as a 'very great constitutional safeguard' in *Trade Practices Commission v Tooth & Co Ltd* (1979) 142 CLR 397, 403 (Barwick CJ).

with a right to trial by jury in the state where the offence was allegedly committed but this can easily be circumvented.[5]

The very absence of things often makes them the subject of intense speculation. Rights within the Australian context are no exception. While he was Solicitor-General of Australia, now Justice Gageler of the High Court of Australia noted that, despite the apparent silence of the Constitution, the 'place of human rights in the structure of our nation's institutions has been debated from the very beginning' since its inception as a federal nation.[6] That reference to a 'place' points to a longstanding reality about rights in Australia. Much of the debate about rights in Australia has long proceeded on the assumption that they deserve a place in Australian law – the difficult question is where. The answer of this book might appear to be the somewhat unsatisfactory one of 'all over the place but nowhere in particular.' Yet the more subtle conclusion suggested by this book is that the absence of a comprehensive, single bill or scheme of rights within the Australian Constitution or legislation is not the end of the story but only its beginning.

The lack of detailed rights within the Australian Constitution has provided the impetus for a multi-layered conception of rights. One is implication. In the absence of express constitutional rights, the High Court has identified a limited collection of what some refer to as 'rights' within Australia's Constitution.[7] Properly understood, these implied rights are not really 'rights' at all, but limits on the powers of legislatures and governments which are necessary to protect the structure of government established by the Constitution. For example, the implied 'right' to freedom of political communication is not a right belonging to individuals, but a limit on the power of Australian legislatures to enact laws which undermine the ability of voters to communicate freely about political matters – a freedom which is necessary in order to protect the system of representative democracy and responsible government that the Constitution establishes.

The other main source of rights is statutory. What is not done directly by the Constitution can largely be done by parliaments. The many statutory rights examined in different chapters of this book suggest that statutes have become the preferred vehicle for the recognition and protection of rights in Australia.[8] Within Australia's federal structure, three jurisdictions have enacted statutory charters of rights. These are each modelled upon on the equivalent instruments of New Zealand, Canada and the UK but each also contains their own modest variations.[9] The influence of those foreign instruments upon Australian charters of rights draws attention to a modern variation of the common law methodology that has long been central to Australian law. That methodology is traditionally conceived as

[5] If legislation does not designate the offence to be an indictable one, the right of jury trial does not apply. Charlesworth has noted that s 80 was based upon an equivalent American requirement, which guarantees a right of jury trial for all federal offences. She argued that the limitation of s 80 to trials in indictment was no accident but was a deliberate drafting choice designed 'precisely to allow the Federal Government to avoid its scope when convenient': Hilary Charlesworth, 'Individual Rights and the Australian High Court' (1986) 4 *Law in Context* 53, 54.

[6] Stephen Gageler, 'Foreword' (2010) 33 *University of New South Wales Law Journal* 1, 1. Gageler made these remarks while he was Solicitor-General of the Commonwealth.

[7] This period of judicial innovation within the High Court is examined by Blackshield in ch 4.

[8] An exemplar is legislative scheme to prevent disability discrimination, examined by Campbell in ch 9.

[9] These are the *Human Rights Act 2004* (ACT), the *Charter of Human Rights and Responsibilities Act 2006* (Vic) and the newly minted *Human Rights Act 2019* (Qld).

a judicial one, in which courts may consider similar principles from similar common law jurisdictions in the development of legal principle. The charters of rights adopted within Australia reflect a statutory equivalent of that process. They are inspired by and draw heavily from similar instruments that exist in similar common law jurisdictions. These statutes also draw attention to a central theme of this book – constitutional restriction can often give rise to statutory innovation.

I. The Constitutional Context – Exceptionalist but also Unexceptional

The aim of this book is to provide a holistic account, as far as is possible, of the novel patchwork of statutes, institutions and discrete bodies of law that comprise Australia's scheme of rights protection. That approach proceeds on the assumption that the Australian system is somewhat unique, but that characteristic can easily become distracting for Australians. When Professor Taggart analysed the exceptionalism of Australian public law, he cautioned that the Australian Constitution should not continue to be regarded as a 'conversation stopper' that was offered as an answer to virtually every question about the past, present and future of Australian public law.[10] He decried the routine and reflexive references to constitutional principles such as the relatively strict Australian conception of the separation of powers as 'too simplistic.' The reason, he explained, was that:

> Like so much Australian constitutional talk it is actually grounded in a more universal common law constitutionalism, which owes much to the writings of A V Dicey.[11]

Taggart's insightful observation was that many of the doctrinal limitations attributed to the Australian Constitution may in fact be more explicable by reference to the influence of the ideas of Dicey upon the development of the Constitution, and to Australian public law more broadly. The absence of express rights in the Australian Constitution is a clear example of that influence and perhaps no surprise. At the time Australia's Constitution was drafted and enacted, nations within the Commonwealth were approaching what nowadays might be termed 'peak Dicey'.[12] One consequence of the influence of Dicey was that the Australian Constitution eschewed the American model, which identified and protected individual rights, and was instead 'built upon confidence in a system of parliamentary Government with ministerial responsibility.'[13] There are three foundational concepts within the system of government created by the Australian Constitution – federalism, the separation of

[10] Michael Taggart, '"Australian Exceptionalism" in Judicial Review' (2008) 36 *Federal Law Review* 1, 11. Taggart's focus, as the title of his paper suggests, was judicial review but his thesis applies equally to other elements of public law.

[11] Ibid.

[12] Though one Chief Justice of Australia has noted that many of the key principles now associated with Dicey were evident in the conduct of Australian colonial officials decades before the rise of Dicey's influence: Murray Gleeson, 'Courts and the Rule of Law' in Cheryl Saunders and Katherine Le Roy (eds), *The Rule of Law* (Annandale, Federation Press, 2003) 178, 179.

[13] *Attorney-General (Cth); Ex rel McKinlay v Commonwealth* (1975) 135 CLR 1, 24 (Barwick CJ).

powers and representative government.[14] The obvious omission is rights. The Australian Constitution contains no unifying theory or vision about rights. The Diceyan explanation for this omission was given by Dawson J, in a case where his Honour dissented against the recognition (or perhaps creation) of the implied freedom of political communication. His Honour explained:

> Those responsible for the drafting of the Constitution saw constitutional guarantees of freedoms as exhibiting a distrust of the democratic process. They preferred to place their trust in Parliament to preserve the nature of our society and regarded as undemocratic guarantees which fettered its powers. Their model in this respect was not the United States Constitution, but the British Parliament, the supremacy of which was by then settled constitutional doctrine.[15]

This argument has a long political pedigree that is now often forgotten. It was present at the nation's founding when the framers deleted a number of rights provisions which formed part of the 1891 original draft of the Australian Constitution. They did so due to their deep (Diceyian) scepticism about formal rights guarantees. And in the late 1960's when much of western society was experiencing a renaissance of rights and activism, the nation's longest serving Prime Minister, Sir Robert Menzies, explained how the talk of modern 'nonsense' such as rights was wisely avoided by the drafters of the Australian Constitution because they had realised:

> … to define rights is to limit them – for in the long run words must be given some meaning – or to express them so broadly that the discipline which is inherent in all government and ordered society becomes impossible.[16]

As with most later references to the wisdom and intention of the authors of the Australian Constitution, these remarks may reveal much more about their own author than the those of the Constitution. The importance of Menzies' remarks and the attitude they embody lies in the strong influence they have exerted over conservative political culture in subsequent decades. Talk about rights in Australia has long assumed a largely partisan political posture. Just as the advancement of rights has become an important part of progressive politics, resistance to rights, whether by their judicial recognition, legislative creation or treaty ratification, has long been equally important to conservative politics.

That same focus has informed two key elements of the modern Australian resistance to any kind of national bill or charter of rights. One is a belief that parliaments are the 'proper institutions under *our* system to decide what rights should be further developed or qualified

[14] In *Nationwide News Pty Ltd v Willis* (1992) 177 CLR 1, 71 (fn 25) Deane and Toohey JJ suggested that the doctrine of responsible government that permeated political practice and many aspects of the Constitution 'can arguably be seen as a fourth main general doctrine underlying the Constitution as a whole.' It has been suggested that another fundamental presumption or general doctrine that underpins the Constitution was the sovereignty of the British Parliament to enact the document and the subject of the legal entity created by the Constitution *to* that very instrument. In other words, the Commonwealth must abide by the rules contained in the instrument of its own creation: Nicholas Aroney, Peter Gerangelos, Sarah Murray and James Stellios, *The Constitution of the Commonwealth of Australia* (Cambridge, Cambridge University Press, 2015) 8–9.

[15] *Australian Capital Television Pty Ltd v Commonwealth* (1992) 177 CLR 106, 186. This case is examined by Blackshield in ch 4.

[16] Sir Robert Menzies, *Central Power in the Australian Commonwealth* (London, Cassell & Co, 1967) 52.

by competing interests.'[17] From a theoretical perspective, this argument echoes Dworkin's distinction between courts and parliaments in which he saw the former as the place for arguments about matters of principle, while the latter was the place for more utilitarian matters such as policy.[18] One consequence of this scheme was the concern that 'rights' might override the community interests as determined by parliaments, hence Dworkin's longstanding concern that rights as applied in the courts might 'trump' those interests recognised by parliaments. In many common law jurisdictions, Dworkin's thesis is essentially rejected by arguments that parliaments can, and often do, carefully weigh different interests in pursuit of a common good.[19] A variation of this argument underpins the persistent Australian refusal to adopt a bill or charter of rights at the federal level. Opponents of such a step implicitly claim that this refusal is a considered, sensible decision of the Parliament rather than the product of political inertia. There is no better modern example in Australia of that inertia than the struggle for marriage equality that is traced by Gabrielle Appleby and Adam Webster in Chapter 14, which those authors make clear was the product of an earlier, considered parliamentary decision to preclude same-sex marriage.[20]

One of the many difficulties with the suggestion that the absence of statutory rights may reflect a considered parliamentary decision, which, by implication, should be respected, is that the opponents of rights in Australia rarely extend that same respect to considered parliamentary decisions to the contrary. A useful example can be drawn from a widely accepted part of Australia's legal framework – legal aid. This is the Australian term for public funding of legal representation to those who cannot afford it. Legal aid has long been supported by state and federal governments of all political persuasions, though its funding has greatly declined in recent years. The value of legal aid is widely accepted but that was not the case when it was proposed during the 1970s. The Chief Justice of Australia described the proposal as 'a serious threat to the administration of law.'[21] A mass meeting of lawyers who opposed the 'communist inspired and unconstitutional' step to employ salaried lawyers to defend the poor made clear that opposition was widespread within the legal profession.[22] That resistance to legal aid eventually faded but it provides a useful reminder of the institutional obstacles that regularly arise in Australia and which may easily frustrate the development of structures and processes intended to protect rights as much as the introduction of substantive rights themselves.

[17] George Brandis, 'The Debate We Didn't Have to Have: The Proposal for an Australian Bill of Rights' in Julian Leeser and Ryan Hadric (eds), *Don't Leave us With the Bill: The Case Against an Australian Bill of Rights* (Menzies Research Centre, 2009) 17, 27 (emphasis added).

[18] We acknowledge that this brief summary greatly simplifies Dworkin's work.

[19] A useful recent example of this argument is contained in Grégoire Webber, Paul Yowell, Richard Ekins, Maris Köpcke Bradley Miller and Fransisco Urbina, *Legislated Rights: Securing Human Rights Through Legislation* (Cambridge, Cambridge University Press, 2018).

[20] We also note that the conservative Prime Minister whose government passed legislation to expressly preclude gay marriage later explained that decision (with obvious pride) by reference to the 'inertia as voluntary political reasoning' logic we have just detailed: John Howard, 'Don't Risk What We Have', in Leeser and Hadric, above n, 17, 69.

[21] [United Kingdom], *Royal Commission on Legal Services* (Cmnd 7648, 1979) – evidence of Sir Garfield Barwick – pg 13.

[22] The virulent conservative resistance to this reform is briefly recounted in the biography of a former federal Attorney-General: Keith Scott, *Gareth Evans* (Sydney, Allen & Unwin, 1999) 88–9.

II. Protecting Institutions Rather than People

The structural focus of the Australian Constitution and the lacuna that has caused for the protection of rights has not gone unnoticed by the High Court, though the more reflective of these views are usually expressed extra-judicially. One former Chief Justice of Australia thought that the institutional focus of the Constitution meant it could be characterised 'as a delineation of government powers rather than as a charter of citizens' rights.'[23] Another Justice similarly suggested that the Constitution 'is *dominated* by the structural pillars of federation and the separation of powers, rather than individual rights …'[24] The implication of such statements is that the Constitution appears to care much more about political and legal institutions than people.

There is a superficial appeal in this suggestion, particularly in light of some of the more recent decisions of the High Court which have focused on the protected nature of judicial power. Although these decisions often leave key doctrinal questions, such as the precise nature of judicial power,[25] uncomfortably vague, they reveal careful attention on the protection of judicial power against legislative intrusion. For example, these cases have led to constitutional principles that essentially prevent Australian Parliaments from placing limits on the supervisory judicial review jurisdiction of courts that might substantively impede access to the courts.[26] In the most significant such case, the High Court stressed the 'centrality, and protective purpose' of the entrenched jurisdiction it was guarding so zealously.[27] That invites the obvious question – protective of what? Before we answer that question, it is useful to note how one consequence of the strong emphasis on institutions and the separation of judicial power has been marshalled as a line of defence against bills and charters of rights.

That defence is a classic common law one of incremental reasoning. The basic proposition is that the Australian Constitution carves out a particular vision of judicial power and the judicial role. The functions allocated to courts and judges in a bill or charter of rights would distort that judicial role and should therefore be rejected.[28] The more sensationalist version of this claim is that a human rights charter would (wrongly) transfer power from the executive to the judiciary. A more neutral variant is that a charter of rights would distort the judicial role, by requiring the issue of advisory opinions (in the form of declarations of incompatibility) and usurp the courts' role in statutory interpretation

[23] Sir Anthony Mason, 'Procedural Fairness: Its Development and Continuing Role of Legitimate Expectation' (2005) 12 *Australian Journal of Administrative Law* 103, 109.

[24] Gageler, above n 6, 4 (emphasis added).

[25] The High Court has frankly acknowledged that this concept cannot be defined exclusively or exhaustively. See, eg, *Precision Data Holdings Ltd v Willis* (1991) 173 CLR 167,188–9.

[26] The foundation case on this was *Plaintiff S157/2002 v Commonwealth* (2003) 211 CLR 276. Subsequent decisions have held that procedural limits which have the substantive effect of impeding access to, and review by the courts are also unconstitutional. See, eg, *Bodruddaza v Minister for Immigration and Multicultural Affairs* (2007) 228 CLR 651 (which involved an inflexible time limit for lodge applications for review, though the logic of the decision could easily extend to exorbitant court fees and other practical impediments).

[27] *Plaintiff S157/2002 v Commonwealth* (2003) 211 CLR 276, [104].

[28] This is a key theme of Dyson Heydon, 'Are Bills of Rights Necessary in Common Law Jurisdictions?' (2014) 130 *LQR* 392. Although Heydon's argument is directed to common law systems in general, his claims on the corrupting effect that bills or charters of rights may have on the judicial function are clearly most informed by an Australian perspective.

(through the interpretive clauses that lie at the heart of charters).[29] However these assumptions are expressed, they lead to an obviously strange position. Any move to a bill or charter of rights that was intended to protect the rights of the Australian people should be avoided because of the danger it presents to some Australian institutions. Put another way, those who claim that the Australian people do not need further rights protection appear to argue that it is in fact institutions which need protection. If one answers the question that we think follows from the High Court's characterisation of its supervisory jurisdiction as protective – which is, protective of what? – the answer is surely the very people those institutions exist to govern, foster and protect.

III. The Failed Attempts to Introduce a Federal Bill or Charter of Rights

There are many now forgotten attempts to either introduce a comprehensive human rights statute or to directly protect some rights in the Australian Constitution.[30] Towards the end of the Second World War, a referendum that sought to introduce constitutional restrictions on federal legislative power to restrict freedom of speech and religion was rejected, fairly narrowly, by popular vote.[31] The wide-ranging reforms contained in these proposed constitutional amendments were perhaps as close as Australia ever came to what Gardbaum recently described as 'revolutionary constitutionalism'.[32] Gardbaum used that term to describe the process in which political revolution of some form is legitimised, and drawn to fruition, by the fashioning or refashioning a national constitution.[33] Australia arguably approached a muted such turning point during the Second World War when it barely survived invasion but also cast aside the key legislative constraint from its British heritage.[34] The timing and content of the 1944 referendum proposals could have enabled

[29] The issue of advisory opinions by courts in Australia is said to involve an impermissible exercise of non-judicial power: *In re Judiciary and Navigation Acts* (1921) 29 CLR 257. This argument was one of the issues raised in *Momcilovic v The Queen* (2011) 245 CLR 1. All of the judges in that case held that making a declaration of inconsistent interpretation – which has no legal effect of the rights or obligations of parties to the dispute – was not an exercise of judicial power. Five judges (French CJ, Gummow, Hayne, Heydon and Bell JJ) held that a declaration is also not incidental to the exercise of judicial power, meaning that it could not be exercised by or conferred on a federal court. Only a slim majority of the court (French CJ, Crennan, Kiefel and Bell JJ) found that the power was not incompatible with the exercise of judicial functions, meaning it could be exercised by state courts.

[30] A useful history of the many (mostly failed) attempts to introduce different forms of rights protection is contained in George Williams, *The Federal Parliament and the Protection of Human Rights* (Parliamentary Research Paper 20, 1998–9).

[31] The proposed amendment was the *Constitution Alteration (Post-War Reconstruction and Democratic Rights) 1944*. The restrictions on legislative power, which were expressed to apply to both state and federal Parliaments, most likely failed because other parts of the amendment sought to extend federal legislative power over a wide range of issues such as air transport, national health, trust laws and employment and unemployment. Extensions to federal parliamentary power have never been well received by Australian voters.

[32] Stephen Gardbaum, 'Revolutionary Constitutionalism' (2017) 15 *International Journal of Constitutional Law* 173.

[33] This metaphor is an inapt description of the adoption of the Australian Constitution because that process was peaceful and democratic. See Aroney, Gerangelos, Murray and Stellios, above n 14, ch 1.

[34] This occurred via the *Statute of Westminster Adoption Act 1942* (Cth), the operation of which was given retrospective effect to 3 September 1939 (the start of World War Two). This adopted the *Statute of Westminster Act 1931* (UK), which provided that British statutes would no longer apply to dominions unless they were expressly given that effect and that operation was expressly consented to by the relevant dominion.

their adoption to be characterised as the culmination of a wider struggle for Australia's survival and independence: but it was not to be.

A more limited proposal that sought to introduce constitutional protection for a right to trial by jury, religious freedom and fair terms for the just acquisition of property was rejected by a far greater popular margin in 1988.[35] These failed attempts to protect rights may simply be particular examples of a much wider Australian mindset against constitutional change in the formal sense.[36] They also illustrate why the focus of efforts for the greater protection of rights in Australia has moved from constitutional amendment to legislative reform.

The most audacious attempt at legislative change came when the reformist Whitlam Labor Government of the 1970's introduced the *Human Rights Bill 1973* (Cth),[37] which sought to enact the *International Covenant on Civil and Political Rights* into Australian law and provide remedies for breach of those rights, including damages in a limited range of circumstances.[38] The Bill also created a wide ranging administrative structure to enforce these rights and foster a culture of rights more generally. The most notable new institutions were a new federal commissioner of human rights and advisory council to assist that new office.[39] While this ambitious Bill lapsed when the government of the day lost office, most of its key elements were gradually introduced in later years. These piecemeal reforms included legislation to prohibit racial discrimination (in 1975), discrimination on the grounds of gender (in 1984) and then disability (in 1992).[40] The administration of these statutes, and the promotion and public discussion rights more generally, was vested in the Australian Human Rights Commission, which was established in 1984.[41] These many individual statutory reforms eventually achieved all that had been proposed by the radical human rights 'big bang' of 1973, except for a national bill of rights. This gradual adoption of legislation to protect rights in a growing number of specific areas, coupled with the creation of an important public agency to oversee those different statutes, may have been a politically wise means by which a rights protective framework could slowly accumulate but it was clearly imperfect. These disparate statutes that operated to protect particular rights or particular groups left many vulnerable people largely unprotected from oppressive legislation and

[35] The proposed amendment was the *Constitution Alteration (Rights and Freedoms) 1988* (Cth). These proposed reforms arose from the *Final Report of the Constitutional Commission* (1988), which considered constitutional reform as part of the 200th anniversary of European arrival to Australia. The 1988 referendum is examined in HP Lee, 'Reforming Australia's Constitution: The Frozen Continent Refuses to Thaw' [1988] *Public Law* 535.

[36] Only eight of 44 of the constitutional amendments that have been proposed have passed the referendum process. On the history of Australian referenda, see George Williams and David Hume, *People Power: The History and Future of the Referendum in Australia* (Sydney UNSW Press, 2010).

[37] The Bill's visionary scope was made clear by the Attorney-General upon its introduction: Hon Lionel Murphy, *Human Rights Bill 1973–Second Reading Speech* (Senate Hansard, 21 November 1973) pp 1971–3, available at https://parlinfo.aph.gov.au/parlInfo/search/display/display.w3p;adv=yes;db=HANSARD80;id=hansard80/hansards80/1973-11-21/0050;orderBy=_fragment_number,doc_date-rev;query=Dataset:hansards,hansards80%20Decade:%221970s%22%20Year:%221973%22;rec=10;resCount=Default.

[38] The Chief Justice of Australia at the time, Sir Garfield Barwick, had been previously been Attorney-General in a conservative government. His 'distaste for the legislation was total': David Marr, *Barwick* (Sydney, Allen & Unwin, 1980) 241.

[39] The Bill also sought to facilitate ratification of the *Convention on the Political Rights of Women* (A/RES/640(VII).

[40] The relevant statutes are the *Racial Discrimination Act 1975* (Cth), *Sex Discrimination Act 1984* (Cth) and the *Disability Discrimination Act 1992* (Cth).

[41] *Human Rights and Equal Opportunity Commission Act 1984* (Cth), which has since been renamed the *Australian Human Rights Commission Act*.

hostile government conduct. The prime example is the lightning rod of recent Australian politics – asylum seekers – whose outlier status is analysed in Chapter 17 by Emma Dunlop, Jane McAdam and Greg Weeks. Yet the successive and ongoing legislative attempts by Australian Governments to limit and sometimes exclude rights to liberty, natural justice, and access to the courts of persons seeking asylum may, at least partly, explain the renaissance of common law rights protection in Australia. This judicial reponse is said to have manifested in the creation of a common law bill of rights.[42]

Another gap in the fragmented scheme of rights protection created by the Commonwealth Parliament was the unclear role of the Parliament itself. There was no clear process by which Parliament and its members were able, or obliged, to consider issues about rights in any systematic manner.[43] There was, in short, no obvious means by which a rights sensitive culture might develop at an institutional level.

That same approach of fragmented statutory reform occurred in the wake of the apparent failure of the most recent attempt to introduce comprehensive human rights protection at the federal level in 2009.[44] That occurred following what was termed a 'National Human Rights Consultation', during which a specialist independent committee considered how best to reform and protect human rights in Australia.[45] The key recommendation of the Consultation Committee report was the adoption of a federal human rights statute, fashioned upon the 'dialogue model' of Canada.[46] This proposal was rejected by the Labor Government of the day, in large part because of the very strong political opposition any such statute would face,[47] but also because of constitutional doubts over the inclusion in any such act of some of the rights drawn from the *International Covenant on Economic, Social and Cultural Rights*.[48]

Another small but potentially far reaching reform, which was also rejected, might have replicated much of this change by indirect means. That was a proposal to amend federal judicial review legislation; to 'make the definitive list of Australia's international human rights obligations a relevant consideration in government decision making,' and provide

[42] These developments are outlined by Meagher in ch 19.

[43] This function was long performed by parliamentary committees on an ad hoc basis, when individual committees considered a specific bill or undertook a particular inquiry that might involve questions of rights, but no single committee had a roving or general brief to consider rights.

[44] The process was announced on 10 December 2008, which was the 60th anniversary of the *Universal Declaration of Human Rights* (GA Res 217A (III), UN GAOR, 3rd sess, 183rd plenary meeting, UN Doc A/Res/217A) (10 December 1948).

[45] [Australia] National Human Rights Consultation Committee, *National Human Rights Consultation Report* (2010).

[46] This description of the Canadian statute is the well known one used in Peter Hogg and Allison Bushell, 'The *Charter* Dialogue Between Courts and Legislatures (Or Perhaps the *Charter of Rights* Isn't Such a Bad Thing After All' (1997) 35 *Osgoode Hall Law Journal* 75.

[47] The submission to the National Consultation made by the opposition Attorney-General, who became Attorney-General in 2013 with a change of government, made clear that the conservative parties formally opposed any federal human rights act: Hon George Brandis, *Submission to the National Human Rights Consultation* (15 June 2009).

[48] Opened for signature 16 December 1966, 993 UNTS 3 (entered into force 3 January 1976). The point of constitutional doubt was whether such rights might lack 'sufficient specificity' to be regarded as supported by the power of the Commonwealth Parliament to enact laws for external affairs (which is invoked for the enactment of treaty related issues): Stephen Gageler and Henry Burmester, *In the Matter of Constitutional Issues Concerning a Charter of Rights: Supplementary Opinion* (Solicitor-General Opinion Nos 40, 68, 2009) para 17.

that a failure to consider rights in decision-making would be a ground of review.[49] Such a change would not directly adopt or enact international rights obligations but would instead have introduced a vastly larger version of the bureaucratic obligation examined in Chapter 6.[50] The definitive list of rights to be used in the bureaucratic 'duty to consider', as part of the exercise of statutory powers, was also important to a further recommendation to amend *Acts Interpretation Act 1901* (Cth) by the introduction of a requirement that all federal legislation be interpreted consistently with that list of rights.[51] As one contributor to this book has previously noted, this ostensibly small legislative proposal was in fact the introduction of a requirement 'functionally identical' to the key interpretive clause of a proposed charter of rights.[52]

The government instead adopted a more limited suite of reforms, the centrepiece of which was establishing a joint federal parliamentary committee for the scrutiny of human rights, which would oversee a greater consideration of human rights in the legislative process.[53] This change may prove more enduring than observers might have first realised. The slow growth of experience in, and hopefully acceptance of, human rights considerations among members of the committee might lead to real cultural change within our parliamentarians.[54] Any such change was clearly stymied, at least in the short term, when a conservative government assumed office in 2013 and left no doubt that its longstanding opposition to a bill or charter of rights was undiminished.[55] This political opposition has almost certainly also frustrated one of the other key recommendations of the National Consultation, which was an initial audit of existing legislation for rights compliance, accompanied by the development of an entirely new administrative culture that embedded the consideration of rights into governmental norms.[56]

IV. The Federal Effect of Non-Federal Charters of Rights

The brief account just given of the continued rejection of a bill or charter of rights at the federal level proceeds on a feature of federalism as it has evolved in Australia that would not

[49] [Australia] National Human Rights Consultation Committee, above n 45, 187 (recommendation 11).

[50] The constitutional and practical obstacles to such a change are analysed in Matthew Groves, 'Judicial Review and Human Rights' (2018) 25 *Australian Journal of Administrative Law* 64.

[51] [Australia] National Human Rights Consultation Committee, above n 45, (recommendation 12).

[52] Edward Santow, 'The Act that Dares Not Speak Its Name: The National Human Rights Consultation Report's Parallel Roads to Human Rights Reform' (2010) 33 *University of New South Wales Law Journal* 8, 22.

[53] Established by the *Human Rights (Parliamentary Scrutiny) Act 2011* (Cth), which is examined by Lisa Burton in ch 8.

[54] A contrary argument was made by opponents to a bill or charter of rights upon the introduction of the ACT and Victorian instruments, which each increased parliamentary involvement in the consideration of rights, such as through scrutiny committees. It was claimed this process might simply lead members of Parliament to simply mouth whatever platitudes and references to case law that might be required to assist the passage of a bill through any human rights scrutiny procedures: James Allan, 'The Victorian Charter of Rights and Responsibilities; Exegesis and Criticism' (2007) 30 *Melbourne University Law Review* 906, 920.

[55] An inadvertent example was the apparent care taken to remove the report of the National Human Rights Consultation Committee from public view. It is not available on the website of the federal Attorney-General. Links to the report in its entry in the catalogue of the National Library of Australia are now disabled.

[56] This possibility is the corollary to the many recommendations in the report of the National Human Rights Consultation Committee, which stressed the importance of greater public education about human rights. An obvious undercurrent in many other recommendations of the report was the need for similar education among parliamentarians.

be easily apparent to many outside observers. That feature is the balance of power, which has, since the time of federation, moved inexorably in favour of the Commonwealth. The Commonwealth largely controls the purse strings, though the twin financial pillars of its dominance over tax revenue,[57] and ability to provide 'tied grants' to the states, which obliges them to spend that federal funding in accordance with federal instructions.[58] These and other principles, which can be traced to evolving constitutional doctrines, have shifted the balance of financial, political and legislative power greatly in favour of the Commonwealth.[59] One of the wider political effects of these changes has been the unspoken cultural assumption that innovation usually arises at the federal level, which the states and territories eventually follow.

The growth of Commonwealth power and influence is, however, subject to inevitable limits by reason of Australia's constitutional structure. This element of federalism has particular resonance in matters of rights protection because, at least in simple terms, conservative social and political elements in Australia have generally opposed the introduction of greater legal protections for human rights. Those same conservative elements have also, as a general rule, opposed the relentless expansion of federal legislative and financial power in part because it comes 'at the expense of the residual legislative powers of the States.'[60] The longstanding concern that the conservative side of Australian politics has professed for the continued existence and political autonomy of the States has had an ironic side effect in the area of rights. Former High Court Justice Dyson Heydon, who has long been the most articulate intellectual opponent of an Australian bill or charter of rights, conceded that this talisman of Australia's federal structure 'permitting diversity' necessarily 'allows its component units to engage in their own legislative experiments.'[61] When writing extra-judicially, Heydon later conceded that this feature of federalism could foster the protection of rights because 'the existence of beneficial institutions in one unit of a federation tends to be noticed by those who live in others, and pressure mounts for an imitation or at least adaptation.'[62] This possibility was described by one commentator as 'laboratory federalism',

[57] This occurred when the federal government seized control of personal income tax payments during the Second World War. The statutes that did so were held constitutionally valid in *South Australia v Commonwealth* (1942) 65 CLR 373 ('the *First Uniform Tax* case).

[58] Section 96 of the Australian Constitution provides that the Commonwealth 'may grant such financial assistance to any State on such terms and conditions as the Parliament thinks fit.' The expansive reading that was given to this power by the High Court in the *First Uniform Tax* case was endorsed by the Court in *Victoria v Commonwealth* (1957) 99 CLR 575 (the '*Second Uniform Tax*' case). This second case left no doubt about federal powers to make 'specific purpose grants' to the states, which essentially enables the Commonwealth to use the states to implement its policies by financial and political blackmail.

[59] A key element of these changes was the expansive reading given to the so-called 'external affairs power' in the Australian Constitution s 51(xxix), which empowers the federal Parliament to legislate with respect to 'external affairs'. This power has been interpreted as supporting the enactment of legislation that implements international treaties acceded to by Australia, the subject matter of which may not be supported by any other head of federal legislative power. The turning pointing in favour of the Commonwealth was *Commonwealth v Tasmania* (1983) 158 CLR 1 (the '*Tasmanian Dams*' case).

[60] Peter Hanks, Frances Gordon and Graeme Hill, *Constitutional Law in Australia* 4th edn (London, Lexis Nexis, 2018) 515. That statement is made in the course of analysis of the expansion of the external affairs power of the Commonwealth, but clearly applies to other federal inroads into state powers.

[61] *Public Service Association and Professional Officers' Association Amalgamated (NSW) v Director of Public Employment* (2012) 250 CLR 343, 369 [61].

[62] Heydon, above n 28, 407–8. This claim was made as part of an argument against the adoption of statutory bills or charters of rights.

by which differing Australian jurisdictions may attempt legislative innovations, within of course, wider constitutional constraints.[63] As with so many metaphors and ideas used in Australian public law, this laboratory metaphor was an adaptation from another federal jurisdiction.[64]

The Australian States and Territories have proved very industrious laboratories. As with the Commonwealth, they have considered the introduction of a bill or charter of rights over the last two decades. The results have not been uniform, but they have been informative to each new consideration of the issues. The first comprehensive such review, in Queensland during the 1990's, concluded that a charter of rights would be burdensome, costly and add little substantive value to the existing framework of rights protection.[65] A subsequent parliamentary inquiry in New South Wales also rejected calls for a charter, but recommended greater parliamentary scrutiny of legislation that could affect basic rights.[66] Similar inquiries conducted in the Australian Capital Territory and Victoria supported the adoption of some sort of charter,[67] and led to the enactment of charters of rights by their legislatures in 2004 and 2006 respectively. The ACT and Victorian charters of rights, and their effects, are each examined in this book.[68] Inquiries in other Australian jurisdictions have recommended the adoption of a charter in some form but not (yet) been adopted,[69] and other inquiries have recommended against human rights legislation, at least in the short term.[70] The most recent such inquiry, the results of which came to fruition just as this book entered production, saw Queensland revisit the issue in a process that split sharply across political lines.[71]

[63] Brendan Lim, 'Laboratory Federalism and the *Kable* Principle' (2014) 42 *Federal Law Review* 519.

[64] The source was *New State Ice Co v Liebmann*, 285 US 262, 311 (1932), where Justice Brandeis spoke of the 'happy incidents of the federal system', in which a 'a single courageous State may, if its citizens choose, serve as a laboratory; and try novel social and economic experiments without risk to the rest of the country.'

[65] [Queensland Parliament] Legal, Constitutional and Administrative Committee, *The Preservation and Enhancement of Individuals' Rights and Freedoms in Queensland* (Report 12, 1998). An earlier report had reached precisely the opposite view: Queensland Electoral and Administrative Review Council, *Report on the Preservation and Enhancement of Individuals' Rights and Freedoms* (1993).

[66] New South Wales Legislative Council, Standing Committee on Law and Justice, *A NSW Bill of Rights* (2001) xiii.

[67] [Australian Capital Territory], ACT Bill of Rights Consultative Committee, *Towards an ACT Human Rights Act* (May 2003); [Victoria], *Rights, Responsibilities and Respect: Report of the Human Rights Consultation Committee*, (November 2005).

[68] Which are examined respectively in ch 10 by Simon Rice and ch 11 by Janina Boughey.

[69] Government of Western Australia, *A WA Human Rights Act: Report of the Consultation Committee For a Proposed WA Human Rights Act* (2007); Tasmania Law Reform Institute, *A Charter of Rights for Tasmania* (Report 10, October 2007); [Australia] Attorney-General's Department, *National Human Rights Consultation Report: Recommendations* (2009).

[70] Legislative Assembly of Northern Territory Standing Committee on Legal and Constitutional Affairs, *Towards Northern Territory Statehood: Issues for Consideration* (2010) iii. This report recommended that the Northern Territory should first gain statehood, which has long been a key political goal of that jurisdiction. The imperative also thwarted the most recent attempt to pursue a charter in the Northern Territory. That occurred when a member of the Territory Parliament introduced a motion that the Parliament acknowledge the UN *Declaration of Rights for Indigenous People*, then enact a charter of rights. The Parliament voted to 'note' the UN Declaration but took no action on a Charter: Stephanie Zillman, 'Northern Territory Bill of Rights Motion Thrown out of Parliament' ABC News, 19 October 2017, www.abc.net.au/news/2017-10-19/northern-territory-parliament-throws-out-bill-of-rights-motion/9067490.

[71] [Queensland] Parliamentary Legal Affairs and Community Safety Committee, *Inquiry into a Possible Human Rights Act for Queensland* (Report 30, 2016). Committee members from the Labor Government favoured a charter, while members of the conservative opposition did not. The report was delivered when the Labor party had formed a tenuous minority government. When it obtained a clear parliamentary majority in a subsequent election, the new Labor Government enacted the *Human Rights Act 2019* (Qld).

The Queensland Parliament passed the *Human Rights Act 2019* (Qld) in March 2019. The Act largely replicates the model of the ACT and Victorian charters, though makes a few potentially significant changes. One of these changes is the conferral of a complaints-resolution function on the Queensland Human Rights Commissioner. If that office is properly resourced and provided with assistance by government agencies in performing its functions, the complaints process has the potential to address one of the most significant limitations of Victoria's charter: the absence of an accessible, cheap and effective mechanism to ensure the executive branch complies with its human rights obligations.[72] Another is its inclusion of a right to health services – a social and economic right which is not included in either of the other sub-national Australian charters. We have not included a separate chapter on the Queensland Act because other than these, and a few other minor, changes, it largely replicates the ACT and Victorian models and we expect that its operation and effect will be similar.

When a federal charter of rights was most recently under consideration, considerable attention was given to the 'downstream' effect that step might have.[73] The slow but clear growth of charters of rights within the states and territories suggests that the current may ultimately flow in the other direction. The states and territories have effectively leap frogged over federal inaction and been informed by each other's experience in this clear break from the federal position.

V. The Outside Experience – Foreign, Global, Transnational or Alien?

As we began this chapter with a literary reference, it seems appropriate to conclude with another, namely the impact upon Australia of what one noted historian described as the 'tyranny of distance'.[74] This influential argument suggested that the great physical distance between Australia and its early colonial master Britain, as well as the other beacons of western democracy in Europe and the US, was an enormous influence on the evolution of Australia's social and political identity. The overt point of this argument was that Australia was long unable to fully interact with the rest of the world. The author suggested that one enduring effect of the long period during which physical distance impeded international communication and travel is an Australian reluctance to engage with the outside world. Whether that was true in legal thinking may not be capable of a single or clear answer,[75] it is plainly no longer the case.[76]

[72] Boughey discusses this in ch 11. See also Janina Boughey and Adam Fletcher, 'Administrative Decision-Making Under Victoria's Charter' (2018) 25 *Australian Journal of Administrative Law* 10.

[73] These issues are thoughtfully examined in Justin Gleeson, 'A Federal Human Rights Act – What Implications for the States and Territories' (2010) 33 *University of New South Wales Law Journal* 110. That author later became Solicitor-General of the Commonwealth.

[74] Geoffrey Blainey, *The Tyranny of Distance – How Distance Shaped Australia's History* (London, Macmillan, 1966). That author became an influential figure in conservative politics, as shown by his involvement in the edited collection of conservative voices against the adoption of a federal charter of rights. See Leeser and Hadric, above n 17.

[75] Two contributors to this book have previously suggested that Australia 'does not have a strong tradition of scholarly analysis of the relationship between international and Australian law': Hilary Charlesworth, Madeline Chiam, Devika Hovell and George Williams, 'Deep Anxieties: Australia and the International Legal Order' (2003) 25 *Sydney Law Review* 423, 425.

[76] See, eg, Justin Gleeson, 'The Increasing Internationalisation of Australian Law' (2017) 28 *Public Law Review* 25. That author argues that the influence of international and foreign law on Australian legal principles is increasing significantly and will only continue to do so.

We think that Australia has always been involved in what is now often referred to as the transnational judicial conversation about rights and related issues.[77] This began in Australia with judicial conversations and exchanges that preceded their modern focus on questions of rights. This earlier iteration occurred in Australia as part of the search for constitutional principles which, by reason of the blend of British and American influences on the design and text of our Constitution, led many judges to draw regularly upon both of those jurisdictions. Sir Owen Dixon, who is widely regarded as the most influential of all Australian jurists, suggested that Australians:

> … stand midway between the two great common law systems … We study them both; we feel that, in some measure, we understand them both, and we seek guidance from them both.[78]

By the time of the centenary of the High Court, Australia's most eminent scholar of constitutional law similarly noted that the Court habitually 'roams the world in search of enlightenment'.[79]

One point that is made clear from several chapters in this book is that much of that roaming has been done in recent times by those states and territories which have adopted a charter or bill of rights. The same can be said, to a somewhat lesser extent, of those jurisdictions which have considered – but decided not to adopt – such an instrument. This journey among the states and territories has placed Australia squarely within the 'new Commonwealth model of constitutionalism' that Stephen Gaurdbaum identified as developing within Commonwealth nations.[80] Gardbaum argues that the human rights charters adopted in Canada, New Zealand, the UK, the ACT and Victoria represent a middle ground between the traditional constitutional rights-protection models of either legislative or judicial supremacy.[81] He posits that this new Commonwealth model – which relies on parliamentary review of legislation and weak-form judicial review for rights protection – is appealing because it 'combines many of the strengths of both traditional polar models whilst avoiding their major characteristic weaknesses'.[82]

Views diverge on whether Gardbaum's optimism about the model is warranted.[83] For instance, the UK's Conservative Government announced a policy to replace the

[77] An expression taken from Christopher McCrudden, 'A Common Law of Human Rights? Transnational Judicial Conversations on Constitutional Rights' (2000) 20 *OJLS* 499. Shipra Chordia's ch 18 in this volume traces one particular rights-based principle, and its translation into Australian law.

[78] Owen Dixon, 'Two Constitutions Compared' (1942) 16 *Australian Law Journal* 192, 194. The outward looking nature of this paper was emphasised by the fact that it was an address delivered to the American Bar Association.

[79] Leslie Zines, 'The Vision and Reality' in Peter Cane (ed), *Centenary Essays for the High Court of Australia* (Chatswood, Butterworths, 2004) 3, 13.

[80] The concept was first explained in Stephen Gardbaum, 'The New Commonwealth Model of Constitutionalism' (2001) 49 *American Journal of Comparative Law* 707, then in greater detail in Stephen Gardbaum, *The New Commonwealth Model of Constitutionalism: Theory and Practice* (Cambridge University Press, 2013).

[81] The newly enacted *Human Rights Act 2019* (Qld) has not been directly considered by Gardbaum but it also fits squarely within his existing analysis.

[82] Gardbaum, *The New Commonwealth Model of Constitutionalism: Theory and Practice*, above n 80, 222.

[83] The best analysis is the nuanced one provided in Scott Stephenson, *From Dialogue to Disagreement in Comparative Righyts Constitutionalism* (Annandale, Federation Press, 2016). At the risk of simplication, Stephenson's approach traces the normative trade offs that occur within the new approaches adopted by Commonwealth nations. He also identifies a 'inter-institutional disagreement' within these new approaches to rights protection. The reasons for, and conseqences of, institutional disagreement are argued to be at least (perhaps more) important than notions of dialogue. This analysis is especially compelling for the Australian context.

Human Rights Act 1998 (UK) c 42 with a scaled-back version which gives less power to the courts;[84] though this proposal has been overtaken by Brexit issues.[85] The particular operation and effects of each of these Commonwealth rights instruments also differs – a topic that one of us has examined at length elsewhere.[86] Nevertheless, as Gardbaum argues, they belong to a distinct family of human rights instruments, which shows that international and overseas developments have been noticed, followed, and adapted to Australian political and legal conditions by state and territory legislatures. Gardbaum has made clear that variation among Commonwealth nations precludes the use of definitive or clear taxonomies.[87] That concession is particularly apt for Australia because of the odd position in which it currently sits. Some jurisdictions have enacted statutory protections for some rights. Others have not. How this may influence the wider Australian Commonwealth remains to be seen.[88]

Hilary Charlesworth has written of 'The Australian Reluctance About Rights'.[89] Insofar as this refers to the history of and attitude towards entrenched constitutional rights, it remains valid. Yet that reluctance is not about the importance of human rights more generally, but how (and by whom) they ought to be protected and promoted. As this book will detail, Australia's legal framework of rights protection is piecemeal, incomplete and largely sub-constitutional. This is both a weakness and a strength. A key strength is the ability of the states and territories to proceed with significant reforms in the face of a stubborn refusal to do so at the federal level. Another strength, which reflects the pecularities of the Australian Constitution, is that legislative change is vastly easier than constitutional change.[90] Statutory bills and charters of rights, as well as other legislative protections for rights, can be enacted with relative ease. The ease with which they can be amended has proven a useful means to broaden the scope of some of the charters of rights, which has been a notable feature of the ACT instrument.[91] The most obvious disadvantage of this piecemeal and largely legislative

[84] The form of these proposals has changed over time and remains fluid. The interation provided at the formation of the Conservative/Unionist Coalition, stated that 'We will not repeal or replace the Human Rights Act *while* the process of Brexit is underway … We will remain signatories to the European Convention on Human Rights *for the duration* of the next parliament': *Forward Together – Our Plan for a Stronger Britain and a Prosperous Future* (Conservative and Unionist Manifesto, 2017) 37 (emphasis added). Such statements signal clearly, but vaguely, that considerable change will shortly come to Britain's human rights regime.

[85] While attention has gone to the *Human Rights Act*, it should also be noted that the status of other human rights instruments also remains unsettled. See Menelaos Markakis, 'Brexit and the EU Charter of Fundamental Rights' [2019] *Public Law* 82.

[86] Janina Boughey, *Human Rights and Judicial Review in Australia and Canada: The Newest Despotism?* (Oxford, Hart Publishing, 2017).

[87] Stephen Gardbaum, 'Reassessing the New Commonwealth Model of Constitutionalism' (2010) 8 *International Journal of Constitutional Law* 167.

[88] Some of the possibilities are explored in Scott Stephenson, 'Federalism and Rights Deliberation' (2014) 38 *Melbourne University Law Review* 709.

[89] Hilary Charlesworth, 'The Australian Reluctance About Rights' (1993) 31 *Osgoode Hall Law Journal* 195.

[90] The Australian Constitution may only be amended by the referendum procedure contained in s 128. The procedure requires that any amendment have the support of a majority of voters in a majority of states. This 'double barrelled' democratic requirement is, arguably, anti-democratic because a referendum can be supported by a majority of voters but not gain that same level of support across four of the six states.

[91] Eight years after its enactment, the *Human Rights Act 2004* (ACT) was amended to include a right to education: *Human Rights Amendment Act 2012* (ACT) s 6 (inserting s 37A into the HRA).

approach is that legislation can be easily undone. Freedoms contained in legislation can be wound back, sometimes to an alarming level.[92]

VI. Reluctant, Exceptional or Unremarkable?

We have stressed the rather odd path taken for the legal protection of rights in Australia. But that should not be taken to mean that we accept without question the repeated suggestions that the Australian approach to rights (or public law more generally) is reluctant, exceptional or any of the other criticisms that are regularly made. In one sense, the variations within the Australian approach to the protection of rights, however imperfect, incomplete and incoherent, arguably reflect some sort of margin of appreciation on these issues within the wider model of western liberal democracies. In the case where this now longstanding feature of European public law was first articulated, the European Court of Human Rights explained that individual states were often better placed to decide many questions about the 'requirements of moral values … By reason of their direct and continuous contact with the vital forces of their countries …'[93] Almost 40 years later, Lord Sales suggested that the margin granted to individual members of the European Union 'is increasingly being replaced by (or subsumed within) a view-point more internal to the constitutional position within contracting states …'[94] The Australian approach within the wider context of western liberal democratic regimes is, we think, a variation along these lines. As many of the chapters of this book make clear, the variation is often as much about *how* rights are protected as it is about *whether* they are protected.

[92] A Conservative Government elected earlier this decade in Queensland enacted a slew of restrictions on rights and freedoms, including legislation that: reversed the presumption of innocence in some instances; removed the right to bail in others; imposed a levy upon those convicted of certain offences; and imposed mandatory minimum sentences upon others. The extraordinary tale of this government is explained in Andrew Trotter and Harry Hobbs, 'The Great Leap Backwards: Criminal Law Reform with The Hon Jarrod Bleijie' (2014) 36 *Sydney Law Review* 1.

[93] *Handyside v United Kingdom* (1976) 1 EHRR 737, [48].

[94] Philip Sales, 'Law Democracy in a Human Rights Framework' in David Feldman (ed), *Law in Politics, Politics in Law* (Oxford, Hart Publishing, 2013) 217, 229.

2

Australia's Constitutional Design and the Protection of Human Rights

GEORGE WILLIAMS*

I. Introduction

One of the most important roles played by the final court of appeal in a democratic nation is to decide cases that bear upon questions of human rights. Such cases are commonplace in nations like the US, where the Supreme Court is often called upon to interpret and enforce rights such as freedom of speech in the First Amendment to its Constitution. The same role is fulfilled in other nations, such as in the UK where the Supreme Court now applies the *Human Rights Act 1998* (UK).

The workload of Australia's High Court also includes many cases that raise important questions of human rights. Recent examples are matters dealing with bikie laws and freedom of association, same-sex marriage, political donations and freedom of speech, compensation for the taking of property and the treatment of asylum seekers. Where the High Court differs from the superior courts of other nations is that it must often resolve such matters without having reference to legal standards of human rights. This is because Australian law does not recognise many of the most significant human rights. As a result, the High Court may need to dispose of issues of human rights by applying other areas of law, whether it be administrative law, constitutional law, or, if no other area of law applies, by rejecting the claim.

Australia's exceptionalism lies in its lack of a national human rights instrument. It is now alone among democratic nations in not having a national bill of rights or human rights act. This chapter sets out Australia's constitutional design when it comes to human rights, and how the nation's High Court determines cases raising questions of human rights in the absence of such a law.

II. Human Rights Protection in Australia

Australia lacks a national instrument of human rights protection, but this is not to say that it is bereft of human rights guarantees and human rights laws. For example, human rights

* This chapter has been adapted from 'The High Court, the Constitution and Human Rights' (2015) 21 *Australian Journal of Human Rights* 1. I thank Zoe Graus for her research assistance.

acts can be found in three subnational jurisdictions, the Australian Capital Territory (ACT), Victoria and Queensland, in the form of the *Human Rights Act 2004* (ACT), *Charter of Human Rights and Responsibilities Act 2006* (Vic) and *Human Rights Act 2019* (Qld).

A broad range of federal, state and territory statutes also protect specific human rights. At the Commonwealth level, such statutes include privacy laws,[1] laws regulating the exercise of administrative power,[2] laws governing evidence and civil and the criminal procedure[3] and employment laws protecting rights such as those related to work conditions and fair wages.[4] Federal laws also protect against several forms of discrimination, such as through the *Racial Discrimination Act 1975* (Cth). On the other hand, a lengthy list of basic rights receives no general legislative protection, including freedom of speech and freedom of association.

Statutes that protect rights are subject to amendment or repeal. For example, the *Native Title Amendment Act 1998* (Cth) implemented the Howard Government's 'ten-point plan' for native title after the High Court's decision in *Wik Peoples v Queensland.* In seeking to achieve, in the words of the Deputy Prime Minister Tim Fischer, 'bucket-loads of extinguishment', the Act overrode the *Racial Discrimination Act.* This was achieved through introducing a new section 7 into the *Native Title Act 1993* (Cth) that expressed an intention that the *Racial Discrimination Act* only overrode the *Native Title Act* where the provisions of the *Native Title Act* were ambiguous. A similar suspension of the *Racial Discrimination Act* was achieved under the legislation that brought about the Northern Territory intervention in 2007 (*Northern Territory National Emergency Response Act 2007* (Cth)).

In 2012, through the *Human Rights (Parliamentary Scrutiny) Act 2011* (Cth), the Commonwealth adopted a new human rights parliamentary scrutiny process. The Act provides for a Parliamentary Joint Committee on Human Rights, the functions of which include examining and reporting to Parliament on the human rights compatibility of bills, legislative instruments and acts and inquiring into human rights matters referred by the Attorney-General. Members of Parliament who propose to introduce a bill must table a 'statement of compatibility' that assesses 'whether the bill is compatible with human rights'. The 'human rights' against which a bill must be evaluated are defined to mean the rights and freedoms declared in several human rights treaties, including the *International Covenant on Civil and Political Rights 1966* and the *International Covenant on Economic, Social and Cultural Rights 1966.*

This scrutiny regime provides a very limited form of human rights protection, and has a limited impact.[5] In fact, the Act does not provide any legal protection for human rights, nor does it vest such rights in individuals. Instead, it merely provides how the federal Parliament can examine proposals for new laws in light of Australia's international human rights obligations. No consequences follow if Parliament chooses to ignore such obligations and so to enact a law identified as being non-compliant. As a result, there is no role for a court to reach any finding in respect of whether human rights have been breached, nor to award a person whose human rights have been infringed a remedy.

[1] See, eg, *Privacy Act 1988* (Cth).
[2] See, eg, *Administrative Decisions (Judicial Review) Act 1977* (Cth).
[3] See, eg, *Evidence Act 1995* (Cth).
[4] See, eg, *Fair Work Act 2009* (Cth).
[5] George Williams and Daniel Reynolds 'The Operation and Impact of Australia's Parliamentary Scrutiny Regime for Human Rights' (2015) 41 *Monash University Law Review* 469.

The limited protection for human rights provided by Australian legislation is mirrored in the terms of the Australian Constitution. The Constitution was drafted at conventions held in 1891 and 1897–98, and then enacted for Australia by the British Parliament. In *Australian Capital Television Pty Ltd v Commonwealth*, Mason CJ noted the 'prevailing sentiment of the framers that there was no need to incorporate a comprehensive Bill of Rights in order to protect the rights and freedoms of citizens. That sentiment was one of the unexpressed assumptions on which the Constitution was drafted'.[6] Chief Justice Mason's statement reflects the widely held view that the framers intended the human rights of the Australian people to be protected by the common law and the good sense of elected representatives, as expressed in the Westminster notion of responsible government.

To the extent that human rights were taken into account by the framers, one concern was to maintain existing race-based distinctions. A majority of the Constitution's framers considered, for example, that a clause that conferred 'equal protection of the laws' was undesirable because it might protect 'Chinamen, Japanese, Hindoos, and other barbarians' in areas such as employment.[7] The racially discriminatory origins of the Constitution remain evident in section 51(xxvi), which provides that the Commonwealth Parliament may legislate with respect to the 'people of any race for whom it is deemed necessary to make special laws'.[8] The original purpose of this section was expressed at the 1898 Convention in Melbourne by Sir Edmund Barton, later Australia's first Prime Minister and one of the first judges of the High Court. He argued that it was necessary to enable the Commonwealth to 'regulate the affairs of the people of coloured or inferior races who are in the Commonwealth'.[9]

The Constitution contains only a few, scattered express protections of human rights. One economic right, section 51(xxxi), which states that federal laws providing for an acquisition of property shall entail just terms, has been given a broad operation by the High Court.[10] On the other hand, the few civil and political rights in the Constitution have, due to a combination of narrow drafting and constrained interpretation by the High Court, had little (if any) effect. For example, the requirement in section 80 that '[t]he trial on indictment of any offence against any law of the Commonwealth shall be by jury' has been interpreted as conferring on Parliament the power to itself determine what offences shall be 'on indictment', and thus subject to a jury trial.[11] Similarly, section 41, which might seem to confer a 'right to vote',[12] has been interpreted as applying only to people who had a right to vote in state elections as at 12 June 1902. The High Court has noted that the

[6] *Australian Capital Television Pty Ltd v Commonwealth* (1992) 177 CLR 106, 136 (Mason CJ).

[7] *Debates of the Australasian Federal Convention*, 1891–1898b, p 1784. See also p 1752, where Dr Quick refers to 'people of any undesirable race or of undesirable antecedents'.

[8] Prior to 1967, this section included the following phrase: 'other than the aboriginal race in any State'. This phrase was deleted by referendum in 1967. Significantly, whilst the intention of voters in 1967 was to enable the Commonwealth Parliament to make laws benefiting the Aboriginal people, it appears that the s 51(xxvi) may also enable the Commonwealth Parliament to make laws which disadvantage Aboriginal people. See *Kartinyeri v Commonwealth* 195 CLR 337 (*Hindmarsh Island Bridge Case*).

[9] *Debates of the Australasian Federal Convention*, 1891–1898a, pp 228–9.

[10] See, eg, *Georgiadis v Australian and Overseas Telecommunications Corporation* 179 CLR 297.

[11] See, eg, *R v Bernasconi* (1915) 19 CLR 629, 637.

[12] This section provides that '[n]o adult person who has or acquires a right to vote at elections for the more numerous House of the Parliament of a State shall, while the right continues, be prevented by any law of the Commonwealth from voting at elections for either House of the Parliament of the Commonwealth'.

'practical effect of s 41 is now spent'.[13] The Constitution also contains a section preserving freedom of religion against Commonwealth laws (section 116), but it has never been applied by the Court to strike down a law.

III. The High Court and Human Rights

How then has the High Court dealt with human rights matters in the context of patchwork legislative protection for human rights and little apparent protection in the Constitution itself? One mechanism employed by the Court (often referred to as the principle of legality) is to develop common law rules regarding the interpretation of legislation so that the infringement of human rights is minimised. For example, the High Court has recognised that 'courts should, in a case of ambiguity, favour a construction of a Commonwealth statute which accords with the obligations of Australia under an international treaty',[14] including any relevant international treaty on human rights.

Another common law rule was set down by Mason CJ and Brennan, Gaudron and McHugh JJ in *Coco v The Queen*: 'The courts should not impute to the legislature an intention to interfere with fundamental rights. Such an intention must be clearly manifested by unmistakeable and unambiguous language'.[15] Hence, 'a statute or statutory instrument which purports to impair a right to personal liberty is interpreted, if possible, so as to respect that right'.[16] This interpretive rule is but one aspect of the development of a principle of legality by the High Court.

Common law principles of this kind can play an important, sometimes decisive, role in enabling the protection of human rights that otherwise lack statutory or constitutional backing. *Evans v New South Wales* provides an example.[17] It concerned a regulation made under the *World Youth Day Act 2006* (NSW), as part of plans for a Catholic youth celebration, that empowered persons to 'direct a person within a World Youth Day declared area to cease engaging in conduct that … causes annoyance or inconvenience to participants in a World Youth Day event'.[18] The applicants intended to protest during the celebrations by distributing T-shirts, leaflets, flyers, stickers, condoms and coat-hangers.

A Full Federal Court comprising French, Branson and Stone JJ applied the principle of legality to read the *World Youth Day Act* in light of the fundamental right to freedom of expression – thereby reducing the scope of the power to make regulations. They pointed out that 'annoyance' was a subjective response and that the regulation could be read as applying regardless of the number of people who might be 'annoyed'.[19] The result was that the regulation of 'annoying' behaviour 'affect[ed] freedom of speech in a way that … [was] not supported by the statutory power'.[20] The effect was that a regulation, which may have

[13] *R v Pearson; Ex parte Sipka* (1983) 152 CLR 254, 280.
[14] *Chu Kheng Lim v Minister for Immigration, Local Government and Ethnic Affairs* (1992) 176 CLR 1, 38 (Brennan, Deane and Dawson JJ).
[15] *Coco v R* (1994) 179 CLR 427, 437 (Mason CJ and Brennan, Gaudron and McHugh JJ).
[16] *Re Bolton; Ex parte Beane* (1987) 162 CLR 514, 523 (Brennan J).
[17] *Evans v New South Wales* (2008) 168 FCR 576.
[18] *World Youth Day Regulations 2008* (NSW) cl 7(1)(b).
[19] *Evans* (n 17) 596 (French, Branson and Stone JJ).
[20] Ibid, 597.

appeared to be within power if the regulation-making power were given its broad, ordinary meaning, was in fact beyond power.

A like approach was adopted by the High Court in *X7 v Australian Crime Commission* (though not in regard to similar issues in the subsequent case of *Lee v NSW Crime Commission*).[21] In *X7*, a majority of the Court held that an examiner appointed under the *Australian Crime Commission Act 2002* (Cth) could not require a person charged with an indictable Commonwealth offence to answer questions before his or her trial about the subject matter of that offence. This result followed from the fact that the person's right to silence had not been abrogated by the statute in clear terms. Without such language, the statute was not capable of effecting a fundamental alteration to the process of criminal justice.

Such cases demonstrate the rise of the principle of legality and how it can be effective where Parliament has not made clear its intention to abrogate human rights. However, the principle has no role to play where such an intent is manifested in 'unmistakeable and unambiguous language'. Such language is not unusual, in part to avoid the application of the principle. Examples are the many amendments made to the *Migration Act 1958* (Cth) directed at asylum seekers seeking to come to Australia by boat. Such amendments are often expressed to deny the human rights of asylum seekers in the clearest terms, such as by providing for their indefinite detention or removing any rights to procedural fairness. Many other instances lie within the field of anti-terrorism law, where for example, control order legislation enables restrictions on a person's movement, communications and liberty without requiring any finding of guilt against them,[22] or where the Australian Security Intelligence Organisation (ASIO) can have non-suspect citizens subjected to coercive questioning for 24 hours and detained for up to a week to gather intelligence about terrorism offences.[23]

In the face of such legislation, only the Constitution can offer protection against the infringement of human rights. Even though the instrument appears to offer little by way of express human rights protection, it can nonetheless resolve such matters in favour of human rights protection in a surprising number of cases. These cases suggest that the Constitution can be conceived of as a rights-respecting instrument even though it lacks anything akin to a bill of rights. This is in large part due to the following three ways in which the High Court has interpreted and applied the document.

IV. Coincidental Protection of Human Rights

There are many examples of the High Court delivering decisions protective of human rights in circumstances where human rights concepts played no role in the reasoning. Typically, protection of such individual interests under the Constitution is merely a consequence of applying constitutional principles that are intended to protect other systemic or public interests. Hence, in vindicating the constitutional interests served by federalism, the separation of powers, representative government and responsible government, the Court will on occasion also end up protecting human rights.

[21] *X7 v Australian Crime Commission* (2013) 248 CLR 92; *Lee v NSW Crime Commission* (2013) 251 CLR 196.
[22] *Criminal Code* (Cth), Pt 5.3, Div 104.
[23] *Australian Security Intelligence Organisation Act 1979* (Cth), Pt III, Div 3.

One well-known example is the High Court's decision in *Australian Communist Party v Commonwealth*, one of the most significant cases ever delivered by the High Court due to its protective effect on a range of democratic rights.[24] The case concerned legislation enacted by the Commonwealth Parliament as part of its attempt to eliminate communism in Australia. The *Communist Party Dissolution Act 1950* (Cth):

(1) declared the Australian Communist Party to be an unlawful association; (s 4)
(2) enabled the Governor-General to declare other organisations whose, in his or her opinion, 'continued existence … would be prejudicial to the security and defence of the Commonwealth or to the execution or maintenance of the Constitution or of the laws of the Commonwealth'; (s 5) and
(3) applying a similar test, enabled the Governor-General to declare any person to be a 'Communist' (s 9).

Such declarations resulted in the dissolution of an organisation and prohibited a person from holding office in the Commonwealth public service or industries declared by the Governor-General to be vital to the security and defence of Australia.

The High Court held the *Communist Party Dissolution Act* invalid in its entirety. However, this finding did not depend upon the Act having breached any constitutional guarantee protective of human rights. Instead, the High Court found that the Act did not fall within any of the heads of Commonwealth legislative power. The Court refused to accept the statement in the recitals to the Act that it fell within the defence power because it was necessary for 'the security and defence of Australia'. It reached this conclusion because sections of the Act imposed 'legal consequences on a legislative or executive opinion which itself supplies the only link between the power and the legal consequences of the opinion'.[25] The attempt by the Commonwealth Parliament in these sections to determine the scope of its own legislative power – by enabling the Governor-General to decide what organisations or persons were 'prejudicial to the security or defence of the Commonwealth' – breached the maxim that 'a stream cannot rise higher than its source'.[26] In other words, it is for the courts rather than the Commonwealth Parliament to determine the scope of the latter's legislative powers under the Constitution.

The *Communist Party* case reflects the importance for the protection of rights of a legal culture based upon the rule of law and enforced by an independent judiciary. It also demonstrates how effective High Court advocacy in the field of human rights can require the invocation of constitutional doctrine that apparently has nothing to do with such interests. In such cases, one common strategy is to align the protection of human rights with some other interest the High Court is prepared to vindicate. A particularly effective approach can be to seek to achieve human rights protection, especially in regard to procedural rights, by way of asserting the High Court's own role in adjudicating the Constitution or other legal disputes in accordance with traditional rule of law principles such as judicial independence. Hence, in *Plaintiff S157/2002 v Commonwealth*, the High Court delivered opinions citing principles such as the rule of law in favour of maintaining its own jurisdiction to

[24] *Australian Communist Party v Commonwealth* (1951) 83 CLR 1.
[25] Ibid, 261 (Fullagar J).
[26] Ibid, 258.

determine the validity of executive action.[27] This decision also had the effect of ensuring that government decisions adverse to the interests of asylum seekers could not be insulated from judicial review.

Another example of coincidental human rights protection is the High Court's decision in *Williams v Commonwealth*, a challenge brought to the federal funding of religious chaplains in schools.[28] Ron Williams brought the case because he wanted his children to have a secular education in a public state school, which he believed was compromised by the presence of chaplains. In the High Court, he sought to assert the separation of church and state by arguing that the scheme breached the guarantee in section 116 of the Constitution that 'no religious test shall be required as a qualification for any office or public trust under the Commonwealth'. This argument was unanimously dismissed by the Court on the basis that the chaplain working at the School held no 'office … under the Commonwealth'. However, he ultimately won the case on an entirely different ground after convincing the Court to adopt a narrow view of Commonwealth executive power in section 61 of the Constitution in a way that invalidated the Commonwealth's entry into the relevant funding agreement. The Commonwealth responded to this decision by reinstituting the scheme using remedial legislation. However, Williams brought a second High Court challenge and succeeded once again in having the scheme struck down based upon principles relating to federalism and executive power.[29]

There are of course severe limitations in relying upon legal rules to protect human rights where those legal rules are not in any way fashioned with a view to vindicating such interests. Human rights protection in such cases is simply a by-product. The legal rules may provide a level of accidental or coincidental protection for human rights, but in other cases will provide no protection at all. This means that there may simply be no constitutional remedy even for the most significant violations of human rights, such as for discrimination on the basis of race.[30] Likewise, in *Al-Kateb v Godwin* a majority of the High Court held that there was no constitutional prohibition on legislation permitting the indefinite detention of asylum seekers.[31] One of the majority judges, McHugh J, described the result as 'tragic' noting that '[e]minent lawyers who have studied the question firmly believe that the Australian Constitution should contain a Bill of Rights'.[32] However, he concluded that 'the justice or wisdom of the course taken by the Parliament is not examinable in this or any other domestic court' since '[i]t is not for courts … to determine whether the course taken by Parliament is unjust or contrary to basic human rights'.[33]

In other cases, the legal rule might be applied to frustrate human rights. For example, federalism principles were applied in the ACT same-sex marriage case to override the recognition of same-sex marriage in that jurisdiction.[34] Or, it may be that the other interest at stake underpinning the legal rule provides only superficial protection for the human right,

[27] *Plaintiff S157/2002 v Commonwealth* (2003) 211 CLR 476.
[28] *Williams v Commonwealth* (2012) 248 CLR 156.
[29] *Williams v Commonwealth (No 2)* (2014) 252 CLR 416.
[30] See *Hindmarsh Island Bridge Case* (n 8).
[31] *Al-Kateb v Godwin* (2004) 219 CLR 562.
[32] Ibid, 581, 594.
[33] Ibid, 595.
[34] *Commonwealth v Australian Capital Territory* (2013) 250 CLR 441.

perhaps because it may be possible to comply with that interest in some other way while still abrogating the right. For example, in the context of the Williams litigation, the federalism interests at stake were ultimately satisfied by directing the funding for religious chaplains in schools via the states in accordance with section 96 of the Constitution.

Furthermore, even where legislation violating human rights is challenged, the cases are not litigated or adjudicated upon within a human rights framework. Instead, complainants are forced to rely upon other features of the Constitution to argue their case. This can transform concerns over human rights into debates about the respective powers of the Commonwealth and the states or about whether the courts are being asked to exercise 'judicial' power, leaving little or no room for concepts that are central to an effective human rights discourse. The result is a decision that may or may not coincidentally involve human rights protection, and which does little to reflect, or be sensitive to, the important human rights interests at stake.

There are a very few exceptions where the High Court has infused human rights principles into a legal rule apparently having nothing to do with human rights. One example was in *University of Wollongong v Metwally*, when Gibbs CJ said that section 109, which provides that federal laws prevail over inconsistent state laws, was of 'great importance for the ordinary citizen, who is entitled to know which of two inconsistent laws he [or she] is required to observe'.[35] Deane J also said that section 109 served a 'function of protecting the individual from the injustice of being subjected to the requirements of valid and inconsistent laws of Commonwealth and State parliaments on the same subject'.[36] More recently, in *Momcilovic v The Queen*, Hayne J, in dissent on this point, held a Commonwealth drug trafficking law to be inconsistent with a state drug trafficking law.[37] He emphasised the role that section 109 played in helping those subject to a law to assess, in advance, their legal obligations.

Such examples are rare. The High Court is more often concerned to make it clear that human rights considerations have played no part in its reasoning, even if the effect of its decision is to ultimately protect those rights. An example is *Commonwealth v Tasmania* (*Tasmanian Dam Case*), in which the Court rejected a challenge by Tasmania to federal legislation blocking the building of a dam on the Franklin River in that State.[38] The case raised important questions of human rights in regard to environmental protection. Today, some other nations would decide such a matter with reference to a constitutionally protected right such as that in section 24 of the South African Constitution, which says that 'everyone has the right … to have the environment protected, for the benefit of present and future generations, through reasonable legislative and other measures that', among other things, 'secure ecologically sustainable development'.

In the absence of any like provision, the High Court decided the matter primarily by reference to the division of legislative power between the Commonwealth and the states. Indeed, any suggestion that the case was decided on grounds relating to environmental

[35] *University of Wollongong v Metwally* (1984) 158 CLR 447, 458.
[36] Ibid 476–7.
[37] *Momcilovic v The Queen* (2011) 245 CLR 1, 124, 133, 143, 146–7.
[38] *Commonwealth v Tasmania* (1983) 158 CLR 1.

protection was explicitly disavowed by the Court. The *Commonwealth Law Reports* contain the following remarkable preface to its report of the case:

> THE COURT published the following statement and the following written judgments were delivered:-
>
> STATEMENT
>
> It seems convenient to state shortly the effect of the answers given by the Court to the questions asked in these actions. The questions concern the validity of certain Commonwealth Acts, regulations and proclamations which have been brought into being for the immediate purpose of preventing the construction of the Gordon below Franklin Dam. They are strictly legal questions. The Court is in no way concerned with the question whether it is desirable or undesirable, either on the whole or from any particular point of view, that the construction of the dam should proceed. The assessment of the possible advantages and disadvantages of constructing the dam, and the balancing of the one against the other, are not matters for the Court, and the Court's judgment does not reflect any view of the merits of the dispute.[39]

Given the prospect that the decision might be perceived to have turned on environmental considerations, the Court took the step of expressly retreating into what former chief justice of the High Court, Sir Owen Dixon famously referred to as 'strict and complete legalism'.[40]

In the face of such an approach, High Court counsel are understandably wary of invoking human rights in relation to provisions that do not appear to serve such interests. In fact, it can be a strategic error to even mention terms such as 'human rights' in written or oral submissions, let alone to engage in the human rights discourse that would apply in the resolution of such matters in other countries. This is because such principles and discourse may not be seen as legitimate tools to use in the application of Australian doctrines and law that is not founded in conceptions of human rights. To seek to do so could suggest a fundamental misunderstanding of those doctrines and law, or an attempt to draw the High Court into areas of political controversy. Deciding not to invoke human rights may also reflect concerns that members of the court are antagonistic to such concepts. An extreme example of this was provided by the dissent of Heydon J in *Momcilovic v The Queen*. In a judgment sharply critical of human rights statutes and human rights principles, he stated at one point in regard to the use of human rights materials from other countries: 'The odour of human rights sanctity is sweet and addictive. It is a comforting drug stronger than poppy or mandragora or all the drowsy syrups of the world. But the effect can only be maintained over time by increasing the strength of the dose'.[41]

V. Implications from the Constitution

The most significant constitutional development for the protection of human rights in Australia has been the inferring of rights by the High Court from the text and structure

[39] Ibid, 58–59.
[40] 'Swearing in of Sir Owen Dixon as Chief Justice' (1952) 85 CLR xi, xiii.
[41] *Momcilovic* (n 37) 183.

of the Constitution. In 1992 the High Court discovered in the Constitution an implied freedom of political communication, and used this to strike down sections of the *Political Broadcasts and Political Disclosures Act 1991* (Cth) which limited political advertising on radio and television during election periods.[42] This freedom has been applied by the High Court to strike down a law only rarely. In 2017 the Court invalidated provisions of Tasmanian legislation which banned participation in protest activities on business premises.[43] Four years earlier it was used to invalidate a NSW law which banned the making of donations to political parties by corporations, unions and individuals not on the electoral roll.[44] In analogous cases relating to the election of federal parliamentarians, the High Court has also protected an implied form of a right to vote.[45]

In addition, Chapter III of the Constitution, which establishes and defines 'federal judicial power' and creates a separation of that power from legislative and executive powers, has been recognised by the High Court as the source of a number of procedural rights.[46] In *Polyukhovich v Commonwealth*, six of the seven members of the High Court held that the Commonwealth Parliament was constitutionally prohibited from enacting a Bill of Attainder; that is, that a declaration of the guilt of a particular person or class of persons by the Commonwealth Parliament would constitute an improper exercise by the Parliament of judicial power.[47] In the same case, however, the limits of the separation of powers as a source for the implication of rights were also demonstrated when the High Court was unable to reach a consensus as to whether the Australian Constitution prohibits the Commonwealth Parliament from making retrospective criminal laws. To date, the High Court has stopped short of inferring substantive rights from the separation of powers provisions.[48] For example, in *Kruger v Commonwealth*, five members of the High Court rejected the existence of an implied guarantee of general legal equality in the Australian Constitution.[49]

Implications of this kind can offer powerful protection to human rights. This is particularly evident in those implications derived from the separation of judicial power. They have, for example, posed a significant barrier to the infringement of human rights in the context of state anti-bikie legislation.[50] In such cases, the constitutional requirement that the independence and integrity of the courts be maintained has had a major impact in requiring that procedural and associated rights be observed in judicial and related proceedings.

The significance of such implications should not be overstated. They are relatively narrow in scope, and are conceived of not as human rights protections, but as expressions of the structural features of the Australian Constitution. Where human rights are protected by such implications, it is not in aid of interests such as personal dignity or autonomy. Rather,

[42] *Australian Capital Television Pty Ltd v Commonwealth* (1992) 177 CLR 106.

[43] *Brown v Tasmania* (2017) 349 ALR 398.

[44] *Unions NSW v New South Wales* (2013) 252 CLR 530.

[45] *Roach v Electoral Commissioner* (2007) 233 CLR 162; *Rowe v Electoral Commissioner* (2010) 243 CLR 1.

[46] In *Re Tracey; Ex parte Ryan* (1989) 166 CLR 518 Deane J suggested that the separation of judicial from legislative and executive power effected by the Constitution is 'the Constitution's only general guarantee of due process' (at 580).

[47] *Polyukhovich v Commonwealth* (1991) 172 CLR 106.

[48] Michael McHugh, 'Does Chapter III of the Constitution Protect Substantive as Well as Procedural Rights?' (2001) 21 *Australian Bar Review* 235.

[49] *Kruger v Commonwealth* (1997) 190 CLR 1, 44–5 (Brennan CJ), 63–8 (Dawson J), 142 (McHugh J) 112–13 (Gaudron J); 153–5 (Gummow J).

[50] See, eg, *South Australia v Totani* (2010) 242 CLR 1.

it is because such a result is demanded by the text and structure of the Constitution, which may be broadly supportive of human rights protection in many cases, but not always.

This approach has important limitations. For example, in the case of the implied freedom of political communication, the structure of the Constitution requires only freedom of communication about such matters. It does not require a general right to freedom of speech. As a result, speech having nothing to do with the choices to be made by electors, such as artistic, commercial or academic speech, receives no constitutional protection. The implied freedom is a protector of systemic public interests and is not an individual right to speak. Hence, the High Court has said that the freedom does 'not confer personal rights on individuals'[51] and that it is not a 'freedom *to* communicate. It is a freedom *from* laws that effectively prevent' political communication.[52] This affects how the freedom is applied, especially in that it focusses the legal question not upon the affected individual but upon the need for communication to be free of government interference so that people are able to elect their federal parliamentary representatives.

Limitations are also evident in regard to implications from the separation of judicial power. These applications might be useful where laws, such as anti-bikie laws, infringe rights like a fair trial or the independence of judicial institutions. However, the implications do not prevent such laws bypassing the courts entirely, such as where control orders are imposed upon bikies by executive fiat, rather than by way of an independent judicial process. As a result, so long as the structural interest in the Constitution is respected, human rights can still be abrogated.

There is also a limit to the extent to which the High Court can infer further doctrines protective of human rights. Such a course, in the absence of a national bill of rights, is contentious and has attracted strong criticism. This gave rise to frequent attacks on the Mason and Brennan Courts of the 1990s with the High Court described as an 'unfaithful servant of the Constitution', a 'pathetic … self-appointed [group of] Kings and Queens', 'gripped … in a mania for progressivism' and guilty of 'plunging Australia into the abyss'.[53] These and other terms of censure were applied whenever politicians, academics or sections of the media perceived a High Court decision to be 'activist', a pejorative term of little content which acts as a statement that a judge has stepped outside the proper bounds of his or her role. The High Court must operate in accordance with the principles of judicial independence, but equally it cannot completely ignore the reactions of the community and other arms of government to its decisions.

VI. Reception of International Law

In one key area of constitutional interpretation, the High Court has not directly recognised the protection of human rights, but has provided a mechanism that can facilitate the enactment of broad-ranging protections by the Federal Parliament. The *Tasmanian Dams* case established a broad view of the Federal Parliament's 'external affairs' power

[51] *Lange v Australian Broadcasting Corporation* (1997) 189 CLR 520, 560.

[52] *Levy v Victoria* (1997) 189 CLR 579, 622 (McHugh J).

[53] These are just a few of the examples collected in Michael Kirby's article, 'Attacks on Judges: A Universal Phenomenon' (1998) 72 *Australian Law Journal* 599.

in section 51(xxix) of the Constitution. That view means that Parliament may pass legislation to implement obligations that Australia has incurred by becoming a party to international instruments such as treaties and covenants. These may be legislated for to the extent that its laws are 'capable of being reasonably considered to be appropriate and adapted' to meeting the treaty obligation.[54]

This interpretation of the power underpins a range of important federal human rights legislation, such as federal anti-discrimination laws. For example, the *Racial Discrimination Act* relies on the International Convention on the Elimination of All Forms of Racial Discrimination and the *Sex Discrimination Act 1984* (Cth) on the Convention on the Elimination of All Forms of Discrimination Against Women.

The power has also been used in an ad hoc fashion to overcome Australia's lack of compliance with international human rights obligations. Nicholas Toonen, a Tasmanian activist, used complaint mechanisms established by the (first) *Optional Protocol of the International Covenant of Civil and Political Rights (ICCPR) 1966*, which came into force in Australia in 1991. Under Article 5(2)(b) of the *Optional Protocol*, anyone within Australian jurisdiction may, after they have 'exhausted all available domestic remedies', make a complaint to the Human Rights Committee that their ICCPR rights have been breached. Toonen complained to the Human Rights Committee that his rights were infringed by the now-repealed sections 122 and 123 of the *Criminal Code Act 1924* (Tas). Section 122 of Chapter XIV ('Crimes against Morality') of the *Code* made homosexual sexual activity between consenting adult males a crime by establishing the offence, punishable by jail, of having 'carnal knowledge of any person against the order of nature'.

The Human Rights Committee upheld Toonen's claim that the law was inconsistent with the right to privacy set out in Article 17 of the ICCPR. The Commonwealth responded by enacting the *Human Rights (Sexual Conduct) Act 1994* (Cth) under the external affairs power so as to override the Tasmanian law. Section 4(1) of that Act provided that '[s]exual conduct involving only consenting adults acting in private is not to be subject, by or under any law of the Commonwealth, a State or a Territory, to any arbitrary interference with privacy within the meaning of Article 17 of the International Covenant on Civil and Political Rights'.

The action taken by the Federal Parliament on this occasion was exceptional. United Nations bodies have found Australia to have violated the *International Covenant on Civil and Political Rights* and other human rights treaties 45 times. Remedy Australia, a non-government organisation that tracks Australia's compliance with United Nations decisions, has calculated that these breaches have been met with an adequate remedy in only 13 per cent of cases.[55]

More broadly, the interpretation reached by the external affairs power opens up the possibility that the power could be used to enact a national bill of rights. Indeed, in anticipating the outcome of the *Tasmanian Dams* case, the Whitlam Government had sought to follow this approach. In 1973, Attorney-General Lionel Murphy introduced the Human Rights Bill into the Federal Parliament. The Bill would have implemented the International Covenant on Civil and Political Rights in Australia by protecting a range of rights, including freedom of expression and movement, and the right to marry. Murphy promoted the Bill on

[54] *Tasmanian Dam* case (n 38) 259–60 (Deane J).
[55] http://remedy.org.au/.

the basis that the Constitution provides scant protection for rights, arguing that 'although we believe these rights to be basic to our democratic society, they now receive remarkably little legal protection in Australia'.[56] He went on:

> What protection is given by the Australian Constitution is minimal and does not touch the most significant of these rights ... Ideally, in my view, a bill of rights should be written into the Australian Constitution ... [T]he enactment of this legislation will be a significant milestone in the political maturity of Australia. It will help to make Australian society more free and more just.[57]

Under section 109 of the Constitution, the rights listed in Murphy's legislation would have overridden inconsistent state legislation. It also provided that Commonwealth legislation would be ineffective if it breached any of the rights listed in the Bill, unless the statute included an express exemption from its operation. The Bill went further than subsequent attempts at a statutory charter of rights by declaring that the listed rights could be enforced not only against governments but also against the private sector. The Human Rights Bill met strong political opposition. Because the International Covenant on Civil and Political Rights had not yet received the necessary number of ratifications to come into force, the government did not press the Bill and it lapsed in early 1974.

Soon after the decision in the *Tasmanian Dams* case, Senator Gareth Evans, Attorney-General in the Hawke Government, prepared a charter of rights that would also have implemented rights recognised in international law. Although the proposal was given cabinet support, it was not introduced into Parliament. Lionel Bowen, who replaced Evans as Attorney-General after the 1984 federal election, introduced in 1985 a redrafted and watered-down bill, the Australian Human Rights Bill. As Bowen indicated in his second reading speech to the Bill, its centrepiece was a self-contained bill of rights 'which further implements [the] International Covenant on Civil and Political Rights' in reliance upon the external affairs power. Although it was passed by the House of Representatives, the Bill was withdrawn from the Senate in 1986.

The Rudd Government established a national human rights consultation chaired by Father Frank Brennan. The report of that committee of September 2009 concluded that 'Australia measures well against many other countries in terms of its human rights protection', and that '[m]any Australians enjoy a standard of living that is at least equal to that in other First World countries and rarely would need to reflect on human rights or whether they are adequately protected'.[58] However, it also stated that Australia's 'record is not perfect', and identified groups of people that needed 'greater protection (or at least assistance in exercising their rights) [such as] children, people with a mental illness, the elderly, people with disabilities, carers, and Indigenous Australians (particularly those in remote areas)'. It made a raft of recommendations, including that the Federal Parliament enact a national human rights act. In making this recommendation, the committee stated:

> **Source of power**
>
> The Federal Parliament's powers to make laws are limited to those specified in the Constitution. Although there is no specific power to make laws in relation to human rights, the external affairs

[56] Commonwealth, *Parliamentary Debates*, Senate, 21 November 1973, 1972.

[57] Ibid, 1972–74.

[58] National Human Rights Consultation Committee, *National Human Rights Consultation Report* (2009) at 97–99.

> power in s 51(xxix) of the Constitution would provide the basis for legislation that implements Australia's obligations under international law.
>
> If a Human Rights Act included provisions that extend beyond Australia's obligations under international law, the provisions would need to be based on a different source of power under the Constitution or on a referral of powers from the states.
>
> The Solicitor-General advised the Committee that the external affairs power would support the enactment of a Human Rights Act that included rights from the International Covenant on Civil and Political Rights only … The Solicitor-General noted, however, that including rights from the International Covenant on Economic, Social and Cultural Rights would be "more problematic", since they could lack "sufficient specificity" to support the making of a law under the external affairs power.

The suggestion here as to the scope to implement the International Covenant on Economic, Social and Cultural Rights by using the external affairs power is surprising, and contentious. It is something that could only be resolved by the question being tested in the High Court. What is clear though is that if Australia is to achieve a national human rights act that extends at least as far as providing comprehensive protection for civil and political rights, the most likely path for this is through the implementation of Australia's international human rights obligations via use of the external affairs power.

VII. Conclusion

Australia has adopted a constitutional design that constrains the High Court in its ability to protect human rights. The Court may do so where a statute provides such protection, but many rights lack any statutory backing, and even where they do, this is subject to amendment or repeal. It has also developed common law mechanisms that enable it to prefer human rights-compliant interpretations of statutes over other approaches. This approach can also prove significant, but is vulnerable to any statute that expresses a clear intent by Parliament to abrogate human rights.

In this context, the Constitution can play a pivotal role. In some cases, a human rights respecting outcome may be reached by way of applying constitutional principles that apparently have nothing to do with human rights protection. In other cases, the High Court may be able to apply an implication from the Constitution protective of human rights, such as the implied freedom of political communication.

These approaches also have their limits and offer no possibility of comprehensive human rights protection. Inevitably, they mean that significant abrogations of human rights will not be remedied in the courts. This is why another aspect of the High Court's interpretation of the Constitution may prove to be of greater significance in the longer term. This is its interpretation of the external affairs power so as to permit the enactment of a domestic national human rights instrument through the implementation of international human rights conventions. It means that Parliament has the capacity to bring about a national bill of rights. If this does occur, the High Court will have a broader canvas upon which to determine human rights matters and may even ultimately come to play a similar role to like courts in other nations.

3

Chapter III of the *Constitution* and the Protection of Due Process Rights

ANTHONY GRAY

This chapter will explore the potentiality of Chapter III of the Australian Constitution to protect due process rights commonly associated with criminal process. The word 'potential' is appropriate because, although there have been a small number of cases which have apparently realised this potential, development of the jurisprudence at this level remains nascent, and the justices' apparent commitment to the protection of due process rights tentative at best. It can only be hoped that a future High Court will nurture and develop the seeds that have been planted by previous and current members of the High Court. The clear reticence among the current court to develop constitutional protection of due process rights is somewhat puzzling.

It is trite to observe that the founding fathers of Australia sought to meld what they considered to be the best features of the two great models they had before them, that of the parliamentary supremacy infused model of the UK, involving an unwritten constitution and a unitary government, and the republican, federalist model of the US, with an express bill of rights. They took what they considered to be the best aspects of the two. Their genius in doing so, providing a platform for a generally very stable system of representative government and democracy, should be acknowledged. On virtually any measure, Australia is a very successful nation. Its foundational constitutional document deserves at least some of the credit.

On the question of rights protection, the founding fathers leaned very heavily towards the UK model of 'rights protection', such as it was. The model was premised on the right of the democratically elected Parliament to pass any law it wished. Under that model, a court could not declare a law to be invalid due to incompatibility with the Constitution.[1] Every law passed by Parliament was, for that reason, valid. Dicey in particular would provide the intellectual heft for such a theory, through his doctrine of parliamentary supremacy.[2] It would also find support through principles of utilitarianism, on the assumption that Parliament would, in general at least, pass laws for the 'greatest good for the greatest number'.

[1] The recent doubts expressed on this principle by members of the UK House of Lords and then Supreme Court were, of course, inconceivable at the time the Australian Constitution was forged: see, eg, *R (Jackson) v Attorney-General* [2006] 1 AC 262, 302 (Lord Steyn) and 303–4 (Lord Hope).

[2] AV Dicey, *An Introduction to the Study of the Law of the Constitution* 8th edn (London, Macmillan, 1915).

It might also find some intellectual roots in the Hobbesian idea of a strong government being needed to curb the 'brutish' citizenry, and maintain strong public order. In such a world, obviously human rights protection is of a relatively minor order.

Of course, Dicey's 'guarantee' of human rights protection was his conception of the rule of law, under which there would be no exercise of state power against an individual without legislative backing, seeking to provide insurance against the kind of exercise of arbitrary, unbridled power of which the British had unhappy experience prior to 1688. It would be supplemented by the principle of legality, under which statutes would (or might) be interpreted in a rights-sensitive manner, including a presumption that Parliament did not intend to abrogate fundamental liberties, in the absence of clearly expressed intention.[3] It would be further supplemented with the claim that the threat of the 'ballot box' would curb any legislature otherwise intent on passing laws invasive of human rights. They would think twice about doing so, because they would likely suffer retribution at election time.

On a personal level, the life experience of the founding fathers was also important. They were members of the elite in colonial society. They would not typically have experienced legal injustice of the kind that might have fired their enthusiasm for rights protection. Obviously, this presents a sharp contrast with the experience of many Americans leading up to the events of 1776, with perceived gross injustice committed on the American people, as the British sought to pay for ruinous wars with punitive taxation arrangements on colonies, together with a lack of parliamentary representation, lack of jury trial rights etc.

Individuals sometimes look at the seating arrangements at functions to determine their status at a particular event. In the Australian Constitution, human rights barely enjoy a seat at the table. They have no table of their own; there are eight chapters (tables) in the Australian Constitution, each devoted to other topics. A few express rights protections are scattered here and there. Their main concern seems to be discrimination against individuals based on their residence, together with a virtually impotent right to freedom of religion, right to trial by jury, and (express) right to vote. There is a right to compensation in cases of property confiscation by the Commonwealth (only).[4] This is of the order of a few chairs at the back of the room, almost as an afterthought. I will not dwell on the interpretation of these 'rights' by the High Court, since that is considered to be beyond the scope of this chapter, but in general terms the High Court's interpretation of these rights has respectfully been somewhat equivalent to the chiselling off of one or two legs of these chairs.[5]

The conversation about implied constitutional rights protection takes place within the context of this generally very modest record of protection of express human rights. Several ironies may be noted here. Firstly, while the High Court's record of interpreting express human rights protections has been modest at best, somewhat perversely its record of developing implied human rights in the Constitution has been stronger.[6] Secondly, when seeking to defend the correctness of the High Court implying principles in the Constitution,

[3] See ch 18.

[4] This right comes in the form of a legislative power granted to the federal parliament to enact laws for the acquisition of property on just terms: Australian Constitution, s 51(xxxi). It follows that any law that enables the acquisition of property on unjust terms, such as by seizure, is invalid.

[5] Anthony Gray, *Criminal Due Process and Chapter III of the Australian Constitution* (Annandale, Federation Press, 2016) 16–18.

[6] The mixed record of the High Court on this issue is explained in ch 4.

one generally cites the likes of early High Court decisions like *R v Smithers*,[7] where the High Court, including the founding fathers, implied concepts into the Constitution. Thus, the founding fathers, heavily infused in the legal positivism of Diceyanism as they were, clearly supported the notion that the Australian Constitution contained implications, in a most un-Diceyan way. Further, another champion of making implications into the Constitution[8] was the 'strict and complete' legalist Sir Owen Dixon.[9] One might respectfully suggest that the making of implications is far from the strict and complete legalism (apparently) espoused by that great judge.

I. Development of Chapter III Jurisprudence

The development of Chapter III jurisprudence can be traced back to the period of the 1930s–1950s. At one level, a battle of two views occurred. The first was that there was no strict separation of powers in the Australian Constitution. In simple terms, this was the Latham CJ view. He attracted a majority to this view in *R v Federal Court of Bankruptcy; Ex Parte Lowenstein* in 1937,[10] where the court upheld the validity of a provision empowering a judge both to charge a person with, and determine the charge of, bankruptcy. This attracted the well-known dissent of Dixon J, together with Evatt J. Here Dixon J espoused the classic separation of powers principle, that judicial power must be reposed only in a judicial body, and vice versa.[11] With the departure of Latham CJ from the court in 1952, and the ascension of Sir Owen Dixon to that position, the Dixon view would soon prevail. Though some version of that position was apparently reached in the 1955 decision in *R v Richards; Ex Parte Fitzpatrick and Browne*,[12] the subsequent *Boilermakers* case is regarded as the landmark case where a bare majority (4:3) of the High Court accepted the twin propositions that judicial power could only be exercised by bodies recognised as courts for the purposes of Chapter III of the Constitution, and that non-judicial power could only be exercised by non-judicial bodies.[13]

As important as this decision was, its effect remained relatively modest. For a period from 1956 until the early 1990s, the potential of that doctrine to protect human rights was completely unrealised. On a personal note, I studied Constitutional Law as an undergraduate student in the year 1990, and at that time the focus of the 'separation of powers' principle was confined to a consideration of what was the nature of judicial power, and whether the body exercising given power was to be recognised as a Chapter III court or not. There was no inkling at this time of the potential for the doctrine to protect fundamental due process rights, either independently or through the prism of protecting fundamental characteristics of courts or judicial process, which include due process.

[7] (1912) 16 CLR 99.

[8] *West v Commissioner of Taxation* (NSW) (1937) 56 CLR 657, 681.

[9] Sir Owen Dixon, 'Address Upon Being Sworn in as Chief Justice' (1952) 85 CLR xiv.

[10] (1937) 59 CLR 556.

[11] Ibid, 585 (Dixon and Evatt JJ, dissenting).

[12] (1955) 92 CLR 157.

[13] *R v Kirby; Ex Parte Boilermakers' Society of Australia* (1956) 94 CLR 254 (Dixon CJ, McTiernan, Fullagar and Kitto JJ; Williams, Webb and Taylor JJ dissenting).

The late 1980s-early 1990s was to be a pivotal time in the development of Chapter III. This was during the era of the Sir Anthony Mason court, where the court was well known for development, sometimes radical, of various areas of common law, and the development of constitutional law doctrine. This is not the place to consider the relative pros and cons of various legal reforms made by the Mason court, but the development of Chapter III jurisprudence in this era is consistent with the Mason court's general tendencies in terms of progressive constitutional interpretation, including implied freedoms/rights, and commitment to law reform.

Thus, in 1989 in *Re Tracey; Ex Parte Ryan*,[14] Deane J classically referred to Chapter III as the Constitution's 'only general guarantee of due process'. He said the consequences of that doctrine were far-reaching, referring to the court's exclusive power over issues like determining guilt or innocence, and whether members of other branches of government have acted within power. He would find an intellectual fellow traveller in Gaudron J, who in cases such as *Polyukovich*[15] in 1991 would affirm her belief that Chapter III protected key features of judicial process. Thus in that case, Deane and Gaudron JJ dissented on the constitutional validity of legislation providing for retrospective criminality for war crimes, on the basis that such a law involved justices in proceedings that were so foreign to typical judicial process so as to make it an affront to justice to require judges to participate in such a process.

Members of the High Court apparently saw the potential of Chapter III to protect key characteristics of judicial process from parliamentary interference, and through this prism, fundamental due process rights. In the very next year in *Leeth v Commonwealth*,[16] Mason CJ, Dawson and McHugh JJ explained that legislation which required a court to depart from principles of natural justice would be invalid because it would be requiring a court to abandon one of its essential attributes and characteristics. In the same year in *Chu Kheng Lim*,[17] Brennan, Deane and Dawson JJ said legislation that required or authorised a court to act in a manner contrary to the essential characteristics of a court or the nature of judicial power was constitutionally invalid. In the same year, a majority of the Court found that an accused had the right to a fair trial at common law, and proceedings could be stayed if this were in peril.[18] At least Deane and Gaudron JJ accorded this constitutional status.[19]

In the important 1995 decision of *Grollo v Palmer*,[20] a majority of the court developed the so-called 'incompatibility' doctrine that had been partly reasoned in earlier cases. The court found that constitutional separation of powers issues would arise if:

(a) Judges were performing non-judicial functions of such a nature that their capacity to perform judicial functions with integrity was being compromised or impaired; or
(b) Judges were performing non-judicial functions of such a nature that public confidence in the integrity of the judiciary as an institution or the capacity of an individual judge to perform their functions with integrity was being diminished.[21]

[14] (1989) 166 CLR 518, 580.
[15] *Polyukovich v Commonwealth* (1991) 172 CLR 501, 703–704.
[16] (1992) 174 CLR 455, 470.
[17] (1992) 176 CLR 1, 27.
[18] *Dietrich v The Queen* (1992) 177 CLR 292.
[19] Ibid, 326 (Deane J) and 362 (Gaudron J). The others did not expressly consider the question.
[20] (1995) 184 CLR 348.
[21] *Grollo v Palmer* (1995) 184 CLR 348, 364–365 (Brennan CJ Deane Dawson and Toohey JJ).

However, it was the landmark decision of *Kable v Director of Public Prosecutions* (NSW)[22] that planted the separation of powers principle on solid ground as a means of rights protection. The case was decided shortly after the departure of Sir Anthony Mason as Chief Justice. Sir William Deane had also just left the court. At the time of the *Kable* decision, William Gummow had recently been appointed, and Michael Kirby had not yet been appointed. Thus, the dynamics of the court had changed in a way that was not yet evident. Two of the leading protagonists in progressive constitutional interpretation and development of Chapter III in due process protection had left the court. It was not clear the extent to which their positions would survive changes on the court. New Chief Justice Sir Gerard Brennan could not be said to have been a leading player in development of Chapter III jurisprudence with a view to due process protection.

The highly unusual legislation at issue named one individual, Gregory Wayne Kable, against whom it was directed.[23] It permitted a state court, upon application by the government, to continue Kable's continued incarceration, if the court believed that it was more likely than not that he would re-offend if released from jail. The ordinary rules of evidence would not apply, and the court was directed that its most important consideration should be community protection. Kable had been in jail for the manslaughter of his wife. He had served his full term, and was due to be released. He had allegedly made threats that he would injure members of his wife's family when he was released. Rather than charge Kable with an offence in relation to these alleged threats, the government proposed legislation unique in Australia's legal history, naming him in the Act. Originally, the proposed legislation was generic, not naming an individual, but the government could only get its proposed legislation through Parliament by restricting it, in the end to one named individual. It was this legislative concession that was to confound the legislation when it was challenged at High Court level. The state Parliament was probably quite confident of the validity of its legislation. A decade earlier, that state's highest court had confirmed there was no separation of powers at state constitutional level.[24]

By a majority of 4:2, the High Court invalidated the legislation.[25] The blandly named *Community Protection Act 1994* (NSW) involved the Supreme Court of New South Wales in a legislative plan to incarcerate a named individual. It sought to use the court's reputation to give legitimacy to the proceedings. The proceedings were highly anomalous. They asked a court to order a person's incarceration based on nothing more than an assessment of the likelihood that they would re-offend. This was the antithesis of the judicial process. Effectively, a person was being punished without any anterior finding of guilt. In terms that would become important in later cases, Gummow J explained that the law was invalid because it undermined the 'institutional integrity' of state courts.[26] The majority overcame past precedents that had apparently found no strict separation of powers at state level by acknowledging an integrated structure of courts in Australia. State courts, or at least state

[22] (1996) 189 CLR 51.

[23] Such legislation is now not so rare: see Matthew Groves, 'A Life Without Hope: Prisoners and the Victorian Charter' (2018) 42 *Criminal Law Journal* 353.

[24] *Building Construction Employees and Builders' Labourers Federation of New South Wales v Minister for Industrial Relations* (1986) 7 NSWLR 372. This holding applied to all State Constitutions.

[25] Toohey McHugh Gaudron and Gummow JJ held the legislation invalid. Brennan CJ and Dawson J dissented.

[26] (1996) 189 CLR 51, 128.

courts capable of exercising federal jurisdiction, were part of that hierarchy. Thus, to that extent the principle of separation of powers was drawn down from the federal level to the state level.

Members of the High Court expressed their reasoning in terms of public confidence in the judiciary.[27] At this juncture, it was said that legislation would be invalid if it caused a loss of public confidence in the judiciary, for instance that the public would wonder about the court's impartiality and independence from government.

Subsequent decisions attempted to articulate the extent to which Chapter III protected features of courts. A leading example is the judgment of Gaudron J in *Nicholas v The Queen*:

> Consistency with the essential character of a court and with the nature of judicial power necessitates that a court not be required or authorised to proceed in a manner that does not ensure equality before the law, impartiality and the appearance of impartiality, the right of a party to meet the case made against him or her, the independent determination of the matter in controversy by application of the law to facts determined in accordance with rules and procedures which truly permit the facts to be ascertained and, in the case of criminal proceedings, the determination of guilt or innocence by means of a fair trial according to law … a court cannot be required or authorised to proceed in any manner which involves an abuse of process, which would render its proceedings inefficacious or which brings or tends to bring the administration of justice into disrepute.[28]

Subsequently, in several decisions the High Court has found that legislation is constitutionally invalid due to a breach of the requirements of Chapter III. For instance, it invalidated legislation in *South Australia v Totani*[29] because the legislation removed all decisional independence from the Magistrates Court of South Australia. The Magistrates Court was required to make a control order against members of an organisation declared to be criminal by the state attorney-general. It had no discretion other than to make the order. In *Wainohu v New South Wales,*[30] the High Court invalidated legislation that precluded the Supreme Court of NSW from giving reasons. The High Court found that it was an essential characteristic of judicial power that judges give reasons for their decisions, such that legislation that precluded them from doing so undermined an essential characteristic of judicial power, and for that reason was invalid. In *International Finance Trust*[31] legislation that cast a reverse onus onto a person accused of wrongdoing, in circumstances where a court was required to hear proceedings in the absence of one of the parties concerned, was held to be invalid. It was generally a requirement of court proceedings that they be open and accessible to the public, and that both parties should be present at the proceeding and able to make submissions. It was also generally the position that the party making accusations had the obligation to prove them, not for the accused to prove innocence. At state level, a court declared invalid legislation that allowed the state attorney general to effectively seek the overturning of a court decision by the head of the executive arm of government.[32]

[27] Ibid, 98 (Toohey J), 107 (Gaudron J) and 116 (McHugh J).

[28] (1998) 193 CLR 173, 208–209; cited with evident approval by six members of the Court in *Bass v Permanent Trustee Co Ltd* (1999) 198 CLR 334, 359 (Gleeson CJ, Gaudron, McHugh, Gummow, Hayne and Callinan JJ).

[29] (2010) 242 CLR 1.

[30] (2011) 243 CLR 181.

[31] (2009) 240 CLR 319.

[32] *Attorney-General (Qld) v Lawrence* [2013] QCA 364; (2013) 237 A Crim R 109.

It should be observed that the High Court's evident primary concern is with the institutional integrity of the courts. Laws that pose dangers to the institutional integrity of courts are those vulnerable to challenge. Some laws that offend the institutional integrity of courts also impact on due process rights. Thus, the protection afforded due process rights by these principles is indirect and derivative in nature. The law has moved to some extent away from the kind of 'public confidence' principles that were evident in *Kable*, though the court has linked public confidence with institutional integrity in saying that whilst damage to institutional integrity is the touchstone of Chapter III invalidity, a law which offends a court's institutional integrity will likely undermine public confidence in the judiciary.

Recently, members of the High Court have emphasised that a standard criminal process is one that is accusatorial, adversarial and usually held in open court.[33] But such statements were characteristically timid, in that the justices who articulated them did not make the obvious connection between them and the requirements of Chapter III, expressly declining to determine whether there was a constitutional limit to their alteration. With respect, this is straining at a gnat. The court has already determined that Chapter III protects fundamental characteristics of court process. If a judge says that a fundamental characteristic of judicial process is that it is accusatorial, adversarial and open, that is surely according them Chapter III protection. But this point is not made clear in those decisions. The judges' reticence, timidity and reluctance in this area is somewhat puzzling.

Public and political perceptions of increased lawlessness within some motorcycle clubs have fed demands for legislative responses.[34] While the High Court held the South Australian version of anti-motorcycle gang legislation invalid in *Totani*, it has rejected two challenges to Queensland's equivalent legislation. The first iteration of these laws in Queensland, the *Criminal Organisation Act 2009* (Qld), permitted the government to seek an order from the courts declaring that an organisation was criminal in nature. The government could then in a subsequent application seek to have a control order made with respect to members of the declared organisation. The court's discretion in that regard helped to save the legislation from invalidity.[35] Of more interest was the use of 'criminal intelligence' material in proceedings under the Act. The court was empowered to declare information said to support the application was 'criminal intelligence'. So declared, that information would be presented in closed court. Neither members of the group that would be affected by the proceedings nor their legal representatives would be present when that evidence was presented. Obviously, the veracity or completeness of the information could not be tested through the traditional rubric of cross-examination.

One might have thought that past statements from the High Court that natural justice was an inherent characteristic of judicial process could mean the legislation was invalid. Clearly, what the legislation contemplated was the antithesis of natural justice. The court justified the validity of the legislation on the basis the court could consider the appropriate weight to place on evidence that had not been the subject of cross-examination.[36]

[33] *X7 v Australian Crime Commission* (2013) 248 CLR 92, 140 (Hayne and Bell JJ), 153 (Kiefel J).

[34] Many such clubs are seen as a form of organised crime – criminal gangs involved in drug trafficking and other related crimes.

[35] *Assistant Commissioner Condon v Pompano Pty Ltd* (2013) 252 CLR 38, 75 (French CJ), 89–90 and 95 (Hayne Crennan Kiefel and Bell JJ), and 115 (Gageler J).

[36] *Assistant Commissioner Condon v Pompano Pty Ltd* (2013) 252 CLR 38.

With a change of government in Queensland, even more extreme legislation was implemented. Despite never having actually used the 2009 version to declare any organisation to be criminal, and despite having successfully defended its constitutionality in the High Court, a new government decided more extreme measures were necessary. Rather than provide for the government to go to the court seeking an order that an organisation should be banned, with the court considering various criteria, the new government rushed through Parliament legislation which simply named and declared 26 organisations to be criminal. No criteria were published explaining why these organisations had been chosen. The court's role in making orders banning organisations had effectively been bypassed. These reforms were coupled with legislation making it a crime for members of declared organisations to be in public together, even though there was no evidence they were meeting for illicit purposes. It included the introduction of a supercharged mandatory sentencing regime, providing for minimum 15- or 25-year jail terms, to be served entirely in correctional facilities, for offences committed as part of the activities of a declared organisation, and Star-Chamber like proceedings by which those thought to have information about the activities of a relevant organisation could be forced, on pain of jail terms, to answer questions. It was specifically not a defence for the person affected to decline to answer questions on the basis they feared reprisals against their family or themselves for doing so.[37]

Now, one might have thought there was a reasonable argument that such legislation was contrary to the requirements of Chapter III of the Constitution. If it was constitutionally acceptable for a court to be asked to declare an organisation to be criminal, based on criteria, could it be constitutionally acceptable for Parliament to simply declare named organisations to be criminal? On one view, the power to declare an organisation to be criminal, with its attendant serious consequences for members, was judicial in nature. It might then be offensive for the same power to be exercised by the legislature, if separation of powers principles were properly applied. However, only Hayne J in dissent accepted this.[38] One might also quibble with legislation providing for mandatory penalties that bear no reasonable relation to the essential criminality of what was involved in the case. However, no member of the High Court invalidated the Queensland legislation on that basis. The relevant legislation provided for a minimum 15-year jail term for any member of a declared organisation proven to have committed various offences pursuant to the association's purposes, and a minimum 25-year jail term if the relevant person was an officer of a declared association.[39] Various offences were included, including simple drug possession. It is suggested most reasonable individuals would find the imposition of a minimum mandatory jail term of 25 years on the secretary of a banned motorcycle club for simple drug possession to be the very antithesis of justice. However, in this case and subsequently, the High Court has rejected any challenge to mandatory sentencing laws based on Chapter III.[40]

[37] The extraordinary content of this legislation is explained in Andrew Trotter and Harry Hobbs, 'The Great Leap Backwards: Criminal Law Reform with the Hon Jarrod Bleijie' (2014) 36 *Sydney Law Review* 1.

[38] Hayne J accepted this on the basis that the legislation treated as being equivalent a judicial decision that an organisation ought to be prescribed and a legislature or executive decision that an organisation ought to be prescribed. He said it was offensive to Chapter III to ask courts to treat these decisions as equivalent: 93.

[39] *Vicious Lawless Association Disestablishment Act 2013* (Qld). This Act was repealed in 2016.

[40] *Magaming v The Queen* (2013) 252 CLR 381.

A brave court might also be tempted to decide that legislation literally providing for guilt by association, still in the Queensland *Criminal Code 1899*[41] but also evident in anti-consorting legislation in other states, is so contrary to our traditions of criminal law, under which guilt is personal and is based on actually committing activity which could justifiably attract criminal sanction, as to be questionable under Chapter III. However, a constitutional challenge to NSW guilt by association legislation, arguing that it is offensive to Chapter III, or is contrary to an implied constitutional freedom of association, was rejected by the High Court.[42]

Space restrictions do not allow a discussion of all of the relevant cases.[43] In summary, it may be said that the High Court has found the following to be essential characteristics of courts that are or may be protected from interference by parliaments because of Chapter III of the Constitution:

(a) natural justice, including the right of both parties to a dispute to present submissions to the decision maker prior to the decision;[44]
(b) procedural fairness;[45]
(c) decisional independence;[46]
(d) the provision of reasons;[47]
(e) hearings in open court, or at least court discretion to hear matters in open court;[48]
(f) courts resolve disputes and controversies between parties;[49]
(g) courts consider matters involving specific allegations of wrongdoing;[50]
(h) courts apply legal standards to resolve factual situations;[51]
(i) courts must have jurisdiction to correct jurisdictional errors of lower courts;[52]

[41] Sections 60A and 60B.

[42] *Tajjour v New South Wales* (2014) 254 CLR 508.

[43] See Anthony Gray, *Criminal Due Process and Chapter III of the Australian Constitution* (Annandale, Federation Press, 2016), Anthony Gray, 'Constitutionally Protected Due Process and the Use of Criminal Intelligence Provisions' (2014) 37 *University of New South Wales Law Journal* 125, and Rebecca Ananian-Welsh and George Williams, 'Judicial Independence from the Executive: A First Principles Review of the Australian Cases' (2014) 40 *Monash University Law Review* 593; Rebecca Ananian-Welsh, 'A Path to Purposive Formalism: Interpreting Chapter III for Judicial Independence and Impartiality' (2012) 39 *Monash University Law Review* 66.

[44] *Bass v Permanent Trustee* (1999) 198 CLR 334, 359 where Gleeson CJ, Gaudron, McHugh, Gummow, McHugh, Hayne and Callinan JJ stated that 'judicial power involves the application of the relevant law to facts as found in proceedings conducted in accordance with the judicial process. And that requires that the parties be given an opportunity to present their evidence and to challenge the evidence led against them'. But it is clear that natural justice can be excluded from the powers conferred on executive agencies and bureaucrats under Ch II of the Constitution. See, eg, *Saeed v Minister for Immigration and Citizenship* (2010) 241 CLR 252.

[45] *Wainohu v New South Wales* (2011) 243 CLR 181, 208 (French CJ and Kiefel JJ), 225–226 (Gummow, Hayne, Crennan and Bell JJ).

[46] *South Australia v Totani* (2010) 242 CLR 1, 20 (French CJ), 66 (Gummow J), 87 (Hayne J), 157 (Crennan and Bell JJ), 172–173 (Kiefel J).

[47] *Wainohu v New South Wales* (2011) 243 CLR 181, 213 (French CJ and Kiefel J), 225 (Gummow, Hayne, Crennan and Bell JJ).

[48] *International Finance Trust Co Ltd v New South Wales Crime Commission* (2009) 240 CLR 319, 366 (Gummow and Bell JJ), 379 (Heydon J).

[49] *Momcilovic v The Queen* (2011) 245 CLR 1, 64–65 (French CJ), 162 (Heydon J), 222–223 (Crennan and Kiefel JJ); *Huddart Parker and Co Pty Ltd v Moorehead* (1908) 8 CLR 330, 357) (Griffith CJ, Barton J agreeing).

[50] *Kirk v Industrial Court* (NSW) (2010) 239 CLR 531, 557–559 (French CJ, Gummow, Hayne, Crennan, Kiefel, and Bell JJ).

[51] *Nicholas v The Queen* (1998) 198 CLR 173, 208–209 (Gaudron J).

[52] *Kirk v Industrial Court* (NSW) (2010) 239 CLR 531.

(j) courts' decisions are final;[53]
(k) courts have power to determine how court proceedings are to be run, including the dress of judges;[54]
(l) the exclusive power to adjudicate and punish criminality;[55]
(m) adversarial nature of proceedings;[56]
(n) accusatorial nature of proceedings.[57]

The following have been determined to not necessarily be considered essential characteristics of courts:

(a) imposition of sentences that bear a reasonable proportionality to the accused's level of criminality;[58]
(b) the power to declare an organisation to be criminal;[59]
(c) that evidence only be derived voluntarily, in the sense that the threat of punishment for failing to answer questions has not been utilised;[60]
(d) that criminal proceedings are only appropriate for acts appropriately classified as criminal, for instance involving mens rea, as opposed to provisions literally criminalising mere association;[61]
(e) open courts – the Court has upheld the validity of provisions by which evidence is given in secret;[62]
(f) cross-examination – the court has upheld the validity of provisions by which evidence has not been tested by cross-examination.[63]

A grey area exists in relation to rules of evidence. There have been suggestions that the Parliament has power to alter rules of evidence. Some argue that the limit of this power is in relation to 'matters of guilt or innocence'.[64] Some argue Parliament can legislate on rules of evidence provided such regulation is 'reasonable'.[65] This means that fundamental rules of evidence such as the burden and standard of proof might be alterable by Parliament. Some have suggested that legislation deeming particular elements of an offence to have been satisfied might be constitutionally invalid.[66] Others have indicated it is fundamental that our legal system is 'accusatorial' and 'adversarial'.[67] These various statements are contradictory. Respectfully, there is not a clear view on the extent to which Parliament can constitutionally alter the rules of evidence, and what limits, if any, exist in relation to Parliament's power to do so.

[53] *Attorney-General (Qld) v Lawrence* [2013] QCA 364; (2013) A Crim R 109.
[54] *Russell v Russell* (1976) 134 CLR 495.
[55] *Chu Kheng Lim v Commonwealth* (1992) 176 CLR 1.
[56] *X7 v Australian Crime Commission* (2013) 148 CLR 92.
[57] Ibid.
[58] *Magaming v The Queen* (2013) 252 CLR 381; *Kuczborski v Queensland* (2014) 254 CLR 51.
[59] *Kuczborski v Queensland* (2014) 254 CLR 51.
[60] Ibid.
[61] *Tajjour v New South Wales* (2014) 254 CLR 508; *Kuczborski v Queensland* (2014) 254 CLR 51.
[62] *Assistant Commissioner Condon v Pompano Pty Ltd* (2013) 252 CLR 38.
[63] ibid.
[64] *Nicholas v The Queen* (1998) 193 CLR 173, 277–278 (dissenting in the result).
[65] Ibid, 190 (Brennan CJ); *Williamson v Ah On* (1926) 39 CLR 95, 116 (Isaacs J, with whom Powers J agreed).
[66] Ibid, 238 (Gummow J).
[67] *X7 v Australian Crime Commission* (2013) 248 CLR 92, 134–135 (Hayne and Bell JJ), 153 (Kiefel J)(only five judges heard the case); *Lee v New South Wales Crime Commission* (2013) 251 CLR 196, 234 (Hayne J), 261 (Kiefel J) and 294 (Bell J).

Having summarised succinctly the current state of play regarding the extent to which Chapter III protects due process rights, I will now consider some specific contexts in which current legislation operates to impinge on fundamental due process rights. The extent of this is the subject of a detailed report by the Australian Law Reform Commission.[68] If Chapter III were applied more robustly than has previously been the case, it could be utilised to strike at the kinds of laws discussed below. Given that Chapter III protects fundamental features of judicial process, history will be even more important than usual. The fact that a particular current feature of our justice system has a long history will, of course, be relevant in determining the extent to which it might be considered 'fundamental' and, by implication, constitutionally protected by Chapter III.

II. Potential for Chapter III to Protect Presumption of Innocence

Legislation in Australia is increasingly abrogating the presumption of innocence. The Institute of Public Affairs, a conservative think tank, counted 48 federal laws that abrogated the presumption. It has been the subject of a specific chapter by the Australian Law Reform Commission in the context of its discussion of traditional rights and freedoms.

The presumption is of ancient vintage. It is apparent in the *Code of Hammurabi* (1792–1750BC).[69] Roman law accepted that the burden of proof lay on the accuser.[70] A fourth century constitution made it clear that the accuser was required to have specific proof of allegations, with doubt to be resolved in favour of the accused.[71] English law did not utilise the presumption at a time when criminal matters were dealt with via trial by ordeal, battle or compurgation, but as these more primitive methods waned, the presumption of innocence was established. Decision makers were wary of the consequences for them, including in the next world, if they made a wrong judgment against someone.[72] Thus, the maxim of when in doubt, acquit took hold. It is evident in the work of Bracton in the thirteenth century,[73] and case reports from that time.[74] Not every court applied it; it was not

[68] Australian Law Reform Commission, *Traditional Rights and Freedoms - Encroachment by Commonwealth Laws* (Report 129, 2015). See also Simon Breheny and Morgan Begg, *The State of Fundamental Legal Rights in Australia: An Audit of Federal Law* (Institute of Public Affairs, 2014).

[69] Allen Godbey, 'The Place of the Code of Hammurabi' (1905) 15 *The Monist* 199, 210: 'it is a fundamental principle of the Code of Hammurabi that the presumption is always in favour of the innocence of the accused: the burden of proof is thrown upon the accuser … not merely is the burden of proof upon the accuser, but in all primitive society (sic) the entire burden of accusation or indictment falls upon him. In this respect, the legal procedure of Babylonia seems to have been that of all early nations'.

[70] Code Just. 2:1:4 'he who wishes to bring an accusation must have the evidence' (Antonin AD 212).

[71] Code Just. 4:19:25.

[72] James Whitman, *The Origins of Reasonable Doubt* (New Haven, Yale University Press, 2008) 4.

[73] James Thayer, 'The Presumption of Innocence in Criminal Cases' (1897) 6 *Yale Law Journal* 185, 190: 'in Bracton, say in 1260, we find it in the most general form - de quolibet homine presumitur quod sit bonus homo donec probetur in contrarium'; Frederick Pollo.ck and Frederic Maitland *The History of English Law II* (Little, Brown and Co, Boston, 1895) 607.

[74] It is reported that a 1293 case in the Court of Common Pleas expresses the presumption: 'felony is never fastened on any person before he is by judgment convicted as guilty of the deed': 2 *Year Books of the Reign of King Edward The First Years XXI and XXII*, Alfred J Horwood (ed) (London, Longman and Co, 1873) 56–57.

utilised in inquisitorial-style courts such as the Court of Star Chamber, or by the ecclesiastical courts,[75] and some put its acceptance in English law much later than the thirteenth century. In any case, it was well-established by the eighteenth century,[76] and by 1935 it was described as the 'golden thread' running through British criminal law.[77] It is sufficient for current purposes to acknowledge that the presumption of innocence is fundamental to our system of criminal justice, and how courts typically approach criminal matters.

No doubt, however, the presumption is very inconvenient for the state, when it believes that an accused is guilty of wrongdoing, but cannot prove it to the requisite standard. Part of the response has been legislation that departs from the presumption of innocence. An example for current discussion purposes is section 302.4 of the *Criminal Code Act 1995* (Cth) creating the offence of drug trafficking. Trafficking is defined in section 302.1 with five examples. All of the examples, apart from one that involves an actual sale, involve a requirement of evidence that the accused intends to sell the drug. However, section 302.5 creates a rebuttable presumption that, where a person possesses more than a certain quantity of drug, they intend to traffic the drug. Thus, the provision effectively casts upon an accused person a requirement to prove their innocence.

The section makes clear that this is a legal, rather than merely evidentiary, onus. This is a key difference. If the onus were merely an evidentiary one, the accused would be able to meet it by raising some evidence of innocence. However, because it is stated to be a legal one, the accused must prove the existence of the defence on the balance of probabilities. If they cannot show that they are not intending to traffic the drug on the balance of probabilities, they will be convicted of trafficking based on possession of the required quantity. While in other jurisdictions high courts have been prepared to read down legislation casting a legal onus upon an accused to be merely an evidentiary onus, in an effort to make the provision consistent with fundamental principles like the presumption of innocence,[78] the High Court has found this is not an option in Australia.[79] The principle of legality is limited. In the case of the above provision, Parliament's intent to cast a legal onus upon the accused is clear. Given the extent of departures from the presumption of innocence, Australian Parliaments seem quite confident that such departures are constitutionally valid.

However, reverse onus provisions have not been treated so generously elsewhere. The example of Canada is apposite here. In one of its leading Canadian Charter decisions in *R v Oakes*,[80] the Canadian Supreme Court actually considered a reverse onus provision very similar to the one described above. It resolved the case by holding that the provision imposed merely an evidentiary, rather than legal, onus upon the accused. Its reasoning for doing so is worthy of reflection. The Court cited leading evidence scholar Rupert Cross in

[75] Anthony Gray, *Presumption of Innocence in Peril* (Lanham, Lexington Books, 2017) 5.

[76] *Regina v Best* (1705) 87 ER 941, 942 (QB) where it was held that 'every man is presumed innocent until the contrary appears'; *Bird v Bird* (1753) 161 ER 78, 79; Allyson May *The Bar and Old Bailey 1750–1850* (University of North Carolina Press, 2003) 233–235; J M Beattie *Crime and the Courts in England 1660–1800* (Princeton University Press, 1986).

[77] *Woolmington v Director of Public Prosecutions* [1935] AC 462, 481 (Viscount Sankey). This rule is subject to the defence of insanity and statutory exceptions.

[78] *R v Director of Public Prosecutions; Ex Parte Kebilene* [2000] 2 AC 326, based on s 3 *Human Rights Act 1998* (UK). In *Momcilovic v The Queen* (2011) 245 CLR 1 the High Court of Australia found that similar interpretive provisions in state human rights instruments could not be utilised in the same way.

[79] *Momcilovic v The Queen* (2011) 245 CLR 1, 55 (French CJ), 184 (Heydon J), 221 (Crennan and Bell JJ), and 244 (Bell J).

[80] [1986] 1 SCR 103.

terms of very strong concern with any criminal provision that effectively contemplated the possibility that an accused could be convicted of a crime despite the existence of reasonable doubt as to their guilt.[81]

However, the Canadian Supreme Court found that such an unacceptable situation was possible if a reverse onus provision were interpreted to impose a legal onus upon an accused. The situation would arise if the accused could provide some evidence of innocence, enough to meet an evidentiary onus and enough to raise a reasonable doubt, but not enough to meet a legal onus. In such cases, according to the Canadian law as framed (and according to the Australian law discussed above), the accused would be convicted of the crime, because they could not meet the legal onus. However, they had raised reasonable doubt as to guilt, and the orthodox view is that they should be acquitted as a result. Neither Rupert Cross nor the Canadian Supreme Court could countenance such a possibility.[82] As a result, under that country's *Charter* and express protection of presumption of innocence, they read down the provision to impose an evidentiary burden only. As a result, an accused could not be convicted although there was reasonable doubt as to their guilt.

What would the Australian High Court do with such a provision? Given the High Court's decision in *Momcilovic*, where the High Court refused to utilise a state human rights instrument interpretive provision to read down a reverse onus provision so as to impose an evidentiary burden only, the limitations of the principle of legality as a protector of rights are apparent. It could not protect the presumption of innocence here in the face of very clear parliamentary intention to the contrary. In such a case, the potential for Chapter III of the Constitution to apply to the situation becomes clear. The argument would be quite simple – the presumption of innocence is one of the most fundamental characteristics of criminal due process. Precedents have confirmed that legislation that undermines fundamental characteristics of judicial process is vulnerable to a Chapter III challenge. Recall that the language the court currently uses to explain its Chapter III precedents is 'institutional integrity'. A law that damages or threatens a court's institutional integrity is vulnerable to a Chapter III challenge. Such a law will likely undermine public confidence in the judiciary.

Consider in this light a law that contemplates the conviction of a person where there is reasonable doubt as to their guilt. A court's reputation for justice and fairness, which is now very well established and which took centuries to establish, would be immediately imperilled. If the public perception were that innocent people were being convicted and punished, the court's institutional integrity would be gravely threatened. Indeed, it is difficult to think of something more likely to threaten a court's institutional integrity than a perception that it might be finding innocent people guilty due to a reverse onus provision. Of course, public confidence in judicial outcomes would be compromised. As a result, it is submitted that the High Court should find that reverse onus provisions, and in particular those that impose a legal burden upon an accused, compromise a court's institutional integrity, and are invalid for that reason due to the requirements of Chapter III. In contrast, a law that imposed only an evidentiary onus upon an accused would not create the danger of convictions in the presence of reasonable doubt as to guilt, and would not be invalid. I must concede that at present

[81] Ibid, 133–4, citing Sir Rupert Cross, The Golden Thread of the English Criminal Law: The Burden of Proof' (paper delivered in the *Rede Lectures*, University of Toronto, Toronto, 1976).

[82] Ibid, [57] (Dickson CJ, Chouinard, Lamer, Wilson and Le Dain JJ).

this is mere argument. The High Court has not found that the presumption of innocence is protected by Chapter III of the Constitution. Nor has it expressed concern with reverse onus provisions, and particularly legal onus provisions, in terms of Chapter III. Frankly, it is time that it did so.[83]

III. Potential for Chapter III to Protect the Right to Silence/Privilege Against Self-Incrimination

Logically, the presumption of innocence and the right to silence run together. If the burden of proof is upon the accuser to prove the truth of their allegations, it would logically follow that the accused is not required to do anything to assist the accuser in this task. In other words, they should be permitted to remain silent in the face of questions and accusations, and simply require the prosecutor to make good their case. If they are not able to prove the elements of the offence, the accused is entitled to be acquitted of the charge. And indeed, the right to silence appears from very early times, from the jus commune phrases *nemo temetur seipsum accusare* (no one shall be required to accuse himself) and *nemo tenetur prodere seipsum* (no one shall be required to betray himself). The ecclesiastical courts and Star Chamber utilised inquisitorial methods, but the common law courts began to insist upon a right to silence. Evidence of this includes a 1568 edict from Lord Chief Justice Dyer issuing a writ of habeas corpus so that a person detained would not be forced to take an oath.[84] Matters came to a head with the trial of John Lilburne, accused of importing seditious books into England. He refused to answer questions about the alleged offence, and was jailed by the Star Chamber for contempt. Community outcry about his treatment led to the abolition of that Chamber in 1641. Statements denouncing anyone being forced to effectively produce evidence against themselves,[85] as well as the efficacy of obtaining 'confessions' by threats and torture appear in the case law of the eighteenth century.[86]

Again, Australian legislation has increasingly diminished the right to silence. Typical are provisions such as section 34L of the *Australian Security Intelligence Organisation Act 1979* (Cth), requiring a person summoned to attend a meeting. It is a crime to fail to attend, and it is a crime to fail to answer questions, if the person is capable of doing so. Similar provisions are found in section 30 of the *Australian Crime Commission Act 2002* (Cth). In past cases, while the High Court has availed itself of the principle of legality to read in a right to silence in cases where the legislation is silent,[87] it quickly folded when the Parliament amended the legislation to specifically abrogate that right in particular cases.[88]

[83] Fiona Wheeler, 'The Doctrine of Separation of Powers and Constitutionally Entrenched Due Process in Australia' (1997) 23 *Monash University Law Review* 248, 272–273; Michael McHugh, 'Does Chapter III Protect Substantive as well as Procedural Rights?' (2001) 21 *Australian Bar Review* 235, 239.

[84] This case is referenced by Lord Coke in *Burrows, Cox, Dyson* (1615) 3 Bulstrode 50; 81 ER 42. See also *Fitzpatrick's Trial* (1631) 3 St Tr 419, 420 (Hyde CJ).

[85] 'There is no rule more established in equity than that a person shall not be obliged to discover what will subject him to a penalty or anything in the nature of a penalty … under the rule, a man is not obliged to accused himself, is implied that he is not to discover a disability in himself': *Smith v Read* (1737) 1 Atk 526, 527 (Lord Hardwicke).

[86] *Rudd's Case* (1775) Leach's Crown Cas 115, 117–118; *Warwickshall's Case* (1783) 1 Leach 263; 168 ER 234; Theodore Barlow *The Justice of Peace: A Treatise Containing the Power and Duty of the Magistrate* (1745) 189.

[87] *Hammond v Commonwealth* (1982) 152 CLR 188.

[88] *Sorby v Commonwealth* (1983) 152 CLR 281.

Notwithstanding this, in several of these cases members of the Court have discussed the threats to the integrity of judicial process posed by regimes of compulsory questioning. This wording is highly material; recall that the High Court has found that legislation that threatens a court's institutional integrity is vulnerable to Chapter III challenge. Several past justices have commented that compulsory process can threaten the integrity of judicial process.[89] It is to be lamented that, so far, no judge has said that compulsory questioning regimes are contrary to Chapter III, because of the threat they pose to a court's institutional integrity.

Most recently, and somewhat encouragingly, members of the High Court have expressed that, fundamentally, a criminal trial is accusatorial and adversarial in nature. I take these words to be highly congruent with a right to silence. In other words, the system is based on accusations, and it is for the one doing the accusing to prove the truth of their accusations, at a level of beyond reasonable doubt, and without any assistance by the accused. Yet frustratingly once again, members of the High Court decline to link this with Chapter III. For example as in *X7*, they might use it as part of the process of statutory interpretation, rather than expressly link it with Chapter III. They apparently are not willing to acknowledge that these supposedly 'fundamental' features of the criminal justice system can only be protected meaningfully at the constitutional level. They must be protected at the constitutional level. And the reasoning exists in previous cases for them to be protected at the constitutional level.[90] Frankly, it is a mystery to this writer as to why the High Court seems reluctant to take this step, and find that they are guaranteed and enshrined at constitutional level.

IV. Potential for Chapter III to Protect Proportionate Sentencing

As law and order campaigns have ramped up in the aftermath of 9/11, debates about border security,[91] and public anxiety over perceived crime in relation to motorcycle clubs, Parliaments have responded with minimum mandatory sentencing regimes. Current examples include section 236B of the *Migration Act 1958* (Cth), which imposes minimum mandatory penalties of between 5–8 years for various so-called 'people smuggling' offences. Section 7 of the *Vicious Lawless Association Disestablishment Act 2013* (Qld) provided for minimum 15-year mandatory jail terms for a range of offences committed pursuant to the association's activities, and a minimum 25-year mandatory jail term if the offender were an executive member of the association. This Act was repealed in 2016.

Again, this is a picture with a detailed background. The history of legal systems taking into account various circumstances of offending in determining an appropriate punishment is evident in Biblical times. Luke 12:47 states that a servant who does not follow their master's orders will be seriously assaulted. Luke 12:48 adds that a servant who 'does not

[89] *Hamilton v Oades* (1989) 166 CLR 486, 502–503 (Deane and Gaudron JJ); *Environmental Protection Authority v Caltex Refinery Co Pty Ltd* (1993) 178 CLR 477, 556 (McHugh J).

[90] *Bass v Permanent Trustee Co Ltd* (1999) 198 CLR 334, 359.

[91] See ch 17.

know' but who acts in a way deserving of punishment will be lightly assaulted. The concept of proportionality of punishment to the wrongdoing is clear. The concept of *lex talionis*, or an 'eye for an eye', was also known in Biblical times. The word talio means equivalent or equal. In English legal history, concern for proportionality in sentencing is evident in *Magna Carta* of 1215[92] and the *Bill of Rights* of 1689 (Eng).[93] A 1689 decision overturned a penalty of £30 000 for assault and battery on the basis it was contrary to Magna Carta, excessive and exorbitant.[94]

Notwithstanding this, it is estimated that in the early nineteenth century approximately 200 crimes in British law carried the death penalty, usually a mandatory punishment. Not surprisingly, various means were found to obviate the gross injustice that might potentially result. They included judicial discretion, finding technicalities to thwart prosecutions, the 'benefit of clergy' claim which was applied initially to members of clergy but then to churchgoers generally, and the so-called 'pious perjury' jurors, who would acquit an accused because they did not believe that the mandatory penalty they would face if found guilty was just, or else they convicted the accused of a lesser charge. By the late 1830s, the number of offences attracting the death penalty was substantially reduced to eight, and those actually executed had dropped to six per year, compared with nearly 100 at the turn of the century. Various law commissions of the 1830s and 1840s recommended more discretion in sentencing, and an abolition of mandatory sentencing. Thus, history should have taught us that cases are all different, presenting great challenges for a system that would assume that the same penalty is always appropriate for any given offence, regardless of circumstances.

Judges of today know this. Mandatory sentencing statutes have been invalidated in Canada,[95] the UK[96] and by the Privy Council,[97] on separation of powers grounds. Five justices of the Australian High Court stated in *Hoare v The Queen* that:

> A basic principle of sentencing law is that a sentence of imprisonment imposed by a court should never exceed that which can be justified as appropriate or proportionate to the gravity of the crime considered in light of its objective circumstances.[98]

[92] Clause 14 provides that 'A man is not to be amerced [fined] for a small offence save in accordance with the manner of the offence, and for a major offence according to its magnitude'.

[93] Section 10 prohibits excessive fines, and cruel and unusual punishment.

[94] *Earl of Devon's Case* (1689) 11 State Trials 133, 136 (KB).

[95] *R v Nur* [2015] 1 SCR 773, 800 where it was stated that 'mandatory minimum sentences by their very nature have the potential to depart form the principle of proportionality in sentencing … they may deprive courts of the ability to tailor proportionate sentences … they modify the general process of sentencing which relies on the review of all relevant factors in order to reach a proportionate result. They affect the outcome of the sentence by changing the normal judicial process of sentencing' (McLachlin CJ, LeBel, Abella, Cromwell, Karakatsanis and Gascon JJ; Rothstein, Moldaver and Wagner JJ dissenting).

[96] *R (Anderson) v Secretary of State for the Home Department* [2003] 1 AC 837, involving a scheme whereby a member of the executive could determine a minimum jail term for a person convicted of a crime. Members of the Court referred to separation of powers difficulties with the legislation, reiterating that sentences could only be imposed by courts: 876 (Lord Bingham, with whom Lords Nicholls, Hobhouse, Scott and Rodger agreed), 886 (Lord Steyn), 899 (Lord Hutton).

[97] *Liyanage v The Queen* [1967] AC 259, 290–291 where the Privy Council held a minimum mandatory sentencing regime on separation of powers grounds. The Council denounced the legislative regulation of sentencing as a 'grave and deliberate incursion into the judicial sphere' whose 'aim was to ensure that the judges in dealing with these particular persons on these particular charges were deprived of their normal discretion as regards appropriate sentencing. They were compelled to sentence each offender on conviction of not less than ten years' imprisonment … even though their part in the conspiracy might have been trivial'.

[98] (1989) 167 CLR 348, 354 (Mason CJ Deane Dawson Toohey and McHugh JJ).

Members of the High Court have referred to the adjudgment and punishment of criminal guilt as an exclusively judicial function.[99] The High Court in *Magaming v The Queen* also seems to acknowledge the importance of proportionality in sentencing:

> The sentence imposed must be proportionate in the sense that it properly reflects the personal circumstances of the particular offender and the particular conduct in which the offender engaged when those circumstances and that conduct are compared with other offenders and offending.[100]

This is ironic because, having acknowledged that the sentence imposed must be proportionate, in the same case a majority of the court, Gageler J dissenting, held valid a minimum mandatory sentencing scheme that clearly contemplates sentences that may be disproportionate, because the judge cannot impose a sentence less than the prescribed minimum, even if the circumstances would warrant a sentence less than that.[101]

The separation of powers' difficulties that should be inherent in any system of mandatory sentencing are well known. They were referred to by the Law Council of Australia in a discussion paper on mandatory sentencing that concluded:

> Mandatory sentencing involves the executive unfairly traversing into an issue of a judicial nature in a different affront to the rule of law and the independence of the judiciary. Mandatory sentencing schemes mean that upon a conviction of guilt, the judiciary in effect acts as a rubber stamp for an executive's penalty policy.[102]

Again, it is submitted that in cases where courts hand out sentences pre-ordained by the legislature, their reputation for justice is at risk. One would have thought that the institutional integrity of a court is in serious peril if it is reduced to rubber-stamping decisions on sentencing made by those in other arms of government, ignorant of the circumstances of a particular offence and a particular offender. The court's apparent aspiration to assert its independence from government and its participation as the fully third arm of government is but a pious dream where the court allows itself to be dictated to by the government in terms of sentences. In other contexts, the Australian High Court has resisted attempts by government to deny it jurisdiction to review decisions.[103] The power of judicial review has been seen as an essential feature of a court, protected by Chapter III. Courts around the world have recognised the serious separation of powers issues involved in mandatory sentencing schemes.[104] The High Court of Australia's meekness in defending its role in administering proportionate sentencing should be seen in sharp, and depressing, contrast.

[99] *Chu Kheng Lim v Minister for Immigration* (1992) 176 CLR 1, 27 (Brennan Deane and Dawson JJ). Their Honours added that this was governed by substance and not form (27). Gaudron J expressed agreement: 53.

[100] (2013) 252 CLR 381, 397 (French CJ, Hayne, Crennan, Kiefel and Bell JJ).

[101] On the facts in *Magaming*, the mandatory minimum sentence of five years was applied, although the original sentencing judge specifically stated that in the ordinary course of things, if the mandatory minimum penalty had not been applicable, he would have viewed the offender's offending here at the very bottom end of the spectrum, not warranting a sentence of five years' jail: (2013) 252 CLR 381, 387.

[102] Law Council of Australia *Policy Discussion Paper on Mandatory Sentencing* (2014); Desmond Manderson and Naomi Sharp, 'Mandatory Sentences and the Constitution: Discretion, Responsibility and Judicial Process' (2000) 22 *Sydney Law Review* 585, 590: 'the act of judgment must involve some degree of independent judicial discretion in determining sentence. A former judge of the New South Wales Supreme Court stated that 'judges must pronounce the mandatory sentence as if it their own and with no discretion, so lending the court's odour of judicial sanctity to the legislature's pre-ordained outcome as adjusted by the discretion of the prosecuting executive': Kim Santow, 'Mandatory Sentencing: A Matter for the High Court?' (2000) 74 *Australian Law Journal* 298, 298–299.

[103] *Plaintiff S157/2002 v Commonwealth* (2003) 211 CLR 476.

[104] *R v Nur* [2015] 1 SCR 773; *Liyanage v The Queen* [1967] AC 259.

V. Potential for Chapter III to Protect the Right to Challenge Evidence and Confront Accusers

Again, the right of a person accused of wrongdoing to face and confront accusers is of ancient vintage. Acts 25:16 reports that 'it is not the manner of the Romans to deliver any man up to die before the accused has met his accusers face to face and has been given a chance to defend himself against the charges'. Emperor Trajan spoke against anonymous accusers. Roman Constitutions written in the second and third centuries refer to the right of an accused to be present at their trial. In Novel 90, written shortly after Justinian's Code of 534, it is stated that during criminal trials, witnesses were required to testify before judges, in the presence of the accused.

It is estimated that inquisitorial processes developed in mainland Europe in the twelfth and thirteenth centuries and have persisted since. Notorious examples include the Spanish Inquisition and the French lettres de cachet, involving punishment without trial. Inquisitorial procedures were adopted in English ecclesiastical courts, and by the Star Chamber and Court of High Commission. The notorious trials of Sir Walter Raleigh, involving unnamed accusers, and Lilburne, tried for sedition, and in the same boat, were pivotal. After the abolition of Star Chamber in 1641, when Lilburne was tried again, the record reflects the judge stating to the accused 'hear what the witnesses say first'. The *Case of the Union of the Realms* in 1604 features statements of Popham CJ to the effect that a defining feature of English criminal trials was the right of the accused to confront accusers.[105] Legal luminaries Sir Matthew Hale,[106] of the seventeeth century, and William Blackstone,[107] of the eighteenth, would laud the openness of English court proceedings as one of their essential attributes. Courts in the UK continue to explain the importance of open proceedings and the right to confront accusers in terms of the fair process,[108] which is itself guaranteed by the European Convention on Human Rights. As has been observed above, the Australian High Court has recognised a fundamental right to a fair trial at common law. The Canadian Supreme Court has also noted potential apprehension around the independence of the judiciary where it only hears from one side in relation to a dispute.[109]

There are various statements in Australian case law that suggest that natural justice is a fundamental feature of the judicial process in Australia, such that departures from it might

[105] (1604) 72 ER 908, 913.

[106] *The History of the Common Law* (6th edn, 1820) 345–346.

[107] *Commentaries on the Laws of England* (1783) 373–374 who, describing English justice, stated that 'this open examination of witnesses viva voce, in the presence of all mankind, is much more conducive to the clearing up of truth, than the private and secret examination taken down before an officer … in the ecclesiastical courts, and all others that have borrowed their practice from the civil law; where a witness may frequently depose that in private, which he will be ashamed to say in public … the occasional questions of the judge, the jury and the counsel, propounded to the witnesses on a sudden, will sift out the truth much better than a formal set of interrogatories previously penned and settled; and the confronting of adverse witnesses is also another opportunity of obtaining a clear discovery which can never be had upon any other method of trial'.

[108] *Home Secretary v AF* (No3) [2010] 2 AC 269, 355: 'strong policy considerations support a rule that a trial can never be considered fair if a party to it is kept in ignorance of the case against him'; *Al-Rawi v Security Service* [2012] 1 AC 531, 577 where Lord Dyson stated that the right to be confronted by accusers was an essential element of a fair trial. Lord Hope (587) and Lord Kerr (591) agreed.

[109] *Charkaoui v Canada* [2007] 1 SCR 350, [35]–[36] (McLachlin CJ, for the Court).

trigger Chapter III issues. The strongest is probably the statement of six justices in *Bass v Permanent Trustee* that:

> Judicial power involves the application of the relevant law to facts as found in proceedings conducted in accordance with the judicial process. And that requires that the parties be given an opportunity to present their evidence and to challenge the evidence led against them.[110]

Despite these apparent assertions that the very essence of the exercise of judicial power involves parties to proceedings being able to see and hear evidence being led against them, and to challenge it, legislation is increasingly removing or abrogating this 'right'. And the High Court has on two occasions rejected constitutional challenges to legislation that contemplated secret proceedings where those who are a party to it may not in fact get to see and hear evidence being led against them.

This has primarily been through the prism of the concept of 'criminal intelligence'. This was first tested in *K-Generation Pty Ltd v Liquor Licensing Court*.[111] There the legislation provided relevantly for an application for a liquor licence. The legislation required that steps be taken to maintain the confidentiality of information pertaining to the application. This was defined as 'criminal intelligence', relating to suspected criminal activity, where disclosure may inhibit an ongoing investigation or compromise the confidentiality of sources. 'Criminal intelligence' was used to reject an applicant's liquor licence application, and the applicant unsuccessfully argued that the proceedings involved a lack of procedural fairness.

Similarly, in *Assistant Commissioner Condon v Pompano Pty Ltd*,[112] discussed above, all members of the High Court rejected a challenge to Queensland anti-association legislation that included the use of 'criminal intelligence' provisions around whether or not an organisation should be declared to be criminal. Such intelligence could be heard in the absence of those who would be affected by the application. They would not be able to test or challenge evidence being led against them. In both cases, the High Court, with the notable exception of Kirby J, held that the use of 'criminal intelligence' against a person's interests was valid, although that person would not know the detail of such evidence or be able to challenge it. It primarily did so on the basis that the court in its discretion could weigh the evidence appropriately; in other words, presumably the evidence would be given less weight, taking into account it had not been tested through the typical rubric of cross-examination.

I have written elsewhere that this is not a convincing justification. How would this practically work? By how much would a judge discount the value of evidence that has not been the subject of cross-examination? How could it accurately judge the likely accuracy and completeness of evidence, when it has not heard the other side? Other scholars have pointed out existing deficiencies in the nature of scientific evidence being presented in our courts.[113] An advocate for the other side can play a meaningful role in bringing these defects to the

[110] (1999) 198 CLR 334, 359 (Gleeson CJ, Gaudron, McHugh, Gummow, Hayne and Callinan JJ).
[111] (2009) 237 CLR 501.
[112] (2013) 252 CLR 38.
[113] Gary Edmond and Andrew Roberts, 'Procedural Fairness, the Criminal Trial and Forensic Science and Medicine' (2011) 33 *Sydney Law Review* 359, 370: 'many of the substantial problems with forensic science and medicine seem to be methodological, statistical or linked to subtle forms of contamination. Whether we can expect lay individuals to follow critiques in these areas, or fully appreciate how they might undermine the probative value of incriminating opinion evidence, is open to doubt … where such evidence is not challenged, we can confidently assume that juries will generally have few, if any, ideas about the evidentiary limitations or magnitude of risks.

attention of the decision maker. Obviously, they cannot do so if they are not present. In *Thomas v Mowbray*,[114] Hayne and Kirby JJ also alluded to these grave difficulties when only one side is heard. However, these were dissenting views, and a majority of the court in *Pompano* would subsequently find the 'criminal intelligence' provisions there, involving the accused not seeing, hearing or being able to test evidence being used against them, to be valid. This was at a time where members of the same court over in *X7* were commenting on the fundamentally 'accusatorial' and 'adversarial' nature of the criminal trial in Australia.[115] Respectfully, it is hard to square a fundamentally accusatorial and adversarial system with secret evidence that is demonstrably not being tested through an adversarial system.

VI. Conclusion

In summary, the record of Chapter III in terms of due process protection is modest. There have been a few 'wins' for those who believe that fundamental human rights in relation to the criminal justice process should have constitutional protection. It is clear that the High Court will frown upon legislation that leaves courts with no discretion (at least in the context of anti-association legislation, though the strong limits on discretion created by minimum mandatory sentencing have been upheld). A court will frown upon legislation that directs it to hear matters in secret in the absence of one of the parties, and legislation that prohibits it from giving reasons. It will not countenance an 'appeal' from a court decision to an office that is non-judicial in nature. And it will be concerned with legislation surrounding court processes such as the wearing of robes in court.

In the bigger picture, these 'wins' are small potatoes. While invalidating the above, the High Court: has not voiced constitutional objections to reverse onus provisions which effectively permit an accused to be convicted despite the existence of reasonable doubt as to their guilt; has not found that the right to silence is so fundamental to criminal proceedings that mandated departures from it cause a court to act in a non-judicial manner; has not found constitutional difficulties with secret hearings where those affected by the proceedings do not get to see, hear or test the evidence being led against them; and has not found a constitutional objection to legislation fundamentally altering typical sentencing procedures by imposing minimum mandatory sentences, crimping the court's duty and responsibility to impose proportionate sentences. In these ways, the criminal justice system has been radically

In many situations, liberal admissibility standards will systematically advantage the state with little evidence of corresponding improvements in the accuracy of decisions'.

[114] (2007) 233 CLR 307, 477–478 where Hayne J pointed out that in many cases the court only heard the view (there anti-terrorism) of the government, meaning the court often would then have little practical choice but to accept the government's view. He emphatically rejected the possibility: 'to the extent that federal courts are left with no practical choice except to act upon a view proffered by the executive, the appearance of institutional impartiality and the maintenance of public confidence in the courts are both damaged. To that extent the judiciary is apt to be seen as but an arm of the executive which implements the will of the legislature'. Kirby J stated, at 435, that 'to expect a court to rely for its decisions solely upon the evidence supplied by the very officers seeking to secure or uphold. The control order is fundamentally inconsistent with adversarial and accusatorial procedures, observed by the Australian judiciary until now in serious matters affecting individual liberty, as contemplated by Chapter III of the *Constitution*'. Both Hayne and Kirby JJ dissented.

[115] *X7 v Australian Crime Commission* (2013) 248 CLR 92, 140 (Hayne and Bell JJ), 153 (Kiefel J).

altered, all in favour of the state, and contrary to the interests of the accused. Fundamental, time-honoured and long-fought for human rights in the criminal justice system have been jettisoned by legislatures in the interests of expediency. The High Court has looked away.

Some might suggest that the arguments about the potential of Chapter III to protect criminal due process rights presented in this chapter are radical in nature. There is nothing necessarily wrong with being radical, but I would have thought that a defence of fundamental civil liberties that have attended criminal processes where the most cherished interests are at stake would essentially be described as a conservative position. It is conceded that the way in which such rights might need to be protected in Australia via Chapter III is somewhat unorthodox. However, it is something of a worry that a position defensive of fundamental criminal due process rights that have existed for centuries is described (presumably, in a pejorative way) as 'radical'. Yet the High Court has, in its tentative way, dropped some seeds for future, more proactive courts to pick up the description of court processes as fundamentally 'accusatorial' and 'adversarial', and to give them real, substantive meaning.

4

The High Court's Implied Rights Experiment

TONY BLACKSHIELD

I. Constitutional Implications

In 1937, six years before his untimely death in a wartime mission over Norway, Richard Latham dismissed the approach to constitutional interpretation in the *Engineers' Case*[1] as 'self-contradictory',[2] in part because of its apparent insistence on textual literalism rather than implications. In the same year Sir Owen Dixon protested that, since the *Engineers' Case*, 'a notion seems to have gained currency that in interpreting the Constitution no implications can be made'. In fact, he said, the case offered no support for such a doctrine – which 'would defeat the intention of any instrument', but especially that of 'a written constitution'.[3]

In December 1912, in *R v Smithers*,[4] the High Court had upheld a challenge to the *Influx of Criminals Prevention Act* 1903 (NSW), as used to create an offence of wrongful entry into New South Wales because of a vagrancy offence in Victoria. Isaacs J relied on section 92 of the Constitution; but neither Griffith CJ nor Barton J did so. Instead, they held that the exclusionary power of the states 'is cut down … by the mere fact of federation'.[5] Both of them invoked the American decision in *Crandall v Nevada*:[6] while a federal government must have freedom of access 'over all this vast country',[7] its citizens must have 'correlative rights'. In *Crandall* this meant access not only to the seat of government, but to seaports and federal agencies throughout the country, 'independent of the will of any State over whose soil he must pass in the exercise of it'.

[1] *Amalgamated Society of Engineers v Adelaide Steamship Co Ltd* (1920) 28 CLR 129.
[2] RTE Latham, 'The Law and the Commonwealth', in WK Hancock, *Survey of British Commonwealth Affairs: Problems of Nationality 1918–1936* (Oxford University Press, 1937) vol 1, 510, 563–4.
[3] *West v Commissioner of Taxation (NSW)* (1937) 56 CLR 657, 681; cf Evatt J at 687. See also Dixon J in *Australian National Airways Pty Ltd v Commonwealth* (1945) 71 CLR 29, 85: in applying a constitution, we should 'avoid pedantic and narrow constructions' and should not 'be fearful about making implications'.
[4] *R v Smithers; Ex parte Benson* (1912) 16 CLR 99.
[5] Ibid, 109.
[6] 73 US (6 Wall) 35 at 44 (1867).
[7] This aspect of *Crandall v Nevada* had already been used in *D'Emden v Pedder* (1904) 1 CLR 91, 119, to support the immunity of the Commonwealth government from any form of state taxation.

More recently,[8] Dixon CJ agreed 'that the constitutional place of the Capital Territory in the federal system of government' must 'necessarily imply the most complete immunity from State interference with all that is involved in its existence as the centre of national government', and hence 'an absence of State legislative power to forbid restrain or impede access to it'. But he held that to apply that implication to the case before him would go 'beyond and outside the constitutional doctrines by which implications are authorized'.

In *Buck v Bavone*,[9] Murphy J used both *Crandall v Nevada* and *R v Smithers* to support his argument that freedom of movement 'across or within State borders' is 'a fundamental right arising from the union of the people in an indissoluble Commonwealth'. He returned to the point repeatedly, always relying on both *Crandall* and *Smithers*. In *McGraw-Hinds (Aust) Pty Ltd v Smith*,[10] he extended the point to 'freedom of communication' as well as 'freedom of movement' – insisting that implied constitutional protections for both of these freedoms could be drawn 'from the nature of our society, reinforced by parts of the written text', since both of them were 'indispensable to any free society'. And in *Miller v TCN Channel Nine Pty Ltd*,[11] in his final judgment, he developed the point even more fully, again citing both *Crandall* and *Smithers*.[12]

Other proposals for implied constitutional freedoms scattered through the judgments of Murphy J attracted only fleeting attention.[13] But his repeated insistence on freedoms of movement and communication, backed by progressively stronger arguments, were harder to ignore. So long as they were presented as a corollary (and an alternative) to his idiosyncratically narrow reading of section 92 of the Constitution, they could be discounted. As Mason J put it in *Miller v TCN Nine*: 'It is sufficient to say that I cannot find any basis for implying a new s 92A into the Constitution.'[14] Yet in the same case Deane J[15] took note of 'the general concept' of implied fundamental freedoms developed by Murphy J, explaining that because the instant case was covered by section 92, 'I do not find it necessary to examine [that idea] in this judgment'.

It is, therefore, not surprising that six years later, when by 6:1 the Court accepted the idea of an implied freedom of (political) communication, it was Deane J (in a joint judgment

[8] *Pioneer Express Pty Ltd v Hotchkiss* (1958) 101 CLR 536, 550.

[9] (1976) 135 CLR 110, 137.

[10] (1979) 144 CLR 633, 670; and see generally 667–670. See also *Ansett Transport Industries (Operations) Pty Ltd v Commonwealth* (1977) 139 CLR 54, 87–8; and *Gallagher v Durack* (1983) 152 CLR 238, 246, treating freedom of expression as 'essential to the achievement and maintenance of a democratic society'.

[11] (1986) 161 CLR 556, 581–5.

[12] He reinforced the effect of *Crandall v Nevada* by reference to other Supreme Court decisions, notably including *United States v Guest*, 383 US 745, 757–8 (1966).

[13] Including an implied exclusion of power to authorise 'cruel and unusual punishment' (*Sillery v The Queen* (1981) 180 CLR 353, 362), or 'to authorize slavery or serfdom' or 'similar vestiges of a feudal society', since ours is 'a Constitution for a free society' (*R v Director-General of Social Welfare (Vic); Ex parte Henry* (1975) 133 CLR 369, 388, and *General Practitioners Society v Commonwealth* (1980) 145 CLR 532, 565).

[14] (1986) 161 CLR 566, 579. See also Gibbs CJ at 569, Dawson J at 637, and Wilson J (agreeing) at 592. Brennan J (at 615) insisted that interstate communication was protected not by any implied freedom but by s 92, and in any event that an implied freedom could hardly prevent regulation (in this case of radio frequencies) on which effective communication depends.

[15] Ibid, 625–6. *Miller v TCN Nine* was one of two cases argued after Murphy J briefly returned to the Court (on 1 August 1986) after disclosing his terminal illness. Judgments in both cases were given on 21 October 1986, in a specially convened emergency sitting (by Gibbs CJ and Brennan J) an hour before Murphy J died. In the other case, *King v The Queen* (1986) 161 CLR 423, Deane J joined Murphy J (in dissent) to read s 80 of the Constitution as a true guarantee.

with Toohey J) who propounded the most ambitious conception of the freedom and its underlying constitutional basis. It was a glorious dawn.[16] But it was not to last.

II. Implied Freedom of Political Communication: Derivation and Consolidation

A. Nationwide News and ACTV

The breakthrough came in two important cases decided on the same day. At issue in *Nationwide News Pty Ltd v Wills*[17] was a provision in the *Industrial Relations Act* 1988 (Cth)[18] prohibiting the use in speech or writing of 'words calculated … to bring … into disrepute' the Industrial Relations Commission or any of its members. The whole Court held the provision invalid, but on different grounds. Mason CJ, Dawson and McHugh JJ held that it was not supported by the incidental power attaching to section 51(xxxv) of the Constitution. Deane and Toohey JJ held that, whether or not the provision was within power, it was invalid because of its limit on political expression. Brennan and Gaudron JJ held that the provision was within power, but invalid for the reason given by Deane and Toohey JJ.

At issue in *Australian Capital Television Pty Ltd v Commonwealth* ('*ACTV*')[19] was the *Political Broadcasts and Political Disclosures Act* 1991 (Cth), which (with limited exceptions) prohibited political advertising on radio or television during federal election periods. Mason CJ, Deane, Toohey and Gaudron JJ held that such restrictions of political communication were wholly invalid, and McHugh J agreed except as to elections held in the Territories. Brennan J also affirmed the implied protection of political communication, but dissented in the result because he thought that, far from undermining the electoral system, the restrictions 'would go far to ensuring an open and equal democracy'.[20] Only Dawson J dissented outright.[21]

In all of the judgments in *ACTV* the discussion was limited to freedom of *political* communication. Mason CJ[22] noted that, even before the adoption in 1982[23] of the Canadian Charter of Rights and Freedoms, the Supreme Court of Canada had recognised[24] 'an implied freedom of speech and expression which may be more extensive' than that accepted in *ACTV*. Gaudron J suggested that similar reasoning might justify 'freedom of movement,

[16] See A R Blackshield, 'The Implied Freedom of Communication', in Geoffrey Lindell (ed), *Future Directions in Australian Constitutional Law* (Annandale, Federation Press, 1994) 232–268; A R Blackshield, 'Reinterpreting the Constitution', in Judith Brett, James Gillespie and Murray Goot (eds), *Developments in Australian Politics* (1994) 23–59.

[17] (1992) 177 CLR 1.

[18] *Industrial Relations Act* 1988 (Cth) s 299(1)(d)(ii).

[19] (1992) 177 CLR 106.

[20] Ibid, 161. This may well have been the preferable view.

[21] Even Dawson J agreed (at 186–87) that legislation by which 'the electors are denied access to the information necessary for the exercise of a true choice' would be invalid. Thus his final position was therefore very close to that of McHugh J.

[22] Ibid, 41.

[23] As Part I of the *Constitution Act* 1982 (Can).

[24] Initially in *Re Alberta Legislation* [1938] SCR 100.

freedom of association … and, perhaps, freedom of speech generally'.[25] But these wider suggestions have never borne fruit.

The far-reaching possibilities envisaged by Deane and Toohey JJ were spelled out most fully in *Nationwide News*. They argued that implications had already been drawn from the Constitution's commitment to federalism and separation of powers because these were 'general doctrines of government which underlie the Constitution and are implemented by its provisions'.[26] They insisted that another such doctrine was that of 'representative government' – with the 'central thesis' that 'the powers of government belong to, and are derived from, the governed', and hence the presupposition of a need for reciprocal communication of 'information, needs, views, explanations and advice' between government and governed, and also for exchange of political information and opinions by 'the people of the Commonwealth … among themselves'. And such information and opinions must extend to 'all aspects' of the Commonwealth Government, 'including the qualifications, conduct and performance of those entrusted (or who seek to be entrusted) with … any part of the legislative, executive or judicial[27] powers of government which are ultimately derived from the people themselves'.

If the rhetoric here was that of Deane J, the underlying conception owed at least as much to Toohey J. In a conference paper delivered five days *after* the judgments in *Nationwide News* and *ACTV*, but written *before* those judgments were published, Toohey J suggested that, rather than persisting in a 'plenary construction' of the legislative powers in section 51 of the Constitution, the courts might apply to those heads of power a presumption similar to that already applied in interpretation of statutes:[28] that is, they might conclude that when legislative powers were conferred by 'the people of Australia, in adopting a constitution', it should be presumed that the people 'did not intend' to authorise any 'invasion of fundamental common law liberties'. As for the legislative will of the Parliament, so for the constituent will of the people: the courts might require that the people 'make unambiguous the expression of their constitutional will to permit Parliament to enact such laws' before holding that such laws are valid.

> If such an approach … were adopted, the courts would over time articulate the content of the limits on power arising from fundamental common law liberties. It would then be a matter for the Australian people whether they wished to amend their Constitution to modify those limits. In that sense, an implied 'bill of rights' might be constructed.[29]

[25] (1992) 177 CLR 1, 212. She saw the idea as based on '[t]he notion of a free society governed in accordance with the principles of representative parliamentary democracy', and referred specifically to various judgments by Murphy J.

[26] Ibid, 69–70.

[27] The inclusion of *judicial* power was to suffer a consistently frosty reception, especially in state courts: see *John Fairfax Publications Pty Ltd v Attorney-General* (NSW) (2000) 181 ALR 694; *Herald & Weekly Times Ltd v Popovic* (2003) 9 VR 1; and *Conservation Council of SA Inc v Chapman* (2003) 87 SASR 62. As to the High Court see *APLA Ltd v Legal Services Commissioner* (NSW) (2005) 224 CLR 322 (below, n 76) and *Hogan v Hinch* (2011) 243 CLR 506 (below, n 88).

[28] That is, what is now called 'the principle of legality' – so referred to in *R v Home Secretary; Ex parte Pierson* [1998] AC 539, 587–9, but commonly cited in Australia by reference to *Maxwell on Statutes* (4 ed by J A Theobald, 1905) 122. As to whether its application *to statutes* might lead to an 'implied bill of rights', see Dan Meagher and Matthew Groves (eds), *The Principle of Legality in Australia and New Zealand* (Alexandria, Federation Press, 2017), and ch 5 below.

[29] John Toohey, 'A Government of Laws, and Not of Men?' (1993) 4 *Public Law Review* 158, 170. Cf Crispin Hull, 'Bill of Rights Implied: Judge', *The Canberra Times*, 6 October 1992, p 5, and Crispin Hull, 'Standing up for basic freedoms', *The Canberra Times*, 7 October 1992, p 11.

It is clear in hindsight that the grandiose vision of Deane and Toohey JJ never had much majority support. In *Nationwide News* Mason CJ, Dawson and McHugh JJ said nothing about the implied freedom. In *ACTV* Dawson J dissented; Brennan J gave the freedom a more limited application; and McHugh J, though joining in the majority result, formulated the freedom (and its constitutional basis) in much more limited terms, focused closely on the explicit textual requirement (in sections 7 and 24 of the Constitution) that the Senate and the House of Representatives be 'directly chosen by the people'. He conceded[30] that these words 'must be construed by reference to the conceptions of representative government and responsible government' (as understood at the time of federation); but his actual decision was confined to a freedom of political discussion during an election period.[31]

At least as to its textual focus, it was this more limited approach that was ultimately to prevail.

B. Theophanous and Stephens

The divisions started to become apparent in 1994. Again two cases were decided together: *Theophanous v Herald & Weekly Times Ltd* and *Stephens v West Australian Newspapers Ltd*.[32] In both cases the plaintiffs were politicians suing a newspaper for defamation.[33] Again the two cases must be read together to understand their effects – which were in any event to be of historical interest only.

In the US a series of cases, beginning in 1964 with *New York Times v Sullivan*,[34] had used the First Amendment's guarantee of freedom of speech to establish a constitutional defence to actions for defamation: neither 'public officials' nor 'public figures' in general could sue successfully for defamation unless they proved 'actual malice' or 'reckless disregard of the truth'. The decisions in *Nationwide News* and *ACTV* had led immediately to speculation on whether, at least for political figures, a similar limit on actions for defamation would now apply in Australia. Unlike the United States Supreme Court,[35] the High Court had a choice: should it use the implied freedom to develop a 'constitutional' defence, or only to modify the common law relating to defamation? In *Theophanous* and *Stephens* a bare majority of the Court did both.

In *Theophanous*, the idea of a constitutional defence was rejected by three judges – Dawson J, who had dissented in *ACTV*; McHugh J, who had given the narrowest explanation for that decision; and Brennan J, who agreed that there is room for judicial development of the common law, but insisted that in interpreting the Constitution, 'judicial policy has

[30] (1992) 177 CLR 106, 229.

[31] Ibid, 231–3. To decide whether the freedom might extend more widely was 'unnecessary for … this case'.

[32] (1994) 182 CLR 104 and (1994) 182 CLR 211 respectively.

[33] Andrew Theophanous, the former chairman of a Parliamentary Committee on Migration, complained of an imputation that his migration policy was biased by his own ethnic background; and in *Stephens* six members of the West Australian Legislative Council complained that their overseas study tour had been criticised as 'a junket of mammoth proportions'.

[34] 376 US 254 (1964).

[35] Which is not a general court of appeal in matters of general law, and had therefore to find constitutional grounds in order to act at all. See Anthony Lewis, *Make No Law: The Sullivan Case and the First Amendment* (New York, Random House, 1991).

no role to play'.[36] By contrast Deane J insisted on a judicial duty to draw implications not only from the 'express terms' of the Constitution, but 'from the fundamental doctrines which they incorporate and implement', lest 'the dead hands of those who framed it' should reach 'from their graves to … deprive what was intended to be a living instrument of its vitality and its adaptability to serve succeeding generations'.[37] His only problem with *New York Times v Sullivan* was that it did not go far enough: in his view, the implied freedom must 'preclude completely' suits for defamation by a member of Parliament 'or other holder of high Commonwealth office'.[38]

Mason CJ, Toohey and Gaudron JJ agreed that the implied freedom gave rise to a constitutional defence, but thought that the *New York Times* test needed further modification. They agreed that publication 'with reckless disregard for the truth' should not be protected, but not that the burden of proof in this respect should be borne by the plaintiff. Instead, it should be for the defendant to prove that the publication had not been 'reckless'. In addition, the defendant should be required to show that it had acted 'reasonably'.[39]

The joint judgment thus fell somewhere in between the position taken by Deane J and that of Brennan, McHugh and Dawson JJ. In order to achieve a result, Deane J indicated (in a written 'Addendum')[40] that although 'quite unable to accept' the conclusions in the joint judgment, he considered it 'appropriate … to lend my support' to the answers there proposed. Accordingly, those answers prevailed by a 4:3 majority. Whether there was a majority *ratio decidendi* remains unclear.

In *Stephens*, the defendants *had* pleaded a constitutional defence, but had failed to foresee the form in which such a defence would be recognised in *Theophanous*. Accordingly, the defendants fell back on an alternative argument, which in fact Mason CJ, Toohey and Gaudron JJ had already spelled out in *Theophanous*:[41] that the effect of the constitutional freedom was to modify the common law, so that the old common law defence of qualified privilege – traditionally understood as applicable only when the allegedly defamatory statement is both made and received pursuant to a legitimate 'interest or duty' – must now be extended. If '[t]he public at large has an interest in the discussion of political matters', then those who make and those who receive communications on such matters must equally have an interest in doing so. Hence any discussion of political matters is an occasion of qualified privilege.

[36] (1994) 182 CLR 104, 143–4: a court created by the Constitution can only 'interpret and apply its text, uncovering implications where they exist'; and the idea of 'developing' the Constitution 'is inconsistent with the judicial power it confers'.

[37] Ibid, 171. He quoted a long passage from Andrew Inglis Clark, *Studies in Australian Constitutional Law* (Charles Maxwell, 1901; reprinted Legal Books, 1997) 21–22, contending that the Constitution must not be read as 'a declaration of the will and intentions of men long since dead'. Compare McHugh J in *Eastman v The Queen* (2000) 203 CLR 1, 50, refusing 'to leave us slaves to the mental images and understandings of the founding fathers'.

[38] (1994) 182 CLR 104, 185. He conceded (at 186) that the defendants thus protected would often be 'large and powerful corporations', but insisted that the protection extended ultimately to the individuals whose opinions were published. (In *Theophanous* the defamatory publication was a letter to the editor.)

[39] Ibid, 137: reasonably 'in the circumstances which prevailed'. The defence thus formulated was so heavily qualified and difficult to prove that it seems never to have been used. See Peter Applegarth, 'Distorting the Law of Defamation' (2011) 30 *University of Queensland Law Journal* 99.

[40] (1994) 182 CLR 104, 187–8.

[41] Ibid, 140.

In *Stephens*, Mason CJ, Toohey and Gaudron JJ accepted and applied such an argument;[42] and Deane J concurred in an extremely brief judgment.[43] Brennan, McHugh and Dawson JJ dissented again, but less strenuously this time. Brennan J saw the existing common law defence as already sufficiently 'flexible' to accommodate such a publication, balancing 'personal reputation' with freedom of speech more effectively than 'the necessary rigidity of constitutional formulae' could do – though in this case the defence would require additional facts to be pleaded.[44] McHugh and Dawson JJ dissented because they thought that, on the facts of this case, the appropriate common law defence was fair comment, rather than qualified privilege – though McHugh J added that, even if a defence of qualified privilege had been appropriate, it would have needed the additional pleadings suggested by Brennan J. He also agreed that the common law defence should be extended to protect 'information about the functions or powers or the performance of duties by public representatives or officials', but attributed this to the growth of bureaucracy rather than to any special operation of the Constitution.[45]

A third decision on the same day as *Theophanous* and *Stephens* again reflected the increasing divisions within the Court. Mason CJ, Deane, Toohey and Gaudron JJ held that the implied freedom extended to the activities of solicitors advising on migration issues, and making submissions to government on such issues. But Brennan, McHugh and Dawson JJ dissented; and Toohey J joined them in upholding the validity of legislation effectively restricting such activities to registered migration agents, since in his view the restrictions were 'not disproportionate' to a legitimate objective.[46]

C. From Dissent to Consensus: *Lange*

How these divisions would have played out had Mason CJ and Deane J remained on the bench, we will never know. In April 1995 Sir Anthony Mason retired;[47] in November, Sir William Deane resigned to become Governor-General. In September, *McGinty v Western Australia*[48] was argued before a Court of six judges; in March 1996 it was decided.[49]

By 4:2 the Court rejected an argument that the Constitution's provisions for choice 'by the people' gave rise to an implied guarantee of equal voting power.[50] Toohey and Gaudron JJ, the only survivors of the majorities in *Theophanous* and *Stephens*, were now

[42] (1994) 182 CLR 211, 234, relying on their earlier discussion of the point in *Theophanous*.

[43] Ibid, 257 where his Honour reasoned that, since his views did not prevail in *Theophanous*, it would be 'inappropriate … to adhere to them'.

[44] Ibid, 255–6, after an exhaustive review of the common law at 237–55.

[45] Ibid, 264–6.

[46] *Cunliffe v Commonwealth* (1994) 182 CLR 272, 383 (Toohey J).

[47] Sir Gerard Brennan replaced him as Chief Justice, and the resulting vacancy was filled by Gummow J.

[48] (1996) 186 CLR 140.

[49] In the same period the Court also considered statutory provisions (at Commonwealth level in *Langer v Commonwealth* (1996) 186 CLR 302, and at State level in *Muldowney v South Australia* (1996) 186 CLR 352) prescribing the procedure for preferential completion of a ballot paper, and prohibiting advocacy of any departure from that procedure. It was held that such provisions were valid. Dawson J unexpectedly dissented in *Langer* (at 324), but not in *Muldowney* (at 371).

[50] (1996) 186 CLR 140, 175 Brennan CJ assumed, without deciding, that such a guarantee might arise under the Commonwealth Constitution, but denied that it could do so under the Constitution of Western Australia.

the only dissenters, while McHugh J mounted a sustained attack[51] on the concept of 'a free-standing principle of representative democracy' in the Constitution. Already in *Theophanous* he had rejected the idea 'that the institution of representative government is a part of the Constitution, independently of its text and structure' – insisting rather that it is 'part of the Constitution only to the extent that the text and the implications to be drawn from the text and structure of the Constitution make it so'.[52] Now, in *McGinty*, he extended his attack to what he called 'top-down reasoning'.[53] It is impermissible to read implications *into* the Constitution; the only legitimate implications are those read *out of* the Constitution.

By this time it seemed increasingly likely that *Nationwide News* and *ACTV* would be overruled; and in *Levy v Victoria*[54] that was formally argued. But the issue was to be resolved sooner. In *Lange v Australian Broadcasting Corporation*,[55] what had seemed to be an increasingly divided Court came together in one unanimous judgment.

The implied freedom was unanimously confirmed, but its logical basis was defined more narrowly. The whole Court effectively adopted the position that McHugh J had taken from the outset: the question is not 'What is required by representative and responsible government?' but 'What do the terms and structure of the Constitution prohibit, authorise or require?'[56]

The textual basis relied upon was now spelled out more fully. Both the Senate (section 7 of the Constitution) and the House of Representatives (section 24) are 'directly chosen by the people'; and since section 64 requires that the federal Ministers be members of Parliament, the executive government ultimately depends on choice by the people as well. Moreover, section 128 provides that '[t]his Constitution shall not be altered' except by a referendum 'submitted to the electors' (that is, to everyone qualified to vote for the House of Representatives). In all these contexts, free and informed choice by 'the people' must 'necessarily' depend on a free flow of information and ideas about political matters.

On the other hand, the joint judgment maintained that the actual scope of the freedom was at least as broad as *Nationwide News* and *ACTV* had said.[57] The 'constitutional defence' from *Theophanous* was ruled to be 'bad in law';[58] but the judgment expressly reaffirmed the modification in *Stephens* of the common law defence of qualified privilege – still attributing the need for such a modification primarily to 'the varied conditions to which McHugh J referred' in *Stephens*, but acknowledging also that it was needed to 'reflect the requirements' of the constitutional text.[59]

Above all, the judgment laid down a clear test of whether a law is compatible with the implied freedom or not. The test involves 'two questions':

> First, does the law effectively burden freedom of communication about government or political matters either in its terms, operation or effect? Second, if the law effectively burdens that freedom,

[51] (1996) 186 CLR, 140, 231–6.

[52] Ibid, 196–7.

[53] Ibid, 232 – citing Richard Posner, 'Legal Reasoning From the Top Down and From the Bottom Up: The Question of Unenumerated Constitutional Rights' (1992) 59 *University of Chicago Law Review* 433.

[54] (1997) 189 CLR 579.

[55] Ibid, 520.

[56] Ibid, 567.

[57] See also McHugh J in *Levy v Victoria* (1997) 189 CLR 579, 622 (note 148).

[58] For the reasons given at (1997) 189 CLR 579, 560 and summarised at 575: the Constitution 'confers no private right of defence and the New South Wales law of defamation … places no undue burden on the freedom'.

[59] 189 CLR at 571.

is the law reasonably appropriate and adapted to serve a legitimate end the fulfilment of which[60] is compatible with the maintenance of the constitutionally prescribed system of representative and responsible government and the procedure prescribed by s 128 for submitting a proposed amendment of the Constitution to the informed decision of the people (hereafter collectively "the system of government prescribed by the Constitution"). If the first question is answered "yes" and the second is answered "no", the law is invalid.[61]

D. The Languors of *Lange*

In other contexts where the High Court has been doctrinally innovative,[62] the original bold declaration has been followed by a period in which the new concept was frequently invoked but rarely applied (at least not directly).[63] So it was with *Lange*.

In *Levy v Victoria*,[64] a planned protest against the Victorian duck hunting season was thwarted by new regulations prohibiting entry to the duck-shooting area. The Court held that the regulations were appropriate and adapted to the legitimate end of protecting public safety, but agreed that, in principle, the intended protest (a televised pile of dead ducks) would have been entitled to protection as political communication[65] – and, indeed, that communication through such a visually arresting image is likely to be particularly effective.

In *Australian Broadcasting Commission v Lenah Game Meats Pty Ltd*,[66] the respondents had sued the ABC for invasion of privacy; but since the privacy claim failed at the outset, a defence relying on the implied freedom was never reached.[67] The case was notable mainly for the vehement denunciation by Callinan J of the whole idea of 'implications from a written constitution'.[68]

[60] In *Coleman v Power*, (2004) 220 CLR 1, 50, McHugh J suggested that this was wrong: the true question is whether the statute pursues its end '*in a manner* which is compatible with' representative and responsible government, and 'both the end and the manner of its achievement' must be thus compatible. Accordingly, the *Lange* test is now sometimes framed as *three* questions: the existence of a 'burden', compatibility of 'purpose', and compatibility of 'manner'.

[61] 189 CLR at 567–68.

[62] As in *Melbourne Corporation v Commonwealth* (1947) 74 CLR 31 or *Kable v Director of Public Prosecutions (NSW)* (1996) 189 CLR 51.

[63] In *Aid/Watch Inc v Federal Commissioner of Taxation* (2010) 241 CLR 539, it was held by 5:2 (Heydon and Kiefel JJ dissenting) that a charitable organisation could claim tax relief despite advocating legislative and political change. The idea that the law would 'stultify itself' by encouraging advocacy of changes to 'the law itself' (*National Anti-Vivisection Society v Inland Revenue Commissioners* [1948] AC 31, 62), was answered (at 556) by invoking *Lange*: communication on government and political matters must now be seen as 'an indispensable incident' of 'the law itself'. The issue remains current: see Mike Seccombe, 'Charitable detonation', *The Saturday Paper*, 19–25 August 2017, p 12.

[64] (1997) 189 CLR 579.

[65] Freedom of 'communication' is thus more obviously inclusive than freedom of 'speech', which has had to be extended in the US by talk of 'expressive conduct' or 'symbolic speech': see, eg, *United States v O'Brien* 391 US 367 (1968) (burning a draft card); *Tinker v Des Moines Independent Community School District* 393 US 503 (1969) (black armbands); *Texas v Johnson* 491 US 397 (1989) and *United States v Eichman* 496 US 310 (1990) (burning the flag).

[66] (2001) 208 CLR 199.

[67] Except by Kirby J, who argued (esp at (2001) 208 CLR 199, 286) that since the constitutional principle must extend to judicial processes, the injunction appealed from should be vacated for want of adequate attention to *Lange*. Gleeson CJ disagreed, holding that the implied freedom 'is not a mere balancing factor in a discretionary judgment' ibid, 220.

[68] Ibid, 331–38, esp at 337.

In *Roberts v Bass*[69] a South Australian politician, defeated at the 1997 election, sued for defamation in respect of material (including a how-to-vote card) distributed in his electorate during the election period. A defence plea of qualified privilege, apparently only in its traditional common law version,[70] led on appeal to a confused discussion of at least three versions of 'qualified privilege': the original common law version; the modified version from *Stephens* and *Lange*;[71] and a newly modified version differing from that in *Stephens* and *Lange*, and clarifying the sense in which (in a political context) qualified privilege will be defeated by 'malice'. The majority[72] applied this final version to hold that there must be a new trial.

Although the majority insisted that *Lange* must be taken into account, the precise extent to which that was so was unclear.[73] Even Kirby J, despite his emphasis on the constitutional context, sought primarily to 'clarify the scope and operation of the "common law privilege" applicable to this case'.[74] The result is that, in later defamation cases, defendants have tended to rely on a common law version of qualified privilege (as clarified or modified by *Roberts v Bass*) with little or no reference to *Lange*.[75]

In *APLA Limited v Legal Services Commissioner (NSW)*,[76] the Court upheld a NSW regulation prohibiting solicitors' advertisements relating to claims for personal injury (including claims in the federal courts). An argument based on *Lange* failed. The advertisements were dismissed as relating merely to 'commercial activity'[77] or to rights and remedies under existing law,[78] while 'government or political matters' were narrowly defined by reference to sections 7, 24, 64 and 128 of the Constitution. At the hearing the plaintiffs' argument had shifted from the freedom of political communication to a parallel freedom said to be implied in Chapter III of the Constitution; but most judges[79] rejected this argument also.

In 2008, Lex Wotton was sentenced to seven years' imprisonment for his role in the Palm Island riots of 2004.[80] In 2010 he was released on parole subject to 22 conditions, including restrictions on his participation in public meetings and a prohibition of unauthorised media contacts (or payments resulting therefrom). The parole conditions were criticised as 'unnecessary, inappropriate and in stark breach of human rights';[81] but in

[69] (2002) 212 CLR 1.

[70] The plea had asserted that publication was limited to persons 'expected to be enrolled as electors', thus apparently seeking to attract the traditional idea of communication to persons having a sufficient interest.

[71] If the *Lange* version is treated as different from the *Stephens* version, *four* versions were now in play.

[72] Gleeson CJ, Hayne and Callinan JJ held that no reasoning based on *Lange* could be considered at all.

[73] Gaudron, McHugh and Gummow JJ insisted (at 29) that *Lange* was 'not concerned with' statements about candidates made during an election period, but also that such statements are 'at the heart' of the constitutional freedom. What *Lange* was thus said to be 'not concerned with' was presumably the conflict between *Braddock v Bevins* [1948] 1 KB 580, and *Lang v Willis* (1934) 52 CLR 637, as to the availability (at common law) of qualified privilege in electoral contexts.

[74] 212 CLR at 58.

[75] See Applegarth, above n 39.

[76] (2005) 224 CLR 322.

[77] Ibid, 351 (Gleeson CJ and Heydon J).

[78] Ibid, 451 (Hayne J).

[79] McHugh and Kirby JJ (in dissent) accepted the argument, but in different versions. McHugh J (at 360, 363) saw the implication from Ch III as entirely separate from *Lange*; Kirby J (at 440) insisted that *Lange* 'could not be confined to protecting Chs I and II of the Constitution', but must also protect 'Ch III and the Judicature for which it provides'.

[80] See Chloe Hooper, *The Tall Man* (Hawthorn, Hamish Hamilton, 2008); Barbara Glowczewski (with Lex Wotton), *Guerriers pour la paix: la condition politique des Aborigènes vue de Palm Island* (Montpellier: Indigène, 2008). And see now *Wotton v Queensland (No 5)* (2016) 352 ALR 146.

[81] Alisa Wicks, 'Due Process and Parole in Queensland: The Case of Lex Wotton' (2010) 7 *Indigenous Law Bulletin* 13, 17.

Wotton v Queensland[82] the Court avoided direct assessment of their validity. Section 200 of the *Corrective Services Act* 2006 (Qld) had authorised such conditions as the parole board 'considers reasonably necessary' to ensure the parolee's good conduct and abstention from further offence. The Court held unanimously[83] that this and other provisions of the Act[84] were compatible with the implied freedom, and that whether or not the parole conditions went beyond what was reasonably necessary was a matter for judicial review, not for constitutional challenge.[85]

In *Attorney-General (SA) v Corporation of the City of Adelaide*,[86] a by-law forbade the use of 'any road' to 'preach, canvass, harangue, tout for business' or conduct an opinion poll without permission. A challenge to its application to Rundle Mall (in the centre of Adelaide) failed: the by-law was reasonably appropriate and adapted to ensuring safety and convenience. In a remarkable judgment Heydon J dissented: while refusing to consider the application of the implied constitutional freedom, he invoked 'the principle of legality' to conclude that the statutory provisions authorising the by-law should be read so as not to abrogate or abridge the 'many common law rights of free speech'.[87]

In *Hogan v Hinch*,[88] the media personality Derryn Hinch (later a one-term Senator) challenged section 42 of the *Serious Sex Offenders Monitoring Act* 2005 (Vic), which permitted orders suppressing the identity of convicted sex offenders. He relied primarily on a supposed implication of 'open justice' in Chapter III of the Constitution, but also on *Lange*. His challenge failed on all points. And in *Day v Australian Electoral Officer (SA)*,[89] the new system of voting 'above the line' in Senate elections was challenged, in part because the ballot paper offered no detailed explanation of how such votes would be scrutinised. This alleged *failure* of communication was said to be inconsistent with the concept of political communication. The Court unanimously held that the argument 'fails at its threshold. The ballot paper does not mislead.'[90]

III. Implied Freedom of Political Communication: Contemporary Issues and Development

A. Civility

In *Coleman v Power*,[91] a student protester appealed against his conviction on a charge of using 'threatening, abusive or insulting words … in any public place or so near to any public place that any person could … view or hear'. He had publicly accused a police

[82] (2012) 246 CLR 1.
[83] Ibid 14 – accepting the argument of Stephen Gageler (as Solicitor-General) at 5–6.
[84] In particular s 132 (prohibiting unauthorised media interviews with prisoners, including those on parole).
[85] Six weeks earlier, the joint judgment in *Wainohu v New South Wales* (2011) 243 CLR 181 had held (at 231) that, once statutory provisions are 'construed conformably with the implied freedom', then 'any particular order' exceeding 'the limit of the implied freedom' does not raise a constitutional issue, but is simply 'reviewable for error'.
[86] (2013) 249 CLR 1.
[87] Ibid, 65–68.
[88] (2011) 243 CLR 506.
[89] (2016) 261 CLR 1.
[90] Ibid, 25.
[91] (2004) 220 CLR 1.

constable of corruption while handing out a pamphlet offensively criticising the police. His appeal was allowed, but only by a 4:3 majority;[92] and of the four majority judges only McHugh J based his decision on the implied constitutional freedom. Gummow, Kirby and Hayne JJ disposed of the case by reading the statutory provision as applicable only to words 'directed to hurting an identified person' and 'either intended to provoke unlawful physical retaliation, or … reasonably likely to do so'.[93] On that reading, they held that the use of insulting words to a police officer would not attract the provision, because '[b]y their training and temperament police officers must be expected to resist the sting of insults directed to them'.[94] Police officers may well take a different view.

Although only McHugh J based his judgment on the implied freedom, the case is notable both for some significant comments on the language of *Lange*,[95] and for a remarkable clash of opinions as to the appropriate degree of tolerance for insulting and offensive language. For Kirby J, such tolerance was built into Australian culture – and especially Australian political debate, which 'has regularly included insult and emotion, calumny and invective'. The Constitution 'does not protect only the whispered civilities of intellectual discourse'.[96] For Heydon J, insulting words 'are generally so unreasonable, so irrational … and so reckless' that they cannot assist informed choice: 'They reflect the vices of intolerance rather than the virtues of tolerance'.[97]

The exchange is unusual because Kirby J, often perceived as judicially liberal, defends the use of insulting or offensive language; and Heydon J, often perceived as judicially conservative, defends legislation against it. The alignment in political debates is usually the other way round.[98] And in *Monis v The Queen*,[99] a similar conflict left a six-judge bench unable to reach any decision.

From 2007 onwards, Man Haron Monis wrote letters to the families of soldiers killed in Afghanistan, accusing the soldiers of murdering innocent civilians, and comparing them to Adolf Hitler. In 2011 he was charged with 13 offences under section 471.12 of the *Criminal Code* (Cth), which makes it an offence to use a postal service 'in a way that reasonable persons would regard as being, in all the circumstances, menacing, harassing or offensive'. He sought to have the indictment quashed on the ground that section 471.12 was incompatible with the implied freedom – not because his letters could themselves be classed as 'political' communication, but because the word 'offensive' made the statutory provision so broad and vague as to burden the freedom unacceptably.

[92] Gleeson CJ, dissented, along with Callinan and Heydon JJ, both of whom consistently maintained while still on the bench that the whole idea of the implied freedom was fundamentally misconceived.

[93] (2004) 220 CLR 1, 74 (Gummow and Hayne JJ); compare Kirby J at 98–99.

[94] Ibid, 79 (Gummow and Hayne JJ); cf Kirby J at 99 (police 'expected to be thick skinned and broad shouldered').

[95] For McHugh J (as to legislation 'in a manner' compatible with the freedom) see above n 60; for Kirby J (as to 'appropriate and adapted') see below n 125.

[96] (2004) 220 CLR 1, 91. Cf his insistence in *Palmer-Bruyn & Parker Pty Ltd v Parsons* (2001) 208 CLR 388 at 431, that the freedom extends to 'expression that is foolish, in bad taste, hurtful, childish and ill-considered'.

[97] Ibid, 126.

[98] Notably in relation to s 18c of the *Racial Discrimination Act* 1975 (Cth), which makes it unlawful (except in private) to do an act which is 'reasonably likely … to offend, insult, humiliate or intimidate' a person or group of people because of race or 'colour or national or ethnic origin'.

[99] (2013) 249 CLR 92.

In the New South Wales courts his argument failed.[100] In the High Court, the six judges hearing the case[101] were evenly divided. Three held that the use of the word 'offensive' widened the scope of the prohibition so much that it would inevitably impede political communication in an unforeseeable 'range of circumstances'.[102] The other three saw the protection of people from 'intrusion of offensive material into their personal domain'[103] as a legitimate purpose, and section 471.12 as a legitimate way to achieve it.

The three judges voting in favour of section 471.12 were women, while the three who found it too restrictive of freedom were men. But in 2017 any suggestion that this might reflect a predictable difference between male and female judges was decisively dispelled by Bell J, who pointed out that when the New South Wales Court of Appeal had upheld section 471.12, all three judges were men. 'I can only marvel', she said, 'at the serendipity of three of the most senior male judges in New South Wales having been gifted with a female sense of justice.'[104]

Since the High Court was evenly divided, the decision of the Court of Appeal was affirmed, and Monis's trial went ahead. On being convicted, he appealed on the same ground as before: that because of the breadth of the word 'offensive', section 471.12 was invalid. He applied for his appeal to be removed into the High Court. French CJ and Gageler J conceded that it raised an important issue, which the earlier 3:3 division had left unresolved; and that this would normally be a compelling reason to hear his appeal. Yet because the earlier proceedings had led to a result *in his case*, the doctrines of *res judicata* or issue estoppel might mean that that result in 2013 was absolutely binding *on him*, so that *he* could not be heard to appeal against it. Noting (though not deciding) the effect of these 'exclusionary principles', the Court did not 'think it appropriate' to order removal.[105] In effect, Monis was told that leave to appeal on the issue would have been granted to anyone in Australia but him.

That was on Friday 12 December 2014. On the following Monday, Monis returned to the Phillip Street area and stormed the Lindt café, a coffee shop frequented by barristers a block away from the Court. At the end of a siege lasting for 16 hours a café employee was killed by Monis, one of the barristers trapped in the siege was killed accidentally by police, and Monis himself was also killed by police.

B. Representative and Responsible Government Reaffirmed

In recent cases the *Lange* formula of 'representative and responsible government' has again been taken seriously – partly because of the chaos over section 44 of the Constitution,[106]

[100] *Monis v The Queen* (2011) 215 A Crim R 64; 256 FLR 28.

[101] Gummow J, who was about to retire, did not sit.

[102] (2013) 249 CLR 92, 134 (French CJ).

[103] Ibid, 207 (Crennan, Kiefel and Bell JJ).

[104] Hon Justice Virginia Bell, 'Examining the Judge' (29 May 2017, launching Issue 40(2) of the *UNSW Law Journal*).

[105] *Monis v The Queen* [2014] HCA Trans 280 (12 December 2014).

[106] See especially *Re Day (No 2)* (2017) 343 ALR 181, 196 (interpreting s 44(v) of the Constitution as 'protective of matters which are fundamental to the Constitution, namely representative and responsible government in a democracy'); and *Re Canavan* (2017) 349 ALR 534, 545 (insisting on the 'constitutional imperative' that in

but also elsewhere.[107] In particular, it has shaped the outcome of challenges to the statutory control of political donations in two decisions – superficially at odds but in fact complementary – arising from amendments in 2010 to the *Election Funding, Expenditure and Disclosures Act* 1981 (NSW).

In 2013 Unions NSW, the peak body for trade unions in New South Wales, challenged two provisions seen as discriminating against trade unions.[108] Section 95G required that, for purposes of enforcing an overall cap on political expenditure, the aggregate expenditure of a political party should include expenditure not only by the party itself, but by any 'affiliated organisation'. Section 96D prohibited political donations by anyone other than an individual elector. Keane J agreed[109] that these provisions were 'discriminatory'. The other five judges found them invalid for a more fundamental reason – not that the restrictions went beyond what was reasonably appropriate to a legitimate purpose, but that they seemed to have no purpose at all.

In particular, the restriction of political donations to those made by individual electors was rejected – not so much as legislative overreach, but simply as pointless. Why should individual electors be the only permissible donors? Others may be affected by political outcomes or make meaningful contributions to political debate. Keane J gave the most telling example:[110] why exclude a not-for-profit group supporting the rights of asylum seekers?

Significantly, the joint judgment drew a contrast with two other examples.[111] A provision banning *all* political donations would clearly be directed towards reducing corruption, and might well be accepted as a reasonable means to that end. And the actual provision in section 96GA of the Act, excluding donations by 'prohibited donors', was also used as a helpful contrast. A 'prohibited donor' was defined by section 96GAA as 'a property developer', 'a tobacco industry business entity', or 'a liquor or gambling industry business entity'. In these cases, the joint judgment implied, it was obvious why such donors might be thought to have 'interests of a kind which requires … an express prohibition'. But no such explanation was possible for the wholesale exclusion of anyone other than individual electors.

This hint that the exclusion of 'prohibited donors' might be valid was borne out in 2015 – when Jeff McCloy, formerly Lord Mayor of Newcastle, challenged the prohibition of donations from property developers.[112] He also attacked the cap on political donations (no more than $5,000 for a political party or $2,000 for a candidate) under section 95A of the Act; in 2014 McCloy had resigned as Lord Mayor after the Independent Commission Against Corruption (ICAC) found that his donations before the 2011 New South Wales election were well in excess of that cap. Finally, he attacked the ban in section 96E on indirect

principle all Australians should be entitled 'to participate in the representative government which the Constitution establishes').

[107] See below ch 5, §VI, emphasising the use of 'representative and responsible government' (as invoked in *Lee v New South Wales Crime Commission* (2013) 251 CLR 196 at 310) to direct attention to 'those rights, freedoms and principles central to the proper functioning of *our* constitutional system of democratic government'. As to *Brown v Tasmania* (2017) 349 ALR 398 see the passages cited below n 142.

[108] *Unions NSW v New South Wales* (2013) 252 CLR 530.

[109] Ibid, 578 (as to s 96D) and 586 (as to s 95G).

[110] Ibid, 530.

[111] Ibid, 559.

[112] *McCloy v New South Wales* (2015) 257 CLR 178. Under s 96GB(1)(b) of the Act, McCloy's association with property development companies meant that he was classified as a 'property developer' himself.

campaign contributions, since ICAC had found that one of his companies had contributed to salary for a candidate's staff.

In all three respects, McCloy's arguments failed. The Court found that the provisions under attack were not only compatible with the implied freedom (and with representative government), but were calculated to preserve and enhance it.[113] As to the exclusion of property developers Nettle J dissented; otherwise the Court was unanimous.

Perhaps through a tendency to take notice of results rather than reasoning, or perhaps through awareness of the corrosive effect of the *Citizens United* decision[114] on elections in the US, the original decision in *Unions NSW* had been perceived as a threat to proposals for more effective legislative limits on political donations. But together the two decisions strike a welcome balance. At a time when legislative proposals include restrictions not only on the financial activities of political parties, but also on those of an expanded conception of their 'associated entities',[115] the Court's insistence in *McCloy* on seeing restrictions on political donations as necessary to the integrity of representative and responsible government,[116] along with its willingness in *Unions NSW* to strike down unreasonable restrictions on political communication, may offer a good combination. Both the joint judgment and Gageler J[117] quoted what Harrison Moore had written in 1902,[118] hailing the 'predominant feature' of the Constitution as 'the prevalence of the democratic principle in its most modern guise', and explaining the absence of guaranteed individual rights by '[t]he great underlying principle … that the rights of individuals are sufficiently secured by ensuring, as far as possible, to each a share, and an equal share, in political power'.

The balance thus struck has been maintained. The insistence in *Unions NSW* that restrictions must be justified has been reaffirmed in *Unions NSW (No 2)*;[119] the willingness in *McCloy* to accept prohibitions where the potential for corruption is obvious has been reaffirmed in *Spence v State of Queensland*.[120]

Moreover, both of the later cases have continued to explore the underlying value of equality. The joint judgment in *Unions (No 2)* again affirmed that the implied freedom 'ensures that the people of the Commonwealth enjoy equal participation in the exercise of political sovereignty', and therefore rejected any suggestion 'that the Constitution impliedly privileges candidates and parties over the electors as sources of political speech'.[121] And even though most judges (unlike Edelman J) accepted that the cap imposed on expenditure by third-party campaigners should be lower than that imposed on political parties (supposedly to ensure that the third party voices should not 'drown out' those of the parties), they

[113] Ibid, 196, 208 (French CJ, Kiefel, Bell and Keane JJ); 221 (Gageler J); 290, 294 and 297 (Gordon J).

[114] *Citizens United v Federal Election Commission* 558 US 310 (2010).

[115] Supposedly including not only trade union support for the Australian Labor Party, as in *Unions NSW*, but independent social media organisations such as GetUp! See Mike Seccombe, 'Turnbull sought help from GetUp! for spill', *The Saturday Paper*, 28 October to 3 November 2017, p 1 at 10, and Mike Seccombe, 'The true story of Cash's union raids', *The Saturday Paper*, 4–10 November 2017, pp 1, 3.

[116] (2015) 257 CLR 178, 223 (Gageler J); cf id 225–233 and *passim*. See also Nettle J at 258, 260–61; Gordon J at 280. French CJ, Kiefel, Bell and Keane JJ spoke repeatedly of the need to protect 'the actual and perceived integrity' of parliamentary institutions: see ibid 196, 204–5 and 212.

[117] Ibid, at 202 and 226 respectively.

[118] W Harrison Moore, *The Constitution of the Commonwealth of Australia* (John Murray, 1902) at 327, 329.

[119] *Unions NSW v New South Wales (No 2)* (2019) 363 ALR 1.

[120] *Spence v State of Queensland* [2019] HCA 15 (15 May 2019).

[121] 363 ALR at 13.

also insisted that the inequality thus introduced should be no greater than 'reasonably necessary'; should still ensure the ability of a third party campaigner 'to present its case to voters';[122] and should not be accepted in the absence of evidence sufficient to persuade the Court that these tests had been satisfied. And among the significant features of *Spence* was its rejection of a submission that a prohibition of donations by property developers would discriminate against the conservative parties, because they received a larger share of such donations than the Labor Party.

C. Proportionality

Initially *McCloy* seemed also to resolve a protracted controversy over the wording of the *Lange* test, which asks whether an impairment of the implied freedom is 'reasonably appropriate and adapted' to a legitimate end. The words 'appropriate and adapted' – themselves appropriated and adapted[123] from a famous American decision[124] – have repeatedly been criticised as clumsy and disingenuous.[125] The alternative usually offered is a 'proportionality' test – derived originally from German law and nowadays widely used in the European Court of Justice and elsewhere,[126] especially as a test for the permissible impairment of guaranteed rights. As between the competing tests the *Lange* judgment was even-handed – noting both tests, but seeing no immediate need to choose between them, and using 'reasonably appropriate and adapted' merely for 'ease of expression'.[127]

In *McCloy v New South Wales*, it seemed that 'proportionality' had won. French CJ, Kiefel, Bell and Keane JJ applied a 'structured proportionality' test, asking (in 'three stages')[128] whether a law is *suitable* ('as having a rational connection to the purpose of the provision'), *necessary* (in the sense that there is no obvious and compelling alternative way to achieve the same purpose with a less restrictive effect on the freedom), and *adequate in its balance* ('a criterion requiring a value judgment, consistently with the limits of the judicial function', describing the balance between the importance of the purpose for the provision and the extent to which it impairs the freedom).[129]

[122] Gageler J at 27–28.

[123] In *Commonwealth v Tasmania* (1983) 158 CLR 1, 259–60, 264–8, Deane J asked whether legislation is 'capable of being reasonably considered to be appropriate and adapted'. The further redaction to 'reasonably appropriate and adapted' came in *Richardson v Forestry Commission* (1988) 164 CLR 261, 303.

[124] *McCulloch v Maryland*, 17 U.S. (4 Wheat.) 316 at 421 (1819): 'Let the end be legitimate … and all means which are appropriate, which are plainly adapted to that end …, are constitutional.' The first Australian citation of the case was in *D'Emden v Pedder* (1904) 1 CLR 91, 111–6. Its first use to enlarge Commonwealth legislative powers came in *Jumbunna Coal Mine v Victorian Coal Miners' Association (No 2)* (1908) 6 CLR 309, 320–2, 343–5 and 357–61.

[125] See, eg, Kirby J in *Coleman v Power* (2004) 220 CLR 1, 90 stating that 'I will never cease to protest at this ungainly phrase 'appropriate and adapted'. Just imagine what non-lawyers must make of it?'

[126] See Tor-Inge Harbo, *The Function of Proportionality Analysis in European Law* (Nijhoff, 2015); Alec Stone Sweet and Jud Mathews, 'Proportionality, Judicial Review, and Global Constitutionalism', in Giorgio Bongiovanni, Giovanni Sartor & Chiara Valentini (eds), *Reasonableness and Law* (Springer, 2009) 171–214; Grant Huscroft, Bradley W Miller and Grégoire Webber, *Proportionality and the Rule of Law* (Cambridge University Press, 2014).

[127] (1997) 189 CLR 520, 562.

[128] See Aharon Barak, *Proportionality: Constitutional Rights and their Limitations* (Cambridge UP, 2012) 303–370.

[129] (2015) 257 CLR 178, 194–5.

In *Murphy v Electoral Commissioner*,[130] most judges refused to extend this test to a question of equal voting rights, yet adhered to their respective positions in *McCloy*. For example, although French CJ and Bell J now saw the 'traditional' formula ('appropriate and adapted') as largely interchangeable with 'the general rubric of proportionality', they insisted that *McCloy* should not be dismissed as 'some exotic jurisprudential pest destructive of the delicate ecology of Australian public law'.[131]

In *Brown v Tasmania*,[132] Nettle J accepts 'structured proportionality', so that it again has the support of four judges,[133] and both sides appear to be seeking a rapprochement.[134] Yet significant differences remain. The idea of proportionality or 'balance' between an impairment of freedom and the justification for the impairment remains heatedly divisive, yet unavoidably shared. In *Brown v Tasmania* Gordon J[135] insists that 'balancing' offers no 'principled answer', yet also that because the prohibited conduct was already unlawful, 'the required justification is less' and 'the law is more readily justified'. Gageler J[136] declines to rely on 'some predetermined all-encompassing algorithm', yet also demands a degree of justification 'calibrated to the nature and intensity of the burden' ('calibrated to the degree of risk'). And the champions of 'structured proportionality' set 'balance' as their ultimate test, yet hope that it need never be reached.

The *Workplaces (Protection from Protesters) Act* 2014 (Tas) had built on existing prohibitions in the *Forest Management Act* 2013 (Tas) by introducing an additional prohibition on entry to 'business premises' (section 6(1)).[137] No penalty was imposed for a prohibited entry, but under section 11(1) a police officer who 'reasonably believes' in the possibility of an offence 'may direct a person … on business premises to leave the premises without delay'. From such a direction various adverse consequences might follow.[138] For Kiefel CJ, Bell and Keane JJ, the first two stages of orderly progress through 'structured proportionality' were sufficient to show that the consequences were unacceptable. Some failed on the test of 'suitability' (having nothing to do with the legitimate purpose of protecting 'forest operations' against 'damage and disruption'); others on the test of 'necessity' (because any possible damage or disruption was already adequately dealt with by the 2013 legislation). The question of 'balance' was never reached.

[130] (2016) 261 CLR 28.

[131] Ibid, 52.

[132] (2017) 349 ALR 398.

[133] French CJ, a party to the joint judgment in *McCloy*, had resigned. Gageler and Gordon JJ continued to prefer 'appropriate and adapted'; and Edelman J, though not reaching the issue, seemed to agree: ibid, 515.

[134] Ibid, 426 where the joint judgment treats its three structural stages as no more than 'methods of analysis'. See also 432, where Gageler J too accepts proportionality as 'a tool of analysis' (though 'not a particularly useful tool').

[135] Ibid, 476.

[136] Ibid, 433–4. At 445 he sees the relevant level of scrutiny as lying on 'a spectrum'. This case involves a 'significant practical burden', so the scrutiny must be 'stringent' and the legislative purpose 'compelling'.

[137] For the joint judgment this lack of definition was crucial. With no way of telling whether any particular part of the forest was 'business premises' or not, a policeman might *mistakenly* direct a protester to abandon a legitimate protest, or the protester might *mistakenly* be deterred from going ahead with a legitimate plan. Thus (at 417), 'some lawful protests [would] be prevented or discontinued' for no legitimate reason; protests would be 'stifled when they should not be'.

[138] The direction could include a 'requirement' not to contravene the Act within the next three months; and a direction to a group bound every member of the group who could reasonably be expected to hear it. It was an offence to disobey such a direction, or to enter a 'business access area' in the next four days. And a police officer who 'reasonably believes' a person to be contravening the Act, or to have done so in the past three months, could make an arrest without warrant.

By contrast, the question for Gageler J was essentially one of 'balance': assuming that the Act had a legitimate purpose, the consequences attached to a direction made under section 11 went far beyond what was reasonably necessary.[139] Nettle J, too, though accepting 'structured proportionality', went directly to the question of 'balance': the consequences of a direction were 'manifestly excessive', 'grossly disproportionate', and went 'far beyond' what was needed.[140]

On the one hand, 'structured proportionality' recognises that judicial decision may ultimately depend on subjective evaluative judgment.[141] On the other hand, it seeks to defer such judgment to the final stage of a schematic routine, apparently in the hope that that final stage may never be reached. The real questions are whether a court can ever escape from the need for evaluative judgment, and whether it should wish to do so.

In any event, *Brown* is a landmark case. *Unions NSW* was the first case since 1992 in which the implied freedom was used to strike down an enacted law; *Brown* does so again, this time to protect the kind of televisual protest recognised in *Levy v Victoria*. And in *Brown*, as in *Unions NSW* and *McCloy*, the freedom of political communication is reaffirmed as an indispensable foundation for responsible and representative government.[142] The languors of *Lange* may have lessened at last.

IV. Right to Vote in Federal Elections

In 2007, the words 'directly chosen by the people' in sections 7 and 24 of the Constitution were relied on to recognise an implied constitutional right to vote – ensuring in principle a universal franchise, with exceptions only for 'substantial reasons'. Such a principle had long been foreshadowed;[143] but the final decision came in response to a legislative amendment in 2006.

Under the *Commonwealth Electoral Act* 1918 (Cth), certain prison inmates are not entitled to vote. Until 1983 the disqualification applied only to those currently imprisoned for one year or more. That period was increased in 1983 to five years; reduced in 2004 to three years; and in 2006 eliminated altogether, so that any person serving any custodial sentence at all was disqualified. By 4:2 (Hayne and Heydon JJ dissenting), that blanket disqualification was held to be invalid – though the previous reference to a sentence for three years

[139] In particular, the penalties for breach of a three-month 'requirement' were 'nothing short of capricious in their temporal duration of three months and nothing short of punitive in their geographical coverage and intensity': 349 ALR at 447–48.

[140] Id 467–68.

[141] See Kai Möller, 'Proportionality: Challenging the Critics' (2012) 10 *International Journal of Constitutional Law* 709; Bonnina Challenor, 'The Balancing Act: A Case for Structured Proportionality under the Second Limb of the *Lange* Test' (2015) 40 *University of Western Australia Law Review* 267.

[142] See, eg, the joint judgment at 419 ('It is necessary to keep firmly in mind that the implied freedom is essential to the maintenance of the system of representative and responsible government'); and Gageler J at 433 ('the entirety of the analytical framework set out in *Lange*' reflects 'the underlying reason for the implication', namely 'the protection of political communication on which depends the efficacy of electoral accountability for the exercise of legislative and executive power within the constitutionally prescribed national system of representative and responsible government').

[143] In *Attorney-General (Cth); Ex rel McKinlay* (1975) 135 CLR 1, 35; *Langer v Commonwealth* (1996) 186 CLR 302, 342; *McGinty v Western Australia* (1996) 186 CLR 140, 201 (Toohey J), 221–22 (Gaudron J) and 287 (Gummow J); and *Attorney-General (WA) v Marquet* (2003) 217 CLR 545, 600 (Kirby J).

or more was accepted, in part because of its correspondence to the three-year electoral cycle.[144]

Three years later another aspect of the 2006 amendments was also struck down. The effect of the amendments was to close the electoral rolls against new enrolments as at 8pm on the day of the issue of the writs, thus effectively eliminating what had formerly been a seven-day grace period. Similarly, for transfers of enrolments, what had been a seven-day grace period was reduced to three days. By 4:3 (Hayne, Heydon and Kiefel JJ dissenting) these amendments were held to be invalid.[145]

On the other hand, when faced with a challenge to the closure of the electoral rolls after the seven-day grace period, the Court was unsympathetic.[146] The plaintiffs had argued that even the so-called 'suspension period', when new enrolments are not accepted (from the closure of the rolls until after the election), was unreasonably restrictive of constitutionally guaranteed voting rights. But the argument was unanimously rejected. As Keane J put it, the closure of the rolls before polling day could be seen as conducive to 'orderly and peaceful' voting, efficient scrutiny of votes, and 'prompt and certain declaration of the poll'.[147]

V. Other Rights and Freedoms

In the first flush of enthusiasm for a 'doctrine' of representative government (with popular sovereignty as its 'rational basis'), it was thought that the freedom of political speech might be matched by other freedoms, including at least those of movement, association and assembly; but from the beginning these subsidiary freedoms were implicated more limply. In *ACTV*[148] Gaudron J envisaged acceptance of 'freedom of movement, freedom of association, and, perhaps, freedom of speech generally'. But in *Kruger v Commonwealth*,[149] only she felt able to hold that the forced removal of Aboriginal children from their families under the *Aboriginals Ordinance* 1918 (NT) had been unconstitutional.[150]

Though treating freedoms of movement and association as merely ancillary to that of political communication, she stressed that they were 'subsidiary only in the sense that they support and supplement that latter freedom'; they were in no way 'inferior to or less robust than it'.[151] Toohey J also recognised freedom of association as 'an essential ingredient of political communication' extending 'to all the people of the Commonwealth', but found it 'not possible to say at this stage' whether the impugned provisions were therefore invalid.[152]

[144] *Roach v Electoral Commissioner* (2007) 233 CLR 162. The case was particularly poignant because the plaintiff was an Aboriginal woman, thus harking back to the period when (until 1962) most Aboriginals were excluded from voting.

[145] *Rowe v Electoral Commissioner* (2010) 243 CLR 1.

[146] *Murphy v Electoral Commissioner* (2016) 261 CLR 28.

[147] Ibid, 89.

[148] (1992) 177 CLR 106, 212.

[149] (1997) 190 CLR 1. When the case was argued Kirby J had only just been appointed, and did not sit.

[150] A claim that the Ordinance was made 'for the purpose of the protection and preservation of persons of the Aboriginal race' was in her view insufficient, though (at 129) she conceded that if it had been possible to say 'that the Ordinance was necessary for the preservation or protection of the Aboriginal race', that would have been sufficient.

[151] 190 CLR at 126.

[152] Ibid 91, 93. He had emphasised (at 73) that the issues were to be decided 'solely on the pleadings'.

McHugh J agreed that the Constitution 'necessarily implies' freedoms of association and movement at the federal level; but he also agreed with Dawson J that section 122 of the Constitution precluded any restriction of legislative powers relating to the territories.[153] Brennan CJ and Gummow J held that even if such a freedom existed, the ostensible purposes of the Ordinance were compatible with it, and in any event that the plaintiffs had shown no 'textual or structural foundation'[154] or 'logical or practical necessity'[155] for the implication of such a freedom.

In *Tajjour v New South Wales*[156] a provision against consorting with convicted offenders[157] was considered (and held to be valid) primarily as a burden on the freedom of political communication, 'consorting' being treated merely as a form of 'communication'. The view of Gaudron J in *Kruger* (that freedom of association is 'subsidiary' to that of political communication, but not 'inferior' or 'less robust') was repeated and reinforced by Gageler J, who again saw association 'for the purpose of engaging in communication' as 'part and parcel of the protected freedom'. He agreed that the provision was valid, but only because in his view it could be read down so as not to apply to 'association for a purpose of engaging in communication on governmental or political matter[s]'.[158] French CJ held (in dissent) that the provision could not be read down, and was therefore wholly invalid; but he based this on the freedom of political communication rather than that of association.[159]

Earlier, in *South Australia v Totani*,[160] French CJ had appeared to look favourably at dicta accepting an implied freedom of association; and Gummow J had noted 'some, but not general, support'[161] for such acceptance. But in *Wainohu v New South Wales*,[162] the subordinate and dependent status of any freedom of association had almost unanimous support. Both in *Totani* and in *Wainohu* (both involving membership of motorcycle clubs) provisions for judicially ordered restrictions on consorting with members of 'declared organisations' were held to be invalid; but that result rested on incompatibility with the exercise of judicial power,[163] rather than on freedom of association or communication.[164]

In *Mulholland v Australian Electoral Commission*,[165] the Democratic Labor Party mounted various challenges to the requirement (under section 124 of the *Commonwealth Electoral Act* 1918 (Cth)) that a political party must have at least 500 members to be eligible

[153] Ibid 69–70(Dawson J), 143 (McHugh J).
[154] Brennan CJ at 45.
[155] Gummow J at 157.
[156] (2014) 254 CLR 508 at 578.
[157] *Crimes Act* 1900 (NSW) s 93x, inserted by the *Crimes Amendment (Consorting and Organised Crime) Act* 2012 (NSW).
[158] 254 CLR at 589.
[159] Ibid 551–56. Earlier at 547, he had also held that the 'principle of legality' (above n 28) could not be used to limit s 93x so as not to impair the *common law* freedoms of speech and association: 'Parliament's choice of language must be respected, even if the unavoidable consequence … is constitutional invalidity.'
[160] (2010) 242 CLR 1, 30 – citing Robin Handley, 'Public Order, Petitioning and Freedom of Assembly' (1986) 7 *Journal of Legal History* 123 at 138–141) to suggest support for such a freedom through 'historical connection' with the right to petition Parliament under the *Bill of Rights* 1689 (1 Wm & Mar Sess 2 c 2).
[161] 242 CLR at 54 (at least as to association for the purpose of political communication).
[162] (2011) 243 CLR 181.
[163] In the sense envisaged by *Kable v Director of Public Prosecutions (NSW)*, above n 62.
[164] Hayne J emphasised in *Totani* (at 84–85) the drastic limits on freedom of association involved; but only because these limits were to follow from the decision *of a court*.
[165] (2004) 220 CLR 181.

for registration, and hence entitled to use its name to identify its candidates on ballot papers. An argument based on freedom of political communication failed, primarily on the ground that purely statutory rights (such as that to identification on a ballot paper) are not protected by the implied freedom. The challenge also relied in part on an implied freedom of association which was said to include 'an associated freedom of political privacy', thus excluding the power of the Electoral Commission (under section 138A of the Act) to seek details of party membership. McHugh and Kirby JJ were 'prepared to accept'[166] that such a freedom could be implied, but not that it had been impermissibly burdened. Most other judges held simply that since any such freedom was merely a 'corollary' of the primary freedom of political communication, any reliance on it must fail along with reliance on that primary freedom itself.

VI. The Wider Context

In continuing to reaffirm her support for freedoms of movement and association, Gaudron J was seeking to give them constitutional force; but her willingness to recognise unwritten rights as having some legal significance was also evident at less exalted levels. In *Teoh's Case*[167] the High Court majority (McHugh J dissenting) found a 'legitimate expectation'[168] that, in proceedings to determine whether Ah Hin Teoh should be deported, the best interests of his children should have been seen as a primary consideration. Mason CJ, Deane and Toohey JJ based this expectation on the Commonwealth's ratification of the Convention on the Rights of the Child,[169] but Gaudron J had a different approach. Initially she found it 'arguable' that, as citizens, both children and parents have 'a common law right' to such an expectation; but since that possibility had not been argued, she did not pursue it. Instead, she agreed that the expectation arose from the Convention – but only because it 'gives expression to a fundamental human right which is taken for granted by Australian society'. In short, the common law right of children to have their interests treated as 'a primary consideration', whether or not it was sufficient to require the Court's conclusion by its own legal force, was a necessary condition of allowing the Convention to have that effect.

In New Zealand during the 1980s Sir Robin Cooke (as he then was) suggested that some common law rights may 'lie so deep that even Parliament could not override them';[170] and when the High Court has been asked to respond to that suggestion, it has repeatedly reserved its opinion.[171] The first reference to 'fundamental common law rights' in the High Court itself came from Deane J in August 1986,[172] three weeks after he had sat for the

[166] Ibid, 277 (Kirby J); McHugh J at 225.
[167] *Minister for Immigration and Ethnic Affairs v Teoh* (1995) 183 CLR 273.
[168] The use of this concept for such a purpose was later disapproved in *Re Minister for Immigration and Multicultural Affairs; Ex parte Lam* (2003) 214 CLR 1, where the dissenting view of McHugh J prevailed.
[169] Opened for signature 20 November 1989, 1577 UNTS 3 (entered into force 2 September 1990).
[170] *Fraser v State Services Commission* [1984] 1 NZLR 116, 121; *Taylor v New Zealand Poultry Board* [1984] 1 NZLR 394, 398.
[171] *Union Steamship Co of Australia Ltd v King* (1988) 166 CLR 1, 10; *Durham Holdings Pty Ltd v New South Wales* (2001) 205 CLR 399, 409–10, 423; *South Australia v Totani* (2010) 242 CLR 1, 29 (French CJ).
[172] *Rohde v Director of Public Prosecutions* (1986) 161 CLR 119, 132.

last time with Murphy J. Since then the phrase has been in frequent use, usually (as on that occasion) as a basis for 'the principle of legality', but occasionally with wider implications. The police officers who in *Plenty v Dillon*[173] had entered private property without permission while attempting to serve a summons were successfully sued for trespass, since neither statute nor common law[174] afforded them the authority to enter. As Gaudron and McHugh JJ put it,[175] 'inconvenience … is not a ground for eroding fundamental common law rights'. That observation was relied on again (along with 'the principle of legality') to justify the conclusion in *Coco v The Queen*[176] that police entry on premises for the undisclosed purpose of installing a listening device had constituted a trespass; that judicial approval of entry for that purpose was wholly void; and that neither state nor federal legislation had authorised that approval.

In cases exploring the limits of the 'inherent jurisdiction' or 'inherent powers' of superior courts, the notion of 'fundamental common law rights' has been less influential.[177] In *NH v Director of Public Prosecutions*,[178] where four defendants had been formally acquitted of murder after the trial judge was *mistakenly* told that a verdict of 'not guilty' had been agreed to by the requisite jury majority, the High Court held that the acquittal must stand: once the acquittal had been perfected by judgment, the Full Supreme Court had no inherent power to interfere. Yet even here, the emphasis was on the limits of a court's 'inherent powers', rather than on the rights of the accused. The case may therefore be merely an illustration of the point made earlier in this book in Chapter 2 by George Williams,[179] with particular reference to the *Communist Party Case*:[180] that protection of human rights may be 'merely a consequence of applying constitutional principles that are intended to protect other systemic or public interests'. In particular, as George Winterton had noted[181] even before the *Kable* decision,[182] the reading of Chapter III of the Constitution as requiring that the exercise of judicial power be consistent 'with the essential character of a court or with the nature of judicial power' will often have the collateral effect of protecting individual rights.

[173] (1991) 171 CLR 635.

[174] The precedents relied on included *Semayne's Case* (1604) 5 Co Rep 91a, 77 ER 194, and *Entick v Carrington* (1765) 19 St Tr 1030.

[175] (1991) 171 CLR 635, 654.

[176] (1994) 179 CLR 427, esp 435–6, 438, 446.

[177] See, eg, *Batistatos v Roads and Traffic Authority of New South Wales* (2006) 226 CLR 256, 297 (Kirby J suggesting that the very terminology of 'inherent' powers might pose an undesirable threat to fundamental common law rights); *Assistant Commissioner Condon v Pompano Pty Ltd* (2013) 252 CLR 37 (noting the decision in *Al Rawi v Security Service* [2012] 1 AC 531 that courts could not use their inherent powers to deny a fundamental common law right to 'open justice', but holding that a statutory provision for a closed hearing was valid); and *Lee v New South Wales Crime Commission* (2013) 251 CLR 196 (permitting a person to be examined under the *Criminal Assets Recovery Act* 1990 (NSW) about conduct which was the subject of pending criminal charges – but with Hayne, Kiefel and Bell JJ dissenting, the latter protesting at 293–94 that the right to silence is 'not a mere forensic advantage' but 'a fundamental common law right').

[178] (2016) 260 CLR 546 (reversing the decision of the Supreme Court of South Australia).

[179] Above ch 2, *sub nom* 'Coincidental Protection of Human Rights'.

[180] *Australian Communist Party v Commonwealth* (1951) 83 CLR 1.

[181] George Winterton, 'The Separation of Powers as an Implied Bill of Rights' in Geoffrey Lindell (ed), *Future Directions in Australian Constitutional Law* (Annandale, Federation Press, 1994) 185, esp at 199–200. Significantly at 204–07, Winterton was concerned to argue that this potential should not be pressed too far.

[182] *Kable v Director of Public Prosecutions (NSW)*, above n 62.

One area in which the protection of rights might arguably be understood as more than merely collateral is that of the right to counsel. A person accused of crime has long had a statutory right 'to be represented by counsel at his own or at someone else's expense', but 'does not have a right to be provided with counsel at public expense';[183] and in *Dietrich v The Queen*[184] the Court insisted that this distinction must stand.[185] Yet the majority also held that an accused has a 'positive right'[186] to receive a fair trial, and that 'in the absence of compelling circumstances'[187] this will normally mean that if an indigent person charged with a serious offence is not represented by counsel, the trial judge should adjourn, postpone or stay the proceedings until representation is provided. This much had already been foreshadowed by Barwick CJ in *McInnis v The Queen*,[188] but what *Dietrich* added was that if the trial was allowed to proceed without representation for the accused, any resulting conviction must be quashed on the grounds of a miscarriage of justice.[189] The analytical focus remains on the elements of a fair trial; but for practical purposes the result is the right of an accused to be represented by counsel, or at least a right not to be convicted in the absence of such representation.[190]

When a written constitution combines the British idea of parliamentary sovereignty with the American idea of judicial review, the resulting distribution of power is inherently unstable – both unpredictable and subject to shifts over time. Not only are the implied power structures mutually incompatible, but they lead to a contradiction 'between the theory that sees Parliament as the source of all law, and the idea that the law may include principles that Parliament has not made'.[191] Since the relative weights to be ascribed

[183] The language is that of Barwick CJ in *McInnis v The Queen* (1979) 143 CLR 575, 579.

[184] (1992) 177 CLR 292 – decided on 13 November 1992, six weeks after *Nationwide News* and *ACTV*. See Jason Pierce, *Inside the Mason Court Revolution: The High Court of Australia Transformed* (Durham, Carolina Academic Press, 2006) 52–3.

[185] For example, Gaudron J insists ((1992) 177 CLR, at 362) that Ch III entrenches a 'fundamental requirement that a trial be fair'; yet three pages later she also insists 'the question whether public funds should be allocated for the legal representation of persons charged with criminal offences is one for governments, not for the courts': 365.

[186] ibid, – but with the caveat that to speak of a 'positive right' was merely a matter of convenience, as explained by Deane J in *Jago v District Court (NSW)* (1989) 168 CLR 23, 56–7.

[187] ibid, at 357 (Tooley J) – or less exigently for Mason CJ and McHugh J (at 311) 'depending on all the circumstances of the particular case'.

[188] Above n 183 (esp at 579) – denying an 'absolute right' to legal aid, but affirming 'that it is in the best interest of the administration of justice' for accused persons to have the 'advantage' of being represented by counsel, so that a trial judge 'ought very seriously to consider whether an accused should be forced on without counsel in any case in which there is a reasonable possibility that he may obtain the services of counsel ... without unbearable delay'. Emphasising the need in such a case 'for the most careful weighing' of all the interests involved, 'and, generally, of the administration of justice', Barwick CJ dealt with the case before him on the assumption that, in refusing an adjournment, the trial judge was in error.

[189] In *McInnis* the majority had held that there was no miscarriage of justice because the evidence against the accused was so strong as to exclude any realistic chance of acquittal, and (with Murphy J dissenting) had refused to hold (as Burt CJ had done in the Western Australian Court of Criminal Appeal) that the decision to proceed without legal representation was itself a miscarriage of justice.

[190] As to the results of this, see Senate Legal and Constitutional Committee, *Inquiry into the Australian Legal Aid System* (Second Report, June 1997, Parliamentary Paper No 113 of 1997) ch 4, available at www.aph.gov.au/Parliamentary_Business/Committees/Senate/Legal_and_Constitutional_Affairs/Completed_inquiries/1996-99/legalaid/report/c07.

[191] Beverley McLachlin, 'Unwritten Constitutional Principles: What is Going On?' (2006) 4 *New Zealand Journal of Public and International Law* 147, 153, paraphrasing David Dyzenhaus, 'The Unwritten Constitution and the Rule of Law', in Grant Huscroft and Ian Brodie (eds), *Constitutionalism in the Charter Era* (London, Lexis Nexis Butterworths, 2004) 383.

to different sources of law must ultimately be determined by the judiciary,[192] one might theoretically expect that under such a constitution the judiciary would emerge as supreme; but at least where the legislature and executive retain significant power, a court which exalts itself too highly is likely to find itself constrained by retaliatory checks and balances. In India, when the Supreme Court ruled that the Parliament did not in fact have unlimited power to amend the constitutionally guaranteed 'Fundamental Rights' whenever they proved inconvenient,[193] the ensuing tensions led in June 1975 to a State of Emergency that lasted until March 1977. Initially, in cases like *ADM Jabalpur v Shivkant Shukla*,[194] it seemed that the Supreme Court had been permanently cowed; but in cases like *Maneka Gandhi v Union of India*[195] the Court reasserted itself so vigorously that it seemed, at least for a time, to emerge as the country's most powerful (and even its most democratic) institution.[196]

In Australia the tensions have been far less dramatic, and certainly less confrontational. The potential scope for judicial review was significantly curtailed at the outset by the decision that the Constitution should not include any comprehensive protection of expressly enumerated rights. It was further confined by the continuing influence of both *D'Emden v Pedder*[197] and the *Engineers Case*[198] – the latter not only as a source of seemingly ingrained judicial adherence to 'strict and complete legalism',[199] but also through its insistence that the Commonwealth's grants of legislative power confer 'authority as plenary and as ample … as the Imperial Parliament in the plenitude of its power possessed and could bestow'.[200] In politically sensitive areas such as immigration – initially in the context of the White Australia policy, and since 1992 in the context of steadily increasing governmental persecution of refugees – the Court's reluctance to interfere has appeared (with some notable exceptions)[201] to cross the fine line that separates 'judicial restraint' from abdication of judicial responsibility. And ironically, in the context of the Parliament's concern with its

[192] Tony Blackshield, 'Fidelity to External (Re)sources' in James Stellios (ed), *Encounters with Constitutional Interpretation and Legal Education: Essays in Honour of Michael Coper* (Annandale, Federation Press, 2018) 94.

[193] Initially in *Golak Nath v State of Punjab*, AIR 1967 SC 1643, and more decisively in *Kesavananda v State of Kerala*, AIR 1973 SC 1461. For the background see AR Blackshield, '"Fundamental Rights" and the Institutional Viability of the Indian Supreme Court' (1966) 8 *Journal of the Indian Law Institute* 139.

[194] AIR 1976 SC 1207.

[195] AIR 1978 SC 597.

[196] See Upendra Baxi, 'Demosprudence versus Jurisprudence: The Indian Judicial Experience in the Context of Comparative Constitutional Studies' (2014) 14 *Macquarie Law Journal* 3.

[197] (1904) 1 CLR 91 – with its emphasis (at 109) that the Commonwealth 'is, within the ambit of its authority, a sovereign State', and (at 110) that the introductory words of s 51 'conferred … sovereign authority, absolute and uncontrolled except … [as] restricted by the Constitution itself' so that 'the Commonwealth is entitled, within the ambit of its authority, to exercise its legislative and executive powers in absolute freedom' subject only to the Constitution itself.

[198] (1920) 28 CLR 129.

[199] As memorably endorsed by Sir Owen Dixon on the occasion of his swearing in as Chief Justice: (1952) 85 CLR xi at xiii. In fact Dixon's position was much more complex: see Owen Dixon, 'Concerning Judicial Method' (1956) 29 *Australian Law Journal* 468; Rachael Gray, *The Constitutional Jurisprudence and Judicial Method of the High Court of Australia: The Dixon, Mason and Gleeson Eras* (Adelaide, Presidian Legal Publications, 2008) 24–30 and 38–41; AR Blackshield, Book Review, *Sydney Morning Herald*, 5 March 1966, p 16; Tony Blackshield, 'Realism', in Tony Blackshield, Michael Coper and George Williams (eds), *The Oxford Companion to the High Court of Australia* (OUP, 2001) 582, 584. Cf generally Stephen Gageler, 'Legalism', id 429.

[200] Id 153, quoting *Hodge v The Queen* (1883) 9 App Cas 117, 132.

[201] Including *Potter v Minahan* (1908) 7 CLR 277 (but with Isaacs and Higgins JJ dissenting in part) and *O'Keefe v Calwell* (1949) 77 CLR 261 (but with Latham CJ and Dixon J dissenting in favour of deportation).

own affairs, the concept of 'exclusive cognisance' has recently been given a more absolutist operation in relation to the Australian Parliament than has ever been accorded to it in relation to the Parliament at Westminster.[202]

Obviously, for a federal government with limited powers, parliamentary sovereignty is impossible. But the currents of Australian constitutional jurisprudence have mostly tended to run in that direction – in part because of the enduring influence of AV Dicey,[203] and in part because the Constitution itself is dependent on Imperial legislation, and thus on the sovereignty of the Imperial Parliament.[204] In the Mason Court of 1987–1995, it appeared that the currents might be starting to run in a different direction;[205] but the result was an inevitable reaction.[206] In context it is hardly surprising that Deane and Toohey JJ met with little success when they sought to counter the idea of parliamentary sovereignty by asserting an alternative model of popular sovereignty; or that the idea of implied constitutional rights has been met at times with outright hostility, and more typically with an awkward timidity.

[202] *Alley v Gillespie* (2018) 353 ALR 1.

[203] Whose *Introduction to the Study of the Law of the Constitution* (1 ed 1885, 10 ed 1959) was the basic textbook on constitutional law in Australian law schools until the 1950s. See Pierce, above n 184 at 62–64.

[204] *Commonwealth of Australia Constitution Act* 1900 (Imp).

[205] See Pierce, above n 184, esp at 157–178.

[206] For a discussion (as at 2006) of the 'retreat' from 'implied rights jurisprudence', see id 248–257.

5

The Reception of International Law in Constitutional Litigation – The *Al-Kateb* Battle and its Aftermath

ADAM FLETCHER

Is the Australian Constitution fit for purpose in the twenty-first century? This is a complex and, for some, emotive question, which I suspect would elicit an affirmative answer from most readers. However, if that purpose is to establish and maintain a democratic polity under the rule of law, the following scenarios warrant consideration:

1. In the wake of a particularly contentious episode of the political panel show *Q&A*,[1] Parliament passes a law prohibiting 'undue' criticism of the Australian Government on both of the national broadcasters – the Australian Broadcasting Corporation and the Special Broadcasting Service.
2. A Bill is introduced into Parliament to prohibit citizens with certain backgrounds or connections from voting in federal elections for ill-specified national security reasons. It is criticised as racially discriminatory by Parliament's own Joint Committee on Human Rights, but passes both Houses rapidly with the support of both major political parties.
3. Parliament passes a law requiring the detention of a specified class of persons, which may include both citizens and non-citizens, on an administrative basis. The detention is to continue until release is authorised by the relevant Minister, and is subject only to judicial (not merits) review.

Nothing express in the Constitution prevents any of these scenarios from eventuating. If it were not for the High Court of Australia having developed the 'implied freedom' doctrines protecting political speech and the right to take part in federal elections,[2] the first two would be far from inconceivable in the current political climate, indeed even today it is not absolutely certain that they would be unconstitutional.[3] There is also no

[1] Q&A is a weekly television programme on the Australian Broadcasting Corporation's Channel 2 which 'focuses mostly on politics but ranges across all of the big issues that set Australians thinking, talking and debating' – see www.abc.net.au/tv/qanda/about.htm.

[2] See Section II below; see also ch 4 in this volume.

[3] On certain accounts of the correct proportionality tests to be employed in the application of the implied freedom doctrines, greater deference to Parliament on political questions such as these might be constitutionally

specific constitutional impediment to the racially discriminatory aspect of the legislation in the second scenario.[4]

The third scenario, at least as it relates to 'unlawful' non-citizens, has already come to pass and been deemed constitutional by the High Court, even though it had previously been found to breach international law by the UN Human Rights Committee.[5] The extension of such an indefinite administrative detention regime to Australian citizens, as long as it is for a constitutional purpose other than punishment, has not been ruled out.[6] This chapter examines the relevant case, *Al-Kateb v Godwin* ('*Al-Kateb*'),[7] and focuses in particular on the minority argument of Kirby J that international law ought to be considered in interpreting the Constitution where it is silent on matters of fundamental rights such as personal liberty – an argument strongly rejected by McHugh J in the majority. However, a brief sketch of the High Court's approach to international law generally, and international human rights law in particular, is necessary to provide some context for this discussion.

I. Background – International Law and the Constitution

The High Court's treatment of international law in constitutional litigation – indeed, in any litigation – might generously be described as wary.[8] Powerful voices within and outside the judiciary seek to guard against 'intrusions from outside' into Australian sovereignty and the original will of the Constitution's drafters – particularly from 'vague and uncertain' principles of international law.[9]

The Constitution itself is silent on how international law should be received in Australia; a result of a decision during the Convention debates to follow the United Kingdom ('UK')

appropriate – see, eg, Dan Meagher, 'The Brennan Conception of the Implied Freedom: Theory, Proportionality and Deference' (2011) 30 *University of Queensland Law Journal* 119. Admittedly, the Commonwealth would need to present robust justifications for this kind of legislation, but restrictions on rights which might be seen as arbitrary under international law cannot be assumed to be invalid in Australia in the absence of a constitutional bill of rights.

[4] See *Kartinyeri v Cth* (1998) 195 CLR 337, 391–392. See also ch 9 in this volume.

[5] *A v Australia*, Communication No 560/1993, UN Doc CCPR/C/59/D/560/1993 (30 April 1997); *C v Australia* Communication No 900/1999, UN Doc CCPR/C/76/D/900/1999 (28 October 2002). On the disjuncture between international and domestic law on this point (albeit before *Al-Kateb* was decided), see Sam Blay and Ryszard Piotrowicz, 'The Awfulness of Lawfulness: Some Reflections on the Tension between International and Domestic Law' (2000) 21 *Australian Year Book of International Law* 1.

[6] *Al-Kateb v Godwin* (2004) 219 CLR 562, 588–589.

[7] Ibid.

[8] Others have used terms such as 'ambivalent' – see Hilary Charlesworth, 'International Law and the High Court' (2005) 68 *Precedent* 20.

[9] See Hilary Charlesworth; Madelaine Chiam; Devika Hovell and George Williams, 'Deep Anxieties: Australia and the International Legal Order,' (2003) 25 *Sydney Law Review* 423, 424 – also Goldsworthy, 'Originalism in Constitutional Interpretation' (1997) 25 *Federal Law Review* 1; Stephen Bouwhuis, 'International Law by the Back Door?' (1998) 72 *Australian Law Journal* 794; the judgments of McHugh and Callinan JJ in *Al-Kateb v Godwin*, above n 6; Dyson Heydon, 'Judicial Activism and the Death of the Rule of Law' (2004) Otago Law Review 2 and his Honour's judgment in *Roach v Electoral Commissioner* (2007) 233 CLR 162, 225. These legal expert voices have been supplemented by influential public figures such as former federal Ministers Julia Gillard, Bob Carr, John Howard, Philip Ruddock and Tony Abbott (for an overview of the tenor of their commentary, see eg Bernard Keane, 'Gillard's 'lashing' of the High Court' *Crikey*, 2 September 2011 and 'Foreign Minister Bob Carr criticises High Court for ruling against 'Malaysia Solution'' *news.com.au*, 28 June 2012 (unattributed)).

rather than the United States ('US') model in this regard.[10] There is no equivalent of Article VI of the US Constitution or the later Article 25 of the German Constitution prescribing the legal force of treaties or other forms of international law. This has resulted in a strictly dualist legal system, whereby treaties to which the Commonwealth is party must be transformed into domestic legislation before they attain the force of law.[11] In addition, the Constitution's silence leaves entry into treaties and other international agreements to Westminster convention, which means that it is at the sole discretion of the executive – albeit with Parliament in an advisory role, at least since reforms in the 1990s.[12]

There is no question that the Constitution is the highest law of the land – a 'special statute' establishing the foundation of our legal system.[13] Australia's obligations under international law, which may not even be sanctioned by Parliament, are of little domestic legal consequence in comparison.[14] Nevertheless, the question arises as to whether the Constitution, and Commonwealth legislation made under it, ought to be *interpreted* with important international law developments in mind. The drafters of the Constitution necessarily drew inspiration from the constitutional law of other nations; particularly the UK and the US.[15] Constitutional jurisprudence from those other jurisdictions, for example to interpret sections 51(xxix) and 92, has therefore been a routine and accepted source upon which the High Court has drawn over the years.[16]

However, the reception of international law has not been consistent, and has tended to depend on the nature of the case at hand. For example, the early case of *Potter v Minahan*[17] saw the court survey principles derived from both foreign and international law in deciding whether a citizen who had been absent for many years could be considered an 'immigrant' for constitutional purposes. The decision cited US, UK and South African jurisprudence, and early guides to relevant transnational law such as *Dicey's Conflict of Laws*.[18] Given the Australian Constitution's structural and contextual roots in US and UK constitutional law, and South Africa's status at the time as a comparable British dominion,[19] the use of these sources of law was entirely orthodox.

International obligations are of course relevant in delineating the scope of the external affairs power, and have been raised in a wide variety of cases concerning other aspects

[10] See Hilary Charlesworth et al, above n 9, 428–429. Note that, at the time of federation, it was arguably assumed that UK law would cover the field in this regard, given Australia's status as a British Dominion.

[11] See, eg, Michael Kirby, 'The common law and international law – a dynamic contemporary dialogue' (2010) 30 *Legal Studies* 30.

[12] See Charlesworth et al, above n 9, 438–444.

[13] See Kristen Walker, 'International Law as a Tool of Constitutional Interpretation' (2003) 28 *Monash University Law Review* 85, 86.

[14] See Charlesworth, above n 8.

[15] See Elisa Arcioni and Andrew McLeod, 'Cautious But Engaged-An Empirical Study of the Australian High Court's Use of Foreign and International Materials in Constitutional Cases,' (2014) 42 *International Journal of Legal Information* 437, 440–442.

[16] Section 51(xxix) is the external affairs power and s 92 is the guarantee of free trade among the states. See Justin Gleeson, 'The Increasing Internationalisation of Australian Law' (2017) 28 *Public Law Review* 25, 28.

[17] (1908) 7 CLR 277.

[18] Ibid at 290–291, where Griffiths CJ cites American and South African jurisprudence. See also 293–294, where Barton J cites *Dicey's Conflict of Laws* on international rules relating to sovereignty and citizenship.

[19] Technically South Africa did not have this status until 1909, but the Anglo-Boer war had concluded the matter, several years before *Potter* was decided.

of the Constitution over many years.[20] In this chapter, I will focus on international law as a limitation on constitutional powers of the executive and Parliament to impinge on individual rights, as this is Kirby J's primary concern in *Al-Kateb* and related cases,[21] and it is also the overarching theme of the present volume.

Nevertheless, a brief discussion of some notable related cases is necessary to frame the discussion. For example, in *Polites v Cth*,[22] the High Court endorsed the common law principle that statutes should be construed compatibly with Australia's relevant international obligations unless Parliament clearly manifests a contrary intention (the 'presumption of consistency'). It was also put in argument in *Polites* that the Constitution ought to be construed consistently with international law, since it was itself an Act of (the Imperial) Parliament. This proposition was rejected by the court. In the words of Dixon J '[i]t is nothing to the point that the Constitution derives its force from an Imperial enactment. It is none the less a constitution.'[23] As applied to Australian statutes, the principle of consistency has been accepted – if not always embraced[24] – by the High Court ever since.[25]

In *Mabo v Queensland (No 2)*,[26] Brennan J described the relationship the court saw at that time between international law and the common law:

> The common law does not necessarily conform to international law, but international law is a legitimate and important influence on the development of the common law, especially when international law declares the existence of universal human rights. A common law doctrine founded on unjust discrimination in the enjoyment of civil and political rights demands reconsideration.[27]

This decision's principal constitutional significance was that it overturned one of the framers' basic legal assumptions – that Australia was unsettled when it was occupied by the British according to the *terra nullius* doctrine.[28] The court did, however, find that English law was still validly received into Australia according to international law at the time of settlement, preserving the existing Australian legal order.[29] The Full Federal Court case of *Nulyarimma v Thompson*[30] discussed the reception of customary international norms, including norms categorised as peremptory or *jus cogens* norms, such as the prohibition on genocide. By a majority of two to one, the Full Court decided that such norms do not form part of Australia's domestic law in the absence of 'transformational' legislation.[31]

[20] See Walker, above n 13, 88.

[21] See also, eg, *Kartinyeri*, above n 4; also *Langer v Cth* (1996) 186 CLR 302, *Re Aird; Ex Parte Alpert* (2004) 220 CLR 308, *Fardon v Attorney-General for the State of Queensland* (2004) 223 CLR 575.

[22] (1945) 70 CLR 60, 68–69, 77, 80–81.

[23] Ibid, 78 (Dixon J). See also 74 (Rich J), 75 (Starke J), 79 (McTiernan J). See further Walker, above n 13, 86.

[24] *Al-Kateb*, above n 6, 590–591.

[25] See further Dan Meagher, 'The Common Law Presumption of Consistency with International Law: Some Observations from Australia (and Comparisons with New Zealand)' (2012) *New Zealand Law Review* 465.

[26] (1992) 175 CLR 1, 42.

[27] Ibid, 42.

[28] Ibid, 45.

[29] See Gerry Simpson, '*Mabo*, International Law, Terra Nullius and the Stories of Settlement: An Unresolved Jurisprudence' (1993) 19 *Melbourne University Law Review* 195. The somewhat hesitant view Brennan J expressed about the influence of international law (Simpson, at 207, terms it the 'deus ex machina' approach) is clearly evidenced in other cases, such as *Dietrich v R* (1992) 177 CLR 292, 321.

[30] (1999) 165 ALR 621.

[31] Amelia Simpson and George Williams, 'International Law and Constitutional Interpretation' (2000) 11 *Public Law Review* 205, 207.

By contrast, in the High Court case of *Polyukhovich v Cth*,[32] Deane and Gaudron JJ considered the international law prohibition on retrospective criminal laws (for example in the European Convention on Human Rights and the International Covenant on Civil and Political Rights ('ICCPR')) to be relevant to the determination of the scope of Parliament's power to pass the *War Crimes Act 1945* (Cth).[33] As is often the case, however, these considerations were not decisive in the result in *Polyukhovich*.

For the time being, Michael Kirby is the sole High Court Justice to have applied international law – meaning treaties and custom binding Australia on the international plane, as opposed to judgments from other common law jurisdictions – directly in constitutional interpretation.[34] Unlike the interpretation of statutes and the development of the common law, this judicial task has been otherwise universally thought of as restricted to a limited range of sources, such as UK constitutional law, the common law, pre-1900 international law, certain statute law and (latterly) the Convention Debates.[35] In *Newcrest Mining v Cth*, his Honour first set out his preferred approach, based on the *Bangalore Principles on the Domestic Application of International Human Rights Norms* – the outcome document of an international judicial colloquium held in 1988:[36]

> Where the Constitution is ambiguous, this Court should adopt that meaning which conforms to the principles of fundamental rights rather than an interpretation which would involve a departure from such rights. …
>
> To the full extent that its text permits, Australia's Constitution, as the fundamental law of government in this country, accommodates itself to international law, including in so far as that law expresses basic rights.[37]

It has been noted that *Newcrest* was perhaps an imperfect vehicle for launching Kirby J's mission to have international human rights law considered a legitimate source in constitutional interpretation. The case concerned property rights of a mining company, and his Honour drew on Article 17 of the Universal Declaration of Human Rights, which is arguably not a binding international law norm, having neither been incorporated into the ICCPR or International Covenant on Economic, Social and Cultural Rights, nor indeed crystallised into custom.[38] Nevertheless, his Honour's subsequent applications of his novel consistency

[32] (1991) 172 CLR 501.

[33] Ibid, 611–612 (Deane J), 699–700 (Gaudron J).

[34] *Roach v Electoral Commissioner*, above n 9, 225 (Heydon J). Heydon J noted that 21 other Justices of the High Court had taken a different position.

[35] See *Al-Kateb*, above n 6, 589 (McHugh J); *Cole v Whitfield* (1988) 165 CLR 360; Sir Owen Dixon, 'The Common Law as an Ultimate Constitutional Foundation' in *Jesting Pilate* (William S Hein & Co, 2nd ed, 1997) 203; Virginia Bell, *Section 80 – The Great Constitutional Tautology*, The Lucinda Lecture, Monash University, 24 October 2013, available at www.hcourt.gov.au/assets/publications/speeches/current-justices/bellj/bellj241013.pdf, 31–34.

[36] The Principles were released as a summary of issues discussed at a Judicial Colloquium on 'The Domestic Application of International Human Rights Norms,' held in Bangalore, India from 24–26 February 1988. They were reprinted in 3 *Commonwealth Secretariat Developing Human Rights Jurisprudence* 151 (see in particular Principles 4 and 7). On their application in Australia, see further Michael Kirby, 'Domestic Implementation of International Human Rights Norms' (1999) 5 *Australian Journal of Human Rights* 109; Glen Cranwell, 'The Bangalore Principles and the Internationalisation of Australian Law' (2002) 32 *Australian Institute of Administrative Law Forum* 1.

[37] *Newcrest Mining (WA) Ltd v Cth* (1997) 190 CLR 513, 657–658. Kirby J had previously used international legal sources in applying the separation of powers doctrine in *Wilson v Minister for Aboriginal and Torres Strait Island Affairs* (1996) 189 CLR 1, but *Newcrest* was the case in which he first devised his general/preferred approach.

[38] See Walker, above n 13, 93–94.

approach, some of which are set out below, drew on less controversial foundations, such as the prohibitions on racial discrimination (common to several international human rights treaties) and arbitrary detention (in Article 9 of the ICCPR).[39]

Kirby J's approach still seems radical (or heretical, depending on one's point of view[40]) today, but repudiations of it[41] often seem to overlook the fact that his Honour always emphasised the primacy of the constitutional text (as in the passage above), cautioned against 'distortion' of constitutional meaning or the 'creation of ambiguities,'[42] and urged consideration of international law only as a subsidiary argument where Australian law produces a result which is inconsistent with fundamental human rights or dignity.[43]

His Honour argued that there is no need to take a hide-bound approach to constitutional interpretation when international law is accepted as a legitimate influence on statutory interpretation – through the presumption of consistency with international obligations ('presumption of consistency') – and on the development of the common law.[44] Kirby J's arguments, as developed in *Al-Kateb*, are explored further below.

Empirical research by Elisa Arcioni and Andrew McLeod on the use of international legal sources in Australian constitutional litigation between 2009 and 2012 revealed it to be more widespread than perhaps might be expected, with more than 80 references in 41 constitutional cases.[45] However, the use of international (as well as foreign) law was found to be 'issue-dependent'.[46] Where it was discussed, as opposed to merely cited, the authors found that the Justices generally engaged with the litigants' submissions on international law, but ultimately found it to be inapplicable in deciding the matters at hand.[47]

The cases studied by Arcioni and McLeod included some dealing with human rights issues, including *South Australia v Totani*,[48] *Rowe v Electoral Commissioner*[49] and *Kirk v Industrial Commission of NSW*,[50] as well as others dealing with proprietary rights and 'just terms' compensation claims.[51] In none of these cases was foreign or international law decisive – although in *Rowe* the engagement was relatively extensive and arguably had some influence.[52] The authors speculate that the High Court's accepted constitutional interpretation process 'imposes a barrier to the adoption of foreign [defined as including

[39] See *Kartinyeri*, above n and *Al-Kateb*.

[40] *Al-Kateb*, above n 6, 589 (McHugh J). It should be noted that critics of the opposite approach (rejecting international law) have also used emotive descriptions such as 'legal xenophobia' – see Noam Kolt, 'Cosmopolitan Originalism: Revisiting the Role of International Law in Constitutional Interpretation' (2017) 41 *Melbourne University Law Review* 182, 184–185.

[41] See, eg, *AMS v AIF* (1999) 199 CLR 160, 180 (Gleeson CJ, McHugh and Gummow JJ) or *Forge v ASIC* (2006) 228 CLR 45, 139–140 (Heydon J). Such repudiations often draw on early statements from *Polites*, above n 22 and *Horta v Cth* (1994) 181 CLR 183 regarding the inapplicability of international law in constitutional interpretation.

[42] See *Kartinyeri*, above n, 417–418; also Kirby, above n 36, 119–120. See further Kolt, above n 40, who terms this the 'construction zone,' in which the court must be wary if use of international law is to remain legitimate (at 216).

[43] *Al-Kateb*, 622–624. See further *Kartinyeri v Cth* (1998) 195 CLR 337, 411; also Charlesworth, above n 8, 21.

[44] See further *Re Aird; Ex Parte Alpert*, above n 21, 344–346 (Kirby J).

[45] Elisa Arcioni and Andrew McLeod, above n 15, 453.

[46] Ibid, 438.

[47] Ibid, 460.

[48] (2010) 242 CLR 1.

[49] (2010) 243 CLR 1.

[50] (2010) 239 CLR 531.

[51] *JT International SA v Cth* (2012) 250 CLR 1 and *ICM Agriculture P/L v Cth* (2009) 240 CLR 140.

[52] See Arcioni and McLeod, above n 15, 466.

international] law.'[53] They give the example of *Momcilovic v The Queen*,[54] in which the High Court considers international legal material extensively in interpreting the *Charter of Human Rights and Responsibilities Act 2006* (Vic), but not at all in considering the constitutional separation of powers question which arose.[55]

In summary, foreign and international law is seen broadly by the High Court as a legitimate influence on the development of the common law, as the basis of a limited interpretive presumption in statutory construction, and – by all but one Justice – as irrelevant to constitutional interpretation.

II. Constitutional Discoveries – Implied Rights and Legitimate Expectations

For a time in the 1980s to early 2000s, the High Court began to show significant interest in Australia's international obligations and their proper influence in the domestic legal arena. However, controversy over the use of international law by the High Court 'ignited' in this period in response to a series of decisions which fired the public imagination, and which some saw as involving radical impositions of 'outside' legal sources on the Australian legal system.[56] These included notably *Koowarta v Bjelke-Petersen*,[57] the *Tasmanian Dams Case*,[58] *Nationwide News*,[59] *Australian Capital Television*,[60] *Lange*,[61] *McGinty*,[62] *Langer*,[63] *Teoh*,[64] and *Mabo No.2*.[65] The first two of these cases expanded the scope of the external affairs power in section 51(xxix) of the Constitution, leading to commentary about a failure to respect the federal balance struck by the framers.[66] These decisions, which favoured the Commonwealth Government, withstood the contemporary controversy and left a lasting legacy with respect to interpretation of the external affairs power.[67]

The High Court was also faced during this period with the question of how to respond to legislation purporting to abrogate basic rights, including freedom of political speech[68] and the right to vote in federal elections.[69] These rights may be considered cornerstones of our

[53] Ibid.
[54] (2011) 245 CLR 1.
[55] Arcioni and McLeod, above n 15, 467.
[56] See Charlesworth et al, above n 9, 426; see also ch 4 in this volume.
[57] (1982) 152 CLR 168.
[58] *Cth v Tasmania* (1983) 158 CLR 1.
[59] (1992) 177 CLR 1.
[60] *Australian Capital Television and NSW v Cth* (1992) 177 CLR 106.
[61] *Lange v ABC* (1997) 189 CLR 520.
[62] *McGinty v Western Australia* (1996) 186 CLR 140
[63] *Langer v Commonwealth*, above n 21.
[64] (1995) 183 CLR 273.
[65] (1992) 175 CLR 1 (discussed above).
[66] Charlesworth et al, above n 9, 426–427.
[67] See Hilary Charlesworth, 'Internal and external affairs: the Koowarta case in context' (2014) 23 *Griffith Law Review* 35.
[68] Relevant cases include *Nationwide News v Wills* (1992) 177 CLR 1; *Australian Capital Television and NSW v Cth* (1992) 177 CLR 106 and *Lange v ABC* (1997) 189 CLR 520.
[69] Relevant cases include *Attorney-General (Cth) (Ex Rel McKinlay) v Commonwealth* (1975) 135 CLR 1 (as precedent); *McGinty v Western Australia* (1996) 186 CLR 140; *Langer v Commonwealth* (1996) 186 CLR 302 and *Roach v Electoral Commissioner* (2007) 233 CLR 162.

constitutional democracy, and on that view their abrogation could be said to undermine the Constitution itself. In the 1990s and 2000s, international human rights law was instrumental in leading the court to conclude that these two rights are implicit in the text and structure of the Constitution. There was a diversity of opinion as to the source of these rights, ranging from common law rights existing at the time of federation[70] to concepts such as representative democracy underpinning the wording of sections 7 and 24, including phrases such as 'directly chosen by the people'.[71] International human rights law arguably formed an influential backdrop to these cases, even if the court at times took pains to emphasise that it had no direct application.[72]

The following five cases in the list above established or laid the groundwork for these implied rights, thereby limiting legislative power where its exercise would deprive individuals[73] of their freedom to express political opinions or to vote. Some dub this period the High Court's 'implied rights experiment,' and it has remained the subject of influential judicial[74] and academic[75] scepticism ever since. Nevertheless, the implied rights cases have also left a lasting legacy, confirmed in more recent cases such as *Aid/Watch*[76] and *Rowe*.[77] The detail of the 'implied rights experiment' is the subject of Chapter 4 in this volume. For present purposes, it is enough to note that it represented a period of opening up to human rights law in particular; an acknowledgment of the global jurisprudential influence of the international human rights movement and of the limitations of the traditional Australian approach of sole reliance on Parliament to protect individual rights.[78]

This brings us to the 1995 case of *Teoh*, which is particularly instructive as to governmental attitudes to international law when it is applied to restrict Commonwealth power. The High Court held that the ratification of international conventions by the Australian Government ought not to be completely meaningless – in the words of Mason CJ and Deane J 'merely platitudinous or ineffectual'[79] – and that individuals had a 'legitimate expectation' in administrative law that decision-makers would take relevant international obligations into account when making decisions affecting their rights. In this case, the relevant international obligation was the 'best interests of the child' principle in the UN Convention on the Rights of the Child,[80] and the issue at stake was family unity.

[70] See, eg, *Nationwide News v Wills*, above n 68, 69 (Deane and Toohey JJ).

[71] See, eg, *Australian Capital Television v Cth*, above n 68, 138 (Mason CJ), 231–2 (McHugh J); also (re voting rights) *Roach v Electoral Commissioner*, above n 69, 198 (Gummow, Kirby and Crennan JJ), 174 (Gleeson CJ).

[72] See, eg, *Nationwide News v Wills*, above n 68, 43–4 (Brennan J); *Roach v Electoral Commissioner*, above n 69, 178–9 (Gleeson CJ), 224–5 (Heydon J). Cf *Australian Capital Television v Cth*, above n 68, in which the judgments of Mason CJ and Brennan J make many references to human rights jurisprudence.

[73] Perhaps not only individuals – corporations and associations may also benefit from these limitations on legislative power – see *Unions NSW v NSW* (2013) 252 CLR 530.

[74] See, eg, *Mulholland v AEC* (2004) 220 CLR 181, 298 (Callinan J); *Monis v The Queen* (2013) 249 CLR 92, 181–182 (Heydon J).

[75] See, eg, Jeffrey Goldsworthy, 'Constitutional Implications and Freedom of Political Speech: A Reply to Stephen Donaghue' (1997) 23 *Monash University Law Review* 362; also 'The High Court, Implied Rights and Constitutional Change' (1995) *Quadrant* 46; James Allan 'Implied Rights and Federalism: Inventing Intentions While Ignoring Them' (2009) 34 *University of Western Australia Law Review* 228.

[76] *Aid/Watch Incorporated v Commissioner of Taxation* (2010) 241 CLR 539.

[77] *Rowe v Electoral Commissioner* (2010) 243 CLR 1.

[78] This approach was characterised in, eg, *Kruger v Cth* (1997) 190 CLR 1, 61 (Dawson J).

[79] (1995) 183 CLR 273, 291.

[80] (1989) 1577 UNTS 3 (entry into force 2 September 1990).

Although it might seem quite reasonable to expect the executive to have some regard to the binding international obligations it has voluntarily assumed,[81] the political reaction to *Teoh* was swift and condemnatory. The Labor Government of the day issued an Executive Statement rejecting the effect of the judgment, as did its Coalition successor (which also introduced supporting legislation).[82] The *Teoh* case and the controversy it generated, as well as the High Court's later retreat from it, are explored fully in Chapter 6, but suffice it to say Australian governments of either political persuasion are exceedingly reluctant to be held to international obligations which have not been transformed into domestic Australian law.

Three years later in *Kartinyeri*,[83] the Commonwealth argued that the 'races power' allowed Parliament to legislate for measures particular to certain races, whether they be adverse or beneficial – evolved international law notions of the evils of racial discrimination notwithstanding. Kirby J remarked that he could not accept that racially discriminatory laws such as those passed in, for example, Nazi Germany or Apartheid South Africa could still be validly enacted under the Australian Constitution – particularly in light of the 1967 referendum aimed at improving the lives of Indigenous Australians.[84] The Commonwealth simply responded that this was a matter for Parliament to determine, not the courts. The Commonwealth's constitutionally orthodox arguments proved persuasive to six of the seven Justices, moving some to declare the relevant constitutional provision (and the Parliament taking advantage of it) racist and out of step with the times.[85] The decision maintained the status quo when it came to interpretation of the Commonwealth's legislative powers.

Various aspects of international human rights law have been invoked to support appellants' arguments in many other High Court cases. Indigenous land rights and the prohibition on racial discrimination,[86] the right to a fair trial[87] and the right to personal liberty[88] have figured prominently.

It is accepted even amongst strong proponents of originalism that the Constitution must be 'capable of flexible application to changing circumstances' – for example through implications in its text and structure.[89] Technological and foreign policy developments have informed such flexible application.[90] In *Langer v Cth*, McHugh J stated that the content of the term 'the people' in the Constitution 'will change from time to time'. His Honour gave an example:

> In the light of the extension of the franchise during this century, for example, it would not now be possible to find that the members of the House of Representatives were "chosen by the people"

[81] Reasonable to an external observer that is – Madelaine Chiam's ch 12 in this volume describes Australia's 'janus-faced' approach to its international human rights obligations, which will be familiar to Australian observers.

[82] Charlesworth et al, above n 9, 437.

[83] (1998) 195 CLR 337.

[84] Ibid, 414–7.

[85] See Debra Jopson, "Worrying Precedent' Threatens All Aboriginal Claims' *The Sydney Morning Herald*, 2 April 1998, 7; Bernard Lane, 'Race to Judgment' *The Australian*, 2 February 1998, 9.

[86] Relevant cases include *Mabo*, above n 65 and *Kruger v Cth*, above n 78.

[87] *Dietrich v R*, above n 29.

[88] Relevant cases include *Chu Kheng Lim v Cth (Minister for Immigration, Local Government and Ethnic Affairs)* (1992) 176 CLR 1; *Al-Kateb*, above n 6; *Plaintiff M61/2010E v Cth* (2010) 243 CLR 319; *Plaintiff M47/2012 v Director-General of Security* (2012) 251 CLR 1; *M76/2013 v Minister for Immigration, Multicultural Affairs and Citizenship* (2013) 251 CLR 322; *Plaintiff M96A/2016 v Cth* [2017] HCA 16; (2017) 91 ALJR 91.

[89] *Australian National Airways v Cth* (1946) 71 CLR 115, 645 Dixon CJ).

[90] See Simpson and Williams, above n 31, 205.

> if women were excluded from voting or if electors had to have property qualifications before they could vote.[91]

Actions of the Australian Parliament, then, in response to changes in society and contemporary politics – even changes in the nature of human rights protections – may alter constitutional meaning. This is seen to be unexceptionable since the changes originate within the Australian politico-legal system. Where the changes are on a global scale, there is far less agreement on how (or indeed whether, in the context of constitutional interpretation) they should influence Australian law. However, where implied rights have already been established, the High Court has recently seemed somewhat more receptive to rights-based reasoning from external sources.[92] We now turn to *Al-Kateb*, which involved an attempt to argue that arbitrary, unreviewable administrative detention was inconsistent with the separation of powers, or at least the principle of legality.

III. *Al-Kateb v Godwin* and the Triumph of Rights Scepticism

The Australian Constitution is neutral when it comes to most matters of human rights and dignity, and will not prevent the executive or Parliament from taking measures which undermine the relevant principles, regardless of the fact that they may have garnered near-universal acceptance in the form of multilateral UN human rights treaties.

As noted above, former High Court Justice Michael Kirby has long been dissatisfied at this state of affairs, and has suggested that international law reflecting fundamental human rights ought to be brought to bear when there is ambiguity in the Constitution on rights matters. Perhaps the epitome of judicial scepticism regarding this approach is McHugh J's judgment, as part of the majority, in *Al-Kateb*. In that case, the High Court held that there was no general right to be free from indefinite detention by the executive government, at least where removal from the country was the ultimate legislative purpose. Only invalidity on some other ground could prevent such a fate if it were authorised by statute – which it was in this instance.[93]

Some factual context for their Honours' debate over international human rights law and constitutional interpretation is required. Ahmed Ali Al-Kateb is a Palestinian man who sought asylum in Australia in December 2000, having arrived by boat. Although he was born in Kuwait and lived most of his life there, he did not hold Kuwaiti, or indeed any other, citizenship at the time of his arrival in Australia.[94] The High Court's decision

[91] *Langer v Cth* (1996) 186 CLR 302, 342

[92] See, eg, *McCloy v NSW* (2015) 257 CLR 178, in which the High Court applied proportionality reasoning derived from European law (at 195–6, French CJ, Kiefel, Bell, and Keane JJ); Cf *Murphy v Electoral Commissioner* [2016] HCA 36; (2016) 90 ALJR 1027, [65] – such reasoning is inapplicable to 'policy or fiscal choices' of Parliament.

[93] *Al-Kateb*, above n 6, 562–563; also 583 (per McHugh J).

[94] Ibid, 596. Mr Al-Kateb has since become an Australian citizen – see David Marr, 'As one, judges show they safeguard liberty' *The Sydney Morning Herald*, 12 November 2010: www.smh.com.au/politics/federal/as-one-judges-show-they-safeguard-liberty-20101111-17pgn.html.

turned on interpretation of the *Migration Act 1958* (Cth), specifically sections 189, 196 and 198. Much has been written on this aspect of the case,[95] and it will not be rehearsed in detail here. Briefly, the majority decided that the sections should be interpreted to permit indefinite executive detention, even in the absence of explicit wording to that effect. Many commentators have cogently argued that the correctness of this decision is doubtful on doctrinal grounds.[96]

However, there was also a constitutional question which the Justices answered (in *obiter*, as it emerged); one which provoked a vehement disagreement between McHugh and Kirby JJ. The question was, if the *Migration Act* did provide for indefinite detention, would that not constitute a breach of the separation of powers? More specifically, would it not constitute punitive detention, which only Chapter III courts may impose after criminal convictions?

The majority answered the constitutional question in the negative, preferring the Commonwealth's argument that administrative detention of aliens for immigration purposes is a well-established exception to the general rule, and is in any case not punitive in nature.[97] In answer to the contention that the purpose had no reasonable prospect of being achieved (since no other country had been found willing to accept Mr Al-Kateb), the majority essentially found that the executive would have to abandon its plans to remove Mr Al-Kateb formally before the purpose could be deemed spent.[98]

The decision of the 4:3 majority *Al-Kateb* has been said to be 'widely regarded as one of the court's worst decisions'[99] and to exemplify 'the "austerity of tabulated legalism" with a vengeance'.[100] Heydon J, one of the four majority Justices, later conceded his approach might be called 'inhumane'.[101] McHugh J also expressed regret about the decision on his retirement.[102] In one author's view, the decision abdicated the High Court's sole authority to determine the scope and operation of the separation of powers doctrine.[103]

The minority, comprising Gleeson CJ and Gummow and Kirby JJ, found that the administrative purpose (in this case detaining aliens pending their removal from the country)

[95] See, eg, Juliet Curtin 'Case and Comment: *Al-Kateb v Godwin*' (2005) 27 *Sydney Law Review* 355; Matthew Groves, 'Immigration Detention vs Imprisonment: Differences Explained' (2004) 29(5) *Alternative Law Journal* 228.

[96] See Dan Meagher, 'The 'tragic' High Court decisions in Al-Kateb and Al-Khafaji: the triumph of the 'plain fact' interpretive approach and constitutional form over substance' (2005) 7(4) *Constitutional Law and Policy Review* 69.

[97] *Al-Kateb*, above n 6, 562–563.

[98] Ibid, 567 (David Bennett for the Commonwealth), 638–639 (Hayne J); 659 (Callinan J), 662 (Heydon J).

[99] See Marr, above n 94.

[100] See James Crawford, 'International Law in the House of Lords and the High Court of Australia 1996–2008' (2009) 28 *Yearbook of International Law* 1, 16. Crawford quotes from Lord Wilberforce in *Minister of Home Affairs v Fisher* [1980] AC 319, 328, commenting on the Constitution of India and the priority which should be given to the rights and freedoms it contains in preference to strict legalism.

[101] See ABC, 'Richard Aedy interview with Justice Dyson Heydon' (*Sunday Profile*, 15 March 2013): www.abc.net.au/radionational/programs/archived/sundayprofile/dyson-heydon/6708644. Interestingly, Heydon did not deal with the difficulties presented by *Al-Kateb* in his article 'Are bills of rights necessary in common law systems?' (2014) 130 *LQR* 392.

[102] See Michael Pelly, 'A higher justice' *The Sydney Morning Herald*, 29 October 2005.

[103] See Meagher, above n 96, 77. As a personal aside, the failure of the highest court in the land to defend one of the most fundamental of individual rights at both common law and international law – that of personal liberty – was perhaps the primary catalyst during this author's law school days to the pursuit of a career in refugee and human rights law.

was in fact no longer achievable, and that consequently the detention could no longer be supported by the *Migration Act*.[104] Gummow J also took a strong stand against dilution of the general constitutional principle that only courts may imprison, stating that whether Mr Al-Kateb's detention was punitive was the wrong question to ask.[105] His Honour noted that detention may be for administrative purposes and yet have punitive aspects, and the fact of deprivation of liberty was the primary constitutional concern. The executive is not free to detain people 'for any purpose selected by Parliament,' and if the constitutionally authorised purpose is spent, the detention becomes unlawful.[106]

Gleeson CJ referred to the principle of legality – that legislation authorising abrogation of fundamental common law rights should be 'clearly manifested by unambiguous language,' otherwise the right in question, in this case personal liberty, should be upheld, and an order in the nature of *habeas corpus* granted.[107] The *Migration Act*, his Honour held, was unclear as to what should happen if a person could not be removed from Australia, and 'indefinite, perhaps permanent, administrative detention is not [a possibility] to be dealt with by implication.'[108] His Honour's judgment represents an elegant and principled disposal of the matter, while remaining within the bounds of Australian legal orthodoxy.

Kirby J, even more so than the other members of the minority, sought to make a broader point about the limits of executive and parliamentary power. Building on arguments he had presented in earlier decisions such as *Newcrest Mining* (in relation to 'just terms' compensation under the section 51(xxxi) acquisition power)[109] and *Kartinyeri* (in relation to racial discrimination),[110] his Honour contended that the Constitution ought to be interpreted 'so far as is possible … in a way that is generally harmonious with the basic principles of international law, including as that law states human rights and fundamental freedoms.'[111] This brought him into direct conflict with McHugh J, who held that it was perfectly possible for the executive to use the aliens power in section 51(xix) of the Constitution to detain without restriction, citing historical precedent.[112] Kirby J noted that the uses cited – National Security Regulations passed during the two World Wars – were exceptional wartime measures, inappropriate as precedent for the immediate decision, which related to incomparable facts in a time of peace.[113] His Honour also noted that they predated modern human rights law – that the 'Constitution was understood and applied in 1945 in a completely different international context from that prevailing today.'[114]

McHugh J relied in particular on the decision of Dixon J in *Polites*, which rejected an argument that an international prohibition on pressing aliens into military service was directly applicable in Australia.[115] His Honour conceded that 'because of political, social

[104] *Al-Kateb*, above n 6, 572 (Gleeson CJ), 608 (Gummow J), 617 (Kirby J).
[105] Ibid, 611–614.
[106] Ibid.
[107] Ibid, 577–580.
[108] Ibid, 577–578.
[109] *Newcrest Mining*, above n 37, 657–658.
[110] *Kartinyeri,* above n, 417–418.
[111] *Al-Kateb*, above n 6, 624.
[112] Ibid, 588–589.
[113] Ibid, 620–622.
[114] Ibid, 624.
[115] Ibid, 589–590.

or economic developments inside and outside Australia, later generations may deduce propositions from the words of the Constitution that earlier generations did not perceive.' However, his Honour went on to state that 'that is a very different process from asserting that the Constitution must be read to conform to or so far as possible with the *rules* of international law.'[116] International law rules, his Honour asserted, amend the Constitution if they are allowed to influence its interpretation – they are too specific to be mere 'context' or 'elucidating factors'.[117] This was a curious argument, as his Honour and at least one other member of the majority had previously declined to apply international law rules in other contexts on the basis that they tend to be insufficiently specific to determine rights and duties in complex cases.[118]

McHugh J also expressed fear that the will and wisdom of those who drafted Australia's Constitution, and in particular their choices of parliamentary sovereignty and the section 128 amendment mechanism, would be thwarted if such rules came to influence its interpretation.[119] With respect, this focus on where the law 'belongs on the continuum of "bindingness"' is misplaced. Its use as additional context in the process of interpretation, as advocated by Kirby J, is far removed from direct application.[120] The weight to be given to any extrinsic source is a matter for the interpreter, and its status in another legal system should not be determinative.

Kirby J's own response to McHugh J was that judicial reinterpretation should not be conflated with amendment contrary to section 128, and that 'from the earliest days of federation both means of adjustment and change have been followed, to the advantage of the Commonwealth and its people.'[121] Adaptation of the Constitution to changing times, including 'finding' rights in its text and structure, as well as other major changes such as shifting the federal balance, has occurred (including with McHugh J's own imprimatur), and will continue to occur.[122]

McHugh J argued further that only international law which was in existence at the time of the Constitution's adoption may be relevant in its interpretation – necessarily excluding the entire body of modern international human rights law.[123] Former Commonwealth Solicitor-General Justin Gleeson has remarked that, at the time of federation, Australia 'was not an independent player on the world stage' and that the 'Imperial Crown would retain the constitutional right to make treaties that would be binding on all parts of the Empire including Australia.'[124] Such a strict approach, if applied to other considerations in

[116] Ibid, 593.

[117] Ibid.

[118] See, eg, *Project Blue Sky v Australian Broadcasting Authority* (1998) 194 CLR 355, 392; also *AMS v AIF*, above n 41, 180; *Western Australia v Ward* (2002) 213 CLR 1, 389 (Callinan J).

[119] *Al-Kateb*, above n 6, 592–593.

[120] See Kolt, above n 40, 243; also Brent Michael, 'International law in constitutional interpretation: A theoretical perspective' (2012) 23 *Public Law Review* 197, 215.

[121] *Al-Kateb*, above n 6, 625.

[122] Ibid, 626–626.

[123] Ibid, 589. The closest analogues at the time were predecessors of modern international humanitarian law, eg, the *Convention for the Amelioration of the Condition of the Wounded in Armies in the Field* [1864] UKTS 04441 (First Geneva Convention) and the *International Convention with respect to the Laws and Customs of War by Land* [1899] UKTS 11, and bilateral treaties vindicating particular rights such as the *Treaty between his Britannic Majesty and his Catholic Majesty, for preventing their subjects from engaging in any illicit traffic in slaves* of 23 September 1817.

[124] Justin Gleeson, 'The increasing internationalisation of Australian Law' (2017) 28 *Public Law Review* 25, 28.

constitutional interpretation such as 'community values and expectations'[125] would see the nation's foundational document truly mired in a time warp.

It is hard to escape the conclusion that the brand of originalism displayed by McHugh J in *Al-Kateb* was exaggerated – indeed his characterisation of international law has been called 'caricature.'[126] However, the motives behind that exaggeration remain unclear. One possible reason is the traditional training of Australian lawyers in strict dualist tradition, which leads to a perception of danger in Kirby J's approach.[127] It has also been suggested that the troubled politics of immigration in Australia may have influenced the majority's thinking – in particular when compared with the decision of the (differently-constituted) majority in *Chu Kheng Lim v Minister for Immigration* a decade prior.[128] In that decision, the High Court found that simply making a law 'relating to aliens' did not suffice to ensure that it was authorised by the relevant head of power in section 51(xix). Some link to the constitutional purpose was required so that the scope of permissible executive detention was not unduly widened.[129] McHugh J was the only Justice to decide both cases. His reasoning remained consistent in both cases while the majority pivoted around him. Gummow J raised a pertinent question in his dissent in *Al-Kateb:*

> Consistently with McHugh J's analysis in *Lim*, it could not seriously be doubted that a law providing for the administrative detention of bankrupts in order to protect the community would be a law with respect to bankruptcy and insolvency (s 51(xvii)), or that a law providing for the involuntary detention of all persons within their homes on census night would be a law with respect to census and statistics (s 51(xi)). If such laws lack validity, it is not by reason of any limitation in the text of paras (xvii) and (xi) but by the limitation in the opening words of s 51, "subject to this Constitution", which attract any limitation required by Ch III.[130]

Gummow J highlights the potential consequence of the *Al-Kateb* majority's decision; that in its apparent eagerness to ensure the executive had the powers needed to deal with 'unlawful non-citizens,' it opened the way for an unwarranted expansion of executive power over citizens and non-citizens alike. This expansion is, or should be, one of the primary drivers for the search for legal principles – such as a broad presumption of consistency with international law and the principle of legality – which might be capable of reigning in future governmental overreach.

IV. Other Jurisdictions and the 'Community of Nations' Justification

The Australian position with regard to the use of international law in constitutional interpretation should be considered in light of the approach of like-minded – particularly

[125] See, eg, *Teoh*, above n 64, 304–305; also John Braithwaite 'Community Values and Australian Jurisprudence' (1995) 17 *Sydney Law Review* 351.

[126] Charlesworth, above n 8, 22.

[127] See Kirby, above n 36, 125.

[128] See, eg, Jessie Hohmann, 'The Thin End of the Wedge: Executive Detention of Non-Citizens and the Australian Constitution' (2006) 9 *Yearbook of New Zealand Jurisprudence* 91.

[129] *Chu Kheng Lim v Minister for Immigration, Local Government and Ethnic Affairs*, above n 88.

[130] *Al-Kateb*, above n 6, 611 (references omitted).

common law – nations.[131] In the US, fears for sovereignty surrounding the influence of foreign law are such that bills have been introduced to ban judicial citation of it, and even to make it an impeachable offence.[132] Nevertheless, the US Supreme Court – which Kirby J pointed out in *Alpert* has been 'long resistant to the use of international law in its constitutional decisions' – has in recent times begun to embrace it despite the fraught political climate.[133] The Australian debate is less heated,[134] although the sovereignty-related fears are still present. Arguably, the majority decision in *Al-Kateb* can be seen as a manifestation of those fears. The UK Parliament, from which the Australian Parliament derives its tradition of sovereignty, is now considerably less free to abrogate fundamental rights and liberties, given the *Human Rights Act 1998* (UK) and jurisprudence relating to it such as the *Al-Jedda* case.[135] Similarly, in jurisdictions such as Canada and New Zealand, bills or charters of rights have 'brought human rights home,' leading to significant decisions on limitation of power to infringe rights.[136]

Depending on one's perspective, Australia is thus lagging behind like-minded nations in maintaining such a strict approach to parliamentary sovereignty, or holding fast against a threatening international trend. In *Newcrest Mining*, Kirby J argued that the *Bangalore Principles* should be applied in interpreting the Australian Constitution because:

> ... the Constitution not only speaks to the people of Australia who made it and accept it for their governance. It also speaks to the international community as the basic law of the Australian nation which is a member of that community.[137]

Is Australia under an obligation to be a 'model global citizen' – in particular to ensure its international obligations are faithfully reflected in its domestic law? Kirby and others argue that it is. The Human Rights Committee and the other UN Treaty Bodies agree.[138] However, others are dubious about this justification.[139] In *Dietrich*, Mason CJ and McHugh J stated:

> On one view, it may seem curious that the Executive Government has seen fit to expose Australia to the potential censure of the Human Rights Committee without endeavouring to ensure that the rights enshrined in the ICCPR are incorporated into domestic law, but such an approach is clearly permissible.[140]

[131] Civil law nations, which tend to have more monist traditions when it comes to the incorporation of international law, are less direct comparators – see further Simpson and Williams, above n 31, 211.

[132] See Arcioni and McLeod, above n 15, 437.

[133] *Re Aird; Ex Parte Alpert*, above n 44, 344–6 (Kirby J). His Honour cites the following authorities: *Atkins v Virginia* (2002) 536 US 304 at 316; *Lawrence v Texas* (2003) 539 US 558 at 572–3, 576–7 (Kennedy J); Harold Koh, 'International Law as Part of Our Law' (2004) 98 *American Journal of International Law* 43; DM Bodansky, 'The Use of International Law Sources in Constitutional Opinion' (2004) 32 *Georgia Journal of International and Comparative Law* 421.

[134] See Arcioni and McLeod, above n 15, 438.

[135] *R (Al-Jedda) v Secretary of State for Defence* [2008] 1 AC 153. See further Crawford, above n 100.

[136] See, eg, *Baker v Canada* [1999] 2 SCR 817 and *Attorney-General v Zaoui* [2005] NZSC 38. To date, Victoria's statutory charter has had a more limited effect; focussing on the powers of the judiciary rather than Parliament– see, eg, Justice Peter Vickery, *Treaties, Human Rights and Statutory Interpretation*, International Commission of Jurists Paper, 19 August 2008, available at: http://icjvictoria.com.au/advocacy/treaties-human-rights-and-statutory-interpretation.

[137] *Newcrest Mining (WA) Ltd v Cth* (1997) 190 CLR 513, 658. See also Al-Kateb, above n 6, 624.

[138] See, eg, Human Rights Committee, *Concluding Observations on Australia*, UN Doc CCPR/C/AUS/CO/5, 7 May 2009, [8].

[139] See, eg, Walker, above n 13, 97.

[140] *Dietrich v R*, above n 29, 305 (Mason CJ and McHugh J).

It is now firmly entrenched in Australian law and politics that it is for Parliament, rather than courts or committees, to decide how and when international obligations are to be 'transformed' into domestic law. Any 'obligation of transformation' at the international level is presently unenforceable, and likely to remain so for the foreseeable future.

In *Teoh*, Gaudron J referred to the fact that the rights under discussion, deriving from the UN Convention on the Rights of the Child, reflected deeply-held values of the Australian community – and it was this fact which could be said to legitimise their use.[141] This, it is submitted, is a more compelling justification for the use of international human rights law as recommended by Kirby J than any obligation to the community of nations at large. Few Australians would demur if the High Court were to insist that Parliament and the executive are obliged to uphold fundamental rights such as freedom of expression, personal liberty, freedom from torture and ill-treatment, fair trial guarantees and the best interests of the child – that is, the kind of rights reflected in multilateral human rights treaties of broad acceptance.[142]

V. Subsequent Related Developments in the High Court's Use of International Law

McHugh J questioned the foundations of the interpretive presumption of consistency in his judgment in *Al-Kateb*:

> No doubt the rule of construction had some validity when the rules of international law were few and well-known. Under modern conditions, however, this rule of construction is based on a fiction. Gone are the days when the rules of international law were to be found in the writings of a few well-known jurists. … [The rationale for the rule] bears no relationship to the reality of the modern legislative process.[143]

Be that as it may, his Honour conceded that the rule was 'too well established to be repealed now by judicial decision.'[144] Although well-accepted in England by 1992, the High Court was still equivocating on the application of this principle in Australia at that time,[145] despite having endorsed it as early as 1908.[146] There is also an ongoing debate about its breadth – whether it applies to all statutes, or merely those which implement international obligations, and whether ambiguity is a condition precedent.[147] Since *Al-Kateb*, in which the presumption was given relatively short shrift, it has been applied in ways which suggest an increasing openness to international law and human rights.[148]

[141] *Teoh*, above n 64, 304–305.
[142] On the subject of which international norms might legitimately be considered, see, eg, Walker, above n 13, 100–102. Cf Michael, above n 120, 215. Michael argues that there are 'few instances where international law could be used [to form evidence of moral truths or community standards].'
[143] *Al-Kateb*, above n 6, 590–591.
[144] Ibid, 591.
[145] *Dietrich v R*, above n 29, 306 (Mason CJ and McHugh J). Cf *Chu Kheng Lim*, above n 88, 38 (Brennan, Deane and Dawson JJ).
[146] *Jumbunna Coal Mine NL v Victorian Coal Miners' Association* (1908) 6 CLR 309, 363.
[147] *Teoh*, above n 64, 287 (Mason CJ and Deane J). See further Charlesworth et al, above n 9, 458.
[148] Anika Gauja and Katherine Gelber, 'High Court Review 2010: The Resurgence of Rights?' (2011) 46 *Australian Journal of Political Science* 683.

As applied, along with the common law principle of legality, to the Migration Act, the presumption of consistency did not prevent four of the Justices in *Al-Kateb* from finding that indefinite detention was legislatively authorised. However, eight years later in *Plaintiff M47/2012 v Director-General of Security*[149] the correctness of the decision in *Al-Kateb* was strongly called into question, although it was not actually overturned. In *M47*, the Commonwealth argued that 'segregating' refugees and asylum seekers – even indefinitely – was authorised by the *Migration Act 1958* (Cth) and a broad definition of 'security' in a related instrument.[150] Moreover, following the majority in *Al-Kateb*, their detention need not be '"appropriate and adapted" or proportionate to the present prospect of removal.'[151] The Commonwealth also argued that the *Al-Kateb* decision should not be re-opened as, among other reasons, it 'had not led to considerable inconvenience'.[152]

The majority in *M47* explicitly linked the *Migration Act 1958* (Cth) with the international instrument on which it is partly based (the *1951 Refugees Convention*[153]), taking into consideration international law principles such as *non-refoulement*.[154] Two Justices also held that personal liberty should have been a stronger consideration in construing the Act's detention provisions in *Al-Kateb*.[155] This case, along with subsequent relevant decisions such as *M76/2013 v Minister of Immigration, Multicultural Affairs and Citizenship*,[156] could be said to suggest a willingness on the part of some Justices to reconsider *Al-Kateb*.[157]

The presumption of consistency in statutory interpretation has evolved further in other jurisdictions, including the UK and New Zealand,[158] to become applicable to statutes with no ostensible basis in international law, and even in the absence of ambiguity.[159] However, neither *M47* nor any subsequent Australian case goes this far. This relative reticence has been convincingly ascribed to differing constitutional cultures; not least the lack of any kind of bill of rights in the Australian federal jurisdiction.[160] The wider significance of migration cases such as these for rights protection is explored in detail in Chapter 17 in this volume.

Dan Meagher suggested in 2012 that the *Human Rights (Parliamentary Scrutiny) Act 2011* (Cth) ('Scrutiny Act') may indicate to the courts that the Australian Parliament is more concerned with the nation's international human rights obligations than was previously the case, and therefore lead to more robust applications of the presumption of consistency.[161] My own research to date, which followed closely the fortunes of the

[149] *Plaintiff M47/2012*, above n 88.

[150] Ibid, 16–20.

[151] Ibid.

[152] Ibid, 15. This argument, of course, refers to inconvenience for those administering the Act.

[153] *Convention Relating to the Status of Refugees* (1951) 189 UNTS 150 (entry into force 22 April 1954).

[154] *Plaintiff M47/2012*, above n 88, see in particular 24–42 (French CJ); 92 (Hayne J); 170–173; and 184–7 (Bell J).

[155] Ibid, 59–61 (Gummow J), 187–194 (Bell J).

[156] (2013) 251 CLR 322.

[157] See further Kellie Robson, 'The State of Personal Liberty in Australia after M47: A Risk Theory Analysis of Security Rights' (2013) 39 *Monash University Law Review* 506, 538.

[158] See Meagher, above n 25.

[159] Ibid, 466. See also Glen Cranwell, 'Treaties and the Interpretation of Statutes: Two Recent Examples in the Migration Context' (2011) 39 *Australian Institute of Administrative Law Forum* 49 – Mason CJ and Deane J in *Teoh* supported this but subsequent Justices appear not to. Cranwell also notes that the Family Court (a separate federal court at the time of writing) has been prepared to apply the principle in respect of UN Convention on the Rights of the Child even to statutes not directly implementing the treaty (at 56).

[160] Meagher, above n 25, 467.

[161] Ibid, 483–485.

parliamentary human rights scrutiny regime from 2012–2016, indicates to the contrary that, several years since its inception, the Scrutiny Act has had a negligible effect on Australian jurisprudence.[162] This issue is canvassed in detail in Chapter 8.

In summary, the Australian courts remain ambivalent about interpreting statutes, at least at the Commonwealth level, consistently with international law. While this remains the case, the prospects for extending the principle of consistency to the Constitution, as urged by Kirby J, are dim.

VI. Is Parliament Interested in Protecting Human Rights?

Federal Court Judge Nye Perram, speaking at a symposium on statutory interpretation in 2016, said that the presumption of consistency:

> … proceed[s] on a premise that, in some ways, it is desirable for municipal law to operate harmoniously with international law, whether customary or public. But modern events cannot leave one with any confidence that this is a shared value at all. …'
>
> [T]he presumption contains an *a priori* notion that the international legal order is something worthwhile. Whilst that is an idea which is attractive to many including myself, it is difficult to avoid the conclusion that it is an opinion lying outside any given legislative text.[163]

In respect of rights and the related interpretive principle of legality, Perram J cited Lord Steyn's dictum from *R v Home Secretary; Ex Parte Pierson*:

> The presumption is not merely a common sense guide to what a Parliament in a liberal democracy is likely to have intended; it is a working hypothesis, the existence of which is known both to Parliament and the courts, upon which statutory language will be interpreted. The hypothesis is an aspect of the rule of law.[164]

Kirby J's call for the *Bangalore Principles* to be applied in interpreting the Australian Parliament's powers might be supported on a similar basis, as long as one is willing to accept that fundamental rights form an essential aspect of the rule of law.[165] Perram J is sceptical of the empirical basis for such a hypothesis. He contends that it reflects a 'certain lawyerly view of how the world should be arranged.'[166] Perram reasoned that 'it would be nice to believe that Parliament shares a commitment to the values which inhere in a modern liberal democracy, but in practice this does not appear to be the case.'[167] His Honour is not alone in this view.[168]

[162] See Adam Fletcher, *Australia's Human Rights Scrutiny Regime: Democratic Masterstroke or Mere Window Dressing?* (Melbourne, Melbourne University Press, 2018).

[163] Nye Perram, *Constitutional Principles and Coherence in Statutory Interpretation*, paper delivered at La Trobe Law School Symposium on the coherence of statutory interpretation, 11 November 2016, 19.

[164] Ibid.

[165] An influential formulation of the rule of law propounded by Tom Bingham sets out eight 'sub-rules' including '(5) The law must afford adequate protection of human rights' – see Bingham, *The Rule of Law* (Allen Lane, 2010) ch 7; also Kirby, above n 36, 120–121; Hilary Charlesworth 'Protecting Human Rights' (1994) 68 *Law Institute Journal* 463. Cf Robert French, 'Rights and Freedoms and the Rule of Law' (2017) 28 *Public Law Review* 109.

[166] Ibid.

[167] Ibid, 21.

[168] See, eg, Brendan Lim, 'The Normativity of the Principle of Legality' (2013) 37 *Melbourne University Law Review* 372.

Perram J did not expand on why he believes Parliament does not necessarily share the mooted 'lawyerly' values, but others including Andrew Lynch, Nicola McGarrity and George Williams have noted that Parliament in recent times has passed some of the most illiberal, rights-limiting laws in Australia's history.[169] These laws give a Minister life-or-death power over asylum seekers at sea;[170] allow for mass surveillance without warrant of almost anyone using the internet;[171] give intelligence officials near-blanket immunity for criminal acts in certain circumstances (including the use of force in questioning suspects);[172] allow for the summary cancellation of passports;[173] extend and expand a control order regime of dubious necessity[174] – among other serious rights restrictions. Even highly critical reports from Parliament's own Joint Committee on Human Rights did not prevent the bills in question from promptly passing into law with support from both major political parties.[175]

Laws, such as those challenged in *Al-Kateb*, authorising administrative detention without meaningful oversight or time limit are hardly the hallmarks of modern democratic government. With Commonwealth laws already in existence, 'unlawful non-citizens' and terrorism suspects are already subject to such detention.[176] If an Australian government decided to apply a similar regime to political opponents on the grounds of 'community protection' or a similar non-criminal formulation, could the authorising legislation be constitutional? On the authority of *Al-Kateb*, as long as it came within a head of legislative power in section 51 of the Australian Constitution, it could.[177] The 'reasonably adapted to the purpose' requirement developed in the *Communist Party Case*[178] appears to have been minimised.[179] This is not a purely hypothetical example – after a visit to Australia in late 2016, the UN Special Rapporteur on the Situation of Human Rights Defenders declared himself:

> … astonished to observe mounting evidence of a range of accumulative measures that have levied enormous pressure on Australian civil society. I was surprised to observe the increasing discrepancy and the lack of coherence between Government's external pronouncements and

[169] See Andrew Lynch, Nicola McGarrity and George Williams, *Inside Australia's Terrorism Laws and Trials: A timely examination of the impact of Australia's anti-terror laws after September 11 and the new 2014 terror laws* (Kensington, NewSouth Publishing, 2015).

[170] Migration and Maritime Powers Legislation Amendment (Resolving the Asylum Legacy Caseload) Bill 2014.

[171] Telecommunications (Interception and Access) Amendment (Data Retention) Bill 2014.

[172] Counter-Terrorism Legislation Amendment Bill (No 1) 2014.

[173] Counter-Terrorism Legislation Amendment (Foreign Fighters) Bill 2014.

[174] Ibid. The necessity for the control order regime was called into question by the former Independent National Security Legislation Monitor – see *Declassified Annual Report*, 20 December 2012: www.dpmc.gov.au/sites/default/files/files/INSLM_Annual_Report_20121220.pdf, 44.

[175] Three of the four example Bills given above passed both Houses after less than a week of debate. The Migration and Maritime Powers Legislation Amendment (Resolving the Asylum Legacy Caseload) Bill 2014 was delayed slightly in the Senate, but still only debated for a total of two days (in both Houses).

[176] *Migration Act 1958* (Cth), ss 189, 196 and 198; *Australian Security Intelligence Organisation Act 1979* (Cth), Division 3, Pt III. See further Lisa Burton, Nicole McGarrity and George Williams, 'The Extraordinary Questioning and Detention Powers of the Australian Security Intelligence Organisation' (2012) 36 *Melbourne University Law Review* 415.

[177] In *Plaintiff M68/2015 v Minister for Immigration* (2016) 257 CLR 42, the plaintiff argued that immigration detention, as practised by the Australian Government (albeit in Nauru), was punitive in nature for several reasons. These arguments were unsuccessful – see 48 (R Merkel QC for the Plaintiff), 69–70 (French CJ, Kiefel and Nettle JJ), 87 (Bell J), 131 (Keane J).

[178] *Australian Communist Party v Cth* (1951) 83 CLR 1, 202–203 (Dixon CJ), 225 (Williams J), 273–274 (Kitto J).

[179] Even in the context of the defence power, the principle developed in the *Communist Party Case* has arguably lost much of its force. See, eg, *Thomas v Mowbray* (2007) 233 CLR 307 (particularly at 503 per Callinan J).

> implementation of human rights obligations internally. … [C]ivil society organizations and journalists have raised concerns about unprecedented anti-protested [sic] laws and intensification of secrecy laws and practices.[180]

Dan Meagher has remarked that Australian judges are concerned about the constitutional legitimacy of applying sources of law external to the Australian legal system.[181] Application of such sources could have implications for the boundaries of judicial power and – in the case of constitutional interpretation – for the integrity of the Constitution itself; little wonder then that judges are cautious in this regard.[182] In addition, the vitriolic reaction to the 'legitimate expectation' doctrine developed in *Teoh* may have made Australian judges 'particularly sensitive' to these legitimacy concerns – and expanding the ambit of the presumption of consistency might be seen as 'having their constitutional cake and eating it too.'[183]

Nevertheless, there must come a point at which the Australian courts, faced with legislation placing increasingly onerous limitations on rights, reconsider their present deference. At that point, they will need to begin to use tools such as these common law interpretive presumptions more robustly, and perhaps even adopt Kirby J's constitutional approach, in order to preserve the rule of law.

The High Court is consistently one of Australia's most trusted institutions, according to opinion polls.[184] This is no doubt in large part because it has remained above the political fray which attends cases involving questions of rights. Whether it can continue to do this indefinitely in the face of a Parliament which accords so little priority to rights protection remains to be seen.

VII. The Way Forward – Evolution or Revolution?

So to return to the question posed at the beginning of this chapter, is the Constitution fit for purpose of underpinning a democratic system of government under the rule of law as we understand it in the twenty-first century?[185] Times have changed since the early twentieth century. The world in which Australia finds itself would no longer be familiar to the Constitution's framers. They were not prophets – as Kirby J stated in *Re Wakim, Ex Parte McNally*, 'the makers of [the Constitution] did not intend, nor did they have the

[180] See *End of mission statement by Michel Forst, United Nations Special Rapporteur on the situation of human rights defenders: Visit to Australia,* Office of the High Commissioner for Human Rights, 18 October 2016: www.ohchr.org/EN/NewsEvents/Pages/DisplayNews.aspx?NewsID=20689&LangID=E. See further *Report of the Special Rapporteur on the situation of human rights defenders on his mission to Australia* (Advance unedited version), UN Doc A/HRC/37/51/Add.3, 28 February 2018.

[181] Meagher, above n 25, 475.

[182] Ibid, 477.

[183] Ibid, 478–479.

[184] See Katy Barnett, 'News: High Court is Australia's Most Trusted Institution' *Opinions on High*, Melbourne Law School, 1 July 2014: https://blogs.unimelb.edu.au/opinionsonhigh/2014/07/01/news-high-court-is-australias-most-trusted-institution.

[185] For an explanation of modern conceptions of the rule of law as it pertains to the Australian Constitution, see Lisa Burton Crawford, *The Rule of Law and the Australian Constitution* (Annandale, Federation Press, 2017).

power to require, that their wishes and expectations should control us who now live under its protection.'[186]

The Constitution was drafted at a time when women and those who held no land could not vote; Australia's Indigenous inhabitants were seen as members of a 'dying race' undeserving of legal recognition,[187] and the 'white Australia policy' was in full effect (the *Immigration Restriction Act 1901* and *Pacific Island Labourers Act 1901* were passed by the first Commonwealth Parliament). Since that time, we have witnessed two world wars, and the advent of the international human rights movement in an effort to avoid such destructive and inhumane conflicts in the future. Bills of rights have arguably been the most important constitutional developments in most Western (and many other) nations since the Second World War. Yet these sweeping changes have largely passed the Australian Constitution by.

In *Kruger v Commonwealth*, Dawson J stated 'The framers [of the Constitution] preferred to place their faith in the democratic process for the protection of individual rights.'[188] So far, this choice has served most Australians well. However, in *Fardon v Attorney-General for the State of Queensland*, Kirby made a plea on behalf of those whom the Constitution ignores, but who are nevertheless owed human rights protections – in the instant case convicted criminals who have served their sentences:

> ... it is in cases of such a kind that the rule of law is tested. As Latham CJ pointed out long ago, in claims for legal protection, normally, "the majority of the people can look after itself": constitutional protections only really become important in the case of "minorities, and, in particular, of unpopular minorities". It is in such cases that the adherence of this Court to established constitutional principle is truly tested, as it is in this case.[189]

In the result in *Fardon*, the High Court approved a legislative scheme to detain 'dangerous' offenders after the expiry of their sentences, similar to the one found to be unconstitutional in *Kable v DPP* (yet sufficiently different to avoid that legislation's fate).[190] Parliament has in recent times also begun to grant the executive ever-broader powers in the name of defence and national security – even reviving offences which had fallen into desuetude such as treason, espionage, treachery and sabotage.[191] There is every indication at present that this trend will continue, with the two major political parties in close accord on national security policy.[192] As such, more Australians may begin to wish

[186] (1999) 198 CLR 511, 600.

[187] See George Williams, 'Recognising Aboriginal and Torres Strait Islander Peoples in the Constitution' (2015) 34 *University of Tasmania Law Review* 114, 117. See also later statements by officials such as the Administrator of the Northern Territory – 'The Australian Aboriginal: A dying race,' *The Cairns Post*, 29 August 1946, 3 (available at https://trove.nla.gov.au/newspaper/article/42508269).

[188] *Kruger v Commonwealth*, above n 78, 61.

[189] *Fardon*, above n 21, 629.

[190] Oscar Roos, '*Baker v The Queen; Fardon v Attorney-General for the State of Queensland*' (2005) 10 *Deakin Law Review* 271.

[191] See, eg, Law Council of Australia Media Release, 'Secrecy of information, treason, espionage and sabotage target of new Bill' (no exact date provided, 2018); also for a summary of national security laws passed in the 44th Parliament, see Monica Biddington, *National security and counter-terrorism laws*, Parliamentary Library Briefing Book 45P (also undated, but issued at the advent of the 45th Parliament in 2016): www.aph.gov.au/About_Parliament/Parliamentary_Departments/Parliamentary_Library/pubs/BriefingBook45p/CounterTerrorism.

[192] See Waleed Aly, 'The problem with 'dangerous times'' *The Sydney Morning Herald*, 7 June 2018, online edition: www.smh.com.au/politics/federal/the-problem-with-dangerous-times-20180607-p4zk0z.html.

that the framers had taken a less faith-based approach, and had instead included more express checks and balances in the Constitution. The applicants in the immigration cases discussed above certainly already do.

It has been observed that one of the reasons for omitting a bill of rights from the Australian Constitution was that such rights would be a product of their time, potentially leading to undesirable consequences in time, like the Second Amendment to the US Constitution.[193] However, it might also legitimately be observed that the very lack of a bill of rights has in some respects frozen the Australian Constitution in time, leaving it out of step with the contemporary international legal context. After *Al-Kateb*, we should all consider whether our Parliament ought to be able to empower the executive branch to detain individuals indefinitely in peacetime – particularly considering the executive's contemporary dominance of the parliamentary agenda.[194] This question evidently troubled McHugh J, who all but called for a bill of rights in his judgment.[195]

In *Polites*, decided before the *Universal Declaration of Human Rights* was adopted by the UN General Assembly, Starke J stated:

> [T]o limit the constitutional power of sovereign States or their subordinate authorities denies the supremacy of those States within their own territory, which is contrary to the principles of the law of nations itself.[196]

In an age requiring international cooperation on issues larger than any one State, including climate change, international crime, mass migration, large-scale security threats and globalised trade and commerce, it is inappropriate for Australian constitutional law to continue to prioritise classical national sovereignty as it did in the twentieth century. The twenty-first century calls for a new 'humanised sovereignty,'[197] taking into account international human rights law, which represents the world's best efforts to prescribe fundamental universal standards of fairness and dignity.

Commentators predicted in the Mason-Brennan era that the High Court would inevitably come to use international human rights law in a 'search for meaningful principles of constitutionalism' in a rapidly globalising era.[198] Their predictions may yet prove accurate, but for the moment fall short. As Hilary Charlesworth and others have noted, international law has a perception problem – its use in the domestic sphere is seen as 'a threatening discourse from outside the Australian legal system,' even though it ought to be seen as 'one that connects us to the rest of the world.'[199]

[193] See, eg, James Lindgren, 'Forward: The Past and Future of Guns' (2015) 104 *Journal of Criminal Law and Criminology* 705.

[194] See, eg, Scott Prasser, Nicholas Aroney and J R Nethercote 'Restraining Executive Government Dominance – Are Upper Houses the Answer?' (2009) *Public Administration Today* 72.

[195] *Al-Kateb*, above n 6, 594–595.

[196] *Polites*, above n 22, 75.

[197] See Bernard G Ramcharan, 'Human Rights as International Constitutional Law' in *For the sake of present and future generations: essays on international law, crime and justice in honour of Roger S. Clark*, Suzannah Linton, Gerry Simpson, William A Schabas (eds) (Leiden, Brill Nijhoff, 2015), 217.

[198] See, eg, Brian Fitzgerald, 'International Human Rights and the High Court of Australia' (1994) 1 *James Cook University Law Review* 78, 101.

[199] Charlesworth et al, above n 9, 465.

It is not suggested that the panoply of international human rights be imported directly into the Australian Constitution. There are very real issues of precision, applicability, legitimacy and consistency with the general scheme of Australian law which will necessarily limit the range of rights suitable for consideration in constitutional interpretation. Such objections are apparent in *Al-Kateb*, and have been covered comprehensively elsewhere.[200] Indeed, Kirby J himself has stated:

> To interpret [the Constitution] as containing a general scheme of protection for fundamental freedoms would compromise the legitimacy of the High Court as the arbiter of the Constitution. … The Court would exceed its brief if it were to go beyond those rights expressed by or necessarily implied in the text.[201]

However, it has already been acknowledged that there is a select range of rights which might be said to be implicit in certain features of the Constitution, such as the structural separation of judicial power or the words 'directly chosen by the people.' A limited right to personal liberty is one which should be held to withstand the typical objections above, and one which is consistent with both the common law and prevailing community values.[202] There may be others, but the 'discovery' of implied right such as this would at least have ameliorated the result in *Al-Kateb*.

Despite Kirby J's robust statement in *Newcrest Mining* and following cases, seemingly amounting to a 'presumption of conformity,' his Honour's actual use of international law in deriving constitutional meaning during his tenure on the High Court was more in the nature of a 'legitimate influence,' using international law 'ideas'[203] to supplement other sources which, in most cases, could have determined the issue without recourse to international law.[204] This is similar to the approach taken in the implied rights cases, including recent decisions such as *Roach*[205] and *McCloy v NSW*.[206] These cases also suggest that the current High Court is increasingly comfortable applying and interpreting international law.[207]

The approach described above is more evolutionary than revolutionary, and should therefore not be dismissed by the moderate originalists of the High Court. There is a global cosmopolitan trend in constitutional interpretation which will become increasingly difficult to ignore in years to come.[208] Kirby J wrote in 1999:

> It will remain to be seen whether this interpretative principle attracts judicial support. One of the lessons of a long judicial life is that today's heresies sometimes become tomorrow's orthodoxy.[209]

[200] See Simpson and Williams, above n 31, 218–227; also Bouwhuis, above n 9; Kirby, above n 36, 119–120.

[201] George Williams, *A Bill of Rights for Australia* (Sydney, University of NSW Press, 2000), 13.

[202] See further Kate Chetty, 'Protection from arbitrary detention in Australia: A proposal for an explicit constitutional right' (2016) 35 *University of Tasmania Law Review* 79.

[203] See Michael, above n 120.

[204] See Walker, above n 13, 97.

[205] *Roach v Electoral Commissioner*, above n 77.

[206] (2015) 257 CLR 178.

[207] See Arcioni and McLeod, above n 15, also Patrick Wall, 'Case Note: A Marked Improvement: The High Court of Australia's Approach to Treaty Interpretation in *Macoun v FCT* [2015] HCA 44' (2016) 17 *Melbourne Journal of International Law* 170.

[208] See Kolt, above n 40, 188, following Jeffrey Goldsworthy in, eg, *Interpreting Constitutions: A Comparative Study* (Oxford, Oxford University Press, 2006).

[209] Kirby, above n 36, 124.

The powers of Parliament and the executive should not be allowed to expand indefinitely, particularly not at the expense of fundamental rights. However, those branches of government have demonstrated little appetite to limit their own powers by prioritising rights,[210] so, if it is to be done, the task falls to the High Court. Since international human rights law and related jurisprudence is of evident assistance in this task – which necessarily involves 'filling the gaps' in Australian law[211] – its influence must surely grow, bearing out Kirby J's prediction.

[210] The Australian Parliament had a robust mandate to introduce a Commonwealth Human Rights Act after one was recommended by the comprehensive *National Human Rights Consultation* in 2009 (See Australian Government, *National Human Rights Consultation Report*, September 2009, Recommendation 18 (the report appears to have been removed from all Government websites, but is archived at: http://webarchive.nla.gov.au/gov/20120316183642/http://www.humanrightsconsultation.gov.au/www/nhrcc/nhrcc.nsf/Page/Report_NationalHumanRightsConsultationReportDownloads).

[211] See, eg, Kolt, above n 40, 233; also Kirby, above n 36, 116–125. Kirby argues that international law pertaining to fundamental rights is at least as 'helpful' in constitutional interpretation as the principles of originalism, though neither can be 'governing' principles. See further Aharon Barak, *The Judge in a Democracy* (Princeton University Press 2009), 122 (fn 1); Ronald Dworkin, *Law's Empire* (1986), 52–53; 62–68.

6

International Law, Administrative Powers and Human Rights: The Legacy of *Teoh*

MATTHEW GROVES*

During the 1990s, in what is called its 'implied rights period', the High Court of Australia delivered a series of radical decisions that either recognised a range of new common law and constitutional rights, or greatly invigorated existing ones.[1] One decision delivered during that period did not do either in any direct sense, and was thus often not included in analyses of implied rights, but it had the indirect effect of creating special rights for government decisions that might adversely affect children. The case was *Minister for Immigration and Ethnic Affairs v Teoh*,[2] in which the High Court held that decision makers contemplating actions that could adversely affect children should give special weight to the effect of their decision on those children. This requirement arose from a novel use of the legitimate expectation doctrine, held to arise from Australia's ratification of the Convention of the Rights of the Child ('the *Convention*').[3] The act of ratification was found to have created a legitimate expectation that officials whose decisions might adversely affect children would either treat the best interests of those children as a primary consideration,[4] or if the decision maker proposed to act otherwise, give affected people notice of this intention and a chance to put contrary arguments.

Teoh provoked strongly divided opinions. The decision was met with intense political criticism and equally strong, though not universal, academic support. This flurry of comment and criticism quickly subsided and the case itself seemed to fall into relative obscurity in later years, when its constituent parts fell away. There was no serious judicial attempt to extend the core reasoning of *Teoh* to other international treaties. The legitimate expectation, upon which much of the case depended, soon vanished from Australian public law.[5] At the same time, however, the key consequence of *Teoh* was actually embraced by

* Thanks are due to Nina Boughey, Dan Meagher and Greg Weeks for helpful comments.

[1] See ch 4 in this volume.

[2] (1995) 183 CLR 273.

[3] *Convention on the Rights of the Child 1989*, done at New York on 20 November 1989.

[4] That requirement for decisions affecting children is contained in Art 3(1) of the *Convention*, which applies to 'all actions … whether taken by public or private social welfare institutions, courts of law, administrative authorities, or legislative bodies …'.

[5] The turning point against the legitimate expectation doctrine was *Re Minister for Immigration and Multicultural and Indigenous Affairs; Ex parte Lam* (2003) 214 CLR 1. Its death knell in Australia was effectively sounded in *Minister for Immigration and Border Protection v WZARH* (2015) 256 CLR 326.

successive governments. The other legacy of *Teoh* was to enhance parliamentary oversight of treaties, which was clearly lacking in earlier times. This chapter explains the rise and fall of *Teoh's* case and the cautionary tale it provides to judicial attempts to draw directly upon international human rights treaties in domestic Australian law.[6]

I. *Teoh* and International Treaties as a Basis for Domestic Procedural Expectations

The modern evolution of Australian administrative law, including natural justice, was fairly typical of the common law world.[7] The scope of government decisions to which supervisory review extended grew steadily, as did the various types of decisions to which the requirements of natural justice applied. The growing reach of fairness during this time was aided by the legitimate expectation principle, which provided a useful conceptual path to extend requirements of fairness to instances where it would not otherwise apply.[8] The earlier approach, which asked whether there was a legal right upon which the duty of fairness could attach, was replaced with a wider presumption that fairness would apply to the exercise of statutory power that could defeat or frustrate a person's rights or interests.[9] In this more expansive approach, references to the legitimate expectation appeared to be rhetorical ones of habit because the breadth of this wider approach protecting interests appeared to remove any practical need for the legitimate expectation.[10] *Teoh* proved otherwise.

Mr Teoh faced deportation because of his criminal convictions for drug smuggling. His main argument against deportation was the devastating impact it would have on his family of seven children, for whom he was the primary carer. The Minister's delegate accepted that the Teoh family faced a 'very bleak and difficult future' if their father was deported, but concluded these 'compassionate claims' were not sufficient reason to waive the character requirements for the grant of a residency visa.[11] That decision was overturned by a majority

[6] The case remains one of several that is regularly cited for the point that statutes should be interpreted, so far as their language permits, in a way that conforms rather than conflicts with international law. See, eg, *CPCF v Minister for Immigration and Border Protection* (2015) 255 CLR 514, 526–7 [8] (French CJ), 627 [385] (Gageler J).

[7] The evolution of this law in Australia over the 20th century is explained in Ian Holloway, *Natural Justice and the High Court of Australia* (London, Ashgate, 2002).

[8] Used in this way, the legitimate expectation helped to answer what was called the 'threshold question' of whether the requirements of fairness applied to a particular circumstance. This and other functions of the doctrine during this time are explained in Graeme Johnson, 'Natural Justice and Legitimate Expectations in Australia' (1985) 15 *Federal Law Review* 39; Pamela Tate, 'The Coherence of "Legitimate Expectations" and the Foundations of Natural Justice' (1988) 14 *Monash University Law Review* 15.

[9] *Annetts v McCann* (1990) 170 CLR 596, 598; *Ainsworth* v *Criminal Justice Commission* (1992) 175 CLR 564, 577. The concept of 'rights' in this context did not mean human rights in any sense but was instead the administrative law notion generally referred to as 'interests'. Compare the proprietary right in *Cooper v Wandsworth Board of Works* (1863) 14 CBNS 180 to the mere interest in ongoing employment in *Ridge v Baldwin* [1964] AC 40.

[10] See, eg, *Teoh* (1995) 183 CLR 273, 311 (McHugh J); cf Sir Anthony Mason, 'Procedural Fairness: its Development and Continuing Role of Legitimate Expectation' (2005) 12 *Australian Journal of Administrative Law* 103, 106–7 (citing the importance of the legitimate expectation concept to deciding cases like *FAI Insurances Ltd v Winneke* (1982) 151 CLR 342).

[11] (1995) 183 CLR 273, 274.

of the High Court because the delegate had not treated the best interests of Teoh's children as 'a primary consideration' as required under the *Convention*.[12] The delegate clearly had not considered the *Convention*, partly because it had not been incorporated into Australian law after its ratification, but also because Mr Teoh had not raised the *Convention* in any way.[13]

The High Court overcame that apparent gap in the effect of the *Convention* by use of the legitimate expectation. Mason CJ, Deane and Toohey JJ held that ratification of the *Convention* by the executive created a legitimate expectation that its administrative officials would honour or consider its terms.[14] Where officials proposed to do otherwise, they were required to give adequate notice of that intention to an affected person and a sufficient opportunity to argue against that intended action.[15] Mr Teoh did not receive that notice, so he was denied natural justice and the resulting decision was invalid. The controversial part of this reasoning was the source of the legitimate expectation. Mason CJ and Deane J explained that the expectation arose because:

> … ratification of a convention is a positive statement by the executive government of this country to the world and to the Australian people that the executive government and its agencies will act in accordance with the Convention. That positive statement is an adequate foundation for a legitimate expectation, absent statutory of executive indications to the contrary, that administrative decision-makers will act in conformity with the Convention.[16]

Their Honours stressed that the expectation was procedural rather than substantive. It could be defeated, with no breach of fairness, if officials gave notice that they proposed to act inconsistently with the *Convention* and also gave an affected person a reasonable opportunity to argue against that course.[17] The majority judges also made clear that the *Convention* was not somehow incorporated into domestic law, so that officials were obliged to follow its terms when exercising discretionary powers.[18]

Gaudron J agreed with Mason CJ and Deane J about the status of the *Convention* in Australian law but held it was 'only of subsidiary significance in this case.'[19] Her Honour stressed that the status of the Teoh children as Australian citizens might provide a stronger foundation for their father's claim. Gaudron J suggested it was:

> … arguable that citizenship carries with a common law right on the part of children *and their parent* to have a child's best interest taken into account, *at least* as a primary consideration in *all* discretionary decisions by governments and government agencies which directly affect that child's welfare.[20]

[12] The Full Federal Court has warned more recently that '*Teoh* does not state more than that, procedurally, the interests of the children are a primary consideration, not the only, or the only primary, consideration.': *Nweke v Minister for Immigration, Multicultural Affairs and Citizenship* [2013] FCAFC 79, [29] (Allsop CJ, Flick and Robertson JJ).

[13] The *Convention* was not raised before the court of first instance and arose late in preparations for an appeal to the Full Federal Court, after leave was granted to raise the issue. The *Convention* proved decisive before the Full Court: *Teoh v Minister for Immigration and Ethnic Affairs* (1994) 49 FCR 409.

[14] (1995) 183 CLR 273, 291–2 (Mason CJ and Deane J), 302–3 (Toohey J).

[15] Ibid, 291–2 (Mason CJ and Deane J), 302–3 (Toohey J).

[16] Ibid, 291. One effect of this 'positive statement' to the wider community was to remove any need for affected people to 'personally entertain the expectation' because it was sufficient that the expectation was 'reasonable in the sense that there are adequate materials to support it': ibid. Toohey J reached a similar view: 301. McHugh J disagreed: 314.

[17] Ibid, 291–2.

[18] Ibid, 291 (Mason CJ and Deane J), 298, 301 (Toohey J).

[19] Ibid, 303.

[20] Ibid (emphasis added).

Gaudron J thought the true relevance of the *Convention* was not that it created any expectation but instead expressed 'a fundamental right which is taken for granted by Australian society'.[21] The ratification of such treaties confirmed their wider social acceptance. Gaudron J did not explain what made rights 'fundamental' in this sense, or the obverse question that arose from the caution that her reasoning 'may not' extend to 'a treaty or convention that is not in harmony with community values and expectations'.[22] While this reasoning avoided any reliance upon a strained version of the legitimate expectation, it arguably transposed that same logical strain upon previously unknown common law citizenship rights. These questions were not explored because the right suggested by Gaudron J did not gain wider support.[23]

McHugh J dissented in a strongly worded judgment that channelled the critical style employed by the late American Justice Antonin Scalia. That dissent contained two key objections to the majority reasoning. One arose from the effect attributed to treaty ratification. McHugh J strongly doubted that ratification could be interpreted as a positive statement by the executive to the Australian community.[24] In a separate but closely related point, he also questioned how people could hold an expectation in any legitimate sense when they were unaware of the very existence of the treaty upon which it was based.[25] McHugh J also drew attention to the impractical nature of expectations that might arise from treaties.[26] Australia had ratified so many different treaties[27] concerning so many different issues that it was 'difficult, if not impossible' to expect that officials 'will necessarily act in accordance with would act in accordance with the terms of a convention that does not have the force of law'.[28]

[21] Ibid, 304–5. Gaudron J did not explain why or how such 'fundamental rights' were to be identified. Her Honour's obscurity on this point was drawn into sharp focus when she suggested that such reasoning would not extend 'a treaty or convention that is not in harmony with community values and expectations': 305. Deciding when and why international instruments are at odds with societal norms, particularly for the purpose of excluding a judicial rule about the relevance of treaties, would be a contentious exercise.

[22] Ibid, 305.

[23] Several later decisions of the Federal Court noted that the suggested right either lacked supporting authority or had simply failed to gain support from the rest of the High Court. See, eg, *Minister for Immigration and Multicultural Affairs v W157/OOA* (2002) 125 FCR 433, 461–2; *Chai v Minister for Immigration and Multicultural and Indigenous Affairs* [2005] FCA 1480, [49]–[65]; *Lam v Minister for Immigration and Multicultural Affairs* (2006) 157 FCR 215, 357–8 [34]–[36].

[24] (1995) 183 CLR 273, 315–7.

[25] A problem amplified by what McHugh J described as the 'almost comic' requirement that the expectation could be evaded if officials informed an affected person that they would not apply a treaty the person did not even know about: (1995) 183 CLR 273, 314.

[26] This point had a curious sequel in the High Court's decision in *Project Blue Sky v Australian Broadcasting Authority* (1998) 194 CLR 355. The issue in that case was how two apparently conflicting provisions in (now repealed) broadcasting legislation might be reconciled. That legislation expressly required the Australian Broadcasting Authority to observe Australia's international obligations in the discharge of its function, but another provision in the statute appeared at odds with those obligations. In its attempts to reconcile provisions, the High Court seemed to doubt that the Parliament could have truly meant what its legislative words had stated about the observance of international obligations. The ironic point that may be taken from the *Blue Sky* case is that parliamentary enactment of treaty obligations is no panacea and may, depending on the clarity or obscurity of legislation, cause more problems than it solves.

[27] McHugh J noted that Australia was a party to over 900 treaties: (1995) 183 CLR 273, 316. This point was repeated in the majority judgment in *Blue Sky*, to which McHugh J was a party: *Project Blue Sky v Australian Broadcast Authority* (1998) 194 CLR 355, 392 [96]. The High Court in *Blue Sky* seemed to accept McHugh J's implication in *Teoh* that treaties cannot be given uniform weight in assessing the scope of their application.

[28] (1995) 183 CLR 273, 317.

The next section of this chapter explains the various official responses to *Teoh* but it is useful first to note briefly some key issues the decision left unclear and an important matter of statutory interpretation that the case did not need to touch upon. Statutory interpretation did not feature greatly in *Teoh* because the key questions were not ones of interpretation, or even whether administrative powers have to be exercised in accordance with the requirements of fairness. By the time *Teoh* was delivered, it was well settled that treaties could inform statutory interpretation, even if the extent to which they could do so was not quite so clear.[29]

Of the many issues *Teoh* left unclear, one was the status of other parts of the *Convention* or rather why the High Court largely focused on a single clause of a single treaty.[30] The High Court's silence on other parts of the *Convention* was curious, especially those parts which expressly anticipate the separation of children from parents in circumstances like those Mr Teoh faced.[31] This incomplete analysis of the *Convention* highlighted the difficulties facing officials. 'If High Court Justices do not attend to such matters', one commentator noted, 'it is surely forlorn to expect administrative decision-makers to do so adequately.'[32] The best reply to this criticism is the honest, but admittedly weak one, that the use of treaties and related principles by domestic courts is often selective, incomplete and conceptually incoherent.[33] *Teoh* was therefore not alone on this issue.

Another issue left unclear by *Teoh* was its potential. Mason CJ and Deane J cautioned that the common law 'must not be seen as a backdoor means of importing an unincorporated convention into Australian law.'[34] But that cautionary remark was made in the course of brief remarks about the incremental nature of common law developments and how international instruments could influence that process.[35] Even those brief references indicate an awareness of the potential of *Teoh* beyond the *Convention*. This potential to apply similar logic to found expectations upon other treaties was the spectre that always followed *Teoh*.

When viewed in combination, the High Court's incomplete consideration of the *Convention* and brief references to common law methodologies, give rise to larger questions. What was special about this particular part of this particular treaty? What was the

[29] This role of treaties was examined with insightful detail a year after *Teoh* was delivered in Kristen Walker, 'Treaties and the Internationalisation of Australian Law' in Cheryl Saunders (ed), *Courts of Final Jurisdiction: The Mason Court in Australia* (Annandale, Federation Press, 1996).

[30] Several parts of the *Convention* other than Art 3(1) were quoted in different judgments but none received detailed attention: (1995) 183 CLR 273, 317.

[31] Article 9(4) anticipates deportation of parents as one of several circumstances in which children may legitimately be separated from their parents. But Art 9(1) provides that separation must have been determined 'necessary for the best interests of the child'. This requirement poses particular difficulty for Australian migration decisions because deportation decisions are typically justified as necessary for the protection of the community, rather than the interests of the deportee's children.

[32] M Taggart, 'Legitimate Expectation and Treaties in the High Court of Australia' (1996) 112 *LQR* 50, 54.

[33] See, eg, Machiko Kanetake, 'UN Human Rights Treaty Monitoring Bodies Before Domestic Courts' (2018) 67 *ICLQ* 201.

[34] (1995) 183 CLR 273, 288. A notable feature of this brief discussion is that Mason CJ and Deane J expressly stated that the case was not concerned with either resolving ambiguity in a statute or developing an *existing* principle of common law: ibid. So what did *Teoh* do? The most likely explanation seems the unconvincing one that it simply applied an existing principle (the legitimate expectation) to novel circumstances.

[35] A widely cited statement to this effect was made in *Mabo (No 2) v Queensland* (1992) 175 CLR 1, 42, when Brennan J stated 'The common law does not necessarily conform with international standards, but international law is a legitimate and important influence on the development of the common law, especially when international law declares the existence of universal human rights.'

normative goal of the High Court? Did it even have one? An exploration of these questions by the High Court could have shed light on a tantalising remark Mason CJ and Deane J made in response to suggestions that treaty ratification was 'merely platitudinous or ineffectual …'.[36] Their Honours dismissed that argument as ill conceived '*particularly* when the instrument evidences internationally accepted standards … dealing with *basic* human rights affecting the family and children'.[37] This remark begs the question of what rights Mason CJ and Deane J thought were 'basic'.[38] In a jurisdiction that lacks an entrenched instrument defining and protecting rights, this question is one of enormous potential consequence.

II. The Official Response to *Teoh*

The Federal Government response to *Teoh* was quick and hostile. Several legislative attempts to reverse the decision lapsed and were eventually not pursued.[39] A more extreme response that gained relatively less public attention than others and faded quickly was the possibility of withdrawal from the *Convention*, so that Australia could ratify it again but with a reservation designed to overcome the effect of *Teoh*. This remarkable proposal fell by the wayside after it became accepted within government that such cynical action could greatly damage Australia's international standing.[40] The supporters of this proposal also seemed unaware that it would have a limited and possibility counterproductive effect. It would be limited in its application to only the *Convention* and would not have precluded similar findings based on other ratified treaties. It might also have been counterproductive by inadvertently suggesting that the lack of equivalent action with the many other unincorporated treaties to which Australia was party was intended to signal, in the terms anticipated by the majority in *Teoh*, that the executive government was content for the courts to draw procedural implications protective of rights from those other treaties. But the possibility of withdrawal was a real one.

Another element of the hostile official response to *Teoh* was the issue of ministerial statements by successive federal governments, stating that ratification of treaties was not, and had never been, intended to be capable of creating the sort of expectation recognised in *Teoh*.[41]

[36] (1995) 183 CLR 273, 291.

[37] Ibid, 291 (emphasis added).

[38] Even this adjective was a slightly curious one to use in the Australian context because it is not one regularly used by judges. Australian judges more commonly refer simply to 'rights and freedoms' rather than 'basic' ones. See, eg, Robert French, 'Rights, Freedoms and the Rule of Law' (2013) 13 *The Judicial Review* 261.

[39] The *Administrative Decisions (Effect of International Instruments) Bill* 1998 (Cth) lapsed upon the calling of the 1999 Federal election. A third Bill was introduced into the House of Representatives on 3 October 1999 but this Bill also failed to pass before the next federal election was called. A similar Bill was enacted in South Australia: *Administrative Decisions (Effect of International Instruments) Act 1995* (SA).

[40] Parliament of Australia, Joint Standing Committee on Treaties, 'United Nations Convention on the Rights of the Child' (17th Report, 1998) at 65–6 (available at www.aph.gov.au/house/committee/jsct/reports/report17/rept17ex.pdf).

[41] One was issued by the Labor Government in power when *Teoh* was decided: Joint Statement by the Minister for Foreign Affairs and the Attorney-General, *International Treaties and the High Court Decision in Teoh*, 10 May 1995. The subsequent Conservative Government issued a similar statement: Joint Statement by the Minister for Foreign Affairs and the Attorney-General and Minister for Justice, 'The Effect of Treaties in Administrative Decision-Making', 25 February 1997. The latter statement is quoted in Edward Cole and Marina Tsirbas, 'Australian Practice in International Law 1997' (1998) 19 *Australian Yearbook of International Law* 183, 224.

These statements built upon the suggestion of Mason CJ and Deane J that procedural rights could arise from treaty ratification in the absence of contrary indication from the executive,[42] and elicited the same divided response from commentators as they had from the High Court in *Teoh* itself.[43] The force of the executive statements remains unsettled in the courts because none of the decisions to consider the statements in any detail reached a clear position.[44] While the uncertain legal effect of the executive statements was undesirable, that uncertainty arguably prevented an open conflict between the courts and the executive.

A different form of executive statement did, however, gain acceptance within the courts. Those more refined statements were administrative directions issued as part of the ministerial power to order deportation of people on what are known as 'character grounds'.[45] After *Teoh* began to be successfully invoked by people resisting deportation decisions,[46] the power was quickly amended to enable the Minister to issue more prescriptive directions limiting the discretionary freedom of migration officials.[47] Directions issued under this power govern the very sort of decision taken in *Teoh*. They have grown relentlessly in detail over time.[48] In one sense, these directions arguably vindicate *Teoh* because they direct officials to consider

[42] *Teoh* (1995) 183 CLR 273, 291. This intended effect of the ministerial statements is at odds with the prevailing legal conception of soft law and policy statements which, in simple terms, denies them the binding force of law. The odd position of the executive statements was that they sought to extinguish the High Court's equally odd ex post facto interpretation of treaty ratification. One decision characterised the statements as something akin to the processes used to create the scientific hoax the 'Piltdown man, which was a fraudulent skull with teeth filed down to frustrate its identification. The ministerial statements were described as taking the further step of attempting to extract all of *Teoh's* teeth and remove it from the historical record: *Yad Ram and Department of Immigration and Ethnic Affairs* [1995] AATA 381, [19].

[43] See, eg, Margaret Allars, 'One Small Step for Legal Doctrine, One Giant Leap Towards Integrity in Government' (1995) 17 *Sydney Law Review* 204, 235–6 (arguing the statements were ineffective) and Elizabeth Handsley, 'Legal Fictions and Confusion as Strategies for Protecting Human Rights: A Dissenting View on *Teoh's* Case' (1997) 2 *Newcastle Law Review* 56, 60–4 (arguing the statements were effective).

[44] See, eg: *Tien v Minister for Immigration and Multicultural Affairs* (1998) 89 FCR 80 101–5 (doubting whether generalised executive statements would overcome *Teoh*); *Department of Immigration and Ethnic Affairs v Ram* (1996) 69 FCR 431, 437–8 (suggestion that executive statements must be made contemporaneously with ratification); *Lam v Minister for Immigration and Multicultural Affairs* (2006) 157 FCR 215, 226 [30] (expressly doubting the point made in *Ram*). These cases are notable for their failure to consider commentary upon the executive statements made by international law scholars, such as Don Rothwell, Stuart Kaye, Afshin Akhtar-Khavari and Imogen Saunders, *International Law – Cases and Materials with Australian Perspectives,* 3rd edn (Cambridge, Cambridge University Press, 2018) 216–227.

[45] The Minister has long been empowered to issue directions governing the performance of virtually all functions and exercise of almost all discretions under the *Migration Act* 1958 (Cth) s 499(1).

[46] This occurred most frequently in the Administrative Appeals Tribunal. See, eg, *Yad Ram and Department of Immigration and Ethnic Affairs* [1995] AATA 381 (decision to refuse visa set aside with heavy reliance on *Teoh*). That tribunal also saw many previously determined applications revived with a new argument based upon *Teoh*. See, eg, *Vaitaiki and Minister of Immigration and Ethnic Affairs* [1995] AATA 331. Even though these application almost always failed, the time and expense in defending them must surely have worried migration officials.

[47] *Migration Legislation Amendment (Strengthening of Provisions Relating to Character and Conduct) Act 1998* (Cth) Sch 1, s 16. The explanatory material that accompanied this amendment left no doubt that it was intended to replace the existing power to issue 'general' directions with one to ensure 'the Minister can specify more *precisely* how a discretion should be exercised': Explanatory Memorandum, Migration Legislation Amendment (Strengthening of Provisions Relating to Character and Conduct Bill 1998 (Cth) para 30 (emphasis added).

[48] The current direction is 33 pages long: [Australia] Minister for Immigration and Citizenship, *Direction No.65 – Visa Refusal and Cancellation Under s501 and Revocation of a Mandatory Cancellation of a Visa Under s501CA* (22 December 2014). This current direction and related ones are explained and criticised in [Australian Parliament] Joint Standing Committee on Migration, *Report of the Inquiry into Review Processes Associated with Visa Cancellations Made on Criminal Grounds* (2019) 8–11.

the best interests of children as a primary consideration in the exercise of these powers.[49] The direction is no longer a vague one from the High Court that is based upon obscure administrative law doctrine. It is now a clear direction, issued by the very Ministers who so vigorously criticised *Teoh* when it was delivered. If this codification of *Teoh* was a victory, it has proved pyrrhic because many other issues important to people facing adverse decisions are either removed from consideration or expressly made considerations of relatively less weight. An example is the impact of such decisions upon the wider family unit, which is a designated consideration for officials, but not a primary one.[50] That means the direction espouses the language of the *Convention* and the status it accords to the interests of children, yet subtly seeks to do otherwise by diminishing the weight given to the impact of decisions on families of those children.[51]

The Ministerial directions also arguably reflect an early suggestion made by Taggart, which was that the many shortcomings of *Teoh* might fade if the case was used as a 'wobbly stepping stone' to the more coherent use of treaty matters as relevant considerations in administrative decision making.[52] No such general approach emerged, though it is useful to note the courts have accepted that the directions prescribe a series of binding relevant considerations that must be weighed in cases to which they apply.[53] That status almost certainly places the directions beyond denunciation by executive statement.[54] But these matters do not apply to the Minister. As the directions apply to delegates empowered to act on the Minister's behalf, they do not extend to a Minister who exercises the powers personally.[55] This limitation has become increasingly important with the growing habit of successive Ministers to exercise many migration powers personally.[56]

Cases that considered the earlier, simpler directions yielded mixed results on the extent to which they bound administrative officials.[57] More recent ones have effectively conceded that the directions create a 'legitimate framework within which the discretion vested in decision-makers is lawfully to be exercised.'[58] While that approach is consistent with suggestions made in *Teoh* that the rights it recognised arose 'absent executive indication to the contrary,'[59] it has also facilitated the practical demise of *Teoh* in this area. The enor-

[49] [Australia] Minister for Immigration and Citizenship, *Direction No.65 – Visa Refusal and Cancellation Under s501 and Revocation of a Mandatory Cancellation of a Visa Under s501CA* (22 December 2014) cl.9.2.

[50] A paradox noted by Australian Human Rights Commission, *Review Processes Associated with Visa Cancellations Made on Criminal Grounds – Submission to the Joint Standing Committee on Migration* (27 April 2018) para 79.

[51] Though it has been held that issues not designated as primary consideration are not necessarily to be treated as lesser or secondary ones. There is a level of discretion on this: *Minister for Home Affairs v HSKJ* [2018] FCAFC 217.

[52] Taggart, above n 32, 50.

[53] *Minister for Immigration and Border Protection v Lesianawai* (2014) 227 FCR 562, 586, [83].

[54] Andrew Edgar and Rayner Thwaites, 'Implementing Treaties in Domestic Law: Translation Enforcement and Administrative Law' (2018) 19 *Melbourne Journal of International Law* 24, 39.

[55] *NBMZ v Minister for Immigration and Border Protection* (2014) 220 FCR 1, 4 [4].

[56] While most migration powers are stated to be vested in the Minister (and then typically delegated), some are expressly stated as exercisable by the Minister alone. See, eg, *Migration Act 1958* (Cth) s 501(3)(4).

[57] Chantal Bostock, 'The Effect of Ministerial Directions on Tribunal Independence' (2011) 66 *AIAL Forum* 33. That author notes that one harsh direction, which removed or lessened the role of factors that might favour applicants, was introduced after its more benevolent predecessor was found partially invalid.

[58] *Minister for Immigration and Border Protection v Lesianawai* (2014) 227 FCR 562, 585 [80] (Perry J, discussing the now repealed Direction No 55).

[59] *Teoh* (1995) 183 CLR 273, 291.

mous detail of the directions has led the courts to concede that 'to the extent that there is *any* inconsistency between the Direction and *any* passage in *Teoh*, the direction *necessarily* prevails.'[60] That outcome has led some commentators to conclude that the 'greater specificity' of successive directions has seen them become a far more effective tool against *Teoh* than the executive statements.[61] This outcome suggests that the directions provide a useful template for officials to deploy against any right akin to the one recognised in *Teoh* that might arise in future cases.

A novel further dimension to the ministerial directions can be found in the less well known rules governing the discretionary powers to grant Australian citizenship to children.[62] The administrative rules that guide the exercise of those powers echo the words of the *Convention*, stating that decision makers must treat the best interests of a child who applies for citizenship as a primary consideration.[63] This aspect of these rules share a common quality with the ministerial directions. They pointedly omit any reference to *Teoh*, yet they codify the very principle that case sought to transmit into administrative decision making by use of the legitimate expectation.[64] Once again, the public denunciation of *Teoh* was followed by the quiet adoption of one of its key consequences.

The most wide ranging institutional official response to *Teoh* was reforms to greatly increase parliamentary and public involvement in the treaty process. A central feature of these reforms was the creation of a Joint Standing Committee on Treaties,[65] which is charged with responsibility to investigate and report upon 'matters arising from treaties'.[66] The Joint Committee has clearly reduced the strength of longstanding complaints about the lack of transparency of the treaty-making process in Australia because its inquiries and reports are public.[67] At the same time, however, many other problems in the treaty process

[60] *Baker v Minister for immigration and Citizenship* [2012] FCAFC 145, [55] (emphasis added). See also *SZRTN v Minister for Immigration and Border Protection* [2014] FCAFC 129, [39].

[61] Edgar and Thwaites, above n 54, 39.

[62] A non-citizen child is eligible for a grant of citizenship if he or she meets certain criteria contained in the *Australian Citizenship Act 2007* (Cth) s 21(5). Satisfaction of the criteria enlivens a discretionary power to grant citizenship under s 24.

[63] These are the *Australian Citizenship Instructions 2014*, which are quoted extensively by Mortimer J in *G v Minister for Immigration and Border Protection* [2018] FCA 1229. Her Honour noted that the *Australian Citizenship Act 2007* (Cth) provides no clear authority for the issue of these rules, which meant they were an executive instrument of policy: [34]. Mortimer J made scathing criticisms of the obscure nature of many rules and noted that many appeared to misunderstand the administrative powers they sought to offer guidance for.

[64] This statement is somewhat speculative because the most recent directions are not publicly available. A previous direction is available in the internet, though with no indication as to who posted it: file:///C:/Users/User/Downloads/acis-may-2012%20(1).pdf. That document is 168 pages long and makes no mention of *Teoh*. The current version is 278 pages long: *G v Minister for Immigration and Border Protection* [2018] FCA 122, [36]. The tenor of Mortimer J's description of the current document suggests it unlikely to include references to the *Convention*.

[65] The operation of the Committee is explained in Joanna Harrington, 'The Role For Parliaments in Treaty-Making' in Hilary Charlesworth, Madelaine Chiam, Devika Hovell and George Williams (eds), *The Fluid State: International Law and National Legal Systems* (Annandale, Federation Press, 2006) 34, 43–9. It is examined from the perspective of politicians in Daryl Williams, 'Establishing an Australian Parliamentary Treaties Committee' (1995) 6 *Public Law Review* 275 and Helen Coonan, 'Signing International Treaties: What do Politicians Think They Are Doing?' (1998) 16 *AIAL Forum* 15.

[66] Australian Parliament, *Resolution of Appointment for a Joint Committee on Treaties*, clause (1)(a), available at www.aph.gov.au/Parliamentary_Business/Committees/Joint/Treaties/Resolution.

[67] The public nature of those processes was almost certainly one reason why the Department of Foreign Affairs and Trade now makes extensive information about the treaty process publicly available: https://dfat.gov.au/international-relations/treaties/treaty-making-process/Pages/treaty-making-process.aspx

remain. Executive governments continue to dominate the treaty process by their practical control over treaty negotiations, which are typically conducted under extreme secrecy that excludes opposing political parties and the public.[68]

There are several practical limitations upon the work of the Joint Committee.[69] A significant one is that its agenda and operation are controlled by the executive government.[70] This strong executive influence extends to the processes that inform the Joint Committee. It applies a 'National Interest Analysis' to treaties under consideration for ratification, which is prepared by the Department of Foreign Affairs and Trade, in conjunction with the department(s) whose activities would be affected by the treaty. The Ministers who control these departments also sit in cabinet with other Ministers involved in treaty negotiations. Such connections may help explain what a cursory inspection of National Interest Analysis reports reveals. They are formulaic, superficial and do little more than repeat generalised statements about the virtue of the treaty under consideration and confirm the diligence with which it has been considered.[71]

These many forms of executive influence impose important substantive limits on the Joint Committee.[72] The role of the Committee normally commences only *after* key domestic political decisions about a treaty are taken by the government. The Committee cannot act of its own motion, such as to recommend the executive consider ratification of a particular treaty. It is reactive and dependent essentially on action by the executive. The Joint Committee also lacks any power to consider wider issues, such as Australia's poor record on the domestic implementation of treaties or its haphazard response to critical reports about its observance of treaty obligations.[73] Another means of executive domination over the Committee arises through its constitution, which requires that a majority of members are drawn from the government.[74] A further limitation upon the Committee's work is the advisory nature of its function. Reports of the Committee do not, indeed cannot, bind the executive.[75]

[68] The typical practice of Australian governments is that senior ministers refer boastfully, but vaguely, to treaty negotiations during press conferences. When politicians are pressed to provide any real detail, they normally refuse by making equally vague references to the sensitive nature of treaty negotiations.

[69] A minor administrative one, which may have significant practical consequence, is the Joint Committee does not appear to have followed the innovative practices adopted by other committees: Carolyn Hendricks, Sue Regan and Adrian Kay, 'Participatory Adaptation in Contemporary Parliamentary Committees in Australia' (2019) 72 *Parliamentary Affairs* 267. There is clear evidence that such changes are vital to the effectiveness of parliamentary committees. See, eg, Cristina Leston-Bandeira, 'Studying the Relationship Between Parliament and Citizens' (2012) 18 *Journal of Legislative Studies* 265.

[70] This executive dominance of the Joint Committee has led to criticisms that the wider treaty process in Australia remains fundamentally anti-democratic. See, eg, Ann Capling, 'Can the Democratic Deficit in Treaty-Making Be Overcome? Parliament and the Australia-United States Free Trade Agreement' in Charlesworth et al, above n 65.

[71] Copies of every National Interest Analysis are available at: www.austlii.edu.au/au/other/dfat/nia/.

[72] Such criticisms apply to parliamentary committees more generally. See, eg, Zoe Hutchinson, 'The Role, Operation and Effectiveness of the Commonwealth Parliamentary Joint Committee on Human Rights after Five Years' (2018) 33 *Australasian Parliamentary Review* 72. That author's careful analysis of the Commonwealth Joint Parliamentary Committee on Human Rights concludes that the shortcomings of that particular committee are an example of a wider problem.

[73] The scope of the Committee's work was also criticised in its early years because it had no clear mandate over human rights, even these are central to many treaties: Ben Saul, 'Administrative Law and Human Rights' in Matthew Groves and HP Lee (eds), *Administrative Law: Fundamentals, Principles and Doctrines* (Cambridge, Cambridge University Press, 2007). This criticism was addressed when the Commonwealth Parliament established the separate human rights committee examined in ch 8.

[74] Australian Parliament, *Resolution of Appointment for a Joint Committee on Treaties*, clause (2).

[75] This limit is somewhat fictional because the nature of Australian politics means there is no real possibility that a parliamentary committee with a majority of members drawn from the government of the day would make recommendations contrary to the wishes of that government.

Most other parliamentary committees exert enormous practical power through their ability to delay or halt the passage of bills before the Parliament. The extra-parliamentary character of treaty ratification deprives the Joint Committee of that power.

There is, however, one important feature of the Committee's work that resonates with the assumptions made in *Teoh* about the presumed acceptance by the executive government of the treaties it ratifies. As formulaic as much of the Joint Committee's work may be, there is no question it has raised awareness within government about treaties, through activities such as National Interest Analyses and public consultation processes.[76] Some of the most compelling criticisms levelled by McHugh J against the use of international treaties as a foundation for procedural rights in domestic law arose from the domestic obscurity of treaties and the artificial nature of suggestions that the act of ratification could signal genuine governmental acceptance of a treaty. These criticisms now have little force unless governments assert that the operation of a parliamentary committee is meaningless. It is one thing to continue to accept that assumption as a matter of practice. It would be quite another for a government to assert it in the courts.

III. The Retreat of the High Court

A cursory glance over federal migration decisions in the years following *Teoh* seemed to reveal that the case was invoked regularly,[77] though rarely with success. One reason might have been the apparent increasing trend by which migration decisions typically contained several paragraphs, which outlined the relevance of *Teoh*, explained how it had been considered in the case at hand and why it did not prevent an unfavourable decision.[78] *Teoh* appeared to have become a box to tick, a hurdle to jump, but one that was rarely insurmountable. That trend may make it all the more surprising that *Teoh* was reconsidered by the High Court in *Lam*,[79] another migration case where a man facing deportation stressed the impact his removal would have on his Australian children. The narrow procedural question before the High Court was whether the failure of migration officials to consult the people caring for Mr Lam's children a final time before making a decision was unfair. The High Court held the decision was not unfair because Lam had provided all the information he could, and nothing would be gained by further consultation. Neither the legitimate expectation nor *Teoh* were in issue but the High Court took the chance to strongly disapprove of both.[80]

[76] The National Interest Analysis reports are posted on the most heavily used legal website in Australia (Austlii) at: www.austlii.edu.au/au/other/dfat/ATNIA/. A recent empirical study of Australian parliamentary committees found that digital outreach with even tedious documents such as these can raise the public profile of committees enormously: Hendricks, Regan and Kay, above n 69.

[77] It is not possible within the confines of this chapter to provide detailed statistics to justify this impression because *Teoh* has been cited in well over 1,000 federal court and tribunal decisions.

[78] I draw this conclusion from having worked in the federal Administrative Appeals Tribunal in the years after *Teoh*, where migration files invariably contained a statement of reasons that addressed these issues in exactly the same terms. The use of template paragraphs may be attributed to a case delivered the year after *Teoh*, where the High Court accepted that the use of standard form paragraphs by officials in decision that raised broadly similar issues was not itself evidence of legal error: *Minister for Immigration and Ethnic Affairs v Wu Shan Liang* (1996) 185 CLR 259.

[79] *Re Minister for Immigration and Multicultural and Indigenous Affairs; Ex parte Lam* (2003) 214 CLR 1.

[80] *Teoh* was not directly relied upon by the applicant. In any case, it was unlikely that *Teoh* would have been overruled by a five-member court. Such a recent case would probably have required a full bench of seven Justices and also a grant leave to pursue this issue (which would also enable the preparation of full arguments).

Teoh's use of legitimate expectation reasoning was disapproved in *Lam* for reasons that echoed the dissenting judgment of McHugh J in *Teoh*. The concept was variously described as 'an unfortunate one, and apt to mislead',[81] now of 'limited utility',[82] that was to be approached with great caution.[83] The unifying thread of these criticisms was that the transitional role of the legitimate expectation had effectively been ended by the expanded scope of fairness. That scope was reflected in the influential judgment of Gleeson CJ, which stressed the 'concern of the law to avoid practical injustice.'[84] That approach was a holistic one that considered whether the procedure was fair as a whole and whether affected people had lost a chance to put their case. Such reasoning contains no obvious place for artificial doctrines such as the legitimate expectation in general, or one based on an obscure treaty. Other members of the High Court focused on the narrower question of whether legitimate expectations could arise from the ratification of treaties. McHugh and Gummow JJ strongly doubted whether treaty ratification itself was a sound basis to impose restrictions or requirements upon the executive government or its officials when exercising discretionary powers.[85] Callinan J expressed similar concerns but also queried whether the judicial recognition of an expectation created by a treaty, particularly one unsupported by domestic legislation, was consistent with the separation of powers.[86]

The impact of *Lam* on the use of international treaties took many forms. The most obvious one was the strong doubt it cast over *Teoh*,[87] which served to both undermine the legitimate expectation in general but also its specific role as a device to compel administrative officials to take account of rights contained in the *Convention*. Another was that it essentially signalled the end of hopes that *Teoh* might provide the template or first example for similar judicial recourse to other rights in other treaties. The case that finally buried the legitimate expectation contained no obvious foothold to consider the possible role of treaties as a source of administrative law principles, though the marginal role accorded to *Teoh* seemed to signal its final demise. That decision was *WZARH*,[88] in which an applicant for refugee status complained that the fragmented hearing of his application was unfair. The initial decision maker had interviewed the applicant but not reached a decision. She then explained to the applicant that she would undertake a fresh hearing. In fact, the case was handed to another official who determined the application without a new hearing. This procedure was found unfair by the Full Federal Court, where the majority justices relied heavily on the legitimate expectation.[89]

[81] (2003) 214 CLR 1, 45 (Callinan J).
[82] Ibid, 16 (McHugh and Gummow JJ).
[83] Ibid, 38 (Hayne J), 45–8 (Callinan J).
[84] Ibid, 13.
[85] Ibid, 31–4.
[86] Ibid, 47–8. His Honour noted that one part of the executive could ratify a treaty and the courts could then essentially require another part of the executive (decision makers) to give effect to it. Callinan J suggested this 'would elevate the Executive over the parliament': 48.
[87] Taggart thought that *Lam* had 'done about as much as judges can by way of *obiter dicta* in a case where the point was not argued to overrule *Teoh*: Michael Taggart, '"Australian Exceptionalism" in Judicial Review' (2008) 36 *Federal Law Review* 1, 17.
[88] *Minister for Immigration and Border Protection v WZARH* (2015) 256 CLR 326.
[89] *WZARH v Minister for Immigration and Border Protection* (2014) 230 FCR 130, 140–2 [23]–[29] (Flick and Gleeson JJ).

The High Court also held that the hearing was unfair but strongly disapproved of any use of the legitimate expectation. Kiefel, Bell and Keane JJ traced the 'tentative acceptance' then 'rejection' of the legitimate expectation in Australian law and held that the concept was not a useful or sound basis for questions about the content of fairness.[90] Their Honours held that the 'real question' was what was 'required in order to ensure that the decision is made fairly in the circumstances having regard to the legal framework within which the decision is to be made'.[91] Gageler and Gordon JJ adopted a broadly similar position.[92] While most analysis of these aspects of *WZARH* has focused on the demise of the legitimate expectation as a discrete element of Australian administrative law,[93] very little attention has been given to the effect of the demise of its role as a means of fostering treaty considerations. That silence is not without meaning.

IV. The Differing International Reception of *Teoh*

The decision in *Teoh* attracted considerable interest from courts and scholars in other countries, though much of that scrutiny did not move beyond hesitant curiosity. The Privy Council has mentioned *Teoh* many times but never gone so far as to adopt its more adventurous aspects.[94] That hesitance mirrors the mixed reception *Teoh* received in English courts. Some English cases appear to have accepted *Teoh*.[95] Others have considered the case but held ratification of the relevant treaty did not create any legitimate expectation.[96] Still others have strongly questioned its reasoning.[97] These divergent authorities may explain why the authors of *de Smith's Judicial Review* have described English law on this point in a way that appears to liken it to a weakened version of *Teoh*. Those authors suggest only that

[90] *WZARH* (2015) 256 CLR 326 334–5 [28]–[30].

[91] Ibid, 335 [30].

[92] Ibid, 342–3 [60]–[63].

[93] See, eg, Naomi Sharp, 'Procedural Fairness: The Age of Legitimate Expectation is Over' (2016) 90 *Australian Law Journal* 797; Matthew Groves, 'Legitimate Expectations in Australia: Overtaken by Formalism and Pragmatism' in Matthew Groves and Greg Weeks (eds), *Legitimate Expectations in the Common Law World* (Oxford, Hart Publishing, 2017).

[94] See *Thomas v Baptiste* [1999] 3 WLR 249, 263; *Fisher v Minister of Public Safety and Immigration (No 2)* [2000] 1 AC 434, 446–7; *Higgs v Minister of National Security* [2000] 2 AC 228, 241; *Naidike v Attorney-General of Trinidad and Tobago* [2005] 1 AC 538, 559–60. The last mentioned case was notable for its total failure to acknowledge the apparent reversal of *Teoh* that occurred in *Lam*. The Privy Council recently lauded the importance of the *Convention*, while also suggesting a more subtle approach for its use: *Seepersad (a minor) v Ayers-Caeser* [2019] UKPC 7, [15]–[16].

[95] *Teoh* was described as 'wholly convincing' by Lord Woolf in *R v Secretary of State for the Home Department; Ex part Ahmed* [1999] IAR 22, 36–7.

[96] See, eg, *Musaj v Secretary of State for the Home Department* [2004] SLT 623, [21]–[23] where Lady Smith held that an expectation of the *Teoh* sort did not arise from ratification of the 'Dublin Convention', which is the *Convention determining the State responsible for examining applications for asylum lodged in one of the member states of the European Community* (15 June 1990, OJ C/254). That document only took full effect as law when ratified by all members of the European Union in 1997, prior to which it had a status not unlike an international instrument which had been ratified but not given full legal effect. The original convention has been replaced more than once by EU rules, the most recent of which Regulation (EU) No 604/2013 ([2013] OJ L/180/31). This rule is known as 'Dublin III'.

[97] Sir John Laws expressed 'some unease' at the cases suggesting ratification of a treaty could itself create a legitimate expectation in *R (on the application of European Roma Rights Centre) v Immigration Officer, Prague Airport* [2004] QB 811, 844.

ratification of a treaty *can* be regarded as a form of conduct or representation that *might* give rise to an expectation that *could* influence the standard expected of public officials and the interpretation of discretionary powers.[98]

The seminal Canadian decision of *Baker*[99] completely ignored *Teoh*, even though each case raised broadly similar issues. The Supreme Court conceded that the *Convention* had not been translated into domestic law but reasoned that 'the values reflected in international human rights law may help inform the contextual approach to statutory interpretation and judicial review.'[100] The Court did not either rely upon the legitimate expectation or suggest the *Convention* might justify recourse of that doctrine. Reliance was instead placed directly on 'the *values* underlying the duty of procedural fairness.'[101] This approach simultaneously removed any need to strain the legitimate expectation concept unduly but also affirmed the value of international instruments and their normative content as a matter of general principle, rather than a narrow exception applicable to a single treaty.[102]

While the Canadian Supreme Court may have ignored *Teoh*, it drew useful guidance from a New Zealand decision that grappled with similar issues a year before *Teoh*. That was the case of *Tavita v Minister for Immigration*,[103] where the New Zealand Court of Appeal was essentially invited to ignore any national obligations that might arise from ratification of the *Convention*, when the Minister for Immigration submitted that administrative powers to order deportation were unaffected by the *Convention*. The Court flatly rejected this 'unattractive' argument, holding that the 'law as to the bearing on domestic law of international human rights declaring them is undergoing evolution.'[104] According to this approach, the rights and values recognised by international instruments could inform but not overwhelm the common law. This reasoning resolved the issues that arose in *Teoh* by suggesting a more modest role for international instruments in general, which contrasted to the stronger role for the *Convention* envisaged by *Teoh*.

The lesser role for international treaties suggested by the Court of Appeal received a measured and positive official reaction. Instead of the political outcry that greeted *Teoh*, the institutional response to *Tavita* was one of quick acceptance that began when the government requested that the New Zealand Law Reform Commission review the treaty making process with particular attention to the role of Parliament.[105] Subsequent changes included extensive reforms to migration procedures to ensure their conformity with New Zealand's

[98] Harry Woolf, Jeffrey Jowell, Catherine Donnelly and Ivan Hare, *de Smith's Judicial Review* (8th edn, 2018) 685–6. An argument for greater use by English courts of treaties as a basis for procedural rights is made in Sanjay Patel, 'Founding Legitimate Expectations on Unincorporated Treaties' [2010] *Judicial Review* 74.

[99] *Baker v Canada (Minister of Citizenship and Immigration)* [1999] 2 SCR 817. The Supreme Court's failure to refer to *Teoh* was all the more remarkable after it had loomed large in the lower courts: *Baker v Canada (Minister of Citizenship and Immigration)* [1997] 2 FC 127.

[100] *Baker v Canada (Minister of Citizenship and Immigration)* [1999] 2 SCR 817, 861.

[101] Ibid, 841 (emphasis added).

[102] A point noted in Janina Boughey, *Human Rights and Judicial Review in Australia and Canada: The Newest Despotism?* (Oxford, Hart Publishing, 2017) 212–4.

[103] [1994] 2 NZLR 257. The wider implications of the decision are analysed thoughtfully in Claudia Geiringer, '*Tavita* and All That: Confronting the Confusion Surrounding Unincorporated Treaties and Administrative Law' (2004) 21 *New Zealand Universities Law Review* 66.

[104] Ibid, 266.

[105] New Zealand Law Reform Commission, *The Treaty Making Process – Reform and the Role of Parliament* (Report 45, 1997). This detailed and thoughtful review was published just two years after *Teoh* but was largely ignored in Australia.

international obligations.[106] The approach taken in *Tavita* and the official response it drew have paved the way for a wider embrace by New Zealand law of international instruments and the rights they seek to protect.[107] The New Zealand experience provides a tantalising hint of the different fate *Teoh* might have met in Australia had its initial reception been different, or perhaps if the High Court of Australia had adopted a more measured and pragmatic approach in its reliance on the *Convention*.

V. Reflections on *Teoh*

Sir Gerard Brennan, who was sworn in as Chief Justice of Australia only weeks after *Teoh* was decided, suggested that the case 'might prove to be a growth point of principle governing the effect of international law on executive power.'[108] He also thought it would be 'no great leap of principle' to assume that the enactment by Parliament of discretionary powers was accompanied by an intention that those powers be exercised consistently with treaty obligations.[109] Such remarks indicate the potential that appeared to lie beyond *Teoh* when the decision was delivered. One can easily see why. The interpretation of legislation in Australia is accompanied by many different interpretive presumptions, which in general operate without significant controversy.[110] That is arguably because most such presumptions have long roots in our common law tradition and can therefore be regarded as a natural part of our heritage. If *Teoh* had somehow become accepted as a general proposition or presumption about statutory interpretation, that took its place as one among many, it could have become an unremarkable part of Australian public law. But this possibility requires the acceptance of assumptions at least as large as the ones it seeks to embed in Australian law.

One of the assumptions was about values. In one sense, if its novel facts are cast aside, *Teoh* was just another example of what Dyzenhaus referred to as the 'normative turn' taken by judicial review in the latter part of the twentieth century.[111] Dyzenhaus was not suggesting that judicial review was traditionally amoral, but rather that it had recently taken greater account of normative considerations and was the better for it. At the same time, however, Dyzenhaus was one of the early sceptics of *Teoh*. In his influential analysis of the increasing

[106] See, eg, *Attorney-General v E* [2000] 3 NZLR 257 (discussing migration procedures that were reformed after *Tavita*) and *Zaoui v Attorney-General* [2004] 2 NZLR 339, 369 (stating that the position of a man facing deportation should be 'assessed conformably' with applicable international instruments that should 'inform construction' of his rights).

[107] An issue examined in Philip Joseph, 'Five Exploratory Questions' [2012] *New Zealand Universities Law Review* 73, 97–102.

[108] Gerard Brennan, 'The Role and Rule of Domestic Law in International Relations' (1998) 10 *Public Law Review* 185, 191.

[109] Ibid, 190.

[110] The challenges of statutory interpretation have caused Pearce and Geddes' *Statutory Interpretation in Australia* to be one of only a few 'books that have for a very long time sat on the shelves of most practising public lawyers in Australia': Justice Stephen Gageler, 'Book Launch: *Delegated Legislation in Australia* (4th edn)' (Canberra, Monday 3 December 2012). See now DC Pearce and RS Geddes, *Statutory Interpretation in Australia* (8th edn) (London, LexisNexis Butterworths, 2014).

[111] David Dyzenhaus, 'The Politics of the Question of Constituent Power' in Martin Loughlin and Neil Walker (eds), *The Paradox of Constitutionalism: Constituent Power and Constitutional Form* (Oxford, Oxford University Press, 2008) 135.

internationalisation of administrative law, which examined the different methods used by different courts of final jurisdiction in the common law world when faced with largely similar cases, Dyzenhaus and his co-authors seemed the least enthusiastic about the methodology of *Teoh*.[112] The doubt essentially arose not from the introduction of the *Convention* as a consideration for administrative officials, but the use of the legitimate expectation as the means to make it so.

Sir Philip Sales, as his Lordship then was, expanded on these criticisms when he argued that the brief flirtation of English courts with *Teoh* was wrong and should end.[113] He and Joanne Clement argued that the legitimate expectation was an 'inapt' means of applying obligations arising from treaties into domestic law, largely because it proceeded upon a false assumption about the nature of treaty ratification. They argued that, where ratification was not followed by domestic legislation, treaties were no more capable of supporting a legitimate expectation than they were a more substantive legal right[114] and also questioned whether the impact of *Teoh*'s reasoning could be confined to a single treaty or part of it, as was done in *Teoh*.[115] According to Sales and Clement, any such principle should apply to all parts of all treaties, or none at all. The unifying theme of these various criticisms was the suggestion that *Teoh* attempted 'too much, too fast'. It was a form of judicial overreach which had the potential to disrupt the balance of power between different arms of government.[116]

This strong rebuttal of *Teoh* from an English perspective does not sit easily with Australian commentators who sought to counter the strong domestic reaction against *Teoh*. In an especially thoughtful analysis of the wider issues surrounding *Teoh*, Charlesworth, Chiam, Hovell and Williams suggested that the adverse reaction to *Teoh* was an example of a wider anxiety about Australia's relationship with both international law and the wider world.[117] Those authors frankly conceded that the practical effect of *Teoh* was to modify the wider general principle that treaties have no direct effect in domestic law unless and until they are implemented by legislation.[118] The deeper change those authors identified within *Teoh* was the challenge it posed to the 'traditional separation between states and individuals in the international community, which sees states as the only actors on the international plane.'[119] This challenge, of course, arose from the High Court's acceptance that ratification of a treaty was a positive statement to both the world and the people of Australia. If one accepts that ratification of a treaty by a government speaks not only to other countries but also to citizens, it is a small doctrinal step to accept those same citizens should have some means by which to give some effect to that statement.

[112] David Dyzenhaus, Murry Hunt and Michael Taggart, 'The Principle of Legality in Administrative Law: Internationalisation as Constitutionalism' (2001) 1 *Oxford University Commonwealth Law Journal* 5.

[113] Philip Sales and Joanne Clement, 'International Law in Domestic Courts: The Developing Framework' (2008) *LQR* 388.

[114] Ibid, 409.

[115] Ibid, 409–10.

[116] On this note, Sales and Clement were particularly alarmed at the prospect that treaty ratification could affect the exercise of prerogative powers: ibid, 412–3.

[117] Hilary Charlesworth, Madeline Chiam, Devika Hovell and George Williams, 'Deep Anxieties: Australia and the International Legal Order' (2003) 25 *Sydney Law Review* 423.

[118] Ibid, 499.

[119] Ibid.

Another way of thinking about *Teoh* is to apply what Karen Knop has described as the 'translation' of international law into domestic law.[120] One of the many reasons Knop used the metaphor of translation was that it helped to convey some of the complexities involved in moving between languages, which involves much more than the task of conveying literal meaning.[121] There is also nuance, context and countless cultural issues. Knop argued that 'the domestic interpretation of international law is not merely the *transmittal* of the international, but a process of *translation* from international to national.'[122] She was mindful that important points can be easily lost in translation, hence her argument that international law scholars should be aware that domestic decisions dealing with international law might be more complex than international lawyers appreciated.[123] Knop's underlying argument is that scholars of international law should give more latitude to the sometimes conceptually unsatisfying attempts of domestic judges and scholars who reach out to their body of law.

Many administrative law commentators writing from domestic perspectives have not been quite so understanding. When Janet McLean considered the translation metaphor, she maintained that administrative law served a 'crucial gate-keeping role' in the implementation of international law.[124] The implication was that principles might bend, but they could not be allowed to break. Some level of structural integrity had to remain around core principles. Paul Daly was not using the translation metaphor when he reached a similar view about the recent evolution of Canadian administrative law.[125] Daly's analysis of the often radical changes to modern Canadian administrative law distinguished procedure from substance, but concluded that procedural changes often had immense substantive effect. Areas where change had been successful, or at least not unduly disruptive, were those where judges had proceeded in a cautious, and incremental manner that respected the different roles of the different arms of government. Daly did not argue against change, but noted that:

> … changes to the procedural law should be made with due appreciation of the dynamic relationship between procedure and substance in the common law tradition, constitutional fundamentals, and the appropriate role of the courts in changing common law.[126]

The central problem of *Teoh* was its failure to recognise these cautions, though one could argue that the full extent of this failure did not become apparent until earlier in the same year that *Lam* was decided. That point was not contained within *Lam* itself but the landmark case of *Plaintiff S157/2002 v Commonwealth*,[127] in which the High Court stridently

[120] Karen Knop, 'Here and There: International Law in Domestic Courts' (2000) 32 *New York University Journal of International Law and Politics* 501, 504. A notable feature of Knop's insightful analysis is that it examines the Canadian case of *Baker* in careful detail but makes no mention of *Teoh*.

[121] This conception of translation as something more than 'word conversion' has been accepted in Australian migration cases. See Matthew Groves, 'Interpreters and Fairness in Administrative Hearings' (2017) 40 *Melbourne University Law Review* 506, 508–12.

[122] Knop, above n120, 506 (emphasis added).

[123] Ibid, 528.

[124] Janet McLean, 'Problems of Translation: The State in Domestic and International Public Law and Beyond' in Charlesworth et al, above n 65, 210, 213.

[125] Paul Daly, 'Updating the Procedural Law of Judicial Review of Administrative Action' (2018) 51 *University of British Columbia Law Review* 705.

[126] Ibid, 737.

[127] (2003) 211 CLR 476.

affirmed the constitutional entrenchment of its supervisory judicial review jurisdiction. One important consequence of that ruling was to signal the practical demise of ouster or privative clauses. This and other parts of that important judgment drew sharp attention to constitutional dividing lines between the arms of Australian government, particularly those which the High Court would not allow the executive and legislative to step past. This decision was a key one in the constitutionalism of Australian administrative law, upon which virtually the entire framework of judicial review doctrine now depends.[128] The more ambitious parts of *Teoh* sat uneasily within this superstructure, providing a clear illustration of Daly's argument of how ostensibly procedural changes may have much wider effect. But *Teoh* can equally be said to have eventually just collapsed under the weight of its own contradictions.

VI. Concluding Observations

The extensive judicial and academic consideration generated by the *Teoh* case and its aftermath focused on the domestic consequences of the High Court's decision. While this chapter has explained some of the decisions of foreign courts that cautiously picked over the reasoning of *Teoh*, it is useful to note that those decisions garnered virtually no attention in Australia. The Australian analysis of *Teoh*, detailed as it was, occurred within a parochial framework. What did this case mean to the assimilation of international treaties in Australia? Was the reasoning of the High Court compatible with the Australian Constitution? These and other questions showed little awareness that the *Teoh* decision might have been symptomatic of wider doctrinal changes occurring in the administrative law principles of other common law jurisdictions. One obvious such instance, though obviously a very different one in many ways, is the suggestion that the *Human Rights Act 1998* (UK) might have provoked a 'righting' of administrative law. The key claim of this argument is that the overall effect of the *Human Rights Act*, which comes from both the substantive rights it incorporates into British law and the procedural fusion of human rights and judicial review claims that it often allows, have led most (if not all) of UK administrative law towards the function of protecting rights.[129] That claim was disputed, if not debunked, by those who noted that the detail of recent UK public law cases simply did not show a wholesale movement towards a rights based conception of administrative law.[130] The very loose parallel that may be drawn between this British experience and the *Teoh* case is that each involved a single, arguably disruptive, factor that might have a transformative effect on administrative law.

[128] See, eg, Cheryl Saunders, 'Constitution As Catalyst: Different Paths Within Australasian Administrative Law' (2012) 10 *New Zealand Journal of Public and International Law* 143.

[129] See, eg, Thomas Poole, 'The Reformation of English Administrative Law' (2009) 68 *CLJ* 142. An extension of this wider claim is the more refined one that human rights principles, such as proportionality, can and should extend to judicial review claims including those not involving rights claims. See, eg, Paul Craig, 'Proportionality, Rationality, Review' [2010] *New Zealand Law Review* 265.

[130] An argument made in Jason NE Varuhas, 'The Reformation of English Administrative Law' (2013) 72 *CLJ* 369. An equivalent point is the central thesis of the analysis of Boughey, above n 102. She explains in careful detail how Canadian administrative law has been influenced, but not consumed, by rights and rights-based reasoning.

Until recently, one might have said that the demise of the *Teoh* case stood in stark contrast to the vigour of the *Human Rights Act* but the fate of that statute looks uncertain in the shadow of Britain's departure from the European Union. Whether the fate of the *Human Rights Act* will hinge on the fate of Britain's membership of the European Union depends largely on whether it is simply repealed, or whether it is replaced with a broadly equivalent document of British rather than European rights (assuming such a distinction in human rights is possible). The *Teoh* case was arguably always in a more vulnerable position because it was a judicial creation. While there was some action by the Executive government, in the form of its decision to ratify the *Convention*, the attempt by the High Court of Australia to invest that act of ratification with a substantive effect in the form of a procedural duty that qualified the exercise of statutory powers was difficult to defend on two grounds. The first was the novel effect ascribed by *Teoh* to the ratification of treaties. The second was the uncertain and unexplained scope of *Teoh*. Why was special effect given to one part of one particular treaty?[131] Where else might the same logic apply? Would it apply to other treaties of particular importance, or to rights of particular importance?

These vital questions were never answered, by either the *Teoh* case itself or by those who sought to justify it. But do they need to be answered in any final sense? Many other chapters in this book explain how Australian courts have recognised and protected rights at common law or by reference to the Australian Constitution. None of the authors of those chapters claim that these rights can be identified with absolute precision. None have pointed to a single point of origin for many of those rights. Put another way, there is much uncertainty about the rights recognised or protected by the Australian Constitution and our common law. Why, then, were the uncertainties that arose in the wake of *Teoh* somehow thought to be fatal to the case? If common law and constitutional doctrine surrounding rights contain much uncertainty, which evolves and generally clarifies over time, why was the same not possible for those rights embodied in international treaties that might have gained some effect by the reasoning in *Teoh*? The most surprising aspect of these difficult questions was not that they were asked, but that they were posed by so many judges, and also used to bury *Teoh*.

[131] There are, however, some relatively narrow instances where recourse to the *Convention* does not raise these problems of selectivity. See, eg, Greg Weeks, *Soft Law and Public Authorities – Remedies and Reform* (Oxford, Hart Publishing, 2016) 133–4. That author discusses several decisions of the New South Wales Court of Appeal that have considered the relevance of the *Convention*, which are notable for involving legislation that somehow appears to anticipate consideration of the *Convention*. Interestingly, that author notes that these cases are not without difficulties such as when and to what extent consideration must be given of treaty issues.

7

The Australian Human Rights Commission

EDWARD SANTOW*

I. Introduction

Like all members of the United Nations (UN), Australia has committed to respect, protect and promote fundamental human rights.[1] This task involves a range of activities. Most obviously, legislation can enshrine and embed human rights by making them enforceable, and this can be supported by government programmes that aim to improve human rights protections, especially for particular groups whose rights might face a special threat. The Australian Human Rights Commission also plays a central role, by providing an authoritative voice on human rights issues that arise in Australia. As in other comparable jurisdictions,[2] Australia's human rights commission is situated within the executive branch of government, but has statutory and other protections of its independence and authority. As Australia's national human rights institution, the Commission has three core responsibilities in advancing human rights. Where an individual believes their human rights have been breached under federal law, the Commission offers an informal mechanism for resolving that complaint. Secondly, the Commission undertakes a range of activities to promote the fulfilment of human rights at the systemic level in Australia. Thirdly, the Commission is active in human rights education and training. This chapter explores how the Commission approaches human rights, how it seeks to perform its functions, and how it operates within a national and international context.

II. Historical Background and Constitution of the Australian Human Rights Commission

Australia ratified the *International Covenant on Civil and Political Rights* (ICCPR) in 1980. The following year, the Australian Parliament established the first incarnation of

* The views expressed in this chapter are my own, and do not necessarily represent those of the Australian Human Rights Commission. I particularly acknowledge my colleague, Phoebe Saintilan, and former Australian Human Rights Commission intern, Rose Dlougatch, who each provided invaluable research assistance, which I relied on in preparing this chapter.

[1] See especially, *Charter of the United Nations* (26 June 1945) Art 1; *Universal Declaration of Human Rights*, GA Res 217A (III), UN GAOR, UN Doc A/810 (10 December 1948).

[2] See, eg, United Kingdom Ministry of Justice, *Rights and Responsibilities: developing our constitutional framework*, CM 7577 (2009) [4.39].

a dedicated, national human rights body for Australia. Its original title was simply the Human Rights Commission. The body has since been re-named twice. On 10 December 1986 – International Human Rights Day – it became known as the Human Rights and Equal Opportunity Commission. Since 2008, it has been known as the Australian Human Rights Commission.[3]

At the time of its establishment, the then Attorney-General, Senator Peter Durack, described the purpose of the Commission as being to promote discussion and understanding of human rights in the community and to recommend to the government and Parliament any changes required to bring law and practice into line with the ICCPR.[4] The early Commission consisted of part-time Commissioners and emphasised education and conciliation as key to promoting human rights in Australia.[5]

Since 1986, when the Commission was established on a permanent basis, the Commission has had the legal status of an independent statutory body. Its objects, powers and functions are set out in the *Australian Human Rights Commission Act 1986* (Cth) (the Australian Human Rights Commission Act). In recognition of the importance of the Commission's mission, the government sought to ensure that it would have a stable, cohesive and effective leadership body, which was constituted by full-time professional Commissioners.[6]

The Commission's President is the senior member of the Commission and is the accountable authority for the purposes of the *Public Governance, Performance and Accountability Act 2013* (Cth).[7] The current Commissioners are the Human Rights Commissioner, Race Discrimination Commissioner, Aboriginal and Torres Strait Islander Social Justice Commissioner, Sex Discrimination Commissioner, Age Discrimination Commissioner, Disability Discrimination Commissioner and the National Children's Commissioner.[8] The President and Commissioners are the statutory office holders who make up the Commission executive and, collectively, are responsible for the Commission's activities. Each of these people is appointed by the Governor-General, on the advice of the Attorney-General and Cabinet. Commissioners are appointed for a fixed term, not exceeding seven years.

The Commission's legislation contains provisions that safeguard the independence of the Commission's statutory office holders. The appointment of the President or a Commissioner may only be terminated in narrow circumstances that are circumscribed by the Act. These include misbehaviour, physical or mental incapacity, or bankruptcy.[9] Since the Commission was established, no President or Commissioner has ever had their appointment terminated, nor is there any public evidence that a government has ever commenced such a termination process.

[3] For simplicity, I have generally referred to all three of these successive bodies compendiously in this chapter as 'the Commission'.

[4] Commonwealth, *Parliamentary Debates*, Senate, 10 March 1981, 422 (Peter Durack, Attorney-General).

[5] Rosalind Croucher, 'National Human Rights Commissions – What's the point?' (Presentation for the International Bar Association, 12 October 2017) www.humanrights.gov.au/news/speeches/national-human-rights-commissions-what-s-point#fnB11.

[6] Commonwealth, *Parliamentary Debates*, House of Representatives, 9 October 1985, 1711 (Lionel Bowen, Attorney-General).

[7] *Australian Human Rights Commission Act 1986* (Cth) s 8A.

[8] Ibid, s 8.

[9] See *Australian Human Rights Commission Act 1986* (Cth) s 41. Special provisions, albeit expressed in similar terms, apply to the termination of appointment for the Aboriginal and Torres Strait Islander Social Justice Commissioner and National Children's Commissioner: see ss 46I and 46MJ.

The Commission administers all federal anti-discrimination legislation: the *Racial Discrimination Act 1975* (Cth), the *Sex Discrimination Act 1984* (Cth), the *Disability Discrimination Act 1992* (Cth) and the *Age Discrimination Act 2004* (Cth).[10] The Commission also has certain responsibilities under the *Native Title Act 1993* (Cth) and the *Fair Work Act 2009* (Cth).

The number of Commissioners has grown incrementally in the three decades since the Australian Human Rights Commission Act came into force. As each Commissioner generally has a designated area of responsibility, the establishment of new Commissioner positions has largely run in parallel to the passage of new federal anti-discrimination legislation.

The most recent statutory role established was the National Children's Commissioner, with the inaugural appointment made in February 2013. From time to time, proposals continue to be made to establish new Commissioner positions. For example, prior to the 2016 federal election, the Australian Labor Party (ALP) committed to establishing a Commissioner role that would focus on the human rights of lesbian, gay, bisexual, transgender and intersex people. The ALP did not win that election and so the position has not been established. More recently, in 2018, the Liberal-National Coalition Government announced its intention to establish a new Freedom of Religion Commissioner, in conjunction with legislative reform to prohibit all forms of discrimination on the ground of religious or other belief.[11] As at June 2019, legislation has yet to be introduced to Parliament with a view to achieving these aims.

III. Role of the Australian Human Rights Commission

The Commission is the *national* body responsible for human rights in Australia. However, its statute was drafted within a federal context, and so the Commission's mandate is primarily focused on federal human rights issues, or such issues that take on a national significance.

The jurisdiction of the Commission has been crafted deliberately to preserve considerable scope for the states and territories to adopt their own legislative and institutional approaches to human rights. The states and territories have done this in their own ways, with all establishing their own human rights agencies, as well as anti-discrimination legislation that is comparable to that which exists federally. Three of these jurisdictions have gone beyond the federal Parliament by enacting human rights acts or statutory charters of human rights.[12]

The Australian Human Rights Commission Act provides that the Commission has a duty to perform its functions with regard to the indivisibility and universality of human rights and the principle that every person is free and equal in dignity and human rights.[13] At one level, this simply may be seen as incorporating an axiomatic principle of international human rights law. Human rights exist in tension with each other, and indeed with

[10] These statutes and their wider implications are examined by Colin Campbell in ch 9.

[11] Australian Government, *Response to the Religious Freedom Review* (December 2018) 5. The review to which the government was responding did not recommend the establishment of this new Commissioner position.

[12] See: *Human Rights Act 2004* (ACT); *Charter of Human Rights and Responsibilities Act 2006* (Vic); *Human Rights Act 2019* (Qld).

[13] *Australian Human Rights Commission Act 1986* (Cth) s 10A.

other legitimate interests. Rather than being a flaw, this is part of the design of the system of international human rights law, in that it anticipates a process of accommodation or balancing when such tensions need to be resolved.

However, minds may differ on the most desirable outcome of any individual accommodation process. This can draw the Commission into difficult but important terrain on issues as diverse as refugee and migration policy, counter terrorism and national security, racial and gender equality, to name only a few. As Australia's most authoritative official voice on human rights, it is central to the Commission's mandate that it provide a sophisticated, nuanced analysis that assists in resolving difficult issues that arise in such areas. But this task is rarely simple.

Like most of the national human rights institutions in other jurisdictions, the Commission has a broad set of responsibilities. They can be divided into the following areas:

(a) complaint handling;
(b) policy and legislative development and reform;
(c) human rights compliance;
(d) intervention in court matters through the exercise of amicus curiae functions;
(e) international engagement; and
(f) education for the purpose of promoting human rights.

These core functions are considered in greater detail later in this chapter. However, it is worth noting that the Commission interacts with the public most directly via its complaint-handling function, which involves a conciliation service for people who believe their human rights have been breached under federal anti-discrimination law or the other related laws within the Commission's jurisdiction.

While the complaint-handling function is directed towards the resolution of *individual* human rights problems, the Commission's other functions focus on improving the *systemic* protection and promotion of human rights. This encompasses a wide range of activities, including public inquiries into human rights issues of national importance; human rights education; providing independent legal input in court matters that engage human rights issues; providing advice, submissions and other input to parliamentary and other inquiries; and researching human rights and discrimination issues.

The Commission's education and training programmes are generally delivered through partnerships with government, community organisations and the private sector. Much of this work aims to improve the way large-scale education programmes address human rights issues. For instance, the Commission has long provided input into processes that set school curricula, as well as providing educational resources that teachers can use when explaining human rights to their classes. In addition, the Commission provides some more targeted training for particular work environments or organisations. Programmes have focused on large groups such as the Australian Public Service, as well as more specialised training for industry groups.

The Commission produces guidelines and other resources that explain particular areas of law – such as in respect of the legal standards under disability discrimination law, or explaining the legal prohibition of discrimination on the basis of sexual orientation, gender identity or intersex status.

While the Commission lacks the resources unilaterally to undertake community-wide awareness-raising campaigns, it does lead and contribute to some public-facing work of that nature. For example, the Commission engaged in a partnership model for a recent national campaign that targeted racism. Entitled 'Racism. It Stops With Me', the campaign enjoyed widespread public engagement, and aimed to equip the community with the knowledge and resources to respond to racial prejudice.[14]

The Commission also speaks publicly about its work, usually through individual Commissioners and often via media and speaking engagements. For example, in 2017–18, the Commission convened 15 major public events, published 141 news stories on its website, responded to 1,037 media enquiries, participated in 483 media interviews and had 17 opinion pieces published. Increasingly, the Commission also uses social media and other digital channels, having generated in this period 26 YouTube videos, 9,606,268 page views on its website, 114,510 Facebook 'likes', and 158,694 Twitter followers.[15] While these statistics provide only limited information about the *impact* of this public engagement, they do show that the Commission prioritises communication with the public at large.

IV. How Does the Commission Approach Human Rights?

Human rights attach to us by virtue of our humanity. They are not accorded, nor can they be removed, by reference to citizenship, good character or some other attribute. Unsurprisingly, therefore, the principal point of reference for human rights law is international. The instruments that lie at the core of the modern incarnation of international human rights law are known colloquially as the 'international Bill of Rights'. This comprises three documents:

(1) the Universal Declaration of Human Rights of 1948;
(2) the International Covenant on Economic, Social and Cultural Rights (ICESCR), which Australia agreed to in 1975;
(3) the International Covenant on Civil and Political Rights (ICCPR), which Australia agreed to in 1980.

In one sense, the role of the Commission – like any national human rights institution (NHRI) – is to take a central role in applying the international Bill of Rights, as well as other sources of international human rights law, to the Australian context.[16] Several of these instruments are scheduled to the Australian Human Rights Commission Act.

There is considerable subtlety and complexity in how a NHRI, such as the Commission, approaches human rights. It involves far more than simply uprooting and planting the foreign sapling of international human rights law in Australian soil.

The concept of human rights is ancient. Throughout history, concepts of ethical behaviour and justice have played critical roles in the development of human societies and can be traced back to the ancient civilisations of Babylon, China and India.[17] Concepts of ethics

[14] See: Australian Human Rights Commission, *Racism. It stops with me* http://itstopswithme.humanrights.gov.au/.

[15] Australian Human Rights Commission, *2017–2018 Annual Report*, 15.

[16] See the broad definition of 'human rights' in *Australian Human Rights Commission Act 1986* (Cth) s 3.

[17] Australian Human Rights Commission, *An Introduction to Human Rights* www.humanrights.gov.au/education/students/get-informed/introduction-human-rights.

and justice also played a key role in the history of Aboriginal and Torres Strait Islander people in Australia and other indigenous societies around the world.[18]

As the origins of our thinking on human rights pre-date the establishment of the nation state of Australia or even its colonial parent, it is natural that Anglo-Australian approaches to human rights have been influenced by philosophical and legal approaches from other places and other times. There has thus been a symbiotic – or perhaps more accurately, a mutualistic – approach to the development of human rights as a body of law.

In the Anglo-Australian legal system, the protection of long-standing human rights principles has generally occurred first or primarily via the common law, with legislation being more piecemeal and more recent.[19] As the Hon James Spigelman AC QC observed, common law human rights protections include rebuttable presumptions that Parliament does not intend:

> To retrospectively change rights and obligations;
> To infringe personal liberty;
> To interfere with freedom of movement;
> To interfere with freedom of speech;
> To alter criminal law practices based on the principle of a fair trial;
> To restrict access to the courts;
> To permit an appeal from an acquittal;
> To interfere with the course of justice;
> To abrogate legal professional privilege;
> To exclude the right to claim self-incrimination;
> To extend the scope of a penal statute;
> To deny procedural fairness to persons affected by the exercise of public power;
> To give executive immunities a wide application;
> To interfere with vested property rights;
> To authorise the commission of a tort;
> To alienate property without compensation;
> To disregard common law protection of personal reputation; and
> To interfere with equality of religion.[20]

The drafters of the Universal Declaration of Human Rights (Universal Declaration) did not seek to develop an entirely new legal approach to human rights. Instead, they set about their task by drawing on the approaches to human rights they considered to be fruitful from their own respective jurisdictions. The UN Commission on Human Rights, which was charged in the mid-1940s with drafting the Universal Declaration, was composed of a remarkably diverse group of people. Professor Mary Ann Glendon noted:

> The Commission [on Human Rights'] Lebanese Rapporteur, Charles Malik, a philosophy professor-turned-diplomat, was the chief spokesman for the Arab League during the Palestine crisis, and would later hold many key posts in the UN, including the presidency of the General Assembly. The French member, René Cassin, was an ardent Zionist, who had served as Charles de Gaulle's wartime legal adviser, and who would receive the Nobel Peace Prize in 1968 for his

[18] Ibid.

[19] This idea is expanded on in an extra-curial speech by the President of the Victorian Court of Appeal. See: the Hon Chris Maxwell, *Address to the Queen's Inn Dinner* (Queen's College, University of Melbourne, 4 May 2012) www.supremecourt.vic.gov.au/contact-us/speeches/judges-and-human-rights.

[20] James Spigelman, *Statutory Interpretation and Human Rights* (University of Queensland Press, 2008) 27–29; see further Meagher in ch 19.

> varied contributions to human rights. Nationalist China's Peng-chun Chang, the vice-chairman of the Commission, was a leading educator-turned-diplomat who had also achieved renown as a poet and playwright. General Carlos Romulo of the Philippines had won a Pullitzer prize for his pre-war articles predicting the end of colonialism. Mrs Hansa Mehta was a veteran of India's struggle for independence and a tireless advocate for women's equality. Alexei Pavlov, nephew of the famed conditioned-reflex scientist, was a powerful orator who, we now know, was under instructions from Moscow to obstruct and delay proceedings. Chile's Hernàn Santa Cruz was an aristocratic man of the left who shared John Humphrey's determination to include social and economic rights in the Declaration along with traditional political and civil liberties.[21]

Specifically, a number of the most influential drafters of the Universal Declaration were highly influenced by their background practising in common law jurisdictions,[22] and so it should be no surprise that many of the common law rights identified by Spigelman find expression also in international human rights instruments.

Similarly, domestic human rights law has always been influenced by comparative and international law. Cases such as *Mabo v Queensland (No.2)*[23] and *Dietrich v The Queen*[24] highlighted the relevance of human rights treaties in statutory interpretation and in developing the common law. In *Mabo v Queensland (No.2)*,[25] Brennan J stated that international law is a legitimate and important influence on the development of common law – particularly in cases where international law recognises the existence of universal human rights.

Returning to the role of the Commission, if it is to fulfil its mandate of enhancing the protection, promotion and fulfilment of human rights in Australia, it must operate with a well-developed understanding of the various sources of human rights law, as well as their inter-relationship. It would be of little value, for instance, for the Commission to pronounce simply that international human rights law requires that the Australian Government improve its protection of freedom of expression, without taking into account the ways in which this freedom is already protected – albeit in limited ways – in practice, at common law, in legislation and by constitutional implication.

As freedom of expression must yield to the protection of other rights, such as privacy and to protect one's reputation, the freedom of expression example reminds us that human rights are rarely absolute. As noted above, where a non-absolute human right is engaged, and it comes into tension with another human right or legitimate interest, international law requires that these be reconciled through a balancing or accommodation process. The method for doing this applies the principles of reasonableness, proportionality and necessity.[26] Given its domestic and international experience, the Commission has developed expertise in applying these principles.

[21] MA Glendon, 'John P Humphrey and the Drafting of the Universal Declaration of Human Rights' (2000) 2 *Journal of the History of International Law* 250, 251. See also discussion by Rosalind Croucher, 'Human Rights are not a foreign language – reflections on the 70th anniversary of the Universal Declaration of Human Rights' (Presentation to the University of Adelaide Faculty of Law, 4 September 2018) 8.

[22] United Nations, *Drafting of the Universal Declaration of Human Rights* http://research.un.org/en/undhr/draftingcommittee.

[23] *Mabo v Queensland (No 2)* (1992) 175 CLR 1.

[24] *Dietrich v The Queen* (1992) 177 CLR 292.

[25] *Mabo v Queensland (No 2)* (1992) 175 CLR 1, 42.

[26] See, especially, *United Nations Economic and Social Council, Commission on Human Rights, Siracusa Principles on the Limitation and Derogation Provisions in the International Covenant on Civil and Political Rights, UN Doc E/CN.4/1985/4, Annex (1985).*

In summary, therefore, the Commission generally seeks to carry out its functions in a way that is at least cognisant of all the sources of human rights law – domestic and international – that bear on the question at issue. This can be seen as contributing to a larger task of applying and adapting international human rights law to domestic Australian conditions.

V. Situating the Commission in the International Framework

As Australia's accredited NHRI, the Commission is the nation's designated government body responsible for protecting and promoting human rights. NHRIs were first discussed in some form in 1946 at the UN Commission on Human Rights (the precursor to the UN Human Rights Council), not long before the proclamation of the Universal Declaration in 1948. As international human rights treaties were developed in the three decades that followed, the international community increasingly shifted its focus to national implementation and monitoring mechanisms, leading the UN Commission on Human Rights to convene a seminar in 1978 encouraging states to establish what came to be known as NHRIs.[27] Today, NHRIs often serve as a bridge between government and civil society, linking the responsibilities of the state to the rights of citizens and others subject to a nation's jurisdiction, while always promoting the implementation of international human rights norms into national law.[28] Although they are funded by the state, NHRIs must be independent, which is essential to maintaining their legitimacy and effective functioning.[29]

The international instrument that sets out the responsibilities, independence and acceptable modes of operation, composition and governance arrangements for NHRIs is *The Principles Relating to the Status of National Institutions*, also known as the Paris Principles. Adopted by the UN General Assembly in 1993, the Paris Principles set broad standards for NHRIs and emphasise the importance of their independence. The key provisions of the Paris Principles include that NHRIs should:

(a) advise the government concerning the promotion and protection of human rights;
(b) promote the harmonisation of national legislation and international human rights instruments;
(c) encourage the ratification and implementation of international human rights instruments;
(d) contribute to Australia's reports to UN bodies and committees;
(e) cooperate with the UN; and
(f) assist with human rights education and raising public awareness of human rights.[30]

[27] *National institutions for the protection and promotion of human rights* (A/Res/33/46 of 14 December 1978); Croucher, above n 6.

[28] Office of the High Commissioner for Human Rights (2010) '*National Human Rights Institutions: History, Principles, Roles, and Responsibilities*,' Training Series No 4 Rev1, OHCHR, HR/P/PT/4/Rev.1. Sales No E.09.XIV.4.

[29] Amrei Muller, Frauke Seidensticker, *The Role of National Human Rights Institutions in the United Nations Treaty Body Process* (German Institute for Human Rights, 2007) 6.

[30] *Principles relating to the Status of National Institutions (The Paris Principles)*, adopted by General Assembly resolution 48/134 of 20 December 1993.

The Paris Principles declare that NHRIs must be independent, autonomous from the government and adequately resourced. They must be pluralist or diverse in their composition, and they must also possess adequate powers of investigation.[31] In practice, the respective mandates and powers of NHRIs around the world vary significantly, but the Paris Principles seek to ensure that NHRIs meet a minimum standard.[32]

The Commission is a bureau member of the Global Alliance of National Human Rights Associations (GANHRI), the international association of NHRIs responsible for accreditation of all NHRIs around the world in accordance with the Paris Principles. GANHRI provides leadership in the protection and promotion of human rights by, for example, facilitating NHRI engagement with the UN Human Rights Council and treaty bodies and encouraging cooperation and information sharing among NHRIs.

The Commission is currently accredited as an 'A status' institution under GANHRI's rating system, which means that Australia's NHRI is in 'full compliance' with the Paris Principles. It has been suggested that the Commission achieving 'A status' may reflect well on the Australian Government's international standing in taking seriously its human rights responsibilities.[33] It is certainly true that, in seeking election to the UN Human Rights Council for 2018–2020, the Australian Government emphasised strong NHRIs and capacity building as one of the five pillars underpinning its candidacy.[34] Professors Byrnes, Durbach and Renshaw have noted:

> The importance – or at least the utility – for governments of having established a national human rights commission can be seen in the many pronouncements of states in international fora, especially when presenting their performance on human rights or defending against criticism of their record. In the recently introduced Universal Periodic Review before the Human Rights Council involving peer review of states by other states, states under review have regularly referred to the existence and work of their commissions to evidence their commitment to human rights.[35]

NHRIs play an important role in supporting and monitoring states' implementation of human rights treaties, including their compliance with UN treaty bodies' concluding observations on a state's performance. More recent human rights treaties have reflected the importance of this cooperation by requiring that states establish national mechanisms for monitoring implementation.[36] Effective cooperation between UN human rights treaty bodies and NHRIs is key to the implementation of international human rights law at the national level.[37]

[31] Ibid.

[32] Office of the High Commissioner for Human Rights (2010) '*National Human Rights Institutions: History, Principles, Roles, and Responsibilities*,' Training Series No. 4 Rev_1, OHCHR, HR/P/PT/4/Rev.1. Sales No E.09.XIV.4.

[33] Croucher, above n 6.

[34] See: United Nations General Assembly, *Note verbale dated 14 July 2017 from the Permanent Mission of Australia to the United Nations addressed to the President of the General Assembly*, 24 July 2017, A/72/212 https://dfat.gov.au/international-relations/international-organisations/un/Documents/ga-doc-a-72-212-voluntary-pledges-hrc-australia.pdf.

[35] Andrew Byrnes, Andrea Durbach and Catherine Renshaw, 'Joining the club: the Asia Pacific Forum of National Human Rights Institutions, the Paris Principles, and the advancement of human rights protection in the region' (2008) 14(1) *Australian Journal of Human Rights* 66; Rosalind Croucher, 'National Human Rights Commissions – What's the point?' (Presentation for the International Bar Association, 12 October 2017).

[36] Muller and Seidensticker, above n 31, 6.

[37] Ibid.

In Chapter 12 of this book, Dr Madelaine Chiam casts a critical eye on the Australian Government's engagement with UN treaty bodies. This criticism is telling. The Australian Government should do more to match human rights rhetoric at international forums with action on the ground in Australia. In any event, the remainder of this section outlines the way in which the Commission, as Australia's NHRI, interacts with those treaty bodies.

NHRIs exercise their role by encouraging states to comply with their reporting obligations, urging the ratification of treaties and removing reservations, encouraging the submission of reports or independent information to treaty bodies, encouraging implementation of concluding observations and assisting governments to prepare reports to treaty bodies.[38]

As an 'A status' NHRI, the Commission engages with the processes conducted by UN treaty bodies. The Commission regularly lodges submissions to support UN treaty bodies to perform their function of periodically reviewing Australia's compliance with human rights treaties. In recent years, the Commission made submissions to and appeared before:

(a) the Committee on the Elimination of Racial Discrimination in relation to Australia's 18th to 20th periodic report
(b) the Committee on the Elimination of Discrimination against Women prior to its adoption of the List of Issues on Australia
(c) the Human Rights Committee in relation to Australia's 6th periodic report
(d) the Committee on the Rights of Persons with Disabilities prior to its adoption of the List of Issues for Australia
(e) the Committee on Economic, Social and Cultural Rights in relation to Australia's 5th periodic report.[39]

In engaging with such treaty-body processes, the Commission aims to provide a fair, impartial, constructive critique of Australia's adherence to the relevant human rights treaty obligations. The Commission's general practice in its engagement with UN processes is to summarise concerns that it has previously raised directly with the Australian Government. It would be very rare indeed for the Commission to raise a concern for the first time with a treaty body, rather than with the relevant Australian Government entity. In taking a 'no surprises approach', UN treaty bodies are given the maximum opportunity to consider all relevant perspectives on the issues raised by the Commission.

By way of example, the Commission's engagement with the UN Human Rights Committee in respect of Australia's compliance with the ICCPR presented an important opportunity to consider Australia's human rights record over a period spanning more than half a decade up until 2017. The Commission's submission to the Committee emphasised some positive developments, such as the Australian Government's then commitment to ratify the *Optional Protocol to the Convention Against Torture and other Cruel, Inhuman or Degrading Treatment or Punishment* (OPCAT) by December 2017, and commence the process of implementation immediately thereafter.[40]

[38] Ibid 36–46.

[39] Australian Human Rights Commission, *Submissions to the United Nations* www.humanrights.gov.au/our-work/legal/submissions/submissions-united-nations.

[40] The Australian Government did indeed ratify OPCAT on 15 December 2017.

However, the bulk of the Commission's submission concentrated on 'priority areas' in which the Commission expressed concern about Australia's compliance with the ICCPR and where significant attention and change were needed. Those areas included:

(1) the Australian Government's lack of success in improving core measures of equality and justice for Aboriginal and Torres Strait Islander Australians, including in the contexts of health, education and the legal system;
(2) the Australian Government's immigration policy (especially as it relates to refugees and asylum seekers);
(3) all Australian governments' compliance with, and implementation of, the recommendations of the Royal Commission into Institutional Responses to Child Sexual Abuse;[41]
(4) the Australian Government's review of counter-terrorism laws to ensure any limitation on human rights is clearly expressed, necessary for the pursuit of a legitimate purpose, reasonable and proportionate.[42]

The Human Rights Committee held a series of formal and informal meetings in October 2017 at which the Australian Government, the Commission and interested civil society representatives could speak to the relevant issues. The Commission representative – literally and figuratively – sat between the Australian Government and civil society representatives in the hearing room. Committee members had an opportunity to question claims made by all relevant stakeholders, with a view to gaining a clear and accurate picture of the human rights issues under consideration. The Committee reported its Concluding Observations in November 2017, with at least 29 of its findings and recommendations substantially endorsing positions set out by the Commission in its engagement with the Committee.[43]

The Committee considered the relationship between the Australian Government and the Commission. While the Commission did not make representations on this issue, some other stakeholders did. The Committee recommended that the Australian Government:

> should refrain from any actions or measures that could undermine the independence of the Australian Human Rights Commission, pursue its stated intention to restore the budget of the Commission, and ensure adequate funding for it to continue to carry out its mandate effectively.[44]

It should be noted that some of the reduction in the Commission's recurrent government funding was indeed restored in the federal budget of 2018.

[41] This royal commission was a large-scale and long-running investigation of the response of official institutions, such as schools, orphanages and religious organisations, to allegations of child sexual abuse within their organisations. This inquiry ran from 2013–2017 and yielded a final report of 17 volumes which contained many recommendations for reform at the federal, state and territory levels: www.childabuseroyalcommission.gov.au/final-report.

[42] Australian Human Rights Commission, *Information concerning Australia's compliance with the International Covenant on Civil and Political Rights (2017)* (18 September 2017) www.humanrights.gov.au/submissions/information-concerning-australia-s-compliance-international-covenant-civil-and-political.

[43] United Nations Human Rights Committee, *Concluding observations on the sixth periodic report of the United Kingdom*, 121st sess, UN Doc CCPR/C/AUS/CO/6 (9 November 2017).

[44] Ibid [14].

VI. The Commission's Role in Human Rights Dispute Resolution

Under the Australian Human Rights Commission Act, complaints alleging unlawful discrimination, harassment and bullying may be lodged with the Commission. The Commission receives complaints under the *Racial Discrimination Act 1975* (Cth), the *Sex Discrimination Act 1984* (Cth), the *Disability Discrimination Act 1992* (Cth) and the *Age Discrimination Act 2004* (Cth). The Commission also has a related jurisdiction to receive complaints under the Australian Human Rights Commission Act itself – this aspect of the Commission's complaint-handling function is dealt with later in this section.

The President is responsible for this aspect of the Commission's functions.[45] This leaves individual Commissioners with greater scope to speak publicly about issues that may arise through the complaint-handling function without prejudicing the impartiality of that function. Nevertheless, Commissioners are generally cautious to speak in a way that avoids any appearance of favouring a particular party to a complaint before the Commission.

The Commission works in the shadow of the law. It does not have the power to determine whether unlawful discriminatory conduct has occurred, instead focusing on alternative dispute resolution.[46] The Commission investigates complaints received and is empowered to perform a conciliation function for the parties involved.[47]

Responsibility for undertaking conciliations rests primarily with the Investigation and Conciliation Service (ICS), a dedicated unit within the Commission. ICS is staffed with experts in conciliation and in the grounds of complaint available under the Commission's legislation. Ordinarily, when the Commission receives a complaint, a staff member from ICS will contact the complainant to discuss the complaint and seek any additional information necessary to process the complaint. Usually, ICS will also contact the individual or organisation against whom the complaint is made in order to provide a copy of the complaint and seek comments and other relevant information.

If the complainant chooses to proceed with the complaint, and the Commission does not form the view that it must terminate the complaint at an early stage (for example, if the complaint were deemed to be lacking in substance or vexatious),[48] the Commission will initiate a conciliation process with the aim of resolving the matter in a way that both parties accept.

Conciliation can take place face to face, through a telephone or video conference, or through an exchange of messages by mail, phone or email. If the process is successful, the complainant and respondent might agree that some further action takes place – such as an apology, a change to a policy, reinstatement to a job or compensation for lost wages. Ultimately, while the Commission can offer its expertise as an impartial expert, it is the parties themselves who must mutually agree to a resolution.

[45] See *Australian Human Rights Commission Act 1986* (Cth) s 46PD.

[46] Australian Human Rights Commission, Submission to Parliamentary Joint Committee on Human Rights, *Inquiry into Free Speech*, 9 December 2016, 35.

[47] See *Australian Human Rights Commission Act 1986* (Cth) Part IIB; Australian Human Rights Commission, Submission to Parliamentary Joint Committee on Human Rights, *Inquiry into Free Speech*, 9 December 2016, 35.

[48] See *Australian Human Rights Commission Act 1986* (Cth) s 46PH.

If the parties do not agree on a course of action, the Commission cannot issue a decision as to whether unlawful discrimination has occurred. Rather, the complaint will be formally terminated. The complainant may choose, but is not obliged, to apply to the Federal Circuit Court or the Federal Court of Australia to have their matter formally determined. The court, unlike the Commission, can decide if unlawful discrimination has occurred.[49] In 2017–18, fewer than three per cent of complaints regarding unlawful discrimination proceeded to court.[50]

The Commission fields inquiries through its National Information Service telephone hotline, which is recognised as a leading source of information about federal human rights and discrimination law. In 2017–18, the Commission received 14,164 enquiries from people seeking information about discrimination and human rights – the majority of these enquiries came through the Commission's hotline. The Commission received 2,046 complaints of alleged discrimination and breaches of human rights in 2017–2018, finalising 2,111 complaints.[51] These figures are typical: over the previous 10 reporting years, the average number of complaints received annually is 2,158 per year.[52] The breakdown of complaints received in 2017–18 by area of discrimination is as follows:

(1) 42% of complaints were lodged under the Disability Discrimination Act;
(2) 27% of complaints were lodged under the Sex Discrimination Act;
(3) 14% of complaints were lodged under the Racial Discrimination Act;
(4) 8% of complaints were lodged under the Australian Human Rights Commission Act;
(5) 8% of complaints were lodged under the Age Discrimination Act.[53]

Of the complaints received in 2017–18, 1,262 proceeded through a conciliation process, of which 74 per cent were successfully resolved. In 31 per cent of conciliations, the conciliation agreements included terms that were of benefit to the wider community.[54] For example, a local business undertook to implement sexual harassment and sex discrimination policies as a term of the conciliation agreement.[55]

Ninety-one per cent of surveyed parties to complaints reported that they were satisfied with the service they received – this comprised 84 per cent of complainants and 98 per cent of respondents.[56] Survey results also indicated that participation in the investigation and conciliation process increased participants' understanding of legal rights and responsibilities, with 77 per cent of respondents indicating that the process helped them understand human rights and responsibilities.[57]

[49] The complaint process for complaints about sex, race, disability and age discrimination is summarised at: Australian Human Rights Commission, *The complaint process for complaints about sex, race, disability and age discrimination* www.humanrights.gov.au/complaint-process-complaints-about-sex-race-disability-and-age-discrimination.

[50] Australian Human Rights Commission, *2017–18 Complaint Statistics*, 2.

[51] Australian Human Rights Commission, *2017–18 Complaint Statistics*, 1–2.

[52] Complaints data are reported by the Commission in its Annual Reports (and from 2015–16 in a separate document on the same webpage as the Annual Report) which are available on its website at www.humanrights.gov.au/our-work/commission-general/publications/annual-reports-index.

[53] Australian Human Rights Commission, *2017–18 Complaint Statistics*, 1.

[54] Ibid 2.

[55] Australian Human Rights Commission, *2016–2017 Annual Report*, 34.

[56] Australian Human Rights Commission, *2017–18 Complaint Statistics*, 2.

[57] Ibid 2.

A typical response from a complainant who had completed the conciliation process was: 'This is a really great service that is not only cost effective but also where normal everyday people don't feel intimidated and can understand.' Similarly, a typical respondent's response to the Commission's post-conciliation survey was: 'I found that everything was explained perfectly and all parties were given a fair hearing.'[58]

A. Complaints Made Under the Australian Human Rights Commission Act

As noted earlier in this section, the Commission has jurisdiction to receive and conciliate complaints that relate to certain other human rights beyond those referred to in the dedicated federal anti-discrimination statutes, such as the *Disability Discrimination Act 1992* (Cth) and *Racial Discrimination Act 1975* (Cth).[59] This gives individuals an opportunity to complain that their human rights have been violated under, for example, the ICCPR, even in circumstances where the relevant provisions of the ICCPR have not been incorporated into Australia's domestic legislation.

Where the President, or her delegate, undertakes this function, she will conclude by issuing a report that may contain findings and/or recommendations. That report must be tabled in Parliament within 15 sitting days. Any recommendations are not binding on the government, and the individual or individuals who lodged their complaint cannot appeal to a court in the event that the government decides not to act on the Commission's recommendations.

This aspect of the Commission's jurisdiction provides a notable contrast to the primarily hostile political response that greeted the High Court's decision in *Teoh*.[60] That decision determined that there existed a limited procedural obligation upon administrative officials when exercising powers that might adversely affect the interests of children. Matthew Groves explains in Chapter 6 that one of the strong criticisms made of that case by politicians arose because Australia had ratified but not incorporated into statute the *Convention on the Rights of the Child*,[61] from which the procedural obligation was drawn. The difference with the just mentioned rights that the Commission may receive and conciliate complaints about is that, while the rights have not been directly incorporated into Australian law, the right to complain about their possible breach has clearly been enacted in Australian law.

B. The Effect of the *Brandy* Decision: Changes Since 2000

The current procedure for dealing with complaints took effect in April 2000. Previously, the Commission could make determinations in response to complaints of unlawful discrimination, which would subsequently be registered with the Federal Court and took the effect

[58] Australian Human Rights Commission, Submission to Parliamentary Joint Committee on Human Rights, *Inquiry into Free Speech*, 9 December 2016, 38–9.

[59] See *Australian Human Rights Commission Act 1986* (Cth) ss 8, 11(1)(f) and 20(1)(b).

[60] *Minister for Immigration and Ethnic Affairs v Teoh* (1995) 183 CLR 273.

[61] *Convention on the Rights of the Child 1989*, done at New York on 20 November 1989.

of an order of the court.[62] However, in *Brandy v Human Rights and Equal Opportunity Commission*,[63] the High Court of Australia held that this procedure purported to empower the Commission to exercise judicial power, contrary to Chapter III of the Constitution.[64] This finding is the inverse of rights or protections contained in Chapter III of the Australian Constitution, which are examined by Anthony Gray in Chapter 3. Gray explains the (perhaps limited) potential of due process rights within Chapter III but it is important to note that the conception of judicial power expounded by the High Court of Australia is in many senses a limiting one. Non-judicial bodies like the Commission cannot exercise judicial functions, such as determining the legal rights and obligations of parties to a human rights complaint.

Parliament responded to the *Brandy* decision by introducing the *Human Rights Legislation Amendment Act (No 1) 1999* (Cth), which amended the *Australian Human Rights Commission Act*, the *Racial Discrimination Act*, the *Sex Discrimination Act* and the *Disability Discrimination Act*. This reform process removed the Commission's power to make determinations about unlawful discrimination, and replaced it with the current conciliation process. The Commission's current process for handling complaints through an alternative dispute resolution mechanism, and the separate judicial process, can thus be considered complementary.[65]

As noted above, in 2017–18 fewer than three per cent of complaints finalised by the Commission proceeded to court. This low number is typical of the statistics in other years. By focusing on conciliation and alternative dispute resolution, the Commission provides complainants with a timely and cost-effective process to resolve discrimination complaints. The high rates of success and satisfaction suggest that the process is effective in achieving its aims. As a relatively cost-effective process, parties avoid the often high costs of going to court, while public spending associated with the administration of court hearings is reduced.[66]

Nevertheless, while these metrics indicate that the conciliation service is successful, concern is expressed from time to time about the Commission's handling of particular complaints. In recent years, a matter that received strong public attention involved a complaint brought under section 18C of the *Racial Discrimination Act 1975* against a number of students from Queensland University of Technology (QUT).[67] This criticism involved concerns raised about some or all of: the Commission's complaint-handling process; its statutory underpinnings in the Australian Human Rights Commission Act; and the legislation that provides the basis of the complaint (such as, in this situation, the Racial Discrimination Act).

[62] Australian Human Rights Commission, Submission to Parliamentary Joint Committee on Human Rights, *Inquiry into Free Speech*, 9 December 2016, 34.

[63] (1995) 183 CLR 245.

[64] Ibid, 264 (Mason CJ, Brennan and Toohey JJ), 271 (Deane, Dawson, Gaudron and McHugh JJ); Australian Human Rights Commission, Submission to Parliamentary Joint Committee on Human Rights, *Inquiry into Free Speech*, 9 December 2016, 34.

[65] Australian Human Rights Commission, Submission to Parliamentary Joint Committee on Human Rights, *Inquiry into Free Speech*, 9 December 2016, 35.

[66] Australian Human Rights Commission, Submission to Parliamentary Joint Committee on Human Rights, *Inquiry into Free Speech*, 9 December 2016.

[67] See, eg, some of the submissions to the Parliamentary Joint Committee on Human Rights 2016–17 *Inquiry into Free Speech*.

Such criticisms, especially connected to the QUT matter, were aired in an inquiry undertaken by the Parliamentary Joint Committee on Human Rights. In 2017, the Committee recommended some legislative reforms and other changes to the complaint-handling process.[68] The vast majority of these recommendations have been implemented.

VII. Promoting Systemic Reform

The Commission undertakes a range of activities in Australia to advance this country's compliance with its international human rights law obligations. This section of the chapter considers three of these activities: the Commission's public inquiry function; its involvement in law reform and policy development processes and its intervention in significant court proceedings.

A. Public inquiries and major projects

While much of the Commission's work to advance human rights in law and policy occurs in response to processes that are led by others, the Commission can and does undertake major work in this area of its own motion. Where it does so, this can be an important way in which the Commission takes a leading role in setting the country's human rights agenda.

Sections 11 and 14 of the Australian Human Rights Commission Act contain a range of powers that, cumulatively, enable the Commission to undertake significant public inquiries, with a broad discretion regarding the gathering of evidence, holding of hearings and so on. For principled and pragmatic reasons, the Commission exercises these powers sparingly. The Commission must first be convinced that a large public inquiry will be an effective means of inquiring into and addressing the relevant human rights issues within the context of its limited resources.

Some of the Commission's public inquiries have been highly influential in investigating and drawing attention to human rights issues in Australia. The *Our Homeless Children* report – the report of the Commission's first national inquiry – estimated that up to 25,000 young Australians were homeless, with many young people abused and exploited.[69] The report recommended changes to income support, health and education, and stressed the need for greater coordination of Commonwealth and state services.[70]

In response to the report and the increased public awareness, the Commonwealth Government committed $100 million over four years for improved accommodation and services.[71] Public inquiries conducted by the Commission have also led to changes in the law. For instance, the Report of the National Inquiry into Racist Violence in 1991 – which

[68] Parliamentary Joint Committee on Human Rights, *Report: Freedom of speech in Australia*, 28 February 2017, 88–94.

[69] Human Rights and Equal Opportunity Commission, *Our Homeless Children: Report of the National Inquiry into Homeless Children* (Final Report, 1989).

[70] Ibid.

[71] Australian Human Rights Commission, *Human Rights 21: Going to the heart of the matter: national inquiries* www.humanrights.gov.au/publications/human-rights-21-going-heart-matter-national-inquiries.

found that racism was ingrained in many institutions – led to legal protection against racism with the amendment of the *Racial Discrimination Act* in 1995.[72] The 1993 report of the national inquiry into the human rights of people with mental illness, also known as the Burdekin Report, is another example of an early Commission inquiry that has had a remarkably enduring influence.

Two other landmark reports published by the Commission include *Bringing them Home* and *The Forgotten Children*.[73] The *Bringing them Home* report was tabled in the Australian Parliament on 26 May 1997 and investigated the forced removal of Aboriginal and Torres Strait Islander children from their families – a group often referred to as the Stolen Generations.[74] The report estimated that as many as one in three Aboriginal and Torres Strait Islander children had been removed from their families between 1910 and the 1970s.[75] The recommendations included a national apology and improved services for the Stolen Generations. It has been a point of consensus that the report opened Australia's eyes to the traumatic and destructive impact of generations of government approved child removal in Australia.[76] Similarly, *The Forgotten Children* report collected powerful evidence that brought the attention of the Australian public to physical and mental health concerns of children in mandatory immigration detention.[77]

Even where the Commission does not exercise the full powers available to it under the Australian Human Rights Commission Act by holding a public inquiry, it can still undertake major investigative projects. This can involve broad community consultation, detailed research and other forms of investigation and analysis. For example, in 2017, the Commission completed a major report, which was led by the Sex Discrimination Commissioner, into the issue of sexual harassment and sexual assault on university campuses.[78] The Commission is also undertaking a major project on human rights and technology, with a final report expected in 2020.

B. Contribution to Law Reform Processes

Separate from its own inquiry-type activities, the Commission frequently participates in the review of existing and proposed legislation, where those reviews are initiated by others, such as parliamentary committees or formal law reform bodies.

[72] Human Rights and Equal Opportunity Commission, *Report of the National Inquiry into Racist Violence in Australia* (Final Report, 1991).

[73] Human Rights and Equal Opportunity Commission, *Bringing them home: National Inquiry into the Separation of Aboriginal and Torres Strait Islander Children from their Families* (Final Report, 1997); Australian Human Rights Commission, *The Forgotten Children: National Inquiry into Children in Immigration Detention* (Final Report, 2014).

[74] Human Rights and Equal Opportunity Commission, *Bringing them home: National Inquiry into the Separation of Aboriginal and Torres Strait Islander Children from their Families* (Final Report, 1997).

[75] Ibid.

[76] Family Matters, *The Family Matters Report 2017: Measuring trends to turn the tide on over-representation of Aboriginal and Torres Strait Islander children in out-of-home care in Australia* (29 November 2018) www.familymatters.org.au/family-matters-state-2017/.

[77] Australian Human Rights Commission, *The Forgotten Children: National Inquiry into Children in Immigration Detention* (Final Report, 2014).

[78] Australian Human Rights Commission, 'Change the course: National Report on Sexual Assault and Sexual Harassment at Australian Universities' (2017) www.humanrights.gov.au/sites/default/files/document/publication/AHRC_2017_ChangeTheCourse_UniversityReport.pdf.

The Commission's engagement typically involves the presentation of a written submission, and the Commission often makes itself available to participate in any public hearing that is established as part of the reform process. In 2017–18, the Commission made 48 submissions to public inquiries, and appeared at 13 public hearings.[79]

Commission submissions are published on the organisation's website, and are often relied on by civil society and other stakeholders that wish to participate in these processes. The Commission also tracks how influential its submissions are by reference to the final reports of these reform processes.

C. Intervening in Court Proceedings

The Commission has a statutory right to intervene in appropriate court proceedings, subject to certain limitations and the inherent powers of the court.[80] In practice, the Commission reserves its exercise of this function for matters that are likely to have a significant societal impact, where the Commission believes it can assist the court on issues related to human rights. This right is a striking exception to the general practice in Australian law, which strongly discourages bodies such as tribunals and commissions from involvement in public law proceedings.[81]

Consequently, the Commission historically has intervened in relatively few matters – 84 times in its history. It is a significant decision for the Commission to intervene in court proceedings. The Anglo-Australian legal system has traditionally been wary of entities that do not have a conventional interest in proceedings to seek to involve themselves. As Lord Denning famously declared, our courts should not make themselves available to the 'busybody … who meddles officiously in other people's affairs'.[82] The High Court of Australia also can be a zealous gatekeeper. In a leading decision, Gibbs CJ said that standing is not generally available merely to

> prevent the violation of a public right if [the applicant] has no interest in the subject matter beyond that of any other member of the public, if no private right of [the applicant's] is interfered with. [The applicant] has standing to sue only if [the applicant] has a special interest in the subject matter of the action.[83]

[79] Australian Human Rights Commission, *2017–2018 Annual Report*, 15.

[80] See *Australian Human Rights Commission Act 1986* (Cth) ss 11(1)(p) and 46PV. Rights of intervention are also granted to human rights agencies under Australia's three statutory charters of rights. See, *Human Rights Act 2004* (ACT) s 36(1); *Charter of Human Rights and Responsibilities 2006* (Vic) s 40(1); *Human Rights Act 2019* (Qld) s 51(1). The ACT provision expressly states that the Human Rights Commission must be granted leave of the court to intervene. The Victorian and queensland provisions have no such requirement, which suggests that the relevant human rights bodies may intervene as of right.

[81] A practice widely known as the 'Hardiman rule' after *R v Australian Broadcasting Tribunal; Ex parte Hardiman* (1980) 144 CLR 13. In that case, the High Court strongly disapproved of the attempt by a statutory tribunal to appear in judicial review proceedings involving one of its decisions. The Court held that the matter should be left to the aggrieved parties who had appeared before the tribunal. This decision has had a chilling effect on the willingness of agencies and tribunals to become involved in review and appeal proceedings.

[82] *R v Inland Revenue Commissioners* [1980] QB 407, 422.

[83] *Onus v Alcoa* (1981) 149 CLR 27, 36.

In addition, the government of the day may, or may not, see the Commission's presence as constructive. As the current President recently remarked: 'At times the Commonwealth Attorney-General also intervenes; at times the Commission's interventions may not always be welcomed with open arms, shall we say.'[84]

For instance, in 2011 the Commission intervened in a case relating to a declaration made by the then Immigration Minister under the *Migration Act 1958* (Cth).[85] The plaintiffs had challenged the declaration, pursuant to section 198A(3) of the *Migration Act 1958* in respect of Malaysia. The Commission was granted leave to intervene in the matter, in relation to an unaccompanied minor (Plaintiff M106/2011), on 22 August 2011. The plaintiffs adopted the Commission's submission, which demonstrates the effectiveness of the Commission's intervention and recognises the expertise of the Commission in this area. Although the judgment did not explicitly refer to the Commission's submissions, its findings on the Minister's duty to provide written consent prior to the removal of an unaccompanied minor was consistent with the Commission's submissions.[86]

The Commission can also intervene in coronial inquests. In late October 2011, the Commission received a request from the family of Ms Andrea Pickett to intervene in the coronial inquest into her death.[87] Through discussions with counsel assisting the Coroner prior to the commencement of the inquiry, the Commission was able to persuade the Coroner to expand the scope of the inquest to look into more systemic issues relating to domestic violence – the first of its kind in Australia. The Commission was granted leave to intervene on 19 December 2011 and the Coroner ultimately made strong recommendations in relation to housing for women and children subject to domestic violence.

VIII. Conclusion

There has always been disagreement about the precise content and operation of human rights law. The advent of the Universal Declaration of Human Rights, or even the 'International Bill of Rights', did not settle that disagreement. Nor did it purport to do so. As previously noted, the constructive working-through of the inherent tensions between specific human rights, and between human rights and other legitimate interests, is central to human rights providing a useful, practical tool to guide human activity.

By their very nature, human rights are expressed in general terms. As such, they cannot anticipate every claim that might be made about how a right is engaged in practice. Only through consideration of how those principles apply in real-world contexts can principled, sensible accommodations be found that put the preservation of individual dignity at the centre.

[84] Rosalind Croucher, '"Rights-mindedness" – making human rights real in public service and community understanding 70 years after the adoption of the Universal Declaration of Human Rights' (Alice Tay Lecture in Law and Human Rights, 25 September 2018) 12.

[85] *Plaintiff M70/2011 v Minister for Immigration and Citizenship; Plaintiff M106 of 2011 v Minister for Immigration and Citizenship* (2011) 244 CLR 144.

[86] Dunlop, McAdam and Weeks note in their introduction to ch 17 (at fn 5) that this High Court decision was one of many that sparked legislative responses from the federal Parliament.

[87] Coroner's Court of Western Australia, *Inquest into the death of Andrea Louise Pickett* (12 June 2009).

The process of dialectic tests each of us to justify our position; to listen to others' perspectives; and to refine our position based on what we hear. The outcome of such a process tends to be more embracing of all the rights and interests that are engaged. It tends to avoid a winner-takes-all approach, and it looks for principled compromise.

On the other hand, from time to time, controversy between the government of the day and a member of the Commission, or the Commission as a whole, can become particularly acute. Without embarking on a detailed analysis of every moment where such tension has arisen, it might be observed generally that *some* tension between an NHRI and the government with which it interacts is common, perhaps even inevitable.[88] A problem arises, however, if this tension impedes the NHRI from fulfilling its core functions.

As with every other area of human relations, *how* we disagree matters. There is always going to be discussion of important human rights issues by all elements of our polity, including the government, elected officials and the Commission itself. That discussion can be robust and marked by divergent perspectives. But, above all, it should seek to advance the principle that lies at the heart of the Commission's statutory mandate: 'that every person is free and equal in dignity and rights'.

[88] See, eg, Croucher, above n 84, 12.

8

The Human Rights (Parliamentary Scrutiny) Act 2011 (Cth): A Failed Human Rights Experiment?

LISA BURTON CRAWFORD*

It is well-known that Australia lacks a constitutional bill of rights. It seems to be less well-known that Australia has a federal human rights act – of sorts.[1] The *Human Rights (Parliamentary Scrutiny) Act* 2011 (Cth) ('*Parliamentary Scrutiny Act*') was enacted in response to the recommendations of the National Human Rights Consultation Committee, which advised that, while Australia generally had a good human rights record, reform was needed.[2] The Committee recommended the enactment of a human rights act of a broadly similar kind to those already in place in the UK,[3] New Zealand,[4] the Australian Capital Territory[5] and Victoria.[6] But the model of rights protection established by the *Parliamentary Scrutiny Act* is not of this kind; indeed, it is unlike any human rights act currently in place in the common law world.[7] It purports to improve Parliament's capacity to protect rights, without involving the courts: it is an *exclusively* parliamentary model of rights protection.[8]

* This chapter draws upon previous research undertaken with George Williams and published as George Williams and Lisa Burton, 'Australia's Parliamentary Scrutiny Act: An Exclusive Parliamentary Model of Rights Protection' in Hayley Hooper, Murray Hunt and Paul Yowell (eds), *Redressing the Democratic Deficit in Human Rights* (Oxford, Hart Publishing, 2015); George Williams and Lisa Burton, 'Australia's Exclusive Parliamentary Model of Rights Protection' (2013) 34 *Statute Law Review* 58. I thank George Williams and Adam Fletcher for helpful discussions on the topic, the editors for their insightful comments and suggestions, and Lilian Frame for excellent research assistance.

[1] Some may well argue that this is not a true 'Human Rights Act' at all. It is commonly said that Australia still has no federal Human Rights Act, eg, George Williams and Daniel Reynolds, 'The Operation and Impact of Australia's Parliamentary Scrutiny Regime for Human Rights' (2015) 41 *Monash University Law Review* 469, 469; Scott Stephenson, 'Rights Protection in Australia' in Cheryl Saunders and Adrienne Stone (eds), *Oxford Handbook of the Australian Constitution* (Oxford, Oxford University Press, 2018) 905.

[2] The *Parliamentary Scrutiny Act* was one part of a new 'human rights framework'; other elements of this framework included new education initiatives, an enhanced role for the Australian Human Rights Commission, and a new 'National Action Plan' on human rights.

[3] *Human Rights Act 1998* (UK) ('*UK Human Rights Act*').

[4] *Human Rights Act 1993* (NZ).

[5] *Human Rights Act 2004* (ACT).

[6] *Charter of Human Rights and Responsibilities Act 2006* (Vic) ('*Victorian Charter*').

[7] The origins of the Act are explained in further detail in George Williams and Lisa Burton, 'Australia's Exclusive Parliamentary Model of Rights Protection' (2013) 34 *Statute Law Review* 58, 70–71.

[8] As defined in ibid.

Read generously, the *Parliamentary Scrutiny Act* represents an experimental attempt to improve Parliament's capacity to protect rights without subjecting it to judicial supervision. That is, the *Parliamentary Scrutiny Act* might be viewed as 'a distinctively democratic way of furthering the implementation of human rights.'[9] If successful, this would have provided a valuable new model for those who insist that responsibility for protecting rights ought to be left in Parliament's hands,[10] but who also recognise that Parliament does not always make decisions about rights in a just and reasonable way.

The democratic objection to a bill of rights has a powerful hold in Australian legal and political discourse. The justice of federal laws and the substantive protection of individual rights is generally seen as the responsibility of the Parliament, and not the courts. While this is undoubtedly a matter of culture and tradition, these ideas do have some footing in the text and structure of the *Constitution*. As a general proposition, the *Australian Constitution* is primarily concerned with distributing power amongst the branches of government, and does not require the federal Parliament to legislate compatibly with human rights norms. It has been suggested that the constitutional distribution of powers constrains the role the courts might play in protecting human rights against legislative incursion.[11] For these reasons, a federal human rights act which provides a more powerful role for the courts has always seemed – and continues to seem – unlikely.

We should also acknowledge that those rights models in place in other jurisdictions which *do* involve the courts have not always worked well.[12] For example, the operation of the *Victorian Charter* has created unexpected problems, and the effect of several of its key provisions remains contested.[13] It also does not seem to have made the impact that many hoped for.[14] In the UK, the *Human Rights Act 1998* has suffered a serious crisis of legitimacy. The reasons for that are complex, and not necessarily justified; they are interwoven with the broader revolt against the European Union. Nonetheless, that experience demonstrates that, rightly or wrongly, judicially enforceable bills of rights can contribute to a loss of faith in the entire human rights project, if they cause rights to be viewed as a tool of defence for the undeserving, or a fetter on democracy. My point here is not to prove that so-called 'strong' or 'weak' forms of rights protection are necessarily flawed[15] – rather, that for various reasons, it was understandable that the Australian Parliament should experiment with a different model.

[9] Tom Campbell and Stephen Morris, 'Human Rights for Democracies: A Provisional Assessment of the *Australian Human Rights (Parliamentary Scrutiny) Act 2011*' (2015) 34 *University of Queensland Law Journal* 7, 8; David Kinley and Christine Ernst, 'Exile on Main Street: Australia's Legislative Agenda for Human Rights' (2012) 1 *European Human Rights Law Review* 58, 69.

[10] See especially Jeremy Waldron, 'The Core of the Case Against Judicial Review' (2006) 115 *Yale Law Journal* 1346.

[11] *Momcilovic v The Queen* (2011) 245 CLR 1, discussed below.

[12] This is not to say that there are not strong principled arguments to be made in favour of such models: Rosalind Dixon, 'The Core Case for Weak-Form Judicial Review' (2017) 38 *Cardozo Law Review* 2193.

[13] As discussed in Janina Boughey's contribution in ch 11. See also the contributions to Vol (2018) 25(1) of the *Australian Journal of Administrative Law*, a special issue dedicated to the complexities of and conundrums posed by the *Victorian Charter*.

[14] The effect of the interpretive provision of the *Victorian Charter* is discussed further in Part III.

[15] I do not make any claims about the accuracy of these labels, either. I will revisit the question of whether a model of rights protection that provides a role for the courts would be constitutionally permissible at the federal level in Part III.

How, then, has Australia's unique model of rights protection fared? Arguably, it has failed. The apparent aims of the *Parliamentary Scrutiny Act* were to enhance parliamentary and public debate about rights, but it does not appear to have done so. This is largely due to the problematic design of the Act which, it was always plain to see, would hinder its operation. For this reason, we may question whether the *Parliamentary Scrutiny Act* represented a careful attempt to improve the legislative process, or a form of 'window dressing' designed to conceal the government's deep-seated apathy for human rights law while notionally meeting long-standing demands for better rights protection.[16]

In Part I of this chapter, I explain the design and purpose of the *Parliamentary Scrutiny Act*. In Part II, I examine its effectiveness. Given much has already been written on this topic,[17] my primary aim is to summarise the results of previous studies, and to examine whether the dynamics identified therein have significantly altered in the period since the last major study was published, by examining the ways in which the Act has influenced parliamentary debate, public discourse and judicial reasoning in the period between 1 January 2016 and 31 December 2017.

My main focus in this chapter is what should now be done about the *Parliamentary Scrutiny Act*, given its lacklustre performance to date. I address this in Part III. I will explain that there are several obvious ways in which the Act could be improved. However, at this point some might argue that the apparent failure of this Act demonstrates that an exclusively parliamentary model of rights protection is fundamentally flawed. I argue that, before abandoning the experiment altogether, it may be most beneficial to amend the way in which the Act defines 'rights', for this seems to be inconsistent with the normative premise of the model, and the root cause of its futility. Either way, it is clear that drastic reform is required to make the *Parliamentary Scrutiny Act* fit for purpose.

I. The Purpose and Design of the Parliamentary Scrutiny Act

The *Parliamentary Scrutiny Act* has three key components.[18] First, it defines 'human rights', to mean 'those rights and freedoms recognised or declared by' the seven key human rights treaties to which Australian is a party, including the International Convention on the Elimination of all Forms of Racial Discrimination, the International Covenant on Economic, Social and Cultural Rights, and the International Covenant on Civil and Political Rights.[19] Each of these recognises a long list of rights and freedoms. This means that the *Parliamentary Scrutiny Act* encompasses 'well over 100 rights and freedoms.'[20] Hence in comparison to other bills of rights, whether statutory or constitutional, the ambit of the *Parliamentary Scrutiny Act* is extraordinarily large.

[16] Adam Fletcher, *Australia's Human Rights Scrutiny Regime: Democratic Masterstroke or Mere Window Dressing?* (Melbourne, Melbourne University Press, 2018).

[17] For an excellent recent overview, see ibid.

[18] The Act is explained in further detail in Williams and Burton, 'Australia's Exclusive Parliamentary Model', above n 7, 70–88.

[19] Section 3.

[20] Kinley and Ernst, 'Exile on Main Street', above n 9, 61.

Secondly, the Act requires that bills and certain legislative instruments be accompanied by a 'Statement of Compatibility' ('SOC'), including 'an assessment of whether the Bill or instrument is compatible with human rights' so defined.[21] This requirement does not apply to legislative instruments that are not disallowable by vote of either House of Parliament.[22] The Act does not explain how a member of Parliament should assess whether a bill or instrument is compatible with rights, or stipulate the details that a SOC should contain. Thirdly, the Act establishes a Parliamentary Joint Committee on Human Rights ('PJCHR'),[23] whose functions include examining the rights-compatibility of bills and acts, and inquiring into other human rights related matters.[24]

As foreshadowed, the legislation does not create or confer any new or additional powers on the courts. For example, there is no equivalent to section 3 of the *UK Human Rights Act*, which directs courts to read legislation in a rights-compatible way, or to section 4 of that Act, which empowers the courts to declare that legislation is incompatible with rights. Insofar as the *Parliamentary Scrutiny Act* could be said to create any form of dialogue, then, it is 'between the *political* arms of government and the Australian public'.[25] The Act does not impose any new limitations on administrative actors, either. For example, there is no equivalent to section 38 of the *Victorian Charter*, which provides that 'it is unlawful for a public authority to act in a way that is incompatible with a human right or, in making a decision, to fail to give proper consideration to a relevant human right' – unless 'the public authority could not reasonably have acted differently or made a different decision.'

The normative premises of the *Parliamentary Scrutiny Act* were not explained in sophisticated detail when it was introduced into Parliament. The explanatory memorandum accompanying the relevant bill was fairly spartan and, in contrast to most contemporary legislation, there is no statement of objects or purposes in the Act itself. In his national address on the subject, the then Attorney-General explained that, contrary to the recommendations of the National Human Rights Consultation Committee, the government had decided not to enact 'a Human Rights Act or Charter' – that is, we may assume, a model of rights protection like that in place elsewhere, which provides a role for the courts – for the following reasons:

> While there is overwhelming support for human rights in our community, many Australians remain concerned about the possible consequences of such an Act. The Government believes that the enhancement of human rights should be done in a way that as far as possible unites, rather than divides, our community. The Government is committed to positive and practical change to promote and protect human rights. Advancing the cause of human rights in Australia would not be served by an approach that is divisive or creates an atmosphere of uncertainty or suspicion in the community.[26]

[21] Sections 8, 9.

[22] Section 9(1).

[23] Section 4.

[24] Section 7.

[25] Dan Meagher, 'The *Human Rights (Parliamentary Scrutiny) Act* and the Courts' (2014) 42 *Federal Law Review* 1, 4. See also Commonwealth, *Parliamentary Debates*, House of Representatives, 30 September 2010, 272 (Robert McClelland, Attorney-General).

[26] Robert McClelland (former Attorney-General), 'Address to the National Press Club of Australia – Launch of Australia's Human Rights Framework' (speech delivered at the National Press Club of Australia, Canberra, 21 April 2010). One may question whether this represents an accurate assessment of the views of the Australian people, given the findings of the Brennan Committee that only 14% of people opposed a human rights act. 87.4%

When the *Parliamentary Scrutiny Act* was introduced in Parliament, there was some suggestion it was intended to actually ensure compliance with international human rights norms.[27] However, this is not reflected in the text and structure of the *Parliamentary Scrutiny Act*. The Act clearly does not prevent Parliament from curtailing human rights. The Act does not provide for any forms of extra-parliamentary supervision or scrutiny either, so there is no mechanism by which Parliament might be told that it 'got it wrong'. Rather, the Act states that '[a] statement of compatibility prepared under [the Act] is not binding on any court or tribunal',[28] and that a failure to comply with the requirement to table a SOC 'in relation to a Bill that becomes an Act does not affect the validity, operation or enforcement of the Act or any other provision of a law of the Commonwealth.'[29] For these reasons, it is difficult to say that the Act was intended to ensure that Parliament would legislate consistently with rights.

Rather, the Act appears to be designed to prevent Parliament from curtailing rights *without adequate deliberation and justification*. More specifically, it apparently aims to enhance parliamentary and in turn public debate about the rights-implications of legislation and legislative instruments, in a way that is public and participatory. Thus the Attorney-General spoke of 'establish[ing] a dialogue between the executive, the parliament and ultimately the citizens they represent', and 'advanc[ing] the concept of participatory democracy by providing additional means for citizens to have input into the legislative process.'[30] Rather than purporting to ensure that Parliament will reach the 'correct' answer on rights questions, the *Parliamentary Scrutiny Act* encourages Parliament to give those questions the attention that they deserve, and to publicly explain and justify its decisions.

Thus the design of the *Parliamentary Scrutiny Act* reflects an understanding of rights which is 'rooted in contestation'.[31] On this view, there is disagreement about what rights are and what they entail, and the circumstances in which they may justifiably be curtailed. Given this, questions about rights are best left to be decided by the branch of government chosen by, and accountable to, the people. It follows that it is not appropriate for courts to decide these questions because they are not representative of the people; as a matter of institutional design, they are ill-suited to resolving polycentric questions that require the balancing of competing rights and interests and broad matters of public policy, as questions about rights tend to do.[32]

of submissions received by the Committee supported a human rights act: Brennan Committee, *National Human Rights Consultation Report* (Canberra, Attorney-General's Department, 2009), 264.

[27] See, eg, Commonwealth, Parliamentary Debates, House of Representatives, 30 September 2010, 271 (Robert McClelland, Attorney-General), 22 November 2010, 3243 (Laura Smyth), 3242 (Graham Perrett). See further Shawn Rajanayagam, 'Does Parliament Do Enough? Evaluating Statements of Compatibility under the *Human Rights (Parliamentary Scrutiny) Act*' (2015) 38 *University of New South Wales Law Journal* 1046, 1056–57.

[28] Section 8(4). See also s 9(3).

[29] Section 8(5). See also s 9(4).

[30] Commonwealth, *Parliamentary Debates*, House of Representatives, 30 September 2010, 271–72 (Robert McLelland, Attorney-General).

[31] Rajanayagam, 'Does Parliament Do Enough?', above n 27, 1058. See also Carolyn Evans and Simon Evans, 'Evaluating the Human Rights Performance of Legislatures' (2006) 6 *Human Rights Law Review* 545, 551.

[32] The leading exposition of this philosophical position is that of Jeremy Waldron in 'The Core of the Case Against Judicial Review', above n 10. See also Jeremy Waldron, *Law and Disagreement* (New York, Oxford University Press, 1999) 11; Jeffrey Goldsworthy, 'Losing Faith in Democracy' (2015) 59(5) *Quadrant* 9. This is obviously but a summary, and there are differences of opinion between those who subscribe to this general view: for example, some argue that certain restrictions on Parliament's ability to restrict rights are needed to maintain the integrity of the democratic system itself.

As I noted at the outset, these ideas have a strong presence in Australian legal and political discourse. Legal protections for rights have long been considered unnecessary and undesirable: unnecessary, as individual rights are adequately protected by the constitutionally prescribed system of representative democracy; undesirable, for the kind of reasons identified above.[33] As Fletcher notes, this view seems to be particularly prominent at the federal level, given several Australian states have enacted, or seriously contemplated, human rights acts which involve the courts.[34] Fletcher is right to note that the democratic objection to human rights law cannot entirely explain the unique design of the *Parliamentary Scrutiny Act*, because it was never seriously suggested that the federal Parliament should enact a human rights act that gave 'final say' over questions of rights to the courts.[35] However, it is not clear whether it is possible to draw such a bright line distinction between 'strong' and 'weak' form rights review. Some argue that 'weak' form review can have a substantive chilling effect on the exercise of legislative power – and for this reason, some strong democrats are wary of this too.[36] The design of the *Parliamentary Scrutiny Act* appears to reflect a far broader aversion to human rights law: a belief that courts should be kept out of the picture *altogether*.

Given its apparent aversion to human rights law, one might question why the federal Parliament bothered to enact the *Parliamentary Scrutiny Act* at all. Yet, even those who ardently believe that the protection of individual rights should be entrusted to Parliament acknowledge that Parliament sometimes does a poor job. One may argue that questions about rights ought to be left to Parliament, yet also argue that mechanisms should be put in place to improve the manner in which Parliament decides them. The democratic objection to human rights law is typically premised upon a well-functioning legislature which, amongst other things, deliberates conscientiously[37] – and for any number of reasons, real-life parliaments may not function quite so well.

One of the least contentious of these reasons is the sheer volume of legislation enacted by contemporary parliaments.[38] Data published by the Australian Parliament reveals that, in the four decades ending 2010, the House of Representatives has passed an average of 170 statutes a year.[39] This represents an enormous jump from the four decades ending 1950, when the average was just 56. These figures do not account for bills considered by

[33] See further Lisa Burton Crawford and Jeffrey Goldsworthy, 'Constitutionalism' in Cheryl Saunders and Adrienne Stone (eds), *Oxford Handbook of the Australian Constitution* (Oxford, Oxford University Press, 2018); Stephenson, 'Rights Protection in Australia', above n 1, 910–11; Fletcher, *Australia's Human Rights*, above n 16, ch 1.

[34] Fletcher, *Australia's Human Rights*, above n 16, 2, 34–36. It is also worth noting that proposals to amend the *Australian Constitution* to include greater protections for individual rights were rejected in referendums in 1944 and 1988.

[35] Ibid, 91.

[36] Aileen Kavanagh, 'What's So Weak About "Weak-Form Review"? The Case of the UK Human Rights Act 1998' (2015) 13 *International Journal of Constitutional Law* 1008, see especially 1023–30. I do not take Kavanagh to be critical of this fact – but others have taken it as a sign to be wary of rights models that involve the courts: eg Goldsworthy, 'Losing Faith in Democracy', above n 32.

[37] Eg, Waldron, 'The Core of the Case Against Judicial Review', above n 10, 1361–62.

[38] This phenomenon is not unique to Australia (for the classic US exposition, see Guido Calabresi, *A Common Law for the Age of Statutes* (Cambridge, Harvard University Press, 1985), though we may question whether it is particularly acute here.

[39] These figures, and the discussion that follows, are drawn from data published by the Parliament of Australia, *House of Representatives Legislation Statistics*, www.aph.gov.au/Parliamentary_Business/Statistics/House_of_Representatives_Statistics.

Parliament but not enacted as law, nor for the disallowable instruments considered by Parliament. Based on these figures, and published data on the sitting hours of Parliament, one might deduce that each Act enacted by the federal Parliament in the past four decades could have received no more than a couple of hours of the House of Representatives' attention.[40] It should also be borne in mind that federal statutes commonly run to hundreds, if not thousands, of pages.[41] The task of reading and formulating an understanding of such complex legislation, or the consequences of making even one small amendment to an existing statute, is clearly an arduous one. Thus it is clear that the rate of legislative activity significantly constrains Parliament's ability to give due consideration to the rights implications of it all. Indeed, many of these implications may go unnoticed in the frenzy of legislative activity.

The question, then, is whether the mechanisms put in place by the *Parliamentary Scrutiny Act* improve the way in which Parliament decides questions about rights, by ameliorating this and the other dynamics which may diminish the quality of its deliberation. As George Williams and I argued shortly after the *Parliamentary Scrutiny Act* was enacted, the greatest challenge facing an exclusively parliamentary model of rights protection was to show that it could prompt Parliament to live up to its full (theoretical) potential without creating any avenue of external scrutiny. There is no legal cost for failing to comply with the *Parliamentary Scrutiny Act*. That is, there are no legal consequences for tabling a perfunctory SOC that does not reflect a genuine assessment of the rights-implication of a bill or legislative instrument. There are no legal consequences for failing to table a SOC at all. The primary forms of 'scrutiny' provided for or contemplated by the Act are the PJCHR, and other Members of Parliament, who may express displeasure at parliamentarians who shirk the requirements of the Act. To this we may add the voting public, who may in theory express their own displeasure at the ballot box if Parliament fails to adequately justify the legislation that it enacts. But none of these mechanisms will be effective (or at least, not very) if there is not a broader rights-respecting culture. In other words, the *Parliamentary Scrutiny Act* will only work if it generates a *political cost* for legislating incompatibly with rights without due deliberation and justification. In this light, the following section explores how the Act has fared.

II. Effectiveness

There are already several comprehensive studies of the effectiveness of the *Parliamentary Scrutiny Act*. Some take a bird's eye perspective;[42] others provide more in-depth case studies

[40] Eg, in the period between 1980 and 2000, the federal Parliament enacted 3,652 statutes, and the House of Representatives sat for a total of 13,477 hours. Not all of this time is devoted to the consideration of legislative proposals. According to the statistics kept of the 45th Parliament, 'government business', which includes consideration of government sponsored legislation and motions (including motions to suspend standing orders) and ministerial statements, and 'private Members' business', which includes legislation and motions (including motions to suspend standing orders) sponsored by private Members and statements by Members comprised 69% of parliamentary business: Parliament of Australia, *House of Representatives Legislation Statistics*, www.aph.gov.au/Parliamentary_Business/Statistics/House_of_Representatives_Statistics.

[41] Eg, as of 1 July 2018, the lengths of the current consolidated versions of the following federal Acts are as follows: *Competition and Consumer Act 2010* (Cth), 1,567 pages; *Social Security Act 1991* (Cth), 2,871 pages; *Corporations Act 2001* (Cth), 3,457 pages; *Income Taxation Assessment Act 1997* (Cth), 5,353 pages.

[42] Fletcher, *Australia's Human Rights*, above n 16; Williams and Reynolds, 'Operation and Impact', above n 1; Williams and Burton, 'Australia's Exclusive Parliamentary Model', above n 7.

of the way the Act influenced the passage of particular statutes.[43] Most reach fairly pessimistic conclusions, while Campbell and Morris strike a more optimistic tone.[44] This section explores the results of these studies, and my own more limited study of the ways in which SOCs and the reports of the PJCHR have influenced parliamentary debate, public discourse and judicial reasoning in the period between January 2016 and December 2017.

There appears to be general agreement that the most effective mechanism created by the Act is the PJCHR. The PJCHR is said to have 'embraced its legislative scrutiny function with great diligence'.[45] Indeed, it appears that the PJCHR has stepped in to pick up the slack created by lacklustre compliance with other components of the Act.[46] Thus the Committee has often questioned implausible claims made in Statements of Compatibility,[47] and requested more information when it perceives a SOC to be inadequate. Fletcher concludes that the reports of the PJCHR 'have, in large part, been detailed, comprehensive and, at times, surprisingly forthright in their assessment of controversial legislation.'[48]

Yet, the operations of the PJCHR have been hindered, by the design of the Act, fluctuations in funding,[49] and the sheer size of its core scrutiny task.[50] The most fundamental of these hurdles appears to be the fact that the *Parliamentary Scrutiny Act* does not require Parliament to wait for the Committee to table its report before voting on a bill or instrument. Given the delays which have inevitably flowed from limitations on resources, many bills and instruments have been enacted before the PJCHR has expressed its view.[51]

On some occasions, it appears that the PJCHR's reports have influenced the design of legislative proposals – for example, where a bill was amended following the PJCHR's report.[52] On many other occasions, the reports of the PJCHR have proven futile.[53] Williams and Reynolds conclude:

> on 73 per cent of the instances where the Committee has made an adverse finding about a Bill or legislative instrument, that conclusion has had no impact on the fate of the legislation in question, while in the remaining 27 per cent of cases in which an impact might have occurred, evidence of this is hard to find.[54]

Of course, it may be legitimate for Parliament to enact legislation without modification, notwithstanding an adverse finding of the PJCHR. It is Parliament, and not the PJCHR, who is ultimately responsible for choosing which legislation should and should not be enacted as

[43] Rajanayagam, 'Does Parliament Do Enough?', above n 27.

[44] Campbell and Morris, 'Human Rights for Democracies', above n 9.

[45] Williams and Reynolds, 'Operation and Impact', above n 1, 476.

[46] See also Williams and Reynolds, 'Operation and Impact', above n 1, 506.

[47] Ibid, 454.

[48] Fletcher, *Australia's Human Rights*, above n 16, 210–11.

[49] Ibid, 180–81.

[50] In particular, this has caused the PJCHR to triage the bills and legislative instruments it will and will not comment on in in its reports in more recent years. The way in which the PJCHR has done this has been criticised. See Fletcher, *Australia's Human Rights*, above n 16, 191–92.

[51] Williams and Reynolds, 'Operation and Impact', above n 1, 476, 501. Williams and Reynolds discuss other difficulties encountered by the PJCHR at 475–83.

[52] Campbell and Morris, 'Human Rights for Democracies', above n 9, 20; Williams and Reynolds, 'Operation and Impact', above n 1, 490, 491–93. Note, Williams and Reynolds question the extent to which some of these events can be attributed to the influence of the PJCHR: 491.

[53] Williams and Reynolds, 'Operation and Impact', above n 1, 491, and sources quoted therein.

[54] Ibid, 494.

law. But given the time pressures facing the contemporary legislature, there is good reason for it to pay close attention to the PJCHR's reports, lest it miss or misunderstand the rights implications of the proposals in question. If Parliament goes on to enact legislation without amendment notwithstanding an adverse report by the PJCHR, one would expect that decision to be clearly explained and justified on the floor of Parliament – but given the relative dearth of references to PJCHR in Hansard, which I explain below, this does not appear to occur.

Most studies indicate that the more novel mechanism created by the Act – the requirement to table a SOC – has been fairly ineffective. Parliamentarians do overwhelmingly abide by the requirement to table a SOC, notwithstanding the fact there are no legal consequences for failing to do so.[55] In this minimal, but important, sense, it appears that the Act is being complied with. Initially, the general standard of Statements of Compatibility was poor.[56] They then appeared to improve.[57] But in his comprehensive study of Statements of Compatibility tabled between 2012 and 2015, Fletcher identifies something of a 'quality plateau': in other words, the quality of Statements of Compatibility has not continued to improve over time, but rather, remains patchy.[58] Some contain detailed examinations of the rights implications of the proposed legislation, and potential alternatives which were considered; others are brief and perfunctory.[59] As explained above, the PJCHR has displayed a determination to follow up on SOCs that it finds unsatisfactory. But of course, if the SOC does not include a sufficient level of detail in the first instance, then it is unlikely to achieve its aim of informing and enhancing parliamentary debate.

One striking feature of the SOCs tabled to date is that, as at the end of 2015, none has ever stated that the relevant bill or legislative instrument was *in*compatible with rights.[60] Campbell and Morris did not find this surprising, or problematic, as 'few treaty-based human rights are absolute and the normal issue, where a human right is thought to be involved, is to determine whether this limitation is morally justified, which will naturally be the opinion of the minister involved.'[61] Others disagree, arguing that there are some claims about rights compatibility that are simply implausible – and that some SOCs tabled to date stretch the boundaries of plausibility.[62] Given the discussion above about the contested nature of rights, and the apparent aims of the *Parliamentary Scrutiny Act*, the key would appear to be that a SOC must clearly articulate the reasons why it is considered to be compatible with rights, especially in the face of an ostensible rights-violation – and hence it is problematic that this is not always done.

[55] Williams and Burton, 'Australia's Exclusive Parliamentary Model', above n 7, 80; Williams and Reynolds, 'Operation and Impact', above n 1, 474; Fletcher, *Australia's Human Rights*, above n 16, 130.

[56] Williams and Burton, 'Australia's Exclusive Parliamentary Model', above n 7, 81–86. Fletcher, *Australia's Human Rights*, above n 16, 134–35.

[57] Williams and Reynolds, 'Operation and Impact', above n 1, 475. Fletcher, *Australia's Human Rights*, above n 16, 136–37.

[58] Fletcher, *Australia's Human Rights*, above n 16, 140.

[59] Rajanayagam, 'Does Parliament Do Enough?', above n 27, 1076–77.

[60] Williams and Reynolds, 'Operation and Impact', above n 1, 18; Fletcher, *Australia's Human Rights*, above n 16, 158.

[61] Campbell and Morris, 'Human Rights for Democracies', above n 9, 18. As Fletcher explains, the experience in other jurisdictions is mixed: in Canada, there has also never been a statement of incompatibility (as of 2015); in New Zealand, such statements are common: *Australia's Human Rights*, above n 16, 158–59.

[62] Rajanayagam, 'Does Parliament Do Enough', above n 27, 1058, 1065.

Just as crucial is the extent to which the devices created by the Act have influenced parliamentary debate, which is, of course, what they were supposed to do. On this point, commentators have reached rather different conclusions. Campbell and Morris argue:

> Hansard searches show considerable engagement with human rights issues from both sides of the chamber. Whether this can be marked down as a direct result of the PJCHR's work or whether such issues were raised regardless is hard to discern. Certainly there are many references to human rights made in Parliament but most of these relate to abuses in foreign countries, and the particular concerns of Representatives for the families of constituents. Nonetheless, there was a steady flow of Hansard references to the PJCHR, its work, and the members own contributions to the debates. Other members of the Parliament occasionally refer to [Statements of Compatibility], while one MP, Janelle Saffin, notes that statements are "one of the first things that I think a lot of members now read".[63]

The authors do not quantify what they consider to be 'a steady flow of references to the PJCHR', nor occasional references to Statements of Compatibility. Williams and Reynolds report that between 2012 and 2016, there were 32 substantive mentions in the House of Representatives between this period, which clearly 'suggest only a very limited impact upon parliamentary debate'.[64] The Senate fared slightly better over the same period of time, 'with a total of 74 substantive mentions'.[65] The authors note that many of these mentions came from the same members of Parliament.[66]

These trends appear to have continued. Between 1 January 2016 and 31 December 2017, 612 bills were presented to the House of Representatives,[67] but there appear to be fewer than a dozen occasions on which a SOC was referred to in the House in the course of debating the substantive merits of a bill.[68] Again, several of these references were made by the same MPs, suggesting patchy interest in, and engagement with, the scrutiny regime.[69]

Many of these discussions were brief. It was typical for a member of the opposition party to express doubt about the cogency of a SOC, where it asserted that the legislation was compatible with rights.[70] On one occasion, a Member of Parliament noted that there was an inconsistency between what was asserted in the SOC, and the report of the PJCHR.[71] On two occasions, the fact that a SOC stated that the Bill was compatible with rights was briefly

[63] Campbell and Morris, 'Human Rights for Democracies', above n 9, 20.

[64] Williams and Reynolds, 'Operation and Impact', above n 1, 487.

[65] Ibid.

[66] Ibid, 488.

[67] Parliament of Australia, *House of Representatives Legislation Statistics*, www.aph.gov.au/Parliamentary_Business/Statistics/House_of_Representatives_Statistics.

[68] I have excluded from this figure the occasions on which the words 'Statement of Compatibility' were mentioned, but to no substantive end – for example, when a member of Parliament stated that a Statement of Compatibility had been tabled. This figure also obviously excludes the occasions on which the Chair of the PJCHR referred to the Statement of Compatibility device in a more general way, which is discussed below.

[69] Three by Andrew Giles MP (Commonwealth, Parliamentary Debates, House of Representatives, 9 November 2016, 3416; 2 February 2016, 91; 22 June 2015, 7061) and two by Graham Perrett MP (Commonwealth, Parliamentary Debates, House of Representatives, 7 September 2017, 9632; 16 August 2017, 8654.)

[70] Commonwealth, Parliamentary Debates, House of Representatives, 9 November 2016, 3416 (Andrew Giles); 2 February 2016, 91 (Andrew Giles); 22 June 2015, 7061 (Andrew Giles). While many have raised the prospect of pro-forma Statements of Compatibility, one may sense here a formulaic way of responding to Statements of Compatibility from this Member of Parliament.

[71] Commonwealth, Parliamentary Debates, House of Representatives, 15 May 2015 (Tony Zappia).

pointed to, as another reason to support the Bill.[72] Two other, more lengthy discussions can be found, in speeches where the SOC was used as the foundation for a relatively lengthy discussion of the scope of the relevant rights at international law – but these appear to be exceptional.[73]

The PJCHR makes far more frequent appearances in Hansard, though in the period studied these primarily consisted of instances where the Chair of the PJCHR rose to table its reports. This was often done in a brief and formulaic way, without explaining the detail of the report on the floor of Parliament, especially in more recent years.[74] On other occasions the Chair did elaborate upon the work of the Committee, or legislative proposals that raised significant human rights implications – though never for much longer than a few paragraphs. It is difficult to characterise these periodic statements as the foundation of a rich and robust human rights dialogue.

The message from these statistics seems clear: SOCs do not play a significant role in guiding, shaping or informing parliamentary debate about the merits of legislative proposals. The PJCHR fares slightly better, but it could not be said to exert a profound influence on parliamentary debate, in large part due to the aspects of the Act's design highlighted above, and revisited below.

Of course, it may be that the scrutiny regime is informing discussions that take place 'behind closed doors', and influencing the initial drafting of bills and legislative instruments before they are presented to Parliament. Fletcher attempted to assess this through a series of interviews with public servants charged with preparing or vetting Statements of Compatibility.[75] As with many other aspects of the regime, the results were patchy. Those interviewed reported that the regime sometimes exerted a positive influence on these backroom activities, but on the whole this was rare. Crucially, those interviewed reported that significant funding cuts had restricted the range of training provided to these staff, which left them less confident of their abilities to properly comply with the regime. Furthermore, while the hidden effects of the Act are important, they are not sufficient, for it removes 'deliberation over questions of human rights protection to a context that is far less public, less political and less participatory' – contrary to the apparent aims of the Act.[76]

A. Public Discourse

One of the apparent aims of the *Parliamentary Scrutiny Act* was to create a broader rights-respecting culture, and a dialogue between Parliament and the people on questions of rights. This reflects the important realisation that the effective protection of human rights

[72] Commonwealth, Parliamentary Debates, House of Representatives, 13 February 2017 (Anthony Albanese); 18 March 2015 (Karen McNamara).

[73] Commonwealth, Parliamentary Debates, House of Representatives, 7 September 2017 (Graham Perrett); Commonwealth, Parliamentary Debates, House of Representatives, 16 August 2017 (Graham Perrett).

[74] For a typical example, see Commonwealth, Parliamentary Debates, House of Representatives, 28 March 2017, 3341 (Ian Goodenough).

[75] Fletcher, *Australia's Human Rights*, above n 16, 155–57.

[76] Rosalind Dixon, 'Comment: A New (Inter)National Human Rights Experiment for Australia' (2012) 23 *Public Law Review* 75, 79. See also Campbell and Morris, 'Human Rights for Democracies', above n 9, 27.

depends in large part upon the social and political culture; that there are limits on the degree of rights-protection that can be afforded by the law alone.[77] Yet, it is a fairly diffuse aim, and one which is difficult to achieve. It is also difficult to assess the progress that has been made. This section explores the way in which the *Parliamentary Scrutiny Act* has influenced public discourse, by examining the extent to which it has been discussed in the media and other online forums.

All major studies on the topic conclude that the Act's effect on media reporting has been small. Campbell and Morris report that:

> media coverage of the contribution of the [Act] has been disappointing. … there has not been a great deal of sustained media attention given to the work of the PJCHR and relatively lukewarm editorial comment on its initiation and impact.[78]

Likewise, Williams and Reynolds conclude that, apart from a handful of instances in which the PJCHR commented on a particularly contentious piece of legislation, the scrutiny regime has attracted limited public attention.[79] The particularly contentious pieces of legislation Williams and Reynolds identify are: the Social Services and Other Legislation Amendment (2014 Budget Measures No 2) Bill 2014 (Cth) (which introduced, amongst other things, a six month waiting period for benefits for job seekers); the Telecommunications (Interception and Access) Amendment (Data Retention Bill) 2014 (Cth) (which required telecommunications providers to retain customers' communication data); and, the Racial Discrimination Bill 2014 (Cth) (which sought to amend the controversial section 18C of the *Racial Discrimination Act 1975* (Cth)). On each of these occasions, the Committee advised that the Bill in question posed significant human rights concerns. Yet, as Williams and Reynolds note, the Committee had made similar findings with respect to numerous other bills which did not arouse the interest of the media.

These trends appear to have continued in the period between 2016 and 2017. A couple of dozen references to the *Parliamentary Scrutiny Act* can be found in online media reports and other public fora during this period. The vast majority concerned one particular, and obvious, rights issue: namely, the debate surrounding freedom of speech and the potential reform of section 18C of the *Racial Discrimination Act*. The discussion of the operation of the Act that does appear is typically brief and superficial. It should be noted that most of this discussion can only be found by specifically searching the records of online newspapers and platforms for public debate. A general internet search reveals very little material on the *Parliamentary Scrutiny Act* from the past five years.

One might therefore conjecture that the *Parliamentary Scrutiny Act* is doing little to expand or alter public discourse about human rights. Where there is a bill that poses an obvious human rights concern, and which the PJCHR has reported on, then the *Scrutiny Act* may enter the public discourse. Where there is a bill that poses a less obvious human rights concern or, for whatever reason, simply does not generate the same degree of public interest, the findings of the PJCHR will not attract much attention. In any event,

[77] See, eg. Victorian Equal Opportunity and Human Rights Commission, *2015 Report on the Charter of Human Rights and Responsibilities*.
[78] Campbell and Morris, 'Human Rights for Democracies', above n 9, 21.
[79] Williams and Reynolds, 'Operation and Impact', above n 1, 496–98.

the handfuls of references to the *Parliamentary Scrutiny Act* that can be found across the years do not demonstrate that it is having a profound effect on public debate.

More generally, Williams and Reynolds note that '[p]ublic awareness of the scrutiny regime appears to be low.'[80] I agree. While it must only be treated as anecdotal evidence, I am always struck by how few lawyers and law students are aware of the existence of the *Parliamentary Scrutiny Act*. Most do not know that it exists at all; those who are aware that it exists rarely have any detailed understanding of its operation. This is a disappointing outcome, for an Act that was lauded as 'the most important piece of human rights legislation in a quarter of a century'.[81]

B. Effect on Judicial Reasoning

When first enacted, there were questions whether and to what extent the *Parliamentary Scrutiny Act* might also inform statutory interpretation. For example, could a SOC which asserted that legislation was compatible with rights be taken by the courts as evidence that they ought to read the legislation in a rights-consistent way? At least one Member of Parliament has suggested that this is how SOCs should be used.[82] The Act stipulates that SOCs are 'not binding on any court or tribunal.'[83] Yet, a SOC is part of the extrinsic material to which a court may have regard, in ascertaining the purpose and meaning of a statute.[84] As Meagher observed:

> When the interpretive duty of the courts is to give the words of a statute the meaning which the Parliament (objectively) intended them to have, a *parliamentary* assessment of legislative human rights compliance is likely to carry some interpretive weight.[85]

Yet, as Meagher continues, it has long been said that the surest guide to parliamentary intention was the statutory text itself.[86] This matter must now be viewed in light of broader developments in the principles and practice of statutory interpretation, that were afoot before the *Parliamentary Scrutiny Act* was enacted but reached their high-water mark thereafter.[87] While there are maddening variations in approach, there have been many strong judicial statements in recent years downplaying the utility and relevance of extrinsic material, and prioritising the ordinary, natural meaning of the statutory text; the purpose of a statute is said to be gleaned *from* the statute, and not external sources. This is one manifestation of a

[80] Williams and Reynolds, 'Operation and Impact', above n 1, 496.

[81] Commonwealth, *Parliamentary Debates*, House of Representatives, 25 November 2011, 9661 (George Brandis).

[82] Commonwealth, Parliamentary Debates, House of Representatives, 13 February 2017, 760 (Anthony Albanese).

[83] Section 8(4), s 9(4).

[84] *Acts Interpretation Act 1901* (Cth) s 15AB. The Explanatory Memorandum accompanying the Human Rights (Parliamentary Scrutiny) Bill 2010 (Cth) stated that it was not intended to exclude the operation of that provision, and that Statements of Compatibility 'could be used by a court to assist in ascertaining the meaning of provisions in a statute where the meaning is unclear or ambiguous.': 5. See also *CIC Insurance Ltd v Bankstown Football Club Ltd* (1997) 187 CLR 384, 408 (Brennan CJ, Dawson, Toohey and Gummow JJ).

[85] Meagher, 'The *Parliamentary Scrutiny Act* and the Courts', above n 25, 2.

[86] Ibid, 6.

[87] See especially Dixon, 'A New (Inter)National Human Rights Experiment', above n 76; Meagher, 'The *Parliamentary Scrutiny Act* and the Courts', above n 25.

deeper shift in judicial attitudes towards parliamentary intention, which was long the guiding principle of statutory interpretation. According to some members of the High Court, parliamentary intention is now seen as something to be *constructed* rather than *found*:[88] the meaning produced by reading the statute in accordance with the established canons of construction is deemed to be that which Parliament 'intended', in a metaphorical sense. On this view, extrinsic material – including SOCs – would seem to carry little weight.

Conversely, it might be argued that a court can read down legislation so as to protect rights, notwithstanding that the SOC states that the statute limits them, if the statutory text is not sufficiently clear.[89] This would prove contentious.[90] Indeed, the application of the principle of legality to federal legislation highlights its contentious normative foundations on a broader level. The principle was traditionally justified on the basis that if a statute was not clear on the matter, the courts should presume that Parliament did not intend to abrogate fundamental common law rights; the thinking was that the rights implications of particular statutes may have escaped Parliament's attention.[91] In a system where the vast majority of statutes are accompanied by a SOC, it seems implausible to assert that the Parliament did not turn its attention to the question of rights – or at least, that category of rights recognised by the *Parliamentary Scrutiny Act.*

Whatever approach is correct in principle, it is clear that, in practice, Statements of Compatibility have not had any marked effect on judicial reasoning. Williams and Reynolds conclude that, as of 4 January 2016, there had been only four cases in which a court had referred to a SOC, or a report of the PJCHR; two of these are insubstantial.[92] Since then, the scrutiny regime has been referred to by the Australian Administrative Appeals Tribunal on two occasions.[93]

III. So: What to Do?

The preceding parts have explained the design and premise of the *Parliamentary Scrutiny Act*, and the minimal influence it has exerted on parliamentary debate and public discourse. As explained above, there are now several studies that have indicated that the *Parliamentary Scrutiny Act* is not producing the effects which it was purportedly designed to achieve.

[88] Richard Ekins and Jeffrey Goldsworthy, 'The Reality and Indispensability of Legislative Intentions' (2014) 36(1) *Sydney Law Review* 39.

[89] The High Court took an analogous position in *Saeed v Minister for Immigration* (2010) 241 CLR 252, 264–65 (French CJ, Gummow, Hayne, Crennan and Keifel JJ). The Court concluded that the legislation in question did not rebut the presumed obligation to afford procedural fairness, notwithstanding the fact that the responsible Minister clearly stated that procedural fairness was not intended to apply in the extrinsic material.

[90] Meagher, 'The *Parliamentary Scrutiny Act* and the Courts', above n 25, 16.

[91] The classic statement is found in *Potter v Minahan* (1908) 7 CLR 277, 304.

[92] Williams and Reynolds, 'Operation and Impact', above n 1, 494–96. The more substantial references can be found in *Wearden v Scotland* [2013] FMCAfam 268 [8]–[9]; *SZVBN v Minister for Immigration* [2015] FCCA 2977 (11 December 2015). The judgment of Gageler J in *R v IBAC* (concerning an SOC produced under the *Victorian Charter*) is also instructive – though his Honour notes that no submissions were made as 'to how the detailed statement of compatibility, laid before the Houses of the Victorian Parliament in respect of the Bill for the [relevant Act] … might bear on the construction of the [Act]': 2016) 256 CLR 459, 478 [72].

[93] *Silva and Minister for Foreign Affairs* [2017] AATA 1285, [14]–[18]; *Waubra Foundation and Commissioner of Australian Charities and Not-for-profits Commission* [2017] AATA 2424, [509].

There are now two questions to be answered. The first is whether the *Parliamentary Scrutiny Act* should be amended, repealed, or replaced. The second is whether the apparent failure of this Act demonstrates that an exclusively parliamentary model of rights protection is an unworkable one.

A. Improving the Parliamentary Model

There are several obvious amendments that could be made to the *Parliamentary Scrutiny Act*, which might enhance its effectiveness. For example, the Act could be amended to stipulate a minimum period of time for the PJCHR to consider each bill, such that a bill could not be enacted as law before the PJCHR had an opportunity to table its report.[94] Given the PJCHR seems to exert some meaningful degree of influence within the Parliament, this seems an entirely reasonable proposal, which may well enhance the effectiveness of the Act. However, as Fletcher notes, this proposal is likely to be resisted on the basis that it would inevitably slow the passage of legislation.[95]

In addition, or in the alternative, the *Parliamentary Scrutiny Act* might be amended to stipulate the level of detail required to be included in SOCs.[96] The Act might also be amended to specify how parliamentarians should assess whether a bill or legislative instrument is or is not compatible with rights. This may assist those designing legislation to think more carefully about its rights implications, and consider alternative, less intrusive means of achieving the same ends. On the other hand, requiring more detailed SOCs would increase the burden of complying with the Act. If the requirement remained self-policing, it remains an open question whether parliamentarians would comply. It is also unclear whether this would enhance the effectiveness of the scheme as a whole, for it is not clear whether the lack of detail found in many SOCs is the reason why they do not feature prominently in parliamentary debate. Would parliamentarians make more use of more detailed SOCs? Would the additional detail discourage them from doing so? Would it simply make no difference, because the device is not perceived as valuable at all? In a similar vein, while it would seem sensible to extend the ambit of the Act so that all legislative instruments are subject to its requirement (thus closing a loophole, whereby Parliament may shift rights-contentious norms into non-disallowable instruments),[97] the substantive benefit of doing so would depend upon the overall effectiveness of the Act. Given SOCs do not presently appear to have a marked effect on parliamentary or public debate, then extending this requirement, in its present form, may make little difference.

I would argue for a far more fundamental change, to the list of rights recognised by the Act itself. Many regard it is as a valuable thing, in and of itself, for there to *be* a statutory definition of human rights at the federal level. This can lend clarity and focus to parliamentary debate on questions about rights, and legitimacy to rights themselves. But the

[94] Williams and Reynolds, 'Operation and Impact', above n 1, 501; Campbell and Morris, 'Human Rights for Democracies', above n 9, 26.

[95] Fletcher, *Australia's Human Rights*, above n 16, 312. See also Williams and Reynolds, 'Operation and Impact', above n 1, 502.

[96] Fletcher, *Australia's Human Rights*, above n 16, 309–10.

[97] ibid 310, see also at 130–31.

Parliamentary Scrutiny Act does not contain a free-standing list of human rights. Rather, it directs the reader to the rights and freedoms recognised by key international treaties. This may have some appeal to those who argue that one of the key problems in Australia's human rights framework is the fact that these international human rights are not given adequate weight in domestic governmental decision-making. But the time and expertise that would be required to properly scrutinise the way in which each bill and legislative instrument intersects with the extensive list of rights and freedoms recognised by the Act is 'staggering'.[98] That is especially so, given the volume of legislative material that the federal Parliament considers each year.

Some might argue the preceding rather misses the point: that the *Parliamentary Scrutiny Act* was intended to slow down the legislative process, to ensure that rights were not sidelined in the rush of legislative activity; if the current pace of legislative activity could not be sustained while also performing proper rights scrutiny, then it is the former that has to give and not the latter. The reasons why legislation is enacted at such a rate is an important one, clearly deserving of further study.[99] Unless and until those dynamics alter, a clearer and more concise list of rights would seem more likely to generate real procedural change.

Of course, '[t]he fact that parliamentarians must learn about a great deal is not a bad thing.'[100] The Attorney-General's Department may, and does, assist by producing various guidelines to assist the process. Yet, the breadth of rights recognised by the Act will surely compromise the depth in which parliamentarians are able to consider each.[101] We must also be realistic about the fact that assessing the rights-compatibility of legislation, while important, is not the only task which parliamentarians must perform: there are a host of other standards against which new legislative proposals must be scrutinised.

The current method of defining rights seems inconsistent with the normative premises of the Act. Given the evident determination of successive Australian Parliaments to reserve questions about rights for themselves, and the aversion to international law that sometimes emanates from that chamber, it is surprising that the list of rights recognised by the *Parliamentary Scrutiny Act* was so indiscriminately drawn. The decision to define rights in this way was not discussed at length in Parliament. The National Human Rights Consultation Committee did conclude that 'unless it has entered a formal reservation in relation to a particular right, any right listed in the seven international human rights treaties [to which Australia is a signatory] should be protected and promoted', and many submissions to the Committee advocated for this approach.[102] Yet, the government was clearly willing to depart from the Committee's recommendations, as the ultimate design of the *Parliamentary Scrutiny Act* shows. Through its extensive community consultations, the Committee gathered information about the rights that the public valued and perceived to be in need of greater protection, which could have been drawn upon to design an Act which would have truly resonated with the Australian people.

[98] Kinley and Ernst, 'Exile on Main Street', above n 9, 61.

[99] In Australia, the issue has received considerable attention in the specific context of national security laws, and the dynamics of 'emergency', but not more broadly. See especially, Kent Roach, *The 9/11 Effect: Comparative Counter-Terrorism* (New York, Cambridge University Press, 2011) ch 6.

[100] Rajanayagam, 'Does Parliament Do Enough', above n 27, 102.

[101] See also Williams and Burton, 'Australia's Exclusive Parliamentary Model', above n 7, 72.

[102] Brennan Committee, above n 26.

Fletcher argues that 'narrowing the definition would send a message that the government prioritises some of its international human rights obligations above others.'[103] I agree that the act of culling the list of rights protected by the Act would send some dubious signals. It would have been far better for the Act to be carefully designed from the start. Still, I would argue that some degree of prioritisation is warranted. However provocative it may sound, it seems implausible to suggest that all of the rights and freedoms presently recognised by the Act – which range from foundational freedoms from torture and slavery,[104] to the rights to 'remuneration for public holidays' and 'the progressive introduction of free [higher education]'[105] – are valued in the same way, or to the same extent.

The current approach is particularly problematic for an exclusively parliamentary model of rights protection. The way in which rights are defined in the Act arguably diminishes its political clout, and hence its capacity to create a proper rights-respecting culture. The political cost for legislating incompatibly with a right is likely to correlate, amongst other things, to the extent to which that right is valued by the voting public. If the political cost of ignoring certain rights recognised by the Act is low, the legitimacy of the Act in its entirety is diminished. To be clear, I do not mean to suggest that a statutory bill of rights must simply correspond with the views and values of the majority of the voting public. Rather, the point is that any catalogue of rights deserving of Parliament's recognition and protection must be carefully designed. The *Parliamentary Scrutiny Act* does not display that requisite degree of care – and this, I argue, is one of the primary reasons why it has not meaningfully influenced parliamentary debate or public discourse.

B. Involving the Courts

Rather than attempting to improve the *Parliamentary Scrutiny Act*, we might abandon the project of an exclusively parliamentary model of rights protection altogether, and incorporate some supervisory role for the courts.[106] Any proposal to do so now would face constitutional hurdles, highlighted by the decision of the High Court in *Momcilovic v The Queen*.[107]

That decision is notoriously complex, and it is difficult to distil the clear ratio of the case. Nonetheless, all judges agreed that the power conferred by section 36 of the *Victorian Charter* – to make a declaration that a statutory provision could not be interpreted consistently with *Charter* rights – is not judicial, nor incidental to the exercise thereof.[108] This did not cause the *Victorian Charter* to fail because, as a matter of Australian constitutional law, a non-judicial power can be conferred on state courts, provided that it is not inconsistent

[103] Fletcher, *Australia's Human Rights*, above n 16, 131.

[104] *International Covenant on Civil and Political Rights*, opened for signature 16 December 1966, 999 UNTS 171 (entered into force 23 March 1976), arts 7 and 8.

[105] *International Covenant on Economic, Social and Cultural Rights*, opened for signature 16 December 1966, 993 UNTS 3 (entered into force 3 January 1976), art 7.

[106] Williams and Reynolds, 'Operation and Impact', above n 1, 507.

[107] *Momcilovic v The Queen* (2011) 245 CLR 1.

[108] *Momcilovic v The Queen* (2011) 245 CLR 1, 60–61 [80], 65 [89] (French C), 94 [178] (Gummow J), 123 [280] (Hayne J), 185 [457] (Heydon J), 222 [584] (Crennan and Kiefel JJ), 241 [661] (Bell J). As to the incidental point, see *Momcilovic v The Queen* (2011) 245 CLR 1, 65–66 [90]–[91] (French CJ), 96–97 [187] (Gummow J), 123 [280]

with the essential and defining characteristics of those courts.[109] In *Momcilovic*, a slender majority concluded that the power conferred by section 36 of the *Victorian Charter* was not so inconsistent, and hence that this provision was valid.[110] But at the federal level, the constitutional rules that constrain the courts are more strict: a power that is not judicial, nor incidental to the exercise thereof, cannot be conferred on a Chapter III court *at all*.

Thus it would appear that the *Parliamentary Scrutiny Act* could not be amended to involve the courts in this way. Any declaration power would have to be designed differently so as to avoid the strictures of Chapter III.[111] For example, a declaration could be made to have some legal consequence, so that it was no longer purely advisory[112] – but it is not clear what those consequences might be, or if there is any political appetite to give the courts such a role. Alternatively, the declaration power could be conferred on a non-judicial body, such as the Australian Human Rights Commission[113] – but this may raise fresh controversies, and would create a different model again from those which are said to involve a dialogue between Parliament and the courts.

The *Parliamentary Scrutiny Act* could also be amended to direct courts to interpret legislation consistently with the rights recognised by that Act, as section 32 of the *Victorian Charter* directs Victorian courts to do. That would not appear to pose any constitutional problems, but the practical benefits of doing so are not entirely clear. Again, there is significant uncertainty, but the decision in *Momcilovic v The Queen* indicates that this provision directs courts to apply a principle of legality-style approach to the catalogue of rights recognised by the *Victorian Charter*.[114] Perhaps due to this modest interpretation, section 32 is rarely used.[115] Fletcher observes that 'only a very small number of Victorian decisions appear to have relied on [section 32], and even then the cases did not necessarily turn on the application s 32.'[116] An equivalent provision could be inserted into the *Parliamentary Scrutiny Act*, yet it would overlap considerably with another well-established canon of construction, which entails that legislation should be read consistently with international law, as well as the principle of legality. A more robust interpretive provision that required courts to modify or alter the words of a statute in order to ensure that it is rights-complaint *would* raise further constitutional concerns.[117] In short, it could be argued that such a provision

(Hayne J), 185 [457] (Heydon J), 241 [661] (Bell J); Crennan and Kiefell JJ dissenting: 227 [600]. See further Will Bateman and James Stellios, 'Chapter III of the *Constitution*, Federal Jurisdiction and Dialogue Charters of Rights' (2012) 36 *Melbourne University Law Review* 1, 18–19.

[109] *Kable v Director of Public Prosecutions (NSW)* (1996) 189 CLR 51; *Forge v Australian Securities and Investments Commission* (2006) 228 CLR 45.

[110] *Momcilovic v The Queen* (2011) 245 CLR 1, 68 [97] (French CJ); 225–56 [597] (Crennan and Kiefel JJ); Gummow, Hayne and Heydon JJ dissenting. See further Bateman and Stellios, 'Chapter III of the *Constitution*', above n 108, 19–26.

[111] As noted by Fletcher, *Australia's Human Rights*, above n 16, 99.

[112] Ibid, 99.

[113] Ibid.

[114] See especially *Momcilovic v The Queen* (2011) 245 CLR 1, 50 [50]–[51] (French CJ); 217 [565]–[566] (Crennan and Kiefel JJ); 250 [684] (Bell J).

[115] Indeed, in its review of the *Victorian Charter*, the Scrutiny of Acts and Regulations Committee asked whether there was much point in retaining s 32 of the *Charter*, given it appeared to add very little to the common law: *Review of the Charter of Human Rights and Responsibilities Act 2006* (Vic), 114–5.

[116] Fletcher, *Australia's Human Rights*, above n 16, 36.

[117] Eg, of the kind required by s 3 of the *UK Human Rights Act*, as interpreted in *Ghaidan v Godin-Mendoza* [2004] UKHL 30, [2004] 2 AC 557.

would purport to vest legislative power in the courts, which would be inconsistent with the separation of powers principles explained above.[118]

The final alternative, then, is a far more fundamental one: to replace the *Parliamentary Scrutiny Act* with a model of 'strong' form review, which empowered courts to invalidate legislation that was found to be inconsistent with rights. This would change the scope of legislative power presently conferred by the *Australian Constitution*, and hence require a national referendum.[119] In light of what has been said here about the prevailing legal and political culture in Australia, it is questionable whether a proposal such as this would ever succeed. If it were, the call to redesign the list of rights recognised and protected by the Act that I have made here would stand – for even if one did desire to empower the courts to strike down legislation on the basis that it was inconsistent with rights, one would probably agree that the catalogue of rights so protected had to be carefully defined. Few would argue, I suspect, that the High Court should be empowered to strike down legislation that it finds to be incompatible with the expansive catalogue of rights and freedoms presently incorporated by the *Parliamentary Scrutiny Act*.

IV. Conclusion

The *Parliamentary Scrutiny Act* could have provided a valuable new model for those who insist that responsibility for protecting rights ought to be left in Parliament's hands, but who also recognise that Parliament does not always make rights-decisions in a just and reasonable way. This is particularly pertinent in Australia, given the apparent constitutional and cultural barriers to the enactment of a bill of rights which provide a more powerful role for the courts. But at this point, we must frankly acknowledge that the experiment has failed.

There are obvious ways in which the Act could be improved, which would seem capable of enhancing its effectiveness. The most substantive of these is, I argue, to redesign the list of rights which the Act recognises and protects. This would serve the practical benefit of reducing the burden imposed by the Act and hence enhancing the prospect of more meaningful compliance; more substantively, it may seriously raise the political cost of enacting legislation or legislative instruments which curtail rights without adequate explanation and justification – which is, in the end, what the Act is supposed to do. But given the general lack of political interest in the Act itself, it is doubtful whether there is sufficient political impetus for these changes to be made.

The broader question is whether the example of the *Parliamentary Scrutiny Act* demonstrates that an exclusively parliamentary model of rights protection – which does not involve the courts in any way – is destined to fail. The claim that Parliament is best placed to protect rights is a serious one. The problems that beset strong form and so-called 'dialogue' models of rights protection are not insignificant. But it is questionable whether the *Parliamentary Scrutiny Act* represents a genuine attempt to enhance Parliament's capacity to protect rights,

[118] As was argued in *Momcilovic v The Queen* (2011) 245 CLR 1. Given the 'narrow' way in which the majority interpreted s 32 of the *Charter*, it was not necessary for their Honours to consider this issue, cf *Momcilovic v The Queen* (2001) 245 CLR 1, 178–82 (Heydon J).

[119] *Australian Constitution* s 128.

or whether, as Fletcher concludes, its unique design is simply the result of long-standing negative attitudes towards human rights law. In other words, there is reason to suspect that the Act is not a 'democratic masterstroke' but an act of 'window-dressing', concealing a deep-seated apathy for human rights.[120] The merits of an exclusively parliamentary model of rights protection remain largely untested, for we simply have not yet seen a well-designed model of this kind in action.

[120] Fletcher, *Australia's Human Rights*, above n 16.

9

The Nature and Limitations of Commonwealth Anti-Discrimination Law

COLIN CAMPBELL

I. Introduction

Understood broadly, anti-discrimination law serves to protect people against decisions that may adversely affect them, and which have been made on the basis of what Moreau calls 'normatively extraneous traits', such as race or gender.[1] The precise underlying basis of anti-discrimination law remains contested,[2] with the principal debate being whether anti-discrimination law should be properly conceived of as, on the one hand, 'equality-based', or, on the other hand, 'liberty-based'. A person wrongly discriminates, according to an equality-based account of discrimination, when they fail to treat those affected by their acts 'as equals'.[3] Thus, this 'understanding of the wrong of discrimination has an essentially comparative dimension'.[4] By contrast, liberty-based accounts are 'non-comparative'. Pursuant to a liberty-based account of discrimination, a person discriminates when they infringe 'on a liberty to which each person is independently entitled'.[5] Examples of both conceptions of anti-discrimination are apparent in Australian law.[6]

There are two main types of discrimination prohibited by Australian anti-discrimination law: direct discrimination and indirect discrimination. Roughly speaking, an act of direct discrimination occurs when a person treats another person less favourably, because of the latter's possession of a protected attribute, than the discriminator would treat someone else without the protected attribute, but who is otherwise in the same circumstances as the person alleging discrimination. Indirect discrimination occurs when a condition or requirement is imposed that must be satisfied if some benefit is to be obtained, and the

[1] Sophia Moreau, 'What is Discrimination?' (2010) 38 *Philosophy & Public Affairs* 143, 152. Henceforth, these 'normatively extraneous traits', to the extent to which they feature in anti-discrimination legislation, will be referred to in the chapter as 'protected attributes'.

[2] Tarunbah Khaitan, *A Theory of Discrimination Law*, (OUP, 2015) 6.

[3] Deborah Hellman, 'Equality and Unconstitutional Discrimination' in Deborah Hellman and Sophia Moreau (eds), *Philosophical Foundations of Discrimination Law* (OUP, 2013) 53.

[4] Ibid.

[5] Ibid, 55.

[6] See Alice Taylor, 'The Conflicting Purposes of Australian Anti-Discrimination Law', (2019) 42(1) *University of New South Wales Law Journal* 1.

condition or requirement is neutral on its face but, in practice, adversely affects people with a protected attribute. The distinction between direct and indirect discrimination, used in Australia (and England) mirrors the distinction, relied on in the US and Canada, between disparate treatment discrimination and disparate impact discrimination.[7]

Anti-discrimination law in Australia (and, indeed, world-wide) is largely a creature of statute. In this sense, the legislature can be seen to have served a valuable purpose in remedying the failure of the common law to protect individuals against adverse treatment due to their possession of the sorts of protected attributes with which anti-discrimination law is concerned.[8] In Australia, there are parallel anti-discrimination regimes: a Commonwealth regime, and regimes that operate in the states and territories. To the extent that there is a conflict between a piece of Commonwealth anti-discrimination legislation and a state or territory enactment, the Commonwealth legislation will prevail.[9] For this reason, and also because the Commonwealth legislation may generally be relied upon by a person in any state or territory, this chapter will focus on the Commonwealth regime (although much of the analysis, particularly in Part II, will also be relevant to anti-discrimination statutes that function at state or territory level).

There are four main pieces of federal legislation, which serve to render discriminatory acts unlawful: the *Racial Discrimination Act 1975* (Cth) (the '*RDA*'); the *Sex Discrimination Act 1984* (Cth) (the '*SDA*'); the *Disability Discrimination Act 1992* (Cth) (the '*DDA*'); and the *Age Discrimination Act 2004* (Cth) (the '*ADA*').[10] It is probably the case that the relatively recent introduction of these enactments is reflective of the fact that general societal concern about discrimination is relatively recent, too. It is also likely that the order in which the Acts were passed is reflective of society's evolving views about areas in which harmful discrimination occurs, and the need to protect against it.

The main purpose of this chapter is to examine some of the ways in which the protection afforded against discriminatory conduct by Commonwealth legislation is limited. The chapter will be divided into two parts. In the first part, consideration will be given to limitations that flow, unequivocally, from the legislation itself. In the second part, an analysis will be made of two important cases that have interpreted anti-discrimination legislation, with a view to determining whether the judges' interpretation of the legislation in those cases was excessively narrow.

[7] See Neil Rees, Simon Rice and Dominique Allen, *Australian Anti-Discrimination Law* 3rd edn (Annandale, Federation Press, 2018) 52–53 for an overview of direct and indirect discrimination, and 85–165 for an in-depth examination of those notions.

[8] Although, note that there have been occasional common law cases that have protected individuals against adverse treatment on the basis of what modern anti-discrimination law would regard as protected attributes. See, eg, *Constantine v Imperial Hotels Ltd* [1944] 1 KB 693; *Nagle v Feilden* [1966] 2 QB 633. For a discussion of the limited extent to which the general law has protected what we might refer to as human rights, see James Spigelman, 'The Common Law Bill of Rights', *Statutory interpretation and human rights: McPherson lecture series* (Brisbane, University of Queensland Press, 2008) vol 3.

[9] See the *Constitution*, s 109. Note, however, that each of the Commonwealth pieces of anti-discrimination legislation contains a provision to the effect that the piece of legislation is not intended to exclude or limit the operation of a state or territory that is capable of operating concurrently with the piece of Commonwealth enactment.

[10] Other federal statutes which protect key rights are the *Australian Human Rights Commission Act 1986* (Cth) and the *Fair Work Act 2009* (Cth).

II. Limitations Flowing Directly from Legislation

Limitations on provisions prohibiting discriminatory conduct, where those limitations flow unequivocally from the legislation containing those provisions, will be considered in three contexts pertaining to anti-discrimination law: firstly, the attributes on the basis of which it is illegal to discriminate; secondly, the 'spheres of activity', within which it is illegal to discriminate; and, thirdly, exemptions which serve to render legal discriminatory conduct which, absent these exemptions, would be illegal.

A. Protected Attributes

To begin, claims in anti-discrimination law can only be made in respect of attributes stipulated in relevant anti-discrimination legislation as being subject to protection.[11] If a particular attribute is not included as a 'protected attribute' in such legislation, then a person cannot normally bring an action on the basis that she has been discriminated against because of her possession of that attribute.[12]

At a Commonwealth level, at least, certain attributes, that one might think should be protected attributes for the purposes of anti-discrimination law, are not. Hence, for instance, a person's physical features (which fall short of disability and are not associated with their race), and any adornments (such as piercings) and clothing they wear, do not generally count as protected attributes.[13] Further, while a person's religious and political beliefs are recognised as protected attributes under Commonwealth anti-discrimination legislation,[14] as is a person's possession of a criminal record,[15] the protection provided against discrimination on the basis of these attributes is limited.[16] And it is only very recently that protection

[11] Or on the basis of characteristics that generally appertain, or are generally imputed, to people who possess those attributes: see, eg, the *SDA* paras 5(1)(b) and (c), 5A(1)(b) and (c), 5B(1)(b) and (c), 5C(1)(b) and (c), 6(1)(b) and (c), 7(1)(b) and (c), and 7AA(1)(b) and (c) and the *ADA* paras 14(b)(ii) and (iii).

[12] However, she may be able to bring such a claim if she is able successfully to argue that the attribute in question is a generally appertaining characteristic of another attribute that *is* included as a protected attribute in legislation. Hence, for instance, prior to the passing of the *Sex and Age Discrimination Legislation Amendment Act 2011* (Cth), 'family responsibilities' was not a protected attribute under the *SDA* in the context of employment. Nonetheless, in *Maxworthy v Shaw* [2010] FMCA 1014, Nicholls FM accepted that childcare commitments were a characteristic generally appertaining to women: at [145]–[154]. Accordingly, Ms Maxworthy was able successfully to argue that she had been directly discriminated against by her former employers, effectively on the basis of her childcare responsibilities, even though 'family responsibilities' was not, at that time, a protected attribute.

[13] But note that 'gender identity' is a protected attribute under the *SDA*, and 'gender identity' is defined under the Act so as to include the 'gender-related … appearance … of a person' (s 4). Also, certain aspects of a person's appearance might be generally appertaining characteristics of age for the purposes of the *ADA*.

[14] See the *Australian Human Rights Commission Act 1986* (Cth) ss 3 and 31(b); the *Fair Work Act 2009* (Cth) s 351(1).

[15] See the *Australian Human Rights Commission Act 1986* (Cth), ss 3 and 31(b); the *Australian Human Rights Commission Regulations 1989* (Cth), reg 4(a)(iii).

[16] Under the *Australian Human Rights Commission Act 1986* (Cth), the Australian Human Rights Commission can (amongst other things) attempt to conciliate claims brought on the basis of a person's religious or political beliefs, or their possession of a criminal record, but cannot make an enforceable order with regard to such claims: see s 31. And while claims made under the *Fair Work Act 2009 (Cth)* can be subject to enforceable orders, such orders can only be made in respect of employees (and not, for example, in respect of, students or the recipients of goods and services) and not all employees, at that: see Beth Gaze and Belinda Smith, *Equality and Discrimination Law in Australia: An Introduction* (Cambridge, Cambridge University Press, 2017) 231 for a summary of those employees who are not covered by the Act.

has been provided with regard to a person's sexual orientation, gender identity and intersex status, by virtue of the insertion, in 2013, of these attributes into the *SDA*.[17]

It may not be going too far to suggest that the absence of certain protected attributes in Commonwealth anti-discrimination legislation, and the presence of others in legislation that affords only limited protection, may have been contributed to, at least in part, by the particular form taken by anti-discrimination legislation at the Commonwealth level. Unlike the position in the states and territories, where each state or territory has one anti-discrimination enactment that contains a broad range of protected attributes,[18] the position at the Commonwealth level is different. As noted above, at the Commonwealth level there are four principal pieces of anti-discrimination legislation,[19] each of which focuses on a particular protected attribute (or, in the case of the *SDA*, a group of protected attributes). It would make no sense for a protected attribute, which bore no obvious connection to any of the attributes currently protected at Commonwealth level – ie race, sex (etc), disability and age – to be inserted into one of the extant Acts. Accordingly, if such a new protected attribute were desired to be introduced – such as, for instance, a person's status as unemployed, or homeless – it would almost certainly have to be the subject of its own piece of legislation.[20] But it may well be more difficult to enact an entirely new piece of anti-discrimination legislation than it would be simply to amend an existing Act so as to insert a new protected attribute, even if the net effect would be the same. And even if, as an empirical matter, the form adopted by Commonwealth anti-discrimination legislation has not, in fact, hindered the enactment of new protected attributes by the legislature, it is nonetheless entirely possible that it will do so in future.

The existence of discrete pieces of legislation, each concerned with a different protected attribute (or group of protected attributes) also hinders the bringing of claims of 'intersectional discrimination'. Intersectional discrimination arises where a person is discriminated against because of their possession, *in combination*, of two or more protected attributes.[21] For instance, an employer may hire white men and Aboriginal women, but may refuse to hire Aboriginal men because he stereotypes them as being lazy and prone to alcohol abuse.[22] Such claims do not fit at all comfortably with the 'single-axis' framework[23] employed by Commonwealth anti-discrimination law.[24]

[17] See the *Sex Discrimination Amendment (Sexual Orientation, Gender Identity and Intersex Status) Act 2013* (Cth).

[18] See, variously, the *Anti-Discrimination Act 1977* (NSW), Pts 2, 3–5; the *Anti-Discrimination Act 1991* (Qld), s 7; the *Equal Opportunity Act 1984* (SA), Pts 3–5B; the *Anti-Discrimination Act* 1998 (Tas) s 16; the *Equal Opportunity Act 2010* (Vic) s 6; the *Equal Opportunity Act 1984* WA, Pts II–IV(C); the *Discrimination Act 1992* (ACT) s 7; and the *Anti-Discrimination Act* 1992 (NT) s 19.

[19] See also the *Australian Human Rights Commission Act 1986* (Cth) and the *Fair Work Act 2009* (Cth).

[20] Or inserted into such general or broad-ranging legislation as was available, even if the protection offered under that legislation were limited.

[21] Iyiola Solanke, 'Putting Race and Gender Together: A New Approach to Intersectionality' (2009) 72 *MLR* 723, 729.The term 'intersectional discrimination' was first coined by Kimberle Crenshaw in 1989: see Kimberle Crenshaw, 'Demarginalising the Intersection of Race and Sex: a Black Feminist Critique of Antidiscrimination Doctrine, Feminist Theory, and Multiple Intersecting Social Inequalities' (1989) *University of Chicago Legal Forum* 139, 140.

[22] This is a (significantly modified) version of an example provided by Ivy Kennedy, 'That Single Mother Element: How White Employers Typify Black Women' (1999) 13 *Gender and Society* 168, 181.

[23] Sarah Hannett, 'Equality at the Intersections: The Legislative and Judicial Failure to Tackle Multiple Discrimination' (2003) 23 *OJLS*, 65, 68.

[24] Julia Mansour, 'Consolidation of Australian Anti-Discrimination Laws: An Intersectional Perspective' (2012) 21 *Griffith Law Review* 533, 538–544.

Nor will the enactment of a single piece of legislation, which contains all of the protected attributes, but without anything more, adequately address the issue of intersectional discrimination. The reason for this is that, without anything more, such 'omnibus'[25] pieces of legislation will still operate by reference to a 'single-axis' framework, with a claim in discrimination only being able to be brought on the basis of a single attribute.[26]

Intersectional discrimination *can* be dealt with, though, by a piece of omnibus legislation that also contains a provision expressly providing for intersectional discrimination. Hence, for example, section 14 (1) of the *Equality Act 2010* (UK) states that 'A person (A) discriminates against another (B) if, because of a combination of two relevant protected characteristics, A treats B less favourably than A treats or would treat a person who does not share either of those characteristics.' However, notwithstanding that the *Equality Act* is an advance, in terms of intersectional discrimination, on legislative schemes that do not provide for intersectional discrimination at all, the fact that it is limited to recognising intersectionality that occurs only on the basis of two protected characteristics, and no more, may undermine its utility. This is because, as Malleson observes, intersectionality frequently encompasses not just two but a number of intersecting characteristics.[27] Accordingly, the approach adopted under *The Canadian Human Rights Act* (RSC, 1985, c H-6), pursuant to which intersectional discrimination is not limited to discrimination which occurs on the basis of just two protected attributes, would seem to be preferable. Section 3.1 of that Act states that 'a discriminatory practice includes a practice based on one or more prohibited grounds of discrimination or on the effect of a combination of prohibited grounds.'[28]

The fact that Commonwealth anti-discrimination law is a creature of statute, with specific protected attributes being stipulated in different pieces of legislation, retards the development of protected attributes in another, more general, fashion. If, for instance, Commonwealth anti-discrimination law were part of the common law, rather than statute, it would be open to the courts to arrive at new protected attributes in two different ways. One way would be for the courts gradually, and incrementally, to develop new protected attributes, based on the close connection between, on the one hand, those new protected attributes, and on the other, protected attributes that currently exist.[29] For instance, it is presently the case, under statute, that discrimination is prohibited on the basis of 'marital or relationship status'.[30] Marital or relationship status, in turn, is defined broadly, so as to mean a person's status as being one of: married; single; married, but living separately and apart from his or her spouse; divorced; the de facto partner of another person; the de facto partner of another person, but living separately and apart from that other person; the former de

[25] This term is used by Julia Mansour, 'Consolidation of Australian Anti-Discrimination Laws, An Intersectional Perspective' (2012) 21 *Griffith Law Review* 533, 547.

[26] See, eg, the *Equal Opportunity Act 2010* (Vic), which operates in this way.

[27] See Kate Malleson, 'Equality Law and the Protected Characteristics' (2018) 81 *MLR* 598, 603, and the sources referred to in note 32.

[28] The draft Human Rights and Anti-Discrimination Bill 2012 (Cth) also contained such a provision. Section 19(1) provided discrimination would occur if a person were accorded unfavourable treatment on the basis of 'a particular protected attribute, or a particular combination of 2 or more protected attributes'.

[29] Some indirect guidance has arguably been given on this by the High Court of Australia. None of the many novel rights recognised by the High Court during the 'implied rights' period, analysed in the chapter by Blackshield, concerned protected attributes. It is possible that intermediate courts could develop new principles in this area but it is also possible they may be more reluctant to do so given the apparent silence on this issue from the High Court.

[30] *SDA*, s 6.

facto partner of another person; and the surviving spouse or de facto partner of a person who has died.[31] It is entirely plausible that if this understanding of what constitutes 'marital status' had been arrived at as a result of the development of the common law, and an appropriate case presented itself, the court might extend the meaning of 'marital status' to include, for instance, a polyamorous relationship. However, because the definition of 'marital status' is included in the *SDA*, and is exhaustive, no such approach is possible.

Another way in which the courts could at least seek to arrive at new protected attributes, if, for example, anti-discrimination law were a creature of the common law rather than being contained in a number of statutes, each dealing with different protected attributes, would be for the courts to attempt to ascertain the concerns underpinning the existing protected attributes, and then, to derive from those concerns, a general principle, by reference to which new protected attributes could be identified.[32] The adoption of such an approach might well also permit the courts to elaborate upon the theoretical underpinnings of anti-discrimination law more generally.

Although these approaches would probably be most naturally employed under the common law, they could be adopted by the courts in respect of prohibitions on discrimination contained in legislation, but only if the definition of what constituted a protected attribute under the legislation was sufficiently (and unusually) broad and flexible (and probably also only if all of the protected attributes were dealt with in the one Act). One jurisdiction in which that is the case is South Africa. In the *Promotion of Equality and Prevention of Unfair Discrimination Act 2000*, part (a) of the definition of 'prohibited grounds' lists a number of standard grounds, such as race, sex and age. However, part (b) of the definition is very different. It states that included amongst the prohibited grounds, for the purposes of the Act are 'any other ground, where discrimination based on that other ground … causes or perpetuates systemic disadvantage; … [or] undermines human dignity; or … adversely effects the equal enjoyment of a person's rights and freedoms in a serious manner …'.

B. Spheres of Activity

The operation of anti-discrimination laws is confined in another way, too. A discriminatory act will be illegal only if it has occurred within one of the 'spheres of activity', again, stipulated in the legislation.[33] On the one hand, it should be acknowledged that these spheres, collectively, cover a broad range of activity. Typically, they include employment (including being an independent contractor and a member of a partnership),[34] the provision of

[31] *SDA*, s 4.

[32] Such a methodology was most famously employed in *Donoghue v Stevenson* [1932] AC 562. Prior to that case, there was no widely accepted general test for determining whether a plaintiff owed a defendant a duty of care. Instead, the courts had simply determined that a duty of care was owed in particular kinds of relationship. In arriving at the 'neighbour principle' Lord Atkin, for the majority, observed that 'in English law there must be, and is, some general conception of relations giving rise to a duty of care, of which the particular instances found in the books are but instances' (580).

[33] But cf *RDA*, s 9 which says that discrimination is illegal if it occurs in 'any field of public life'. It may be, however, that s 9 must be read subject to ss 11–16 which state that discrimination will be illegal if it occurs in certain spheres.

[34] See the *RDA*, s 15; the *SDA*, ss 14–17; the *DDA*, ss15–21B; the *ADA*, ss 18–25.

education,[35] the provision of goods, services and facilities[36] (whether for a fee or not),[37] the provision of accommodation,[38] membership of clubs,[39] and the sale of land.[40] Furthermore, there is also a certain breadth within each sphere. Hence, the spheres eschew any distinction between 'public' and 'private'.[41] Thus, there is no reference, for instance, in the provisions prohibiting discrimination in the context of the employment, to 'public employment' or 'private employment' but, rather, simply to 'employment'.[42] The same is the case with the provision of goods, services and facilities, and the other areas of endeavour within which discrimination is illegal. Accordingly, a consideration of whether the discriminatory act in question, the entity that carried it out, or the context in which it occurred, is somehow public or private will simply be irrelevant to the issue of whether the discriminatory act falls within one of the spheres.[43]

On the other hand, some areas of endeavour are conspicuously not covered by anti-discrimination law. Hence, a person's ability to engage in volunteer work, or to do an unpaid internship, may both provide her with a degree of 'self-respect'[44] and contribute to her possession of an 'adequate range of valuable opportunities',[45] both 'basic goods' that we might think should be protected by anti-discrimination law.[46] So, too, would a person's being a member of an amateur orchestra or theatrical society. But none of these is a stipulated sphere of activity for the purposes of anti-discrimination law in Australia. Accordingly, any discrimination that occurs within these spheres will not be illegal.

Whilst as observed above, there is a certain breadth within the stipulated spheres of activity, there is a kind of narrowness, too. Prohibitions on discrimination within the spheres are 'unidirectional'. Hence, for instance, an employer (or would-be employer) can commit an act of illegal discrimination against her employee, but not vice versa.[47] Similarly, the provider of goods, services or facilities can commit an act of illegal discrimination against the recipient (or would-be recipient) of those goods, services or facilities but, again, not vice-versa.[48] Each of the spheres of activity is unidirectional in this fashion. Presumably the idea is that only the party to the relationship that will typically be regarded as the more powerful party should bear a justiciable duty of non-discrimination.[49]

[35] See the *SDA*, s 21; the *DDA*, s 22; the *ADA*, s 26.

[36] See the *RDA*, ss 11, 13; the *SDA*, ss 22; the *DDA*, ss 24; the *ADA*, s 28.

[37] See the *SDA*, s 22; the *DDA*, s 24; the *ADA*, s 28.

[38] See the *RDA*, s 12; the *SDA*, s 23; the *DDA*, s 25; the *ADA*, s 29.

[39] See the *SDA*, s 25; the *DDA*, s 27.

[40] See the *RDA*, s 12; the *SDA*, s 24; the *DDA*, s 26; the *ADA*, s 30.

[41] Although note that many of the exemptions in the legislation appear to be based on some conception of that which is somehow 'private': see the discussion under 'Exemptions' below.

[42] Note that the definition of employment doesn't import any notion of publicness or privateness either.

[43] This makes for a stark contrast with, for example, the law of judicial review, where, under the general law at least (as opposed to statutory review regimes), the issue of whether the relevant exercise of power can be characterised as 'public' – or at least in possession of a public element – is crucial to the question of whether review is available. See, eg, *R (Holmcroft Properties)* v *KPMG LLP* [2016] EWHC 323 (Admin); *TH* v *Chapter of Worcester Cathedral* [2016] EWHC 1117. But note *RDA*, s 9, discussed briefly in n 33 above.

[44] Tarunbah Khaitan, *A Theory of Discrimination Law* (OUP, 2015) chs 4 and 5.

[45] Ibid.

[46] Ibid.

[47] See the *RDA*, s 15; the *SDA*, ss 14–17; the *DDA*, ss15–21B; the *ADA*, ss 18–25.

[48] See the *RDA*, ss 11, 13; the *SDA*, ss 22; the *DDA*, ss 24; the *ADA*, s 28.

[49] Tarunbah Khaitan, *A Theory of Discrimination Law* (OUP, 2015) 208.

This restriction on what constitutes illegal discrimination is troubling for at least two reasons. Firstly, it is not necessarily the case, in any given relationship, that the party whose actions are capable of constituting illegal discrimination (according to the legislation) will, in fact, be the more powerful party in the relationship, with the party whose actions are not capable of constituting illegal discrimination being the less powerful party. For instance, imagine a scenario where a person refuses to purchase goods or services from a particular provider, upon discovering that that provider is gay. The provider would be unable to sue the (non) customer under the *SDA* because, under that Act (and, indeed, under most anti-discrimination enactments world-wide) only a would-be recipient of goods or services may sue a provider, and not the other way around. However, there is no reason to assume that a provider of goods or services, operating as a sole trader or a modestly-sized concern, in a competitive market, will be in some way more powerful than even an individual (non) customer.

Secondly, even if, in a particular situation, the party whose actions are not able to constitute illegal discrimination (eg, the employee, or the (possible) recipient of goods) is, in some sense related to the market, the weaker party to the relationship, it remains possible that such a party may nonetheless discriminate against the stronger party on the basis of a protected attribute, causing the stronger party, if nothing else, at least dignitarian harm.[50] It is not particularly outlandish, for instance, to imagine that a person who is racist against (say) Asian people might decline an offer of employment from a (potential) employer who was of Asian descent, even if jobs are in short supply. It is acknowledged that where discrimination occurs in one of the stipulated spheres of activity, it is much more likely that the stronger party to the particular relationship will discriminate against the weaker, rather than the reverse. But where the less powerful party to a relationship in one of the stipulated spheres of activity *does* discriminate on the basis of a protected attribute, it is not entirely clear why their activity should not be illegal. This is especially the case, given that the purpose of anti-discrimination legislation is invariably to eliminate discrimination of the specified kind.[51]

C. Exemptions

The prima facie breadth of the spheres of activity is also undermined by the substantial number of exemptions contained in each of the pieces of Commonwealth anti-discrimination

[50] For an instance of a very well developed dignitarian theory of anti-discrimination law, see Deborah Hellman, *When is Discrimination Wrong?* (Cambridge, Harvard University Press, 2008).

[51] Hence, the long title of the *RDA* is 'An Act relating to the Elimination of Racial and other Discrimination'. And see the objects of, variously, the *SDA*, (s 3), the *DDA*, (s 3) and the *ADA*, (s 3). It is acknowledged that it may often be difficult to prove that a person has declined to purchase the goods, or use the services, of a particular provider because of the provider's possession of a protected attribute, or has declined to accept a job with an employer because of the employer's possession of a protected attribute. However, there is no reason to think that these matters could not be proved in at least some cases. Furthermore, acts of discrimination, generally, are extremely difficult to prove under Australian law: see Beth Gaze, 'Context and Interpretation in Anti-Discrimination Law' (2002) 26 *Melbourne University Law Review* 325, fn 17; Dominique Allen, 'Reducing the Burden of Proving Discrimination in Australia' (2009) 31 *Sydney Law Review* 579. Accordingly, the fact that it may be difficult to prove instances of discrimination against the providers of goods or services, or against employers, would not seem to justify the uni-directional nature of the legislation.

legislation.[52] It is not possible, because of constraints of space, to consider all of these exemptions here.[53] However, an examination will be made of two exemptions that the author considers especially egregious: the exemption in the *SDA* in favour of single-sex clubs,[54] and the exemption in the *SDA*, the *DDA* and the *ADA* in respect of 'domestic duties'.[55]

i. Single-sex clubs

As noted above, 'clubs' are a stipulated sphere of activity for the purposes of the *SDA*. Hence, sub-sections 23(1) and (2) render it illegal to discriminate against someone on the basis of, inter alia, their sex in, respectively, determining who can join the club, and then, broadly, the way in which a person is treated once they are a member. However, an exemption is provided in section 23(3). This provides that '[n]othing in subsection (1) or (2) renders it unlawful to discriminate against a person on the ground of the person's sex if membership of the club is available to persons of a different sex only.' In other words, if a club accepts both men and women as members, it will be illegal for the club to (for instance) decline membership to a particular woman, on the basis that she is a woman. However, if a particular club permits only (say) men to join, then it will not be illegally discriminatory to refuse membership to a particular woman on the basis that she is a woman.

Although this exemption is, in form, symmetrical (in the sense that it permits the existence of 'female-only' clubs as well as 'male-only' clubs), in substance it operates asymmetrically to the detriment of women.[56] The (male) members of male-only clubs are typically drawn from the legal, business and political elite, with the clubs traditionally being places 'where contacts are made and deals are clinched'.[57] Even if the discussion of business is banned at certain clubs[58] – and the ban is adhered to – it remains the case that the clubs facilitate the formation of important networks, membership of which will assist with the advancement of men's careers in various ways.[59]

By being excluded from male only clubs, women are largely excluded, in turn, from those networks, and so deprived of the benefits which membership of the networks may confer.[60] Moreover, to the extent that membership of male-only clubs suggests members

[52] See *RDA*, s 8, *SDA*, ss 30–47, *DDA*, ss 45–58, *ADA*, ss 33–47.

[53] For an overview of these exemptions, see Beth Gaze and Belinda Smith, *Equality and Discrimination Law in Australia: An Introduction* (Cambridge, Cambridge University Press, 2017) 155–64.

[54] See s 25(3).

[55] See, *SDA*, s 14(3), *DDA*, s 15(3), and *ADA*, s 19(3). Note also the corresponding, but much broader, exemption in the *RDA*, s 15(5).

[56] Note that women-only gyms will not normally be regarded as 'clubs' for the purposes of the *SDA* to begin with. Hence a body will only be a 'club' in the requisite sense if it 'sells or supplies liquor for consumption on its premises' (s 3). Accordingly, s 21(3) will not serve to render women-only gyms legal in circumstances where they would otherwise have been illegal by virtue of being 'clubs'.

[57] Mai Chen, 'Self-Regulation or State Regulation? Discrimination in Clubs' (1992–3) 15 *New Zealand Universities Law Review* 421, 423.

[58] Melanie Schleiger, 'Men-only clubs: entitled to discriminate?' (2010) 16 *Australian Journal of Human Rights*, 105, 108.

[59] James Stacey Taylor, 'Executives, Professionals, and the Morality of Single-Sex Clubs' (2004) 23 *Business and Professional Ethics Journal* 93, 98–100.

[60] Melanie Schleiger, 'Men-only clubs: entitled to discriminate?' (2010) 16 *Australian Journal of Human Rights*, 105, 121.

have achieved a high level of career success, women, by being denied membership, are denied such hallmarks of achievement.[61]

The existence of female-only clubs, and clubs which both men and women may join, does not cure the adverse impact, on women, of male-only clubs. In circumstances where women are still very significantly under-represented in the upper echelons of the legal and business communities, and in politics,[62] the networks to which women may gain access in female-only clubs will be significantly less beneficial to them than the networks to which men may gain access through membership of male-only clubs.[63] Nor do clubs which may be joined by both men and women 'enjoy the same exclusive and powerful membership of male-only clubs'.[64]

Two main arguments are commonly advanced in support of the notion that male-only clubs should not fall foul of prohibitions in sex discrimination legislation. One is that such clubs are essentially akin to the home, and, given that activities which occur there are generally not subject to justiciable duties of non-discrimination, nor should male-only clubs be subject to such duties either.[65] The other argument (which overlaps, to an extent, with the first) concerns freedom of association. If male-only clubs are prohibited by anti-discrimination laws, so the arguments goes, men's freedom of association would be impermissibly restricted.[66]

Neither of these arguments is persuasive. With regard to the first (and putting aside the issue of whether activities that occur in the home *should* be immune from the reach of anti-discrimination law)[67] any analogy sought to be drawn between, on the one hand, the home, and, on the other, clubs (at least as they are defined in the *SDA*), would be extremely forced. Hence, in order to be a 'club' for the purposes of the Act, an association must have no fewer than 30 members, must have 'facilities', and must sell or supply 'liquor for consumption on its premises'[68] (and so presumably be licensed to do so).

The second argument, concerning freedom of association, is even weaker. It is true that, in the absence of an exemption of the kind contained in section 23(3), anti-sex discrimination legislation would impinge upon men's freedom of association by rendering male-only clubs illegal, at least in enactments where 'clubs' were a stipulated sphere of activity. But impinging upon freedom of association is one of the principal outcomes of effect being given to anti-discrimination legislation. Within each of the stipulated spheres of activity, the bearer of the anti-discrimination duty is forbidden from declining to engage in various ways with a person, on the basis of that person's protected attribute. But so forbidding the duty-bearer impinges upon the duty bearer's freedom of association. Hence, for instance, when

[61] Mai Chen, 'Self-Regulation or State Regulation? Discrimination in Clubs' (1992–3) 15 *New Zealand Universities Law Review* 421, 452.

[62] Melanie Schleiger, 'Men-only clubs: entitled to discriminate?' (2010) 16 *Australian Journal of Human Rights* 105, 121.

[63] Ibid, 121

[64] Ibid, 122.

[65] See *Roberts v United States Jaycees* 468 US 609 (1984), referred to in Mai Chen, 'Self-Regulation or State Regulation? Discrimination in Clubs' (1992–3) 15 *New Zealand Universities Law Review* 421, 425.

[66] Mai Chen, 'Self-Regulation or State Regulation? Discrimination in Clubs' (1992–3) 15 *New Zealand Universities Law Review* 421, 424–426.

[67] See below, the text accompanying note 54.

[68] *SDA*, s 4.

an employer is prevented from not employing someone, because of that person's protected attribute, the employer's freedom of association is impinged upon. The same is true when a provider of (for example) goods is prevented from declining to provide those goods to a person, on the basis of their protected attribute. And this is the case throughout each of the stipulated spheres of activity.[69]

Hence, the fact that men's freedom of association would be impinged upon by anti sex discrimination legislation, in the absence of an exemption for men-only clubs, hardly seems a justification for such an exemption. This is especially the case, given the strong adverse impact, discussed above, that men-only clubs may have on women, including upon their career opportunities.

By contrast, female-only clubs are quite defensible in the context of legislation, whose purpose is to eliminate discrimination on the basis of sex. Most anti sex discrimination enactments recognise the importance of substantive – as well as just formal – equality, at least to an extent. This recognition occurs through the inclusion of provisions prohibiting indirect discrimination, and permitting, in certain circumstances, the adoption of 'special measures'.[70] Accordingly, female only groups – which seek to help women achieve substantive equality with men – should not be offensive to such legislation (at least until such equality has been achieved).[71]

ii. Domestic duties (and other work)

As noted above, 'employment' is a stipulated sphere of activity under Commonwealth anti-discrimination legislation. However, each of the *SDA*, the *DDA* and the *ADA* contains an exemption to the effect that it will not be illegal to discriminate against someone on the basis of, respectively, their sex,[72] disability or age in engaging (or, more accurately, declining to engage) the person to undertake 'domestic duties'.[73] The term 'domestic duties' is not defined in any of the pieces of legislation, but, presumably, it refers to the activities that were undertaken in Victorian times by domestic servants – namely, cleaning of the dwelling (whether a house or a flat) and the washing of clothes.

There is a corresponding, but broader, provision in the *RDA*. It states that '[n]othing in this section [the section indicating that employment is a stipulated sphere] renders unlawful an act in relation to employment, or an application for employment, in a dwelling house or flat occupied by the person who did the act …'.[74] Unlike the provisions in the other pieces

[69] Australian Law Reform Commission, *Traditional Rights and Freedoms – Encroachment by Commonwealth Laws* (Report 129, December 2015) which recognised that anti-discrimination law may conflict with freedom of association, but considered this issue in only a limited fashion: see paras [6.133]–[6.143].

[70] *SDA*, s 5(2) and s 7D.

[71] Mai Chen, 'Self-Regulation or State Regulation? Discrimination in Clubs' (1992–3) 15 *New Zealand Universities Law Review* 421 at 455–458.

[72] But, interestingly, not any of the other protected attributes contained in the *SDA1992* (Cth).

[73] See n 35 above. Interestingly, the exemptions do not extend to an alleged discriminator's conduct *after* they have engaged the complainant. Presumably the idea is that the alleged discriminator cannot have it both ways: if the alleged discriminator is sufficiently unperturbed the complainant's possession of a protected attribute to engage them, the alleged discriminator cannot, then, discriminate against the complainant, on the basis of that protected attribute, with impunity.

[74] See the *RDA*, s 15(5).

of legislation, this exemption is not limited to the engaging of someone (so it extends to the treatment they receive once they are engaged) and is not confined to domestic duties – it presumably covers all kinds of paid work that might be done in a dwelling house or flat (such as work done by an electrician or plumber).

Presumably, these exemptions would be sought to be justified, in large part at least, by virtue of the supposedly 'private' nature of the home. However, that justification is undermined immediately when we appreciate that, in this context, the home of the alleged discriminator is the complainant's workplace. More generally, we should be extremely cautious about any reliance on the so-called 'private' nature of the home as a basis for rendering things that occur within the home immune from the law's reach. Such a conception of the home was historically – and, to some extent, still is – the reason for the authorities' failure to investigate and then prosecute, cases of domestic violence.[75]

The question then arises as to whether there are any other bases on which the exemption may be justified. One possible such basis, in the context of the *SDA*, is personal safety. The argument might be made that a woman – and especially a woman who lives alone – is rendered more vulnerable if she has a male working in her house than a female, and so should be entitled to have work done by a female. Whatever the merits of this argument, the fact that the exemption applies only to discrimination on the basis of sex, and not in respect of any of the other protected attributes in the Act – for example, sexual orientation, or gender identity – suggests that a concern with safety might underlie the 'domestic duties' exemption in the *SDA*. At the same time, however, the fact that the exemption applies only to domestic duties, and not to other work done in the house, undermines this suggestion somewhat. So, too, does the fact that the exemption may be relied on not only by females but by males, in respect of claims that may be brought not only by males, but by females, too.

With regard to the *DDA*, it might be argued that the 'domestic duties' exemption is justified because some people with disabilities may not be able to undertake particular domestic duties. However, such an argument is unpersuasive. If a person was unable to perform the required domestic duties due to her possession of a disability, and, for that reason, was not hired, the alleged discriminator would be able to avail herself of the inherent requirements defence. Pursuant to this defence, it is not unlawful to decline to engage a person because of their possession of a disability, if the disability would render them unable to meet the inherent requirements of the job in question.[76]

Another possible justification for the 'domestic duties' exemption, in the context of the *DDA*, might be the burden imposed on a 'domestic' employer by the Act's stipulation that, in certain circumstances, an employer will discriminate against a worker with a disability by failing to make 'reasonable adjustments' for the worker.[77] However, this, too, is unconvincing. In determining whether the adjustments in question are reasonable, the relevant court or tribunal must take into account, inter alia, both the financial circumstances of the alleged discriminator, and the cost of the adjustments.[78]

[75] See, eg, Elizabeth M. Schneider, *Battered Women and Feminist Lawmaking*, (London, Yale University Press, 2000) 87–97.

[76] *DDA*, s 21A.

[77] See *DDA*, ss 5(2) and 6(2). A failure, for instance, to provide a ramp so that a worker in a wheelchair can surmount some steps and enter her workplace might be a failure to make reasonable adjustments.

[78] *DDA*, s 4, s 11. Note that, with regard to the inherent requirements defence, a person will be unable to meet the inherent requirements of a job only if she is unable to meet the inherent requirements once reasonable adjustments have been made to assist her: s 21A.

It might be claimed, somewhat more plausibly, that it is simply too difficult for mere 'domestic' employers to ascertain what is required to make 'reasonable adjustments' in particular cases. But even if that view were to be accepted,[79] the 'domestic duties' exemption would be overly wide. This is because it would operate as an exemption in respect of a person declining to hire a person who was disabled because of their disability, even where hiring the person would not require any adjustments, reasonable or not, to be made. That would be the case, for instance, where a person simply disliked the idea of someone with a disability working in their house, in circumstances where the person with a disability was perfectly capable of doing the required tasks without any adjustments being made for them.

Nor is there any plausible argument in favour of the domestic duties exemption in the *ADA*. The only possible justification would be that people past a certain age may not be able effectively to undertake the relevant domestic duties. However, the *ADA*, like the *DDA*, contains in inherent requirements defence.[80] The availability of that defence would deal with situations of the sort described where, because of their advanced years, a person was unable to undertake particular domestic tasks.

And there is simply no justification whatsoever for the broader exemption that is present in the *RDA*. The presence of that exemption is entirely unjustified, and simply permits effect to be given to grotesque bigotry.

III. Limitations Arising as a Result of the Courts' Interpretation of Legislation

So far, an examination has been made of various ways in which the legislation that imposes prohibitions on discrimination in Australia, itself clearly restricts the operation of those prohibitions. However, the prevailing view amongst Australian commentators is that the approach of the courts, in interpreting the relevant legislative provisions, also restricts the operation of Australian anti-discrimination law. Hence, Gaze, for example, has claimed that 'Australian judges most often give a literal or narrow reading of specific provisions or terms' of anti-discrimination legislation,[81] while Thornton has described the High Court's approach to interpreting anti-discrimination legislation in recent years as 'narrow and formalistic',[82] permitting the Court to 'to slough off not only all knowledge of discrimination as a social phenomenon, but interdisciplinary perspectives and the non-discrimination aims of the legislation as well.'[83] Rice has stated that the 'High Court's anti-discrimination jurisprudence is a sad example of the failure to have regard to the aims of the legislation'[84]

[79] And it is not clear that it should be. In other areas – say taxation – it may be difficult for individuals to know what they have to do in order to comply with relevant laws. However, that difficulty is not generally accepted as a reason in support of changing the laws so that individuals are not subject to them.

[80] See ss 18(4) and (5).

[81] Beth Gaze, 'Context and Interpretation in Anti-Discrimination Law' (2002) 26 *Melbourne University Law Review* 325, 333.

[82] Margaret Thornton, 'Disabling discrimination legislation: The High Court and judicial activism', (2009) 15 *Australian Journal of Human Rights* 1, 21.

[83] Ibid.

[84] Simon Rice, 'And which 'Equality Act' Would that Be?' in Margaret Thornton (ed), *Sex Discrimination in Uncertain Times* (Canberra, ANU Press, 2010) 204.

and has commented, more generally, upon the 'Australian judiciary's persistently technical and curmudgeonly approach to the beneficial aims of discrimination legislation', in interpreting that legislation.[85]

And it is not only commentators who seem to hold such views. In a series of dissenting judgments, Kirby J expressed concern about the narrow approach to interpreting anti-discrimination legislation that was being adopted by the High Court. In *Amery v New South Wales*, for instance, decided in 2006, the judge observed that in 'no decision of this Court in the past decade … has a party claiming relief on a ground of discrimination succeeded'.[86] He suggested that such outcomes may have been due to 'considerations of approach',[87] and contrasted the situation that concerned him with the position that had been adopted by the High Court earlier, when the judges adopted 'a beneficial interpretation to the laws in question'[88] and, as a result, applicants in discrimination law cases before the High Court were often successful.[89]

It is not possible here to engage in a comprehensive examination of whether these claims about the approach of Australian courts to anti-discrimination law are correct.[90] What will be done, is to analyse two cases, each concerning the *DDA*, and each decided relatively recently, in which the court adopted a very narrow approach to the interpretation of the relevant legislation. One, is a decision of the High Court, *Purvis v New South Wales*.[91] The other is a decision of the Full Court of the Australian Federal Court, *Sklavos v Australasian College of Dermatologists*.[92]

A. Purvis

In *Purvis*, a claim in direct discrimination was brought on behalf of an intellectually disabled 12-year-old, Daniel Hoggan, whose disabilities manifested themselves, from time to time, in aggressive behaviour such as hitting or kicking. He entered year seven at South Grafton High School, and over the ensuing months was suspended five times for hitting and kicking other students and staff members. Eventually he was expelled. His legal guardian brought an action under the *DDA*, claiming that, in being expelled, he had been treated less favourably, because of his disability, than someone would have been who was not disabled.

The school argued, first of all, that any less favourable treatment had not been accorded because of Daniel's disability, but, rather, because of the manifestations of that disability (which, the school argued, was a different thing). The Court rejected that argument, saying

[85] Ibid 225.
[86] (2006) 230 CLR 174, 200.
[87] Ibid, 201.
[88] Ibid, 200.
[89] Ibid. See also *IW v City of Perth* (1997) 191 CLR 1, 52 (Kirby J); *X v Commonwealth* (1999) 200 CLR 177, 211 (Kirby J).
[90] Although in this regard, see Thornton's analysis of a number of relatively recent decisions of the High Court of Australia concerning anti-discrimination law: Margaret Thornton, 'Disabling discrimination legislation: The High Court and judicial activism' (2009) 15 *Australian Journal of Human Rights* 1, 8–20.
[91] (2003) 217 CLR 92.
[92] (2017) 347 ALR 78. An application for special leave to appeal this decision was denied by the High Court on 7 February 2018: see *Sklavos v Australasian College of Dermatologists* [2018] HCASL 7.

that for the purposes of ascertaining whether treatment that was accorded *because* of a person's disability, the manifestations of the disability would count as the disability.[93]

However, the Court was more receptive to another argument made by the school. In order for a claim of direct discrimination, under section 5(1) of the *DDA* to be made out, it must be the case that the alleged 'discriminator treats, or proposes to treat, the aggrieved person less favourably than the [alleged] discriminator would treat a person without the disability in circumstances that are not materially different' from those of the aggrieved person.

The majority in *Purvis* said that in making that assessment for the purposes of the *DDA*, the manifestations of the complainant's disability must be regarded as part of his circumstances, to be attributed to the comparator.[94] The question therefore becomes whether the alleged discriminator treated the complainant (and who has a disability) less favourably than he would have treated someone without a disability but with all of the manifestations of the disability. Therefore, in this particular case, the question became did the school, in expelling Daniel Hoggan, treat him less favourably than it would have treated someone who was not disabled, but who had the manifestations of his disability, ie, was violent?[95]

The High Court held that in this case, the requirements of less favourable treatment were not made out. Just as the school expelled Daniel Hoggan, whose disability manifested in violent actions, the school would have expelled a student who was not disabled, but who was similarly violent.[96]

This approach, whereby, for the purposes of ascertaining whether there is less favourable treatment, the manifestations of the complainant's disability are treated as part of his circumstances, to be attributed to the comparator, is extremely problematic. This is because it comes very close to attributing the protected attribute to the comparator. The whole point of the comparison process in direct discrimination is to see how the person accused of discrimination treated the person alleging discrimination, who has a disability, compared with how he would have treated someone without disability. Therefore the comparator cannot have the disability. If the comparator has the disability, the comparison central to the determination of whether there is direct discrimination is rendered pointless. But in saying that the manifestations of the complainant's disability are part of his circumstances, to be attributed to the comparator, the Court is coming very, very close to giving the comparator the disability.

The practical consequence of coming so close to giving the comparator the protected attribute is that it will be extremely difficult for the complainant to show that the alleged discriminator treated them less favourably than he would have treated the comparator. This is because, as far as possessing the disability is concerned, the complainant and the comparator will be in essentially the same position. They will both effectively have the disability, insofar as it manifests. That being the case, there will almost always be no reason to suppose that the alleged discriminator would treat the complainant – who has the disability – less favourably than he would treat the complainant who, while not having the disability, has the

[93] Ibid, 156–57 (Gummow, Hayne and Heydon JJ), 175 (Callinan J).
[94] Ibid, 161 (Gummow, Hayne and Heydon JJ), 175 (Callinan J).
[95] Ibid.
[96] Ibid.

manifestations of the disability, ie the annoying and problematic aspects of the disability.[97] Indeed, almost all claims of direct discrimination brought under the *DDA* since *Purvis* have failed, for the very reason that has just been explained.[98] Thus, in interpreting section 5(1) of the *DDA* in the way that it did, the Court effectively eviscerated the prohibition on direct discrimination in the *Disability Discrimination Act*.

It is acknowledged that there have been a few cases, decided since *Purvis*, where the claim of direct discrimination on the basis of disability has been successful.[99] However, if anything, these cases just emphasise the damage done to the prohibition on direct discrimination by *Purvis*. This is because in those cases, the complainant was successful only because the decision-maker did not apply *Purvis* – so in other words, it ignored High Court authority – or the decision-maker misapplied *Purvis*.

An example of the former type of case (ie where the decision-maker simply did not apply *Purvis*) is *Gordon v Commonwealth of Australia*.[100] The applicant's provisional employment with the Australian Tax Office was withdrawn on the basis that he was imputed to have hypertension (ie high blood pressure), with the result that it was thought that he would be unable to satisfy one of the conditions of his employment, namely the ability safely to drive a motor vehicle for lengthy periods. In finding in favour of the applicant's claim under section 5 of the *DDA*, Heerey J stated that the 'comparator for the purposes of s 5(1) is a hypothetical person who does not have hypertension but has Mr Gordon's qualifications and experience ….'[101] It followed, according to the judge, that there could 'be no doubt that such a person would … not have got the employment offer withdrawn'[102] and that, accordingly, by 'withdrawing the offer of employment, the respondent had treated Mr Gordon less favourably than it would have treated such a hypothetical person.'[103]

Heerey J's analysis here does not conform to the reasoning of the majority of the High Court in *Purvis*. As has been seen, pursuant to that approach and its logic (such as it is), the comparator should be placed in as close a position to the complainant as is possible, without

[97] One possible exception is where there is particular stigma that attaches to the disability such that the stigma would apply to a person who actually had the disability, but perhaps not to a person with all of the manifestations of the disability, but not the disability itself. See, eg, *Power v Aboriginal Hostels Ltd* (2003) 133 FCR 254, 259 (Selway J). For an excellent examination, more generally, of the manner in which a person's behaviour may constitute a disability, and the implications of characterising a person's behaviour in that way, see Isabel Karpin and Karen O'Connell, 'Stigmatising the "Normal"' The Legal Regulation of Behaviour as Disability', (2015) 38 *University of New South Wales Law Journal* 1461.

[98] See, eg, *Y v Human Rights & Equal Opportunity Commission* [2004] FCA 184 (Unreported, Finkelstein J, 4 March 2004) [24]–[28]; *Fetherston v Peninsula Health* [2004] FCA 485 (Unreported, Heerey J, 23 April 2004) [86]–[90]; *Forbes v Australian Federal Police (Commonwealth of Australia)* [2004] FCAFC 95 (Unreported, Black CJ, Tamberlin, Sackville JJ, 5 May 2004) [78]–[82]; *Hollingdale v North Coast Area Health Service* [2006] FMCA 5 (Unreported, Driver FM, 20 January 2006) [150]; *Tyler v Kesser Torah College* [2006] FMCA 1 (Unreported, Driver FM, 20 January 2006) [106]–[107]; *Thompson v IGT (Australia)* (2008) 173 IR 395, 410 (Goldberg J); *Razumic v Brite Industries* [2008] FCA 985 (Unreported, Ryan J, 30 June 2008) [72]; *Zhang v University of Tasmania* (2009) 174 FCR 366, 386 (Jessup and Gordon JJ); *Flanagan v Murdoch Community Services* (2010) 188 FCR 300, 318–20 (Gordon J); *Gibbons v Commonwealth of Australia* [2010] FMCA 115 (Unreported, Burnett FM, 24 February 2010) [112]–[120]; and *Walker v State of Victoria* [2012] FCAFC 38 (Unreported, Gray, Flick and Reeves JJ, 22 March 2012) [73], [79].

[99] Note that these cases are not akin to *Power*. In these cases, it was not the position that a stigma attached to the complainant, but not the comparator.

[100] [2008] FCA 603 (Unreported, Heerey J, 6 May 2008).

[101] Ibid, [56].

[102] Ibid, [56].

[103] Ibid, [56].

actually possessing the complainant's disability, even to the extent of possessing the manifestations of the complainant's disability. Accordingly, if the approach of the majority in *Purvis* were being adhered to, the comparator in *Gordon* should have possessed those manifestations of, and risks pertaining to, Mr Gordon's (imputed) hypertension that resulted in the relevant officials at the Tax Office thinking it unsafe for Mr Gordon to drive a car for extended periods. But if that were so, less favourable treatment would not have been made out, and Mr Gordon's claim would have failed.[104]

An example of the latter type of case (ie where the court misapplied *Purvis*) is *Maxworthy v Shaw*.[105] In that case, the applicant claimed that she had been discriminated against in various ways by her employer as a result of the fact that she suffered from Crohn's disease and was required to carry a colostomy bag. Nicholls FM paraphrased the relevant portion of *Purvis* and outlined the characteristics of the appropriate comparator. His Honour stated, correctly in accordance with the majority approach in *Purvis*, that the comparator 'did not have Crohn's disease', but did, nonetheless 'carr[y] a colostomy bag'.[106] However, Nicholls FM subsequently concluded that the applicant had been discriminated against contrary to section 5 because she received the treatment of which she complained as a result of carrying 'a colostomy bag', to which the respondent had referred 'in deprecating terms'.[107]

But, by Nicholls FM's own account, the comparator, too, carried a colostomy bag. Accordingly, it is difficult to understand how a finding of less favourable treatment could have been made out conformably with the approach of the majority in *Purvis* – there is no reason to think that the comparator's carrying of a colostomy bag would have generated any different reaction in the respondent than would the applicant's carrying of such a bag due to Crohn's disease. It therefore appears that, in determining whether there was less favourable treatment, Nicholls FM either ignored the fact that the comparator carried a colostomy bag or, alternately, determined that there was discrimination not on the basis of less favourable treatment making use of a comparator, but, rather, on the basis that the applicant had simply been treated unjustly. In either case, however, the approach of the majority in *Purvis* was not ultimately relied on in determining whether the claim of direct discrimination under the *Disability Discrimination Act* was made out.[108]

It should be emphasised that it is not the purpose of the preceding analysis in this section of the chapter to criticise the decision-makers in *Gordon* or *Maxworthy*, or any like cases. It is not apparent, for instance, whether any of those decision-makers realised that they were misapplying, or failing to apply, the approach of the majority in *Purvis*. And even if

[104] Interestingly, in an earlier case, *Fetherston v Peninsula Health* [2004] FCA 485 (Unreported, Heerey J, 23 April 2004), Heerey J did properly apply *Purvis*, with the consequence that less favourable treatment was not made out. In *Fetherston*, the complainant had diabetes-related visual impairment. Although the comparator in that case did not, according to Heerey J, have that disability, he nonetheless suffered from sub-standard sight: see [86]. Other cases decided under the *DDA* in which *Purvis* seems to have been entirely ignored for the purposes of determining whether there was less favourable treatment are *Wiggins v Department of Defence* (2006) 200 FLR 438 [173] (McInnis FM) and *GAMA v Qantas Airways Ltd (No 2)* [2006] FCMA 1767 (Unreported, Raphael FM, 8 December 2006) [100]

[105] [2010] FMCA 1014 (Unreported, Nicholls FM, 24 December 2010).

[106] Ibid, [69].

[107] Ibid, [104], [107].

[108] Other cases involving the misapplication of *Purvis* are *Trindall v NSW Commissioner of Police* [2005] FMCA 2 (Unreported, Driver FM, 11 March 2005) and *Ware v OAMPS Insurance Brokers Ltd* [2005] FCMA 664 (Unreported, Driver FM, 29 July 2005).

they did know exactly what they were doing, their actions must be seen in the proper legal context – namely that the majority approach in *Purvis* is almost certainly legally wrong,[109] and, if accurately applied, renders the direct discrimination provision of the *DDA* very largely inoperative, with all of the unfortunate consequences that follow from such a lack of operation.

Interestingly, especially given the concern of the first part of this chapter about the limited nature of the protections afforded against discrimination in legislation, it is possible that the problems posed for the operation of direct discrimination under the *DDA* by *Purvis* have been cured by legislation, although, ultimately, it is unlikely that this is the case.

In 2009, the Commonwealth Government made various amendments to the *Disability Discrimination Act*.[110] One amendment was the inclusion of the following words into section 4 of the Act:

> To avoid doubt, a ***disability*** that is otherwise covered by this definition includes behaviour that is a symptom or manifestation of the disability.[111]

As was indicated above, in the discussion of the Court's reasoning in *Purvis*, the disability/manifestations distinction arises in two contexts. One is in the context of what is commonly referred to as 'causation', where the Court determines whether the complainant was treated as they were 'on the ground of' their disability (the 'causation context'). As mentioned above, the Court in *Purvis* held that, in the causation context, there is no distinction between a disability and its manifestations – the manifestations of the disability are, in that context, part of the disability. Accordingly, it will not be open to an alleged discriminator to say 'I didn't treat the complainant as I did because of her disability, I treated her as I did because of the manifestations of her disability. (And therefore, I am not liable).'

The other context in which the disability/manifestations distinction arises – and which has been the focus of this part of the chapter – is the context of the comparator, and the circumstances of the complainant's case which are attributed to the comparator. And in this context, as has been explained, *Purvis* says that there can be a distinction between, on the one hand, the disability, and on the other hand, its manifestations. While the comparator cannot, by definition, have the disability, the manifestations of the complainant's disability are regarded as part of his circumstances, to be attributed to the comparator.

So the addition to section 4 – which states that a disability includes its manifestations – could be referring to the disability/manifestations distinction in the causation context, or the comparator context, or both. It is only if it applies in the comparator context that the problems caused to direct discrimination in the context of the *DDA* by *Purvis* will be cured.

It is suggested that the words added to section 4, and extracted above, apply to the disability/manifestations distinction only in the causation context, rather than the comparator context. This is because 'To avoid doubt', which prefaces the words in question, suggests that an already existing position is being confirmed, rather than that a position is being changed. And, as has been explained, *Purvis* had made it clear that the manifestations of a disability were part of the disability in the causation context, but not in the comparator context.

[109] Kate Rattigan, 'Purvis v New South Wales (Department of Education and Training A Case for Amending the *Disability Discrimination Act 1992*' (2004) 28 *Melbourne University Law Review* 532, 548; Colin Campbell, 'A Hard Case Making Bad Law: *Purvis v New South Wales* and the Role of the Comparator under the *Disability Discrimination Act 1992* (Cth)' (2007) 35 *Federal Law Review* 111, 113–18.

[110] *Disability Discrimination and Other Human Rights Legislation Amendment Act 2009* (Cth) sch 2, s 6.

[111] Bolding and italics appear as they do in the amending legislation.

That interpretation is consistent with the position set out in the Explanatory Memorandum to the *Disability Discrimination and Other Human Rights Legislation Amendment Act 2009* (Cth). Paragraph 21 of the Explanatory Memorandum states that the amendment to section 4 'reflects the current status of the law as pronounced by the High Court in *Purvis* …' and was made only 'for the avoidance of doubt'.[112]

This view, that the added words do not apply to the disability/manifestations distinction, in the comparator context, seems to have been confirmed by Mortimer J in *Watts v Australian Postal Corporation*.[113] In that case, as part of a discussion in which she acknowledged that the Court in *Purvis* held that the manifestations of a disability were not, in the comparator context, part of the disability, her Honour discussed the effect of the added words. Mortimer J observed that 'the 2009 amendments did not purport to modify the language used in s 5(1) (which was the subject of the decision in *Purvis*) to describe the comparison required'.[114]

B. Sklavos

The case of *Sklavos* involved the operation of section 5(2) of the *DDA*. That sub-section (along with section 6(2)) was incorporated into the *DDA* by the *Disability Discrimination and other Human Rights Legislation Amendment Act 2009* (Cth) Schedule 2, pursuant to comments made by the Court in *Purvis*. As explained in the Explanatory Memorandum to the Amendment Act, prior to the decision in *Purvis*, 'the general view, including in the case law, was that the [*DDA*] impliedly impose[d] a duty to make [reasonable] adjustments if such adjustments [were] necessary to avoid unlawful discrimination – subject to the defence of reasonable hardship'.[115] However, some doubt was cast on the existence of that duty by the majority in *Purvis*, when it stated that the *DDA*, unlike disability discrimination legislation in the UK and the US did not 'explicitly oblige persons to treat disabled persons differently from others in the Community'.[116] It did not, for instance, 'contain provisions … which expressly oblige employers and educational institutions to make "reasonable adjustments" to accommodate disabled persons'.[117] Accordingly, section 5(2) and 6(2) were introduced to put the matter beyond doubt.[118] Section 5(2) states that:

> For the purposes of this Act, a person (the ***discriminator***) also discriminates against another person (the ***aggrieved person***) on the ground of a disability if: (a) the discriminator does not make

[112] Indeed, para 21 of the Explanatory Memorandum, in its terms, gives effect to recommendation 11.1 of the Productivity Commission Inquiry Report No 30, *Review of the Disability Discrimination Act* 1992, 30 April 2004. That recommendation states that 'A note should be added to the Act to explain that behaviour that is a symptom or manifestation of a disability is part of the disability for the purposes of the Act.' The preceding text states that the 'status of behaviour that is a consequence or manifestation of a disability … has been addressed by the High Court in the Purvis case', with the result that the amendment 'is a clarification, and not an extension, of the meaning of 'disability' in the DDA.'

[113] (2014) 222 FCR 220.

[114] Ibid, 277.

[115] *Explanatory Memorandum, Disability Discrimination and other Human Rights Legislation Amendment Bill 2008*, para 38.

[116] *Purvis v New South Wales* (2003) 217 CLR 92, 155.

[117] Ibid.

[118] *Explanatory Memorandum, Disability Discrimination and other Human Rights Legislation Amendment Bill 2008*, paras 39, 41(iii)(7).

> … reasonable adjustments for the person; and (b) the failure to make the reasonable adjustments has … the effect that the aggrieved person is, because of the disability, treated less favourably than a person without the disability would be treated in circumstances that are not materially different.

Mr Sklavos was a medical practitioner who was training to be a dermatologist under the training programme run by the Australian College of Dermatologists. In order to be admitted as a Fellow of the College – and so be admitted to practice as a dermatologist – Sklavos (like all trainees) was required to pass the College's final written and clinical examinations. However, Sklavos suffered from a relevant disability, namely a psychiatric disorder in the nature of a phobia of being assessed by the College that 'would have a disabling effect on his capacity and performance, were he to attempt … to participate in the written and oral components of the College's examination.'[119] Sklavos requested that the College admit him as a Fellow without passing the final examinations. Upon the College's refusal Sklavos brought action, including a claim that the College had directly discriminated against him under section 5(2) of the Act.

Sklavos' claim in this respect was unsuccessful. Bromberg J, with whom, in this regard, Griffiths and Bromwich JJ agreed, held that in order for a claim under section 5(2) to be made out, it was necessary that the complainant show that their disability was, while not necessarily the sole reason, at least a reason, for the respondent's failure to make reasonable adjustments in favour of the plaintiff.[120]

We might well be forgiven for thinking that the Court's interpretation of section 5(2) in *Sklavos* is another example of the judicial approach to anti-discrimination law described by commentators including Gaze, Thornton and Rice, and referred to above. Hence his interpretation accorded to section 5(2) in *Sklavos* is *extremely* narrow, and limits drastically the circumstances in which section 5(2) will be made out. It is not unreasonable to suggest that in most cases where a respondent has refused to make reasonable adjustments, this will not be because of the plaintiff's disability, but will be because of, for instance, the expense and inconvenience involved in making those adjustments. But, in such cases, section 5(2), at least as interpreted by the Court in *Sklavos*, will have no operation.

That the Court in *Sklavos* incorrectly interpreted section 5(2) is further suggested by the fact that that interpretation does not fit at all comfortably with the language of the sub-section. In limb 'b' of the sub-section, the words 'because of the disability', read most naturally, do not refer to the discriminator's reason or reasons for refusing to make reasonable adjustments. Rather, read most naturally, they refer to the reason why the failure to make reasonable adjustments will have an adverse impact on the aggrieved person (ie 'because of' the aggrieved person's disability).[121]

Interestingly, the Court's interpretation of section 5(2) in *Sklavos* limits the operation of that provision in a way that is comparable to the way in which *Purvis* limited the scope of section 5(1). It will be recalled that, pursuant to *Purvis*, one of the few circumstances in which a breach of section 5(1) could be made out would be if the disability in question carried with it a particular stigma. If that were the case, it might plausibly be argued that

[119] *Sklavos v Australian College of Dermatologists* (2017) 347 ALR 78, 80 [4]

[120] Ibid, 86–87 [30] (Bromberg J), Griffiths J 120 [179], Bromwich J 131–32 [213].

[121] The Court recognises that there is at some possible ambiguity in this regard (see ibid 86–87 [30]), but argues that the words 'because of' here do relate to the (alleged) discriminator's reasons (see: ibid, 87–89 [30]–[43]).

the alleged discriminator treated the plaintiff less favourably than they would have treated a comparator who did not possess the disability, but who nonetheless was presented with the disability's manifestations. The position with regard to section 5(2), as a result of *Sklavos*, is very similar. Pursuant to the narrow interpretation accorded to section 5(2) in *Sklavos*, one of the few circumstances in which the section might be breached is if there were a stigma attached to the disability. If that were the case, then the plaintiff might plausibly be able to contend (in some instances at least) that their disability was a reason for the respondent's failure to make reasonable adjustments.

IV. Conclusion

Commonwealth anti-discrimination legislation plays a very important role in filling a gap left by the common law. However, because of the particular form taken by the legislation, the protection afforded by it is at least somewhat limited. That protection would be stronger if the Commonwealth enactments were consolidated into an 'omnibus' piece of legislation, and if that omnibus piece of legislation provided specifically for intersectional discrimination, as well as the development, by the courts, of new grounds of discrimination, and 'multi-directional' discrimination. The protection would be strengthened also if exemptions in the legislation that lack a firm normative basis – like those in respect of single-sex clubs, and domestic duties – were removed.

However, whatever form the legislation takes, its ability to afford protection to those adversely affected by discriminatory treatment will remain subject to the interpretation accorded to the legislation by the courts. In at least some cases – like, for instance, *Purvis* and *Sklavos* – that interpretation will significantly undermine the protection that is able to be afforded.

10

'Culture, What Culture?' Why We Don't Know if the ACT Human Rights Act is Working

SIMON RICE

I. Introduction

The human rights project in the Australian Capital Territory ('ACT') is travelling steadily, within its modest bounds. Its focus is the *Human Rights Act 2004* (ACT) ('*HRA*'), which comes up in courts occasionally, is mentioned in legislative debates from time to time, and is a standard against which new legislation is assessed. While this activity is all, technically, in the public sphere, none of it is actually very public; it is almost exclusively the business of politicians (of whom there are 25), lawyers and administrative officials. Any public profile that human rights have is the work of the ACT Human Rights Commission, principally through its community engagement and education activity.

The vision for human rights in the ACT was not for a law that would generate headline cases, David and Goliath legal battles, and remedies for the oppressed, but for a law and associated mechanisms that would create a 'human rights culture', creating a rights-respecting community among the small population of the ACT. But there was never a plan. Politicians, bureaucrats and lawyers knew what to do with the law, and any larger awareness of human rights, let alone a culture, was expected to follow. There is little evidence that it did and, more tellingly, no effort to know if it did. One of the most significant public policy initiatives in Australia in the early part of the century, and its real intended effect, is unmonitored and unassessed. Only numbers are reported: how often something happened, not what difference it made.

That is the story I tell here: what was promised, what has happened, and how little we know about whether and how the ACT community has changed as a result.

II. Getting to the Human Rights Act

The ACT has a human rights law because the leader of the ACT Labor Party, Chief Minister and Attorney-General, John Stanhope, wanted one.[1]

[1] For an account of the party policy origins of the *HRA*, see John Stanhope, 'Reflections on the History of the *Human Rights Act*', speech to the conference *Ten Years of the ACT Human Rights Act Continuing the Dialogue*

Stanhope paved the way for the *HRA* with an ostensibly credible 'programme of community consultation'[2] – it was led by recognised experts in the field, conducted over a long period, and accessible to the community.[3] The Consultative Committee's Terms of Reference asked 'whether it is appropriate and desirable' to enact a human rights law in the ACT and, if so, what form it should take.[4] So the form of the *HRA*, with its modest legal mechanisms and ambitious aims, follows from the reasons why the *HRA* is appropriate and desirable at all.

The Committee did recommend 'the adoption of a bill of rights',[5] but also a 'community-wide education campaign' to promote the 'cultural and symbolic value' of such a law,[6] and 'a broad, ongoing education programme that brings [that law] and its implications to the attention of the public sector and the ACT community'.[7] Neither these formal recommendations, nor the text of the report that supports them, clearly spell out the extent to which the ACT was aiming for cultural transformation. It is implicit in the Committee's response to its review of then-existing rights protections in the ACT that it saw rights protection as deriving not from laws alone, saying that:

> Even if it were possible to argue that a combination of international, constitutional, Commonwealth, territorial and common law provided adequate coverage for human rights in the ACT, the fragmented nature of the coverage would remain a serious barrier to the development of a human rights-conscious culture.

This is the first mention in the report of 'a human rights-conscious culture', under the heading *An accessible statement of community values*, and the Committee explained what it understood to be the real meaning of human rights protections in the ACT:[8]

> much of the real value of a bill of rights lies in the *cultural change that takes place beyond the public gaze*, in the backrooms where bureaucratic practices are reformed and legislation is scrutinised to ensure compliance with human rights. A successful bill of rights should *permeate a community's bureaucratic and civic culture* so that breaches of rights become less frequent.

Recognising that 'a bill of rights cannot of itself create a human rights culture', the Committee saw that ensuring observance of such a law:[9]

> … would mean devoting resources to educating those who administer government programmes, from the agency chiefs right through to the newest recruits. It would mean making education a

10th Anniversary of the Human Rights Act, Australian National University, 1 July 2014, www.hrc.act.gov.au/res/J Stanhope Human Rights Act Speech.pdf; see also Hilary Charlesworth, 'Australia's First Bill of Rights: The Australian Capital Territory's *Human Rights Act*' in Tom Campbell, Jeffrey Goldsworthy and Adrienne Stone (eds), *Protecting Rights Without a Bill of Rights: Institutional Performance and Reform in Australia*, (Farnham, Ashgate, 2006) 289, 289–290.

[2] *Towards an ACT Human Rights Act: Report of the ACT Bill of Rights Consultative Committee*, May 2003, Australian Capital Territory, Canberra 2003, 13.

[3] See Alice Donald, *Developing a Bill of Rights for the UK. Project Report* (Equality and Human Rights Commission, UK, 20100 10–12. On sound processes of public consultation, see Helena Catt and Michael Murphy, 'What voice for the people? categorising methods of public consultation' (2003) 38 *Australian Journal of Political Science*, 407, 408.

[4] *Towards an ACT Human Rights Act: Report of the ACT Bill of Rights Consultative Committee*, May 2003, Australian Capital Territory, Canberra 2003, 12.

[5] Ibid, Recommendation 1, 42.

[6] Ibid, Recommendation 2, 42.

[7] Ibid, Recommendation 6, 60.

[8] Ibid, 36 (emphasis added).

[9] Ibid, 37.

> formal, permanent part of each agency's corporate plan. In essence, it would mean building a public sector where a "rights-respecting culture" would imbue decision-making at every level.

As a result, the Committee said that it:[10]

> ... believes that the introduction of a bill of rights must be accompanied by a commitment - and a plan - to see *cultural change implemented across government agencies*, and a commitment to *a long-term programme of community education and awareness-raising.*

I come back below to the reference to 'a plan'. Further, the Committee said that:[11]

> ... education would need to occur in the classrooms, where young people would be first taught to regard themselves and each other as holders of rights, and in the community, where that status would need to be reinforced and restated throughout an individual's lifetime.

It is unclear what relationship the Committee saw between a human rights law and cultural change. The Committee stated that 'a bill of rights cannot of itself create a human rights culture' and that education towards cultural change is necessary, but then placed law at the centre of that cultural change, stating that the 'primary purpose' of a human rights law 'should be to encourage the development of a human rights-respecting culture in ACT public life and in the community generally'.[12] So when the Terms of Reference asked whether to enact a human rights law in the ACT, the Committee's answer was, in substance, more than the simple 'Yes' of Recommendation 1; it was, effectively, 'Yes, *but only if* measures are taken to establish a human rights-respecting culture in ACT public life and in the community generally'.

A. The Dialogue Model

The bulk of the Committee's report considers cultural change within the legislature, executive and judiciary, recommending the 'dialogue' model of human rights as 'a relatively weak form of rights-based judicial review'[13] which would 'create a dialogue about the best way to protect rights in the ACT between all branches of government'.[14] The Committee's intention was that the *HRA* would 'be directing the executive and the judiciary to conduct their business in a particular way',[15] giving the legislature the 'last say'.[16] The Committee's focus was on the institutions of government. Only the statutory position of a Human Rights Commissioner, and arguably the executive's annual reporting, are directed towards public awareness of human rights issues, which I discuss below.

The Committee saw aspects of the *HRA* dialogue as creating a human rights culture beyond the institutions of government: limiting remedies would 'more effectively build a

[10] Ibid, 37 (emphasis added).
[11] Ibid, 37.
[12] Ibid, 41.
[13] Nicholas Barry and Tom Campbell, 'Towards a Democratic Bill of Rights' (2011) 46 *Australian Journal of Political Science* 71, 72.
[14] *Towards an ACT Human Rights Act*, above n 2, 56.
[15] Ibid, 61.
[16] Ibid, 61.

culture of respect for human rights in the ACT',[17] and open standing would 'chang[e] behaviour and build[] a rights culture'.[18] But the report says nothing about how this human rights culture was to emerge; it seems to have been an article of faith that the creation of the human rights dialogue will contribute more generally to a culture of human rights consciousness, and of respect for and observance of human rights.

When Stanhope introduced the Human Rights Bill into the ACT Legislative Assembly he had little to say about a human rights culture, and much to say about the Human Rights Bill.[19] He needed to sell the idea of a human rights law,[20] repeatedly referring to the Legislative Assembly's law-making role,[21] and only twice to the *HRA*'s having an effect outside the Assembly: the Supreme Court's 'declaration of incompatibility' power,[22] and government departments' annual reporting obligation.[23] The introduction of the Bill suggests that the legislators did not have uppermost in their minds, or at all, the Committee's view that 'a bill of rights cannot of itself create a human rights culture'.[24]

III. What We Know About Activity Under the HRA

Much has been reported on quantitative indicators, 'the more visible (albeit fairly narrow)'[25] examples of ACT human rights activity that tell us what the legislature, executive and judiciary have done under the *HRA*.

A. Legislature

In the first year of the *HRA*, the ACT Legislative Assembly was reported to have engaged in an 'intense "pre-enactment dialogue" prior to the passing of a Bill' – 'nearly a hundred bills were assessed for human rights compatibility' – and the Legal Affairs Committee experienced 'a new focus and workload'.[26] Research shows that over the next four years the *HRA* was increasingly referred to in debates in the Legislative Assembly,[27] was the basis of serious debate regarding a range of policy issues,[28] and continued to be a standard against which the Standing Committee on Legal Affairs scrutinised and reported on bills.

[17] Ibid, 81.
[18] Ibid, 82.
[19] Legislative Assembly for the ACT: 2003 Week 12 Hansard (18 November), 4244–4250.
[20] The whole of the Human Rights Bill was opposed by Opposition party in the Assembly; see, eg, Legislative Assembly for the ACT, Hansard, 2 March 2004, 442–465, 501–586.
[21] Legislative Assembly for the ACT, Hansard, 18 November 2003, 4245–4249.
[22] Ibid, 4248.
[23] Ibid, 4249.
[24] *Towards an ACT Human Rights Act*, above n 3, 37.
[25] Jeremy Gans, 'The Impact of the *Human Rights Act 2004* (ACT) on Other Australian Jurisdictions', speech to the conference *Ten Years of the ACT Human Rights Act Continuing the Dialogue* 10th Anniversary of the Human Rights Act, Australian National University, 1 July 2014, 4.
[26] Department of Justice and Community Safety, *Human Rights Act 2004 Twelve-Month Review – Report*, Department of Justice and Community Safety, Canberra, June 2006, 15.
[27] ACT Human Rights Act Research Project, *The Human Rights Act 2004 (Act): The First Five Years of Operation, A Report to the Act Department of Justice and Community Safety*, The Australian National University, May 2009, 27.
[28] Ibid, 28.

This last mechanism, the scrutiny reports, does suggest a degree of human rights awareness on the part of the government: some bills were amended in light of criticisms in the Committee's reports, and some of the Committee's comments on bills gave rise to an exchange of correspondence and views between the Committee and the government.[29] The government responded to most if not all reports by the Committee[30] and even when, as was usually the case, the government defended its views on compatibility, it did so in the context of providing additional justification in response to the Committee's concerns.[31]

In its 2014–2015 Annual Report, the ACT Human Rights Commission claimed that 'Human rights legislation in the ACT has had a significant beneficial impact',[32] citing regular human rights arguments in debates on new laws in the Legislative Assembly, routine reference in Legislative Assembly debates to reports of the Scrutiny of Bills Committee, the proposing of amendments to bills in response to Committee comments, and frequent consultation with the Commission in the early stages of policy and law development.

There is here a suggestion of a degree of stagnation in human rights engagement on the part of the government's engagement, as if the levels that were reached were sufficient. For example, the government rejected a recommendation by the Five Year review that the Scrutiny Committee be required to report on subordinate legislation,[33] saying that such an amendment was unnecessary and could be burdensome,[34] and merely gave 'in-principle' support to a recommendation – already made in the Twelve-Month review[35] – that 'a statement of reasons should be included with each compatibility statement'.[36] In 2015 Costello and Thilagaratnam reported 'signs that the HR Act has made a genuine cultural difference to the way the ACT Legislative Assembly goes about its work', citing frequent references in parliamentary debates to the Act and to scrutiny reports, and noting that 'close to 100 government amendments in relation to 7 bills were moved, ostensibly in response to comments made by the [scrutiny] Committee'.[37] Costello and Thilagaratnam speculate that this human rights-related activity in the Legislative Assembly 'may be a reflection of the robust policy process human rights legislation imposes on the executive and legislature',[38] but without any formal evaluation mechanism, that is really all that is available to us, speculation and inference from conduct.

B. Judiciary

The dialogue model in the ACT is intended to limit the role of the courts, preserving for the legislature the final say in human rights policy.[39] The *HRA* does not give courts in the ACT

[29] Ibid, 31.
[30] Ibid, 30.
[31] Ibid, 31.
[32] ACT Human Rights Commission, *Annual Report 2014–2015*, Australian Capital Territory, Canberra, 11.
[33] *The First Five Years*, above n 26, 33.
[34] Ibid, 22–23; compare *Subordinate Legislation Act 1994* (Vic), s 21(1)(ha), *Human Rights Act 2019* (Qld), s 41.
[35] *Twelve-Month Review*, above n 26, 22.
[36] *The First Five Years*, above n 27, 37.
[37] Sean Costello and Renuka Thilagaratnam, 'Reinvigorating the human rights dialogue', (2015) 128 Precedent 16, 16; and see *Annual Report 2014–2015*, above n 31, 11.
[38] Costello and Thilagaratnam, above n 37, 17.
[39] This model and its implications are considered by Scott Stephenson, in ch 20.

the power, for example, to invalidate legislation for want of human rights compatibility.[40] The interpretive power in section 30 of the *HRA* could, however, be used in a way that 'sits a long way towards the "law-making" end of the spectrum',[41] and the later-enacted right of action against public authorities[42] has the potential to render government agencies accountable to the courts rather than the legislature. But, as it happens, the ACT courts have made little use of the *HRA*, and litigants have afforded the courts few opportunities.

The Twelve-Month review observed that 'the courts and tribunals have arguably been the least affected by the HRA'. But of course more time was needed. Many cases decided in that period would have commenced before the *HRA* did, and for those cases that did engage the Act there would have been a degree of caution in pleading and arguing human rights principles for the first time in any Australian court.

After the first twelve months numbers picked up, even if real impact did not. In the first five and half years of the *HRA* to 2010 the Act was 'mentioned' in at least 122 decisions in ACT courts and tribunals, in 86 in the ACT Supreme Court and in 12 in the Court of Appeal.[43] But Watchirs and McKinnon report that the *HRA* was generally 'applied conservatively ... and ... tended to reinforce important common law principles, rather than significantly expanding them'.[44] Watchirs and McKinnon call this a 'slow start', and opine that it reflected in part 'the lack of considered human rights arguments being made by the ACT legal profession'.[45]

After ten years, the ACT Chief Justice Helen Murrell noted a declining rate of reliance on the *HRA* in the Supreme Court and said that, in her view 'the HRA has had little direct impact on the outcome of cases despite the significant number of cases in which the HRA has been mentioned, there are very few in which it has made a difference to the outcome'.[46] The Chief Justice echoed Watchirs and McKinnon from almost ten years earlier, suggesting that 'the amount of jurisprudence is partly dependent on the willingness of counsel to raise the *HRA*'.[47]

Nothing has happened in the Court's jurisprudence to change the views of Watchirs and McKinnon that the Court's approach to the *HRA* is conservative, and of Chief Justice Murrell that the *HRA* has had little direct impact on the outcome of cases. Perhaps the limited and largely unremarkable jurisprudence under the *HRA* is explained by the warning of London barrister Murray Hunt in anticipation of the *Human Rights Act 1998* (UK): 'if the ... prevailing legal culture is not to act as a strong brake on progress towards [the type of human rights culture envisaged by the Human Rights Act]', then judges 'will need to be

[40] A declaration of incompatibility is expressly stated as not affecting the 'validity, operation or enforcement of the law': *HRA*, s 32(2)(a).

[41] Barry and Campbell, above n 13, 75.

[42] Part 5A of the *HRA*.

[43] Helen Watchirs and Gabrielle McKinnon, 'Five Years' Experience of the *Human Rights Act 2004* (ACT): Insights for Human Rights Protection in Australia', (2010) 33(1) *UNSW Law Journal* 136, 142, quoting cases compiled in the ANU ACT Human Rights Act Research Project case database as at 13 April 2010: Australian National University, *Australia's First Bill of Human Rights* (2010) ACTHRA Project and ACT ESCR Project http://acthra.anu.edu.au.

[44] Ibid, 146.

[45] Ibid, 147.

[46] Chief Justice Helen Murrell, 'The Judiciary and Human Rights', speech to the conference *Ten Years of the ACT Human Rights Act Continuing the Dialogue* 10th Anniversary of the Human Rights Act, Australian National University, 1 July 2014.

[47] Ibid, 23.

alert to the ability of the prevailing legal culture to absorb change by an invisible assimilative process'.[48] It may be that conventional approaches in the ACT have indeed assimilated the opportunities for adventurous judicial activity offered – or threatened[49] – by the *HRA*, and what was a slow start has become a very slow journey.

C. Executive – Bureaucracy and Agencies

Human rights issues arise most directly for people in the delivery of public services provided by the executive, such as in health, policing, incarceration, education and housing. In the National Human Rights Consultation in 2009 most community forum participants said that when their rights were not upheld it was due to systemic problems with service delivery.[50] It is appropriate, therefore, that the balance of the 'dialogue' measures in the *HRA* are directed to the executive.

But human rights in the ACT executive got off to a difficult start. McKinnon reports on opposition to the Consultative Committee's proposal 'that emerged from within the ACT Cabinet and at the most senior levels of the bureaucracy'.[51] Legal advice within government departments 'predicted serious consequences for departmental budgets and policy making', and McKinnon credits that internal opposition for a Human Rights Bill that did not include economic, social and cultural rights, did not impose a direct duty on government officials to comply with human rights, and did not provide for a specific remedy for a breach of human rights.[52] It is unsurprising that in 2006 there was 'only a thin ACT human rights culture' within government.[53] After just a year of the HRA's operation, however, the Twelve-Month review claimed that the scrutiny process had resulted in the executive showing 'a marked increase in the awareness of human rights principles',[54] engaging in 'fruitful' conversation',[55] and 'a great deal of debate and talk'.[56] Significantly, the Review addressed the issue of 'Building a Human Rights Culture' and stated, in a way that had not been done previously, culture-oriented objectives for the *HRA*, including 'to promote cultural change within the executive by ensuring that decision makers work within the internationally agreed framework of human rights standards'.[57] The Review gave examples of '[v]arious

[48] Murray Hunt, 'The Human Rights Act and Legal Culture: The Judiciary and the Legal Profession', (1999) 26 *Journal of Law and Society*, 86, 102.

[49] Barry and Campbell, above n 13, 73–78.

[50] Colmar Brunton, 'Devolved consultation report: summary', Appx C in *National Human Rights Consultation Report*, Commonwealth of Australia, 2009, 395–396.

[51] Gabrielle McKinnon, 'Giving Meaning to a 'Culture of Human Rights', Working Paper No 3, September 2006, RegNet, ANU, 6.

[52] Ibid.

[53] Charlesworth, above n 1, 301–302.

[54] *Twelve-Month Review*, above note 26, 13, citing Dr Helen Watchirs, 'Review of the first year of operation of the Human Rights Act 2004', *Democratic Audit of Australia*, June 2005, p 5.

[55] Ibid, 13, citing Elizabeth Kelly, 'Government in the ACT: a Human Rights Dialogue', paper presented to ANU Conference *Assessing the First Year of the ACT Human Rights Act*, June 2005, p 2.

[56] Ibid, 14, citing Peter Bayne, 'Pre-Enactment dialogue about proposed laws under the influence of the Human Rights Act 2004', paper presented to ANU Conference *Assessing the First Year of the ACT Human Rights Act*, June 2005, p 1.

[57] Ibid, 34.

measures … taken to promote this cultural change and awareness'; in the Department of Justice and Community Safety these measures were a toolkit for developing new legislation and policy, a strategy for auditing and reviewing existing legislation and policy, and funding for training of staff, police and judicial officers; in the Human Rights Office these measures were education, training, forums and publications; and in the community the measures were a range of conferences and forums.[58]

These measures amounted to a disparate collection of local activity; what was lacking was any overall plan for achieving change. A 'plan' for developing a human rights culture was envisaged by both the Consultative Committee in 2003[59] and the 2008 report *Creating a human rights culture within the ACT Government.*[60] But there continues to be no apparent plan. In 2019 the ACT Audit Office reported its finding that '[t]he Justice and Community Safety Directorate does not have a human rights-specific policy or action plan'.[61]

McKinnon argues that an essential aim of the dialogue model is 'to foster a "culture of human rights" within the executive', but that 'the content of such a culture is generally left implicit, or is seen as self evident'.[62] She proposes a 'tentative definition for a human rights culture within the executive government':[63]

> A pattern of assumptions shared by government officers, and taught to new officers; that human rights must be considered and respected in carrying out all government functions and in developing new law and policy.

McKinnon suggests there is as an evaluation tool, a 'hierarchy of development of a human rights culture within the executive': awareness, engagement, and commitment.[64] Although 'a survey of individual attitudes is likely to provide a useful reflection of shared cultural norms',[65] McKinnon warns that 'such results may not tell the full story[66]', and says that 'to provide a richer assessment it may also be useful to monitor other more tangible evidence of culture'.[67] McKinnon and her colleagues carried out her proposed 'survey of individual attitudes' in 2006–2008, interviewing officers from eleven government departments and agencies 'to test the predictions about the effect of the *HRA* on work practices and culture within the government'.[68] Their report formed part of a larger report on 'the first five years' of the *HRA*.[69]

[58] Ibid, 34–35.

[59] *Towards an ACT Human Rights Act*, above n 2, 37.

[60] ACT Human Rights Act Research Project, *Creating a human rights culture within the ACT government: Report on interview research assessing the impact of the* Human Rights Act 2004 *on the ACT Public Service*, ANU, October 2008, 3.

[61] ACT Audit Office, ACT Auditor–General's Report: Recognition and Implementation of Obligations under the Human Rights Act 2004, Report No 2/2019, Australian Capital Territory, Canberra 2019, 42.

[62] McKinnon, above n 51, 1.

[63] Ibid, 4; this definition was later adopted in research into culture in the ACT bureaucracy: see pp 204–5 below.

[64] Ibid, 4–6.

[65] Ibid, 6.

[66] See, eg, Cooper MD, Towards a definition of Safety Culture, Safety Science 36 (2000) 111–136, who suggests that issues related to situational constraints and the actual behaviour of people are as important as their attitudes and beliefs in measuring safety culture.

[67] McKinnon, above n 51, 6.

[68] *Creating a human rights culture*, above n 60, 2.

[69] *The First Five Years*, above n 27.

On the question of awareness, interviews indicated that 'most ACT government officers across all roles and areas of government have a general awareness of the *HRA*'.[70] However, only a third had received any training on the *HRA* before or in the four years after its introduction,[71] and there was confusion about who was responsible for the training.[72]

Reporting 'across all roles and areas of government' is of limited use. Keeping in mind the 'service' dimension of human rights, it is important to understand where in the bureaucracy a human rights culture is developing. McKinnon was concerned that the Act was 'having less impact in developing a human rights culture in those areas of government that do not have direct involvement in the legislative process, but are responsible for decision making and the application of laws'.[73] As McKinnon had feared, the research for the *Creating a human rights culture* report showed a clear divide in human rights awareness and understanding between those of the executive engaged in the institutional dialogue, and those engaged in service provision.

Perception among officers of the relevance of the *HRA* to their work was higher among those 'who were involved in the development or scrutiny of legislation'.[74] On the other hand, '[o]fficers who were not directly involved in legislative development perceived the *HRA* to be less relevant to their work, and the *HRA* did not appear to have led to any real changes in their approach or decision-making'.[75] Even though the *HRA* obliges anyone 'working out' the meaning of a Territory law to interpret the law to be consistent with human rights,[76] the interviewees who were involved in 'the front-line implementation of policy' saw the *HRA* to be 'of little or no relevance'.[77] Overall, the research indicated that 'the interpretive obligation in the *HRA* has not had a significant impact on the work practices or perceptions of those involved in frontline implementation of policy and decision making'.[78]

To make progress towards a human rights culture in the ACT Government, the Five Year review made some recommendations 'as a starting point for devising a framework to measure the impact of the HRA on the protection of human rights in the ACT'.[79] The government's response to these recommendations was unenthusiastic. Outright support was given only to two of the nine recommendations: an accessible online resource, which has not eventuated,[80] and a bilateral dialogue with Victoria.[81] The government merely noted, and has not since acted on, measures that might establish a credible and continuing basis for measuring and monitoring indicators of human rights culture: a 'longitudinal study of human rights awareness in the ACT'; an extended list of issues on which public agencies must report annually; the setting by public agencies of benchmarks and progressive goals

[70] *Creating a human rights culture*, above n 60, 6.
[71] Ibid, 7.
[72] Ibid, 8.
[73] McKinnon, above n 51, 6.
[74] Ibid, 10.
[75] Ibid, 2.
[76] *HRA*, s 30.
[77] *Creating a human rights culture*, above n 60, 10.
[78] Ibid, 12.
[79] *The First Five Years*, above n 27, 44.
[80] See p 194 below.
[81] Bi-monthly phone conferences, including officers of the Commonwealth Attorney-General's Department, took place for a short period but did not continue.

for their performance; and continuing five-year reviews by the Attorney General of the operation of the *HRA*.[82]

There has been no formal review of the *HRA* since the Five Year review in 2008. After ten years, in 2015, the ACT Human Rights and Discrimination Commissioner wrote that the impact of the *HRA* on departmental practices and culture is 'difficult to assess, due in part to the absence of any ongoing or systematic initiative by the Government to measure the HR Act's influence in this area'.[83] The Commissioner pointed out that there are 'few public examples to draw on, as to whether the HR Act is genuinely a starting point for Government agencies when developing policies, programmes and procedures that do not require a legislative expression'.[84]

An example that suggests a persistently weak human rights culture in the ACT bureaucracy is the long-promised Toolkit, repeatedly acknowledged by the government 'as being a key resource that would be available for ACT Government agencies'.[85] The resource would, for example, include 'a web-based information sheet, to form part of the human rights related resources maintained by the HRU … [and] to be circulated to community sector organisations … [and] private industry through, for example, the ACT Business Council'.[86] In 2014 the ACT Human Rights and Discrimination Commissioner observed that almost three years after the Toolkit was promised, 'these materials have not yet been made available'.[87] In 2019 the ACT Audit Office reported that the Toolkit 'has not been developed or made available to ACT Government agencies to assist them in recognising and implementing the requirements of the *Human Rights Act 2004*'.[88]

Not only the Toolkit is missing. In 2019 the human rights pages on the government's website[89] are in the same state as they were when the Commissioner noted in 2014 'that [the Department's] online presence is represented in the main by HR Act publications that were developed some ten years ago, and which are no longer current', and that links to resources have not been updated. It is hard not to wonder at the priorities and culture of even a very small human rights capacity within a government department, when the public profile of human rights is so neglected.

IV. Other Indicators

McKinnon makes the point that a survey of individual attitudes may not tell the full story, and suggests looking at 'other more tangible evidence of culture'.[90] Some such evidence is

[82] *The First Five Years*, above n 27, Recommendations 23–6.

[83] ACT Human Rights and Discrimination Commissioner, *Look Who's Talking A Snapshot Of Ten Years Of Dialogue Under The Human Rights Act* 2004 (ACT, 2014) 16.

[84] Ibid, 17.

[85] ACT Audit Office, above n 61, 32.

[86] ACT Government, *Government Response to the ANU Human Rights Research Project Report, The Human Rights Act 2004 (ACT): The First Five Years of Operation* (2009), March 2012, 28–31.

[87] *Look Who's Talking*, above n 87, 19.

[88] ACT Audit Office, above n 61, 32.

[89] www.justice.act.gov.au/protection_of_rights/human_rights_act.

[90] McKinnon, above n 51, 6.

the human rights accountability of public agencies, public agencies' annual reports, the conduct of human rights audits, and education of the executive.

A. Public Agencies' Accountability to the Courts

There is an accountability mechanism in the *HRA* that obliges public authorities to act and to make decisions, consistently with human rights, and that exposes them to accountability in the courts.[91] But public authorities have scarcely been held to account at all for non-compliance with the *HRA*. At the time of writing, in over 10 years of operation, Part 5A of the *HRA* has been dealt with substantively in only a few cases, and no reliance on it has been successful. Claims under Part 5A have commonly been dismissed on technical grounds.[92]

In its 2014–2015 Annual Report, the ACT Human Rights Commission called for amendments that would allow individuals to make Part 5A claims in the simpler, cheaper and easier jurisdiction of the ACT Civil and Administrative Tribunal (ACAT). The government, however, rejected such calls[93] and, as a result, access to the means of holding public authorities accountable for their human rights compliance remains limited, thereby limiting the extent to which this mechanism can operate to develop a human rights culture.

B. Annual Reports of Public Agencies

The *Annual Reports (Government Agencies) Act 2004* (ACT) obliges an administrative unit to 'include a statement describing the measures taken by the administrative unit during the reporting year to respect, protect and promote human rights'.[94] Presumably the thinking is that if a public authority has to publish the steps it has taken to promote awareness of, engagement with, and commitment to human rights, it will indeed take those steps. But reliance on annual reports for this purpose may be misplaced. Research has found 'a relatively low level of usage of public sector annual reports',[95] and it seems that while some policy makers are placing 'increased reliance on the annual report … to discharge their accountability obligations to a diverse group of stakeholders', others discount the importance of annual reporting, arguing that 'in spite of the considerable resources consumed to produce these reports there is no public interest in them'.[96]

[91] *HRA*, Pt 5A.

[92] *Strano v Australian Capital Territory* [2016] ACTSC 4; *Chaloner & Anor. v Australian Capital Territory* [2013] ACTSC 269; *Concerned Citizens of Canberra v Chief Planning Executive* [2014] ACTSC 165; *Stewart v Wreck Bay Aboriginal Community Council* [2014] ACTSC 334; *Ezekiel-Hart v Reis* [2018] ACTSC 264; *Islam v Director-General, Justice and Community Safety Directorate* [2015] ACTCA 60; *Director of Public Prosecutions v Close and Close* [2015] ACTSC 10; *Miles v Director-General of the Justice and Community Safety Directorate* [2016] ACTSC 70; *Director of Public Prosecutions v Close and Close* [2015] ACTSC 10; *C v Chief Psychiatrist and anor* [2011] ACTSC 195; *ACT Director of Public Prosecutions v Nikro* [2017] ACTSC; *R v Davis* [2015] ACTSC 101.

[93] *Look Who's Talking*, above n 83, 7.

[94] *Annual Reports (Government Agencies) Act 2004* (ACT), s 6(2).

[95] Janet Lee 'Preparing Performance Information In The Public Sector: An Australian Perspective' (2008) 24(2) *Financial Accountability & Management* 117, 125.

[96] Christine Ryan and Janet Mack, (2007) 20 (2) 'Is there an audience for public sector annual reports: Australian evidence?', *International Journal of Public Sector Management* 134.

Research suggests that, in annual reports, regulators 'need to differentiate content prescription depending on entity type … [and] tailor the information provided to stakeholders'.[97] For human rights reporting, for example, an ACT public authority might reflect on who its audience is, what story needs to be told, and how is that best conveyed, rather than simply providing quantitative data generated by its own activity.

The question of what story is told, and how it is best told, is a vexing one for annual reporting: there are 'difficulties in developing appropriate indicators, such as specifying relevant outcomes, measuring quality and impact, multiple objectives confronted by governments and slow progress in developing effectiveness measures'[98] and, as the discussion below shows, these difficulties are especially acute for human rights reporting. Lee warns that 'an emphasis on quantitative performance information can result in insignificant factors being elevated to a primary focus while crucial variables expressed in qualitative terms may be ignored'.[99]

As well as the statutory obligations on administrative units in their annual reporting,[100] the Minister must make a direction about annual reports, with which an annual report must comply. The directions first suggested,[101] then required[102] matters for reporting: '… implementation strategies and progress in incorporating human rights standards into their operations', with reference to education and training of staff, internal dissemination of information to agency staff, liaison with the Bill of Rights Unit, and human rights audits of existing legislation. The direction became more specific in 2007 and thereafter but covered the same essential points, adding to the list any human rights cases before courts or tribunals.[103] In 2017–18 the direction, in the same terms, was made not to 'agencies' but to the Directorates, each of which would report for the agencies for which it is responsible,[104] which means that eleven public sector bodies now provide information to the Justice and Community Safety Directorate for inclusion in its report.[105]

[97] Ibid, 143.

[98] Lee, above n 95, 124.

[99] Ibid, 125, quoting J. Guthrie and L.D. Parker 'Managerialism and Marketisation in Financial Management Change in Australia', in O. Olson, J. Guthrie and C. Humphrey (eds.), *Global Warning! Debating International Developments in New Public Financial Management* (Cappelen Akademisk Forlag as, Oslo, 1998) 49, 60.

[100] *Annual Reports (Government Agencies) Act 2004* (ACT), s 6(2).

[101] Australian Capital Territory Annual Reports (Government Agencies), Notice 2005, Notifiable instrument NI2005-237.

[102] Australian Capital Territory Annual Reports (Government Agencies), Notice 2006, Notifiable instrument NI2006-279.

[103] Australian Capital Territory Annual Reports (Government Agencies), Notice 2007, Notifiable instrument NI2007-206; Australian Capital Territory Annual Reports (Government Agencies), Notice 2008 (No 1), Notifiable instrument NI2008-225; Australian Capital Territory Annual Reports (Government Agencies), Notice 2009 (No 1), Notifiable instrument NI2009-283; Australian Capital Territory Annual Reports (Government Agencies), Notice 2010 (No 1), Notifiable instrument NI2010-308; Australian Capital Territory Annual Reports (Government Agencies), Notice 2011 (No 1), Notifiable instrument NI2011-311; Australian Capital Territory Annual Reports (Government Agencies), Notice 2012 (No 1), Notifiable instrument NI2012-293; Australian Capital Territory Annual Reports (Government Agencies), Notice 2013, Notifiable instrument NI2013-243; Australian Capital Territory Annual Reports (Government Agencies), Notice 2014, Notifiable instrument NI2014-319.

[104] Australian Capital Territory Annual Reports (Government Agencies), Notice 2015, Notifiable instrument NI2015-207; Australian Capital Territory Annual Reports (Government Agencies), Notice 2017, Notifiable instrument NI2017–280.

[105] ACT Audit Office, above note 61, 36.

There was no change to the terms of the direction in response to a recommendation of the Five Year review in 2009 that agencies should be strongly encouraged to use the annual reporting framework to initiate a process for benchmarking their performance and setting progressive goals with the view to continuous improvement.[106]

In 2014 the ACT Human Rights Commission commented that 'Directorates have … for most part continued to provide only perfunctory accounts of their efforts to implement the HR Act in their respective annual reports, despite the promulgation of directions requiring more detailed information'.[107] This criticism is mild compared to the 2019 report of the ACT Audit Office, which examined ACT public agencies' annual reporting of 'implementation strategies and progress in incorporating human rights standards into their operations', and found that:

> [t]he quality and comprehensiveness of this reporting are varied. This results in difficulty in assessing what progress, if any, is being achieved by ACT Government agencies in meeting their human rights obligations and in the development of a human rights culture in ACT Government agencies.[108]

The ACT Audit Office recommends that future Annual Report Directions 'specify minimum standards and formats' for reporting human rights activities, and that they 'identify additional, meaningful information required to be reported by agencies that allows for an assessment of the development of a human rights culture in each agency'.

On 'the strategic and organisational mechanisms within the Justice and Community Safety Directorate and the Community Services Directorate to support the development of a human rights culture', the ACT Audit Office is highly critical, saying there is no human rights-specific policy or action plan; policies and documents inconsistently reference human rights and the relevance of human rights; no explanation is given for what it means to 'embed human rights in the legal system, executive and community'; no guidance is provided on the relevance of human rights to the Directorate's activities; and overall there is reliance on documents that 'are not incompatible with a human rights culture'.[109]

This ACT Audit Office report is an indictment of the commitment of the ACT executive to developing and promoting a human rights culture. Perhaps a report from the ACT Audit Office will move the government to act where previous independent, academic, reviews have failed.

C. Human Rights Audits

The activities of the ACT Human Rights Commission demonstrate the effectiveness of a formal audit of a public agency's human rights activity. Barry and Campbell – making their argument that 'dialogue' with the judiciary is not necessary – point out that the ACT Human Rights Commission's 2005 human rights audit of the Quamby juvenile detention facility[110]

[106] *The First Five Years*, above n 27, 46.
[107] *Look Who's Talking*, above n 61, 16–17.
[108] ACT Audit Office, above n 63, 23.
[109] Ibid, 42.
[110] ACT Human Rights Commission, *Human Rights Audit of Quamby Youth Detention Centre*, 2005.

'resulted in a number of reforms which improved human rights practices at the Centre'.[111] Other Commission audits are on the treatment of women at the Alexander Maconochie Centre,[112] on the Bimberi Youth Justice Centre,[113] and on the Operation of ACT Correctional Facilities under corrections legislation.[114]

D. Education of the Executive

The Chief Minister and champion of the *HRA*, John Stanhope, outlined to the Legislative Assembly measures proposed in the ACT for educating public officials, making information available online for the public and departmental staff, conducting judicial education, and empowering the Human Rights Commissioner to engage in community education.[115] This resolve was borne out to an extent in the examples cited in the Twelve-Month review of initiatives of the Department of Justice and Community Safety and the Human Rights Office,[116] but momentum slowed.

In relation to government agencies, the Annual Report Directives do not expect any report on their conduct of human rights education in the community; they are concerned only with 'education and training of agency staff', and then only with on 'the number of training sessions … a description of the staff who attended … [and] who provided the training'.[117] In her ten year 'snapshot' of progress under the *HRA* the ACT Human Rights and Discrimination Commissioner observed on 'the continued lack of systematic education inside the bureaucracy',[118] to which I would add the bureaucracy's reliance only on quantitative indicators, with no measurement of enhanced understanding and implementation of human rights principles.

V. Into the Community

As the ACT Human Rights Commissioner's annual report, discussed below, makes clear, taking human rights into the community requires resources, and resources are scarce, for this purpose at least, in the ACT. With that in mind, two matters I discuss here, the symbolic value of the *HRA* and voluntary accountability under the *HRA*, are notable for not actually being a cost to the state.

[111] Barry and Campbell, above n 13, 81, citing Helen Watchirs 'The ACT Human Rights Act 2004: An Overview of its Operation.' (2007) 43 *Just Policy* 11, 13.

[112] ACT Human Rights and Discrimination Commissioner, *Human Rights Audit on the Conditions of Detention of Women at the Alexander Maconochie Centre*, ACT Human Rights Commission, April 2014.

[113] ACT Human Rights Commission, *The ACT Youth Justice System: A Report to the ACT Legislative Assembly*, 2011.

[114] ACT Human Rights Commission, *Human Rights Audit on the Operation of ACT Correctional Facilities under Corrections Legislation*, July 2007.

[115] Legislative Assembly for the ACT, Hansard, 2 March 2004, 532.

[116] *Twelve-Month Review*, above n 26, 34–35.

[117] See pp 195–6 above.

[118] *Look Who's Talking*, above n 83, 19.

A. The Symbolic Value of the *HRA*

There are consistent claims for the 'symbolic value' of the *HRA*,[119] even to the extent that it 'resembles the *Magna Carta*.'[120] But beyond the rhetoric, we do not know what symbolic force there actually is in the *HRA*, or what any such symbolic force does to advance a human rights culture.

Law can proclaim and maintain symbols – 'values, ideals and ways of thinking about government and society – to which individuals can adhere',[121] and can be intentionally instrumental, designed to achieve a particular goal.[122] Although law can be both at once – 'symbolic legislation is not the antithesis to instrumental legislation'[123] – the *HRA* is instrumental only to a limited degree, principally through the later addition of Part 5A.[124] It can fairly be said of the *HRA* that it is 'not merely a set of rules, but it is also a symbol for something higher, more valuable. It gives expression to values which are fundamental for the community, for example human dignity [and] equality'.[125] But whether symbolic law such as the *HRA* can communicate values to the community without the need for rule enforcement is the subject of unresolved debate. Perhaps the most that can be said is that symbolic legislation 'communicates … values to its members, expecting that they will take these values as guidelines.'[126]

B. Community Human Rights Education

From the outset reliance was placed on 'education' as a means of achieving the aims of the *HRA*. Quite apart from education for 'those who administer government programmes',[127] the Consultative Committee recommended both a 'community-wide education campaign' to promote the 'cultural and symbolic value' of such a law,[128] and 'a broad, ongoing education programme that brings [that law] and its implications to the attention of the public sector and the ACT community'.[129] This required 'a commitment to a long-term programme of community education and awareness-raising',[130] in the classrooms and in the community.[131]

[119] See, eg, *Towards an ACT Human Rights Act*, above n 2, Recommendation 2, 42; *The First Five Years*, above n 27, 71; Murrell, above n 46, 22.

[120] The Honourable Justice Margaret McMurdo AC President, Court of Appeal, Supreme Court of Queensland 'A Human Rights Act for Queensland?', University of the Sunshine Coast Inaugural Law Oration, 23 September 2015.

[121] Roger Cottrell, *The Sociology of Law*, Butterworths, London 1984, 108, quoting TW Arnold, *The Symbols of Government*, Harcourt and Brace, New York, (1935) 1962.

[122] See Stephen Bottomley and Simon Bronitt, *Law in Context* 4th edn (Annandale, Federation Press, 2012) 310–311.

[123] Bart van Klink, 'Symbolic Legislation: An Essentially Political Concept', in Bart van Klink, Britta van Beers and Lonneke Poort, (eds.), *Symbolic Legislation Theory and Developments in Biolaw* (Cham, Springer Publishing, 2016) 19–35, 23.

[124] See p 195 above.

[125] van Klink above n 123, 24.

[126] Ibid, 27.

[127] *Towards an ACT Human Rights Act*, above n 2, 37.

[128] Ibid, Recommendation 2, 42.

[129] Ibid, Recommendation 6, 60.

[130] Ibid, 37.

[131] Ibid.

It is apparent that from the beginning the idea of 'education' had two quite different parts to it: human rights education in the community, and human rights education within the public sector and among the judiciary. In the area of community education there seem to be two approaches: education about human rights generally, and promoting public awareness of the operation of the *HRA*, which is seen as having educative potential in itself.[132]

Human rights education for the community is the province of the ACT Human Rights Commission.[133] 2013 was a bad year for human rights education in the ACT: 'on-going resource constraints' saw the Commission not fill its Community Engagement Officer position, discontinue its on-line quarterly newsletter, discontinue the ACT Human Rights Commission Art Award, cease training on the *Health Records (Privacy & Access) Act 1997*, and reduce the provision of scheduled and tailored training.[134] The ACT Human Rights Commissioner and her staff provided only '10 sessions of formal training to government, private sector and broader community'.[135] They spoke at a number of public forums, and in the news media, and the Commission maintained a public presence through a range of community education and engagement activities such as speeches and presentations; consultation activities with children and young people; outreach; launches; and forums, stalls and public events. That type and level of community human rights engagement has persisted.[136]

Human rights education is a well-established, well-developed global discipline.[137] A definition of human rights education is:[138]

> … education, training, awareness raising, information, practices and activities which aim, by quipping learners with knowledge, skills and understanding and developing their attitudes and behaviour, to empower learners to contribute to the building and defence of universal human rights in society with a views to the promotion and protection of human rights and fundamental freedoms.

This is not an elegant definition, but it conveys some of the ambition and scope of what human rights education strives for. For want of resources, the activities of the ACT Human Rights Commission fall well short of this ambition and scope, and of the 'broad, ongoing education programme', and 'long-term programme of community education and awareness-raising' in the classrooms and in the community that the Consultative Committee envisaged.

[132] Ibid, 58.

[133] *Human Rights Commission Act 2005* (ACT), s 27(2)(a).

[134] ACT Human Rights Commission, *Annual Report 2012–2013*, Australian Capital Territory, Canberra, 65.

[135] Ibid, 48, 50.

[136] See, eg, ACT Human Rights Commission, *Annual Report 2017–2018*, Australian Capital Territory, Canberra, 18.

[137] See, eg, Monisha Bajaj (ed), *Human Rights Education: Theory, Research, Praxis* (Philadelphia, University of Pennsylvania Press, 2017); Michalinos Zembylas, André Keet (eds), *Critical Human Rights, Citizenship, and Democracy Education: Entanglements and Regenerations* (London, Bloomsbury Publishing, 2018); *International Journal of Human Rights Education*, University of San Francisco.

[138] André Keet, 'Crisis and Critique: Critical Theories and the renewal of Citizenship, Democracy and Human rights Education, in Michalinos Zembylas, André Keet (eds), *Critical Human Rights, Citizenship, and Democracy Education: Entanglements and Regenerations* (London, Bloomsbury Publishing, 2018) 17–34, 28, quoting David Kerr, *The Council of Europe Charter on Education for Democratic Citizenship and Human Rights Education (EDC/HRE): and its Implementation* Citizenship Foundation/University of Bristol, December 2013.

C. Non-government Audits

The mechanism in the *HRA* that exposes public authorities to accountability in the courts for human rights compliance also enables private entities to opt in to such accountability.[139] An entity that is not a public authority 'may choose to be subject to obligations of public authorities' and request the Minister to make a declaration (a notifiable instrument) to that effect.[140]

The take-up for volunteering into the public authorities' human rights regime has been very slow, almost insignificant.[141] Despite the ACT Attorney General's 'calling on both community and commercial groups in Canberra to "opt in"',[142] only seven entities have made the election, all of them operating not-for-profit: Companion House Inc,[143] Women's Legal Centre (ACT and Region) Inc,[144] Centre for Australian Ethical Research,[145] Relationships Australia Canberra and Region Inc,[146] Amnesty International Australia Inc,[147] ACT Disability, Aged and Carer Advocacy Service Inc (ADACAS),[148] and Advocacy for Inclusion Inc.[149]

The director of Companion House explained the gesture, saying that opting in 'was an important way for Companion House to publicly express our commitment to the human rights principles that are the foundation of our work'.[150] But opting in is not a step to be taken lightly. Prudence requires an entity to be prepared for the accountability to which they will be subject, so that Women's Legal Centre, for example, reported that opting in to the *HRA* 'was a large task as the Centre needed to ensure all of its policies and procedures were human rights compliant', and that it engaged a human rights expert to assist.[151]

No commercial entities have opted in. It is not hard to see human rights principles in commercial activity; the Australian Human Right Commission, for example, lists labour rights, rights of indigenous peoples, and rights to life, security, health, housing and an adequate standard of living.[152] But the fact that businesses have not opted in suggests that they neither see human rights principles as the foundation of their work, nor see the need to be, or to show that they are, human rights compliant, further indicating a low level of 'human rights culture' in the broader ACT community.

[139] *HRA*, Pt 5A; see p 195 above.

[140] *HRA*, s 40D.

[141] Mr Bill Stefaniak, a vocal opponent of the *HRA* (see, eg, *Legislative Assembly for the ACT: 2004 Week 2 Hansard (2 March)*, 443–452), was presumably being sardonic when he referred to 'the honour of being included in 40D' in *Thornthwaite and Commissioner for Social Housing* [2012] ACAT 11, [18].

[142] Media Release: *Attorney General calls for ACT business industry to embrace human rights*, 21 June 2010.

[143] *Human Rights (Private Entity) Declaration* 2009, Notifiable instrument NI2009-239.

[144] *Human Rights (Private Entity) Declaration* 2010 (No 1), Notifiable instrument NI2010-68.

[145] *Human Rights (Private Entity) Declaration* 2010 (No 2), Notifiable instrument NI2010-59.

[146] *Human Rights (Private Entity) Declaration* 2012, Notifiable instrument NI2012-230.

[147] *Human Rights (Private Entity) Declaration* 2012 (No 2), Notifiable instrument NI2012-276.

[148] *Human Rights (Private Entity) Declaration* 2012 (No 3), Notifiable instrument NI2012-621.

[149] *Human Rights (Private Entity) Declaration* 2013, Notifiable instrument NI2013-531.

[150] Media Release, above n 144; and see research on 'The reasons for 'opting-in' in Louis Schetzer, *Human Rights and the Hollowed-Out State: How Human Rights Charters Apply to Contracted-Out Public Services*, unpublished PhD thesis, University of New South Wales Faculty of Law, 2018, ch 11, available at www.unsworks.unsw.edu.au.

[151] Women's Legal Centre (ACT and Region) Inc, *Annual Report 2009–2010*, 7.

[152] Australian Human Right Commission, *Fact Sheet: Integrating human rights into Australian business practice*, November 2014.

VI. Measuring Cultural Change

While we know what has been happening under the *HRA*, we know very little about what effect that activity has had in bringing about changes in public attitudes and behaviour. Gibson cautions that '[i]nstitutions and cultures are two separate entities, and the question of whether one reinforces and supports the other is a vital empirical question'.[153]

Tracking the operation of the *HRA* in its institutional context – the legislature, courts and executive – is fairly straightforward, as the largely descriptive and quantitative accounts above show, but tracking the development in the ACT of a culture of human rights consciousness is much more difficult. Yet it is exactly that culture that was said by the Consultative Committee to represent 'much of the real value of a bill of rights'.

The search for indicators of human rights progress, as for indicators of social progress generally, is both longstanding and much debated.[154] For some time the template has been provided by the United Nations High Commissioner for Human Rights.[155] But there has been very little by way of human rights measurement in Australia. As part of the development of Australia's 2012 National Human Rights Action Plan,[156] the then government conducted what it called a 'Baseline Study',[157] to 'survey the status of human rights in Australia … [and] help with identifying priority areas for the Action Plan'.[158] Although the Plan had 355 actions, policies and programmes 'to improve human rights' in Australia, it lacked any overarching evaluative mechanism, and offered no means of measuring the hoped-for 'improvement' apart from some quantitative measures (eg, '40 per cent representation of both women and men on Australian Government Boards[159]). I do not agree with Zifcak and King that 'The Plan provides a benchmark against which future progress with human rights may fairly be assessed';[160] all that could be said if the Plan were implemented is that certain actions, policies and programmes had happened; to what effect would remain unknown.

[153] James Gibson, 'Truth, Reconciliation, and the Creation of a Human Rights Culture in South Africa' (2004) 38 *Law & Society Review* 5, 8.

[154] See, eg, David McGrogan, 'Human Rights Indicators and the Sovereignty of Technique' (2016) 27(2) *European Journal of International Law*, 385, 390; Sally Engle Merry, 'The Problem of Human Rights Indicators', unpublished, 2012, www.law.uvic.ca/demcon/2012%20readings/Chapter%203%20Problem%20of%20HR%20indicators.pdf; Sally Engle Merry, *The Seductions of Quantification: Measuring Human Rights, Gender Violence, and Sex Trafficking* (Chicago, University of Chicago Press, 2016); Ramona Vijeyarasa and Jose Miguel Bello y Villarino, 'The Indicator Fad: How Quantifiable Measurement Can Work Hand-in-Hand with Human Rights – A Response to Sally Engle Merry's the Seductions of Quantification' (2018) 50(3) *New York University Journal of International Law and Politics*, 985; and more generally Kevin Davis, Benedict Kingsbury and Sally Engle Merry, 'Introduction: The Local-Global Life of Indicators: Law, Power and Resistance', and David Nelken, 'Conclusion: Contesting Global Indicators', in Sally Engle Merry, Kevin Davis, and Benedict Kingsbury, *The Quiet Power of Indicators: Measuring Governance, Corruption, and Rule of Law* (Cambridge, Cambridge University Press, 2015).

[155] Office of the United Nations High Commissioner for Human Rights, *Human rights indicators: A guide to measurement and implementation*. Geneva, 2012; see, eg, Equality and Human Rights Commission, *Measurement Framework for Equality and Human Rights* (Manchester, 2017); Jean Candler, Holly Holder, Sanchita Hosali, Anne Maree Payne, Tiffany Tsang and Polly Vizard, *Human Rights Measurement Framework: Prototype panels, indicator set and evidence base* (Manchester, 2011).

[156] *Australia's National Human Rights Action Plan 2012*, Commonwealth of Australia, 2012; this, Australia's most recent Plan, is noted by the United Nations to be 'no longer current': www.ohchr.org/en/issues/plansactions/pages/plansofactionindex.aspx.

[157] *National Human Rights Action Plan Baseline Study*, Commonwealth of Australia 2011.

[158] Ibid, 1.

[159] Ibid, 38.

[160] Spencer Zifcak and Alison King, *Human Rights: For and Against*, (The Australian Collaboration, 2013) 72.

More promising is the activity in Victoria related to the *Charter of Rights and Responsibilities.*[161] The 2011 review of the Charter offered an account of 'benefits' that the Charter offered,[162] providing anecdotal reports of, for example, 'increased focus on human rights' by parliamentary counsel,[163] 'greater emphasis on human rights issues and accountability throughout Victoria Police',[164] a 'substantive effect on the way in which services are delivered' in schools, among police, and in prisons,[165] and alteration of service provision by community sector organisations 'to better protect the rights of clients'.[166] These examples suggest indicators that are not mere quantitative measures, but give a sense of what is actually changing in public awareness, understanding and behaviour. This aspect of the report did not, however, translate into recommendations for a continuing and developed approach to assessing the effects of the Charter, and recommendations in the 2015 Review[167] were of the 'action, policy and programme' type: proposing things to do, rather an evaluation of result.[168]

An assessment of law's power to effect social change looks more broadly than the legislation itself, to 'the law in practice in courts, bureaucratic settings, and other settings … not only [in] the formal language of the statute, but also how that language is implemented, interpreted, and understood by institutional actors in the state or by individuals in everyday life'.[169] More broadly still, law 'is constructed through social interaction, wherein people mobilise legal concepts and language outside the courts to negotiate conflict or to interpret their experiences'.[170] The research and related literature on assessing the 'social change effectiveness' of law is vast, most of it from the US, and much of it focussed on court decisions[171] and social movements.[172] But the *HRA*, differently from the 'rights' legislation subject to analysis in the US jurisprudence, is, largely, not justiciable. There simply are not and cannot be causes of action and decisions around which to build public campaigns for change. The social change effectiveness of the *HRA* has to come from other aspects of its operation.

[161] *Charter of Rights and Responsibilities 2006* (Vic).

[162] Scrutiny of Acts and Regulations Committee, *Review of the Charter of Human Rights and Responsibilities Act 2006*, Parliament of Victoria, Australia 2011, 131–141.

[163] Ibid, 131.

[164] Ibid, 134.

[165] Ibid, 137.

[166] Ibid, 137.

[167] Michael Brett Young, *From Commitment to Culture: The 2015 Review of the* Charter of Human Rights and Responsibilities Act 2006, State of Victoria, 2015, v–xi.

[168] See, eg, Victorian Equal Opportunity and Human Rights Commission, *2015 Charter Review Recommendations – Implementation Progress*, www.humanrightscommission.vic.gov.au/human-rights/the-charter/review.

[169] Catherine Albiston and Gwendolyn Leachman, 'Law as an Instrument of Social Change', in: James Wright (ed), *International Encyclopedia of the Social and Behavioral Sciences* 2nd edn (London, Elsevier, 2015) Vol 13, 542–549, 542.

[170] Ibid, 543.

[171] See, eg, the renowned Rosenberg/McCann debate, including Gerald Rosenberg, *The Hollow Hope: Can Courts Bring About Social Change?*' (Chicago, University of Chicago Press, 1991); Gerald Rosenberg, 'Hollow Hopes Other Aspirations: A Reply to Feeley and McCann', (1992) 17(4) *Law and Social Inquiry*, 761; Gerald Rosenberg, 'Positivism, Interpretivism, and the Study of law: McCann's *Rights at Work*', (1996) 21 *Law and Social Inquiry* 435; Gerald Rosenberg, 'Knowledge and Desire: Thinking About Courts and Social Change', in David Schultz (ed) *Leveraging the Law: Using Courts to Achieve Social Change*, Peter Lang, New York, 1998, 251–291; Michael McCann, 'Reform Litigation on Trial', in 'Symposium: The Supreme Court and Social Change' (1992) 17 *Law and Social Inquiry* 715; Michael McCann. *Rights at Work: Pay Equity Reform and the Politics of Legal Mobilization* (Chicago, University of Chicago Press, 1994); Michael McCann 'Causal versus Constitutive Explanations (or, On the Difficulty of Being so Positive) (1996) 21 *Law and Social Inquiry* 457.

[172] See, eg, McCann 1994, above n 171, and the recent work of Scott Cummings: 'Movement Lawyering', [2017] *University of Illinois Law Review*, 1645; 'Law and Social Movements: Reimagining The Progressive Canon', [2018] (3) *Wisconsin Law Review*, 441.

A. Evaluating a Human Rights Culture

Research from South Africa offers insights into how to investigate whether a 'culture respectful of human rights has been created'.[173] Gibson proposed that 'one way of looking at the question … is to examine the attitudes and values of ordinary South Africans. How much value do ordinary people attach to human rights?'.[174]

Gibson set out an indicative, inclusive list of values that might guide an empirical inquiry into attitudes toward human rights. In the South African context, his research focused on support for the rule of law,[175] while in an Australian context research could focus on, for example, rights consciousness. In an intense period over the summer of 2000–2001, Gibson surveyed over 3,700 South Africans. The sample was representative of the entire adult South African population,[176] and the research controlled a variety of variables such as class, gender, urban-rural differences, literacy and education, media consumption and interest in politics.[177] While the findings are of interest, they are particular to South Africa, and the time. It is the method that is instructive: a way of investigating whether a culture respectful of human rights has been created.

Nothing of that nature and scale has been attempted in the ACT. Early assessments of the effectiveness of the *HRA* focussed on activity and conduct. For example, to assess 'the development of a human rights culture within government agencies' the Twelve-Month Review of the *HRA* reported on what information had been disseminated and what training had been offered, rather on what people within the agencies knew and thought.[178]

Subsequently, more attention was paid to knowledge and attitudes when, for example, interviews explored the human rights sensibilities of ACT public servants[179] and, using an online instrument,[180] the ACT Human Rights Commission asked ACT public servants and the ACT public to comment on their awareness of and attitudes to human rights.[181] That was an opportunity missed: the Five-Year review recommended 'that the [ACT] Human Rights Commission's public survey on the impact of the HRA should be used as the basis for a longitudinal study of human rights awareness in the ACT',[182] but the government merely noted the recommendation, saying 'the availability of resources for this would need to be balanced against other needs of the community in a budget context'.[183]

Research I conducted with colleagues in 2009 proposed a basis for measuring cultural change over time.[184] We collected data to measure awareness, understanding and use of

173 Gibson, above n 153, 5.

174 Ibid, 9.

175 Ibid, 9–10.

176 Ibid, 14; and see 'Appendix A: The Design of the Survey' in James Gibson, *Overcoming Apartheid: Can Truth Reconcile a Divided Nation?* (Russell Sage Foundation, 2004).

177 Ibid, 27.

178 *Twelve-Month Review*, above n 26, 35.

179 *Creating a human rights culture*, above n 60, 2.

180 See www.surveymonkey.com.

181 ACT Human Rights Commission, *Submission to the National Human Rights Consultation*, 15 June 2009, Annexure 3: ACT Human Rights Commission Survey of ACT Government; Annexure 4: ACT Human Rights Commission Survey of the ACT Community.

182 *The First Five Years*, above n 27, 45.

183 ACT Government, *Government Response: ACT Human Rights Act Research Project Report, The Human Rights Act 2004 (Act): The First Five Years of Operation* (Canberra, March 2012), 32.

184 Simon Rice, Denise Meyerson and Kate Ogg 'Are we there yet? Measuring human rights sensibilities', (2014) 20(1) *Australian Human Rights Journal* 67.

human rights legislation among a relevant cohort so as to demonstrate that benchmarks can be set as a basis for evaluating the effectiveness of human rights legislation over time. We surveyed social service providers and legal practitioners because the ACT research had already focussed largely on government actors; those professionals have the opportunity to bring human rights considerations into their work; and other research[185] suggests that the effectiveness of human rights laws is partly dependent on the extent to which lawyers and civil society understand and are committed to human rights norms.

Our research indicated that 'degrees of internalisation of human rights norms can be measured',[186] and that [c]hanges can be tracked by periodically revisiting these measures, thus providing the basis for an informed assessment of the long-term success of human rights legislation'.[187] We concluded that surveys such as those we administered 'offer a way to evaluate over time the extent to which legislated rights have been internalised as community values'.[188]

VII. Conclusion

What was hoped for, if not promised, with the new Act in 2004 was 'a public sector where a "rights-respecting culture" would imbue decision-making at every level', and a 'long-term programme of community education and awareness-raising ... where young people would be first taught to regard themselves and each other as holders of rights ... reinforced and restated throughout an individual's lifetime'.[189]

Hoped for, but not planned for. We do not know if the ACT is on track for that vision, because there has been little effort at all, and certainly no sustained and systematic effort, to monitor and measure the creation and maintenance of a human rights culture. As Parts III, IV and V above show, there are plenty of quantitative indicators that report how the *HRA* is being used within the institutions of government, and in the community. It is just that there is little basis on which to infer that that activity is translating into a rights-consciousness; we do not know how far the ACT has progressed to seeing human rights imbue decision-making at every level, or how close we are to young people regarding themselves and each other as holders of these rights.

As I discuss above in Part VI, although measuring cultural change is difficult, there are precedents for such an activity and approaches to measurement have been piloted and reported on independently. But few recommendations of independent reviews of progress under the *HRA* after twelve months, five years and ten years – including a recommendation for long term monitoring of change under the *HRA* – have been accepted or acted on by the ACT Government.

As a result, the intended effect of a bold social experiment – achieving a human rights respecting culture – is unmonitored and unassessed. But there is still time, if there is the will.

[185] Charles Epp, *The Rights Revolution: Lawyers, Activists, and Supreme Courts in Comparative Perspective* (Chicago, University of Chicago Press, 1998).

[186] Rice, Meyerson and Ogg, above n 184, 92.

[187] Ibid, 93.

[188] Ibid.

[189] *Towards an ACT Human Rights Act*, above n 2, 77.

11

The Victorian Charter: A Slow Start or Fundamentally Flawed?

JANINA BOUGHEY*

Victorian lawyers reacted enthusiastically to the Supreme Court of Victoria's 2017 decision in *Certain Children v Minister for Families and Children (No 2)*;[1] saying that it reflected the *Charter of Human Rights and Responsibilities Act 2006* (Vic) ('*Charter*') finally 'gaining teeth'.[2] The case was only the second occasion, and the first in six years, on which the Supreme Court has found administrative action to be substantively incompatible with *Charter* rights and issued a remedy which prevented the government from continuing to breach those rights.[3] It also represents a clear example of the *Charter* having an effect in its own right, rather than simply adding to the arguments and remedies that would already have been available at common law.

However, the history of that case arguably reveals a less rosy story about the *Charter*'s effectiveness. The decision found to be unlawful in the *Barwon Prison Case* – to establish a youth detention facility within the grounds of a maximum security adult prison – had already been found to be unlawful by the Supreme Court and Court of Appeal.[4] The first instance decision found that the decision breached the *Charter*; the Court of Appeal had not needed to answer that question on appeal as they found it unlawful on non-*Charter* grounds. The government simply re-made the same decision correcting the procedural errors that the courts had identified, before the Supreme Court ruled it unlawful again. The Ombudsman had also previously investigated the practice of placing youths in adult prison facilities, and

* My thanks to Lisa Burton Crawford and Bruce Chen for helpful discussions and to Matthew Groves and Dan Meagher for their comments on a draft of this chapter.

[1] (2017) 52 VR 441 ('*Barwon Prison Case*').

[2] Tessa Van Duyn, 'Gaining Teeth' (2018) *Law Institute Journal*, 1 March 2018, 44. See also Bobbi Murphy, 'Victorian Supreme Court finds establishment of youth justice centre at Barwon adult prison contrary to human rights and unlawful', *Human Rights Law Centre Blog*, 11 May 2017 www.hrlc.org.au/human-rights-case-summaries/2017/6/30/victorian-supreme-court-finds-establishment-of-youth-justice-centre-at-barwon-adult-prison-contrary-to-human-rights-and-unlawful; Victorian Equal Opportunity and Human Rights Commission (VEOHRC), *Growing a Human Rights Culture: 2016 Report on the operation of the Charter of Human Rights and Responsibilities* (2017), 47–49 ('VEOHRC 2016 Report').

[3] The other case was *PJB v Melbourne Health* (2011) 39 VR 373. There have been other cases in which courts have found that the procedural limb of s 38 has been breached, resulting in the relevant decisions being remitted to the decision-maker to be remade giving 'proper consideration' to the affected person's rights.

[4] *Arthur v Minister for Families and Children* (2016) 51 VR 473; *Minister for Families and Children v Arthur* (2016) 51 VR 597.

observed that the practice breached the *Charter* and made recommendations to prevent it from occurring.[5] This history indicates that the government had fair warning that detaining young people in a facility designed for high risk adult prisoners was a breach of their human rights, but pursued the strategy anyway, without implementing sufficient measures to minimise the harm to young prisoners. This suggests that the *Charter* might not yet be gaining real traction within the Victorian Government or influencing decision-making, at least not in all cases.

A story of the *Charter*'s limited effectiveness would be no great surprise to those who have read some of the reviews of the instrument. In the first statutory review of the *Charter* conducted by the Scrutiny of Acts and Regulations Committee (SARC) in 2011, a majority of SARC recommended that large parts of the *Charter* be scrapped because they were ineffective or had adverse effects.[6] The second statutory review, conducted by Barrister Michael Brett Young in 2015, found some reasons for optimism about the *Charter*, but also found that there are major barriers to its effectiveness.[7] Crucially, many of these barriers are the same ones identified in the first review; which have not yet been addressed by Parliament despite the government's acceptance of them. The lack of action by governments from both major parties on these issues to date suggests that these important changes will not be made soon. Annual reviews by the Victorian Equal Opportunity and Human Rights Commission (VEOHRC) suggest that on many measures, the *Charter* appears to be decreasing in its effectiveness.[8] Each of these reviews will be considered further in this chapter.

The aim of this chapter is to examine how effective the *Charter* has been at achieving its aims, and whether optimism about it gaining teeth is warranted. The first section explores what the desired effects of the *Charter* are and explains the 'dialogue model' of rights that it aims to implement in Victoria. The following two sections examine evidence of the *Charter*'s impact on the substantive protection of rights in Victoria and on creating a dialogue between the branches of government and between government and the public about rights respectively.

I. What is the Desired Effect of the *Charter*?

The stated purpose of the *Charter* is 'to protect and promote human rights …'.[9] The language of 'protection and promotion' was also used in the Explanatory Memorandum.[10] This suggests that the *Charter*'s main objective is to improve the extent to which individuals enjoy rights in Victoria, and under Victorian law.[11] This objective was confirmed by the

[5] Victorian Ombudsman, *Investigation into children transferred from the youth justice system to the adult prison system* (2013).

[6] Scrutiny of Acts and Regulations Committee, Parliament of Victoria, *Review of the Charter of Human Rights and Responsibilities Act 2006* (2011) ('SARC Review').

[7] Michael Brett Young, *From Commitment to Culture: The 2015 Review of the Charter of Human Rights and Responsibilities Act 2006* (2015).

[8] See VEOHRC, Charter Reports, www.humanrightscommission.vic.gov.au/home/our-resources-and-publications/charter-reports. The details of these reports are discussed below.

[9] *Charter of Human Rights and Responsibilities Act 2006* (Vic), s 1(2).

[10] Explanatory Memorandum, Human Rights and Responsibilities Bill 2006, 1.

[11] I am assuming here that 'promote' means 'to advance the interests of' and further progress of, rather than any of its other meanings: see Oxford English Dictionary (OUP, 3rd edn, 2007).

second reading speech, in which then Attorney-General the Hon Rob Hulls explained that the *Charter* 'fulfils [the government's] commitment to provide better protection for human rights for all people in Victoria'.[12]

However, the *Charter*'s aims are not quite so singular or straightforward. The fact that the *Charter*, like many human rights charters in similar jurisdictions, includes a clause stating that rights can be subject to reasonable limits indicates that its objective is not simply to increase the level of rights protection at any cost.[13] Rather, it is to protect rights to the extent possible while allowing the government and Parliament to pursue policies and make laws that further the public interest. Furthermore, the *Charter*'s objects clause provides that its aim of protecting and promoting rights is to be achieved *by the mechanisms* set out in therein. Thus, the *method* via which the *Charter* seeks to protect rights is also relevant in explaining its desired effects.

Crucially, the Victorian *Charter* establishes a scheme for the protection of rights which attempts, insofar as is possible, to maintain the existing constitutional functions of, and relationships between, the three branches of government. As Hulls explained:

> Importantly, it is nothing like the United States Bill of Rights. This bill promotes a dialogue between the three arms of the government – the Parliament, the executive and the courts – while giving Parliament the final say. Unlike the United States, courts will not have the power to strike down legislation.[14]

The *Charter* seeks to create the 'dialogue' that Hulls described by requiring the executive to provide information and analysis to the legislature about how proposed legislation will affect rights, and by requiring scrutiny of that information by the legislature. When the executive (or, in fact, any member of Parliament) introduces a bill into Parliament, they must table a Statement of Compatibility (SoC) setting out whether and how the bill is compatible with the human rights protected by the *Charter* and if it is not compatible, 'the nature and extent of the incompatibility'.[15] A similar requirement applies to the introduction of subordinate legislation.[16] The SARC is then required to scrutinise bills and statutory rules and report to Parliament on whether they are incompatible with human rights.[17] These mechanisms are designed to 'create new and innovative forms of deliberation and interaction for law, policy and politics as they relate to human rights'.[18] Specifically, the hope was that they would: cause the government to consider rights in developing policies and legislation; improve the information available to Parliament about the rights implications of new legislation; and cause Parliament to actively consider rights in making law.[19]

The courts are also involved in rights dialogue via their functions of interpreting legislation and reviewing the lawfulness of administrative action. With respect to the first of these functions, the *Charter* expressly provides that: 'So far as it is possible to do so consistently with their purpose, all statutory provisions must be interpreted in a way that is

[12] Victoria, *Parliamentary Debates*, Legislative Assembly, 4 May 2006, 1289 (Rob Hulls, Attorney-General).

[13] *Charter of Human Rights and Responsibilities Act 2006* (Vic), s 7(2).

[14] Victoria, *Parliamentary Debates*, Legislative Assembly, 4 May 2006, 1290 (Rob Hulls, Attorney-General).

[15] *Charter of Human Rights and Responsibilities Act 2006* (Vic), s 28.

[16] *Subordinate Legislation Act 1994* (Vic), s 12D.

[17] *Charter of Human Rights and Responsibilities Act 2006* (Vic), s 30.

[18] George Williams, 'The Victorian Charter of Human Rights and Responsibilities: Origins and Scope' (2006) 30 *Melbourne University Law Review* 880, 902. Williams was the chair of the Victorian Human Rights Consultation Committee.

[19] Ibid. Brett Young, above n 7, 4.

compatible with human rights'.[20] In the early years of the *Charter*, there was a view amongst some judges and scholars that section 32 permitted courts to adopt a 'remedial' approach to interpreting legislation, as occurred in the UK House of Lords' decision in *Ghaidan v Godin-Mendoza*.[21] That is, to strain the meaning of the words used in legislation so as to make the legislation consistent with human rights. Since the High Court's (train wreck of a) decision in *Momcilovic v The Queen*[22] – in which six members of the Court found that section 32 does not replicate the interpretive mechanism in the UK *Human Rights Act 1998* (UK) c 42 – Victorian courts have taken the view that section 32 simply codifies the common law principle known in Australia as the 'principle of legality' and extends its application to a wider range of rights.[23] Though, as Chen argues, this view 'seems to be based on the judgment of French CJ' and it is not clear whether it reflects the positions of the other five justices in *Momcilovic*.[24]

Where the Supreme Court finds that a statutory provision cannot be interpreted consistently with human rights, it can issue a declaration of inconsistent interpretation under section 36 of the *Charter*. This has no impact on the validity or operation of the law[25] but requires the Attorney-General to table a written response in Parliament.[26] This is said to create a dialogue about rights between the judiciary and the political branches, with Parliament ultimately retaining the final say.

The *Charter* also imposes obligations on public authorities to comply with and consider protected rights. Section 38 places two obligations on public authorities: a procedural obligation to 'give proper consideration' to rights; and a substantive obligation not to act in a manner incompatible with rights unless there is no other way the authority could reasonably have acted. The Supreme Court is empowered to determine whether these legal obligations have been complied with, and if they have not been, to issue remedies which the aggrieved person would otherwise have been able to seek for unlawfulness.[27] The precise nature and operation of the *Charter*'s remedies in this respect remains uncertain.[28] However, it is clear that review of a public authority's compliance with the section 38 requirements looks much like judicial review of any other legal requirement.[29] Thus, although dialogue between the courts and executive was not mentioned in any of the explanatory material associated with the *Charter*, it is arguable that judicial review can result in a dialogue of sorts between the courts and the executive; whereby courts establish the parameters of executive power within which the executive is free to act and adopt lawful policies.

[20] *Charter of Human Rights and Responsibilities Act 2006* (Vic), s 32.

[21] [2004] 2 AC 557. See, eg, *Kracke v Mental Health Review Board* (2009) 29 VAR 1, 54–55 [214]–[216]; Simeon Beckett, 'Interpreting Legislation Consistently with Human Rights' (2008) 58 *AIAL Forum* 43.

[22] (2011) 245 CLR 1 ('*Momcilovic*').

[23] See Bruce Chen, 'Making Sense of *Momcilovic:* the Court of Appeal, Statutory Interpretation and the *Charter of Human Rights and Responsibilities Act 2006* (2013) 74 *AIAL Forum* 65.

[24] Bruce Chen, 'Section 32(1) of the *Charter*: Confining Statutory Discretions Compatibly With *Charter* Rights' (2016) 42 *Monash University Law Review* 608, 610. See Tate JA's comments in *Victoria Police Toll Enforcement v Taha* (2013) 49 VR 1, 62 [189] which support this.

[25] *Charter of Human Rights and Responsibilities Act 2006* (Vic), s 36(5)(a).

[26] Ibid, s 37.

[27] Ibid, s 39.

[28] Mark Moshinsky, 'Charter Remedies' in Matthew Groves and Colin Campbell (eds), *Australian Charters of Rights a Decade On* (Annandale, Federation Press, 2017) 69; Brett Young, above n 7, 119–121.

[29] For an analysis and critique of this approach see Matthew Groves, 'Judicial Review and Human Rights' (2018) 25 *Australian Journal of Administrative Law* 64.

The notable thing about this model of rights protection that the *Charter* establishes is that it does not in fact demand that the legislative and executive branches increase rights protection in their decision-making. Rather, it encourages the political branches to 'squarely confront' what they are doing when they limit rights 'and accept the political cost'.[30] The executive must explain limits on rights to Parliament when proposing legislation, and to the courts when judicial review of its actions is sought. Parliament is encouraged to consider and debate the appropriateness of limits on rights in proposed legislation. The executive must demonstrate that it has considered rights and reached a reasonable balance between rights and public interests when it makes decisions. The courts are generally unable to limit the policy choices of either branch,[31] but can express an opinion that rights have been unreasonably transgressed by the political branches.

It has also been suggested on occasion, and emphasised by VEOHRC, that this model is intended to create dialogue and engagement with the general public about rights;[32] though the public's involvement is not generally mentioned in the academic work explaining the dialogue model of rights protection.[33] The general idea seems to be that the executive branch may choose to consult the public in developing legislation to ensure that limits on rights are regarded as 'reasonable', and in SARC inquiries about the human rights issues raised by certain bills.

Thus, I suggest that the *Charter* has two central, overlapping objectives, each of which must be considered to assess how 'effective' it has been. The first is substantive rights protection. The second is the extent to which it creates a meaningful dialogue about rights between branches of government, and between government and the community, thereby requiring the political branches to 'squarely confront' limits on rights. In the sections that follow, I examine the extent to which the *Charter* has met each of these objectives, and whether there are signs of its impact increasing.

II. Has the *Charter* Succeeded at Improving Rights Protection in Victoria?

As SARC noted in its 2011 review of the *Charter*, it is probably impossible to accurately 'measure' the *Charter*'s impact on human rights protection.[34] Even in situations where it seems relatively clear that the *Charter* has resulted in a change to legislation to make it

[30] To adapt Lord Hoffmann's phrase regarding the purpose of the principle of legality from *R v Secretary of State for the Home Department; Ex parte Simms* [2000] 2 AC 115, 131.

[31] Except when courts apply the proportionality test under the substantive limb of s 38, see: Janina Boughey and Adam Fletcher, 'Administrative Decision-Making under Victoria's Charter' (2018) 25 *Australian Journal of Administrative Law* 10, 19–20.

[32] See, eg, SARC Review, above n 6, 79–80; VEOHRC, *Making Progress: The 2009 Report on the operation of the Charter of Human Rights and Responsibilities* (2010), 11 ('VEOHRC 2009 Report'); VEOHRC, *Talking Rights: 2010 report on the operation of the Charter of Human Rights and Responsibilities* (2011), 11 ('VEOHRC 2010 Report'); VEOHRC 2016 Report, above n 2, 8, 9

[33] See, eg, Peter W Hogg and Alison A Bushell, 'The *Charter* Dialogue between Courts and Legislatures (Or Perhaps the *Charter of Rights* isn't Such a Bad Thing After All)' (1997) 35 *Osgoode Hall Law Journal* 75, 79–82; Kent Roach, 'Dialogic Judicial Review and its Critics' (2004) 23 Sup. Ct. L. Rev. (2d) 49; Scott Stephenson, *From Dialogue to Disagreement in Comparative Rights Constitutionalism* (Annandale, Federation Press, 2016) 102–106.

[34] SARC Review, above n 6, 75–77.

more compliant with rights, there may be other forces at play. For example, SARC observed that amendments to the onus of proof in the *Fair Trading Act 1999* (Vic) were explained as intended to better protect *Charter* rights,[35] 'would have been enacted in any event the following year as part of Victoria's adoption of the *Australian Consumer Law*'.[36] Furthermore, it is not clear how you would go about measuring the extent to which rights are protected in Victoria now, and what you would try to compare that with. Comparing the level of rights protection in Victoria now prior to the *Charter*'s enactment (assuming this were even possible) might overlook other changes that have occurred over time. For example, the threat posed by terrorism might have increased over that period, necessitating more reasonable limits on rights. A better method might be to compare rights protection in Victoria with that in *Charter*-lacking states. Though it may be that any differences are explained not by the presence of the *Charter*, but by other factors, especially political differences. So all one can really do to attempt to assess the effectiveness of the *Charter* in improving rights protection is to rely on case studies and examples that appear to speak to that question, while being cautious to highlight other possible influences and reasons for change or lack thereof. This is the approach that VEOHRC's annual reports on the effectiveness of the *Charter* tend to take; though they also involve surveys and statistical data which I draw on in this chapter.

As a starting point, it is useful to consider how the *Charter* might have the effect of increasing rights protection, in order to assess whether this has in fact occurred. There seem to be four main ways in which the *Charter* might increase rights protection. First, the processes of reporting on the rights compatibility of bills, scrutiny of bills by Parliament might cause new or existing legislation to impose fewer limits on rights than it otherwise would have. This could occur either at the drafting stage or via amendments in the Parliament.

There have been few examples of the latter: of parliamentary scrutiny resulting in legislation being amended to make it more compatible with human rights. This has not changed over time. The limited capacity of SARC reports to lead to amendments was commented on in the early years of the *Charter*'s operation,[37] as well as the most recent reviews of the *Charter*.[38] It is also not an issue unique to the Victorian *Charter*. As Janet Hiebert has observed in the UK context, 'the government is unlikely to change its mind on the basis of a single but contrary parliamentary committee report'.[39] This does not, however, necessarily mean that SARC scrutiny has no effect on the content of legislation. There are rare occasions in which it does seem to have had a clear impact, such as the *Mental Health Act* (2014),

[35] Explanatory Memorandum, Statute Law Amendment (Charter of Human Rights and Responsibilities) Bill 2009, 2–3.

[36] SARC Review, above n 6, 81.

[37] See, eg, Carlo Carli MP, 'Scrutiny and the Charter of Rights and Responsibilities', (Paper presented at the Australia–New Zealand Scrutiny of Legislation Conference: Scrutiny and Accountability in the 21st Century, Parliament House, Canberra, 6–8 July 2009), available at: www.aph.gov.au/~/media/Committees/Senate/sl_conference/papers/carli.pdf?la=en. Note Carlo Carli was, at the time, the Chair of SARC. See also James B Kelly, 'A Difficult Dialogue: Statements of Compatibility and the Victorian *Charter of Human Rights and Responsibilities Act*' (2011) 46 *Australian Journal of Political Science* 257.

[38] VEOHRC 2016 Report, above n 2, 43; Laura Grenfell and Sarah Moulds, 'The Role of Committees in Rights Protection in Australia' (2018) 41 *UNSW Law Journal* 40, 66–67.

[39] Janet Hiebert, 'Legislative Rights Review: Addressing the Gap between Ideals and Constraints' in Murray Hunt, Hayley J Cooper and Paul Yowell (eds), *Parliament and Human Rights: Redressing the Democratic Deficit* (Oxford, Hart Publishing, 2015) 39, 52.

discussed below. Furthermore, as Carlo Carli MP, the first chair of SARC after the *Charter's* introduction, explained:

> In our experience SARC has had little influence over the content of legislation once the bill has been presented to Parliament. However there is evidence that the Committee's functions and reports influence the drafting of bills. Generally the Committee's experience is that there is reluctance by the executive to amend bills once introduced.[40]

Thus, it is possible that the very existence of the scrutiny process has caused governments to be more vigilant in protecting rights at the policy development and drafting stages.[41] However, whether this has occurred is a more difficult thing to assess, as it largely relies on self-reporting by government departments. As one might expect, the government's self-reporting on how the *Charter* has influenced the development of legislation has tended to be very optimistic, suggesting that robust procedures have been put in place to ensure that only reasonable limits are placed on protected rights.[42]

The second way in which the *Charter* might result in legislation being more rights-protective than it otherwise would have been is via the judicial processes under sections 32 (interpretation) and 36 (declarations of inconsistent interpretation). It is clear that these processes have not had a significant impact on the extent to which rights are protected in Victorian legislation. The *Momcilovic* decision bears a large portion of the blame for this.[43] As discussed above, the judgments have been read as finding that the interpretive function in section 32 is simply an extended version of the common law principle of legality. The result is that courts have tended to rely on the far more settled common law interpretive principles where they are available – which they often are.[44]

The High Court's judgment in *Minogue v Victoria*[45] provides a good example. Craig Minogue is a prisoner convicted for the 1986 bombing of the Melbourne Police Headquarters. In 2016, the Victorian Parliament enacted legislation providing that the Parole Board cannot order the parole of any prisoner convicted and sentenced to imprisonment for the murder of a police officer unless the Board is satisfied that the prisoner is:

> in imminent danger of dying, or is seriously incapacitated and, as a result, the prisoner no longer has the physical ability to do harm to any person; and has demonstrated that the prisoner does not pose a risk to the community …[46]

Minogue challenged the validity of the provision in the High Court, and argued that both common law canons of construction and the *Charter* required that the provision be read

[40] Carli, above n 37.
[41] See also Grenfell and Moulds, above n 38, 67.
[42] See, eg, VEOHRC 2009 Report, above n 32, 33–34; VEOHRC 2010 Report, above n 32, 35.
[43] See generally Claudia Geiringer, 'Inside and Outside Criminal Process: the Comparative Salience of the New Zealand and Victorian Human Rights Charters' (2017) *Public Law Review* 219, 224, 229.
[44] Though there is evidence of this pre-*Momcilovic* as well (eg *Hogan v Hinch* (2011) 243 CLR 506).
[45] (2018) 92 ALJR 668.
[46] *Justice Legislation Amendment (Parole Reform and Other Matters) Act 2016*, inserting s 74AAA into the *Corrections Act 1986* (Vic). Note that parole board are exempt from the *Charter* (*Charter of Human Rights and Responsibilities (Public Authorities) Regulations 2013* r 5), but legislation empowering parole boards is not exempt unless there is an express provision overriding the *Charter* included in the legislation. The exemption of parole boards from the *Charter* is controversial, and distinguishes the Victorian *Charter* from human rights instruments in the UK, Canada and New Zealand: see Matthew Groves, 'The Second Charters of Prisoners' Rights' in Matthew Groves and Colin Campbell (eds), *Australian Charters of Rights a Decade On* (Annandale, Federation Press, 2017) 187, 196–97.

narrowly such that it did not apply to him. The Court found that the ordinary principles of construction (particularly the principle that penal statutes should be construed strictly, and the principle of legality) yielded the narrow interpretation for which Minogue argued, and did not need to rely on the *Charter*.[47] Gageler J described the *Charter* question as 'important' and said that he was 'not without hesitation' in taking this approach.[48]

Similarly in *Victoria Police Toll Enforcement v Taha*,[49] the Court was able to rely on ordinary principles of construction to interpret a provision permitting a court to order that a person with outstanding infringements be imprisoned as subject to consideration of the person's personal circumstances as set out in later sub-sections.[50] It was therefore unnecessary to rely on section 32 of the *Charter*. Nevertheless, Tate JA discussed the effect of section 32 and concluded that it both supported and mandated the conclusion.[51] This, and other post-*Momcilovic* cases dealing with section 32 reveal that Australian courts seem to be much more comfortable relying on the established common law principles of construction – some of which have rather tenuous links to parliamentary 'intention'[52] – than a direct mandate from the Victorian Parliament to interpret statutes consistently with *Charter* rights.

Similarly, the only declaration of inconsistent interpretation that the Supreme Court has issued was in *Momcilovic*, which was subsequently overturned.[53] This should not necessarily be read as an indication that all Victorian law is compatible with the *Charter*. Rather, as I will discuss below, it probably reflects the limited use of the *Charter* in court proceedings, and the lack of incentive to seek a remedy which will have no impact on the outcome of one's case. Thus, it cannot be said that the judicial functions of interpreting legislation and declaring it incompatible with rights have had a direct and meaningful impact on the extent to which Victorian legislation protects human rights.

The third way in which the *Charter* might improve the protection of rights in Victoria is through its application to court proceedings. As Geiringer has noted, perhaps the most potent effect of the *New Zealand Bill of Rights Act 1990* (NZ) has been on the criminal process.[54] The same cannot be said of the Victorian *Charter*. In part this is due to its design: the designers of the *Charter* deliberately excluded courts from section 38, meaning that courts are not required to consider or comply with *Charter* rights when exercising their judicial functions (and nor are tribunals when exercising judicial functions).[55] The reason

[47] *Minogue v Victoria* (2018) 92 ALJR 668, 678–79 [47], [48], 680 [56] (Kiefel CJ, Bell, Keane, Nettle and Edelman JJ); 683 [80], 684 [88] (Gageler J).

[48] *Minogue v Victoria* (2018) 92 ALJR 668, 683 [80]. Other members of the Court appeared not to have any such hesitation, see, eg, [102][103] (Gordon J).

[49] (2013) 49 VR 1.

[50] *Victoria Police Toll Enforcement v Taha* (2013) 49 VR 1, 10 [18] (Nettle JA), 48 [144]–[147] (Tate JA).

[51] Ibid, 61–73 [186][216]. See also *Nigro v Secretary to the Dept of Justice* (2013) 41 VR 359, 383 [85].

[52] See generally Dan Meagher, 'The "Modern Approach" to Interpretation, Statutory Text and Fundamental Rights: An Issue of Coherence?' 46 *Federal Law Review* 397.

[53] The Court of Appeal of Victoria had found that s 5 of the *Drugs, Poisons and Controlled Poisons Act 1981* (Vic), which deemed a person to be in 'possession' of drugs when drugs were found on their property, and reversed the onus of proof, was inconsistent with the right to be presumed innocent. The Court of Appeal held that it was not possible to interpret s 5 in a manner compatible with that right so issued a declaration of inconsistent interpretation. A majority of the High Court held that s 5 did not apply to the offence Ms Momcilovic had been charged with and convicted of, and the trial court had erred in applying it. It was therefore not necessary to consider whether s 5 was incompatible with the *Charter* or issue a declaration of inconsistent interpretation. For a coherent explanation of the quite incoherent High Court judgments see: Will Bateman and James Stellios, 'Chapter III of the Constitution, Federal Jurisdiction and Dialogue Charters of Rights' (2012) 36 *Melbourne University Law Review* 1.

[54] Geiringer, above n 43.

[55] *Charter of Human Rights and Responsibilities Act 2006* (Vic), s 4(1)(j).

for this exclusion was to avoid Victorian common law from developing differently to the common law in other Australian jurisdictions, which might have put the constitutional validity of the *Charter* at risk.[56] However, somewhat confusingly, section 6(2)(b) of the *Charter* provides that the *Charter does* apply to courts and tribunals 'to the extent that they have functions under Part 2 …' (which is the Part of the *Charter* that sets out rights). This raises the interpretive question of when courts are required to comply with rights in exercising their judicial functions. The position that Victorian courts have taken seems to be that they are only required to comply with those rights that relate to court proceedings – most notably the right to a fair hearing contained in section 24,[57] and rights of accused persons in criminal proceedings contained in section 25. In certain circumstances other *Charter* rights may also be relevant to judicial decision-making, such as equality (section 8) and cultural rights (section 19) in decisions to transfer proceedings to the Koori Court (a court which sentences Indigenous Australians).[58] However, the right to a fair hearing under the *Charter* does not appear to add anything to existing common law principles[59] and nor do any other *Charter* rights seem to have had any effect on the criminal justice process in Victoria.[60]

The fourth process through which the *Charter* might improve the protection of rights is via judicial review of administrative action. Specifically, the requirement that rights be 'considered' in the administrative decision-making process, and that public authorities act in a manner consistent with rights, as well as the threat and impacts of judicial review, might result in administrative decisions being made that better protect rights. As with the drafting of legislation, it is difficult to know whether this has in fact occurred. The (small) number of judicial review applications cannot necessary be read as evidence that administrative decisions are generally compatible with rights, because the cost and effort of making such an application is so prohibitive. It really seems to come down to whether the *Charter* has created a 'human rights culture' within government, which is a much more difficult thing to measure. The following sections examine the limited evidence and case studies which speak to the questions of whether the *Charter* has resulted in legislation and administrative decisions respectively being more compatible with rights.

A. Rights Compatibility of Legislation

With respect to the first of these questions – whether legislation is more compatible with rights than it otherwise would have been – the evidence is mixed. Early on in the *Charter*'s life, the Parliament enacted the *Statute Law Amendment (Charter of Human Rights and*

[56] Human Rights Consultation Committee, Rights, *Responsibilities and Respect: The Report of the Human Rights Consultation Committee* (2005) 59.

[57] *Victoria Police Toll Enforcement v Taha* (2013) 49 VR 1, 81 [248] (Tate JA). See further, Bruce Chen, 'How Does the Charter Affect Discretions?' (2018) 25 *Australian Journal of Administrative Law* 28, 44–50.

[58] *Cemino v Cannan* [2018] VSC 535, [100] ff.

[59] See statements to this effect in *Matsoukatidou v Yarra Ranges Council* (2017) 51 VR 624, 660–661 [111]–[112] (Bell J states that the *Charter* 'magnifies the force' of the common law, but does not identify any differences between the two); *Taha v Broadmeadows Magistrates' Court* [2011] VSC 642, [71]; *Russell v Yarra Ranges Shire Council* [2009] VSC 486, [42].

[60] In *Cemino v Cannan* [2018] VSC 535 Ginnane J held that equality and cultural rights did not add anything to the statutory discretion of the Magistrates Court to transfer proceedings to the Koori Court. See generally, Jeremy Gans, 'The Charter and Law and Order' in Matthew Groves and Colin Campbell (eds) *Australian Charters of Rights A Decade On* (Annandale, Federation Press, 2017) 169.

Responsibilities) Act 2009 (Vic), which amended several existing Acts with the objective of ensuring that those Acts are compliant with human rights.[61] It followed a government review of existing statutes for compatibility with rights. As noted above, at least some of these changes would have been made anyway. Other existing Acts were not amended via this process, because the government reached the view that they could be interpreted in a way which was consistent with rights, using section 32.[62] However, as discussed above, section 32 has not had quite the effect that many expected or hoped. In addition, none of the seven pieces of legislation that were amended included those that have the most significant impact on rights, or that are the most contentious in terms of the balance struck between rights and public interests. For example, no amendments were made to existing corrections, mental health treatment, police powers, or social housing legislation though the process.

A re-write of Victoria's mental health treatment laws did, however, occur several years later, in 2014.[63] The Act made a range of important changes to the laws relating to involuntary treatment and detention of persons with severe mental illness, which are widely regarded to have improved patients' rights and autonomy.[64] The changes followed an extensive community consultation process, which was applauded by VEOHRC.[65] The SoC reported that these changes were driven by a desire to comply with the *Charter*.[66] For instance, while the Act permits significant limits on the rights of persons with severe mental illness, it incorporates obligations to ensure that these restrictions are justified as well as oversight mechanisms.[67] Bell J's decision in *Kracke v Mental Health Review Board*,[68] finding that the Mental Health Review Board had breached Mr Kracke's *Charter* rights by failing to review his involuntary treatment orders and highlighting the significant rights implications of such orders, was also reported to be a driver of the changes to the Act.[69] Several amendments to the original Bill were made in Parliament, following the SARC report on the Bill, to better protect rights, such as amendments to clarify that a person's gender identity is not a mental illness.[70] In short, the legislation seems to provide an example of all elements of the process set out in the *Charter* working together in order to improve the rights of a vulnerable group of people.

There are other examples of legislative change which purport to have been driven, at least in part, by the *Charter*. These include the *Equal Opportunity Act 2010* (Vic), which provides in its objects clause that one of its purposes is 'to further promote and protect the right to equality set out in the Charter of Human Rights and Responsibilities'.[71] Interestingly, other examples which improve the rights compatibility of legislation have mentioned that protecting rights generally is a motive, but have not specifically referred to the *Charter*.[72]

[61] *Statute Law Amendment (Charter of Human Rights and Responsibilities) Act 2009* (Vic), s 1.

[62] VEOHRC, *Emerging change: The 2008 report on the operation of the Charter of Human Rights and Responsibilities* (2009) 31, 34 ('VEOHRC 2008 Report').

[63] *Mental Health Act 2014* (Vic).

[64] See, eg, Leslie Cannold, 'Victoria a true leader in mental health reform' *The Drum*, 2 July 2014 www.abc.net.au/news/2014-02-28/cannold-victoria-a-true-leader-in-mental-health-reform/5289940.

[65] VEOHRC, *2014 report on the operation of the Charter of Human Rights and Responsibilities* (2015), 62 ('VEOHRC 2014 Report').

[66] Victoria, *Parliamentary Debates*, Legislative Assembly, 20 February 2014, 458–470 (Mary Wooldridge, Minister for Mental Health).

[67] VEOHRC 2014 Report, above n 64, 57.

[68] (2009) 29 VAR 1.

[69] VEOHRC 2009 Report, above n 32, 34.

[70] Victoria, *Parliamentary Debates*, Legislative Council, 28 March 2014, 841 (Colleen Hartland).

[71] *Equal Opportunity Act 2010* (Vic), s 3.

[72] Eg neither the explanatory memorandum nor second reading speech for the *Adoption Amendment (Adoption by Same-Sex Couples) Act 2015* (Vic) referred to the *Charter*.

However, there are just as many examples of Victorian legislation which place considerable limits on rights, and do so in the same controversial ways as those laws in other states without human rights charters. Of particular note are Victorian statutes which target specific prisoners and prevent them from being released on parole. One such provision has already been mentioned – section 74AAA of the *Corrections Act 1986* (Vic), which was the subject of the High Court's decision in *Minogue v Victoria*.[73] The SoC, Explanatory Memorandum and SARC report on that amendment did not acknowledge that section 74AAA was directed to Minogue, but this was discussed in parliamentary debates.[74] The SoC frankly acknowledged that:

> it may be argued that [the provision] is incompatible with the [right to be free from cruel, inhuman and degrading treatment or punishment] …, in light of the particularly severe retrospective effect the limitation will have on certain individual offenders and the potential availability of less restrictive alternative measures.[75]

Despite this, there was no provision included in the amending legislation stating that the *Charter* did not apply. Such 'overrides' are expressly permitted by the *Charter*, section 31(7) of which places a five year 'sunset' on override declarations. Following the High Court's decision, the Victorian Parliament amended section 74AAA, and added a new section 74AB to the *Corrections Act* which expressly applies to Minogue. The new provision is identical to that which applies to Julian Knight, and which survived a High Court challenge (discussed below). The amendments contain a clear *Charter* override provision which also overrides the *Charter*'s sunset clause.[76]

A similar provision (section 74AA) was inserted into the *Corrections Act 1986* (Vic) in 2014, but it applies only to one named prisoner – Julian Knight, also known as the 'Hoddle Street killer', who murdered seven people and injured 19 others in a mass shooting in 1987. The section is headed 'Conditions for Making a Parole Order for Julian Knight', and prohibits Knight's release unless the Parole Board is satisfied that he is either dying or incapacitated and no longer presents a risk to the community or any person.[77] The SoC relating to section 74AA said that the legislation does not limit Knight's liberty because it has no effect on his head sentence, just the conditions on which he may be granted parole; and there is no 'right' to parole.[78] However, the SoC noted that the courts might take a different view, and so the amending Act also included an override provision of both the *Charter* and of its sunset clause.[79] The SoC also referred to the fact that NSW (a state which has no charter of rights) has similar legislation in place as demonstrating the reasonableness of the limit placed on Knight's *Charter* rights.[80] SARC's report on the amendments noted that there may be less restrictive ways of preventing Knight from endangering the community than denying him

[73] (2018) 92 ALJR 668.

[74] Victoria, *Parliamentary Debates*, Legislative Assembly, 7 December 2016, 4850 (Robert Clark).

[75] Victoria, *Parliamentary Debates*, Legislative Assembly, 6 December 2016, 4725 (Lisa Neville, Minister for Police).

[76] *Corrections Amendment (Parole) Act 2018* (Vic), s 4.

[77] *Corrections Act 1986* (Vic), s 74AA(3)(a).

[78] Victoria, *Parliamentary Debates*, Legislative Assembly, 13 March 2014, 745 (Kim Wells, Minister for Police and Emergency Services).

[79] This override meant that Knight did not raise the *Charter* in his challenge to the validity of the law, see: *Knight v Victoria* (2017) 91 ALJR 824.

[80] Victoria, Parliamentary Debates, Legislative Assembly, 13 March 2014, 745 (Kim Wells, Minister for Police and Emergency Services).

parole, but did not recommend any amendments or that the Bill not be passed.[81] SARC's report was very briefly mentioned in the debate over the amendments, but not engaged with.[82]

Victoria also has laws permitting the detention of suspected terrorists without charge for community protection,[83] providing for the continued detention of serious sex offenders after their prison sentence,[84] and making it an offence to associate with certain convicted criminals.[85] All have been introduced or amended in ways that impose further limits on rights since the enactment of the *Charter*. These laws are very similar, sometimes identical, to those in place in other Australian jurisdictions without charters of rights. While the *Charter* tends to be mentioned in law reform and policy documents at the development stage as a factor that needs to be considered in developing the legislation,[86] it does not seem to have resulted in Victorian legislation being significantly different from that in many other states. There are many possible explanations for this. One is that these laws limit the rights of unpopular groups of people and so are generally unlikely to cause much controversy within the electorate even if those limits are incompatible with the *Charter*.[87] Another is that perhaps governments in other states weigh rights into their formulation of policies and legislation even where there is no charter directing them to do so. That is, a government will only ever propose limits on rights where, in its view, it is reasonable and necessary to do so in order to protect the public interest. Whatever the reason, the *Charter* does not appear to have had a significant impact in these policy areas, and frequently seems to be treated as a procedural hurdle that requires an explanation of why the legislation is justified, rather than as something that should be seriously engaged with at the design stage. Interestingly, as noted above, explanations as to why legislation is justified often refer to the fact that it is in place in other non-charter states.

B. Rights Compatibility of Administrative Decision-making

As with the rights compatibility of legislation, it is impossible to accurately 'measure' whether administrative decision-making has become more rights compatible as a result of the *Charter*. There have only been a small number of applications for judicial review of decisions made by public authorities on *Charter* grounds.[88] There have been more instances in which *Charter* issues have been raised in Victorian Civil and Administrative Tribunal (VCAT) appeals, but the Court of Appeal's 2011 decision in *Director of Housing v Sudi*[89]

[81] SARC, *Alert Digest*, No 3 of 2014, 11 March 2014, 6.

[82] Victoria, *Parliamentary Debates*, Legislative Council, 11 March 2014, 592 (David O'Brien).

[83] *Terrorism (Community Protection) Act 2003* (Vic), Pt 2A.

[84] *Serious Sex Offenders (Detention and Supervision) Act 2009* (Vic).

[85] *Criminal Organisations Control Act 2012* (Vic), Pt 5A.

[86] See, eg, Expert Panel on Terrorism and Violent Extremism Prevention and Response Powers, *Report 1*, (2017) 35, 59, 63, 81.

[87] This suggestion has been made by Grenfell and Moulds, above n 38, 41, 44.

[88] My audit found fewer than 30 cases over the decade in which the *Charter* has been in force, however the number depends on how you count. Sometimes claims that a public authority has breached its charter obligations are raised in the context of a criminal defence (eg the DPP), or in merits review proceedings in VCAT. I have not included either of these in my count.

[89] *Director of Housing v Sudi* (2011) 33 VR 559.

held that VCAT has no general merits review jurisdiction with respect to the *Charter* and can only consider *Charter* issues where it has otherwise been conferred review or decision-making functions.

The limited number of judicial review applications (and the even more limited number of successful applications) cannot be taken as evidence that public authorities are generally complying with the *Charter*. There are considerable barriers to people accessing the courts to challenge administrative action on *Charter* grounds. The first and most obvious is the cost and complexity of judicial review proceedings. This is especially problematic for vulnerable people at most risk of their *Charter* rights being impinged.[90] The complexity of a judicial review application is amplified under the *Charter* due to its unclear and restrictive 'remedies' provision – section 39. Subsection 39(1) states:

> If, otherwise than because of this Charter, a person may seek any relief or remedy in respect of an act or decision of a public authority on the ground that the act or decision was unlawful, that person may seek that relief or remedy on a ground of unlawfulness arising because of this Charter.

Section 39 then goes on to provide that damages are not available for a breach of the *Charter*. The problems with this section of the *Charter* have been well-explored elsewhere.[91] In short, they include uncertainties resulting from its ambiguous language and unclear interaction with section 38, the fact that it over-complicates the process of applying for a remedy for breach of the *Charter*, and its possible effect of denying remedies to many persons whose *Charter* rights have been breached. Many, including Brett Young, have recommended it be repealed or redrafted.[92]

In addition, lawyers have not generally been particularly zealous in exploring *Charter* issues in litigation. There is a view amongst practitioners that 'the time and effort involved in raising [the *Charter*] has often outweighed the beneficial effect it has had for those relying on it.'[93] The *Charter* is perceived as remedially weak and procedurally complex.[94] There is also a perception that judges are, on the whole, not especially enthusiastic about *Charter* arguments.[95] However, even where judges encourage litigants to consider *Charter* arguments, former Chief Justice Warren and Justice Tate have said that:

> Despite the encouragement of courts, and the support of individual judges, we continue to see reluctance on the part of practitioners to raise arguments under the Charter.[96]

[90] Brett Young, above n 7, ch 4.

[91] Moshinsky, above n 28; Justice Pamela Tate, 'Special Issue on the Charter' (2018) 25 *Australian Journal of Administrative Law* 1, 6; Mark Aronson, 'Judicial Review and the Charter' (2018) 25 *Australian Journal of Administrative Law* 52. Unfortunately, Queensland's new *Human Rights Act 2019* (Qld), s 59 essentially replicates s 39 of the Victorian Charter.

[92] Brett Young, above n 7, 119–133.

[93] Emrys Nekvapil, 'Using the Charter in Litigation' in Matthew Groves and Colin Campbell (eds), *Australian Charters of Rights a Decade On* (Annandale, Federation Press, 2017) 84, 84. The litigation in Nassir Bare's case is a good example. After protracted and complex litigation (made more complex by the presence of a privative clause and lengthy discussion of whether a breach of s 38 is a 'jurisdictional error'), the Independent Broad-based Anti-corruption Commission ultimately found that his allegations of police brutality and racism were unsubstantiated. See: *Bare v Independent Broad-based Anti-corruption Commission* (2015) 48 VR 129; 'Nassir Bare's allegations of police brutality and racism 'unable to be substantiated', IBAC finds', *ABC Online*, 18 May 2016 www.abc.net.au/news/2016-05-18/allegations-of-police-brutality-racism-not-substantiated-court/7424470.

[94] Brett Young, above n 7, 49; Chen, 'How Does the Charter Affect Discretions?', above n 57, 31–34.

[95] Geiringer, above n 43, 224.

[96] Chief Justice Marilyn Warren AC and the Hon Justice Pamela Tate, 'Editorial' (2014) 2 *Judicial College of Victoria Online Journal: Human Rights Under the Charter: The Development of Human Rights Law in Victoria* 2, 3.

Thus, there are barriers to using the main method that the *Charter* provides to remedy *Charter* breaches by public authorities. There are other formal avenues through which individuals can raise claims that a public authority has breached their *Charter* rights, including the Ombudsman[97] and the Independent Broad-based Anti-corruption Commission.[98] However, as Adam Fletcher and I have argued elsewhere, neither avenue is well-known to the public, and each has significant limitations.[99]

With the absence of accessible and effective enforcement, the extent to which public authorities consider *Charter* rights in decision-making and act in ways that are compatible with rights depends largely on the existence of a 'human rights culture' within the public sector.[100] This has been acknowledged in *Charter* reviews from the outset,[101] and continues to be the focus of recommendations in the most recent reports of VEOHRC and Brett Young.[102] But how can the strength of a human rights culture be measured? Self-reporting by the government has consistently asserted that the *Charter* has had a positive impact on decision-making, and resulted in such a culture.[103] And VEOHRC's early reports tended to agree, finding promising signs in the fact that public authorities had developed operational policies which incorporated human rights, and implemented training for staff.[104] Two thirds of agencies now mention human rights in their vision and value statements.[105] However, the views of community groups and individuals about whether this is mere lip service, or whether rights are taken into account in decision-making have tended to be more mixed. A 2010 survey of community organisations and individuals conducted for VEOHRC's annual review found that while there may be reference to rights in department planning and policy documents, it was not clear that this had 'fully filtered through to the front line'.[106] The survey also revealed a perception that the presence of a rights culture within government was 'patchy' – meaning that while some agencies and departments fared well, others did not.[107]

[97] *Ombudsman Act 1973* (Vic), s 13(2).

[98] *Independent Broad-based Anti-corruption Commission Act 2011* (Vic), s 15(3)(b)(iii).

[99] Boughey and Fletcher, above n 31, 22–24. There are also unexplored possibilities for the courts to have a greater impact on rights via their role in interpreting administrative discretion: see Chen, 'How Does the Charter Affect Discretions?', above n 57.

[100] Enforcement is one area where Queensland's *Human Rights Act 2019* (Qld) makes important improvements on the Victorian model. In particular, it provides for the investigation and conciliation of complaints about agency actions by the Queensland Human Rights Commissioner (in Pt 4). This has the potential to provide an effective, efficient, accessible remedy for individuals affected by government decisions which breach their human rights. But it is yet to be seen how the Queensland model will operate in practice.

[101] VEOHRC, *First steps forward: The 2007 report on the operation of the Charter of Human Rights and Responsibilities* (2008) 63–67 ('VEOHRC 2007 Report').

[102] Brett Young, above n 7, ch 1; the VEOHRC 2016 Report is titled 'Growing a human rights culture'.

[103] See, eg, VEOHRC 2009 Report, above n 32, 57; VEOHRC, *Protecting us all: 2012 report on the operation of the Charter of Human Rights and Responsibilities* (2013), 14–16 ('VEOHRC 2012 Report'); VEHORC 2014 Report, above n 64, 45–55.

[104] See, eg, VEOHRC 2008 Report, above n 61, 3; VEOHRC 2009 Report, above n 32, 5–6; VEOHRC 2010 Report, above n 32, 9.

[105] VEOHRC 2016 Report, above n 2, 24.

[106] VEOHRC 2010 Report, above n 32, 15.

[107] Ibid.

These have been recurring themes in VEOHRC's subsequent reports as well as in the statutory reviews of the *Charter*.[108] It seems, for instance, that staff in core departments tend to have more understanding of rights compared with local councils.[109] Brett Young's review of the *Charter* also found that:

> Over time, implementation of the Charter has helped to build a greater consideration of and adherence to human rights principles by the public sector, Parliament and the courts in key areas. But this progress has stalled.[110]

Brett Young explained that his consultations 'highlighted a deprioritisation of the Charter in recent years, which has set back the development of a human rights culture in Victoria'.[111] This is supported by VEOHRC's survey of government employees for its 2016 report, which found that a considerable percentage (almost 40 per cent) still did not have a good understanding of their duties under the *Charter*.[112] VEOHRC's survey also revealed that *Charter* training programmes may not be particularly effective.[113]

The case studies in VEOHRC's reports over the last decade describe many instances in which the *Charter* has had a positive, rights promoting impact on both individual decision-making and policy making. A common feature of many of these case studies is that they have involved direct action by community organisations, advocacy groups or community legal centres. There are countless examples in the reports of these organisations raising rights issues with public authorities, and this resulting in reconsideration of the decision or policy with a more rights-protective result, without resort to the courts.[114] Many of the case studies tell the story of an advocacy group acting on behalf of an aggrieved person or social group, and communicating directly with a public authority to effect change. These case studies give an impression that one of the most effective mechanisms of ensuring that administrative decisions and actions protect rights is via advocacy. Perhaps the threat of litigation provides an incentive for public authorities to engage with advocacy groups on these issues.

Thus, as with the rights-compatibility of legislation, the evidence of whether the *Charter* has resulted in more rights compatible actions by public authorities is mixed. There does seem to be a reasonable awareness of rights within government, according to self-reporting surveys. Though this knowledge differs from agency to agency. There were signs of a 'human rights culture' developing in the *Charter*'s early years, but progress seems to have slowed more recently. However, the *Charter* does seem to be a useful tool for advocacy groups to effect change in relation to particular decisions and policies. On the whole, it seems that the *Charter* has either directly caused, or been useful in persuading many public authorities to act in ways that are more rights compatible at least some of the time.

[108] See, eg, VEOHRC 2012 Report, above n 101, 3; VEOHRC, *2013 Report on the operation of the Charter of Human Rights and Responsibilities* (2014), 18–19 ('VEOHRC 2013 Report'); Brett Young, above n 7, 22.
[109] VEOHRC 2016 Report, above n 2, 25.
[110] Brett Young, above n 7, 22.
[111] Brett Young, above n 7, 23.
[112] VEOHRC 2016 Report, above n 2, 19. This includes those who said they strongly disagreed, disagreed, or neither agreed nor disagreed with the statement 'I understand how the Charter of Human Rights and Responsibilities applies to my work'.
[113] VEOHRC 2016 Report, above n 2, 30.
[114] See, eg, VEOHRC, *Rights in focus: 2011 Report on the operation of the Charter of Human Rights and Responsibilities* (2012), 9–10 ('VEOHRC 2011 Report'); VEOHRC 2009 Report, above n 32, 87; VEOHRC 2014 Report,

III. Has the *Charter* Succeeded in Creating a 'Dialogue' About Rights?

While the *Charter* appears to have had some (albeit patchy) success in improving the level of rights protection in legislation and administrative decisions, it has been less successful in creating a meaningful dialogue about rights between the three branches of government, and between government and the public. There are a few examples of the *Charter's* dialogue model being successful. Reforms to Victoria's mental health laws, which were discussed above, are one example. Another is the Legislative Council's amendment to the *Adoption Amendment (Adoption by Same-Sex Couples) Act 2015* (Vic) to exempt religious bodies from anti-discrimination law when deciding who to place a child with. The original Bill contained a clause which provided that, despite the general exemption of religious bodies from the *Equal Opportunity Act 2010* (Vic), religious bodies could not discriminate in respect of adoption decisions. SARC raised concerns that this provision might interfere with the freedom of religion of biological parents.[115] A vigorous debate about the balance between the freedom from discrimination and right to religion followed in the Council, and the opposition successfully amended the Bill to remove the relevant clause.[116] The government reluctantly passed the amended Bill in the Assembly.[117] It is clearly debatable as to whether this second example of dialogue strengthened the protection of rights. Nevertheless, it is one of the relatively rare examples of a SARC report being discussed in Parliament, and this parliamentary debate about rights then resulting in amendments to legislation.

For the most part, however, it is agreed that the impact of the SoC and SARC process on parliamentary debate about rights has been disappointing. With respect to SoCs, this may in part be due to their quality. Although the quality of SoCs has improved significantly since SARC's criticisms in 2010,[118] it remains inconsistent.[119] Kelly has also argued that, at least in the first three and a half years of the *Charter's* operation, the Cabinet engaged in deliberate strategies to reduce the dialogic impact of SoCs, such as relying on assertions that no less restrictive means were available to achieving the same objective to justify limits on rights.[120] With respect to SARC, there does not seem to be a quality problem with its reports. Nevertheless, SoCs and SARC reports are rarely mentioned in parliamentary debate. Furthermore, where *Charter* issues are discussed in parliamentary debate, they tend to be discussed by Greens MPs, and not the major parties.[121] Though this does seem to have changed over time. In its 2009 report, VEOHRC reported that there had been an 'active exchange' about rights on more than a third of bills introduced that year.[122] Although SARC's 2010 review suggests that this represents only a small increase on the pre-*Charter* position, when SARC

above n 64, 51, 66; VEOHRC, *2015 report on the operation of the Charter of Human Rights and Responsibilities* (2016), 42 ('VEOHRC 2015 Report'); Brett Young, above n 7, 51.

[115] SARC, *Alert Digest*, No 13 of 2015, 20 October 2015, 4–6.

[116] Victoria, *Parliamentary Debates*, Legislative Council, 12 November 2015, 4323–65.

[117] Victoria, *Parliamentary Debates*, Legislative Assembly, 9 December 2015, 5443 (Martin Foley, Minister for Equality).

[118] SARC Review, above n 6, 87–88.

[119] Brett Young, above n 7, 186–87.

[120] Kelly, above n 37, 268.

[121] Grenfell and Moulds, above n 38, 66.

[122] VEOHRC 2009 Report, above n 32, 84.

already reported to Parliament on the extent to which bills interfered with fundamental common law rights.[123] More recently, VEOHRC reported that in 2016 'parliamentarians only referred to SARC reports during debate a handful of times'.[124] Despite SARC reports apparently having a greater impact on debate in the *Charter*'s early years, in his survey of the *Charter*'s impact over its first three and a half years, Kelly reached the conclusion that the *Charter*'s 'dialogic promise' remained 'unfulfilled'.[125] He explained that 'there is very limited evidence of parliamentarians using SARC reports to challenge a SoC introduced by a minister', despite the fact that SARC was more willing to disagree with statements of compatibility in the early years.[126]

Several reasons have been given for the lack of parliamentary debate on SARC reports. Grenfell and Moulds compared the impact of scrutiny committees in the federal and several state legislatures on rights limiting legislation. They concluded that it was 'difficult to trace much impact [of SARC] on the deliberative process' in rights-limiting anti-motorcycle gang legislation.[127] Grenfell and Moulds' comparative study revealed that certain attributes distinguished more effective parliamentary committees from less effective committees. One of these attributes is the type of scrutiny undertaken by the committee – with policy committees (which comment on the balance legislation strikes between competing interests and objectives) being more successful than technical scrutiny committees (which offer technical guidance to Parliament regarding compliance).[128] The former type of scrutiny tends to involve more public engagement, as well as recommendations for amendments; the latter tends to 'note' or bring matters to Parliament's attention rather than make strong recommendations to Parliament.[129] SARC sees its role as involving technical scrutiny – continuing its pre-*Charter* functions[130] – despite its apparent mandate to engage with policy issues in reporting on whether a limit on rights is 'reasonable'.[131] As a consequence, SARC rarely engages with the public in relation to its scrutiny role, for which it has been criticised.[132] As Brett Young explained:

> Meaningful human rights scrutiny by SARC relies on the Committee members, but also on the broader culture of the Parliament, public involvement in the scrutiny process (so it is relevant for members of Parliament).[133]

SARC also seems to have become less likely over time to comment that a bill is incompatible with the *Charter*.[134] Further reasons that have been given for SARC's lack of impact on parliamentary dialogue include the lack of education and support provided to the committee, the short timeframes it is sometimes given to examine contentious bills, and

[123] SARC Review, above n 6, 85.
[124] VEOHRC 2016 Report, above n 2, 43.
[125] Kelly, above n 37, 270.
[126] Ibid.
[127] Grenfell and Moulds, above n 38, 66.
[128] Ibid 73.
[129] Ibid 51.
[130] SARC Review, above n 6, 2.
[131] Brett Young, above n 7, 176; Grenfell and Moulds, above n 38, 73.
[132] Brett Young, above n 7, 178; VEOHRC 2016 Report, above n 2, 44.
[133] Brett Young, above n 7, 178. See also Grenfell and Moulds, above n 38, 69.
[134] Brett Young, above n 7, 177–78.

the composition of the committee as a two-party committee dominated by the Legislative Assembly.[135]

It should be noted that SARC does frequently write to Ministers asking for clarifications in performing its scrutiny role. This constitutes a form of dialogue, and Ministers tend to respond promptly, despite the fact that there is no statutory requirement for them to do so. However, Grenfell and Moulds are sceptical of this engagement, suggesting that it may in fact be a deliberate strategy by the executive to avoid parliamentary scrutiny. They argue that:

> One Coalition strategy appears to be that of giving prompt ministerial responses to ensure that any debate is highly scripted by the government and thus to shut down any potential questions that might be posed in Parliament.[136]

It cannot be said that the dialogue between the judiciary and the political branches has been any more effective. As noted above, the Supreme Court has only issued one statement of incompatibility, and this was overturned on appeal. And its use of the interpretive function in section 32 has been equally weak. Thus there has been no cause for the legislature to revisit legislation and engage in dialogue as a result of either a declaration of inconsistent interpretation or a judicial interpretation of a statute under section 32.

With respect to judicial review of administrative decisions on *Charter* grounds, it is not clear whether the *Charter* intends for there to be any dialogue between the judiciary and executive, and if so, how this would operate. As noted above, it is arguable that judicial review on human rights grounds may result in a dialogue of sorts. For example in some Canadian cases courts have said that the *Canadian Charter of Rights and Freedoms*[137] requires administrative decision-makers to justify limitations on rights; but provided the justification given is reasonable, courts will defer to the executive branch.[138] This might be regarded as a form of dialogue, as it involves the executive providing the courts with an explanation, and courts determining whether it is sufficiently convincing. However, the Victorian Supreme Court has taken a different approach, due largely to the absence of a doctrine of deference in Australia. The approach of Victorian courts is to treat the question of whether a public authority's actions comply with the *Charter* as a legal question for the courts to decide on a 'correctness' basis.[139] That is, a reviewing court will undertake its own assessment of whether any limits placed on rights are reasonable and justified, and whether less restrictive means of achieving the same objective were available.

Dixon J's judgment in the *Barwon Prison Case* provides a good example.[140] His Honour concluded that the government's decision to designate part of an adult maximum security prison as a youth justice centre and remand centre, and decisions to transfer young

[135] Ibid 178–79; Grenfell and Moulds, above n 38, 69.

[136] Grenfell and Moulds, above n 38, 68.

[137] *Canada Act 1982* (UK) c 11, Sch B, Pt 1.

[138] See, eg, *Doré v Barreau du Quebec* [2012] 1 SCR 395. On this approach see: Janina Boughey, 'Rights, Review and Reasonableness: The Implications of Canada's New Approach to Administrative Decision-Making and Human Rights for Australia' (2013) 35 *Sydney Law Review* 283. Note that the approach the Supreme Court of Canada takes to administrative decisions which limit *Charter* rights is not consistent.

[139] See Janina Boughey, 'Re-evaluating the Doctrine of Deference in Administrative Law' (2017) 45 *Federal Law Review* 597, 622–23.

[140] For a fuller discussion see Boughey and Fletcher, above n 31.

prisoners there, were incompatible with the prisoners' human rights under section 17(2) (the right of every child to such protection as is in his or her best interests) and section 22(1) (the right of persons deprived of liberty to be treated with humanity and with respect for the inherent dignity of the human person) of the *Charter*.[141] His Honour approached this question by reviewing the evidence for himself to reach a conclusion that the limits the decisions placed on the prisoners' rights were not justified. Of particular relevance is his finding that the government could have allocated considerably more resources to improving accommodation at Barwon Prison, or reducing delays in the criminal justice system, both of which would have reduced the severity of the impact of the decision on young prisoners' rights.[142] Thus, there were less restrictive means of reaching the government's objective, meaning that the limit on the prisoners' rights was not reasonable under section 7(2) of the *Charter*.

Dixon J considered a submission from the government that he ought to give a 'margin of appreciation' to the government's views on the question of whether the limits were justified. However, he dismissed this submission, stating that:

> Proportionality ... must be judged objectively, by the court. No greater degree of "weight and latitude" can be given to a public authority's acts and decisions for to do so would be for the court to defer in its review to the balance struck by the public authority.[143]

While this may be the correct approach in law, following the High Court's rejection of deference in *City of Enfield v Development Assessment Commission*,[144] it does not appear to leave any scope for dialogue between the executive and judiciary with respect to the scope and application of rights in administrative decision-making.

Finally, dialogue between government and the public with respect to rights has been one of the most disappointing aspects of the *Charter*. The lack of consultation and engagement with the public – in both the design of bills, and in the parliamentary scrutiny process – has been a consistent theme in VEOHRC's annual reports and in the two statutory reviews of the *Charter*'s operation.[145] Of course there are exceptions. Brett Young undertook considerable public consultation in his 2015 review of the *Charter*.[146] There are also instances where there has been considerable public engagement in the development or scrutiny of legislation. But such instances also existed prior to the *Charter*, and there is no evidence that the *Charter* has increased the level of dialogue between government and the public about rights issues specifically. The SoC and SARC reports certainly do mean that there is more information available to the public about the justification for limits that legislation places on rights. In a sense, therefore, the political branches do now 'squarely confront' and explain why limits on rights are necessary and justified. However, there are very few examples of this resulting in any kind of public debate about the scope of rights, balancing rights, or whether

[141] *Barwon Prison Case* (2017) 52 VR 441, 581 [476].

[142] Ibid 580–81 [471]–[473].

[143] Ibid 508 [218].

[144] *City of Enfield v Development Assessment Commission* (2000) 199 CLR 135, [44] (Gleeson CJ, Gummow, Kirby and Hayne JJ); [2000] HCA 5. See also Gageler J's more recent comments in *Minister for Immigration and Border Protection v SZVFW* [2018] HCA 30, [54]–[55].

[145] VEOHRC 2009 Report, above n 32, 33; VEOHRC 2010 Report, above n 32, 14; VEOHRC 2012 Report, above n 101, 26; VEOHRC 2014 Report, above n 64, 64–65; VEOHRC 2015 Report, above n 112, 31; VEOHRC 2016 Report, above n 2, 25, 35, 44; SARC Review, above n 6, 132; Brett Young, above n 7, 183–85,

[146] Brett Young, above n 7, Appendix.

limits on rights are justified.[147] There are also only a handful of instances in which either SARC reports or SoCs have been mentioned in either *The Age* or the *Herald Sun* (Victoria's two major newspapers). It is therefore difficult to conclude that the *Charter* has had any significant impact on public debate about rights, or resulted in the political branches being held to account for the decisions they make about limits on rights.

IV. Conclusions

The *Charter* was intended to both improve the protection of rights in Victoria, as well as to create a dialogue between the branches of government, and between government and the public, about the scope of rights and when they ought to be limited. It was intended that Parliament would retain the final say on rights questions, but would be required to justify its decisions to the public. An analysis of the two reviews of the *Charter* and VEOHRC's nine annual reports, case law, legislative practice, and academic and professional commentary on the *Charter* reveals that it has had some success in achieving these aims over the past decade. Interestingly, however, this success has not tended to be achieved directly through the mechanisms set out in the *Charter* – of parliamentary scrutiny and judicial interpretation and review. As I have argued in this chapter, both of those mechanisms have fundamental flaws which make them less successful in protecting rights than many hoped. Instead, many of the best examples of legislation and administrative decision-making protecting rights to a greater extent than they likely would have without the *Charter* have been achieved within the executive branch alone, as a result greater cognisance about rights in developing legislation and policy, and through advocacy by lawyers and community groups on behalf of specific individuals or groups. While the threats of parliamentary scrutiny and judicial review very likely play a role in the effectiveness of this advocacy, and in building a 'human rights culture' within government, they have rarely directly resulted in Victorian law and administrative decisions being more rights protective.

On law and order issues which involve the rights of politically unpopular social groups – such as prisoners and bikies – comparison with jurisdictions without charters of rights suggests that the *Charter* has not resulted in less rights restrictive approaches being adopted in Victoria.[148] This may be because Australian Parliaments tend only to limit rights to the extent necessary irrespective of whether a charter of rights requires this. Nevertheless, it suggests that in these circumstances, the *Charter* has not been especially successful at altering the balance that laws and decisions strike between rights and competing public interests.

[147] A search of *The Age* digital editions reveals five topics on which there was any level of analysis of *Charter* rights issues in the past two years. (Mere mentions are excluded from this count.) Only one could be considered detailed independent analysis – reporting on the Barwon Prison cases. The others were all one or two paragraphs suggesting that *Charter* rights might be engaged by a policy. All related to administrative action, not the balance struck by legislation. A search of the *Herald Sun* digital editions reveals five such articles which involved any analysis of the *Charter* in the past two years, none of which could be considered detailed.

[148] In relation to prisoners generally, the *Charter* seems to have had limited effect in part due to the fact that there was already a prisoners' charter of rights in Victoria, which the *Charter* does not significantly add to. See Groves, 'The Second Charters of Prisoners' Rights', above n 46.

With respect to its other objective, of creating a 'dialogue' about rights, the *Charter* has been fairly disappointing overall. There are striking examples of success. But these are few and far between. On the whole, and with the exception of Greens MPs, parliamentarians have not used the enormous quantity of information they now receive through the SoC and SARC processes to engage in debate about the appropriate limits on rights. And, largely as a result of the *Momcilovic* decision, courts have not found it necessary or possible to play a role in any rights dialogue with respect to legislation. With respect to administrative decision-making, courts have treated *Charter* questions as questions of law, leaving no scope for any dialogue with the executive branch. Nor has the *Charter* had much of a noticeable effect on public dialogue about whether the political branches have reached the right balance between rights and public interests.

Thus, the *Charter* is probably best described as a partial success, with significant flaws preventing it from fully achieving both its rights protection and dialogic objectives. There is nothing to indicate that the *Charter*'s influence is overcoming these problems and picking up steam over time. Indeed in some respects, such as SARC's influence and the training of government officials it has gone backwards. So, the *Charter* is likely to remain only partially successful unless and until its most significant flaws are fixed via legislative amendment.

12

International Human Rights Treaties and Institutions in the Protection of Human Rights in Australia

MADELAINE CHIAM*

I. Introduction

Australia is party to the major international human rights treaties, and to many of the protocols attached to those treaties, but it has not implemented the majority of those obligations into domestic law. Successive Australian governments have nevertheless maintained that Australia complies with its international human rights obligations, primarily through many of the mechanisms described in this book. Australian governments have held these positions even as international human rights treaty bodies have continued to identify violations by Australia of international human rights obligations. In 1995, Hilary Charlesworth described as 'Janus-faced' the Australian practice of presenting itself as committed to human rights protections internationally, while failing to protect those same rights domestically.[1] In the decades since then, observers of human rights protections in Australia have made similar critiques, including describing Australia's commitment to international human rights standards as embodying exceptionalism,[2] or as an 'ornament of foreign policy'.[3] International bodies too have noticed this characteristic of Australian human rights practice. In 2018, the report of the Special Rapporteur on the Situation of Human Rights Defenders

* Thanks to the editors, Alison Duxbury and Emma Henderson for their comments on earlier drafts of this chapter, and to Stephanie Falconer for her always excellent research assistance.

[1] Hilary Charlesworth, 'Australia's Split Personality: Implementation of Human Rights Treaty Obligations in Australia' in Philip Alston and Madelaine Chiam (eds), *Treaty-Making and Australia: Globalisation versus Sovereignty?* (Annandale, The Federation Press, 1995) 129.

[2] Dianne Otto, 'From "Reluctance" to "Exceptionalism": The Australian Approach to Domestic Implementation of Human Rights' (2001) 26 *Alternative Law Journal* 219.

[3] Devika Hovell, 'The Sovereignty Stratagem: Australia's Response to UN Human Rights Treaty Bodies' (2003) 28 *Alternative Law Journal* 297. See also Hilary Charlesworth, *Writing in Rights – Australia and the Protection of Human Rights* (Sydney, UNSW Press, 2002); Sarah Joseph, 'The Howard Government's Record of Engagement with the International Human Rights System' (2008) 27 *Australian Yearbook of International Law* 45; Ben Saul, 'Dark Justice: Australia's Indefinite Detention of Refugees on Security Grounds under International Human Rights Law' (2012) 13 *Melbourne Journal of International Law* 685; Hilary Charlesworth & Gillian Triggs, 'Australia and the International Protection of Human Rights' in Donald R Rothwell and Emily Crawford (eds), *International Law in Australia*, 3rd edn (Melbourne, Thomson Reuters, 2017).

in Australia expressed astonishment at what he described as 'the increasing discrepancy and incoherence between the Government's external pronouncements … and the domestic implementation of its human rights obligations'.[4]

This chapter builds on these observations to examine Australia's attitudes towards the international human rights system, with a focus on events after 2010.[5] Using examples of Australian government responses to international criticisms of its domestic human rights protections, this chapter argues that in many respects Australia has lessened its tendency to display a Janus-face in relation to human rights protections. This is not however because Australian governments have improved records of compliance with international human rights standards. Rather, Australian governments' skepticism of the application of international human rights standards domestically has resulted in repeatedly hostile responses to the views of international human rights bodies. Australian governments have minimised the Janus-faced approach through their open rejection, both internationally and domestically, of the views of international human rights bodies. This attitude has meant that the determinations and recommendations of these international bodies have had minimal impact in Australia.

This chapter proceeds in four parts. Part 2 outlines the international human rights regime, with a particular focus on the protections offered to Australians by that system. Part 3 examines Australian interactions with the human rights scrutiny mechanisms under the Human Rights Council and the committees established under the human rights treaties. In part 4, this chapter explores the individual complaints mechanisms that are open to Australians under some human rights treaties. Parts 3 and 4 use examples of Australian interactions with the international human rights system to highlight the guarded, and often combative, nature of Australia's approach to international assessments of Australia's human rights compliance. Part 5 of this chapter asks what purpose is served – what human rights are protected – by Australia continuing to participate in the international human rights regime, when its reception to those bodies is so consistently hostile.

II. Australia and the International Human Rights Regime

The essential features of the international human rights regime are well documented.[6] This section describes them only briefly and focuses on those aspects most closely related to the legal protection of rights in Australia. Australia is a party to all of the major human rights treaties including, most recently, the *Convention on the Rights of Persons with Disabilities* 2006 ('CRPD'), which Australia ratified in 2008.[7] It has thus accepted international legal

[4] Michel Forst, *Report of the Special Rapporteur on the Situation of Human Rights Defenders on his Mission to Australia*, UN Doc A/HRC/37/51/Add.3 (28 February 2018).

[5] For a comprehensive account of events up to 2013, see Kate Eastman, 'Australia's Engagement with the United Nations' in Paula Gerber and Melissa Castan (eds), *Contemporary Perspectives on Human Rights Law in Australia* (Melbourne, Thomson Reuters, 2013).

[6] The entire system is described at www.ohchr.org/EN/Pages/Home.aspx. Australia's interactions with it are described in the Department of Foreign Affairs and Trade Human Rights Manual (4th edn, 2017), available at: http://dfat.gov.au/about-us/publications/Pages/human-rights-manual-fourth-edition.aspx. More critical views are available in, eg, Charlesworth & Triggs, above n 3; Joseph, above n 3; and Eastman, above n 5.

[7] The main international human rights treaties are: *International Covenant on Civil and Political Rights*, opened for signature 16 December 1966, 999 UNTS 171 (entered into force 23 March 1976), Australian ratification 13 August 1980 ('ICCPR'); *International Covenant on Economic, Social and Cultural Rights*, opened for signature

obligations to protect the rights contained in the major human rights treaties. In some cases, this acceptance has been modified by reservations issued at or after ratification.[8] Australia has a reservation under article 37(c) of the *Convention on the Rights of the Child* ('CRC'), for example, that modifies its obligations to keep children and adults separate in prisons.[9] Australia has also maintained reservations to the *Convention on the Elimination of All Forms of Discrimination Against Women* ('CEDAW') in relation to paid maternity leave, even though legislative changes in Australia mean that this reservation is no longer necessary.[10]

Australia has also made statements in relation to some of the treaties that it has termed 'declarations'. In relation to the *International Covenant on Civil and Political Rights* 1966 ('ICCPR') and CEDAW, for example, Australia has issued declarations about Australia's federal system, the terms of which are as follows:

> Australia has a federal constitutional system in which legislative, executive, and judicial powers are shared or distributed between the Commonwealth and the constituent States. The implementation of the treaty throughout Australia will be effected by the Commonwealth, State and Territory authorities having regard to their respective constitutional powers and arrangements concerning their exercise.[11]

These 'Federal Statements' were attached to the ICCPR and CEDAW in the aftermath of the High Court's decision in the *Tasmanian Dams* case,[12] and should be understood in the political and legal context of that time. As 'declarations', the Federal Statements were not intended to have any legal effect. Indeed, under international law they can have no legal effect as a state cannot invoke its internal law as a reason not to implement international

16 December 1966, 993 UNTS 3 (entered into force 3 January 1976); Australian ratification 10 December 1975 ('ICESCR'); *International Covenant on the Elimination of Racial Discrimination*, opened for signature 21 December 1965, 660 UNTS 195 (entered into force 4 January 1969), Australian ratification 30 September 1975 ('ICERD'); *Convention on the Elimination of All Forms of Discrimination Against Women*, opened for signature 1 March 1980, 1249 UNTS 13 (entered into force 3 September 1981), Australian ratification 28 July 1983 ('CEDAW'); *Convention against Torture and Other Cruel, Inhuman or Degrading Treatment or Punishment*, opened for signature 10 December 1984, 1465 UNTS 85 (entered into force 26 June 1987), Australian ratification 8 August 1989 ('CAT'); *Convention on the Rights of the Child*, opened for signature 20 November 1989, 1577 UNTS 3 (entered into force 2 September 1990), Australian ratification 17 December 1990 ('CRC') *Convention on the Rights of Persons with Disabilities*, opened for signature 30 March 2007, 2515 UNTS 3 (entered into force 3 May 2008); Australian ratification 17 July 2008 ('CRPD'). The two human rights treaties that Australia has not ratified are the *International Convention on the Protection of All Migrant Workers and Members of their Families*, opened for signature 18 December 1990, 1616 UNTS 120 (entered into force 1 July 2003), and *International Convention for the Protection of All Persons from Enforced Disappearances*, opened for signature 6 February 2007, UN Doc A/61/488 (entered into force 23 December 2010).

[8] Under Art 1(d) of the *Vienna Convention on the Law of Treaties*, opened for signature 23 May 1969, 1155 UNTS 331 (entered into force 27 January 1980), a reservation is a 'unilateral statement … made by a State … that purports to exclude or modify the legal effect of certain provisions of the treaty in their application to that State'.

[9] Reservation made on ratification. The Committee on the Rights of the Child considers this reservation to be unnecessary, see Committee on the Rights of the Child, *Concluding Observations: Australia*, UN Doc CRC/AUS/C0/4 (28 August 2012), para 9.

[10] See Australian Human Rights Commission, 'Factsheet: Scope of International Obligations' www.humanrights.gov.au/sites/default/files/1.%20Scope%20of%20international%20obligations%20Final_1.pdf.

[11] *Convention on the Elimination of All Forms of Discrimination Against Women*, opened for signature 18 December 1979, (1983) ATS 9 (entered into force for Australia 27 August 1983), Statement by Australia (available at http://www.austlii.edu.au/au/other/dfat/treaties/1983/9.html).

[12] *Commonwealth v Tasmania* (1983) 158 CLR 1. See Madelaine Chiam, '*Tasmanian Dams* and Australia's Relationship with International Law' (2015) 24 *Griffith Law Review* 89; Jon Piccini, *Human Rights in Twentieth Century Australia* (Cambridge, Cambridge University Press, forthcoming 2019).

obligations.[13] Nevertheless, Australia has never withdrawn the Statements, despite being urged by the treaty bodies to review them, and notwithstanding that none of the treaty ratifications after 1984 had similar Federal Statements appended.[14] The continued presence of the Federal Statements and the treaty reservations points to Australia's longstanding determination to protect human rights in its own way; an attitude that emerges in Australia's responses to determinations of the treaty bodies that are discussed below.

Australia's acceptance of human rights obligations internationally has not translated into the application or enforcement of these obligations domestically. Australia's legal dualism means that international law has no direct effect without the passage of implementing legislation.[15] As the chapters in this book attest, Australia's domestic implementation of its international human rights obligations has been, at best, inconsistent.[16] Certain obligations under CEDAW and CERD have, for example, been expressly implemented via the *Sex Discrimination Act 1984* (Cth) and the *Racial Discrimination Act 1975* (Cth),[17] while the *Australian Human Rights Commission Act 1986* (Cth) gives effect to a limited number of obligations under a number of human rights treaties and declarations, including the ICCPR.[18] The bulk of Australia's international human rights obligations remain unincorporated via legislation, however, with Australian governments consistently maintaining that Australia meets its human rights obligations through a combination of common law protections, statutory interpretation, domestic legislation and parliamentary processes.[19] In the absence then of comprehensive protection for human rights that a federal human rights Act might provide, Australian residents are peculiarly reliant on the international human rights system for the establishment of domestic human rights standards. This is evident, for example, in the process for human rights scrutiny of bills introduced into the Commonwealth Parliament under the *Human Rights (Parliamentary Scrutiny) Act 2011* (Cth). Under that Act, the Parliamentary Joint Committee on Human Rights assesses the compliance of Australian laws against the seven core international human rights treaties, rather than under a comprehensive national human rights act.[20] It is also highlighted by the reliance of Australian residents on the international human rights reporting and complaints mechanisms to secure some level of transparency about Australia's human rights protections.

The two key scrutiny and complaints mechanisms are the reporting requirements under the various human rights treaties to the Human Rights Council and the individual

[13] *VCLT*, Art 27.

[14] See, eg, Human Right Committee, *Concluding Observations on the Sixth Periodic Report of Australia*, UN Doc CCPR/C/AUS/CO/6 (1 December 2017), paras 7--8. The practice of no longer issuing Federal Statements appears to have been because they were no longer considered necessary at either a domestic or international level. Henry Burmester, 'Federal Clauses: An Australian Perspective' (1985) 34 *The International and Comparative Law Quarterly* 522.

[15] See, eg, Hilary Charlesworth, Madelaine Chiam, Devika Hovell and George Williams, 'Deep Anxieties: Australia and the International Legal Order, (2003) 25 *Sydney Law Review* 423. See ch 6 in this volume.

[16] An issue explained in chapter 2 by Williams and chapter 17 by Dunlop, McAdam and Weeks.

[17] See the *Sex Discrimination Act 1984* (Cth), s 3; and the preamble of the *Racial Discrimination Act 1975* (Cth).

[18] *Human Rights Commission Act 1986* (Cth), schs 1, 2, 3, 4 and 5. A full list of the treaties that have been partially implemented into Australian law, and the implementing statutes, is available at www.humanrights.gov.au/our-work/legal/legislation.

[19] See, eg, *National Report of Australia Universal Periodic Review Second Cycle 2015*, paras 16–19, available at www.ag.gov.au/RightsAndProtections/HumanRights/United-Nations-Human-Rights-Reporting/Documents/UPR-National-Report-of-Australia-2015.pdf.

[20] See *Human Rights (Parliamentary Scrutiny) Act 2011* (Cth), sections 3–7.

complaints mechanisms under the human rights treaties. Australia is subject to the monitoring mechanisms established under each of the human rights treaties.[21] There are differences in process between the treaty monitoring bodies – with respect to the regularity of state party reporting for example – but the key functions of assessing compliance and hearing complaints are the same. As a Member State of the UN, Australia also participates in the Universal Periodic Review ('UPR') process. As its name suggests, the UPR is the periodic review of the human rights records of all of the UN Member States. It is conducted by the Human Rights Council, which meets three times a year. Australia was elected to the Council for 2018–2020, and has been reviewed twice by the UPR. Finally, Australia has acceded to the relevant Protocols or made the necessary treaty declarations to allow individuals to bring international complaints of violations under five treaties: the ICCPR, CEDAW, the CRPD, the *Convention Against Torture and Other Cruel, Inhuman or Degrading Treatment or Punishment* 1987 ('CAT'), and the *Convention on the Elimination of Racial Discrimination* ('CERD'). The treaty complaints mechanisms have been particularly important, both as a way for individuals to seek redress from the Australian Government and as a means to assess Australia's human rights compliance. Neither the complaints nor the monitoring mechanisms create rights that are directly enforceable in Australian law; all rely on the willingness of Australian governments to accept and implement the determinations or recommendations of treaty bodies or the Human Rights Council. The next sections consider the ways in which Australian governments have responded to the assessments of international human rights bodies.

III. Australian Interactions with International Human Rights Monitoring Mechanisms

A. The Human Rights Council and the Universal Periodic Review

The Human Rights Council is charged with the promotion and protection of human rights around the world.[22] Unlike the treaty bodies, whose mandate over a state requires the state to be party to the particular treaty, all UN Member States are subject to the procedures of the Human Rights Council. The key Council mechanisms for monitoring human rights standards are the UPR, a Council complaints procedure for consistent patterns of human rights violations by states,[23] and other special procedures, which include Special Rapporteurs and

[21] *ICCPR*, art 28; *ICERD*, art 8; *CEDAW*, art 17; *CAT*, art 17; *CRC*, art 43; *CRPD*, art 34. The Committee on Economic, Social and Cultural Rights was established under ECOSOC Resolution 1985/17 (1985).

[22] The Human Rights Council was established by GA Res 60/251, UN GAOR, 60th sess, UN Doc A/RES/60/251 (3 April 2006). For a general overview of the role of the Council, see www.ohchr.org/EN/HRBodies/HRC/Pages/Home.aspx.

[23] See HRC Res 5/1, 5th sess, UN Doc A/HRC/RES/5/1 (18 June 2007). The procedure for the Council complaints procedure is set out at www.ohchr.org/EN/HRBodies/HRC/ComplaintProcedure/Pages/HRCComplaintProcedureIndex.aspx. This procedure has not been widely used, see Human Rights Council, *List of Situations Referred to the Human Rights Council under the Complaint Procedure Since 2006* (1 October 2014) Office of the High Commissioner for Human Rights, www.ohchr.org/Documents/HRBodies/ComplaintProcedure/SituationsConsideredUnderComplaintProcedures.pdf.

independent experts working on specific thematic issues or countries.[24] The Council itself consists of 47-Member States, with membership elected via General Assembly procedures. The Council was designed to replace, and address the limits of, the Human Rights Commission, which by the time of its demise had become mired in accusations of political bias and ineffectiveness.[25] While not as condemned as the Commission, the Human Rights Council has not escaped criticism. US governments have been especially sceptical of the Council, with the administration of George W Bush voting against its establishment in 2006,[26] and President Donald Trump withdrawing from membership in 2018, citing political bias.[27]

In a posture that is consistent with Australia's 'Janus-faced' approach to human rights protections, Australia has supported the international institution of the Council from its inception.[28] Australia's actions in relation to the Human Rights Council do not create enforceable rights for Australians domestically. They do, however, indicate Australia's attitude towards human rights protections internationally, which may then form the basis of domestic human rights advocacy. Australia considers the work of the Council important enough that it sought and was subsequently elected to the Council for the period from 2018–2020. Australia campaigned for Council membership on a five-pronged platform of gender equality, good governance, freedom of expression, the rights of Indigenous peoples and strong national human rights institutions and capacity building.[29] The Australian Government positions Australia as providing a 'unique Indo-Pacific perspective' on the Council. Then Foreign Minister Julie Bishop has stated that it was in Australia's national interest to 'shape the work of the Council and uphold the international rules-based order'.[30] Australia has, thus far, been an active member of the Council.[31] One indication of Australia's priorities in this role was its vote in relation to the Council's resolution to establish an independent commission of inquiry into the May 2018 violence in the Gaza Strip.[32] Australia and the US were the only Council Members to vote against the resolution.[33]

[24] For the work of the special procedures, see www.ohchr.org/EN/HRBodies/SP/Pages/Welcomepage.aspx. For an analysis of the Council's work, see Ted Piccone and Naomi McMillen, 'Country-Specific Scrutiny at the United Nations Human Rights Council' (Working Paper, Brookings Institution, May 2016).

[25] For an overview, see Philip Alston, 'Reconceiving the UN Human Rights Regime: Challenges Confronting the New UN Human Rights Council', (2006) 7 *Melbourne Journal of International Law* 185.

[26] United Nations, 'General Assembly Establishes New Human Rights Council by vote of 170 in Favor to 4 Against, with 3 Abstentions' (Press Release, GA/10449, 15 March 2006), www.un.org/press/en/2006/ga10449.doc.htm.

[27] Julian Borger, 'US Quits UN human Rights Council – "A Cesspool of Political Bias"', *The Guardian* (online) 20 June 2018 www.theguardian.com/world/2018/jun/19/us-quits-un-human-rights-council-cesspool-political-bias. See also Philip Alston, 'The Populist Challenge to Human Rights' (2017) 9 *Journal of Human Rights Practice* 1.

[28] United Nations, 'General Assembly Establishes New Human Rights Council', above n 23.

[29] These 'pillars' are described in detail at http://dfat.gov.au/international-relations/international-organisations/un/unhrc-2018-2020/pillars-and-priorities/Pages/pillars-and-priorities.aspx.

[30] See, eg, Minister for Foreign Affairs, 'United States Resigns from the UN Human Rights Council', (Media Release, Department of Foreign Affairs and Trade, 20 June 2018).

[31] See, eg, Marta Maurás, *Report of the Human Rights Council on its Thirty-Seventh Session*, UN Doc A/HRC/37/2 (14 June 2018). See also the series of Australian statements to various Council bodies, at http://dfat.gov.au/international-relations/international-organisations/un/unhrc-2018-2020/statements/Pages/hrc-statements.aspx.

[32] *Violations of International Law in the Context of Large-Scale Civilian Protests in the Occupied Palestinian Territory, Including East Jerusalem*, HRC Res S-28/1, UN GAOR, 28th sess, UN Doc A/HRC/RES/S-28/1, (22 May 2018).

[33] Australia's explanation of its vote is here: http://dfat.gov.au/international-relations/international-organisations/un/unhrc-2018-2020/statements/Documents/explanation-of-vote-for-the-resolution-on-violations-of-international-law.pdf.

As noted earlier, the primary Human Rights Council monitoring mechanism is the UPR: a state-to-state peer review system, which creates a periodic record of a state's human rights protections and allows other Member States to express their views about specific human rights issues in that country.[34] In order not to duplicate the treaty review processes, the UPR process measures a state's compliance with human rights obligations under the UN Charter and customary international law obligations under the Universal Declaration of Human Rights, as well as specific obligations under the human rights treaties, voluntary human rights commitments of states and any applicable international humanitarian law.[35]

Australia has experienced two UPR review cycles, one in 2011 and one in 2015. Australia's interactions with the UPR process have generally been positive. At the end of the 2011 cycle, for example, the Australian Government accepted in part or in full over 90 per cent of the recommendations made by the UPR Report. These included recommendations in relation to the over-representation in prisons of Aboriginal and Torres Strait Islander peoples, streamlining federal anti-discrimination legislation, reviewing federal offences in relation to people trafficking and slavery, and gender pay equity.[36] Acceptance of the recommendations did not, however, translate into comprehensive domestic action. Australia's appearance in the 2015 UPR, which measured Australia's human rights standards against the 2011 report, led to the conclusion that less than 10 per cent of the recommendations accepted in 2011 had been fully implemented.[37] Australia was also less open to the recommendations of the 2015 UPR process. Of the 291 recommendations made in 2015, 150 were accepted, 50 were noted to consider further and 90 were noted but not considered further.[38] In addition, Australia accepted many of the recommendations 'on the basis of existing law, policy and action'.[39] A significant number of the recommendations in relation to migration, refugees and asylum were accepted on this basis, including for example, recommendations to 'improve conditions of reception and detention of refugees and migrants in accordance with international standards' and 'review its immigration laws and policies and ensure compliance with its international obligations, especially regarding the rights of children'.[40]

It is not clear what the formulation of acceptance 'on the basis of existing law, policy and action' means. One possibility is that it allows Australia to interpret the UPR recommendations in a way that asserts the primacy of Australian law and policy, and of Australian views of international human rights standards. Australia, for example, considers that its treatment of refugees and migrants complies with international human rights standards, even if the recommendations through the UPR process and other experts have expressed contrary

[34] For a detailed description of the UPR process, see www.ohchr.org/EN/HRBodies/UPR/Pages/UPRMain.aspx. See also Eastman, above n 5.

[35] See United Nations Human Rights Council, *Basic Facts about the UPR* (Factsheet, Office of the High Commissioner for Human Rights, 1 November 2008), www.ohchr.org/en/hrbodies/upr/pages/basicfacts.aspx.

[36] See Human Rights Council, *Report of the Working Group on the Universal Periodic Review: Australia*, UN Doc A/HRC/17/10 (24 March 2011); Australia's response is available at www.ag.gov.au/RightsAndProtections/HumanRights/United-Nations-Human-Rights-Reporting/Pages/Australias-Universal-Periodic-Review.aspx.

[37] Charlesworth & Triggs, above n 3, 135.

[38] Human Rights Council, *Report of the Working Group on the Universal Periodic Review: Australia Addendum*, UN Doc A/HRC/31/14/Add.1, (29 February 2016).

[39] Ibid, paras 53, 62 and 65.

[40] See Human Rights Council, *Report of the Working Group on the Universal Periodic Review: Australia*, UN Doc A/HRC/31/14 (13 January 2016), Recommendations 136.243 (Uzbekistan) and 136.245 (Fiji).

views.[41] Maintaining that it has implemented the UPR recommendations on the basis of 'existing law, policy and action' may thus enable Australia to characterise its refugee and migration policies as consistent with Australia's interpretations of international standards, and thus make no changes to those policies. It is notable, for example, that two years after the 2015 UPR recommendations, the Human Rights Committee continued to recommend that Australia should 'bring its legislation and practices relating to immigration detention' into compliance with the ICCPR.[42] Australia's resistance to the recommendations of the UPR is consistent with its rejections of the findings of individual violations of human rights that are discussed in part 4. It also undermines Australia's claims that it 'strongly supports the UPR process',[43] and calls into question Australia's good faith in interactions with the Human Rights Council.

B. Reports of the Treaty Bodies

Each of the human rights treaties establishes a committee to monitor compliance with that treaty. States' parties to the treaties are required to submit regular reports to the treaty committees, and Australia thus has reporting obligations under each of the human rights treaties to which it is a party. Australia has had a fractious relationship with the treaty bodies. The relationship became openly hostile in 2000 when the CERD committee issued a report that was critical of Australia's race relations. The report was rejected by the Conservative Howard Government, with the Attorney-General, Daryl Williams, issuing a statement accusing the Committee of failing 'to grapple with the unique and complex history of race relations in Australia' and of paying 'scant regard to the Government's input'.[44] It was 'unacceptable', the Minister said, that Australia, 'a model member of the UN, [was] being criticized in this way for its human rights record'.[45] As a consequence, the Howard Government undertook a review of the ways that the UN treaty body system affected Australia,[46] the results of which included insisting that Australia's 'strategic engagement' with the system ensured a 'better deal from the UN treaty committees' for Australia.[47] In the years immediately following this decision, Australia withdrew from interacting with the treaty bodies, including by failing to comply with the reporting requirements under the treaties.[48]

Since 2010, Australia has re-engaged with the treaty body reporting mechanisms, including by submitting its overdue reports.[49] Australian responses to the treaty body

[41] See further ch 17 in this volume.

[42] Human Right Committee, *Concluding Observations*, above n 13, para 36.

[43] Universal Periodic Review Working Group, 23rd Session, Opening Statement by Australia, 16 March 2017.

[44] Attorney-General, The Hon Daryl Williams AM QC MP, 'CERD Report Unbalanced', (Media Release, Attorney-General's Department, 26 March 2000).

[45] Ibid.

[46] Minister for Foreign Affairs, Alexander Downer, 'Government to Review UN Treaty Committees', (Media Release, Department of Foreign Affairs, 30 March 2000).

[47] Australian Minister for Foreign Affairs, Alexander Downer, Attorney-General, The Hon Daryl Williams AM QC MP, Minister for Immigration and Multicultural Affairs, The Hon Philip Ruddock MP, 'Improving the Effectiveness of United Nations Committees', (Joint Media Release, 29 August 2000).

[48] See, eg, Charlesworth & Triggs, above n 3, 131–133.

[49] These include, eg, Committee on the Elimination of Racial Discrimination, *Eighteenth to twentieth periodic reports of States Parties Due in 2014: Australia*, UN Doc CERD/C/AUS/18-20 (15 March 2016); and Committee

reporting mechanisms retain something of the Janus-face however. Internationally, the general tenor of Australia's reports to the treaty bodies has been cooperative, as has been the mode of Australian representatives' appearances before the treaty committees. Thus, in 2014/15, Australia submitted its overdue reports to the Committee Against Torture, and also complied with requests for follow-up reports from the Committee.[50] Australia provided further information in relation to the Committee's queries on violence against women, indigenous people in the criminal justice system, the mandatory detention of asylum-seekers and Australia's commitment to its *non-refoulement* obligations.[51] Similarly, having used a CERD report as the impetus for Australia's withdrawal from the treaty body process in 2000, Australia submitted its overdue reports in 2010 and 2016.[52] Australian representatives appeared before the CERD committee in 2017 in a professed spirit of 'a long record of engaging closely with UN Human Rights Treaty Bodies' and in the interests of 'advancing human rights at home'.[53]

Despite this language, Australia's cooperation with the treaty bodies has not resulted in substantive changes in human rights protections in Australia. Australia's treaty body reports display the same kind of chauvinism about the superiority of Australia's domestic regime on human rights grounds that appear in its UPR reporting. The interaction between Australia and the CAT committee noted above, for example, included Australia resisting the Committee's concerns about the mandatory detention of asylum-seekers by insisting that the treatment of *non-refoulement* obligations within the 'protective framework' of the domestic *Migration Act 1958* (Cth) was sufficient, despite this framework being precisely the system about which the Committee had expressed concern.[54] Indeed, in the same period that Australia was acting cooperatively with the CAT Committee, the UN Special Rapporteur on Torture issued findings that components of Australia's asylum-seeker regime violated the right of individuals to be free from torture.[55] The then Prime Minister Tony Abbott expressed fury about the Special Rapporteur's report, rejecting his findings on the basis that 'Australians are sick of being lectured to by the United Nations'.[56] Echoing the justifications for Australia's withdrawal from the treaty bodies after 2000, Abbott insisted that the UN had failed to take proper account of Australia's achievements, and that the UN representatives 'would have a lot more credibility if they were to give some credit to the Australian government' for 'stopping the boats … [and having] ended the deaths at sea'.[57]

Thus, while Australian governments characterise themselves as having a long history of cooperation with the human rights monitoring mechanisms, they periodically

Against Torture, *Fourth and Fifth Periodic Reports of States Parties due in 2012: Australia*, UN Doc CAT/C/AUS/4-5 (9 January 2014).

[50] Committee Against Torture, *Periodic Reports*, above n 46.

[51] See Committee Against Torture, *Information Received from Australia on Follow-up to the Concluding Observations*, UN Doc CAT/C/AUS/4-5/Add.1 (18 August 2016).

[52] See CERD, *Periodic Reports*, above n 46, paras 2–4.

[53] Lachlan Strachan, 'Australia's Appearance Before the Committee on the Elimination of Racial Discrimination', Opening Statement, 27 November 2017.

[54] CAT, *Information Received from Australia*, above n 48, paras 20–27.

[55] Juan E Mendez, *Report of the Special Rapporteur on Torture and other Cruel, Inhuman or Degrading Treatment and Punishment, Addendum*, UN Doc A/HRC.28/68/Add. 1 (6 March 2015), 7–9.

[56] Ben Doherty and Daniel Hurst, 'UN Accuses Australia of Systematically Violating Torture Convention', *The Guardian* (online), 10 March 2015 www.theguardian.com/australia-news/2015/mar/09/un-reports-australias-immigration-detention-breaches-torture-convention. See also ch 17 in this volume.

[57] Ibid.

resist – and have sometimes openly rejected – the findings made under those systems. Even where Australia has accepted the recommendations of the human rights body, that acceptance has rarely translated into systematic human rights reform domestically. In these circumstances, it is unclear what impact, if any, the international human rights scrutiny mechanisms have on the protection of human rights in Australia. The next section considers this question in relation to the human rights complaints system.

IV. Australian Interactions with International Human Rights Complaints Mechanisms

A. The Individual Complaints Process

As one of two ways in which individuals under Australia's jurisdiction can have complaints of rights violations assessed by a competent body, and the only mechanism that can hear complaints about the full range of human rights, the complaints processes with respect to Australia under the international human rights treaties have been well-used.[58] The Human Rights Committee, which hears complaints of violations of the ICCPR rights, has for example received over 150 communications about Australia.[59] According to Human Rights Committee statistics, only four states have had more individual complaints made about them.[60] Being a member of the top five most-complained about states to the Human Rights Committee does not mean that Australia is amongst the top five most egregious abusers of human rights. Canada, for example, also numbers amongst the most-complained about states, despite its generally strong commitment to domestic human rights protections.[61] In addition, many states are not party to the ICCPR individual complaints process, and of those that are, there are different reasons that individuals may not use the complaints procedure, including lack of access to the resources and expertise required bring a complaint.[62]

The process for making a complaint (or 'communication') to a treaty body is relatively straightforward.[63] Any individual can bring a complaint to a treaty body, as long as the state that is the subject of the complaint has recognised the competence of the treaty committee

[58] There are also complaints mechanisms available under the Australian Human Rights Commission processes and the equivalent state bodies, but these are limited to complaints about discrimination or harassment. See ch 7 in this volume.

[59] Human Rights Committee, *Statistical Survey of Individual Complaints Dealt With by the Human Rights Committee under the Optional Protocol to the International Covenant on Civil and Political Rights*, Office of the High Commissioner for Human Rights, (March 2016), www.ohchr.org/Documents/HRBodies/CCPR/StatisticalSurvey.xls.

[60] These are Belarus, Canada, Denmark and Jamaica, *CCPR Statistical Survey*, above n 56.

[61] See, eg, Human Rights Watch, *Human Rights Report 2018: Canada*, www.hrw.org/world-report/2018/country-chapters/canada.

[62] For example, the series of complaints filed against Jamaica and Trinidad & Tobago in the mid-1990s were almost all prepared by British law firms or independent human rights organisations: Laurence R Helfer, 'Overlegalizing Human Rights: International Relations Theory and the Commonwealth Caribbean Backlash Against Human Rights Regimes' (2002) 102 *Columbia Law Review* 1832, 1874–1879. See also Sarah Joseph and Melissa Castan, *International Covenant on Civil and Political Rights: Cases, Materials and Commentary* 3rd edn (Oxford, Oxford University Press, 2013), paras 1.138–1.145; General Assembly, *Strengthening and enhancing the effective functioning of the human rights treaty body system*, UN Doc A/RES/68/268 (21 April 2014).

[63] A simplified version of this process is set out at www.ohchr.org/EN/HRBodies/TBPetitions/Pages/IndividualCommunications.aspx#theprocedure.

to hear complaints. As noted above, this is the case for Australia in relation to five of the human rights treaties. The complaints are subject to admissibility and merits criteria, and the committees tend to hear both arguments together. Complaints are regularly rejected by treaty bodies on admissibility grounds, which can include that a complainant has failed to exhaust domestic remedies, or has failed to substantiate a complaint sufficiently. Approximately one-quarter of the complaints filed against Australia in the Human Rights Committee have been found to be inadmissible.[64] If a complaint is admissible, the relevant committee also then considers the merits of the complaint. The materials that the committee has when considering the merits include the original complaint, a response by the state, and a further response by the complainant to the state's reply.

If a committee finds that an individual's rights have been violated, it can make recommendations as to how the violation can be remedied, including through the award of reparations. A state found to be in violation is usually given 180 days to report on the steps it has taken to remedy the violation. Committees have follow-up procedures under which they maintain dialogue with a state about violations and the case remains open until the state has implemented measures considered 'satisfactory' by the committee. The jurisprudence of the committees – that is, their determinations on admissibility and merits – is public, as are any ongoing follow-up measures taken by the committees. All of the publicly available material for complaints can be found at the webpages for each of the treaty bodies. In line with the requirement that determinations of the treaty committees be made public in the relevant state, unless there are confidentiality reasons not to do so, the Australian Attorney-General's Department maintains a webpage that records the treaty body determinations in relation to complaints made against Australia.[65] The page also provides information about how to make a complaint, and includes links to the different treaty body webpages, where the processes for making a complaint to a human rights treaty body are set out. The page does not, however, provide a guide to when and how human rights violations determined by the treaty bodies have been remedied, presumably because the Australian Government has accepted so few findings that Australia has violated human rights standards.

The large number of communications about Australia that have been made to the Human Rights Committee, and the fewer though not insignificant number made to the other treaty bodies,[66] have opened up Australia's human rights protections to international scrutiny across a range of issues. Some of the matters that have been considered by the individual complaints mechanisms include Australia's mandatory detention of asylum-seekers;[67] the indefinite detention of individuals who have received negative security assessments from Australian security services;[68] Australia's refugee assessment procedures, including

[64] *CCPR Statistical Survey*, above n 56.

[65] Attorney-General's Department, *Human Rights Communications* www.ag.gov.au/RightsAndProtections/HumanRights/Pages/HumanRightsCommunications.aspx.

[66] As at February 2019, there have been over 40 complaints submitted against Australia to the *Committee Against Torture*, 11 complaints submitted to *the Committee on the Elimination of All Forms of Racial Discrimination* and 7 complaints submitted to the *Committee on the Rights of Persons with Disabilities*. The treaty bodies established under *CEDAW*, *ICESCR* and *CRC* have not had any complaints submitted against Australia.

[67] *M.G.C v Australia*, Communication No 1875/2009, UN Doc CCPR/C/113/D/1875/2009 (2 April 2015); *Nasir v Australia*, Communication No 2229/2012, UN Doc CCPR/C/119/D/2216/2012 (1 November 2017).

[68] *F.K.A.G v Australia*, Communication No 2094/2011, UN Doc CCPR/C/108/D/2094/2011 (20 August 2013); *M.M.M v Australia*, Communication 2136/2012, UN Doc CCPR/C/108/D/2136/2012 (20 August 2013); *F.J v Australia*, Communication No 2233/2013, UN Doc CCPR/C/ 116/D/2233/2013 (18 April 2016).

its approach to returning individuals to places where they may be at risk of torture;[69] the rights of individuals with disabilities to participate in aspects of everyday life such as jury duty;[70] and Australia's marriage equality laws.[71] The number of complaints that have been made against Australia also mean that the treaty bodies have made a relatively large number of determinations that Australia has breached international human rights standards. For example, according to the Human Rights Committee statistics that include complaints made up until March 2016, 48 complaints against Australia were assessed on their merits. Of those, Australia was found to have violated ICCPR standards in 39 cases, or 80 per cent of the instances.[72] By way of comparison, in the same time period, of the 39 complaints against Canada that were assessed on their merits, violations were found in 21 cases, or 53 per cent of instances.[73]

B. Australia's Responses to Findings of Human Rights Violations

Determinations of the treaty body committees are not legally binding on states. The treaty bodies have made clear, however, that they consider their determinations to be authoritative interpretations of the treaty concerned. This position was expressed for example by the Human Rights Committee in its General Comment 33, where it stated that:

> The views of the Committee … represent an authoritative determination by the organ established under the Covenant itself charged with the interpretation of that instrument. These views derive their character, and the importance which attaches to them, from the integral role of the Committee under both the Covenant and the Optional Protocol.
>
> …
>
> A duty to cooperate with the Committee arises from an application of the principle of good faith to the observance of all treaty obligations.[74]

Australia has a different view of the weight attached to determinations of the human rights treaty bodies. In its response to an earlier draft of General Comment 33, Australia described the Human Rights Committee as '"an" authentic interpreter of the [ICCPR]'.[75] States parties to that treaty, Australia insisted, 'are of course also capable of providing authentic interpretations to that treaty'.[76] Australia's view is that 'the accurate legal position remains that, although the views of the Committee are not regarded as formally binding in law, they are

[69] *H.K v Australia*, Communication No 701/2015, CAT/C/60/D/701/2015 (15 June 2017); *M.K.M v Australia*, Communication No 681/2015, CAT/C/60/D/681/2015 (30 June 2017).
[70] *G.B v Australia*, Communication No 11/2013, CRPD/C/15/D/11/2013 (25 April 2016); *M.L. v Australia*, Communication No 13/2013, UN Doc. CRPD/C/15/D/13/2013 (25 April 2016).
[71] *C v Australia*, Communication No 2216/2012, CCPR/C/119/D/2216/2012 (3 August 2017).
[72] 'CCPR Statistical Survey', above n 56.
[73] Ibid.
[74] Human Rights Committee, *General Comment 33 – The Obligations of State Parties under the Optional Protocol to the International Covenant on Civil and Political Rights*, UN Doc CCPR/C/GC/33 (5 November 2008), paras 13 and 15.
[75] Australian Permanent Mission to the UN, *Views of the Australian Government on draft General Comment 33: 'The Obligations of States Parties under the Optional Protocol to the International Covenant on Civil and Political Rights*, Note Verbale 234/2008 (3 October 2008).
[76] Ibid.

to be considered in good faith.'[77] Thus while the Committee has reserved for itself the status of authoritative interpreter of the rights in the ICCPR, Australia insists that states parties can equally make authoritative interpretations of treaty-based human rights standards. The difference between the Committee's view of its authority and Australia's view underpins the whole of Australia's approach to the individual complaints processes.

Australia has consistently disagreed with committee interpretations of rights, rejecting them in favour of Australian interpretations of those same rights. None of the 15 available Australian Government responses to findings of violations dating from 2010 accept the determination of the international body. Australia did provide a remedy in relation to one claim arising from Australia's then lack of marriage equality laws. This remedy was, however, a result of domestic political imperatives rather than the recommendation of the Human Rights Committee.[78] Australia's response to the Committee in that claim was drafted in a way that did not accept any finding of violation on Australia's part. Rather, the response stated that the government was 'pleased to advise' that Australia had introduced marriage equality laws that provided the complainant with access to the divorce proceedings that she had been seeking.[79]

Two examples illustrate the style of response to treaty body determinations that has become a reflex of Australian governments. The first is the 'Response of the Australian Government to the Views of the Human Rights Committee in Communication No 2233/2013 (*F.J. v Australia*)'.[80] This was a claim arising from Australia's policy to indefinitely detain refugees about whom adverse security assessments have been made. The complainants argued that their detention, without access to information about their security assessments or merits review processes, violated a number of Convention rights, including the right not to be arbitrarily detained. The complainants' cases had been reviewed by the Independent Reviewer of Adverse Security Assessments,[81] but this process did not appear to convince the Committee that existing procedures provided adequate protection of the complainants' rights.[82] The Committee agreed that articles 9 and 7 of the ICCPR had been violated and directed Australia to provide an effective and enforceable remedy for the complainants. Australia's response opened with the diplomatic language of giving 'careful consideration' to the views of the Committee and closed with similarly careful 'assurances of [Australia's] highest consideration'.[83] In between these expressions of courtesy, however, was language

[77] Ibid.

[78] See, eg, Paul Karp, 'Australia says yes to same-sex marriage in historic postal survey', *The Guardian*, 15 November 2017; Paul Karp, 'Marriage equality law passes Australia's parliament in landslide vote', *The Guardian*, 7 December 2017.

[79] Response of the Australian Government to the Views of the Human Rights Committee in Communication No 2216/2012 (*C v Australia*), *Attorney-General's Department* www.ag.gov.au/RightsAndProtections/HumanRights/Documents/c-v-australia-2216-2012-aus-gov-response.PDF.

[80] *F.J v Australia*, above n 64.

[81] For details on the Independent Reviewer of Adverse Security Assessments, see www.ag.gov.au/NationalSecurity/Counterterrorismlaw/Pages/IndependentReviewofAdverseSecurityAssessments.aspx.

[82] Both parties made arguments with respect to the role Independent Reviewer of Adverse Security Assessments. The Committee did not engage with these arguments. The Committee's determination of the various breaches suggests instead that the Committee did not consider the Independent Reviewer process to be an adequate protection for the complainants' rights. See *F.J v Australia*, ibid, paras 4.1 and 5.2.

[83] 'Response of the Australian Government to the Views of the Human Rights Committee in Communication No 2233/2013 (*F.J. v Australia*)', *Attorney-General's Department*, paras 2 and 22 www.ag.gov.au/RightsAndProtections/HumanRights/Documents/fj-et-al-v-australia-2233-2013-australian-government-response.pdf.

that rejected the assessments of the Committee. Australia emphasised its entitlement to 'take measures, including detention, to uphold … national security', in which context Australia considered that the Committee 'failed to give adequate weight to various processes and policy developments outlined in Australia's submissions'.[84] Australia stated that it 'disagrees with' or 'does not accept' the Committee's view on the breaches of ICCPR article 9 (on arbitrary detention); considered that the Committee's interpretation of an Australian High Court decision was 'not the correct conclusion to reach from these circumstances'; and submitted that 'the treatment of the [complainants] is not such that it has reached the threshold necessary to satisfy a finding of a violation of article 7'.[85] The government did not respond to the Committee's determination that Australia should provide 'rehabilitation and adequate compensation' for their detention in violation of the ICCPR.[86]

The second example is the 'Response of Australia to the Views of the Committee Against Torture in Communication No 681/2015 (*M.K.M v Australia*)'. The complainant in this case had argued that there were substantial grounds for believing that he would be at risk of torture if he were returned to Afghanistan, and thus that returning him would violate Australia's *non-refoulement* obligation under article 3 of the CAT. The complainant's case had been through the complex Australian refugee tribunal and federal court processes, resulting in a final appeal rejection from the Federal Circuit Court in January 2013.[87] The CAT Committee determined that Australia had an obligation not to forcibly return him to Afghanistan.[88] The Australian Government again rejected all of the findings of human rights violations by the treaty body. Australia in this case 'respectfully' disagreed with the 'findings and reasonings' of the CAT Committee,[89] while assuring the Committee of Australia's 'highest consideration'.[90] These discursive niceties bookended an even more trenchant rejection of a committee's views than those expressed in *F.J. v Australia*. In this response, Australia described the CAT Committee as having made determinations 'erroneously' and 'selectively';[91] and as having not explained its findings adequately or at all.[92] Australia 'disagree[d] with the Committee's reasoning', and asserted that the Committee had provided 'very few linkages between the legal principles … and the factual circumstances of the case'.[93] Australia reiterated the primacy of its 'robust domestic processes' and remained of the view that 'the return of the [complainant] to Afghanistan would not constitute a violation of article 3'.[94] As a consequence, Australia did not 'accept the Committee's view that Australia is obliged to refrain from returning the [complainant] to Afghanistan' and he remained 'subject to Australia's domestic migration processes'.[95]

[84] Ibid, para 5.
[85] Ibid, paras 2, 9, 10, 15.
[86] *F.J v Australia*, above n 64, para 12.
[87] *M.K.M v Australia*, above n 72 paras 2.1–2.6.
[88] *M.K.M v Australia*, above n 65.
[89] 'Response of Australia to the Views of the Committee Against Torture in Communication No. 681.215 (*M.K.M v Australia*)', *Attorney-General's Department*, para 4 www.ag.gov.au/RightsAndProtections/HumanRights/Documents/mkm-v-australia-6812015-australian-government-response.PDF.
[90] Ibid, para 31.
[91] Ibid, paras 5(c) and 11.
[92] Ibid, paras 13, 24 and 26.
[93] Ibid, para 11.
[94] Ibid, para 28.
[95] Ibid, paras 29 and 30.

The fundamental characteristic of these Australian responses is a conviction that Australian legal processes and interpretations of human rights standards are superior to those of the international bodies. As part 3 argues, this chauvinism about Australian law is characteristic of Australian interactions with international human rights bodies in general. For Australian complainants to the human rights treaty bodies, this chauvinism has resulted in a process that may highlight Australian practices that infringe human rights standards but does not achieve effective remedies for the vast majority of complainants. While some of the earliest complaints to the treaty bodies resulted in changes to Australian law or practice,[96] Australia's overall record of providing remedies for human rights breaches determined by the treaty bodies is poor. The non-government organisation 'Remedy Australia' has estimated, for example, that Australia has remedied only 13 per cent of complaints upheld against it.[97]

The human rights treaty bodies have been consistently critical of Australia's attitude towards the views of the committees. In its 2009 Concluding Observations on the fifth periodic report of Australia, for example, the Human Rights Committee expressed concern at Australia's 'restrictive interpretation of, and failure to fulfill its obligations' under the complaints process, and also 'at the fact that victims have not received reparation'.[98] The Committee considered that Australia's attitude 'would call into question [its] commitment to the complaints process'.[99] The Committee reiterated these concerns during Australia's appearance before it for its sixth periodic report in 2017. Yuval Shany, then vice-chair of the Committee, was especially scathing, describing it as:

> [U]nacceptable for a State party to routinely fail to implement [the Committee's Views] and to take a position that in essence challenged multilateral, expertise-based treaty monitoring by declaring the power to self-assess its own record of compliance and to pick and choose which obligations to implement.[100]

Shany also noted that Australia has the lowest compliance grade of all states parties to the ICCPR, even in comparison with states with far worse overall human rights records.[101] The eventual language of the 2017 Concluding Observations was more measured than Shany's. The Committee emphasised that it 'regards implementation of the remedies indicated in its Views as an important part of the obligations of States parties' under the ICCPR and urged Australia to 'promptly and fully' implement all of the Committee's views.[102]

There is a good argument that Australia's consistent refusal to accept the determinations of any of the human rights treaty bodies means that it is failing to act in good faith to uphold its obligations under the human rights treaties. While determining what it means to

[96] *Toonen v Australia*, Communication No 488/1992, UN Doc CCPR/C/50/D/488/1992 (31 March 1994); Wayne Morgan, 'Identifying Evil for what it is: Tasmania, Sexual Perversity and the United Nations (1994) 19 *Melbourne Law Review*, 740; Emma Henderson, 'Of Signifiers and Sodomy: Privacy, Public Morality and Sex in the Decriminalisation Debates' (1996) 20 *Melbourne University Law Review* 1023; Hovell, 'The Sovereignty Stratagem' above n 3; Otto, From '"Reluctance" to "Exceptionalism"' above n 2.

[97] See http://remedy.org.au/.

[98] Human Rights Committee, *Concluding Observations*, UN Doc CCPR/C/AUS/CO/5 (7 May 2009), para 10.

[99] Ibid.

[100] Human Rights Committee, *Consideration of Reports Submitted by States Parties*, UN Doc CCPR/C/SR.3418 (24 October 2017), para 14.

[101] Ibid.

[102] Human Rights Committee, *Concluding Observations*, above n 13, paras 9 and 10.

implement obligations in good faith is contested,[103] it is hard to see how it can be consistent with the good faith implementation of treaty obligations to reject nearly all of the determinations of the bodies authorised to interpret that treaty. The Human Rights Committee appears to have been close to drawing this conclusion in both 2009 and 2017, restraining its final expressions of concern out of a diplomatic imperative not to make its criticisms of Australia too strident. In doing so, the Committee appeared to decide that it was preferable to keep Australia within the complaints system, rather than make a criticism that might provoke Australia into the kind of withdrawal that occurred in the early 2000s. The weighing of these competing considerations is an ongoing question in the legal protection of international human rights, and is discussed in the next section.

V. Tensions in Human Rights Protections

Two tensions emerge from the analysis in this chapter. The first arises from the purpose and value for residents of Australia in having their government continue to participate in the international human rights regime. What protections can the international human rights system be said to provide when complainants about Australia's human rights violations receive no remedy and Australian governments refuse to alter either laws or practices in line with treaty body findings? The widespread reliance on treaties in international law proceeds on an understanding that it is better for the international community to have the capacity to discipline states within a treaty regime (however imperfectly), than for states to be outside that regime and potentially beyond reach.[104] With respect to human rights treaties, this argument holds that it is better for Australian residents that their state is a participant in the human rights regime than not. Australia's resistance to the human rights complaints mechanisms, however, raises a serious question over whether and how this justification continues to apply. Given that it is unlikely that they will receive an individual remedy, participants in the complaints mechanisms have to find value in forcing Australian governments to continue to defend publicly practices that infringe international human rights standards. It is difficult to know whether the individuals who continue to bring complaints against Australia do so with the hope of a remedy or in a mode of strategic advocacy, or both. The high number of complaints against Australia suggests that complainants engage in the treaty body process in the hope that treaty body scrutiny will have some impact, however minimal.

The question of treaty body scrutiny leads to the second and related tension in this chapter: a challenge to the idea that making transparent a state's human rights violations is of value in itself. It is a longstanding pillar of the international human rights regime that human rights transparency and the consequent public condemnation can influence change within states.[105] Civil society organisations and others who participate in human

[103] Sarah Joseph and Melissa Castan argue that 'rejection of [Human Rights Committee] decisions is good evidence of a State's bad faith attitude', see Sarah Joseph and Melissa Castan, *The International Covenant on Civil and Political Rights: Cases, Materials, and Commentary* 3rd edn (Oxford, Oxford University Press, 2013), para 1.61.

[104] Eg, the structure of the reservations scheme under the *Vienna Convention on the Law of Treaties* is designed to encourage as widespread participation in treaties as possible. See, eg, Anthony Aust, *Treaty Law and Practice* (Cambridge, Cambridge University Press, 2007). Note that all states are subject to human rights obligations that exist under customary international law, although it is only the treaty regimes that give rise to specific complaints mechanisms.

[105] Ibid. See also Rosalyn Higgins, 'Some Thoughts on the Implementation of Human Rights' (1990) 5 *Interights Bulletin* 52.

rights monitoring processes must have some faith that regular and transparent reporting will influence Australian law and policy-making, if not immediately then in the longer term. But Australian governments have been rejecting human rights monitoring reports and determinations for over 20 years. Their actions challenge the idea that states, and in particular Western liberal democracies, can be scrutinised into human rights compliance. Australian governments' responses to the findings of treaty bodies suggest indeed precisely the opposite – they have refused to implement reforms and proclaimed the superiority of Australian interpretations and processes over international ones. Australian governments appear to remain unmoved by public pronouncements that Australia has breached human rights standards, suggesting that the views of the treaty bodies and the Human Rights Council hold no persuasive power for them.

There is an argument that Australian governments of different political persuasions have been more open than others to the international human rights regime. The examples in this chapter suggest however that not too much emphasis should be placed on political differences when it comes to assessing the protection of rights in Australia. The rejection of the findings of human rights treaty bodies has been consistent under both Labor and Liberal/National governments. Further, as section 3 argues, the Labor Government's acceptance of the UPR recommendations in 2011 did not translate into substantive change in domestic law or practice. In any event, agreeing to adopt UPR recommendations merely tinkers at the edges of human rights protection in Australia. The most profound way that human rights could be protected in Australia is by the adoption of a federal human rights Act,[106] and governments of both stripes have consistently refused to do so.[107]

VI. Conclusion

This chapter questions the capacity of international human rights law and policy to achieve structural change in domestic societies, particularly in the face of governments that are as openly reluctant as Australia's. This analysis shares a concern with many of the different critiques of human rights of the last two decades about the utility of human rights discourse and policy for individuals and communities fighting for change.[108] Human rights, some critics argue, have been not the counterpoint but the handmaiden to ongoing structural inequalities.[109] On this basis, those seeking societal change should discard emphasis

[106] See ch 2 in this volume.

[107] The processes introduced via the *Human Rights (Parliamentary Scrutiny) Act 2011* (Cth), noted earlier, are an ineffectual substitute for a comprehensive human rights act. See, eg, ch 8 in this volume; Adam Fletcher, *Australia's Human Rights Scrutiny Regime: Democratic Masterstroke or Mere Window Dressing?* (Melbourne, Melbourne University Press, 2018).

[108] For various iterations of this critique, see, eg, Samuel Moyn, *The Last Utopia: Human Rights in History* (Cambridge, Harvard University Press, 2010) and Samuel Moyn, *Not Enough: Human Rights in an Unequal World* (Cambridge, Harvard University Press, 2018); Jessica Whyte, 'Human Rights and the Collateral Damage of Neoliberalism' (2017) 20(1) *Theory and Event* 137–151; Ben Golder, 'Beyond Redemption? Problematising the Critique of Human Rights in Contemporary International Legal Thought' (2014) 2 *London Review of International Law* 77–114; David Kennedy, *The Dark Sides of Virtue: Reassessing International Humanitarianism* (Princeton, Princeton University Press, 2005); Naomi Klein, *The Shock Doctrine* (London, Allen Lane, 2007); Susan Marks, 'Human Rights and Root Causes' (2011) 74 *MLR* 1.

[109] On this point, see in particular Whyte, 'Human Rights and the Collateral Damage of Neoliberalism', above n 100; and Jessica Whyte, 'Powerless Companions or Fellow Travelers? Human Rights and the Neoliberal Assault

on 'human rights protections' in favour of different emancipatory forms and ideas. These claims are contested in a variety of ways,[110] but underlying all of them is a concern about the dominance of human rights as *the* language of emancipation. Nearly all commentators accept that, for better or worse, 'human rights' has become the dominant language in which individuals and communities can make their claims for a better life intelligible to those in power.[111]

The example of Australia sits uncomfortably within this narrative. Human rights, as language, law or policy, is not dominant in Australia and the few human rights claims that have been made of Australian governments have almost always been rejected. Australia remains one of the few states, and the only liberal democracy, without national human rights legislation. The examples from this chapter – and indeed from this book – suggest that framing claims in the language and law of human rights provides little assistance to individuals and groups in Australia seeking to alleviate abuses of their human rights. Australians have somehow missed out on the benefits of the human rights heyday. We find ourselves in a time where doubts about the value of human rights protections are in the ascendancy, but without having experienced any of the gains (however limited) that were achieved in other places using human rights law and policy.

Yet despite the attitude of Australian governments to international human rights treaties and scrutiny, Australian human rights advocates and lawyers continue to make claims in the language of human rights, and individuals continue to bring complaints to the human rights treaty bodies.[112] It may be that there remains value in maintaining international scrutiny of Australian human rights standards precisely because of Australian recalcitrance in relation to the international human rights mechanisms and the lack of enforceable domestic protections. Treaty body reviews and determinations on human rights issues give Australians additional information when considering, for example, the relationships between national security and 'border protection' on the one hand, and individual freedoms of speech and association and rights to be free from torture on the other. Access to international scrutiny and complaints mechanisms opens up the possibility of different conversations for Australian residents when they are considering human rights issues. Having at least some information about the human rights abuses being perpetrated by Australian governments may in turn enable Australian voters to make more informed decisions in domestic democratic processes. And the examples in this chapter suggest that Australian residents need these returns, however meagre they may be.

on Post-Colonial Economic Justice' (2018) 2(02) *Radical Philosophy* 13, www.radicalphilosophy.com/article/powerless-companions-or-fellow-travellers.

[110] Philip Alston has been especially vigorous in resisting these arguments, see, eg, Philip Alston, 'Does the Past Matter? On the Origins of Human Rights' (2013) 126 *Harvard Law Review* 2043. Alston is also the UN Special Rapporteur on Extreme Poverty and Human Rights and has a long record of arguing for role of human rights in addressing poverty and inequality, see, eg, Philip Alston, 'Out of the Abyss: The Challenges Confronting the new U.N. Committee on Economic, Social and Cultural Rights', (1987) 9(3) Human Rights Quarterly 332; Philip Alston, 'Human Rights Under Siege' (2017) 14(25) *International Journal on Human Rights* 267.

[111] See, eg, Sally Engle Merry, *Human Rights and Gender Violence: Translating International Law into Local Justice* (Chicago, University of Chicago Press, 2006).

[112] Michel Forst, *Report of the Special Rapporteur* above n 4.

13

The Recognition and Protection of Indigenous Rights

EDWARD SYNOT AND DYLAN LINO

I. Introduction

The establishment of the Australian settler-colonial state and its legal apparatus is premised on the colonisation and dispossession of Aboriginal and Torres Strait Islander peoples. Like other settler-colonial states around the world, Australia has struggled to determine what is owed – and in particular, what is owed as a matter of law – to those peoples whose dispossession is the basis for its own existence. And like other Indigenous peoples around the world, Aboriginal and Torres Strait Islander peoples have since the beginning of the colonial encounter made claims upon and against the settler-colonial state to redress grievances stemming from its foundational disregard of their immemorial occupation of their territories and ancient forms of political organisation, as well as from its oppressive treatment of them over centuries of settler-colonial rule. The question of what is owed to Aboriginal and Torres Strait Islander peoples by the Australian state is one that can be usefully understood – and indeed, has frequently been understood by both Aboriginal and Torres Strait Islander peoples and the Australian state – as a matter of Indigenous rights.

In this chapter, we focus on two ways in which Indigenous rights have been historically articulated against the Australian state, by both Indigenous and non-Indigenous actors. The first category comprises those rights afforded to Aboriginal and Torres Strait Islander people (historically) as British subjects and (subsequently) as Australian citizens. These are rights premised on Aboriginal and Torres Strait Islander peoples' incorporation as individual members of the settler political community. The second category comprises those rights afforded to Aboriginal and Torres Strait Islander peoples as peoples. These rights are premised on Aboriginal and Torres Strait Islander peoples' historical and contemporary existence as collective political agents, as sovereign political communities in their own right. To the (now considerable) extent that the Australian state has been willing to grant the former, this has overwhelmingly been conditional on transforming Aboriginal and Torres Strait Islander peoples into governable subjects, mostly expected to leave their Indigeneity behind. To the (very limited) extent that the Australian state has been willing to grant the latter, this has been in a way that reaffirms the state's unitary sovereign authority while incorporating Aboriginal and Torres Strait Islander peoples within it.

II. Rights as Subjects and Citizens

A major battleground in the struggles of Aboriginal and Torres Strait Islander peoples against settler domination has been in the domain of settler citizenship and the rights (and burdens) attached to it. To be more accurate, these struggles have been about Indigenous membership in the political communities – imperial, colonial, state and federal – that British settlers have established on the lands of Aboriginal and Torres Strait Islander peoples since 1788 in the country now known as Australia. That membership has not always come within the legal or ideological frameworks of citizenship. Indeed, Australian citizenship as a formal legal status was only established in 1948 (and Aboriginal and Torres Strait Islander people automatically possessed it).[1] In the preceding century and a half, British subjecthood rather than settler citizenship provided the formal basis of membership within the settler and imperial political communities.[2] That being said, even before the advent of citizenship as a legal status, citizenship could and did form a discursive framework for imagining and debating such membership. For all the important differences that may exist between subjecthood and citizenship in theory and practice, our account here assumes and emphasises their continuities.[3]

For the hundreds of peoples occupying the Australian continent at the time of British colonisation, the extension over them of British subjecthood represented in the first instance their subjection to alien rule. Prior to British colonisation, Aboriginal peoples had for millennia lived autonomously and in relation to one another under their own complex legal systems. Accordingly, they resisted as the colonial frontier pressed outwards into the territories they had possessed and governed for generations, with violent clashes a common and frequently fatal result.[4] That Aboriginal people were British subjects according to the common law was a position haltingly reached by colonial officials over the first half-century of colonisation.[5] Their recognition as British subjects heralded, at least formally, the end of their autonomy and their forced incorporation into a regime of overriding imperial sovereignty. The leading edge of this incorporation was the criminal law.[6] As Bruce Kercher has explained:

> For the native people of Australia, the primary effect of becoming British subjects was that they were thrust before the courts as defendants. Far from the law protecting them, it usually victimised them. Its main impact was to coerce them into obeying a law that they had not agreed to observe and which they often knew nothing about.[7]

[1] *Nationality and Citizenship Act 1948* (Cth).

[2] John Chesterman, 'Natural-Born Subjects? Race and British Subjecthood in Australia' (2005) 51 *Australian Journal of Politics and History* 30.

[3] For a recent treatment of these and other questions in historical, comparative and theoretical perspective, see Frederick Cooper, *Citizenship, Inequality, and Difference: Historical Perspectives* (Princeton, Princeton University Press, 2018).

[4] See, eg, Henry Reynolds, *The Other Side of the Frontier: Aboriginal Resistance to the European Invasion of Australia* rev edn (Sydney, UNSW Press, 2006); Howard Pedersen and Banjo Woorunmurra, *Jandamarra and the Bunuba Resistance* rev edn (Broome, Magabala Books, 2016); Libby Connors, *Warrior: A Legendary Leader's Dramatic Life and Violent Death on the Colonial Frontier* (Crows Nest, Allen & Unwin, 2015).

[5] Bruce Kercher, *An Unruly Child: A History of Law in Australia* (St Leonards, Allen & Unwin, 1995) 3–12; Lisa Ford, 'Indigenous Policy and Its Historical Occlusions: The North American and Global Contexts of Australian Settlement' (2008) 12 *Australian Indigenous Law Review* 69.

[6] Lisa Ford, *Settler Sovereignty: Jurisdiction and Indigenous People in America and Australia, 1788–1836* (Cambridge, Harvard University Press, 2010). For a perspective on North America, see Heidi Kiiwetinepinesiik Stark, 'Criminal Empire: The Making of the Savage in a Lawless Land' (2016) 19 *Theory and Event*.

[7] Kercher (n 5) 12.

As discussed later in the chapter, since the colonial authorities in Australia ultimately refused to formally recognise Indigenous forms of political organisation, Aboriginal and Torres Strait Islander peoples' incorporation as subjects within the settler legal order also meant that their own claims to sovereignty and peoplehood were disregarded.[8]

Of course, the expansive British claims to territorial sovereignty over the Australian continent, and concomitant claims to jurisdiction over Aboriginal 'subjects', were belied by the much patchier and piecemeal reality of colonial settlement and the far-from-total territorial reach of its governing institutions. Well into the twentieth century, some Aboriginal peoples in remoter parts of the country, especially in the north and centre, could still live relatively autonomously from settler authority, though they were formally considered under settler law to be British subjects or, later, Australian citizens.[9] And whenever and wherever settler institutions have tightened their grip over Indigenous lands and lives, Indigenous legal orders have frequently persisted as a lived reality, even as they have been forced to adapt to colonial conditions and operate in the absence of formal settler recognition.[10]

Throughout the colonial era, the ostensible benefits of British subjecthood – in particular, the formal equality of basic civil and political rights under settler law – were often denied to Aboriginal people, either by explicit or de facto legal exclusions or by failures of enforcement. The most conspicuous and egregious failures of colonial authorities to uphold their own law concerned the subjection of Aboriginal people to wanton and habitually deadly frontier violence.[11] Rather than punish such violence as crimes infringing the liberty and security of British subjects, settler authorities typically condoned it and not infrequently authorised or perpetrated it.[12] Less egregious but still a significant issue in some colonies throughout the nineteenth century was the inadmissibility of Aboriginal evidence in colonial courts. This made it even easier for settler crimes against Aboriginal people to go unpunished and even harder for Aboriginal defendants to obtain some semblance of a fair trial.[13] As for the most fundamental political right within settler institutions, the right to vote, only a minority of colonial governments – Queensland and Western Australia – ever expressly denied this right to Aboriginal and Torres Strait Islander people on the face of the law.[14] However, in jurisdictions without formal bars on Indigenous voting, Indigenous people were often effectively denied the franchise on other bases. For instance, in New South Wales, Aboriginal people living on missions and reserves were denied the right

[8] PG McHugh, *Aboriginal Societies and the Common Law* (Oxford, OUP, 2004) 159–64.

[9] This is a major theme of Tim Rowse, *Indigenous and Other Australians Since 1901* (Sydney, UNSW Press, 2017).

[10] The most comprehensive study of Indigenous law remains Australian Law Reform Commission, *Recognition of Aboriginal Customary Laws*, (Report No 31, 1986).

[11] See, eg, Reynolds (n 4); Lyndall Ryan, 'Settler Massacres on the Port Phillip Frontier, 1836–1851' (2010) 34 *Journal of Australian Studies* 257; Timothy Bottoms, *Conspiracy of Silence: Queensland's Frontier Killing Times* (Crows Nest, Allen & Unwin, 2013); Nicholas Clements, *The Black War: Fear, Sex and Resistance in Tasmania* (St Lucia, University of Queensland Press, 2014); Chris Owen, *Every Mother's Son is Guilty: Policing the Kimberley Frontier of Western Australia, 1882-1905* (Crawley, UWA Press, 2016).

[12] See, eg, Amanda Nettelbeck and Robert Foster, 'Colonial Judiciaries, Aboriginal Protection and South Australia's Policy of Punishing "With Exemplary Severity"' (2010) 41 *Australian Historical Studies* 319; Amanda Nettelbeck, '"Equals of the White Man": Prosecution of Settlers for Violence Against Aboriginal Subjects of the Crown, Colonial Western Australia' (2013) 31 *Law and History Review* 355.

[13] Heather Douglas and Mark Finnane, *Indigenous Crime and Settler Law: White Sovereignty After Empire* (New York, Palgrave Macmillan, 2011) 55–9; Kercher (n 5) 15–17.

[14] Julie Evans and others, *Equal Subjects, Unequal Rights: Indigenous Peoples in British Settler Colonies, 1830–1910* (Manchester, Manchester University Press, 2003) 137–9.

to vote on the basis that they were in receipt of aid from the state or charitable institutions – a formal ground for disenfranchisement until 1926.[15]

From the late nineteenth century, the grip of settler law over Indigenous lives tightened, deploying regimes of control and exclusion that deprived Aboriginal and Torres Strait Islander people of the basic civil rights enjoyed by other subjects.[16] These schemes were rationalised as being in Indigenous people's best interests by protecting them from the depredations of white society or facilitating their biological or cultural assimilation.[17] Indigenous governance was a matter for each individual colony, and after federation in 1901, for each state, with the Federal Government assuming responsibility for the Northern Territory in 1911. Aboriginal and Torres Strait Islander people governed under these exclusionary regimes were usually segregated on government settlements or church-run missions. The regimes varied, both between jurisdictions and across time, in the people they applied to and in their precise operation and effect. But they typically imposed restrictions on Indigenous people's family life (especially marriage and custody of children), freedom of movement, finances and property, employment and access to alcohol.[18] The most notorious legacy of these governing arrangements is the Stolen Generations, the thousands of Indigenous children forcibly removed from their families over the course of a century from the late 1800s.[19]

Alongside restrictions on the civil and political rights of Aboriginal and Torres Strait Islander people, as the Australian welfare state expanded over the first half of the twentieth century, Aboriginal and Torres Strait Islander people (at least those defined as having more than half 'Aboriginal blood') were also denied the new social rights that broadened the entitlements of citizenship.[20] When invalid and old-age pensions were introduced by the Federal Government in 1908, Indigenous people were expressly excluded from eligibility, an exclusion repeated four years later with the maternity allowance.[21] Aboriginal and Torres Strait Islander people likewise did not receive the benefits of the Australian welfare state's extension in the early 1940s: the child endowment, widows' pension and unemployment and sickness benefits.[22] Indigenous people's disqualification from social rights at the federal level also went hand in hand with their disqualification from voting in national elections. From the moment the Federal Parliament determined the franchise in 1902, it followed Queensland and Western Australia in disenfranchising Indigenous people.[23]

While British subjecthood and Australian citizenship were in the first place the legal means by which sovereign and independent Indigenous polities were subjected to alien

[15] Adrian Brooks, 'A Paragon of Democratic Virtues? The Development of the Commonwealth Franchise' (1993) 12 *University of Tasmania Law Review* 209, 213; ibid 65–70, 83–4; Murray Goot, 'The Aboriginal Franchise and Its Consequences' (2006) 52 *Australian Journal of Politics and History* 517, 519.

[16] John Chesterman and Brian Galligan, *Citizens Without Rights: Aborigines and Australian Citizenship* (Melbourne, CUP, 1997) chs 1, 2, 4.

[17] See, eg, Katherine Ellinghaus, 'Absorbing the "Aboriginal Problem": Controlling Interracial Marriage in Australia in the Late 19th and Early 20th Centuries' (2003) 27 *Aboriginal History* 183; Rowse (n 9) ch 3.

[18] Chesterman and Galligan (n 16) chs 1, 2, 4; Ellinghaus (n 17).

[19] Human Rights and Equal Opportunity Commission, *Bringing Them Home: National Inquiry into the Separation of Aboriginal and Torres Strait Islander Children from their Families* (Sydney, Human Rights and Equal Opportunity Commission, 1997).

[20] On blood quantum as a determinant of these rights, see Chesterman and Galligan (n 16) ch 4.

[21] Ibid 85–6.

[22] Ibid 117.

[23] *Commonwealth Electoral Act 1902* (Cth) s 4.

rule, subjecthood and citizenship also provided resources for Aboriginal and Torres Strait Islander people to advance their political and legal claims once they had been effectively incorporated, however violently and unjustly, within the compass of settler institutions. Subjecthood and citizenship afforded Aboriginal and Torres Strait Islander people a formal legal basis for making claims upon settler and imperial governments. They supplied rhetorical frameworks, including through associated discourses such as protection and equality, that lent Indigenous claims valuable ideological support. At different times and places, Aboriginal and Torres Strait Islander people drew on their status as subjects or citizens to seek greater autonomy over their families, communities and lands, the dismantling of settler regimes of control, and the extension of civil, political and social rights.[24] Until the final third of the twentieth century, virtually the sole means for this activism was political agitation rather than litigation. Often appealing to the language of subjecthood or citizenship as the basis for fairer treatment, Aboriginal and Torres Strait Islander peoples confronted settler and sometimes imperial authorities by writing letters, sending delegations, creating petitions, giving evidence to inquiries, staging protests and going on strike.[25]

But even as Indigenous activists took up subjecthood and citizenship as the basis for making rights claims against the settler state, they resolutely rejected the idea that assimilation was the necessary price of their inclusion in the settler political community. Here, they sharply conflicted with governments. Especially from the late 1930s through to the early 1970s, assimilating Indigenous individuals, families and communities into settler society, with a view to 'their ultimate absorption by the people of the Commonwealth', emerged as the central goal of government policy in Indigenous affairs.[26] As part of their policies of Indigenous assimilation, Australian governments posited the eventual extension of full citizenship rights to Aboriginal and Torres Strait Islander people, but only once sufficient Indigenous acculturation to settler norms had taken place – and Indigenous norms had been largely destroyed.[27] Aboriginal and Torres Strait Islander people, however, overwhelmingly repudiated efforts to premise their attainment of citizenship rights on the loss of their distinct identities and cultures. While Aboriginal and Torres Strait Islander people increasingly saw great value in gaining full citizenship rights and achieving material equality with other Australians, they staunchly resisted the cultural assimilation underpinning governmental attempts to achieve those ends.[28]

[24] See, eg, John Maynard, *Fight for Liberty and Freedom: The Origins of Australian Aboriginal Activism* (Canberra, Aboriginal Studies Press, 2007); Bain Attwood and Andrew Markus, *The Struggle for Aboriginal Rights: A Documentary History* (St Leonards, Allen & Unwin, 1999); Sue Taffe, *Black and White Together: FCAATSI: The Federal Council for the Advancement of Aborigines and Torres Strait Islanders 1958–1973* (St Lucia, University of Queensland Press, 2005).

[25] See the sources in the previous footnote.

[26] Commonwealth of Australia, *Aboriginal Welfare: Initial Conference of Commonwealth and State Aboriginal Authorities* (Canberra, Commonwealth Government Printer, 1937) 2 https://aiatsis.gov.au/sites/default/files/catalogue_resources/20663.pdf. See further CD Rowley, *Outcasts in White Society* (Canberra, Australian National University Press, 1971) ch 18; Tim Rowse (ed), *Contesting Assimilation* (API Network, Perth 2005); Russell McGregor, 'Nation and Assimilation: Continuity and Discontinuity in Aboriginal Affairs in the 1950s' in Julie T Wells, Mickey Dewar and Suzanne Parry (eds), *Modern Frontier: Aspects of the 1950s in Australia's Northern Territory* (Darwin, Charles Darwin University Press, 2005).

[27] See the sources in the previous footnote.

[28] See, eg, Taffe (n 24) 53–5, 82; Bain Attwood, 'Rights, Racism and Aboriginality: Critics of Assimilation in the 1950s and 1960s' in Tim Rowse (ed), *Contesting Assimilation* (Perth, API Network, 2005); Russell McGregor, 'Arguing About Assimilation: Aboriginal Policy and Advocacy in Australia' in Bain Attwood and Tom Griffiths (eds),

By the late 1960s, the formal extension of Indigenous citizenship rights and the dismantling of exclusionary regimes of Indigenous governance had taken place across most Australian jurisdictions.[29] Queensland was the glaring exception to this trend, with a racially discriminatory governing regime remaining in place for Aboriginal and Torres Strait Islander people living on Queensland reserves into the 1980s.[30] But even in Queensland, Aboriginal and Torres Strait Islander people had been afforded the right to vote by 1965 (the last jurisdiction to grant it).[31] A crucial ingredient in achieving these reforms was activism by Aboriginal and Torres Strait Islander people and their supporters, as they successfully waged local, state and national campaigns for equal rights.[32] Also crucial was the post-war international environment. With a growing number of states in Asia and Africa newly liberated from colonial rule, the surge of powerful anti-colonial and anti-racist movements worldwide, and the ramping up of Cold War rivalry between the USSR and Western states for moral superiority, it became much harder for Australia to ignore Indigenous demands to overturn racially discriminatory laws.[33]

The 1967 constitutional referendum marked the symbolic highpoint of Indigenous struggles for political and legal recognition of equal citizenship, as well as precipitating a constitutional shift that now positioned the Federal Government as the ultimate guarantor of Indigenous citizenship.[34] Symbolically, the referendum deleted references to Indigenous people embedded in the original Constitution that discursively excluded them from the political community. Through popularly endorsed changes to an important civic symbol of the Australian body politic, the referendum publicly affirmed Aboriginal and Torres Strait Islander people's citizenship, not in the sense of conferring a formal legal status or bundle of rights but in the sense of acknowledging 'a form of collective identity and sentiment'.[35] Bound up with this symbolism was a constitutional shift that conferred on the Federal Government a national responsibility for securing Indigenous citizenship legally and materially, including against resistant state governments. This constitutional shift was partially the result of formal constitutional change – the extension of the Federal Parliament's law-making power in Indigenous affairs – but also the result of a change in constitutional culture that the referendum and the activism surrounding it had effected.[36]

Frontier, Race, Nation: Henry Reynolds and Australian History (Australian Scholarly Publishing, 2009) 268–75; Dylan Lino, 'The Indigenous Franchise and Assimilation' (2017) 48 *Australian Historical Studies* 363.

[29] Chesterman and Galligan (n 16) ch 6; John Chesterman, *Civil Rights: How Indigenous Australians Won Formal Equality* (St Lucia, University of Queensland Press, 2005).

[30] Rosalind Kidd, *The Way We Civilise: Aboriginal Affairs – The Untold Story* (St Lucia, University of Queensland Press, 1997) chs 8–10; Garth Nettheim, *Out Lawed: Queensland's Aborigines and Islanders and the Rule of Law* (Sydney, Australia and New Zealand Book Co, 1973); Garth Nettheim, *Victims of the Law: Black Queenslanders Today* (Sydney, George Allen & Unwin, 1981).

[31] Chesterman and Galligan (n 16) 145.

[32] See, eg, Chesterman (n 29); Taffe (n 24).

[33] See, eg, Jennifer Clark, *Aborigines & Activism: Race, Aborigines and the Coming of the Sixties to Australia* (Crawley, UWA Press, 2008); Chesterman (n 29) chs 2–3; Anna Haebich, *Spinning the Dream: Assimilation in Australia 1950–1970* (North Fremantle, Fremantle Press, 2008) 194–211.

[34] Dylan Lino, *Constitutional Recognition: First Peoples and the Australian Settler State* (Sydney, Federation Press, 2018) ch 5.

[35] Linda Bosniak, 'Citizenship Denationalized' (2000) 7 *Indiana Journal of Global Legal Studies* 447, 455. See further Frances Peters-Little, 'Remembering the Referendum with Compassion' in Frances Peters-Little, Ann Curthoys and John Docker (eds), *Passionate Histories: Myth, Memory and Indigenous Australia* (Canberra, ANU E Press, 2010) 75, 88–94.

[36] Lino (n 34) ch 5.

Partly in belated fulfilment of its new constitutional mandate in Indigenous affairs, the Federal Government in 1975 passed the *Racial Discrimination Act 1975* (Cth) (RDA), which remains the legal centrepiece for protecting Indigenous citizenship rights from discriminatory government action.[37] Although the RDA is a general piece of legislation that implements the 1965 *Convention on the Elimination of All Forms of Racial Discrimination* into domestic law, it has from its inception held a special relevance for Aboriginal and Torres Strait Islander people. The RDA's enactment had been prompted by a decade of Indigenous activism and by the Whitlam Government's determination to overcome Queensland's discriminatory reserve system.[38] Key early litigation under the RDA involved tussles over Aboriginal rights in Queensland – the 1982 *Koowarta* decision and the first *Mabo* decision in 1988, both cases that were narrowly resolved in favour of Aboriginal rights.[39] In addition to outlawing racially discriminatory actions by private actors and government decision-makers, the RDA – alone among Australia's suite of anti-discrimination legislation – includes a guarantee of equality before the law.[40] When combined with the supremacy of federal law over state and territory law in the event of an inconsistency, the RDA's guarantee of equality before the law operates effectively as a constitutional prohibition, rendering racially discriminatory state and territory laws inoperative.[41] Somewhat ironically, the RDA's signal achievement with respect to Indigenous peoples has been in protecting native title – a distinct Indigenous right based on pre-colonial ancestral connection to land – from state government incursions rather than in protecting Indigenous citizenship rights.[42]

If the extension of Indigenous citizenship rights won since the mid-twentieth century for a time seemed irreversible, reversals would nonetheless begin to occur in the new millennium, and they continue in various guises today. The winding back of Indigenous citizenship rights emerged amidst growing scepticism among governments of Indigenous people's personal capacities to behave responsibly and thus of their worthiness of full citizenship.[43] The most dramatic policy manifestation of this neo-paternalism was the Federal Government's 2007 'Intervention' into Northern Territory Aboriginal communities, which imposed a range of restrictions on individuals and communities and which continues today, albeit in a modified guise, under the banner of 'Stronger Futures'.[44]

[37] Ibid, ch 6.

[38] Ibid.

[39] *Koowarta v Bjelke-Petersen* (1982) 153 CLR 168; *Mabo v Queensland* (1988) 166 CLR 186.

[40] RDA, s 10.

[41] Constitution, s 109; Anne Twomey, 'Inconsistency Between Commonwealth and Territory Laws' (2014) 42 *Federal Law Review* 421. The section also purports to constrain Commonwealth laws, but if a later Commonwealth law is inconsistent with the RDA, the RDA will simply be repealed to the extent of the inconsistency.

[42] State legislation that treats native title less favourably than other property rights has been held to infringe the guarantee of equality before the law in s 10 of the RDA. See especially *Mabo v Queensland* (1988) 166 CLR 186; *Western Australia v Commonwealth* (1995) 183 CLR 373.

[43] Elizabeth Strakosch, *Neoliberal Indigenous Policy: Settler Colonialism and the 'Post-Welfare' State* (New York, Palgrave Macmillan, 2015); Will Sanders, 'Changing Agendas in Australian Indigenous Policy: Federalism, Competing Principles and Generational Dynamics' (2013) 72 *Australian Journal of Public Administration* 156, 162–8.

[44] Rosie Scott and Anita Heiss (eds), *The Intervention: An Anthology* (Sydney, NewSouth Publishing, 2016); Jon Altman and Melinda Hinkson (eds), *Coercive Reconciliation: Stabilise, Normalise, Exit Aboriginal Australia* (North Carlton, Arena Publications, 2007); Will Sanders, 'Sorry, But the Indigenous Affairs Revolution Continues' in Chris Aulich and Mark Evans (eds), *The Rudd Government* (Canberra, ANU E Press, 2010) 221, 226–9.

One of the citizenship rights most heavily impacted by this neo-paternalist turn has been the right to social security. This right has been especially undermined through federal policy measures that control Aboriginal and Torres Strait Islander people's social security income. Income management for Aboriginal and Torres Strait Islander people was first introduced as one of the centrepieces of the Northern Territory Intervention, though it has since been extended in a range of different forms and to select sites outside the Northern Territory.[45] Income management measures, while now ostensibly racially neutral, continue to disproportionately impact upon Aboriginal and Torres Strait Islander people, especially in the Northern Territory. For instance, of more than 22,000 people on income management in the Northern Territory in 2018, 82 per cent were Indigenous.[46] Another significant federal policy intervention conditioning Indigenous welfare rights is a remote-area work-for-the-dole scheme, first introduced in 2013 and since 2015 known as the Community Development Program (CDP).[47] The CDP's more than 30,000 clients are over 80 per cent Indigenous.[48] This scheme places substantially more onerous work requirements on its recipients than other work-for-the-dole schemes.[49] Moreover, the penalty burden for failing to satisfy work requirements – including up to eight weeks of payment suspension – has disproportionately fallen on CDP recipients: they have received 95 per cent of all penalties while only comprising 5 per cent of the entire work-for-the-dole clientele.[50]

The other citizenship right heavily impacted in the neo-paternalistic policy turn has been the 'right to drink' – an amalgam of basic civil rights to property and freedom of contract. If not a classic citizenship right, the right to drink alcohol is an entitlement with deep resonance for Aboriginal and Torres Strait Islander people as a marker of civic inclusion.[51] It is vital to note that many Indigenous communities, especially in remote areas, have for decades sought to reduce alcohol-related harms through the imposition of alcohol restrictions on themselves, as an exercise in self-determination.[52] The neo-paternalist era, however, has seen the rise of alcohol restrictions imposed on Aboriginal communities by government with questionable or no community involvement.

[45] Shelley Bielefeld, 'Government Mythology on Income Management, Alcohol, Addiction and Indigenous Communities' (2018) 38 *Critical Social Policy* 749.

[46] Australian Government, 'Income Management and Cashless Debit Card Summary' (31 March 2018) https://data.gov.au/dataset/income-management-summary-data/resource/986ef7fe-1ba8-460e-b1c4-2cf00145a948?inner_span=True accessed 23 September 2018. See also ibid 5.

[47] Senate Finance and Public Administration References Committee, Parliament of Australia, *Appropriateness and Effectiveness of the Objectives, Design, Implementation and Evaluation of the Community Development Program (CDP)* (2017) ch 2; Lisa Fowkes and Will Sanders, 'Financial Penalties Under the Remote Jobs and Communities Program' (Centre for Aboriginal Economic Policy Research Working Paper No 108, 2016) 10–11; Lisa Fowkes, 'Impact on Social Security Penalties of Increased Remote Work for the Dole Requirements' (Centre for Aboriginal Economic Policy Research Working Paper No 112, 2016).

[48] Senate Finance and Public Administration References Committee (n 47) 5; Department of Prime Minister and Cabinet, Australian Government, 'The Community Development Programme Regions' (June 2018) www.pmc.gov.au/sites/default/files/publications/cdp-regions_25-June-18.pdf accessed 23 September 2018.

[49] Fowkes and Sanders (n 47); Fowkes (n 47).

[50] Fowkes (n 47) 1.

[51] Maggie Brady, 'Equality and Difference: Persisting Historical Themes in Health and Alcohol Policies Affecting Indigenous Australians' (2007) 61 *Journal of Epidemiology and Community Health* 759, 760; Russell McGregor, *Indifferent Inclusion: Aboriginal People and the Australian Nation* (Canberra, Aboriginal Studies Press, 2011) 147–51.

[52] See, eg, Maggie Brady, 'Law Reforming Lawyers and Aboriginal Social Controls: The Case of the Western Australian *Aboriginal Communities Act*' (2013) 17 *Australian Indigenous Law Review* 38.

The Queensland Government was the first to go down this path in 2002, followed by the Federal Government in 2007, which imposed alcohol restrictions in the Northern Territory with the Intervention.[53] Government-imposed alcohol restriction regimes remain in place in both jurisdictions.[54]

As safeguards against the winding back of Indigenous citizenship rights, the two apparently strongest protections – the 1967 constitutional amendments and the RDA – have proven vulnerable. Though the 1967 referendum had occasioned a shift in constitutional culture that positioned the Federal Government as guarantor of Indigenous citizenship rights, there was clearly another constitutional shift under the Howard Government, which eroded the Commonwealth's protective role and retrenched some of the gains made on Indigenous rights in the preceding half-century.[55] For their part, the courts have to date declined to impose any significant constraints on the power that the Federal Parliament gained over Indigenous affairs in 1967.[56] When it comes to the RDA, since it is only ordinary legislation, it has been possible for the Federal Parliament to simply wind back its guarantees of equal treatment for Aboriginal and Torres Strait Islander people – either explicitly, as occurred under the original Northern Territory Intervention, or implicitly, as has arguably occurred with the neo-paternalist policies that have followed in the Intervention's wake.[57] Even where the RDA's guarantee of equality before the law promises to have the most bite – at the state and territory level – the courts have shown considerable deference to neo-paternalist policies. Thus, in a series of challenges to the discriminatory nature of Queensland's alcohol restrictions, the courts, including the High Court, have upheld these as valid 'special measures' that appropriately remediate Indigenous dysfunction and disadvantage.[58]

To many, the fragility of existing protections of Indigenous citizenship rights has strongly suggested the need for constitutional reform. One longstanding proposal for reform has been to impose judicially enforceable constitutional limits on the capacity of Australian governments to racially discriminate against Aboriginal and Torres Strait Islander peoples. There are different models for how this might be done, from a general prohibition on racially discriminatory legislative and executive action by all levels of government, to a narrower constraint on the Federal Parliament's power to make Indigenous-specific laws.[59] Another common proposal is for the creation of an Indigenous representative body entrenched within the Australian Constitution. The idea for a 'First Nations Voice' was most prominently put forward in the 2017 Uluru Statement from the Heart, a historic document of Indigenous advocacy endorsed by more than 200 Indigenous delegates at a National First Nations Constitutional Convention.[60] While a First Nations Voice is designed

[53] Peter d'Abbs, 'Widening the Gap: The Gulf Between Policy Rhetoric and Implementation Reality in Addressing Alcohol Problems Among Indigenous Australians' (2015) 34 *Drug and Alcohol Review* 461, 461–2.

[54] Ibid.

[55] Lino (n 34) ch 5.

[56] See especially *Kartinyeri v Commonwealth* (1998) 195 CLR 337.

[57] Lino (n 34) ch 6.

[58] *Aurukun Shire Council v Chief Executive, Office of Liquor, Gaming and Racing in the Department of Treasury* (2010) 237 FLR 369; *Maloney v The Queen* (2013) 252 CLR 168.

[59] See, eg, Joint Select Committee on Constitutional Recognition of Aboriginal and Torres Strait Islander Peoples, Parliament of Australia, *Final Report* (June 2015) xiii–xv.

[60] 'Uluru Statement from the Heart' (25 May 2017) www.referendumcouncil.org.au/sites/default/files/2017-05/Uluru_Statement_From_The_Heart_0.PDF accessed 23 September 2018; Megan Davis, 'To Walk in Two Worlds', *The Monthly* (Melbourne), July 2017, 8.

to be an institutional fulfilment of the Indigenous peoplehood right of self-determination – guaranteeing Aboriginal and Torres Strait Islander peoples greater collective autonomy within the Australian political process – many have also seen it as a politically potent prophylactic against the passage of racially discriminatory laws seeking to deny Indigenous citizenship rights.[61]

But if Aboriginal and Torres Strait Islander people's individual rights as Australian citizens remain vulnerable to rescission, especially as a means for governments to make Aboriginal and Torres Strait Islander people into more easily governable subjects, their collective rights as peoples remain minimally recognised at all and resolutely cabined within the bounds of a unitary settler sovereignty.

III. Rights as Peoples

An overwhelming emphasis of the majority of Indigenous advocates in Australian history has been recognition and protection of their rights as Aboriginal and Torres Strait Islander peoples.[62] That means recognition and protection of rights that inhere in their sovereignty and existence as political entities according to their own cultures, laws and traditions. This aspect of Indigenous rights advocacy – the Indigenous peoplehood aspect – has also proven to be one of the biggest points of contention between Indigenous and non-Indigenous approaches to the recognition and protection of Indigenous rights. Further to this point, Australia lacks any foundational agreement or authoritative mechanism to negotiate its relationship with Aboriginal and Torres Strait Islander people other than incorporation into its already existing hierarchical legal system and polity. This lack has also meant a failure to recognise the sovereign rights of Aboriginal and Torres Strait Islander people.

From the beginning of European imperial expansion, European political traditions have been unwilling to recognise Indigenous societies as peoples equal in standing and rights to the colonisers.[63] When liberalism's founding doctrines were written, it was the bodies and landscapes of the colonised practiced upon, demarcating what it was to be savage, justifying also what is was to be civilised.[64] Identified as savages, barbarians, natives and so forth, Indigenous peoples were denied the same rights as others and treated in a manner that dismissed their interests and claims.[65] This system of differentiation projected fragile representations onto the colonised as more or less civilised, justifying their level of protection and treatment according to settler-colonial standards. These descriptions came to represent the colonised as a 'people' or 'non-people' entitled to certain treatment, as much as they did

[61] See, eg, Noel Pearson, 'A Rightful Place: Race, Recognition and a More Complete Commonwealth' (2014) 55 *Quarterly Essay* 1, 64–7.

[62] See, eg, Larissa Behrendt, *Achieving Social Justice: Indigenous Rights and Australia's Future* (Sydney, Federation Press, 2004); Aileen Moreton-Robinson (ed), *Sovereign Subjects: Indigenous Sovereignty Matters* (Crows Nest, Allen & Unwin, 2007); Bain Attwood and Andrew Markus, *Thinking Black: William Cooper and the Australia Aborigines' League* (Canberra, Aboriginal Studies Press, 2004).

[63] See, eg, Peter Fitzpatrick, *The Mythology of Modern Law* (London, Routledge, 2002); Paul Keal, *European Conquest and the Rights of Indigenous Peoples* (Cambridge, CUP, 2003).

[64] Ibid; Kay Anderson, *Race and the Crisis of Humanism* (London, Routledge, 2007) 11–32; Anna Haebich, 'Marked Bodies: A Corporeal History of Colonial Australia' (2008) 7 *Borderlands* 2.

[65] Barry Morris, 'Frontier Colonialism as a Culture of Terror' (1992) 35 *Journal of Australian Studies* 72.

the inherent fragility of an expansive colonial authority attempting to project control over contested space.[66]

The foundational non-recognition of Indigenous peoplehood was not total, however, especially in situations where on-the-ground bargaining power between Indigenous and colonial actors was more evenly balanced. Especially in North America, some Indigenous peoples entered treaty relationships with colonial authorities, wherein the collective political authority of each party was mutually recognised.[67] To be sure, these agreements were often regarded as mere formalities by their European signatories. Eroded over time or ignored for their meaning to Indigenous peoples, treaties were used by colonists to manipulate circumstances in favour of ensuring settler-colonial progress, or disregarded by administrative approaches toward Indigenous affairs that would see Indigenous people disappear in favour of a settler-colonial future.[68] Those early recognitions, if only limited, have however formed the foundations of a key translation of Indigenous rights into contemporary political discourse. For many they formed a tradition of legal protection now embedded in constitutional protections that continue to provide a discourse for Indigenous rights that inhere as a result of their peoplehood.[69]

Although the Australian colonies, alone among British settler colonies, did not conclude foundational treaties with Aboriginal and Torres Strait Islander peoples, colonial and imperial authorities at least initially struggled to determine whether Aboriginal peoples came within a singular settler sovereignty or existed separately from it. And even when that question seemed to be officially resolved by the courts – in favour of a denial of Indigenous sovereign peoplehood – by the 1840s,[70] Aboriginal and Torres Strait Islander people continued to operate under their own laws, cultures and traditions, many of which are now recognised to varying degrees in the Australian legal and political system.[71] This history of the management of Indigenous affairs – not especially the rights of Indigenous people, but rather their protection, relations and amenability to British law – can be traced to a time before the colony of New South Wales had begun. While Indigenous people had been minimally considered as part of the Beauchamp Commission into Transportation of 1785 as to whether they would offer any resistance to settlement,[72] it is the instructions issued to

[66] See, eg, Lauren Benton, *A Search for Sovereignty: Law and Geography in European Empires 1400–1900* (Cambridge, CUP, 2010); Ford (n 6).

[67] James Tully, *Strange Multiplicity: Constitutionalism in an Age of Diversity* (Cambridge, CUP, 1995) 116–39.

[68] See, eg, Patrick Wolfe, 'Settler Colonialism and the Elimination of the Native' (2006) 8 *Journal of Genocide Research* 4, 387–409.

[69] Such as Canada's s 35. See, eg, Patrick Macklem and Douglas Sanderson (eds), *From Recognition to Reconciliation: Essays on the Constitutional Entrenchment of Aboriginal and Treaty Rights* (Toronto, University of Toronto Press, 2016).

[70] A number of early colonial judgments were decided during this time with respect to the amenability of Aboriginal and Torres Strait Islander people to Crown authority and English law. These were most often cases dealing with criminal law and the questions often turned on whether Indigenous people were liable for inter se crimes along with those committed against non-Indigenous British subjects. See, eg, *R v Murrell and Bummaree* (1836) 1 Legge 72; *R v Ballard or Barrett* (Unreported, New South Wales Supreme Court, Forbes CJ, 21 April 1829) http://classic.austlii.edu.au/au/cases/nsw/NSWSupC/1829/26.html accessed at 23 September 2018; Douglas and Finnane (n 13).

[71] Rowse (n 9).

[72] See, eg, Bruce Buchan, *The Empire of Political Thought: Indigenous Australians and the Language of Colonial Government* (London, Routledge, 2008).

Arthur Phillip, in April of 1787, for the establishment of a settlement in New South Wales that represent a more nuanced understanding of the development of British attitudes toward Indigenous peoples.[73] The draft and final instructions stated:

> You are to endeavour by every possible means to open an Intercourse with the ~~savages~~ natives, and to conciliate their affections, enjoining all Our Subjects to live in amity and kindness with them. If Our Subjects shall wantonly destroy them, or give them any unnecessary Interruption in the exercise of their several occupations, it is Our Will and Pleasure that you do cause such offenders to be brought to punishment according to the degree of the Offence. You will endeavour to procure an account of the Numbers inhabiting the Neighborhood of the intended settlement, and report your opinion to one of Our Secretaries of State in what manner Our Intercourse with their People may be turned to the advantage of this Country.[74]

Two points are key: the first being where 'savages' is replaced by 'natives', and second where Phillip is encouraged to avoid wanton destruction and unnecessary interruption so that the relationship may be turned to the advantage of the country. Both instances indicate a consideration of differentiations between 'native' and 'savage', suggesting a desire to soften the approach toward Indigenous peoples. Yet the instructions also implicitly approve of what would inform 'wanton destruction' or 'unnecessary interruption' – that is the need for *deliberate* and *necessary* destruction and interruption of Indigenous peoples. Early New South Wales case law illustrates this indifference toward Indigenous people further, while also highlighting the challenge of relations between Indigenous and non-Indigenous peoples and the difficult difference of this reality to the Colonial Office instructions issued at distance. Judgments oscillated between statements that the 'Englishman has no right wantonly to deprive the savage of any property he possesses or assumes a dominion over',[75] to assessments that found that the 'various tribes had not attained at first settlement of the English people amongst them to such a position in points of numbers and civilisation, and to such a form of Government and laws, as to be entitled to be recognized as so many sovereign states governed by laws of their own'.[76]

The development of these opinions is reflected further again in the 1837 House of Commons Select Committee on Aborigines (British Settlements) Commission report.[77] While noting that British morality required a responsibility to those lesser people as a response to reported deprivations against them,[78] the Commission reserved particular judgement for the 'aborigines of New Holland'.[79] The Commission reported that 'in their original condition' the New Holland Aboriginal 'was the most degraded of the human race', adding further that the 'territorial rights of the natives were not considered, and very little care has since been taken to protect them from the violence or the contamination of the dregs of our countrymen'.[80] Adding to this explanation of the fact that Indigenous

[73] Governor Phillip's Instructions, *Historical Records of New South Wales*, Vol 2, Pt 2, CO 201/1, 29–45, author accessed and viewed original Colonial Office files at The National Archives, UK.

[74] Ibid.

[75] See the reasoning of Forbes CJ in *R v Ballard or Barrett* (n 70).

[76] See the reasoning of Burton J in *R v Murrell and Bummaree* (n 70).

[77] House of Commons, *Report of the Parliamentary Select Committee on Aboriginal Tribes (British Settlements) Commission* (Aboriginal Protection Society, 1837).

[78] Ibid, 1–4.

[79] Ibid, 125–126.

[80] Ibid.

territorial rights had not been considered, the Commission also reported that the 'barbarous state of these people' meant that they were 'so entirely destitute … of the rudest forms of civil polity, that their claims, whether as sovereigns or proprietors of the soil, have been utterly disregarded'.[81]

The Commission's report reconciled this position with their moral duty to protect the barbarous of New Holland as part of a growing British humanism, committing to a 'policy of Great Britain' that would 'influence the character and the destiny of millions of the human race'.[82] For Aboriginal and Torres Strait Islander people this wedged their treatment between religious instruction and education for civilisation as part of a protection regime, or justifiable destructions and interruptions as part of progressing settler-colonial interests.[83] This variance represented a ceiling to the achievement of rights for Indigenous people in Australia that continues to exist today. Particular emphasis was placed on treatment that would force Indigenous people to give up their Indigeneity – something belonging to the past – and become part of a settler-colonial future.[84] Even today most measures available to Indigenous people continue this trajectory and are aimed at amelioration of the negative impacts of colonialism in order for Aboriginal and Torres Strait Islander people to achieve the same level of subjecthood and citizenship as other Australians.[85]

This denial of Indigenous peoplehood was cemented in the common law by the 1889 judgment of *Cooper v Stuart*,[86] an otherwise innocuous case that established authority for the reception of English law in New South Wales. On appeal from the Supreme Court of New South Wales, the Privy Council was asked whether a Crown reservation of 10 hectares of land as part of an original 1824 grant of 1,400 hectares was valid.[87] Lord Watson drew on Blackstone's Commentaries to determine the extent to which English law would apply to new colonies and whether the reservation was valid. This consideration drew on a characterisation of the nature of that land and its inhabitants. Lord Watson, applying Blackstone, wrote:

> The extent to which English law is introduced into a British Colony, and the manner of its introduction, must necessarily vary according to circumstances. There is a great difference between a colony acquired by conquest or cession, in which there is an established system of law, and that of a colony which consisted of a tract of territory practically unoccupied, without settled inhabitants or settled law, at the time when it was peacefully annexed to the British dominions. The Colony of New South Wales belongs to the latter class.[88]

This narrative of the reception of English law simultaneously formalised the erasure of Indigenous peoplehood. *Cooper v Stuart* also became authority for the doctrine of the silent

[81] Ibid.

[82] Ibid, 1.

[83] See, eg, Russell McGregor, *Imagined Destinies: Aboriginal Australians and the Doomed Race Theory, 1880–1939* (Carlton, Melbourne University Press, 1993).

[84] See, eg, Bob Reece, 'Inventing Aborigines' (1987) 11 *Aboriginal History* 14; Jeremy Beckett, 'Aboriginality, Citizenship and Nation State' (1988) 24 *Social Analysis* 3.

[85] See, eg, Virginia Watson, 'Liberalism and Advanced Liberalism in Australian Indigenous Affairs' (2004) 29 *Alternatives* 577; Marjo Lindroth, 'Indigenous Rights as Tactics of Neoliberal Governance: Practices of Expertise in the United Nations' (2014) 23 *Social & Legal Studies* 341.

[86] *Cooper v Stuart* (1889) 14 App Cas 286.

[87] *Cooper v Stuart* (1886) 7 LR (NSW) Eq 1.

[88] *Cooper v Stuart* (1889) (n 86) 5–6.

operation of constitutional principles, and while not explicitly acknowledged, it is arguable that the founding silent operating principle of Australian constitutionalism became the erasure of Indigenous peoplehood, as this act of erasure itself formed the factual calculation and authorising justification of the Crown's claim.[89]

Much has changed both internationally and domestically in the recognition and protection of Indigenous peoplehood rights since the late nineteenth century. Following the end of World War II, developments such as those represented by the work of the International Labour Organization and the United Nations Working Group and Permanent Forum on Indigenous Issues reflected struggles occurring in many decolonising and continuing settler-colonial nations where Indigenous self-determination was beginning to be recognised. These developments saw the proliferation of other forms of protections ensuring more aspects of Indigenous peoples, lives such as protection from racial discrimination and protection for cultural heritage. These changes ultimately saw removal of the last vestiges of discriminatory regimes prohibiting Indigenous enjoyment of equal citizenship rights, but recognition also of their rights as Indigenous peoples through an inherent right to self-determination. These developments also included a basic recognition of Indigenous peoplehood when the High Court in *Mabo (No 2)* would claim to overturn *Cooper v Stuart*'s century-old precedent that, upon colonisation, Australia was 'without settled inhabitants or settled law'.[90]

And yet the progress made in the Australian recognition of Indigenous peoplehood rights remains sharply circumscribed. Thus, while the High Court in *Mabo (No 2)* recognised that the assessments of Indigenous peoplehood made in *Cooper v Stuart* could no longer be supported, there was nonetheless a ceiling reaffirmed to Indigenous rights that remains unchallengeable in Australian courts today. Justice Brennan explained this ceiling when noting that the:

> Court is not free to adopt rules that accord with contemporary notions of justice and human rights if their adoption would fracture the skeleton of principle which gives the body of our law its shape and internal consistency.[91]

This variance between recognition of Indigenous rights and protecting the skeleton principle of the Australian legal system remains the simultaneous founding authority of British law in the Australian colonies and the erasure of Indigenous peoplehood. Justice Brennan further addressed, and in a way explained, the centrality of dispossession when noting:

> The proposition that the Crown became the beneficial owner of all colonial land on first settlement has been supported by more than a disregard of indigenous rights and interests.[92]

Yet those other supporting propositions cannot be understood without a characterisation of Indigenous peoplehood as inferior to Crown interest or as not sufficiently developed to register as a legitimate claim at the time of 'peaceful annexation'.[93] Justice Brennan indicates this himself when noting that 'the peace and order of Australian society is built on the legal

[89] See, eg, *Commonwealth v Queensland* (1975) 134 CLR 298, 333.
[90] *Mabo v Queensland (No 2)* (1992) 175 CLR 1.
[91] Ibid, 29.
[92] Ibid, 43.
[93] *Cooper v Stuart* (1889) (n 86) 5.

system',[94] and that the system 'can be modified to bring it into conformity with contemporary notions of justice and human rights', yet warns that 'it cannot be destroyed'.[95] However in reconfirming that ceiling on Indigenous peoplehood, Australian jurisprudence, and it seems significant popular political opinion, remains ardent in its belief of singular sovereignty resting in the Crown.[96]

Yet the Australian continent is a contested space, a contestation that due to an unflinching faith in the indivisibility of Crown sovereignty requires the perpetual myth of the Crown's radical title to be protected by a skeleton of principle that erases Indigenous peoplehood. This results in the paradoxical position from which Indigenous people can be singled out as an administrative category – such as for the administration of criminality, government programmes, grant processes and those other actions aimed at alleviating disadvantage or celebrating diversity – but any positive suggestion of a sovereign right is anathema to the Australian nation-state that continues to cling to the anxious fragility of its own projected sovereign authority over contested space.

While those Indigenous peoples that did enter formal agreements with settler colonialists are not without their continued and serious issues in being able to ensure the protection of their rights, there exists at least a foundational recognition between peoples that provides some form of shape and consistency to the continuing relationship between those peoples. The Australian approach as demonstrated however has been one that has progressed via successive attempts at transforming Aboriginal and Torres Strait Islander people into governable subjects via an incorporation into the Australian polity without serious recognition for those claims borne from Indigenous sovereignty.[97] Even the 1967 referendum, imbued with the significant symbolism that it was, can be understood to be more a vote for Indigenous people in the sense of ensuring their participation in the Australian polity and the alleviation of their disadvantage rather than any attempt to licence the recognition and protection of their sovereign rights.[98]

Challenges have of course been brought by Indigenous people to the erasure of their peoplehood. One such instance was *Coe v Commonwealth* that challenged the Crown's claim while also asserting Indigenous sovereignty.[99] While Justice Murphy was willing to recognise the injustice of the denial of Indigenous peoplehood 'as having been made in ignorance or as a convenient falsehood to justify the taking of aborigines' land',[100] it was Gibbs J's insistence that the 'contention that there is in Australia an aboriginal nation exercising sovereignty, even of a limited kind, is quite impossible in law to maintain' that reconfirmed again the legal erasure of Indigenous peoplehood.[101] Justice Gibbs continued in *Coe v Commonwealth* to note that 'it is fundamental to our legal system that the

[94] *Mabo v Queensland (No 2)* (n 90) 30.

[95] Ibid.

[96] See, eg, Michael Mansell, *Treaty and Statehood: Aboriginal Self-determination* (Sydney, Federation Press, 2016) ch 1, 5.

[97] See, eg, Behrendt (n 62); Moreton-Robinson (n 62); Douglas and Finnane (n 13); Chesterman and Galligan (n 16).

[98] Bain Attwood and Andrew Markus, *The 1967 Referendum: Race, Power and the Australian Constitution* (Canberra, Aboriginal Studies Press, 2007) 65–87.

[99] *Coe v Commonwealth* (1979) 53 ALJR 403.

[100] Ibid, 412 [E].

[101] Ibid, 408 [E]

Australian colonies became British possessions by settlement and not by conquest' in a similar movement to that of Brennan J some two decades later in *Mabo (No 2)* that protected the singular sovereign authority of the Australian state.[102] While *Mabo (No 2)* of course addressed many of the concerns stemming from two centuries of erasure, the High Court also reconfirmed its commitment to the sovereign fiction that underpins the Australian legal system by recognising a radical title that rested with the Crown, that all other claims remain vulnerable to.

To this end, the ceiling on Indigenous peoplehood remains where even the hypothetical entertainment of the idea of Indigenous sovereign rights is anathema to dominant understandings of Australian state sovereignty and law, and to the deeply entrenched sense of a unitary political and legal authority existing over the Australian continent, embodied in Australian citizenship. This commitment has developed over time to infect even the very nature of reconciliation and Indigenous rights based programmes in Australia, where much of the emphasis continues to be placed on reaching a state of final reconciliation between Indigenous and non-Indigenous citizens, rather than on reforming a relationship that continues to allow Indigenous peoplehood to be erased through denial, ignorance or incorporation.[103] This predominant approach of the past 30–40 years of reconciliation in Australia, especially within the last decade of focus on constitutional recognition, has been one focused on making space for a people that are recognised to have unique cultures, law and traditions, but in a way that is informed by and assessed from the point of view of dominant legal, social and political traditions without risking or piercing that same skeleton or ceiling of Australian state sovereignty.[104]

This particular point surrounding Indigenous peoplehood is one that not many understand. It has taken a decade to come to the fore in the constitutional recognition debate in Australia. This reluctance to understand Indigenous peoplehood is part of this history of the approach to Indigenous rights in Australia that continues to result in Indigenous people existing in the precarious position of having no guaranteed protections at the constitutional level.[105] These concerns exist not just for peoplehood rights that have long been denied, but also for the hard-fought citizenship and subjecthood rights as detailed above that have been under consistent attack over the past two decades. Indigenous people and rights remain ultimately susceptible to the legislative whim of the government of the day, and are rights, along with a peoplehood status, that have long been anathema to the popular settler-colonial narrative and prevailing approaches to Indigenous claims within Australian jurisprudence.[106]

This is also why constitutional amendment remains a paramount imperative for the future of Indigenous peoplehood in Australia. The Australian Constitution remains that authoritative place where proper recognition and protection of Indigenous peoplehood and

[102] Ibid, [F].

[103] See, eg, Penelope Edmonds, *Settler Colonialism and (Re)conciliation: Frontier Violence, Affective Performances, and Imaginative Refoundings* (Hampshire, Palgrave Macmillan, 2016) 90–125.

[104] Ibid. See also Tim Rowse, 'The Ontological Politics of "Closing the Gaps"' (2009) 2 *Journal of Cultural Economy* 33.

[105] See, eg, Megan Davis and George Williams, *Everything You Need to Know About the Referendum to Recognise Indigenous Australians* (Sydney, NewSouth Publishing, 2015); Simon Young, Jennifer Nielsen and Jeremy Patrick (eds), *Constitutional Recognition of First Peoples in Australia* (Sydney, Federation Press, 2017).

[106] See especially *Kartinyeri v Commonwealth* (n 56); Scott and Heiss (n 44).

rights can be ensured where they have not been before. The key problem remains however that the demand for that recognition and protection continues to run against the continually reaffirmed ceiling on Indigenous peoplehood. It is for these reasons also that the historic Uluru Statement from the Heart marked an important call for a transformation in the history of the relationship between Indigenous and non-Indigenous Australians.[107] Recognising the diversity within Aboriginal and Torres Strait Islander people, but also speaking from a position of solidarity with respect to Indigenous sovereignty, the Uluru Statement from the Heart was an invitation to the Australian people, not just its legal and political institutions, to hear Indigenous voices and understand the justice of their demands. This was an important transformation of the past decade of development toward constitutional recognition, despite the various responses it was met with, as it moved considerations from being a possibility of further incorporations within a strict hierarchy, to the potential for a re-imagination of the relationship between peoples based in the justice of their respective demands.[108] For these reasons, and including the fact that the High Court has proven itself unwilling to entertain other 'political' measures outside of its closed authority, constitutional entrenchment and amendment remains the first and most necessary step forward for the negotiation of a new relationship and the realisation of the recognition and protection of Indigenous peoplehood.

IV. Conclusion

Aboriginal and Torres Strait Islander people have fought long and hard for the recognition and protection of their people and rights. Too often a common liberal rights narrative progresses along the lines of a recognition of past behaviour and treatment as not acceptable by contemporary standards of human rights and justice, and that society can now rest safe in the knowledge that those deprivations and lack of protections are a thing of the past. For the most part, Australians may be willing to accept this narrative as representative of the progress of Indigenous rights in their own country. Yet surrounding the fragile veneer of contemporary reconciliation politics and law, a practice and belief that is triumphant in its own achievements, are the lived experiences and realities of Aboriginal and Torres Strait Islander peoples that continue to suffer inordinately compared to their non-Indigenous counterparts, and that continue to be denied their sovereign right as peoples. These lived experiences and realities are those same aspects of Indigenous peoples' lives that have been denied since the beginning of relations between Indigenous and non-Indigenous Australians. They are also those same recognitions, experiences and realities that have in practice already fractured and destroyed the skeleton of principle that holds together the Australian legal system and the ceiling that has been applied to Indigenous peoplehood. The continued inference otherwise remains nothing but a crude majoritarian play of power combined with the myth it conjures, from one generation to the next, of a renewed denial of Indigenous peoplehood based in further fabrications of the status of Indigenous claims, and the self-justification of the rights of the Crown.

[107] 'Uluru Statement from the Heart' (n 60).

[108] See, eg, Shireen Morris (ed), *A Rightful Place: A Road Map to Recognition* (Carlton, Black Inc, 2017); Megan Davis and Marcia Langton (eds), *It's Our Country: Indigenous Arguments for Meaningful Constitutional Recognition and Reform* (Carlton, Melbourne University Press, 2016).

14

Federalism, Public Interest Advocacy and Marriage Equality in Australia

GABRIELLE APPLEBY AND ADAM WEBSTER*

I. Introduction

In this chapter, we explore the relationship between federalism and the progress towards law reform, particularly in relation to rights protection, in the Australian federation. We start by considering the complicated traditional understanding of the relationship between federalism and the protection and promotion of human rights and other public interest causes. While our consideration of this relationship draws on the more traditional study of the inter-political relationship between the federal and state polities, it goes further to consider the perspective of the influence of federalism on the strategy of public interest advocates in the areas of rights protection, First Nations rights and self-determination and environmental protection. As Claussen, Grogg and Russell have observed in the US context, the federal structure must 'affect[] the shape and content of public interest advocacy.'[1] As Goluboff explains, it is only with an appreciation of advocacy and reform below the national level that the full range of actors that propelled historic and celebrated law reform forward is appreciated.[2] It is also true that the federal structure has affected the ways through which reform has been opposed.

As Dorsen and Herman have observed, 'one cannot assume acontextually that either national or state laws would secure individual rights.'[3] In Australia, there are certainly instances of public interest achievements through lobbying for state-based policy experimentation that have led to central consolidation and national adoption. Equally, we have also seen successful instances of progress achieved through the lobbying of federal governments to adopt and mandate reforms in the face of state defiance.

* We would like to thank George Williams, Andrea Durbach and Paul Kildea for comments they provided on earlier drafts of this chapter.

[1] Kathleen Clausssen, Adam Grogg and Sarah French Russell, 'Action across the landscape of federalism' in *Why the Local Matters: Federalism, Localism and Public Interest Advocacy* (Liman Public Interest Program, Yale Law School, and National State Attorneys General Program, Columbia Law School, 2010) 1.

[2] Risa Goluboff, 'Civil Rights History Before, and Beyond, Brown' in *Why the Local Matters*, above n 1, 11. Note also in that collection the essays on the place of cities in progressive policy innovation, which is not explored in this chapter.

[3] Norman Dorsen and Susan N Herman, 'American Federalism and the American Civil Liberties Union', in *Why the Local Matters*, above n 1, 21.

By using the case example of how marriage equality was achieved in Australia in 2017,[4] we even further problematise the influence of federalism on public interest advocacy. We argue that in Australia's federal constitutional system, public interest and rights advocates are often navigating constitutionally uncertain areas of federal law; that is, areas in which state and federal responsibility and jurisdiction are unclear. Advocates for change engaged with this constitutional uncertainty and resulting complexity deploy it as a further point of political leverage, a particular achievement in the face of attempts by opponents to use it to thwart reforms on constitutional rather than substantive grounds.[5] This last point highlights that the federal system is engaged with and deployed not just by advocates for reform, but also by opponents of it.

Ultimately, we argue that federalism will sometimes provide an important point of political leverage for advocates in Australian seeking progress towards rights protections, and other public interest causes. However, this will require at least some understanding of, and patience with, the constitutional dynamics of Australia's federal system.

II. Federalism and Public Interest Advocacy

There is no linear and inevitable relationship between federal governance structures and greater human rights protections. Indeed, federal systems have often been the location of the cause and continuation of rights violations. Historical examples of federalism as a rights-violative tool abound, from the American experience of federalism-enabled state-slavery policies and state perpetuation of Jim Crow,[6] to the Australian experience of state protectionist and assimilationist policies towards their Aboriginal populations.[7]

Nonetheless, there remains a standard theoretical thesis that asserts a relationship between federalism and human rights. According to this thesis, federal structures provide the opportunity for human rights advancement in three key ways.[8] Montesquieu proffers

[4] We are not the first to use the progress towards marriage equality in Australia as a case study of the relationship between federalism and rights. Scott Stephenson, 'Federalism and Rights Deliberation' (2014) 38 *Melbourne University Law Review* 709, also uses a same-sex marriage case study to prove his thesis that federalism creates opportunities for more deliberation about rights in legislative reform processes. We deploy same sex marriage in a different way, to look at how individuals and groups have leveraged federalism to create productive tensions for their causes.

[5] For further explanation of constitutional uncertainty, and how it can be used by politicians in rights-reform debates, see Gabrielle Appleby and Adam Webster, 'Parliament's Role in Constitutional Interpretation' (2013) 37 *Melbourne University Law Review* 255 and Gabrielle Appleby and Anna Olijnyk, 'Parliamentary Deliberation on Constitutional Limits in the Legislative Process' (2017) 40 *University of New South Wales Law Journal* 976.

[6] For a discussion of the system of the racial segregation that existed in the US during significant parts the 19th and 20th centuries (often referred to as 'Jim Crow' or 'Jim Crow laws'), see, eg, Michael J Klarman, *From Jim Crow to Civil Rights: The Supreme Court and the Struggle for Racial Equality* (Oxford, Oxford University Press, 2006), Leslie V Tischauser, *Jim Crow Laws* (ABC-CLIO, 2012).

[7] See [Australian] Human Rights and Equal Opportunity Commission, *Bringing Them Home: Report of the National Inquiry into the Separation of Aboriginal and Torres Strait Islander Children from Their Families* (1997) Pt 2. See also *Kruger v Commonwealth* (1997) 190 CLR 1, 33–40; *Trevorrow v South Australia (No 5)* (2007) 98 SASR 136, 236–239 [422]–[431].

[8] We have taken this tripartite classification from Robyn Hollander and Haig Patapan, 'Deliberative Federalism', in Ron Levy, Hoi Kong, Graeme Orr and Jeff King (eds) *The Cambridge Handbook of Deliberative Constitutionalism* (Cambridge, Cambridge University Press, 2018) 101, 102.

the first and most traditional view of this relationship, in which federalism, by offering additional restrictions on state power in a single governance system, defrays and disperses power across that system so as to decrease a single group or faction from harnessing the state's power to deploy it in a corrupt or tyrannous way.[9] While this thesis appears attractive, in a federal system such as Australia's[10] – where there is fluidity between the jurisdictions of the states and the central Parliament, with a tendency towards central dominance in overlapping spheres of competence[11] – Montesquieu's conceptions of defraying and dispersion no longer holds the force it might once have.

The second provides the justification for more modern federal systems, in which heterogenous groups are able to come together in a single state while maintaining their cultural, ethnic, social and political diversity. Federalism thus offers protections for these otherwise minority groups within a single governance system. While this arrangement may result in greater legalistic pluralism,[12] there is no necessary correlation between this and liberalism.

Third, federalism, at least in theory, provides sub-national laboratories for policy experimentation, providing 'spaces for deliberation in which minority voices can be heard, facilitating the advancement of human rights.'[13] The concept of voice is paired with that of exit:[14] individuals and groups have the ability to choose between jurisdictions in search of a jurisdiction that best coalesces with their policy desires, including around rights.

Despite evidence of the rights-regressive effect that these smaller spaces can have (for instance, making it easier for one group or faction to gain control over state apparatus)[15] and the potential costs associated with the concept of exit, proponents of laboratory federalism argue that progress towards rights protection is at least facilitated by certain federal designs. Depending on the politics that prevail at the state versus the national level, this can manifest in different ways, as the different levels provide different political access points for public interest advocates.[16]

[9] Charles-Louis de Secondat, Baron de Montesquieu, *The Spirit of the Laws* (1748) vol 1, book 9, ch 1. This argument was adopted by Alexander Hamilton prior to the ratification of the *United States Constitution*: see Alexander Hamilton, *Federalist No 9: The Union as a Safeguard Against Domestic Faction and Insurrection* (21 November 1787) in *The Federalist Papers* (Benediction Classics, 2016) 14.

[10] This might be contrasted to federal systems in which there is greater distinction and exclusivity between the responsibilities and jurisdictions of the national and sub-national governments.

[11] See a description of the different phases and trajectory of Australian federalism in Gabrielle Appleby, Nicholas Aroney and Thomas John, 'Australian Federalism: Present, Past and Future Tense' in Gabrielle Appleby, Nicholas Aroney and Thomas John (eds), *The Future of Australian Federalism* (Cambridge, Cambridge University Press, 2012) 1.

[12] John Griffiths, 'What is Legal Pluralism' (1986) 24 *Journal of Legal Pluralism* 1.

[13] Hollander and Patapan, 'Deliberative Federalism', above n 8, 102. See also David L Shapiro, Federalism: A Dialogue (Evanston, Northwestern University Press, 1995) 91–2.

[14] See further Albert Hirschman, *Exit, Voice and Loyalty: Responses to Decline in Firms Organisations and States* (Cambridge, Harvard University Press, 1970).

[15] For an analysis of the regressive use of laboratory federalism, driven by state politicking around law and order policies and the desire to be seen to be 'tough on crime' in the anti-bikie sphere, and what this reveals about failures of federalism theory in relation to rights protection, see Gabrielle Appleby and Brendan Lim, 'Democratic Federalism' in Rosalind Dixon (ed), *Constitutional Values* (Oxford, Hart Publishing, 2018) 221, 235; Gabrielle Appleby, 'The High Court and *Kable*: A Study in Federalism and Rights Protection' (2014) 40 *Monash University Law Review* 673.

[16] See further, eg, Erwin Chemerinsky, 'The Values of Federalism' (1995) 47 *Florida Law Review* 499, 539.

First, states can be lobbied to agree to enact experimental policies, that is, agree to be used as 'laboratories'. Majorities can be garnered more easily in these smaller spaces, particularly where political opinion is not evenly distributed around the federation, and so certain jurisdictions with stronger support for particular policies naturally exist. It is also the case that in a federal system, with a greater multitude of jurisdictions, there is an increased likelihood that the necessary preconditions for reform will align: popular support, government support and a political champion. In these situations, policies might be implemented more quickly in a particular sub-national government. According to Sagar, from this starting point national reform will progress in three stages: *invention*, where one or more states embraces a rights-progressive policy; *propagation*, where other states will start to adopt the policy; and *consolidation*, where federal intervention finally occurs (legislatively or judicially) and uniform adoption of the policy occurs across all remaining recalcitrant states.[17] In Australia, we have seen this, for instance, in the decriminalisation of homosexuality across the states, starting with South Australia in 1975.[18] The other states gradually followed and the Australian federal Parliament finally passed legislation to overturn the criminalisation of homosexuality in Tasmania in the mid-1990s,[19] at which point full consolidation was achieved.

Hollander and Patapan problematise the cleanliness of Sager's model, arguing by using the case example of marriage equality reform in the US that the relationship between federalism and human rights is far more complicated. Federalism in the US allowed discrimination against same-sex couples to co-exist with marriage equality for a significant period before reform was achieved. The move towards moral progression across the American federation was not a foregone conclusion. The initial moves in some states towards marriage equality sparked rights-regressive legislative and constitutional retaliations in other states and in the federal sphere with the passage of the *Defense of Marriage Act*. The intervention of the US Supreme Court in the *Obergefell v Hodges*[20] decision was also far from inevitable. It was the subject of strident dissents from Chief Justice Roberts, among others. Following the retirement of the lead judgment author Justice Kennedy, and the nomination by President Donald Trump of a generally perceived more socially conservative Brett Kavanagh, Roberts now occupies a more powerful swing position on future cases seeking to further advance the rights of LGBTI people. Relatedly, Hollander and Patapan warn against the presumption of ongoing consolidation of same-sex marriage reforms, which, they say, might be undermined by the court's approach to future conflicts, particularly between claims to religious freedom rights and equality advocates.

Second, where the states are less politically sympathetic to rights reform, lobbying can turn directly to the federal government to overturn regressive policies in the states. This, for instance, was evident in the 1967 referendum campaign in Australia to provide legislative power to the federal Parliament by amending the races power (section 51(xxvi) of the Constitution) to extend to Aboriginal and Torres Strait Islander peoples. It was hoped,

[17] Lawrence G Sager, 'Cool Federalism and the Life-Cycle of Moral Progress' (2005) 46 *William & Mary Law Review* 1385.

[18] *Criminal Law (Sexual Offences) Amendment Act 1975* (SA).

[19] *Human Rights (Sexual Conduct) Act 1994* (Cth). For the effect of this on the Tasmanian legislation, see *Croome v Tasmania* (1997) 191 CLR 119.

[20] 576 US __ (2015).

although not necessarily immediately realised, that the federal Parliament would be more sympathetic to the plight of Aboriginal people than successive state governments had proven.[21] The federal Parliament has also historically been the target of environmentalists seeking federal action to override regressive state policies, such as with the passage of the *World Heritage Properties Conservation Act 1983* (Cth) in the face of the Tasmanian Government's attempt to dam the Franklin River system.[22]

In this chapter, we explore a different dimension of the relationship between federalism and public interest advocacy, one that draws on Hollander and Patapan's earlier thesis on the essential *pragmatism* of the practice of modern Australian federalism.[23] Hollander and Patapan explain that the practice of federalism at any moment is characterised by the pressing problem, the policy agenda and the prevailing political dynamic. This is consistent with the constitutional argument made by Stephen Gageler that within Australia's highly centralised federation in which political constitutionalism continues to hold particular loyalty, it is political bargaining between the central and state governments that determines the practice of federalism, and not, as AV Dicey predicted,[24] the jurisprudential limits asserted by the judiciary against the political branches.[25]

Hollander, Patapan and Gageler posit their theses in the context of struggles over policy control between the central and state governments, and the push and pull between the centripetal and centrifugal forces that these governments and parliaments represent. Similarly, in Stephenson's thesis that federalism affects legislative deliberation about rights, he is focused on the links the federalism creates between governments rather than the links between governments and the citizens.[26] Although, of course, much of their discussion of the political agendas that emerge in these institutional actors are driven by citizens and citizen-led groups.

In this chapter, we explicitly turn our attention beyond the Commonwealth and the states as institutional government actors, towards the leverage that federalism gives individuals and advocacy groups pursuing public interest reform. In this way, we follow the work of Stephenson in focusing on the intersection between rights and federalism in Australia as a pivotal question of process rather than outcome.[27]

We argue that public interest advocates can benefit greatly from a keen understanding of the constitutional dimensions and dynamics of our federal system, and the different

[21] Gabrielle Appleby and Gemma McKinnon, 'Lessons of 1967 referendum still apply to debates on constitutional recognition', *The Conversation,* 22 May 2017, https://theconversation.com/lessons-of-1967-referendum-still-apply-to-debates-on-constitutional-recognition-76725.

[22] See further *Commonwealth v Tasmania* (1983) 158 CLR 1 ('*Tasmanian Dam Case*').

[23] Robyn Hollander and Haig Patapan, 'Pragmatic Federalism: Australian Federalism from Hawke to Howard' (2007) 66 *Australian Journal of Public Administration* 280.

[24] As Dicey noted, '[f]ederalism means … legalism – the predominance of the judiciary in the constitution': Albert V Dicey, *Introduction to the Study of the Law of the Constitution* 8th edn (London, Macmillan, 1915) 170. Examining the position in the US, Dicey argued that '[c]ourts become the pivot on which the constitutional arrangements of the country turn': 170.

[25] Stephen Gageler, 'Beyond the Text: A Vision of the Structure and Function of the Constitution' (2009) 32 *Australian Bar Review* 138, 152; Stephen Gageler, 'Foundations of Australian Federalism and the Role of Judicial Review' (1987) 17 *Federal Law Review* 162; Stephen Gageler, 'The Federal Balance' in Gabrielle Appleby, Nicholas Aroney and Thomas John (eds), *The Future of Australian Federalism* (Cambridge, Cambridge University Press, 2012) 27.

[26] Stephenson, above n 4, 724.

[27] Ibid, 711.

position of the federal legislative, executive and judicial institutions, the state institutions and those of the self-governing territories. Of course, a similar understanding of the federal system is equally beneficial for those opposing reform. Advocates have already learned to harness federalism in its more accepted forms to advance public interest reforms. Whether that has been by lobbying successive state governments and bringing actions to achieve consolidation as we saw in the decriminalisation of homosexuality, or realising the need to engage the central government to act in the case of Indigenous rights and environmental protection.

However, we demonstrate that this type of advocacy is often more complicated and requires greater understanding of the constitutional system than either of these traditional theses suggest. We explore our thesis through the case study of the achievement of marriage equality in the Australian federal system, in which Australian states and territories initially pursued marriage equality reform in the face of federal opposition to do so. In a situation where the level of overlap between the Commonwealth and state spheres was uncertain, there were more complicated federal and state strategies deployed by advocates and state polities to maintain political momentum and pressure, as well as to leverage the federal-political tensions to their full potential, and ensure they were not deployed against the cause.

III. Australian Marriage Equality Reform and Federalism

> *In that environment we always have a new path forward, if a federal law is blocked, going through the states, if a state law is blocked – vice versa. We are always bubbling along.*
>
> Rodney Croome, Australian Marriage Equality[28]

The achievement of marriage equality in Australia has taken considerable effort: countless bills have been drafted and debated in the Commonwealth Parliament as well as the parliaments of the states and territories; there have been calls for a constitutional referendum, two legal challenges in the High Court, a failed attempt at holding a plebiscite, and the conducting of a postal survey. Bringing about marriage equality in Australia involved parliaments, governments and courts across the national, state and territory levels in a long process of public interest reform.[29] Thus, an examination of the history of attempts to legislate for marriage equality in Australia reveals the importance of public interest advocates understanding the constitutional framework within which the politics of an issue will play out.

With Australia's unique constitutional arrangements, including a federal system but lacking a constitutional bill of rights, marriage equality reform had to be achieved

[28] Quoted in Bridgid Delaney, 'Personal, political, persistent: how the campaign for marriage equality learned the hard way', *The Guardian* (online), 30 November 2015 www.theguardian.com/australia-news/2015/nov/30/personal-political-persistent-how-the-campaign-for-marriage-equality-learned-the-hard-way.

[29] For a personal account from two key individuals intimately involved with this campaign as part of Australian Marriage Equality, see Alex Greenwich and Shirleene Robinson, *Yes Yes Yes: Australia's Journey to Marriage Equality* (Sydney, NewSouth Publishing, 2018).

differently from its progress in other countries whose debates and reforms occurred in advance of ours, including the US,[30] the UK,[31] and Ireland.[32] In the following part of this chapter we explain how the Australian constitutional framework, with its absence of a bill of rights but entrenchment of federalism, provided novel points of political tension that were successfully leveraged by advocates to achieve marriage equality.

A. The Commonwealth's *Marriage Act 1961*

The *Australian Constitution* provides the Commonwealth Parliament with the power to make laws with respect to 'marriage'.[33] Despite being given this power, for the first 60 years after federation, marriage law was left to the states. This changed in 1961 with the passage of the *Marriage Act 1961* (Cth), which created a national scheme for marriage with the states continuing to maintain marriage registers.[34]

The *Marriage Act 1961* initially did not expressly define 'marriage'. However, following a request from two same-sex couples who had been married in Canada to have their marriages recognised in Australia,[35] in 2004 the conservative Howard Government inserted a definition of 'marriage' within the Act, which excluded same-sex marriage.[36] After the 2004 amendments, marriage was expressly defined within the Act as 'the union of a man and a woman to the exclusion of all others, voluntarily entered into for life'.[37] The amendments also made it clear that same-sex marriages conducted overseas were not recognised in Australia.[38]

According to then Attorney-General Philip Ruddock, there was 'significant community concern about the possible erosion of the institution of marriage'.[39] The purpose of the amendment was to ensure 'same sex relationships cannot be equated with marriage'.[40] The Labor Party, under the leadership of Mark Latham, supported the Howard Government amendments,[41] and as a result the amendments passed through the federal Parliament

[30] A federal system with a bill of rights. See further Hollander and Patapan, 'Deliberative Federalism', above n 8.

[31] A unitary system with no written constitutional limitations.

[32] Constitutional referendum *required* to achieve marriage equality.

[33] Australian Constitution, s 51(xxi).

[34] *Marriage Act 1961* (Cth), s 6.

[35] Jacqueline Tomlins, 'When I do becomes you can't', *The Age* (online), 3 September 2004 www.theage.com.au/articles/2004/09/02/1093939067726.html; Farah Farouque 'Gay "Husbands" to Test their Marriage in Court', *The Age* (online), 4 February 2004 www.theage.com.au/articles/2004/02/03/1075776059590.html; Commonwealth, *Parliamentary Debates*, House of Representatives, 24 June 2004, 31 460 (Nicola Roxon, Shadow Attorney-General). Pt VA of the *Marriage Act 1961* (Cth) gives effect to the Convention on Celebration and Recognition of the Validity of Marriages, allowing marriages conducted overseas to be recognised under Australian law.

[36] See *Marriage Amendment Act 2004* (Cth).

[37] *Marriage Act 1961* (Cth), s 5(1).

[38] *Marriage Act 1961* (Cth), s 88EA.

[39] Commonwealth, *Parliamentary Debates*, House of Representatives, 24 June 2004, 31 459. Opposition to same-sex marriage from conservative parliamentarians stemmed from the belief that limiting marriage to heterosexual couples was 'vital to the stability of our society and provides the best environment for the raising of children': at 31 459. See also Commonwealth, *Parliamentary Debates*, Senate, 12 August 2004, 26 512 (Ron Boswell).

[40] Explanatory Memorandum, Marriage Amendment Bill 2004 (Cth).

[41] Commonwealth, *Parliamentary Debates*, House of Representatives, 24 June 2004, 31460 (Nicola Roxon, Shadow Attorney-General).

without any great scrutiny or deliberation.[42] There was some political opposition to the move.[43] Greens leader Bob Brown, long-term LGBTI campaigner and a veteran advocate in the reforms to decriminalise homosexuality in his home State of Tasmania, moved an amendment to change the name of the Bill from the Marriage Amendment Bill to the Marriage Discrimination Bill, at least attempting to bring some transparency to the reforms. While the issue was not yet a mainstream one among the Australian public, in the lead up to and immediately following these amendments, marriage equality advocacy organisations emerged, including Australian Marriage Equality, which would go on to become a key player in driving the reform agenda.

Following the 2004 amendments, Australian Marriage Equality launched national and state-based campaigns. Over the following six years, attempts were made federally by the Greens and the Democrats to amend the *Marriage Act 1961* to allow for same-sex marriage.[44] However, without the support of the major parties, these bills either lapsed or did not proceed.

B. Attention Turns to the States and Territories

With the prospect of achieving marriage equality at a federal level seeming unlikely, those advocating for same-sex marriage turned their attention to the states and territories. In 2005, and following advice from constitutional expert Professor George Williams,[45] Australian Marriage Equality launched a national campaign to try to change state and territory laws.[46] This saw bills introduced by The Greens in Tasmania,[47] and attempts to do so in other states and territories.[48] At that time, state Premiers were unsupportive of the move, claiming that marriage laws needed to be uniform across the Commonwealth, and that it was something that was most appropriately dealt with by the federal Parliament, not state legislation.[49] However, this argument ignored the constitutional reality that the power to make laws with respect to marriage was a power that was held *concurrently* between the federal and state governments. The federal law would only prevail over a state law if the courts were to find that it was inconsistent under section 109 of the Constitution. With the federal *Marriage Act* now explicitly excluding same-sex marriage from its remit, there was a strong argument that the court would find the federal Act, and a state Act legislating for same-sex marriage, consistent.

[42] The Marriage Amendment Bill 2004 (Cth) was introduced into the Parliament on 24 June 2004. The Act received royal assent on 16 August 2004. See further discussion in Greenwich and Robinson, above n 29, 12–14.

[43] See further discussion in Greenwich and Robinson, above n 29, 14–15.

[44] Same Sex Relationships (Enduring Equality) Bill 2004, Same-Sex Marriage Bill 2006, Marriage (Relationships Equality) Amendment Bill 2007, Marriage (Relationships Equality) Amendment Bill 2008, Same-Sex Marriage Bill 2008, Marriage Equality Amendment Bill 2009, Marriage Equality Amendment Bill 2010.

[45] George Williams, 'Advice Regarding the Proposed Same-Sex Marriage Act' (2006) 9 *Constitutional Law and Policy Review* 21. Similar advice was provided by other constitutional experts later in the campaign, see below n 76.

[46] 'Campaign launched for gay marriages', *The Sydney Morning Herald* (online), 1 May 2005 www.theage.com.au/news/National/Campaign-launched-for-gay-marriagess/2005/05/01/1114886242426.html.

[47] Same Sex Marriage Bill 2005 (Tas), developed with the Tasmanian Gay and Lesbian Rights Group.

[48] See further discussion in Greenwich and Robinson, above n 29, 23.

[49] George Williams, 'State of Same-Sex Union: Federal Defeat Won't Spell End of Debate', *The Sydney Morning Herald* (online), 5 June 2012 www.smh.com.au/politics/federal/state-of-same-sex-union-federal-defeat-wont-spell-end-of-debate-20120604-1zs1j.html.

Ultimately, the move towards reform came from a series of political steps taken between 2006–2013 in the Australian Capital Territory by successive Labor Governments, with the support of the ACT Greens. While each individual piece of legislation that was introduced in that jurisdiction was short-lived, the ACT proved an important jurisdiction in the federation for shaping the national debate for a number of reasons.

The first was that the ACT, which during that time had demonstrated itself to be jurisdictionally sympathetic to greater legal protections for rights through, for instance, the enactment of the *Human Rights Act 2004* (ACT), provided a smaller forum in which marriage equality voices could be heard. As Stephenson explained, it 'lower[ed] the threshold for minorities to place issues on the political agenda'.[50] Unusually in Australia, the ACT is also a unicameral system making legislative change relatively easier than in most other jurisdictions. However, marriage equality advocates needed more than just to convince the ACT to introduce marriage equality reforms and sit back for other states to adopt them. Indeed, because of the unique characteristics that made it an ideal forum to introduce marriage equality reforms, this meant wider state adoption was not necessarily guaranteed. Marriage equality advocates needed to use the voice they were able to achieve in ACT to leverage wider state and national reform. A number of challenges stood in their way, including lack of public awareness of the importance of full marriage equality reform (in contrast to, for instance, legal rights equality for same-sex couples,[51] or recognition through civil unions[52]), and constitutional uncertainty at the federal level as to whether the Commonwealth Parliament had the legislative power to introduce marriage equality. A sophisticated understanding of Australia's federal system and the role of the High Court allowed marriage equality advocates to leverage the reforms in the ACT to meet both of these challenges.

C. Civil Unions in the Australian Capital Territory

In 2006, the ACT Parliament was the first jurisdiction to allow both same-sex and heterosexual couples to enter into 'civil unions' through the passage of the *Civil Unions Act 2006* (ACT). A civil union was to be treated as equivalent to marriage for the purpose of ACT law.[53] At the time, the federal government had the power to override territory laws and the Howard Government used this power to veto the *Civil Unions Act 2006*.[54] The Commonwealth

[50] Stephenson, above n 4, 751.

[51] Reforms in this area themselves used the facilitation that federalism offers, with states moving first to recognise de facto relationships and equalise rights to those couples. See further Michael Kirby, 'Same Sex Relationships – Some Australian Legal Developments' (1999) 19 *Australian Bar Review* 4; HREOC, *Same Sex: Same Entitlements – National Inquiry into Discrimination Against People in Same-Sex Relationships: Financial and Work-Related Entitlements and Benefits* (May 2007).

[52] See, eg, Stephenson, above n 4, 738.

[53] *Civil Unions Act* (ACT), s 5(2).

[54] The *Civil Unions Act 2006* (ACT) was disallowed under s 35 of the *Australian Government Territory (Self-Government) Act 1988* (Cth). The Governor-General, acting on the advice of the Federal Executive Council disallowed the *Civil Unions Act 2006* (ACT) on 13 June 2006: see 'Australian Capital Territory (Self-Government) Act 1998 – Disallowance: Civil Unions Act (ACT)' (13 June 2006) www.legislation.gov.au/Details/F2006L01810. At the time, s 35 provided the federal government to veto legislation of the ACT Parliament. That veto power has since been repealed: *Territories Self-Government Legislation Amendment (Disallowance and Amendment of Laws) Act 2011* (Cth). Of course, this was not the first time that the Commonwealth had interfered with the law-making power of the territories. After the Northern Territory had passed legislation legalising euthanasia in 1995, the Commonwealth Parliament passed legislation revoking the power of the governments of the Northern Territory,

objected to the ACT law because it equated civil unions with marriage, thereby undermining the Commonwealth's attempts to limit marriage to heterosexual couples.[55] In response to the government's actions, Greens Leader Senator Bob Brown introduced a Private Members Bill that would have removed the ability of the executive to disallow or amend an enactment of the ACT.[56] Brown's Bill was defeated at this time, but demonstrated a nuanced understanding of the then Commonwealth-Territory constitutional and legal relationship that prevented policy experimentation through the ACT.

Undeterred by the Commonwealth's veto, the ACT Government introduced the Civil Partnership Bill into the Parliament later that same year. The Bill allowed same-sex and heterosexual couples to enter into 'civil partnerships', which would be equivalent to a 'domestic partnership' under ACT law.[57] A 'domestic partnership' – often referred to as a '*de facto*' relationship – was already defined in ACT law as a relationship 'between 2 people, whether of a different or same sex, living together as a couple on a genuine domestic basis'.[58] While the Bill removed the references to 'marriage' and used 'partnership' rather than 'union' (to remove any confusion with marriage), the Commonwealth Attorney-General Philip Ruddock stated that if the Bill were to pass the ACT Parliament, the Commonwealth would again block the law, stating that the ACT law would 'undermine the institution of marriage'.[59] One of the objections that the federal government still had was that the Civil Partnership Bill would allow same-sex couples to hold a ceremony not dissimilar to a marriage ceremony.[60]

With a change in government at a national level in late-2007, the ACT Government reintroduced legislation recognising civil partnerships. However, the fact that Labor was now in power at both the territory and federal levels did not make marriage equality reform easier overnight. The Rudd Government was initially reluctant to allow civil unions that 'mimic marriage'.[61] Like the previous federal government, the Rudd Government objected to the possibility of civil partnerships being solemnised by a celebrant. Taking the federal government's objections into account, the ACT Bill was amended to allow for the registration of

the Australian Capital Territory and Norfolk Island to make laws with respect to euthanasia: see *Euthanasia Laws Act 1997* (Cth). Despite recent attempts to repeal this Act, this restriction remains in place.

[55] 'PM Will Not Allow "Marriage By Another Name"', *The Sydney Morning Harald* (online), 30 March 2006 www.smh.com.au/news/national/pm-will-not-allow-marriage-by-another-name/2006/03/30/1143441269545.html; David Humphries, 'Same-sex Laws Face Federal Resistance', *The Sydney Morning Herald* (online), 31 March 2006 www.smh.com.au/news/national/samesex-laws-face-federal-resistance/2006/03/30/1143441281190.html.

[56] Australian Capital Territory (Self-Government) Amendment (Disallowance Power of the Commonwealth) Bill 2006.

[57] Civil Partnership Bill 2006 (ACT), cl 6(3). This followed a similar approach that had been adopted earlier in Victoria, which introduced the concept of 'domestic partner' in 2001, to remove distinctions between married spouses and domestic partners across a range of statutory regimes. The term included people of the same or different genders. While not introducing the concept of civil partnership, it achieved many of the same outcomes as the ACT regime: see further *Statute Law Amendment (Domestic Relationships) Act 2001* (Vic).

[58] *Legislation Act 2001* (ACT), s 169.

[59] 'ACT Move to Legalise Gay Marriage Vetoed', *The Sydney Morning Herald* (online), 6 February 2007 www.smh.com.au/news/national/act-move-to-legalise-gay-marriage-vetoed/2007/02/06/1170524092401.html.

[60] Kenneth Nguyen, 'Ceremony Not for Gays, Says Ruddock', *The Age* (online), 8 February 2007 www.theage.com.au/news/national/ceremony-not-for-gays-says-ruddock/2007/02/07/1170524164173.html. The Civil Partnership Bill 2006 (ACT) allowed civil partnerships to be entered into by two people 'making a declaration before the civil partnership notary and at least 1 other witness': cl 12. While there was no reference in the Bill to a ceremony, there was also nothing expressly preventing the declaration being made as part of a civil partnership ceremony similar to a wedding.

[61] 'Government Won't Budge on Civil Unions Marriage', *The Sydney Morning Herald* (online), 1 August 2009 www.smh.com.au/national/government-wont-budge-on-civil-unions-marriage-20090801-e4wf.html.

civil partnerships but the ceremonial aspects of the policy were removed.[62] The amendments also required both parties to be at least 18 years of age and at least one of the parties to the civil partnership to reside in the ACT.[63]

In 2009 the ACT Greens, with the support of the ACT Labor Government, introduced a Bill to amend the *Civil Partnerships Act* that would allow civil partnership ceremonies for same-sex couples.[64] The Commonwealth maintained some reservation to the amendments and had not ruled out vetoing on the ACT law.[65] However, after talks between the ACT and federal governments, the Rudd Government decided it would not block the amendments and civil partnership ceremonies for same-sex couples were able to take place.[66]

In 2011, a reform was achieved at the federal level that would prove significant in the longer campaign for marriage equality reform. Senator Brown was successful in his attempt to remove the Commonwealth's power to veto territory legislation, citing as examples the federal override of the ACT's civil partnership laws as well as the override of euthanasia laws in the Northern Territory.[67]

In 2012, the ACT Labor Government went a step further by allowing civil unions which were to be 'treated for all purposes under territory law in the same way as marriage'.[68] The civil union laws passed with the support of the ACT Greens, although the Greens were initially reluctant to support reforms, as they were concerned they might undermine attempts to achieve marriage equality at the national level.[69]

The new ACT law was carefully drafted to distinguish civil unions from marriage,[70] presumably so the ACT law stood a better chance of operating in harmony with the *Marriage Act 1961* (Cth). This was reinforced in the explanatory memorandum of the Bill, which explained that civil unions would 'enable couples who are unable to marry under the Commonwealth *Marriage Act 1961* to enter into a legally recognisable relationship'.[71] While the ACT Government no longer had to be concerned with the Commonwealth Government vetoing its same-sex marriage reforms, the Commonwealth still had the power to challenge the ACT law on the basis that it was inconsistent with the *Marriage Act 1961*

[62] *Civil Partnerships Act 2008* (ACT). See also Supplementary Explanatory Statement, Civil Partnerships Bill 2006 (ACT). Cf the original Civil Partnerships Bill 2006 (ACT), cl 12, which had allowed for a declaration of civil partnership to be made before the civil partnership notary and at least 1 other witness.

[63] *Civil Partnerships Act 2008* (ACT), s 6.

[64] *Civil Partnerships Amendment Act 2009* (ACT), s 6A. The declaration of civil partnership before a civil partnership notary was only available to same-sex couples and not to couples who may marry under the *Marriage Act 1961* (Cth): see *Civil Partnerships Amendment Act 2009* (ACT), s 6A.

[65] Karlis Salna, 'Rudd Mulls Veto of Same-Sex Civil Unions', *The Sydney Morning Herald* (online), 24 November 2009 www.smh.com.au/national/rudd-mulls-veto-of-samesex-civil-unions-20091124-jfdj.html. See also ABC News, 'No Word: Commonwealth Quiet on New Same-Sex Laws' (16 November 2009) www.abc.net.au/news/2009-11-16/no-word-commonwealth-quiet-on-new-same-sex-laws/1143728; ABC News, 'Rudd Undecided on Same-Sex Civil Unions' (23 November 2009) www.abc.net.au/news/2009-11-22/rudd-undecided-on-same-sex-civil-unions/1153054.

[66] ABC News, 'Commonwealth Accepts Gay Ceremonies' (26 November 2009) www.abc.net.au/news/2009-11-26/commonwealth-accepts-gay-ceremonies/1158012.

[67] *Territories Self-Government Legislation Amendment (Disallowance and Amendment of Laws) Act 2011* (Cth).

[68] *Civil Union Act 2012* (ACT), s 6.

[69] 'ACT Passes New Laws Allowing Same-Sex Civil Unions', *The Australian* (online), 23 August 2012 www.theaustralian.com.au/national-affairs/act-passes-new-laws-allowing-same-sex-civil-unions/news-story/1bfd0cf2218eb1808f977c980214d875.

[70] The Act expressly stated that 'a civil union is different to marriage': *Civil Unions Act 2012* (ACT), s 6.

[71] Explanatory Memorandum, Civil Union Bill 2011 (ACT).

(Cth),[72] or by direct legislative intervention. No such challenge or intervention was, at that time, forthcoming.

Over the previous seven years the ACT Government had made some progress in affording same-sex couples similar recognition of their relationship to married couples despite significant legal and political challenges. As Stephenson points out, in this way, the ACT provided an important forum of rights deliberation where bicameralism at the federal level had failed to provide a meaningful forum for debate because of the agreement of both major parties on the issue. The reforms in the ACT kept the issue on the public agenda, and kept the pressure on successive federal governments. Intergovernmental debate thus played an important role where the effects of bicameralism on the debate were less pronounced.[73]

D. The Same-Sex Marriage Case

In 2011, the Labor Party had introduced a conscience vote on the issue for its members,[74] although the Liberal/National Coalition was still maintaining a tied vote against marriage equality. Since 2007, the ACT Government had managed to find a way to negotiate with the federal government and slowly progress its same-sex marriage policy agenda. In 2013 the ACT Parliament took the final leap towards legislating for same-sex marriage and passed the *Marriage Equality (Same Sex) Act 2013* (ACT). At the same time, a number of state legislatures were also considering introducing same-sex marriage legislation.[75] While previous legislation had danced around the issue of the Territory legislating 'marriage', the 2013 Act squarely raised the legal question of whether the Territory might be legislating within the scope of the Commonwealth's 'marriage power'. Indeed, the 2013 ACT Act raised this question acutely. It took a different form from the proposed state laws, which had been carefully drafted so as to distinguish same-sex marriage from federal heterosexual marriage.[76] In contrast, the ACT Act connected and equated same-sex marriage in the Territory with marriage under the federal *Marriage Act*. This, in George Williams' words, 'gave rise to a heightened possibility of inconsistency'.[77] This appeared to be of great concern to marriage equality advocates. Australian Marriage Equality announced that while the carefully drafted state laws were likely to pass constitutional muster, the ACT statute was likely to be found invalid.[78] But in the face of advocacy pressure, the ACT held firm on its legislative course,

[72] *Australian Capital Territory (Self-Government) Act 1988* (Cth), s 28.

[73] Stephenson, above n 4, 724–8.

[74] See further discussion in Greenwich and Robinson, above n 29, 79.

[75] Same-Sex Marriage Bill 2013 (NSW), Same Sex Marriage Bill 2013 (SA), Same-Sex Marriage Bill 2012 (Tas), Marriage Equality Bill 2012 (Vic), Same-Sex Marriage Bill 2013 (WA).

[76] These laws had been the subject of intensive debate, with leading constitutional experts and barristers agreeing that they would not be inconsistent with the federal *Marriage Act*. See, eg, Patrick Parkinson, Submission No 102 to Standing Committee on Social Issues, Parliament of New South Wales *Inquiry into Same sex marriage law in NSW*, 2 February 2013; Bret Walker, Chris Young and Perry Herzfeld, 'In the Matter of the Same-Sex Marriage Bill 2012 (Tas): Memorandum of Advice' (11 October 2013), Bret Walker and Perry Herzfeld, 'In the Matter of the Same-Sex Marriage Bill 2013 (NSW): Memorandum of Advice' (22 October 2013).

[77] George Williams, 'Same-Sex Marriage and the Australian States' (2015) 40 *Alternative Law Journal* 4, 6.

[78] Rodney Croome, 'Marriage Equality at Last in the ACT', *New Matilda* (online), 22 October 2013 https://newmatilda.com/2013/10/22/marriage-equality-last-act/. See also reflections from Anna Brown of the Human Rights Law Centre in Victoria, as quoted in Greenwich and Robinson, above n 29, 102.

making some changes but these were largely viewed as insufficient to meet the legal concerns that had been identified.[79]

Shortly after the passage of the *Marriage Equality (Same Sex) Act*, there was a change in government at a federal level. The Coalition was back in power and Tony Abbott was now Prime Minister, a former Howard Cabinet Minister, and known for his deep Catholic faith. Within a month of taking office, the Abbott Government confirmed it would challenge the ACT's same-sex marriage law in the High Court.[80] Unlike most constitutional challenges that pertained to inconsistency with federal laws,[81] no other state or territory Attorney-General intervened in the case.[82] Australian Marriage Equality appeared as amicus curiae.

The Commonwealth's challenge to the *Marriage Equality (Same Sex) Act 2013* (ACT) raised the issue of whether the ACT's same-sex marriage law could operate concurrently with the *Marriage Act 1961* (Cth). In short, the effect of section 28 of the *Australian Capital Territory (Self-Government) Act 1988* (Cth) was that the ACT Act would have no effect if it was inconsistent with the *Marriage Act 1961* (Cth).[83] Somewhat in the face of their refusal to change their laws as advocated by marriage equality groups, the ACT Government's argument was that the Territory and federal laws were capable of operating concurrently – the Commonwealth was legislating for heterosexual marriage and the Territory was legislating for same-sex marriage.[84]

Ultimately, the case provided a strategic vehicle of a different kind for marriage equality. It allowed marriage equality advocates to close off one of the tropes that federal politicians had been using to avoid engagement with the issue: that the federal Parliament did not have legislative power to bring about marriage equality.[85]

In resolving the dispute, the Commonwealth's written submissions were that it was unnecessary for the High Court to determine the scope of the Commonwealth's legislature power with respect to 'marriage' (and specifically whether it included same-sex marriage).[86] Similarly, the ACT Government did not assert that the Court necessarily needed to decide the scope of the Commonwealth's marriage power to determine the issue in its favour.[87]

[79] Williams, above n 77, 6.

[80] Lisa Cox, 'Same-Sex Marriage Law High Court Challenge Confirmed', *The Sydney Morning Herald* (online), 10 October 2013 www.smh.com.au/politics/federal/same-sex-marriage-law-high-court-challenge-confirmed-20131010-2vaqe.html.

[81] Even accounting for the difference between s 109 inconsistency and inconsistency between laws of the Commonwealth and laws of the territories.

[82] They have a right to do so in any case arising under the Constitution or involving its interpretation: s 78A of the *Judiciary Act 1903* (Cth).

[83] For a discussion of inconsistencies between law of the territories and the Commonwealth see Anne Twomey, 'Inconsistency Between Commonwealth and Territory Laws' (2014) 42 *Federal Law Review* 421.

[84] *Commonwealth v Australian Capital Territory* (2013) 250 CLR 441, 449 (K L Eastman SC) (in argument). For a discussion of the case see: Patrick Parkinson and Nicholas Aroney, 'The Territory of Marriage: Constitutional Law, Marriage Law and Family Policy in the ACT Same Sex Marriage Case' (2014) 28 *Australian Journal of Family Law* 160; Margaret Brock 'Commonwealth v Australian Capital Territory' (2014) 25 *Public Law Review* 157; Anne Twomey, 'Same-Sex Marriage and Constitutional Interpretation' (2014) 88 *Australian Law Journal* 613; Shipra Chordia, 'The High Court, Same-Sex Marriage and Federalism' (2014) 39 *Alternative Law Journal* 84.

[85] See further discussion in Greenwich and Robinson, above n 29, 104.

[86] Commonwealth of Australia, 'Annotated Submissions of the Plaintiff', Submission in *Commonwealth v Australian Capital Territory*, C13/2013, 13 November 2013, [35].

[87] Australian Capital Territory, 'Annotated Submissions of the Australian Capital Territory', Submission in *Commonwealth v Australian Capital Territory*, C13/2013, 13 November 2013, [19].

In contrast, it was Australian Marriage Equality, as amicus curiae, who submitted that it was 'necessary to determine whether federal regulation of marriage of same-sex couples would be within the marriage power.'[88]

Despite the position taken in the written submissions, when pushed during oral argument the Commonwealth Solicitor-General accepted that the better view was a broad interpretation of section 51(xxi) to include same-sex marriage.[89] The Court concluded that it was necessary to determine whether the Commonwealth's 'marriage power' included the power to legislate for same-sex marriage. The Court explained:

> This Court must decide whether s 51(xxi) permit the federal Parliament to make a law with respect to same sex marriage because the ACT Act would probably operate concurrently with the *Marriage Act* if the federal parliament had no power to make a national law providing for same sex marriage.[90]

In a rare unanimous decision, the High Court held that the federal Parliament had the power to legislate for same-sex marriage,[91] and that the *Marriage Act* was a 'comprehensive and exhaustive statement of the law with respect to the creation and recognition of the legal status of marriage'.[92] The whole of the *Marriage Equality (Same Sex) Act 2013* (ACT) was inconsistent with the *Marriage Act* and the ACT Act was, therefore, of no effect.[93]

Framing the case in such a way that the scope of section 51(xxi) needed to be determined placed the Commonwealth in a difficult position. If the Commonwealth did not have power to legislate with respect to same-sex marriage, it increased the likelihood that the Court would accept that the ACT law could sit alongside, supplementary or complementary to the *Marriage Act*. If the Commonwealth accepted that the scope of the 'marriage' power included same-sex marriage, the Commonwealth Government was accepting that same-sex marriage was an issue for the federal Parliament. This would then put the issue back on the federal agenda, and prevent future parliamentarians from avoiding the issue by hiding behind the Constitution.[94]

Some members of the Abbott Government were more comfortable in maintaining the uncertainty over the meaning of 'marriage' within section 51(xxi) of the Constitution. The constitutional uncertainty could be used as a 'shield' to avoid the Parliament having to confront the issue of same-sex marriage.[95] Further, section 128 of the Constitution

[88] Australian Marriage Equality Inc, 'Submissions of Australian Marriage Equality Inc', Submission in *Commonwealth v Australian Capital Territory*, C13/2013, 13 November 2013, [10](a).

[89] *Commonwealth v Australian Capital Territory* (2013) 250 CLR 441, 444 (J T Gleeson SC) ('*Same-Sex Marriage Case*'). See also *Commonwealth v Australian Capital Territory* [2013] HCATrans 299 (3 December 2013) (J T Gleeson SC).

[90] *Same-Sex Marriage Case* (2013) 250 CLR 441, 454 [9].

[91] Ibid, 463 [38].

[92] Ibid, 467, [57].

[93] Although, as George Williams noted, this would not have prevented a state or territory passing same-sex marriage laws. It is just that had such laws passed, they were likely to have no effect given the positional the federal government had taken on legislating for marriage. Had the Commonwealth not ultimately legislated for same-sex there might have been political reasons for a state Parliament re-introducing a same-sex marriage bill into the state Parliament: Williams, above n 77, 8.

[94] As Michael Kirby describes it, the ACT might have lost the battle but won the 'constitutional war': Michael Kirby, 'The ACT Marriage Equality Case – Losing the Battle but Winning the Constitutional War' (2016) 18 *Southern Cross University Law Review* 79, 91.

[95] For a discussion of how constitutional uncertainty and the referendum process may be used as a 'shield' and a 'sword' by parliamentarians see Appleby and Webster, above n 5, 282.

could be used as a 'sword' by parliamentarians to avoid considering the issue of same-sex marriage despite considerable community support.[96] As the dissenting Coalition Senators noted in Senate Legal and Constitutional Affairs Legislation Committee's 2012 report on the *Marriage Equality Amendment Bill 2010*:

> However, if there is a deficiency – or a reasonable fear that such a deficiency might exist – in the constitutional power of the Commonwealth to legislate for same-sex marriage, a remedy is available. The founding fathers recognised that the specified powers set out in the Constitution should not be immutable forever, but provide a mechanism in section 128 to ensure that any change to the powers set out in the Constitution should be subject to the will of the people and not the mere convenience of the Parliament from time to time.[97]

As is well known, section 128 creates a difficult hurdle,[98] especially without bipartisan support.[99] Here it appeared that a referendum was being used as a political tool in an attempt to ensure the failure of the reform. In June 2013, just months before the ACT Parliament passed its marriage equality legislation Labor Prime Minister Kevin Rudd, who had by then changed his own position on marriage equality, had offered marriage equality advocates the possibility of holding a constitutional referendum on the issue. This was rejected, on the basis it would create fear-mongering and division within the community against LGBTI people, and it would be unnecessarily expensive.[100]

In this dimension of the same-sex marriage debate, the High Court of Australia played an important role. By clarifying the scope of the Commonwealth 'marriage' power, the Court's decision in the *Same-Sex Marriage Case* disarmed those parliamentarians relying on the constitutional uncertainty and the possible need for a referendum. The Court's decision in the *Same-Sex Marriage Case* shifted the focus back to the federal level. While neither the Commonwealth nor the ACT had argued that it was necessary to determine the scope of the Commonwealth's marriage power, accepting the arguments of Australian Marriage Equality, the High Court held that it needed to be determined. Although the first sentence of the Court's judgment made it clear that 'the only issue which this Court can decide is a legal issue',[101] the Court would have been well aware of the political consequences of its decision. By defining the scope of the power to include same-sex marriage, the Court had firmly placed the issue in the hands of the federal Parliament. The effect of the Court's decision was

[96] In 2012 reports indicated that over 60 per cent of Australians support the rights of same-sex couples to enter into marriage: see Milanda Rout and Matthew Denholm, 'Poll Shows Support of Gay Marriage at High', *The Australian* (online), 7 August 2012 www.theaustralian.com.au/national-affairs/state-politics/poll-shows-support-of-gay-marriage-at-high/news-story/e5d01c4e1fefeaa62dbc78f78159569f?sv=47aafda7077cf7f47b2ec73a2fe61ac4. For earlier figures, see Australian Marriage Equality, 'Marriage Equality and Public Opinion' (Fact Sheet, 7 November 2012) www.australianmarriageequality.com/wp/who-supports-equality/a-majority-of-australians-support-marriage-equality/.

[97] Senate Legal and Constitutional Affairs Legislation Committee, Parliament of Australia, *Marriage Equality Amendment Bill 2010* (2012) 77 [1.53]–[1.54].

[98] Scott Bennett, 'The Politics of Constitutional Amendment' (Research Paper No 11, Parliamentary Research Service, Commonwealth Parliament, 23 June 2005) 5.

[99] Ibid. See also George Williams and David Hume, *People Power: Thee History and Future of the Referendum in Australia* (Sydney, University of New South Wales Press, 2010).

[100] Ashley Hall, 'Kevin Rudd's Gay Marriage Referendum Offer Dismissed By Advocates', *ABC News*, 29 June 2013 www.abc.net.au/news/specials/rudd-returns/2013-06-28/kevin-rudd-gay-marriage-referendum-dismissed-by-advocates/4788796.

[101] *Same-Sex Marriage Case* (2013) 250 CLR 441, 452 [1].

to strip away the legal uncertainty surrounding same-sex marriage and made it now a purely *political* and *federal* issue. The focus of marriage equality advocates must therefore pivot.

Had the Court avoided the question regarding the scope of the 'marriage' power, any future federal legislation on same-sex marriage would have been open to legal challenge. The legal uncertainty would have continued and no-doubt some federal parliamentarians would have continued to use this constitutional uncertainty as a 'shield' and the need for a referendum as a 'sword'. As then National Director of Australian Marriage Equality Rodney Croome (who had been involved in the campaign to decriminalise homosexuality in Tasmania and was appointed Director of Australian Marriage Equality in 2012) said after the High Court decision, for marriage equality advocates, the decision was only a 'temporary defeat'.[102]

Indeed, the effect of the case was to 'funnel future deliberation about same-sex marriage exclusively into the federal sphere.'[103] The courts were no longer the necessary site of advocacy; rather, marriage equality advocates pivoted into other forums, lobbying politicians, deploying media strategies and forging alliances across society.[104] The political and social landscape by this stage was very different from that in 2004 when the amendments were introduced. Public understanding of the issue and support for it had reached significantly higher levels, and a number of states and territories had demonstrated themselves willing to act on the wishes of their electors. Australian Marriage Equality reported that it had been employing a strategy of targeting individual federal parliamentarians so as to build the numbers of both sides of politics willing to act on their conscience should a free vote finally be put.[105]

In the face of these developments, and particularly the growing support for reform from federal parliamentarians on all sides of politics, marriage equality reform was still a way off: it would take an attempt at a plebiscite on the issue, and then a postal survey, before a bill would be substantively debated on the floor of the federal Parliament and passed. With these changing political conditions, it is unlikely that the Coalition's attempt to conduct a plebiscite and then the conduct of the postal survey were ever seriously considered likely to stop the move towards marriage equality. However, they represented a tactic of delay, and were also the manifestation of a compromise that was forged in the Coalition party room over an issue that remained highly divisive on the conservative side of Australian politics.

E. The Plebiscite and Postal Survey

From 2012 to 2015 a number of private members bills seeking to amend the *Marriage Act* to allow for same-sex marriage were introduced into the federal Parliament, from across the

[102] Lauren Wilson, 'High Court Strikes Down Gay Marriage Law', *The Australian* (online), 12 December 2013 <https://www.theaustralian.com.au/national-affairs/high-court-strikes-down-act-gay-marriage-law/news-story/3c41ce4007872e1a4b8ebcb5399a34f2>.

[103] Stephenson, above n 4, 738.

[104] See further discussion in Greenwich and Robinson, above n 29, chapter 105–121 ('Communities and Corporates').

[105] Brigid Delaney, 'Personal, political, persistent: how the campaign for marriage equality learned the hard way', *The Guardian* (online), 30 November 2015 <https://www.theguardian.com/australia-news/2015/nov/30/personal-political-persistent-how-the-campaign-for-marriage-equality-learned-the-hard-way>.

political spectrum.[106] In June 2015 the Leader of the Opposition, Bill Shorten, introduced a private member's bill to allow for same-sex marriage.[107] This was followed by a group of cross-party MPs, including Liberals Warren Entsch and Teresa Gambaro, announcing that they would introduce a bill into the Parliament.[108] Despite the High Court holding in 2013 that there was no constitutional impediment for the Commonwealth Parliament, the bills were either defeated or lapsed. The hurdle was now very much political. The Labor Party had given its members a free vote on the issue, but the Liberal-National coalition members were not given a conscience vote and voted in accordance with the Coalition's policy to oppose same-sex marriage.[109]

In mid-2015, the announcement of a Bill with cross-party support being introduced into the federal Parliament caused tensions within the Liberal-National coalition. After a lengthy meeting of Coalition members, Prime Minister Abbott announced that a plebiscite would be held on the issue of same-sex marriage.[110] Shortly after this announcement, the Coalition Government had a change in leadership. Malcolm Turnbull was elected leader of the Liberal Party on 14 September 2015 and became Prime Minister on 15 September 2015. Prime Minister Turnbull maintained the Liberal-National coalition's commitment to a plebiscite, despite being a supporter of same-sex marriage and having previously questioned the need for a plebiscite.[111] The Coalition Government was returned at the 2016 election and following the election a Bill allowing for a plebiscite on same-sex marriage was introduced into the Parliament by Prime Minister Turnbull.

Critics of the Coalition's position attacked the proposed plebiscite on a number of bases, arguing it was a further attempt by the Coalition Government to deflect or delay the issue and deny the federal Parliament the opportunity to vote on it. The first argument was that the plebiscite was not constitutionally or legally required to give effect to marriage equality, and thus could be distinguished on some level from the earlier calls for a referendum where there was genuine constitutional uncertainty as to the federal Parliament's capacity to pass laws for marriage equality. Further, it was argued that there was no principled reason for putting the issue to the people. Rather, critics argued that the plebiscite would provide a platform for hurtful discrimination against LGBTI people, causing unnecessary division and harm in the community. Further, it was argued that questions of equality and rights of minority groups within the community should be shielded from majoritarian impulses that

[106] Marriage Amendment Bill 2012 (Cth); Marriage Equality Amendment Bill 2012 (Cth); Marriage Equality Amendment Bill (No 2) 2012 (Cth); Marriage Equality Amendment Bill 2013 (Cth); Marriage Equality Amendment Bill 2013 (Cth); Recognition of Foreign Marriages Bill 2014 (Cth); Freedom to Marry Bill 2014; Marriage Amendment (Marriage Equality) Bill 2015 (Cth). See further discussion in Greenwich and Robinson, above n 29, 82–84.

[107] The Marriage Amendment (Marriage Equality) Bill 2015 (Cth) was introduced on 17 August 2018.

[108] Marriage Legislation Amendment Bill 2015 (Cth).

[109] Simon Cullen, 'Lower House votes down same-sex marriage bill', *ABC News*, 19 September 2012 www.abc.net.au/news/2012-09-19/same-sex-marriage-bill-voted-down/4270016.

[110] Judith Ireland, 'Tony Abbott Flags Plebiscite on Same-Sex Marriage in Bid to Defuse Anger', *The Sydney Morning Herald* (online), 12 August 2015 www.smh.com.au/federal-politics/political-news/tony-abbott-flags-plebiscite-on-samesex-marriage-in-bid-to-defuse-anger-20150811-giwygl.html.

[111] Daniel Hurst, 'Turnbull Says Plebiscite on Gay Marriage will Overshadow Coalition's Messages', *The Guardian* (online), 12 August 2015 www.theguardian.com/australia-news/2015/aug/12/malcolm-turnbull-says-plebiscite-on-marriage-equality-will-keep-issue-alive.

a plebiscite might reflect. This was before the question of the significant and unnecessary costs was even raised.

When introducing the Plebiscite (Same-Sex Marriage) Bill into the House of Representatives, Prime Minister Turnbull stated: 'If ever there was an issue to be put to a plebiscite, this is one that can be and should be, because it is a very straightforward question'.[112] Beyond simplicity, on taking the mantle of Prime Minister from Abbott, he had previously explained that a plebiscite was a 'legitimate and democratic way' of dealing with the question of marriage equality.[113] Others argued that it was an issue involving a deeply divided moral issue over which parliamentarians should first gain guidance directly from their electorate.[114] However, as Kildea has argued, Australians have a very weak tradition of direct democratic participation.[115] Indeed, the plebiscite was inconsistent with the Coalition's previous approach to amending the *Marriage Act*: the Howard Government never sought to consult the people before amending the Act in 2004 to include a definition of marriage which excluded same-sex marriage.

In the lead up to the introduction of the plebiscite to the Parliament, Croome quit his job as National Director of Australian Marriage Equality.[116] This was reported as being on the basis that while Croome understood the need for Australian Marriage Equality to work with the government on the form and wording of the plebiscite, he would continue to work to stop the plebiscite and try for a free vote in the Parliament.

When the Senate rejected the legislation authorising the plebiscite,[117] the government then promised to achieve the same outcome through a 'postal survey', conducted under existing legislation. The government used existing powers to instruct the Australia Bureau of Statistics to conduct the postal survey,[118] and to fund the survey.[119] Marriage equality advocates saw a further opportunity to defeat the idea of a popular vote on the question, and rather increase the pressure to have the issue determined on the floor of the Parliament. A technical challenge to the postal survey launched by Australian Marriage Equality, Independent MP Andrew Willkie and Parents and Friends of Lesbians and Gays advocate Felicity Harlowe, was rejected by the High Court.[120] It was not decided until after the campaign for

[112] Commonwealth of Australia, *Parliamentary Debates*, House of Representatives, 14 September 2016, 847 (Malcolm Turnbull).

[113] Anna Henderson, 'Malcolm Turnbull keeps same-sex marriage, climate change policies on first day as Prime Minister', *ABC* News, 15 September 2015 www.abc.net.au/news/2015-09-15/malcolm-turnbull-keeps-same-sex-marriage-climate-change-policies/6777416.

[114] Matthew Knott and Sarah Whyte, 'George Brandis slaps down Scott Morrison over proposal to hold same-sex marriage referendum', *The Sydney Morning Herald* (online), 13 August 2015 www.smh.com.au/politics/federal/george-brandis-slaps-down-scott-morrison-over-proposal-to-hold-samesex-marriage-referendum-20150813-giy9vy.htm>.

[115] Paul Kildea, 'Same-sex marriage – Don't let the people decide' on *UK Constitutional Law Association* (6 October 2015) https://ukconstitutionallaw.org/2015/10/06/paul-kildea-same-sex-marriage-dont-let-the-people-decide/.

[116] Chloe Booker, 'Rodney Croome quits Australian Marriage Equality role over plebiscite', *The Sydney Morning Herald* (3 August 2016) www.smh.com.au/national/rodney-croome-quits-australian-marriage-equality-role-over-plebiscite-20160802-gqjl8n.html.

[117] The Commonwealth Government proposed to hold the same-sex marriage plebiscite on 11 February 2017: Plebiscite (Same-Sex Marriage) Bill 2016 (Cth). However, the government did not hold a majority in the Senate and the Plebiscite (Same-Sex Marriage) Bill 2016, which established the legislative framework for the plebiscite, was defeated in the Senate: See Commonwealth, *Parliamentary Debates*, Senate, 7 November 2016, 2058.

[118] *Census and Statistics Act 1905* (Cth), s 9.

[119] *Appropriation Act (No. 1) 2017–2018* (Cth), s 10.

[120] *Wilkie v Commonwealth* (2017) 91 ALJR 1035.

the survey had already commenced, largely undercutting the desire of the marriage equality campaign to reduce the likelihood of traumatic and harmful public debate.[121]

The survey took place between 12 September and 7 November 2017. The survey result was 61.6 per cent in favour of changing the law to allow same-sex marriage. It reflected opinion poll data that had been conducted as early as five years before, which showed over 60 per cent of Australians supported allowing same-sex marriage.[122]

After the result of the postal survey was announced, former Prime Minister Tony Abbott declared that the vote 'should be respected – respected by the community, respected by the parliament'.[123] However, when the vote on the Marriage Amendment (Definition and Religious Freedoms) Bill 2017 took place in the House of Representatives, Abbott and a number of other members of the Coalition continued to shield themselves from the issue and abstained from voting.[124] In December 2017 the Commonwealth Parliament passed the *Marriage Amendment (Definition and Religious Freedoms) Act 2017* (Cth), amending the *Marriage Act 1961* to allow same-sex couples to marry.

IV. Conclusions: Public Interest Advocacy within a Federal System

Central to the way in which the politics surrounding the issue of same-sex marriage played out was an understanding by those advocating for marriage equality of the *Constitution* and the federal system it creates. This has operated as a stricture within which the debate and reform advocacy must be staged, as well as an opportunity for its advancement.

Those advocating for marriage equality needed to be astute political operators, as well as have a strong understanding of the legal landscape and engage competent legal counsel. It is unsurprising, therefore, that two of the key advocates for marriage equality – Rodney Croome from Australian Marriage Equality, and Bob Brown from The Greens – had both previously been involved in public interest advocacy.[125] And more than that, they were both familiar with the way in which litigation between the Commonwealth and states could be used as an important tool in furthering reform objectives.[126] They were thus able to be deft in determining when litigation in the courts was the most appropriate way to progress reform, and when they should deploy their energies into other forums.

[121] Although note the reflections of Greenwich and Robinson, above n 29, 199, that the case 'was critical in buying time. It was also important for advocates to know they had given everything to stop the postal survey from proceeding.'

[122] See above n 96.

[123] Ean Higgins, 'Same-sex Marriage: Abbott Pledges to Respect Warringah's Vote', *The Australian* (online), 16 November 2017 www.theaustralian.com.au/national-affairs/samesex-marriage-abbott-pledges-to-respect-warringahs-vote/news-story/9c7ccd377a8912ae3cccc656a28e3a2e.

[124] Judith Ireland and Latika Bourke, 'Same-sex Marriage: Tony Abbott, Barnaby Joyce, Scott Morrison and the Other MPs Who Didn't Vote "Yes" or "No"', *The Sydney Morning Herald* (online), 8 December 2017 www.smh.com.au/politics/federal/samesex-marriage-tony-abbott-barnaby-joyce-scott-morrison-and-the-other-mps-who-didnt-vote-yes-or-no-20171207-h00kwo.html.

[125] Rodney Croome had previously been involved in the decriminalisation of homosexuality in Australia: see above n 19. As is well known, Bob Brown led the campaign to stop the construction of the Franklin Dam.

[126] See respectively *Croome v Tasmanian* (1997) 191 CLR 119 and *Tasmanian Dam Case* (1983) 158 CLR 1.

The legal uncertainty over the definition of 'marriage' within the Constitution meant that at least some of the states and territories were willing to attempt to legislate in this area at a time when the Commonwealth Government was outright opposed to being involved in progressive reform. At that stage, the support from both major parties for the status quo meant that the opportunities that was often available to advocates through the bicameral parliamentary structure was unhelpful. Equally, this uncertainty provided the Commonwealth with some justification for avoiding the issue. In a federal system, with this level of constitutional uncertainty over the scope of the Commonwealth's power, there was an opportunity to push for reform at a sub-national level where there was inaction at a national level. The federal system provided a further set of forums within which to discuss and leverage reform opportunities.

Further, in Australia, with different levels of sympathy for such reform across the different jurisdictions, the ACT offered marriage equality advocates a forum in which they could speak loudly and persuasively to achieve legal reform. They could bring issues onto the national agenda and spark a national debate and awareness campaign of an issue successive federal governments were unwilling to engage with.

Further, through reform in the ACT, marriage equality reformers were able to force the High Court to remove a significant national hurdle to reform: uncertainty around the scope of the federal marriage power. Once this had been achieved through constitutional litigation, it was natural for the focus of reform to move from the states to the federal level. By then, a number of states had indicated their own willingness to adopt marriage reforms, there was increasing public awareness and momentum behind national adoption, and targeted advocacy work by marriage equality campaigners of federal parliamentarians meant individual reform leaders were emerging across the political spectrum. While the Coalition Government deployed the plebiscite and then postal survey to at least delay this reform, it would eventually be achieved. It was a long, complex fight across the entire federation, won by advocates who understood and were able to deploy and respond to the Constitution in a way that traditional theoretical descriptions of the relationship between federalism and law fail to capture.

15

Freedom of Religion

NICHOLAS ARONEY AND BENJAMIN B SAUNDERS

I. Introduction

Freedom of religion is universally recognised as a fundamental, non-derogable human right.[1] The right to religious freedom is typically partnered with the rights to freedom of thought, conscience and belief. Indeed, these rights are closely related. A person's religion is an expression of beliefs which impact to a greater or lesser extent the way he or she views and lives within the world. There is a close connection between religion and morality, with many religions expressing or stipulating ethical codes and ways of life. The internalisation of such moral norms shapes the conscience, 'an individual's inward conviction of what is morally right or morally wrong'.[2] Freedom of religion thus includes freedom to manifest religious belief – not only individually, but also in community with others, and not only in private, but also in public.[3] For this reason, freedom of religion is inextricably linked with other human rights, including freedom of expression, freedom of assembly and freedom of association.[4]

At face value, religion and freedom of religion hold an important place in Australian law. The Constitution begins with an acknowledgment of God and limits the Commonwealth's power to curtail the free exercise of religion.[5] The three jurisdictions which have enacted statutory charters of rights all include freedom of religion and belief,[6] and religions are protected in important ways in ordinary law, such as exemptions clauses in anti-discrimination statutes,[7] and recognition of religion as a legitimate field of charitable activity, which provides the basis for concessional taxation treatment.[8] Given the increasing

[1] *International Covenant on Civil and Political Rights* opened for signature 16 December 1966, 999 UNTS 171 (entered into force 23 March 1976) art 18 ('ICCPR').

[2] *R v AM* (2010) 5 ACTLR 170, 177 [32], quoting *Grondal v Minister of State for Labour and National Service* (unreported, Supreme Court of Western Australia, Dwyer CJ, 11 September 1953).

[3] ICCPR, art 18.1.

[4] ICCPR, arts 19, 21, 22.

[5] *Commonwealth of Australia Constitution Act 1900* (UK) preamble; Australian Constitution, s 116.

[6] *Charter of Human Rights and Responsibilities Act 2006* (Vic), s 14 ('*Charter Act* (Vic)'); *Human Rights Act 2004* (ACT), s 14; *Human Rights Act 2019* (Qld), s 20.

[7] See below, Parts III.C and IV.

[8] Eg, *Australian Charities and Not-for-profits Commission Act 2012* (Cth), s 25-5 (entities with a purpose of advancing religion are entitled to registration with the Australian Charities and Not-for-profits Commission); *Charities Act 2013* (Cth), ss 7(e) (the purpose of advancing religion is presumed to be for the public benefit), 12(1)(d) (the purpose of advancing religion is a charitable purpose).

secularisation of Australian society,[9] why does freedom of religion continue to be accorded such importance? Mason ACJ and Brennan J offered an answer in the *Scientology Case*: 'Freedom of religion, the paradigm freedom of conscience, is of the essence of a free society' and the legal definition of religion marks out 'an area within which a person subject to the law is free to believe and to act in accordance with his belief without legal restraint'.[10] The respect accorded to freedom of religion and belief 'is closely related to the degree of tolerance and respect for diversity within a society'.[11] Respect for another person's religious and other beliefs is 'one of the hallmarks of a civilised society'.[12]

Despite the lack of a constitutional bill of rights – a fact which has been often commented on – Australians enjoy a relatively high level of religious freedom.[13] Religious freedom is, however, coming under pressure, in ways which may undermine the importance seemingly accorded to it. The principal sources of this pressure are, first, an argument that religious freedom should be limited to the extent it conflicts with other rights, especially rights to equality and non-discrimination, and secondly, the argument that religion should not be afforded privileged treatment in a secular society. Many submissions to the recent Ruddock review on religious freedom[14] called for the removal of religious exemptions to anti-discrimination laws and the removal of public funding and taxation concessions unless religious bodies adhere to the principle of non-discrimination.[15] If Australia follows developments overseas,[16] these calls are likely to become more vocal.[17] This is compounded by the fact that the regulation of religion and religious freedom in Australia has developed as a series of compromises among different political beliefs and world views,[18] and so a principled basis for resolving the conflicts between such beliefs, and conflicting rights, has struggled to emerge. There have been few cases in Australia involving freedom of religion, and therefore questions of conflicts of rights represent largely uncharted territory.[19]

Law may interact with religion in a number of ways.[20] These include expressly protecting the right to freedom of religion or belief, for example by means of a guarantee contained in a constitutional document or human rights statute. A second way is by exempting religion from the operation of a particular law, for example religious exemptions to anti-discrimination legislation. A third way is simply to leave an area unregulated, for example the approach

[9] See, eg, Stephen Chavura, John Gascoigne and Ian Tregenza, *Reason, Religion and the Australian Polity: A Secular State?* (Abingdon, Routledge, 2019) ch 11. Note, however, that secularisation is a complex and contested phenomenon.

[10] *Church of the New Faith v Commissioner of Pay-roll Tax (Vic)* (1983) 154 CLR 120, 130.

[11] Ahmed Shaheed, *Report of the Special Rapporteur on Freedom of Religion and Belief*, UN Doc A/HRC/37/49 (28 February 2018) [88].

[12] *R v Secretary of State for Education and Employment; ex parte Williamson* [2005] UKHL 15 [15] (Lord Nicholls of Birkenhead).

[13] Renae Barker, *State and Religion: The Australian Story* (Abingdon, Routledge, 2018) 38.

[14] *Religious Freedom Review: Report of the Expert Panel* (May 2018) ['Expert Panel'].

[15] Eg, Discrimination Law Experts, Submission No 14 926 to Expert Panel, *Religious Freedom Review* (14 February 2018); Rodney Croome, Submission No 14 866 to Expert Panel, *Religious Freedom Review* (14 February 2018).

[16] The Expert Panel on Religious Freedom was cautious about drawing conclusions from the experience in other jurisdictions with different legal arrangements: Expert Panel (n 14) 10.

[17] See, eg, Rex Ahdar and Ian Leigh, *Religious Freedom in the Liberal State* 2nd edn (Oxford, Oxford University Press, 2013) ch 1.

[18] Carolyn Evans, *Legal Protection of Religious Freedom in Australia* (Sydney, Federation Press, 2012) 19.

[19] *Christian Youth Camps Ltd v Cobaw Community Health Services Ltd* (2014) 50 VR 256, 262 [14] (Maxwell P).

[20] Evans (n 18) ch 5.

adopted by Australian law in relation to head coverings for Muslim women.[21] A final way that law may interact with religion is by not providing sufficient protection for religious freedom, including the freedom to hold a religion or belief, or more commonly, not providing sufficient protection for the manifestation of religious belief. Numerous submissions to the Ruddock review argued that religious freedom is being threatened in Australia in diverse ways, including discrimination against individuals on the basis of religious dress or observance, instances of intolerance against religious minorities and instances 'where people of faith experienced adverse consequences as a result of expressing views in favour of same-sex marriage or as a result of their sexual orientation or gender identity'.[22]

This chapter examines the state of religious freedom in Australia by assessing legislation and key cases in the light of international human rights instruments. A focus of this chapter is to examine how conflicts between religious freedom and other rights are resolved and to unpack the underlying conception of religion evident in both legislation and relevant cases.

II. International Human Rights Law

International human rights law is relevant to an understanding of the right to freedom of religion for several reasons. First, Australia is a party to key international covenants such as the *International Covenant on Civil and Political Rights* ('ICCPR') and is required to give effect in domestic law to the obligations contained in those instruments.[23] Secondly, the statutory human rights acts which have been enacted in Australia provide that international law relevant to a human right may be taken into account when interpreting legislation.[24] International jurisprudence has been influential in key decisions relating to religious freedom.[25] As such, an accurate understanding of international human rights law provides an important benchmark against which to assess the effectiveness of the Australian protections for religious freedom.

The leading international provision on religious freedom is Article 18 of the ICCPR, which provides:

1. Everyone shall have the right to freedom of thought, conscience and religion. This right shall include freedom to have or to adopt a religion or belief of his choice, and freedom, either individually or in community with others and in public or private, to manifest his religion or belief in worship, observance, practice and teaching.
2. No one shall be subject to coercion which would impair his freedom to have or to adopt a religion or belief of his choice.
3. Freedom to manifest one's religion or beliefs may be subject only to such limitations as are prescribed by law and are necessary to protect public safety, order, health, or morals or the fundamental rights and freedoms of others.

[21] See discussion in Renae Barker, 'Rebutting the Ban the Burqa Rhetoric: A Critical Analysis of the Arguments for a Ban on the Islamic Face Veil in Australia' (2016) 37 *Adelaide Law Review* 191.

[22] Expert Panel (n 14) 98–9.

[23] *International Covenant on Civil and Political Rights*, opened for signature 16 December 1966, 999 UNTS 171 (entered into force 23 March 1976) art 2.

[24] *Charter Act* (Vic), s 32(2); *Human Rights Act 2004* (ACT), s 31; *Human Rights Act 2019* (Qld), s 48(3).

[25] *Christian Youth Camps Ltd v Cobaw Community Health Services Ltd* (2014) 50 VR 256, 394 [535] (Redlich JA).

4. The States Parties to the present Covenant undertake to have respect for the liberty of parents and, when applicable, legal guardians to ensure the religious and moral education of their children in conformity with their own convictions.[26]

The *Declaration on the Elimination of All Forms of Intolerance and of Discrimination Based on Religion or Belief* states that the right to freedom of thought, conscience, religion or belief includes the freedom to worship or assemble in connection with a religion or belief, to establish and maintain appropriate charitable or humanitarian institutions, to write, issue and disseminate publications, to train and appoint appropriate leaders consistent with the requirements and standards of any religion or belief, among other things.[27] The ICCPR also enshrines various other rights relevant to religion and religious practice, such as the right to be free from discrimination, the rights to free expression and freedom of association.[28] All such human rights are 'universal, indivisible and interdependent and interrelated'.[29] Accordingly, the relevant international instruments do not recognise a hierarchy of rights and it cannot be said that some rights are more fundamental than others.[30] However, one indication of the relative importance of the right to freedom of religion and belief in comparison with other rights is that freedom of religion is one of the few rights listed in the ICCPR from which derogation is not permitted in time of public emergency.[31] Freedom of thought, conscience and religion are rights which are 'not derogable under any conditions'.[32]

Article 18 recognises a distinction between the right to hold a religion and the right to manifest that religion. Freedom of thought and conscience, and the right to have or adopt a religion or belief, sometimes referred to as the '*forum internum*', is an absolute right that simply cannot be limited. The right to manifest a religion, by contrast, is subject to limitation, where such limitations are 'necessary to protect public safety, order, health, or morals or the fundamental rights and freedoms of others'.[33] This distinction, though fundamental, needs to be understood carefully. The *forum internum* 'falls primarily within the domain of the inner faith and conscience of an individual', with the implication that 'any intervention from outside is not only illegitimate but impossible'.[34] The internal forum is thus protected principally by the prohibition on any coercion that would impair the freedom of each person to adopt, maintain or change a religion or belief of his or her choice.[35] Such coercion can occur

[26] ICCPR, art 18.

[27] *Declaration on the Elimination of All Forms of Intolerance and of Discrimination Based on Religion or Belief*, GA Res 36/55, UN GAOR, 36th sess, 73rd plen mtg, Supp No 51, UN Doc A/RES/26/55 (25 November 1981) art 6.

[28] ICCPR, arts 2, 26 (equality of all persons before the law and the right to be free from discrimination), 19 (right to hold opinions and free expression), 20 (prohibition of religious hatred and incitement to violence), 21 (right to peaceful assembly), 22 (freedom of association), 25 (right to take part in public affairs) and 27 (rights of religious minorities).

[29] *Vienna Declaration and Programme of Action*, UN GAOR, World Conf on Human Rights, 48th Sess., 22d plen mtg, part I, ¶ 5, UN Doc A/CONF.157/24 (1993) [5].

[30] Chris Sidoti, Human Rights Commissioner, 'Introducing Human Rights Law' (Speech, Hanoi, 2 May 1997) www.humanrights.gov.au/news/speeches/introducing-human-rights-law-chris-sidoti-1997.

[31] ICCPR, art 4.2; Human Rights Committee, *General Comment 22: The Right to Freedom of Thought, Conscience and Religion* (Art 18), 48th sess, UN Doc CCPR/C/21/Rev.1/Add.4 (30 July 1993) ('General Comment 22') [1].

[32] United Nations Commission on Human Rights, *Siracusa Principles on the Limitation and Derogation of Provisions in the International Covenant on Civil and Political Rights*, UN Doc E/CN.4/1985/4 (28 September 1984) [58] ('*Siracusa Principles*').

[33] ICCPR, art 18.3.

[34] Arcot Krishnaswami, Special Rapporteur, *Study of Discrimination in the matter of Religious Rights and Practices*, UN Document E/CN.4/Sub.2/200/Rev.1 (1960) 23.

[35] ICCPR, art 18.2. See General Comment 22, [3].

not only through the imposition of punishments or sanctions, but through the imposition of detriments in a discriminatory manner; and it can also occur by requiring individuals to act in ways that are in direct contradiction to the requirements of their religious beliefs, for this can amount to requiring them to recant their religion through their actions.[36] Furthermore, the *forum internum* has an additional 'indirect' aspect requiring states to respect the religious convictions and conscientious beliefs of individuals. It thus includes the liberty of parents to ensure the moral and religious education of their children in accordance with their own convictions,[37] a right that is also absolute and cannot be limited.[38]

Although the ICCPR permits states to limit the manifestation of religion, limitations are permitted in narrowly prescribed ways, and international law imposes a very high threshold on the imposition of limitations on the manifestation of religion.[39] Under Article 18.3 of the ICCPR, limitations may be imposed only on the grounds permitted by the terms of the ICCPR; limitations clauses must be 'interpreted strictly and in favour of the rights at issue'; when a limitation is required by the ICCPR to be 'necessary', this requires that the limitation must be based on one of the grounds recognised by the relevant article of the ICCPR, must respond to a 'pressing public or social need', pursue a 'legitimate aim', and be 'proportionate to that aim'; and a state must use 'no more restrictive means than are required for the achievement of the purpose of the limitation'.[40] Limitations may be imposed 'only for those purposes for which they were prescribed' and they must be 'directly related and proportionate to the specific need on which they are predicated'.[41] In this respect it is important to note that while such limitations may be imposed to protect the rights of others not to be discriminated against as guaranteed by articles 2 and 26 of the ICCPR, the UN Human Right Committee has observed that this does not mean that individuals must be accorded 'identical treatment in every instance', for 'not every differentiation of treatment will constitute discrimination, if the criteria for such differentiation are reasonable and objective and if the aim is to achieve a purpose which is legitimate under the Covenant'.[42]

According to article 18.1, one of the ways in which religion may be manifested is through 'teaching', a concept which embraces not only the 'private' instruction that may be given to children within families, and to religious adherents in the context of religious gatherings, but also the 'public' sharing or promulgation of religious beliefs in the form of what is commonly known as evangelism or proselytism.[43] In this way, freedom of religion overlaps with the freedom of expression protected under article 19, which cannot be limited except under strict conditions similar to those that apply to freedom of religion. In this

[36] Evans (n 18) 102.

[37] ICCPR, art 18.4.

[38] General Comment 22, [8]. See Paul M Taylor, *Freedom of Religion: UN and European Human Rights Law and Practice* (Cambridge, Cambridge University Press, 2005) 177–82.

[39] See also Human Rights Committee, *General Comment 27: The Right to Freedom of Movement* (Art 12), 67th sess, UN Doc CCPR/C/21/Rev.1/Add.9 (2 November 1999) [11], [14]; Human Rights Committee, *General Comment 34: Freedoms of Opinion and Expression* (Art 19), 102nd sess, UN Doc CCPR/C/GC/34 (12 September 2011) [22].

[40] *Siracusa Principles*, [10]–[11].

[41] General Comment 22, [8].

[42] Human Rights Committee, *General Comment 18: Non-discrimination* (Arts 2 and 26), 37th sess UN Doc. HRI/GEN/1/Rev.8 (10 November 1989) [8], [13].

[43] General Comment 22, [5]. For a detailed study of the right to convert, the right not to be forced to convert, and the right to try to convert others by means of non-coercive persuasion, see Heiner Bielefeldt, *Interim Report of the Special Rapporteur on Freedom of Religion and Belief*, UN Doc A/67/303 (13 August 2012).

connection, article 20.2 of the ICCPR further requires that 'any advocacy of national, racial or religious hatred that constitutes incitement to discrimination, hostility or violence' must be prohibited by law. An Expert Workshop convened by the UN High Commissioner for Human Rights in 2013 concluded that article 20(2) establishes a 'high threshold' because 'as a matter of fundamental principle, limitation of speech must remain an exception'. Articles 19 and 20.2 require that any restriction on freedom of expression must be 'clearly and narrowly defined', 'least intrusive', 'not overly broad' and 'proportionate', and must accord closely with the restrictive language of article 20.2.[44] Similar observations about articles 19 and 20.2 have been made by the UN Human Rights Committee in its General Comments on the ICCPR and in its Reports assessing the compliance of particular countries with the ICCPR, including its 2009 Report on Australia.[45]

These comments are an important reminder that too ready a limitation of the right to manifest religion is apt to 'erect a barrier between one's conscience and actions manifesting that conscience'.[46] The Special Rapporteur on Freedom of Religion has accordingly warned that states which attempt to 'sanitize' the public sphere from the expression of religious views may contravene 'their duty to respect the right to manifest one's religion or belief'.[47]

III. Freedom of Religion in Australian Law

A. Constitutional Fundamentals

The right to freedom of religion has a complex relation to Australian law. Much of this complexity lies in the multiple senses in which rights and freedoms can be said to exist in law generally. Following the approach advanced by Glanville Williams, it is arguable that the condition of liberty is one of the most fundamental presuppositions of the law in this sense: one is free to do or decline to do anything unless that act or omission is the subject of a legal duty.[48] Liberties are expressly referred to in the law usually in order to indicate the limits of a duty, and they are usually invoked where the line between duty and liberty is in dispute.[49] In this sense, religious freedom is a fundamental presupposition of the law: one is free to believe anything, and to act on those beliefs, provided such actions are not specifically prohibited by law. The principle of legality supports this fundamental principle of liberty through the proposition that the courts will not impute to a legislature an intention to interfere with fundamental rights or liberties unless such an intention is clearly manifested by

[44] *Rabat Plan of Action on National, Racial or Religious Hatred* (*Report of the United Nations High Commissioner for Human Rights on the expert workshops on the prohibition of incitement to national, racial or religious hatred*, Appendix) (11 January 2013) UN Doc A/HRC/22/17/Add 4, [18], [21].

[45] Human Rights Committee, *Consideration of Reports Submitted by States Parties under Article 40 of the Covenant: Concluding Observations of the Human Rights Committee: Australia* (7 May 2009) UN Doc CCPR/C/AUS/CO/5 [26].

[46] Sheldon Leader, 'Freedom and Futures: Personal Priorities, Institutional Demands and Freedom of Religion' (2007) 70 *MLR* 713, 730.

[47] Shaheed (n 11) [49].

[48] Glanville Williams, 'The Concept of Legal Liberty' (1956) 56(8) *Columbia Law Review* 1129. Williams puts it this way: 'When I get up in the morning, dress, take breakfast, and so on, I am exercising liberties, because I do not commit legal wrongs. Since the commission of legal wrongs is relatively infrequent, almost every act is the exercise of a liberty': ibid 1129.

[49] Ibid, 1130.

unambiguous language.[50] Recent decisions have suggested that freedom of religion is one of these fundamental rights and freedoms,[51] and that this freedom, following article 18 of the ICCPR, extends to the 'freedom of people to adhere to the religion of their choice and the beliefs of their choice and to manifest their religion or beliefs in worship, observance, practice and teaching'.[52] The common law's recognition of the right to freedom of religion does not mean, however, that Australian Parliaments lack the legislative power to enact laws which interfere with freedom of religion.[53] The constitutional provisions in Australia which protect freedom of religion are limited. Section 46 of the Tasmanian *Constitution Act 1934* provides that:

> (1) Freedom of conscience and the free profession and practice of religion are, subject to public order and morality, guaranteed to every citizen.
> (2) No person shall be subject to any disability, or be required to take any oath on account of his religion or religious belief and no religious test shall be imposed in respect of the appointment to or holding of any public office.

These protections arguably control and limit the scope of lawful executive action within Tasmania. However, section 46 is not constitutionally entrenched, which means that it can be amended by a subsequent statute which is simply inconsistent with it.[54]

Religion played an important part in the enactment of the Australian Constitution: the preamble recites that the people of the colonies agreed to unite to form the federal Commonwealth 'humbly relying on the blessing of Almighty God'[55] and the churches were influential in securing acceptance of the draft Constitution Bill in the colonies.[56] The Constitution nevertheless contains limited protection for religious freedom. Section 116 provides:

> The Commonwealth shall not make any law for establishing any religion, or for imposing any religious observance, or for prohibiting the free exercise of any religion, and no religious test shall be required as a qualification for any office or public trust under the Commonwealth.[57]

Reflecting the pragmatic origins of section 116,[58] its clauses have been interpreted narrowly by the High Court as a limitation on Commonwealth legislative power rather than an individual right.[59] In no case has a law been held to contravene section 116. The 'free exercise'

[50] *Coco v The Queen* (1994) 179 CLR 427, 437 (Mason CJ, Brennan, Gaudron and McHugh JJ); Murray Gleeson, 'The Meaning of Legislation: Context, Purpose and Respect for Fundamental Rights' (2009) 20 *Public Law Review* 26, 33.

[51] *Canterbury Municipal Council v Moslem Alawy Society Ltd* (1985) 1 NSWLR 525, 544 (McHugh JA).

[52] *Evans v New South Wales* (2008) 168 FCR 576, [8], [79].

[53] *Grace Bible Church v Reedman* (1984) 36 SASR 376.

[54] *Corneloup v Launceston City Council* [2016] FCA 974, [38]. See, generally, *McCawley v The King* [1920] AC 69; (1920) 28 CLR 106.

[55] *Commonwealth of Australia Constitution Act 1900* (UK) preamble.

[56] Alan Atkinson, *The Europeans in Australia* (Sydney, UNSW Press, 2014) vol 3, ch 9.

[57] Australian Constitution, s 116.

[58] Luke Beck, *Religious Freedom and the Australian Constitution: Origins and Future* (Abingdon, Routledge, 2018) 120.

[59] *Attorney-General (Vic); Ex rel Black v Commonwealth* (1981) 146 CLR 559, 605, 609, 615, 616, 652–3, ('*DOGS*'); Stephen McLeish, 'Making Sense of Religion and the Constitution: A Fresh Start for Section 116' (1992) 18 *Monash University Law Review* 207; Reid Mortensen, 'The Unfinished Experiment: A Report on Religious Freedom in Australia' (2007) 21 *Emory International Law Review* 167; Carolyn Evans, 'Religion', in Cheryl Saunders and Adrienne Stone (eds), *The Oxford Handbook of the Australian Constitution* (Oxford, Oxford University Press, 2018); Carolyn Evans, 'Religion as Politics not law: The Religion Clauses in the Australian Constitution' (2008) 36 *Religion, State and Society* 283.

clause has been given a restricted interpretation – sometimes dismissively so[60] – with the Court readily finding that the free exercise of religion is subject to and may be overridden by other legitimate interests such as the protection of the community.[61] When interpreting the 'establishment' clause the High Court has not followed the US approach[62] but has rather held that indirect funding of religious schools does not amount to an 'establishment' of religion, thereby permitting a much greater degree of government support for religious schools and other religious entities.[63] There has been limited consideration of the observance and religious tests clauses, which also have been interpreted narrowly.[64]

B. Human Rights Acts

Each of the human rights statutes in Australia contains a right to freedom of religion, in almost identical terms. For example, the recently passed *Human Rights Act 2019* (Qld) provides:

(1) Every person has the right to freedom of thought, conscience, religion and belief, including—
  (a) the freedom to have or to adopt a religion or belief of the person's choice; and
  (b) the freedom to demonstrate the person's religion or belief in worship, observance, practice and teaching, either individually or as part of a community, in public or in private.
(2) A person must not be coerced or restrained in a way that limits the person's freedom to have or adopt a religion or belief.[65]

Consistently with the international human rights treaties, these provisions recognise a distinction between holding a religion or belief, and demonstrating such a belief in certain listed ways. However, the charters diverge in three important ways from the relevant international jurisprudence. First, the stringent requirements relating to limitations on the right are replaced by considerably weaker protections. Under the ICCPR, the internal right to freedom of religion cannot be limited to any extent while the external freedom to manifest one's religion or beliefs 'may be subject only to such limitations as are prescribed by law and are necessary to protect public safety, order, health, or morals or the fundamental rights and freedoms of others'.[66] By contrast, the charters provide that all rights – including freedom of religion – may be subject to 'such reasonable limits as can be demonstrably justified in

[60] *Krygger v Williams* (1912) 15 CLR 366.

[61] *Adelaide Company of Jehovah's Witnesses Inc v Commonwealth* (1943) 67 CLR 116. For criticism, see Alex Deagon, 'Liberal Assumptions in Section 116 Cases and Implications for Religious Freedom' (2018) 46 *Federal Law Review* 113.

[62] See *Lemon v Kurtzman*, 403 US 602, 612–13 (1971).

[63] *A-G (Vic) (ex rel Black) v Commonwealth* (1981) 146 CLR 559; *Hoxton Park Residents Action Group Inc v Liverpool City Council* (2010) 344 ALR 101.

[64] *Williams v Commonwealth* (2013) 248 CLR 156, [109]–[110], [443]–[447].

[65] *Human Rights Act 2019* (Qld), s 20; see also *Charter Act* (Vic), s 14(1); *Human Rights Act 2004* (ACT), s 14(1) (omitting 'belief' from the scope of the right).

[66] ICCPR, art 18.3.

a free and democratic society based on human dignity, equality and freedom'.[67] Secondly, notwithstanding the emphatic terms in which the charters protect the freedom to have or adopt a religion or belief,[68] it appears that limitations on the *forum internum* may nonetheless be subject to limitations pursuant to the general limitations clause, even though under the ICCPR the internal right to freedom of religion is an absolute right that simply cannot be limited. A third glaring difference is that there is no equivalent in the Queensland or Victorian charters of article 18.4 of the ICCPR, which guarantees the liberty of parents and guardians 'to ensure the religious and moral education of their children in conformity with their own convictions'.[69] These significant divergences detract significantly from the claim that the human rights charters were enacted to give effect to Australia's obligations under the ICCPR and other relevant international human rights standards.

To the extent that the right to religious freedom as enshrined in these human rights statutes has any substantive legal effect, this occurs by means of two provisions. First, the statutes require that all statutory provisions must be interpreted in a way that is compatible with human rights to the extent that it is possible to do so consistently with their purpose.[70] In *Momcilovic* the High Court declined to follow the approach to comparable interpretive provisions taken in other countries,[71] holding instead that the task imposed by section 32(1) of the *Charter Act* (Vic) is consistent with ordinary principles of statutory construction.[72] These interpretation provisions do not, therefore, authorise courts to depart in significant ways from orthodox approaches. Whether this will enable Australian courts to interpret statutes in a manner that accords with Australia's obligations under art 18.3 of the ICCPR remains to be seen.

Secondly, the statutes provide that it is unlawful for a public authority 'to act or make a decision in a way that is not compatible with human rights' or 'in making a decision, to fail to give proper consideration to a human right relevant to the decision'.[73] The Queensland legislation exempts from this provision bodies established for a religious purpose 'if the act or decision is done or made in accordance with the doctrine of the religion concerned and is necessary to avoid offending the religious sensitivities of the people of the religion'.[74] In Victoria and Queensland, there is no freestanding right to bring proceedings against a public authority on the basis of unlawfulness under these provisions; any such action must 'piggy back' on another claim for relief on the basis of unlawfulness.[75] The *Human Rights*

[67] *Charter Act* (Vic), s 7(2); *Human Rights Act 2019* (Qld), s 13(1); *Human Rights Act 2004* (ACT), s 28(1) (omitting the words 'based on human dignity, equality and freedom').

[68] *Charter Act* (Vic), s 14(2); *Human Rights Act 2004* (ACT), s,14(2); *Human Rights Act 2019* (Qld), s 20(2).

[69] ICCPR, art 18.4. See *Human Rights Act 2004* (ACT), which provides: 'to ensure the religious and moral education of a child in conformity with the convictions of the child's parent or guardian, the parent or guardian may choose schooling for the child (other than schooling provided by the government) that conforms to the minimum educational standards required under law'.

[70] *Charter Act* (Vic), s 32(1); *Human Rights Act 2019* (Qld), s 48(1) (which provides: '[a]ll statutory provisions must, to the extent possible that is consistent with their purpose, be interpreted in a way that is compatible with human rights'); *Human Rights Act 2004* (ACT) s 30.

[71] See especially *Ghaidan v Godin-Mendoza* [2004] 2 AC 557.

[72] *Momcilovic v The Queen* (2011) 245 CLR 1, 47–8 [46], 50 [50]–[51], 55 [62] (French CJ), 85 [146] (step (v)), 92–3 [170]–[171] (Gummow J), 123 [280] (Hayne J), 210 [544]–[545] (Crennan and Kiefel JJ), 250 [684] (Bell J).

[73] *Charter Act* (Vic), s 38(1); *Human Rights Act 2019* (Qld), s 58(1); *Human Rights Act 2004* (ACT), s 40B(1).

[74] *Human Rights Act 2019* (Qld), s 58(3).

[75] *Charter Act* (Vic), s 39(1); *Human Rights Act 2019* (Qld), s 59. For analysis, see Jeremy Gans, 'The Charter's Irremediable Remedies Provision' (2009) 33 *Melbourne University Law Review* 105.

Act 2004 (ACT) enables a person who claims that a public authority contravened and who alleges that he or she is or would be a victim of the contravention to commence proceedings in the Supreme Court against the authority. The Supreme Court has power to grant any relief it considers appropriate except damages.[76]

We discuss a selection of the few freedom of religion cases decided in the context of the human rights charters in Part IV below.

C. Anti-discrimination Laws

Discrimination laws are relevant to religion in two ways. First, many jurisdictions prohibit discrimination on the basis of religious belief or activity. In all states and territories other than New South Wales and South Australia, discrimination on the basis of religious belief or activity is unlawful.[77] The legislation varies from jurisdiction to jurisdiction and typically prohibits discrimination in areas such as employment,[78] accommodation,[79] the provision of goods and services,[80] and other contexts.[81] The New South Wales Law Reform Commission in 1999 recommended that religious beliefs and practices be included as a ground of discrimination but the *Anti-Discrimination Act* has not been amended to reflect this.[82] The South Australian legislation prohibits discrimination on the basis of 'religious appearance or dress'.[83] The only protection against discrimination on the ground of religion in Commonwealth law is contained in the *Fair Work Act 2009*, which prohibits an employer from taking adverse action against an employee, or prospective employee, because of the person's religion.[84] The Ruddock review recommended that the Commonwealth, New South Wales and South Australia should amend their respective anti-discrimination laws to render it unlawful to discriminate on the basis of a person's 'religious belief or activity', including on the basis that a person does not hold any religious belief.[85]

Secondly, discrimination laws typically provide exemptions or exceptions to religious individuals and bodies to enable them to discriminate lawfully in certain circumstances. While these exemptions are controversial, they are considered necessary to prevent people

[76] *Human Rights Act 2004* (ACT), s 40C.

[77] *Anti-Discrimination Act 1991* (Qld), s 7(i); *Anti-Discrimination Act 1992* (NT), s 19(1)(m); *Anti-Discrimination Act 1998* (Tas), ss 16(o), (p); *Discrimination Act 1991* (ACT), ss 7(1)(u), 8; *Equal Opportunity Act 1984* (WA), s 53(1); *Equal Opportunity Act 2010* (Vic), s 6(n).

[78] *Anti-Discrimination Act 1991* (Qld), ss13–36; *Anti-Discrimination Act 2004* (NT), ss 31–37A; *Anti-Discrimination Act 1998* (Tas), s 22(1)(a); *Discrimination Act 1991* (ACT), ss 10–17; *Equal Opportunity Act 1984* (WA), ss 11–17; *Equal Opportunity Act 2010* (Vic), ss 16, 18, 21, 30–31.

[79] *Anti-Discrimination Act 1991* (Qld), ss 82–84; *Anti-Discrimination Act 2004* (NT), ss 38–39; *Anti-Discrimination Act 1998* (Tas), s 22(1)(d); *Discrimination Act 1991* (ACT), s 21; *Equal Opportunity Act 1984* (WA), ss 21–21A; *Equal Opportunity Act 2010* (Vic), ss 52–57.

[80] *Anti-Discrimination Act 1991* (Qld), ss 45–51; *Anti-Discrimination Act 2004* (NT), s 41; *Anti-Discrimination Act 1998* (Tas), s 22(1)(c); *Discrimination Act 1991* (ACT), s 20; *Equal Opportunity Act 1984* (WA), s 20; *Equal Opportunity Act 2010* (Vic), s 44.

[81] See Expert Panel (n 14) 131–2.

[82] New South Wales Law Reform Commission, *Review of the Anti-Discrimination Act 1977 (NSW)*, Report No 92 (1999) recommendation 38.

[83] *Equal Opportunity Act 1984* (SA), ss 85T, 85U, 85ZD.

[84] *Fair Work Act 2009* (Cth), s 351(1). See also s 153(1), which provides that modern awards must not include provisions that discriminate against an employee because of religion.

[85] Expert Panel (n 14), recs 15 and 16.

from being compelled to act contrary to their genuinely held religious beliefs,[86] and to enable religious groups to exist as distinctive religious entities.[87] Exemptions typically are available in relation to the training, ordination or appointment of ministers of religion or members of a religious order, thereby giving religious groups the power of internal control over their leadership. Exemptions also typically apply in relation to acts or practices 'of a body established for religious purposes' that 'conforms with the doctrines, beliefs or principles of the religion' or 'is reasonably necessary to avoid injury to the religious sensitivities of adherents of the religion'.[88] When proposing that religious discrimination should be made unlawful in all Australian jurisdictions, the Ruddock review recommended that consideration be given to providing for appropriate exceptions for religious bodies, religious schools and charities to enable them to exercise their religion.[89]

The drafting technique often employed to create exemptions for religious bodies makes those exemptions inherently vulnerable.[90] An exemption creates the impression that the protections are special privileges afforded to certain groups and not others, allowing them to engage in conduct which would otherwise be unlawful. In addition, exemptions can be readily removed without otherwise disturbing the operation of the legislation. However, the exemptions exist to further the legitimate purpose of protecting freedom of religion and, as noted above, not all discrimination is unlawful or morally objectionable.[91] For instance, while refusing to employ a person because of their political beliefs would ordinarily constitute unlawful discrimination, it is uncontroversial that political parties and members of Parliament should be (and are) entitled to discriminate on the basis of political beliefs or activity when employing their staff.[92]

There have been a number of cases involving discrimination or alleged discrimination on the basis of religious belief or activity. Some religious adherents have had success in establishing such discrimination. In *Queensland v Mahommed* the Queensland Anti-Discrimination Tribunal held that the failure to provide a Muslim prisoner with fresh Halal meat constituted unfavourable treatment based on his religious beliefs or religious activity, and this was upheld on appeal to the Supreme Court of Queensland.[93] *Christian Family Schools Association v Public Transport Corporation* concerned a requirement imposed by the Public Transport Corporation that, in order to obtain a concession card to travel on public transport, a child had to be enrolled at a school or be recognised as a student on a list maintained by the Ministry of Education. The complainant home schooled his children and, for religious reasons, was not prepared to submit the education of his children to the authority

[86] Victoria, *Parliamentary Debates*, Legislative Assembly, 4 May 1995, 1254 (Jan Wade, Attorney-General).

[87] Reid Mortensen, 'A Reconstruction of Religious Freedom and Equality: Gay, Lesbian and De Facto Rights and the Religious School in Queensland' (2003) 3 *Queensland University of Technology Law and Justice Journal* 320, 323.

[88] *Anti-Discrimination Act 1977* (NSW), s 56; *Anti-Discrimination Act 1991* (Qld), s 109; *Anti-Discrimination Act 2004* (NT), s 51; *Anti-Discrimination Act 1998* (Tas), ss 27, 51, 51A, 52; *Discrimination Act 1991* (ACT), s 32; *Equal Opportunity Act 1984* (WA), s 72; *Equal Opportunity Act 1984* (SA), s 50; *Equal Opportunity Act 2010* (Vic), s 82, see also s 84.

[89] Expert Panel (n 14) recs 15 and 16.

[90] See, eg, *Equal Opportunity Act 1984* (WA), s 72; *Equal Opportunity Act 2010* (Vic), s 82. See critique of this approach in Neil Foster, 'Freedom of Religion and Balancing Clauses in Discrimination Legislation' (2016) 5 *Oxford Journal of Law and Religion* 385.

[91] General Comment 18, [8], [13].

[92] *Equal Opportunity Act 2010* (Vic), s 27; *Anti-Discrimination Act 1991* (Qld), s 25(1).

[93] *Queensland v Mahommed* [2007] QSC 18.

of the Ministry. The Victorian Equal Opportunity Board held that the requirement imposed by the Corporation was discriminatory on the basis that the complainant could not comply with the condition due to his religious beliefs, and it was unreasonable for the Public Transport Corporation not to provide alternative methods of proving that a child was a student.[94]

Other claims have not been successful. In *Coulson v Austereo Pty Ltd* the Queensland Industrial Relations Commission held that it was not unreasonable for the operator of a radio business to require an employee to work occasionally on Sundays, given the seven day, twenty-four hour nature of the industry.[95] In *D'Urso v Peninsula Support Service Inc* the Victorian Civil and Administrative Tribunal ('VCAT') held that refusing to allow the complainant to hold a prayer meeting during office hours on the employer's property did not constitute unfavourable treatment on the basis of her religion or religious beliefs.[96] Thus, a claim that an employer must accommodate an employee's religious beliefs will not always succeed; the issue will depend on matters such as the reasonableness of the claim, the nature of the employer's business and the employee's role. This is perhaps analogous to the requirement to make 'reasonable adjustments' to accommodate a person's disability under the *Disability Discrimination Act 1992* (Cth).[97]

There have been several cases in which a religious body has claimed the benefit of religious exemptions. In Part IV we discuss two of the leading cases – the *Cobaw*[98] and *Wesley Mission* cases.[99] In some situations, apparently religious bodies have had some difficulty in demonstrating that they were 'religious bodies' entitled to the protection of the religious exemptions. In *Walsh v St Vincent de Paul Society Queensland (No 2)* the complainant, who was not a Roman Catholic, had volunteered for many years with the St Vincent de Paul Society, and after some years became its President. Subsequently, the fact that she was not Roman Catholic became 'a point of contention for some members of the Society', and she was asked to become a Roman Catholic, resign her position or leave the Society.[100] The Queensland Anti-Discrimination Tribunal held that this was unfavourable treatment, thereby amounting to discrimination on the basis of religious belief or activity.[101] Although there was an exemption relating to 'the selection or appointment of people to perform functions in relation to, or otherwise participate in, any religious observance or practice',[102] the Tribunal held that this did not apply because the Society was not a 'religious body' (even though the provision did not contain a reference to 'religious body'). The Tribunal adopted a narrow conception of 'religious body', considering that even though the Society was a society of lay faithful which was closely associated with the Catholic Church, and one of the

[94] *Christian Family Schools Association of Australia v Public Transport Corporation* (1990) EOC ¶92–300.

[95] *Coulson v Austereo Pty Ltd* (2003) 173 QGIG 1034.

[96] *D'Urso v Peninsula Support Service Inc* [2005] VCAT 871 [36]–[39].

[97] More precisely, the failure to make reasonable adjustments for a person with a disability which has the effect that the person with the disability is treated less favourably than a person without the disability constitutes unlawful discrimination: *Disability Discrimination Act 1992* (Cth), s 5(2); see also s 6(2).

[98] *Cobaw Community Health Services v Christian Youth Camps Ltd* [2010] VCAT 1613; *Christian Youth Camps Ltd v Cobaw Community Health Services Ltd* (2014) 50 VR 256.

[99] *V v QZ (No 2)* [2008] NSWADT 115 [35]–[60], [65]; *Members of the Board of the Wesley Mission Council v OV and OW (No 2)* [2009] NSWADTAP 57; *OV and OW v Members of the Board of Wesley Mission Council* (2010) 79 NSWLR 606.

[100] *Walsh v St Vincent de Paul Society Queensland (No 2)* [2008] QADT 32 [53].

[101] Ibid [67].

[102] *Anti-Discrimination Act 1991* (Qld), s 109(1)(c).

main objectives of the Society was 'a spiritual one, involving members bearing witness to Christ by helping others on a personal basis and in doing so endeavouring to bring grace to those they help and earn grace themselves for their common salvation', that was not sufficient to make the Society a religious body.[103] By contrast, the Victorian Equal Opportunity Board held in *Hazan v Victorian Jewish Board of Deputies* that the North Eastern Jewish War memorial Centre was a 'body established to propagate religion'.[104] In *Burke v Tralaggan* the complainant had applied to rent a property, but the owners, who were Christians, refused to let the premises on the basis that the complainant was in an unmarried relationship. The New South Wales Equal Opportunity Tribunal held that this constituted unlawful discrimination and that the respondents were not able to claim the benefit of the religious exemptions because the relevant provision applied to religious orders or bodies and '[did] not operate to allow the members of any religion to impose their beliefs on secular society, so as to exempt them from the operation of the law'.[105]

In other cases, religious bodies have had difficulty in establishing that particular action was required by the doctrines or tenets of their religion. In *Griffin v Catholic Education Office* the complainant had been refused classification as a teacher by the respondent because she was convenor of the Gay and Lesbian Teachers and Students Association, and because of her public statements on lesbian lifestyles, with the consequence that she could not be employed as a teacher in Catholic schools. She brought a complaint to the Human Rights and Equal Opportunity Commission under the *Human Rights and Equal Opportunity Commission Act 1986* (Cth) arguing that the refusal constituted discrimination on the grounds of sexual preference.[106] The Catholic Education Office ('CEO') argued that it was entitled to rely on the 'religious institutions exception', which provided an exception for conduct 'made in good faith in order to avoid injury to the religious susceptibilities of adherents' of a religion.[107] The Commission held that the CEO's approach was premised on assumptions about the complainant's sexual practices and her promotion of gay or lesbian lifestyles, for which there was no evidence.[108] The CEO's actions in refusing classification to the complainant was not consistent with the Catholic Church's doctrines and beliefs. The Commission noted:

> Religious institutions can claim quite properly a margin of appreciation or discretion in making distinctions under this exception. Religious believers have the right to determine what are or are not the doctrines, tenets, beliefs or teachings of their religion. The state and state institutions have no entitlement or authority in human rights law or domestic law to define those. But in applying laws that recognise the doctrines, tenets, beliefs or teachings of a religion the state and state institutions are entitled to rely upon what religious believers say are their doctrines, tenets, beliefs and teachings. Indeed they have no option but to do so.[109]

[103] *Walsh v St Vincent de Paul Society Queensland (No 2)* [2008] QADT 32 [76]. The Society also argued that it was an inherent requirement of the role that the President of the Society be a Roman Catholic, which was also unsuccessful.

[104] *Hazan v Victorian Jewish Board of Deputies* (1990) EOC ¶92-298.

[105] *Burke v Tralaggan* (1986) EOC ¶92-161, 76 588.

[106] *Griffin v Catholic Education Office* (1998) EOC ¶92-928, contained in Human Rights and Equal Opportunity Commission, *Report of an Inquiry into a Complaint of Discrimination in Employment and Occupation: Discrimination on the Ground of Sexual Preference* (HRC Report No 6, 1998).

[107] *Human Rights and Equal Opportunity Commission Act 1986* (Cth), s 3 (definition of 'discrimination').

[108] Human Rights and Equal Opportunity Commission (n 106) 20–22.

[109] Ibid 23.

In two cases, the body claiming the benefit of the religious exemption had acted inconsistently, or at least had not made clear that the complainant was expected to adhere to a particular requirement. In *Walsh v St Vincent de Paul Society Queensland*, which was discussed above, the complainant had served for many years as a volunteer, member, officer and finally President of the Society without concern being raised, but was later asked to relinquish her leadership role unless she became a Roman Catholic. In a second case, *Thompson v Catholic College, Wodonga*, the applicant, a teacher in a Catholic College, had been living in a de facto relationship when she became pregnant. She was dismissed from her employment upon returning from maternity leave on the basis that her lifestyle was contrary to the Catholic Church's teaching on marriage. The Conciliation and Arbitration Board found that the termination was harsh, unjust and unreasonable, concluding that a reasonable person in the position of the applicant could not have been aware of the requirements as to her lifestyle which the employer expected of her. The expectation was never presented to her, giving her no opportunity to accept or reject it.[110]

The requirement that religious organisations act consistently with their professed beliefs and standards of conduct and that they ensure that those who work for them clearly understand their expectations is an important one. In proposing that exceptions for religious schools continue to be maintained in Australian law, the Ruddock review recommended that existing and prospective employees and contractors be provided with written copies of the organisation's policy in relation to such matters.[111]

We discuss the interpretation and application of religious freedom exemptions in more detail in Part IV below.

D. Religious Vilification Laws

Four jurisdictions in Australia have religious vilification laws. Legislation in Victoria, Queensland, Tasmania and the Australian Capital Territory makes it an offence to engage in conduct which incites 'hatred towards, serious contempt for, or severe ridicule of' a class of persons on the ground of their religion or religious activity (or other listed attribute).[112] In Tasmania, in addition, it is unlawful to engage in any conduct 'which offends, humiliates, intimidates, insults or ridicules another person' on the basis of a specified attribute.[113] There is an exception or defence in each jurisdiction which applies where a person's conduct was engaged in reasonably and in good faith for a 'genuine academic, artistic, scientific or research purpose', or for a purpose that is in the public interest.[114] These could be seen as

[110] *Thompson v Catholic College, Wodonga* (1988) EOC ¶92–217.

[111] Expert Panel (n 14) recs 5 and 7.

[112] *Racial and Religious Tolerance Act 2001* (Vic), s 8(1) (religious belief or activity); *Anti-Discrimination Act 1991* (Qld), s 124A(1) (race, religion, sexuality or gender identity); *Anti-Discrimination Act 1998* (Tas), s 19 (race, disability, sexual orientation or lawful sexual act, religious belief or affiliation or religious); *Discrimination Act 1991* (ACT), s 67A(1)(f) (disability, gender identity, HIV/AIDS status, intersex status, race, religious conviction or sexuality).

[113] *Anti-Discrimination Act 1998* (Tas), s 17(1).

[114] *Anti-Discrimination Act 1991* (Qld), s 124A(2); *Anti-Discrimination Act 1998* (Tas), s 55; *Racial and Religious Tolerance Act 2001* (Vic), s 11(1). Defences also apply in relation to 'a fair report of a public act' and several

both a protection for religious freedom, by protecting religious groups from having hatred or ridicule incited against them, and also a potential threat to religious freedom, by limiting the ability to discuss the merits of religious views.[115]

The Victorian laws were the subject of one notorious case, *Islamic Council of Victoria v Catch the Fire Ministries Inc.*[116] In that case Pastor Scot, the director of Catch the Fire Ministries ('CTF') presented a seminar at which he made numerous comments strongly critical of aspects of Muslim teaching and practice, and CTF published a newsletter written by Pastor Nalliah and a further article on its website, both of which discussed the nature of Islam in critical terms. The Islamic Council of Victoria instituted proceedings against CTF, Pastors Scot and Nalliah alleging that the conduct incited hatred against, serious contempt for, or revulsion or severe ridicule of the Islamic faith, contrary to s 8 of the *Racial and Religious Tolerance Act 2001* (Vic). VCAT held that the seminar and publications breached section 8 of the Act and that the statements were not made reasonably and in good faith, and so the respondents could not obtain the benefit of the defence in section 11.

The Victorian Court of Appeal upheld an appeal by the respondents, holding that the Tribunal had incorrectly interpreted section 8(1) and had mischaracterised the statements made at the seminar. Section 8(1) provides:

> A person must not, on the ground of the religious belief or activity of another person or class of persons, engage in conduct that incites hatred against, serious contempt for, or revulsion or severe ridicule of, that other person or class of persons.[117]

The Tribunal had held that the phrase 'on the ground of the religious belief or activity' requires that there be a causal connection between the impugned conduct and the religion of the person alleged to have contravened section 8(1). In other words, the religious beliefs of the person must have moved or caused the alleged offender to engage in the relevant conduct.[118] The Court of Appeal rejected this construction, holding that the correct construction of section 8(1) is that it prohibits conduct which incites hatred towards (or serious contempt for, or revulsion or severe ridicule of) a class of persons on the basis of *their* religious beliefs or activities. That is, section 8(1) is concerned with whether the audience 'was incited to hatred (or other relevant emotion) of another group, because of that group's religious beliefs', rather than whether the alleged incitement was prompted by the religious belief of the alleged perpetrator.[119]

The members of the Court came to different conclusions on whether it was necessary to determine whether the seminar was a 'balanced presentation' and whether a distinction should be drawn between vilification of a person and criticism of their beliefs. The Tribunal had held that the seminar was not a balanced discussion of Islam, but consisted of 'taking literal translations from the Qur'an and making no allowance for their applicability

other grounds: *Racial and Religious Tolerance Act 2001* (Vic), s 11(1)(a), (c); *Anti-Discrimination Act 1991* (Qld), s 124A(2); *Anti-Discrimination Act 1998* (Tas), s 55.

[115] See Rex Tauati Ahdar, 'Religious Vilification: Confused Policy, Unsound Principle and Unfortunate Law' (2007) 26 *University of Queensland Law Journal* 293.

[116] *Islamic Council of Victoria v Catch the Fire Ministries Inc* [2004] VCAT 2510; *Catch the Fire Ministries Inc v Islamic Council of Victoria* (2006) 15 VR 207.

[117] *Racial and Religious Tolerance Act 2001* (Vic), s 8(1).

[118] *Catch the Fire Ministries Inc v Islamic Council of Victoria* (2006) 15 VR 207, 211 [10], 218 [30].

[119] Ibid 218 [30], 251 [141].

to modern day society'.[120] However, Nettle JA considered that it is essential 'to keep the distinction between the hatred of beliefs and the hatred of their adherents steadily in view'. He said that section 8 'goes no further in restricting freedom to criticise the religious beliefs of others than to prohibit criticism so extreme as to incite hatred or other relevant emotion of or towards those others'.[121] As such, whether the seminar was a balanced presentation of Islam was irrelevant to the question of whether the statements were such as to incite hatred against Muslims on the ground of their religious beliefs. Further, for a secular tribunal 'to attempt to assess the theological propriety of what was asserted at the seminar' was 'calculated to lead to error'.[122] Nettle JA was prepared to afford a wide margin of latitude, informed by community standards, in assessing what was reasonable speech for the purposes of the Act. Our society is a 'polytopic multicultural society' which accords freedom to persuade others to one's point of view. 'It is only when what is said is so ill-informed or misconceived or ignorant and so hurtful as to go beyond the bounds of what tolerance should accommodate that it may be regarded as unreasonable'.[123]

By contrast, Neave JA considered that the question of balance was not an irrelevant consideration. Misleading and unbalanced statements about a particular religion could have the effect of inciting hatred against a class of persons, and so may be relevant to a determination of breach of section 8(1) of the Act.[124] Her honour also placed less emphasis on the distinction between a person and their religious views. Adherence to a particular racial or religious group, particularly a minority one such as Islam, 'may be portrayed by some and seen by others as a characteristic which determines their identity'. Ascribing characteristics to people based on their group membership 'is the essence of racial and religious prejudice', and so statements attacking Muslim religious belief could be capable of inciting hatred, contempt, revulsion or ridicule of Muslim persons themselves.[125]

Given the divergent interpretations of the Victorian Act, and the far-reaching scope of the Tasmanian Act, it is questionable whether these laws are consistent with Australia's obligations under articles 19 and 20.2 of the ICCPR noted in Part II.[126]

E. Abortion Protest Control Laws and Exemptions for Conscientious Objection to Abortion

The regulation of abortion is another issue which directly implicates freedom of religion. This is so in two principal ways. Legislation in several Australian jurisdictions creates 'safe access zones' around premises at which abortions are provided. Within these zones certain types of conduct are prohibited. The safe access zones are typically the 150 metre area surrounding any part of the premises of a clinic at which abortions are provided.[127]

[120] *Islamic Council of Victoria v Catch the Fire Ministries Inc* [2004] VCAT 2510 [384].
[121] *Catch the Fire Ministries Inc v Islamic Council of Victoria* (2006) 15 VR 207, 219 [34].
[122] Ibid, 220–1 [36].
[123] Ibid, 241–2 [94]–[98].
[124] Ibid, 259 [178]–[180].
[125] Ibid, 258 [176]–[177].
[126] See, in particular, *Rabat Plan of Action* (n 44).
[127] See, eg, *Public Health and Wellbeing Act 2008* (Vic), s 185B(1) (definition of 'safe access zone'); *Public Health Act 2010* (NSW), s 98A (definition of 'safe access zone').

The conduct typically prohibited in these zones includes harassing, intimidating or obstructing a person accessing or leaving premises at which abortions are provided, communicating in relation to abortions in a manner which is reasonably likely to cause distress or anxiety, and intentionally recording another person accessing or leaving premises at which abortions are provided.[128]

One interesting feature of the enactment of the bills which introduced these legislative schemes is the treatment of the right to religious freedom. It is uncontroversial that those who seek to protest or present an alternative view, or offer support or counselling to women seeking access to abortions[129] are often motivated by religious convictions about the sanctity of life. Prohibiting certain conduct which would otherwise be lawful is therefore a significant incursion, not only on the freedoms of movement and of speech, but also a person's right to manifest his or her religion.

However, the right to freedom of religion was given little weight in the relevant debates that accompanied the enactment of these laws. In four jurisdictions those introducing the relevant bills made no mention at all of religious freedom; debate focused instead on the rights of women accessing abortion services.[130] In Victoria the statement of compatibility required by the *Charter Act* acknowledged that the Bill impacted the right in section 14(1)(b) to demonstrate his or her religion. However, it was said that the fact that communication is motivated by religious concerns 'does not diminish the impact upon the rights of persons accessing lawful abortion services or the stress and harm they may experience', and that the prohibition on the relevant conduct was therefore 'reasonable and necessary in order to protect the rights of persons accessing lawful abortion services'.[131] One member in New South Wales noted that '[t]he protesters can act in accordance with their private and personal religious beliefs and faith without impinging on the private and personal rights of women to make their own personal and private decisions'.[132] Constitutional challenges to the Victorian and Tasmanian laws on the ground that they impermissibly burden the implied freedom of political communication were recently rejected by the High Court.[133] Religious conviction was considered irrelevant to the case because, as Nettle J put it, a communication directed to persuading a woman as to whether or not to have an abortion is not political communication but rather a communication concerning an entirely personal decision informed by medical considerations, personal circumstances and personal religious and ethical beliefs.[134]

[128] *Public Health and Wellbeing Act 2008* (Vic), s 185B(1) (definition of 'prohibited behaviour'); *Public Health Act 2010* (NSW), ss 98C–98E; *Health Act 1993* (ACT), s 85 (definition of 'prohibited behaviour'); *Reproductive Health (Access to Terminations) Act 2013* (Tas), s 9 (definition of 'prohibited behaviour'); *Termination of Pregnancy Act 2018* (Qld), s 15.

[129] It is also frequently alleged that women are subjected to harassment, intimidation and verbal abuse: see, eg, Victoria, *Parliamentary Debates*, Legislative Assembly, 22 October 2015, 3973 (Jill Hennessy).

[130] New South Wales, *Parliamentary Debates*, Legislative Assembly, 7 June 2018; Explanatory Statement, Health (Patient Privacy) Amendment Bill 2015 (ACT); Explanatory Statement, Termination of Pregnancy Law Reform Bill 2017; Tasmania, *Parliamentary Debates*, Legislative Assembly, 16 April 2013, 44–52 (Michelle O'Byrne). In Queensland the Explanatory Statement contained two brief references to freedom of thought, conscience and religion: Queensland, *Parliamentary Debates*, Legislative Assembly, 22 August 2018, 1962 (Yvette D'Ath).

[131] Statement of Compatibility, Public Health and Wellbeing Amendment (Safe Access Zones) Bill 2015 (Vic), Victoria, *Parliamentary Debates*, Legislative Assembly, 22 October 2015, 3972–4 (Jill Hennessy).

[132] New South Wales, *Parliamentary Debates*, Legislative Assembly, 7 June 2018 (Jenny Aitchison).

[133] *Clubb v Edwards; Preston v Avery* [2019] HCA 11 (10 April 2019).

[134] Ibid [253].

The second way that the regulation of abortion directly implicates freedom of religion is the referral requirement imposed on medical practitioners. For example, the *Abortion Law Reform Act 2008* (Vic) provides:

> If a woman requests a registered health practitioner to advise on a proposed abortion, or to perform, direct, authorise or supervise an abortion for that woman, and the practitioner has a conscientious objection to abortion, the practitioner must—
>
> (a) inform the woman that the practitioner has a conscientious objection to abortion; and
> (b) refer the woman to another registered health practitioner in the same regulated health profession who the practitioner knows does not have a conscientious objection to abortion.[135]

The purpose of this requirement to refer was to promote 'the woman's right to make decisions about her own health care'.[136] The Act also imposes an overriding obligation on a medical practitioner to perform an abortion in an emergency situation where necessary to preserve the life of the pregnant woman, notwithstanding any conscientious objection to abortion.[137] The question of abortion is exempted from the *Charter Act*,[138] so it was considered that there was no requirement to scutinise the human rights implications of the Abortion Law Reform Bill.[139] The singling out of abortion as an area of law exempt from *Charter* analysis is difficult to square with Australia's obligations to protect the full array of human rights referred to in the ICCPR.[140]

The effect of these requirements is to compel health practitioners to cooperate in an act which, according to the teaching of many religious traditions is in many circumstances an immoral one. This amounts to a significant intrusion on the religious and conscientious rights of health practitioners who adhere to such moral and religious beliefs.[141] In both types of legislation considered in this section, notwithstanding that freedom of religion is considered a fundamental, non-derogable right at international law, it is evident that religious freedom has been readily displaced in favour of other rights.

IV. Conceptions of Religion in Two Key Cases

In this section we consider two leading cases for the purpose of examining the underlying conception of religion and its implications for the outcome in each case.

In *OV & OW v Members of the Board of Wesley Mission Council* a same sex couple contacted Wesley Dalmar Child and Family Care, an entity within the umbrella of the Uniting Church of Australia, to enquire about becoming foster carers. They were informed that

[135] *Abortion Law Reform Act 2008* (Vic), s 8(1).
[136] Victoria, *Parliamentary Debates*, Legislative Assembly, 19 August 2008, 2953–4 (Maxine Morand).
[137] Ibid, 8(3).
[138] *Charter Act*, s 48; see also *Human Rights Act 2004* (ACT), s 9(1); *Human Rights Act 2019* (Qld), s 106.
[139] *Charter Act*, s 28; Victoria, *Parliamentary Debates*, Legislative Assembly, 19 August 2008, 2950, 2952 (Maxine Morand).
[140] ICCPR, arts 2 and 3.
[141] Michael Quinlan, 'When the State Requires Doctors to Act Against their Conscience: The Religious Freedom Implications of the Referral and the Direction Obligations of Health Practitioners in Victoria and New South Wales' [2016] *Brigham Young University Law Review* 101.

the Wesley Mission did not support same sex couples, and so refused to allow them to become foster carers. The couple lodged a complaint under the *Anti-Discrimination Act 1977* (NSW) alleging discrimination on the ground of homosexuality. The respondents argued that they were entitled to rely on the 'religious exemption' in section 56 of the Act.[142] At first instance the New South Wales Administrative Decisions Tribunal held that the refusal constituted unlawful discrimination.[143] The crucial issues at first instance and on appeal were whether the respondent was a body established for religious purposes and, if so, what were the relevant doctrines of the particular religion which the respondent was established to propagate.

Although the terms of the exemption are arguably narrower than those contained in similar legislation in other jurisdictions,[144] the Tribunal took a more generous approach to the issue of whether the respondent was able to claim the benefit of the religious exemption than has been taken in other cases. The tribunal held that the exemption provisions did not require that the 'propagation of religion' must be a body's sole purpose, but that a body may have other complementary purposes, and that in this case '[t]he evidence tendered by the respondents amply demonstrate[d] the linkage between evangelism and charitable works'.[145] However, the Tribunal identified the relevant religion of the respondent as Christianity, rather than more specifically identifying the religion by reference to the denominational distinctives of the Wesley Mission.[146] Given that there are a diversity of views within the Christian tradition on the subject of homosexuality, the respondents were not able to establish that the belief that 'monogamous heterosexual partnership within marriage is both the norm and ideal' was a doctrine of the Christian religion.[147] Given this diversity of views, the Tribunal held that the 'prohibition against homosexual foster carers applied by Wesley Mission cannot be said to be necessary to avoid injury to the religious susceptibilities of the adherents of the Christian religion'.[148]

The Appeal Panel overturned the Tribunal's decision, holding that there had been an error of law in the manner in which the Tribunal had interpreted the word 'religion' in section 56.[149] The Appeal Panel considered that the Tribunal should have identified the nominated religion in accordance with the beliefs of the 'Wesleyan (or Methodist) understanding of Christianity'.[150] The Tribunal's interpretation had the effect of making 'acts or practices which conform to the doctrines of Christianity (or the religion of the Uniting Church) lawful and making acts or practices which conform to the doctrines of discrete

[142] The relevant section provides: '[n]othing in this Act affects: … (c) the appointment of any other person in any capacity by a body established to propagate religion, or (d) any other act or practice of a body established to propagate religion that conforms to the doctrines of that religion or is necessary to avoid injury to the religious susceptibilities of the adherents of that religion': *Anti-Discrimination Act 1977* (NSW), ss 56(c), (d).

[143] *OV & OW v QZ (No 2)* [2008] NSWADT 115 [26]–[27]; *Anti-Discrimination Act 1977* (NSW), ss 49ZG(1)(a), 49ZP(a).

[144] The provision refers to 'a body established to propagate religion' (*Anti-Discrimination Act 1977* (NSW), ss 56(c), (d)) whereas legislation in other jurisdictions refers to 'a body established for a religious purpose' (*Equal Opportunity Act 2010* (Vic), s 81(a) (definition of 'religious body'), see also s 81(b)).

[145] *OV & OW v QZ (No 2)* [2008] NSWADT 115 [69]–[70].

[146] Ibid, [90], [115].

[147] Ibid, [127]–[128].

[148] Ibid, [142].

[149] *Members of the Board of the Wesley Mission Council v OV & OW (No 2)* [2009] NSWADTAP 57 [39].

[150] Ibid [18].

belief systems within Christianity or the religion of the Uniting Church unlawful' and such an anomalous interpretation was to be avoided.[151]

On further appeal, the New South Wales Court of Appeal also rejected the approach taken by the Tribunal. The Court considered that section 56 of the Act required 'identification of a relevant body, responsible for the act or practice, which must be one "established to propagate religion"'.[152] This enabled a more specific identification of the relevant religion than had been undertaken by the Tribunal. Accepting the evidence presented to the Tribunal, the Court considered that the relevant doctrines and beliefs were those of the Methodist Church, derived from the teachings of John Wesley.[153] Indeed, the Court considered that it would even be an error to assume that the Wesley Mission had been formed to propagate teachings 'common to *all* branches of the Uniting Church'.[154] For the purpose of section 56 is not to protect 'some lowest common denominator of Christianity' regardless of the specific beliefs and teachings of the relevant body.[155]

The effect of the approach adopted by the New South Wales Court of Appeal is to afford more freedom to religious bodies to determine their own beliefs and doctrines so as to receive the protection of the exemptions clauses in the *Anti-Discrimination Act*. A very different approach was adopted, however, by the Victorian Court of Appeal in *Christian Youth Camps Ltd v Cobaw Community Health Services Ltd*.

Christian Youth Camps Ltd v Cobaw Community Health Services Ltd concerned the refusal of a camp site operator to allow an organisation to hire a camping resort for the purposes of providing support to same sex attracted young people.[156] The *Equal Opportunity Act 1995* (Vic) ('1995 Act') made it unlawful for a person to discriminate against another person by refusing to provide goods or services to another person, by subjecting that person to detriment in connection with the provision of goods or services, or by refusing the other person's application for accommodation, on the basis of a protected attribute such as sexual orientation.[157] One of the key issues at first instance and on appeal was whether the owner of the camp could claim the benefit of one or more of the religious exceptions in Part 4 of the 1995 Act. Section 75(2) of the Act provided that anything done 'by a body established for religious purposes' that 'conforms with the doctrines of the religion' or was 'necessary to avoid injury to the religious sensitivities of people of the religion' was not unlawful discrimination.[158] In addition, any discrimination which was necessary for a person to comply with his or her 'genuine religious beliefs or principles' was not unlawful.[159] At first instance VCAT held that the camp operator could not rely on the religious exemptions, a decision which was upheld by the Court of Appeal.[160]

[151] Ibid [38].
[152] *OV & OW v Members of the Board of Wesley Mission Council* (2010) 79 NSWLR 606, 616 [33] (Basten JA and Handley AJA, Allsop P agreeing at 610–11 [9]).
[153] Ibid 617 [35].
[154] Ibid 619 [45] (emphasis added).
[155] Ibid 618 [40]–[41].
[156] *Christian Youth Camps Ltd v Cobaw Community Health Services Ltd* (2014) 50 VR 256.
[157] *Equal Opportunity Act 1995* (Vic), ss 6 (definition of 'attribute'), 42(1)(a), (c), 49 ('1995 Act').
[158] 1995 Act, s 75(2).
[159] 1995 Act, s 77.
[160] *Cobaw Community Health Services v Christian Youth Camps Ltd* [2010] VCAT 1613; *Christian Youth Camps Ltd v Cobaw Community Health Services Ltd* (2014) 50 VR 256 (Maxwell P and Neave JA, Redlich JA dissenting). Leave to appeal to the High Court was refused: *Christian Youth Camps Limited v Cobaw Community Health Services Limited* [2014] HCATrans 289.

The Court of Appeal's judgment indicates some very important aspects of its conception of religion and the legitimate expression of religion in the commercial sphere. These preconceptions influenced the manner in which it interpreted the religious exception clauses of the Act.

The first aspect was the sharp distinction that was drawn between 'religious' and 'secular' activity. The majority of the Court of Appeal[161] referred to *Roman Catholic Archbishop of Melbourne v Lawlor*,[162] where Dixon J considered that religious purposes (in the context of charity law) must be purposes that were 'directly and immediately religious', involving 'the spread or strengthening of spiritual teaching within a wide sense, the maintenance of the doctrines upon which it rests, the observances that promote and manifest it'. For an activity to be religious 'it is not enough that an activity or pursuit in itself secular is actuated or inspired by a religious motive'.[163] The majority considered this distinction to be crucial: an activity that is 'in itself secular' is not religious, even if 'inspired by a religious motive'.[164] Adopting this reasoning, the majority held that '[m]uch of the camping business conducted by CYC at the Resort [was] secular: school camps, corporate camps and groups with no explicit religious connection'.[165] Religious purposes were to do with 'propagating or advancing the religion'; being established as a 'commercial accommodation provider' which engaged in 'strategic planning and marketing' meant that the body was not established for religious purposes.[166] At the heart of the protection accorded by section 75(2) were 'the activities of churches and like institutions in which, or by which, religious observance is carried out'.[167] 'Quite different questions arise', it was said, 'if the body in question engages in an activity which is wholly secular'.[168]

The following passage is revealing:

> The conduct in issue here was an act of refusal in the ordinary course of the conduct of a secular accommodation business. It is not … conduct of a kind which Parliament intended would attract the attention of s 75(2). Put simply, CYC has chosen voluntarily to enter the market for accommodation services, and participates in that market in an avowedly commercial way. … That step – of moving from the field of religious activity to the field of secular activity – has the consequence … that in relation to decisions made in the course of the secular undertaking, questions of doctrinal conformity and offence to religious sensitivities simply do not arise.[169]

As such, the camp operator fell outside the protection of section 75(2). Had the camp operator existed 'for *the sole purpose* of providing facilities for camps and conferences' which were 'held for the purpose of religious instruction, discussion or inquiry', the position might have been different.[170]

A second aspect of the Court's treatment of religion was the characterisation of the objection by the camp operator to the use of their facilities, and a refusal to accept the claims of the respondents about what was necessary to conform to their own beliefs.

[161] Maxwell P, Neave JA agreeing on this point.
[162] (1934) 51 CLR 1.
[163] *Roman Catholic Archbishop of Melbourne v Lawlor* (1934) 51 CLR 1, 32.
[164] *Christian Youth Camps Ltd v Cobaw Community Health Services Ltd* (2014) 50 VR 256, 315 [232].
[165] Ibid, 310 [216].
[166] Ibid, 318 [250].
[167] Ibid, 313 [227].
[168] Ibid, 321 [265].
[169] Ibid, 322 [269].
[170] Ibid, 318 [249] (emphasis added).

The respondents argued that the refusal of the booking was justified under section 75(2) of the Act on the basis of their religious doctrines and beliefs. The Court refused to accept this, holding that the wrongfulness of homosexual activity was not a doctrine of the respondents' religion[171] and that the refusal was not necessary to conform with that doctrine. Moreover, even if it was a doctrine, the belief as to the wrongfulness of homosexual activity was a 'rule of private morality', which carried no 'obligation to interfere with, or obstruct, or discourage, the expression by other persons of their sexual preferences'.[172]

This characterisation of the situation differs significantly from the respondents' own understanding of why they refused the booking. According to the respondents, their refusal was not based on the sexual orientation of the potential campers, or a desire to interfere with the expression of their sexuality, but with allowing the use of their facilities to express a particular view about sexual orientation.[173] However, the Court rejected any distinction between, on the one hand, objecting to sexual orientation as such, and, on the other, promoting the view that certain forms of sexual orientation and their expression were natural and healthy. The Tribunal had stated that:

> the respondents' attempts to distinguish between homosexuality and promoting homosexuality fail. Mr Rowe's objection to promotion of homosexuality is, in truth, an objection to same sex attraction, or as the respondents characterised it, homosexuality.[174]

This characterisation of the respondent's actions was affirmed by the Court of Appeal. Maxwell P considered that '[w]hat Mr Rowe described as "promotion" was, in truth, affirmation of same sex attraction as "a natural part of the range of human sexualities"'.[175]

A final significant feature of the case was the asymmetry in the treatment of various rights. Much was made of the centrality of sexual orientation to a person's identity. For example, the Tribunal, drawing on similar statements in overseas jurisprudence,[176] held that:

> Sexual orientation, like gender, race and ethnicity, [is] part of a person's being, or identity. The essence of the prohibitions on discrimination on the basis of attributes such as sexual orientation, gender, race or ethnicity is to recognise the right of people to be who or what they are. … To distinguish between an aspect of a person's identity, and conduct which accepts that aspect of identity, or encourages people to see that part of identity as normal, or part of the natural and healthy range of human identities, is to deny the right to enjoyment and acceptance of identity.[177]

This was upheld by the Court of Appeal.[178] The Tribunal also referred to a statement of Baroness Hale in *Ghaidan v Godin-Mendoza* to the effect that sexual orientation goes beyond mere attraction, and necessarily results in the expression of that orientation with another

[171] At first instance the respondents argued that the relevant doctrine was plenary inspiration; on appeal they argued that the doctrines were: 'sexual activity must be confined to marriage; and sexual activity between members of the same sex is against God's will': *Christian Youth Camps Ltd v Cobaw Community Health Services Ltd* (2014) 50 VR 256, 323 [272].

[172] Ibid, 325 [281], 326 [284].

[173] Ibid, 269–70.

[174] *Cobaw Community Health Services v Christian Youth Camps Ltd* [2010] VCAT 1613 [190].

[175] *Christian Youth Camps Ltd v Cobaw Community Health Services Ltd* (2014) 50 VR 256, 274 [59]–[60].

[176] *R (Amicus) & Others v Secretary of State for Trade and Industry* [2004] EWHC 860 [28].

[177] *Cobaw Community Health Services v Christian Youth Camps Ltd* [2010] VCAT 1613 [193].

[178] *Christian Youth Camps Ltd v Cobaw Community Health Services Ltd* (2014) 50 VR 256, 274 [57].

person.[179] Other jurisdictions have also affirmed that sexual orientation is an important aspect of a person's identity.[180]

These things, of course, are equally true of religion. For a religious adherent, their religion is a deeply-held expression of their identity and fundamental beliefs. It defines their place in, and interaction with the world. Religious adherence has implications for many, and potentially all, areas of a person's life, including family, parenting, education, work, politics, sexuality, and many other things. Religion is as fundamental to a person's identity as sexual orientation: indeed, given that sexual morality is a deeply embedded aspect of almost every major religion, adherence to a religion typically shapes and even defines the way in which a person understands their sexual identity. To prevent a religious person from acting on the tenets of his or her religion is no less a denial of 'the right to enjoyment and acceptance of identity' than unlawful discrimination on the basis of attributes such as sexual orientation, gender, race or ethnicity. And yet these points are rarely made in relation to religion. Australian courts seem to have been reluctant to concede that religion is a core part of a person's beliefs and identity, shaping the way a person interacts with the world, similar to the role sexual orientation may play for a person.

It is unclear why this asymmetry between different categories of rights exists in Australian law and jurisprudence. Possible explanations include a belief that sexual orientation is more fundamental than religion, or a belief that the right to be protected from unlawful discrimination on the basis of sexual orientation is more worthy of protection than religious freedom. Certainly, this approach is out of step with international jurisprudence which recognises no hierarchy of rights, but considers all rights to be of equal importance.

Underlying the judgment, therefore, are several assumptions about the nature of religion and religious belief, and the legitimacy of acting in the commercial sphere on the basis of religious beliefs. For the majority, there is a binary distinction between secular and religious, and engaging in secular business removes it from the sphere of the 'religious'. Certain religious beliefs have no place in the commercial sphere: once a religious person moves beyond the pulpit or the seminary, their religious beliefs must give way to the rights of others. The religious exception provisions are to be interpreted according to a presumption that Parliament intended to protect an act of refusal in the course of a secular accommodation business.[181] But this, of course, is not what the religious exception provisions of the 1995 Act stated, and is directly contrary to the stated purpose of the religious exceptions clauses, namely to prevent people from being compelled to act contrary to their genuinely held religious beliefs.[182] Being forced to act contrary to one's religious beliefs is as objectionable in the 'commercial sphere' as in the seminary or pulpit. At the heart of this decision is an extremely narrow conception of religious belief, and the legitimate protection in law of religious belief, namely that it ought to be protected only to the extent that it is privatised and internal, with little impact beyond the *forum internum*.

[179] (2004) 2 AC 557, 142. See also *Preddy v Bull* [2013] 1 WLR 3741, 3755 [52].

[180] *Christian Youth Camps Ltd v Cobaw Community Health Services Ltd* (2014) 50 VR 256, 274 [57]; *R v Ministry of Defence; ex parte Smith* [1996] QB 517, 564; *R v Secretary of State for Trade and Industry; ex parte Amicus* [2004] EWHC (Admin) 860 [192]; *Egan v Canada* [1995] 2 SCR 513, 528; *Living Word Distributors Ltd v Human Rights Action Group (Wellington)* [2000] 3 NZLR 570, 588 [67]; *Obergefell v Hodges*, 576 US ___, 1–2 (2015) (Kennedy J).

[181] *Christian Youth Camps Ltd v Cobaw Community Health Services Ltd* (2014) 50 VR 256, 322 [269].

[182] Victoria, *Parliamentary Debates*, Legislative Assembly, 4 May 1995, 1254 (Jan Wade, Attorney-General).

Two closely-related aspects of Australia's anti-discrimination laws contribute to this approach. The first is that the laws have as their expressed purpose the elimination of discrimination and the promotion of equality.[183] The second is that the whole scheme of the laws is to achieve this purpose by defining the nature of discrimination and the forms in which it can be manifest, the grounds upon which discrimination is made unlawful, and the areas of activity in which such discrimination is made unlawful.[184] In such statutory schemes, freedom of religion is protected only by way of special, narrowly-defined exceptions, and there is no mention in the statutes that the purpose of such exceptions is to protect the internationally recognised right to freedom of religion. However, international human rights law deliberately juxtaposes rights to equality and non-discrimination (articles 2 and 26 of the ICCPR) with corresponding liberty rights to freedom of religion, expression, assembly and association (articles 18, 19, 21 and 22 of the ICCPR) and suggests no hierarchy between them. None of these rights in their practical manifestation is absolute: not every act of differentiated treatment is prohibited discrimination and not every limitation on the protected rights is a contravention of human rights, but such limitations must meet the exacting standards set out in the ICCPR. As the UN Commission on Human Rights has emphasised, such limitations must be prescribed by law, they must be interpreted strictly and in favour of the rights at issue, and they must be no more restrictive than is required to achieve the purpose of the limitation.[185] Recognising these problems, the Ruddock review recommended that all Australian jurisdictions should have regard to the Siracusa principles when drafting laws that would limit the right to freedom of religion and should consider the use of objects clauses in anti-discrimination laws to reflect the equal status of all international human rights, including freedom of religion.[186]

V. Conclusion

While at face value freedom of religion is afforded a significant place in Australian law, the legislation and cases discussed above demonstrate that there are significant pressures on religion, stemming in particular from situations where religion conflicts with other rights. Further, the materials discussed reveal an underlying conception of religion and its relation to other rights which will likely lead to further incursions on religious freedom unless legislative changes are made to address the issue. Courts and legislatures have adopted a conception of religion that is private and narrowly confined.[187] The manifestation

[183] Eg, *Equal Opportunity Act 1995* (Vic), s 3; *Equal Opportunity Act 2010* (Vic), s 3.

[184] Remarkably, the Victorian *Equal Opportunity Act*, s 4 defines 'religious belief or activity' as—

> (a) holding or not holding a lawful religious belief or view;
> (b) engaging in, not engaging in or refusing to engage in a lawful religious activity.

It is extraordinary that the Act should contemplate the possibility that the holding of certain religious beliefs could be unlawful, bearing in mind the fundamental principle of international human rights law that freedom of belief is an absolute right that cannot be limited. The definition of 'political belief' makes the same fundamental mistake.

[185] UN Commission on Human Rights, *Siracusa Principles on the Limitation and Derogation Provisions in the International Covenant on Civil and Political Rights*, UN Doc E/CN.4/1985/4 (28 September 1984) [10], [11].

[186] Expert Panel (n 14) recs 2 and 3.

[187] See Deagon (n 61) 4–6, 8–9.

of religion in the pulpit, the pew and the seminary will be protected, but there is a strong resistance to the public manifestation of religion, particularly in the commercial sphere, and particularly where religion conflicts with other rights. Anti-discrimination exemptions designed to protect religious freedom are often defined narrowly. Courts have adopted a binary distinction between 'religious' and 'secular'; activities beyond religious instruction and other similarly confined activities are afforded little protection. Often there appears to be a pre-conceived assumption relating to the proper balance between different rights which influences the way legislation is interpreted: religion readily gives way to other rights, whether these rights be recognised in the ICCPR or not.

There is an asymmetry in how the right to freedom of religion is characterised as compared with the way other rights are spoken of. The many and varied protected attributes contained in anti-discrimination laws are often fundamental to an individual's identity. However, while this is as true of religion as it is of the other protected attributes, there is little judicial or legislative acknowledgement of this. Harms are readily ascribed to the possessors of other rights but there is little recognition of the harm done by forcing religious people to act contrary to their conscience, especially when that is considered legitimate to achieve other important ends. Much of this is at variance with international law, which lays down strict limitations on the restriction of religious freedom. While it may be that, to date, numerically few examples of incursions on religious freedom have occurred,[188] this approach to religion and religious freedom represents fertile ground for significantly diminishing the protections afforded to religious freedom in the future.

We conclude with some modest proposals. First, in light of the well understood principle that there is no hierarchy of rights, there should be greater acknowledgment that the right to freedom of religion is of equal importance to other rights. There should be no automatic expectation that the right to freedom of religion must give way to other rights such as the right to equality or the right to be free from discrimination. Religion is not something to be readily dispensed with upon the identification of another right or desirable social good.

Secondly, there needs to be greater recognition of the wrongness of compelling someone to act contrary to their conscience. We noted above the close connection between religion, belief, thought and conscience. Indeed, religious exemptions clauses in anti-discrimination statutes have been expressly drafted with this purpose. When introducing the Equal Opportunity Bill 1995 into the Victorian Parliament, the Attorney-General noted that the religious exemption clauses were based on the principle that 'it is not acceptable to compel a person to act in a way that would compromise his or her genuinely held religious beliefs'.[189] To the extent that such clauses are read narrowly and do not prevent religious adherents from being compelled to act contrary to their conscience, that fails to give effect to the intention of Parliament.

Thirdly, there is a need for greater nuance in the employment of the 'harm principle' in the resolution of rights conflicts. Calls for the restriction of freedom of religion (for example by removing or limiting religious exemptions to anti-discrimination laws) are often based on the harm caused to persons negatively affected by that conduct.[190] However, the harm

[188] Cf Expert Panel (n 14) 98–9.

[189] Victoria, *Parliamentary Debates*, Legislative Assembly, 4 May 1995, 1254 (Jan Wade, Attorney-General).

[190] Eg, Human Rights Law Centre Ltd, Submission No 11 126 to Expert Panel, *Religious Freedom Review* (14 February 2017 [sic]) 20–4; Victorian Gay & Lesbian Rights Lobby, Submission No 14 946 to Expert Panel, *Religious Freedom Review* (14 February 2018) 5–8.

principle cannot do the work it is being called upon to do, but simply restates the conflict between competing rights in different language. Discrimination can indeed cause great harm to those discriminated against. On the other hand, forcing a person to act contrary to their conscience, even if necessary to achieve a legitimate purpose such as preventing discrimination, causes harm to that person. Preventing parents from being able to educate their children in accordance with their moral and religious convictions is likewise harmful. Preventing a person from being able to manifest his or her religious beliefs is harmful (and should only occur if necessary, and in a proportionate way). However, the way the harm principle is often employed seems to rest on an implicit 'hierarchy of harms' in which there is an assumption that certain harms are more worthy of prevention than others. We argue that when called upon to decide questions of conflicts between rights, courts and legislatures should give greater recognition to the harm done when religious adherents are forced to act contrary to their conscience – even if the person's moral beliefs are not widely shared, or are considered unacceptable by many in society.

This point is also relevant to a matter touched on earlier, namely the need for greater symmetry in discussions of various rights. Religion is a deeply significant aspect of a person's identity; although this may vary from person to person, religion is of comparable importance to many people as sexual orientation or gender identity. 'For some religious believers or those who hold a comprehensive philosophical view of the world, their religion or belief is part of almost every decision and action that they take'.[191] Moreover, just as sexual orientation necessarily results in the expression of that orientation, religious beliefs require expression to be meaningful. Again, as with sexual orientation, that expression cannot simply be confined to the prayer closet or private sphere, but requires expression in ways that are public, such as the commercial sphere. Denying a person the ability to hold or express a religious belief is a denial of a core part of that person's identity. Our point is not that all manifestations of religious belief must be protected, but simply that courts and policymakers ought to give greater recognition to the importance of religion for a religious adherent, no less so than a person to whom sexual orientation is a core aspect of their identity.

We also argue that a distinction needs to be recognised between discriminating against a person on the basis of an attribute, and engaging in an activity which implies acceptance of, or support for, something that a person considers morally wrong. As noted above, this distinction was resisted by VCAT and the Victorian Court of Appeal in *Cobaw*.[192] But it is a valid one. For instance, it is uncontroversial that refusing to provide services to a person because of their sexual orientation is unlawful discrimination. However, being required to provide services in such a way as to imply affirmation, support or celebration of a homosexual marriage – something intimately linked to sexual orientation – is not the same thing. For person A to refuse to allow another person B to use A's premises for the purpose of promoting beliefs and ideas which are contrary to A's religious doctrines and beliefs (for example, that same sex attraction is a normal and natural part of the range of human sexualities) is not the same thing as for A to refuse to allow B to stay on A's premises merely because of B's sexual orientation. To the extent that religious persons are required by law to act in ways

[191] Evans (n 18) 36.

[192] *Cobaw Community Health Services v Christian Youth Camps Ltd* [2010] VCAT 1613 [190]; *Christian Youth Camps Ltd v Cobaw Community Health Services Ltd* (2014) 50 VR 256, 274 [59]–[60].

which are tantamount to promoting, celebrating or endorsing a viewpoint contrary to their religious beliefs, the vitality of the protection accorded to religious freedom is in jeopardy.

Lastly, it needs to be recalled that the human rights to freedom of thought, conscience and religion, to freedom of association, to freedom of assembly and to freedom of expression are rights enjoyed by all persons no matter what the content of their beliefs and no matter what the nature of their sexualities. While many of the cases have involved what appear to be contests between religion and sexuality, the underlying human rights principles exist for the benefit of everyone. Narrow interpretations of freedom of religion, particularly in its expressive and associational dimensions, restrict the rights of everyone to the same freedoms. Too much of the debate in this field has been conducted in a manner that exacerbates polarisation in our society, rather than in a manner that affirms the indivisibility, interdependence and universality of human rights and which has respect for the unifying principle of the dignity of all humans.[193]

All of this highlights the urgent need to develop a principled basis by which to resolve apparent conflicts of rights. The harm principle is incapable of solving them of itself, for it merely restates the underlying issues in a different way. There is no hierarchy of rights, and so the right to freedom of religion must be treated with as much respect as the right not to be discriminated against. Religion can be as significant an aspect of a person's identity as sexual orientation or gender identity. Forcing someone to act or prohibiting them from acting in a manner that conflicts with their conscientious beliefs, their moral convictions or their sexual orientation can cause significant harm and distress and should be avoided at all costs. The crucial task facing courts and policymakers is to develop a principled basis by which to resolve apparent conflicts of rights, taking into account these considerations. In undertaking that exercise a more balanced and accurate understanding of international human rights law may be beneficial, in particular a recognition that all rights are of equal importance, and greater attention to the proposition that limitations on human rights should be the exception and not the rule, and may only be imposed where strictly necessary, in a proportionate manner.

[193] *Universal Declaration of Human Rights*, GA Res 217A (III), UN GAOR, 3rd sess, 183rd plen mtg, UN Doc A/810 (10 December 1948), preamble.

16

A Fair Trial for Accused Terrorists

REBECCA ANANIAN-WELSH*

Australia may lack a constitutional due process clause, but fair trial principles are protected by common law rules, numerous statutes, the principle of legality, the inherent powers of courts and, implicitly at least, the constitutional separation of powers. These layers of protection reflect the centrality of the fair trial to the liberal democratic system grounded in the rule of law. They have also evolved out of centuries of judicial responsiveness to the 'limitless ways in which the due administration of justice can be delayed, impeded or frustrated'.[1]

This chapter focuses on three key challenges to the fair trial that have arisen in the criminal trials of accused terrorists. It examines how courts have responded to these concerns by 'balancing' fairness and security. I draw in particular on Australia's largest terrorism prosecution to date: the 2007–2008 trial of Abdul Nacer Benbrika and his 11 co-accused. In this trial, secret evidence, courtroom security measures and severe conditions of imprisonment (amongst other things) undermined the fair trial rights of these accused people. From this analysis, the inherent jurisdiction of courts emerges as a particularly effective, practical and useful vehicle for the protection of fair trial rights. However, this loosely defined, highly discretionary set of powers is not without its weaknesses.

I. The Fair Trial

The requirement for disputes to be determined by a fair process is globally recognised as a fundamental human right. Article 14(1) of the *International Covenant on Civil and Political Rights* states:

> All persons shall be equal before the courts and tribunals. In the determination of any criminal charge against him, or of his rights and obligations in a suit at law, everyone shall be entitled to a fair and public hearing by a competent, independent and impartial tribunal established by law.[2]

* Senior Lecturer, TC Beirne School of Law, University of Queensland. The author is indebted to Sophie Philip for her excellent research assistance.

[1] K Mason, 'The Inherent Jurisdiction of the Court' (1983) 57 *Australian Law Journal* 449, 449.

[2] International Covenant on Civil and Political Rights (adopted 16 December 1966, entered into force 23 March 1976) 999 UNTS 171 (ICCPR). See also Universal Declaration of Human Rights (adopted 10 December 1948 UNGA Res 217 A(III) (UDHR) art 10); Convention for the Protection of Human Rights and Fundamental Freedoms (European Convention on Human Rights, as amended) (ECHR), art 6.

Similar entitlements have been incorporated in human rights instruments the world over, including in the US,[3] the UK,[4] Canada,[5] New Zealand,[6] and in Australia's three human rights charters: the Victorian *Charter of Human Rights and Responsibilities Act*[7] ('the *Charter*') the ACT *Human Rights Act*[8] and the Queensland *Human Rights Act*.[9]

The absence of a national bill or charter of rights in Australia has inhibited the development of a constitutional due process jurisprudence of the kind that exists in, for example, the US.[10] The Australian Constitution provides merely for the trial of indictable Commonwealth offences to be by jury, although this provision has been interpreted to grant the Commonwealth Parliament the sole power to determine which offences are subject to jury trial.[11] Andrew Inglis Clark's attempt to include a due process and equal protection clause in the Constitution did not survive the 1898 convention.[12] Nonetheless, as former Chief Justice of Australia Robert French observed, 'procedural fairness' is 'deeply rooted in our law',[13] having been recognised 'from the very earliest colonial times'[14] as a concept which 'lies at the heart of the judicial function and conditions the exercise of a large array of administrative powers affecting the rights, duties, privileges and immunities of individuals and organisations'.[15]

While procedural fairness and the related, if not synonymous,[16] notions of a fair trial and natural justice remain elusive, there is nonetheless 'a recognised core of meaning',[17] comprised of the hearing rule *audi alteram partem* (hear the other side) and the bias rule *nemo debet esse judex in propria sua causa* (no one can be a judge in their own cause).[18] Together, these rules give procedural fairness a two-pronged definition which requires that 'people be afforded a hearing that is *fair* and *without bias* before decisions which affect them are made'.[19]

[3] US Const. amend. V, XIV.

[4] *The Human Rights Act 1998* (UK), s 1(1).

[5] *Canadian Charter of Rights and Freedoms*, Part I of the *Constitution Act*, 1982, being Schedule B to the *Canada Act 1982 (UK)*, 1982, c 11, s 7.

[6] *Bill of Rights Act 1990* (NZ), s 27(1).

[7] *Charter of Human Rights and Responsibilities Act 2006* (Vic), s 24(1).

[8] *Human Rights Act 2004* (ACT), s 21(1).

[9] *Human Rights Act 2019* (Qld), s 31–33.

[10] W Bateman, 'Procedural Due Process under the Australian Constitution' (2009) 31 *Sydney Law Review* 411, 415; K Rubenstein, 'Towards 2001: An Assessment of the Possible Impact of a Bill of Rights on Administrative Law in Australia – Part II' (1994) 1 *Australian Journal of Administrative Law* 59, 64.

[11] Australian Constitution, s 80; G Williams and D Hume, *Human Rights under the Australian Constitution*, 2nd edn (Melbourne, Oxford University Press, 2013) 356.

[12] Williams and Hume, (n 11) 66.

[13] Chief Justice Robert S French, 'Procedural Fairness – Indispensable to Justice?' (Speech at the Sir Anthony Mason Lecture, University of Melbourne, 7 October 2010) www.hcourt.gov.au/assets/publications/speeches/current-justices/frenchcj/frenchcj07oct10.pdf 1.

[14] Ibid, 18.

[15] Ibid, 1. See also I Holloway, *Natural Justice and the High Court of Australia: A Study in Common Law Constitutionalism* (Aldershot, Ashgate Publishing, 2002) 2–3; K Rundle, 'The Stakes of Procedural Fairness: Reflections on the Australian Position' (2016) 23 *Australian Journal of Administrative Law* 164, 165; *Kioa v West* (1985) 159 CLR 550, 614.

[16] J Edelman, 'Why Do We Have Rules of Procedural Fairness?' (2016) 23 *Australian Journal of Administrative Law* 144, 144.

[17] R Creyke, J McMillan and M Smyth, *Control of Government Action: Text, Cases and Commentary*, 4th edn (Chatswood, LexisNexis Butterworths Australia, 2015) 634.

[18] Ibid.

[19] M Aronson, M Groves and G Weeks, *Judicial Review of Administrative Action and Government Liability*, 6th edn (Sydney, Lawbook Co, 2017) 403 (emphasis added).

Beyond this vague standard, the High Court has acknowledged that defining the specific attributes of procedural fairness – including in the context of the criminal trial – is neither possible nor desirable.[20] As such, these requirements have been left to the ad hoc determinations of judges, taking into account the unique and varied circumstances of each particular case, as well as prevailing social values and community expectations.[21] Nonetheless, a range of 'widely accepted general attributes' of procedural fairness have emerged from this piecemeal and dynamic approach, which include but are not limited to:[22]

(1) The independence of the court.
(2) A public trial.
(3) The presumption of innocence.
(4) That the defendant is informed of and understands the charge against him or her.
(5) That the defendant has adequate time and facilities to prepare a defence and instruct counsel.
(6) That the trial should be conducted without undue delay.
(7) A right to a lawyer.
(8) The right to examine witnesses.

II. Layers of Protection

As former Chief Justice of New South Wales James Spigelman observed, in Australia the 'principle of a fair trial is based on the inherent power of a court to control its own processes and, particularly, on its power to prevent abuse of its processes'.[23] This is a power 'which a court has simply because it is a court of a particular description'[24] and it has both positive and negative aspects; it may be 'invoked to facilitate the proper conduct of legal proceedings, or to overcome practices or devices which tend to delay, impede or frustrate judicial functioning'.[25] In other words, it may be invoked to promote fairness or to prevent unfairness.

The courts' inherent jurisdiction expands well beyond powers related to the fair trial. Writing in 1983, well before his ascension to the Presidency of the New South Wales Court of Appeal, Keith Mason observed that '[t]he concept resists analysis in view of judicial claims to exercise the jurisdiction wherever necessary for the administration of justice'.[26] Mason went on to identify four roles served by the inherent jurisdiction, namely: ensuring convenience and fairness in legal proceedings, preventing steps from being taken that

[20] *Dietrich v R* (1992) 177 CLR 292, 300 (Mason CJ and McHugh J), 364 (Gaudron J); *Jago v District Court (NSW)* (1989) 168 CLR 23, 57 (Deane J); J Spigelman, 'The Truth Can Cost Too Much: The Principle of a Fair Trial' (2004) 78 *Australian Law Journal* 29, 33–34, 43–46.

[21] *Dietrich v R* (1992) 177 CLR 292, 364 (Gaudron J); Spigelman (n 20) 43.

[22] Australian Law Reform Commission, *Traditional Rights and Freedoms- Encroachments by Commonwealth Laws*, Interim Report No 127 (2015), 279–280, referring to common law, Parliamentary reforms, international treaties, conventions, human rights statutes and bills of rights, but particularly citing: *International Covenant on Civil and Political Rights*, opened for signature 16 December 1966, 999 UNTS 171 (entered into force 23 March 1976) art 14.

[23] Spigelman (n 20) 31.

[24] *R v Forbes; Ex parte Bevan* (1972) 127 CLR 1, 7 (Menzies J).

[25] Mason (n 1) 449.

[26] Ibid, 449.

would render judicial proceedings inefficacious, preventing abuse of process, and acting in aid of superior courts and in aid or control of inferior courts and tribunals.[27] By focussing on the inherent jurisdiction as a mechanism for protecting fair trial rights, this chapter concerns only part of this large set of powers.

There is a fantastic breadth of circumstances that may challenge the fairness or efficacy of a court proceeding or amount to an abuse of process. Likewise, there is a vast array of potential remedies that may be required in an exercise of the court's inherent jurisdiction. Thus, Master I H Jacob described the inherent jurisdiction as 'so amorphous and ubiquitous and so pervasive in its operation that it seems to defy the challenge to determine its quality and to establish its limits'.[28] Moreover, while the scope of the inherent jurisdiction may, at least in theory, be altered by clear statutory words,[29] it 'may be asserted even though the conduct complained of may be in literal compliance with some statute or rule of court'[30] – so strong is the imperative that courts maintain control of trial proceedings and prevent abuse of process.

In a more concrete sense, a broader notion of procedural fairness that applies to administrative as well as judicial decisions finds protection through common law principles of statutory interpretation.[31] In *S10/2010 v Minister for Immigration and Citizenship*, the High Court held:[32]

> "[T]he common law" usually will imply, as a matter of statutory interpretation, a condition that a power conferred by statute upon the executive branch be exercised with procedural fairness to those whose interests may be adversely affected by the exercise of that power.[33]

As a rule of statutory interpretation founded in the common law, this protection is subject to alteration by statute.[34] However, as the High Court observed in *Saeed v Minister for Immigration and Citizenship*, the courts presume 'it is highly improbable that Parliament would overthrow fundamental principles' of natural justice 'without expressing its intention with irresistible clearness', a presumption which derives from the principle of legality.[35]

Notwithstanding this enhanced degree of protection, common law principles of procedural fairness may be altered by implication,[36] or when legitimate public policy interests would be frustrated if the ordinary incidents of procedural fairness were to apply.[37]

[27] Ibid, 449–457.

[28] I H Jacobs, 'The Inherent Jurisdiction of the Court' (1970) 23 *Current Legal Problems* 23, 23.

[29] *Cameron v Cole* (1944) 68 CLR 571, 589 (Rich J).

[30] Mason (n 1) 449.

[31] *S10/2010 v Minister for Immigration and Citizenship* (2012) 246 CLR 636, 666 [97] (Gummow, Hayne, Crennan and Bell JJ).

[32] Ibid.

[33] In this ruling, the High Court avoided the former debate as to whether principles of natural justice conditioning the exercise of statutory power are founded in common law rights or arise as a matter of statutory construction, which was first conducted between Brennan and Mason JJ in *Kioa v West* (1985) 159 CLR 550. The position is now that the root of the obligation is ultimately irrelevant, with both analyses leading to the same result; see also *Plaintiff M16/2010E* (2010) 243 CLR 319, 352 [74].

[34] *S10/2010 v Minister for Immigration and Citizenship* (2012) 246 CLR 636, 666 [97] (Gummow, Hayne, Crennan and Bell JJ).

[35] *Saeed v Minister for Immigration and Citizenship* (2010) 241 CLR 252, 259 [14]-[15] (French CJ, Gummow, Hayne, Crennan and Kiefel JJ).

[36] See, eg, *Plaintiff S10/2011 v Minister for Immigration and Citizenship* (2012) 246 CLR 636.

[37] See, eg, *Kioa v West* (1985) 159 CLR 550, 584 (Mason J), citing *Salemi v Mackellar (No 2)* (1977) 137 CLR 396, 452 (Jacobs J); *Botany Bay City Council v Minister for Transport and Regional Development* (1996) 66 FCR 537, 553–555.

This has occurred in the context of adverse security assessments by the Australian Security Intelligence Organisation (ASIO). Adverse security assessments are relevant to administrative decisions on visa status and may have serious results. For instance, they may result in visa cancellation – as happened to Sheik Mansour Leghaei in 2004. In *Leghaei v Director General of Security*, the Court found that there existed a common law 'duty to afford such degree of procedural fairness in the making of an adverse security assessment as the circumstances could bear, consistent with a lack of prejudice to national security'.[38] However, in balancing the public interest in security against the duty to disclose, the primary judge found the content of procedural fairness was 'reduced, in practical terms, to nothingness'.[39] The notion that the content of natural justice is so flexible that it may, in appropriate circumstances, be reduced to 'nothingness' rather than including an irreducible minimum,[40] is one that has generated significant academic debate.[41]

Fair trial rights may be undermined or bolstered by statute. Charters of rights in Queensland, the ACT and Victoria grant specific protection to fair trial rights,[42] and require that legislation be interpreted 'so far as possible … in a manner consistent with human rights'.[43] In the event that a provision 'cannot be interpreted [by the Supreme Court] consistently with a human right', the legislative incursion will stand and the court may issue a declaration of inconsistent interpretation, signalling the inconsistency to the sovereign Parliament.[44]

Across Australia, rules of evidence and procedure play a vital role in maintaining the fairness of judicial proceedings. For instance, civil procedure rules bolster courts' inherent jurisdiction by adopting the just and expeditious resolution of disputes as their guiding ethos.[45] Likewise, the uniform Evidence Acts permit the court to refuse to admit evidence if its probative value is 'substantially outweighed' by the risk that the evidence might be unfairly prejudicial, mislead or confuse, or unduly waste time.[46]

Inglis Clark may have failed in his attempt to give Australia a constitutional due process and equal protection clause, but over the course of the twentieth century the High Court gradually interpreted Chapter III of the Constitution to extend a degree of protection to fair trial rights. Today, it is well-accepted that Chapter III lends constitutional protection

[38] *Leghaei v Director General of Security* [2005] FCA 1576 (10 November 2005) [83].

[39] Ibid, [88]. On appeal, the Full Federal Court considered that the balance struck by the primary judge was correct: *Leghaei v Director-General of Security* [2007] FCAFC 37 (23 March 2007) [51]–[55]. See also *Plaintiff M47/2012 v Director General of Security* (2012) 251 CLR 1.

[40] See, eg, *Kioa v West* (1985) 159 CLR 550, 615 (Brennan J), citing G Johnson, 'Natural Justice and Legitimate Expectation in Australia' (1985) 15 *Federal Law Review* 39, 71; *CPCF v Minister for Immigration and Border Protection* (2015) 255 CLR 514, 622 [367] (Gageler J).

[41] See, eg, G Johnson, 'Natural Justice and Legitimate Expectations in Australia' (1985) 15 *Federal Law Review* 39, 71; P Tate, 'The Coherence of "Legitimate Expectations" and the Foundations of Natural Justice' (1988) 14 *Monash University Law Review* 15, 69–71; B Dyer, 'Determining the Content of Procedural Fairness' (1993) 19 *Monash University Law Review* 165, 199–201.

[42] *Human Rights Act 2019* (Qld), ss 31–33; *Charter of Human Rights and Responsibilities Act 2006* (Vic), s 24(1); *Human Rights Act 2004* (ACT), s 21(1).

[43] *Human Rights Act 2019* (Qld), s 48 which uses the phrasing: 'All statutory provisions must, to the extent possible that is consistent with their purpose, be interpreted in a way that is compatible with human rights'; *Charter of Human Rights and Responsibilities Act 2006* (Vic), s 32(1); *Human Rights Act 2004* (ACT), s 30.

[44] *Human Rights Act 2019* (Qld), s 53; *Charter of Human Rights and Responsibilities Act 2006* (Vic), s 36; *Human Rights Act 2004* (ACT), s 32.

[45] See, eg *Uniform Civil Procedure Rules 1999* (Qld) r 5; *Civil Procedure Act 2005* (NSW), s 56; *Civil Procedure Act 2010* (Vic) s 7; *Rules of the Supreme Court 1971* (WA) rr 1.4A, 1.4B. See also *Aon Risk Services Australia Ltd v Australian National University* (2009) 239 CLR 175.

[46] *Evidence Act 1995* (Cth), s 135.

to the actual and perceived independence and impartiality of all federal, state and territory judges.[47] Thus, the 'bias rule' aspect of procedural fairness is constitutionally entrenched, at least with respect to matters presided over by a judge (whether sitting as a court or in a personal capacity). Moreover, the institutional integrity of the courts and their processes is protected by Chapter III, and the High Court has recognised that procedural fairness is closely entwined with this notion.[48] Finally, procedural fairness has been – albeit vaguely – identified as an 'immutable characteristic' of 'courts' and therefore subject to constitutional protection.[49]

While this expression of the principle provides some protection to principles of natural justice in courts, it offers no protection to persons appearing before tribunals. For example, the cancellation of Leghaei's visa was affirmed in the Security Division of the Administrative Appeals Tribunal. In this Tribunal, key aspects of fairness including principles of open justice and the right to see all the evidence are drastically curtailed and, in some instances, removed entirely by statute.[50] It is constitutionally permissible to negate procedural fairness in tribunals because they do not exercise judicial power, and therefore are not entitled to the same 'immutable characteristics' as courts. This inherent limitation on the reach of procedural fairness protections is especially important given the role of administrative procedures and sanctions in achieving national security aims (for instance, in the immigration context).

The distinct avenues of constitutional protection appear to exist alongside one-another, further adding to the complexity of Chapter III jurisprudence. What is more, the High Court has avoided stipulating that any particular fair trial requirements are constitutionally entrenched. Instead constitutional jurisprudence tends to reflect courts' broader appreciation of the fair trial as a vital but amorphous set of principles that is best considered on a case by case basis.[51] This has led some scholars, such as Wendy Lacey and myself, to suggest that it is not the fair trial as such that is protected by Chapter III, but the courts' inherent powers to control proceedings, including to preserve a fair trial and prevent abuse of process.[52]

Whether and how the common law, statutory and constitutional protections for a fair trial outlined above are invoked will depend on the factual and legal context of each case. It will also turn upon more pragmatic, strategic factors such as whether the client is well-resourced, whether there is any urgency to be considered, whether there is an advantage

[47] See, eg, *North Australian Legal Aid v Bradley* (2004) 218 CLR 146, 163 [29]–[30] (McHugh, Gummow, Kirby, Hayne, Callinan and Heydon JJ); F Wheeler, 'Due Process, Judicial Power and Chapter III in the High Court' (2004) 32 *Federal Law Review* 205. This protection extends to judges vested with functions in their personal capacities: *Grollo v Palmer* (1995) 184 CLR 348, 376 (McHugh J), 365 (Brennan CJ, Deane, Dawson and Toohey JJ); *Wainohu v New South Wales* (2011) 243 CLR 181, 208 [43] (French CJ and Kiefel J); R Ananian-Welsh and G Williams, 'Judges in Vice-Regal Roles' (2015) 43 *Federal Law Review* 119, 140–141.

[48] *Attorney-General (NT) v Emmerson* (2014) 253 CLR 393, 426 [44] (French CJ, Hayne, Crennan, Kiefel, Bell, and Keane JJ); *Gypsy Jokers Motorcycle Club Incorporated v Commissioner of Police* (2008) 234 CLR 532, 560 [39] (Gummow, Hayne, Heydon and Kiefel JJ); *South Australia v Totani* (2010) 242 CLR 1, 52–53 [82]–[83] (French CJ), 63 [132] (Gummow J), 82 [204], 88–89 [226] (Hayne J), 158 [428] (Crennan and Bell JJ).

[49] *Assistant Commissioner Condon v Pompano Pty Ltd* (2013) 252 CLR 38, 105 [177] (Gageler J); Williams and Hume (n 11) 375–376.

[50] See *Administrative Appeals Tribunal Act* 1975 (Cth), ss 35AA, 39B.

[51] *International Finance Trust Co Ltd v New South Wales Crime Commission* (2009) 240 CLR 319, 354 [54] (French CJ); G Appleby, 'Protecting Procedural Fairness and Criminal Intelligence: Is There a Balance to Be Struck?' in G Martin, R Scott Bray and M Kumar (eds), *Secrecy, Law and Society* (Abingdon, Routledge, 2015) 75, 84–86.

[52] W Lacey, 'Inherent Jurisdiction, Judicial Power and Implied Guarantees under Chapter III of the Constitution' (2003) 31 *Federal Law Review* 57, 59; R Ananian-Welsh, '*Kuczborski v Queensland* and the Scope of the *Kable* Doctrine' (2015) 34 *University of Queensland Law Journal* 47, 67.

in the particular methodology of, say, advancing a Charter argument over the principle of legality and, simply, what will achieve the best outcome for the affected party. It may be that a combination of arguments is appropriate in the circumstances. Ultimately however, as *Leghaei* demonstrates, there is a high degree of risk that fairness will be trumped by national security concerns as a court balances community interests against personal rights.[53]

III. The Benbrika Trial

Leghaei reflects the whittling down of fairness for the sake of national security in the administrative decision-making context. However, even in the fair trial heartland of criminal proceedings keen threats to fairness have arisen, requiring courts to weigh fair trial principles against the community interest in security. Rather than attempt a sweeping analysis of how this balance has been struck across terrorism trials, the remainder of this chapter considers how three specific threats to the fair trial arose in Australia's largest terrorism prosecution to-date: the trial of Abdul Nacer Benbrika and his 11 co-accused in 2007–2008. In this case the court grappled with a range of threats to fair trial principles that, whilst not confined to terrorism proceedings, were highly likely to arise in this context. Moreover, as one of Australia's first terrorism trials the court had relatively scant assistance from precedent in navigating a path through competing fairness and security concerns. Accordingly, these proceedings have played an important role in shaping the conduct of later terrorism trials.

Following raids on various properties around Melbourne on 8 November 2005, 10 men were arrested and charged with a variety of terrorism offences, including membership and support of an alleged terrorist organisation led by Abdul Nacer Benbrika. A further three men were arrested on 31 March 2006, bringing the total to 13. The following month, Izydeen Atik (who had been arrested in the initial raids) pleaded guilty to being a member of a terrorist organisation, and to providing resources, namely himself, to that organisation. Atik's five-and-a-half-year sentence reflected his willingness to assist the prosecution as its key witness against the remaining 12 men, although in sentencing those accused Bongiorno J gave no weight to Atik's evidence,[54] but described him to the jury as 'a liar, a cheat and a fraudster of significant accomplishment'.[55] The remaining 12 men pleaded not guilty to 27 counts against them.

Over the course of 2007 the Court dealt with a considerable number of pre-trial applications, and applications continued throughout the trial proper. The six-month trial of the accused commenced in February 2008. The trial concluded and jury deliberations commenced on 20 August 2008. During this period none of the men were released on bail. This was to be expected, as a grant of bail for a person accused of a terrorism offence is only permitted in 'exceptional circumstances'.[56] The accused being denied bail and charged with

[53] For discussion of how this has played out in the respect of constitutional rights, see: Rebecca Ananian-Welsh and Nicola McGarrity 'National Security: A Hegemonic Constitutional Value' in *Australian Constitutional Values* (Rosalind Dixon ed), (Oxford, Hart-Bloomsbury, 2018) 276.

[54] *R v Benbrika* (2009) 222 FLR 433, 443 [42]–[43].

[55] Ibid, 442 [40].

[56] *Crimes Act 1914* (Cth), s 15AA.

terrorism offences appear to be the primary factors behind their classification as A1 prisoners, the most severe classification in the Victorian prison system.[57] As A1 prisoners the men were held in Barwon maximum security prison and subject to a raft of onerous conditions, outlined in some detail below.

On 15 September 2008, almost three years after the initial raids, the jury returned verdicts against 10 of the men. Four were acquitted of all charges (Hany Taha, Shoue Hammoud, Bassam Raad and Majed Raad). The remaining six, including Benbrika, were found guilty of various terrorism and terrorist organisation offences. The verdicts in relation to Amer Haddara and Shane Kent would have been delivered the following day, but for a statement made by the Federal Attorney-General praising the initial raft of verdicts.[58] This prompted an application that the jury be dismissed on the basis that it had been influenced by these comments. Whilst Bongiorno J strongly criticised the Attorney-General's statement, his Honour refused the application and the jury returned a verdict of guilty in relation to Haddara only.[59] It was unable to reach a verdict in relation to Kent who would later plead guilty to two charges before he could be retried.[60]

IV. Secret Evidence: The *NSI Act*

It is a basic principle of the accusatorial system of justice that court proceedings are open, both to the public and to those whose rights are at stake. In addition, a fair criminal trial is contingent upon the accused having the opportunity to confront his or her accusers, knowing and having an opportunity to test the case against him or herself, and enjoying the benefits of 'equality of arms' in court. These basic requirements of the fair trial have clear links to the presumption of innocence and the right to an impartial arbiter. As with all aspects of a fair trial, these are not absolute requirements. There may be circumstances in which the administration of justice requires *in camera* or private proceedings,[61] and the doctrine of public interest immunity has long existed to permit the exclusion of relevant and admissible evidence on public interest grounds.[62]

Post-9/11, the fairness and openness of trial proceedings has been challenged by an increased reliance on national security information as evidence. Such information is more likely to be in the form of intelligence, which may have been obtained covertly in the course of an intelligence operation, never have been intended for public dissemination, and form a 'patchy' picture of predicted events.[63] Traditional evidence, on the other hand, is collected after a crime has been committed, for the purpose of being adduced and tested in a public trial to prove guilt beyond reasonable doubt. As Kent Roach has observed, terrorism

[57] *R v Benbrika (Ruling No 12)* [2007] VSC 524 (12 December 2007) [17]–[19] (Bongiorno J); *R v Benbrika (Ruling No 20)* (2008) 18 VR 410, 420 [40] (Bongiorno J).

[58] *R v Benbrika (Rulings No 35.01-35.11)* [2009] VSC 142 (8 April 2009) [120]–[121] (Bongiorno J).

[59] Ibid, [121]–[125].

[60] *R v Kent* [2009] VSC 375 (2 September 2009) [1].

[61] Mason (n 1) 452.

[62] *Evidence Act 1995* (Cth), s 130; Australian Law Reform Commission, *Uniform Evidence Law*, Final Report No 102 (2006), 544–546.

[63] K Roach, 'The Eroding Distinction between Intelligence and Evidence in Terrorism Investigations' in N McGarrity, A Lynch and G Williams (eds), *Counter-Terrorism and Beyond: The Culture of Law and Justice After 9/11* (New York, Routledge, 2010), 48.

offences enacted after 9/11 'reflect an intelligence mindset that focuses on threats, risk, associations and suspicion as opposed to an evidence or criminal law mindset that focuses on acts, accomplices and guilt'.[64]

In this context, the Australian Government introduced the *National Security Information (Criminal and Civil Proceedings) Act 2004* (Cth) ('*NSI Act*'). This Act creates a scheme by which information relating to national security may be adduced and relied upon as evidence in a court proceeding, but seen only by the prosecution and the presiding judge – thus avoiding the risks associated with placing national security information in the public eye, whilst preserving its evidential value. In short, it permits secret evidence in court.[65]

The *NSI Act* is intended to be a comprehensive legislative framework for the handling of national security information in court proceedings. The Act defines 'national security' as 'Australia's defence, security, international relations or law enforcement interests'.[66] In a closed hearing, within the context of a criminal trial, the court will be called upon to determine the disclosure of national security information based on:[67]

(a) whether, having regard to the Attorney-General's non-disclosure or witness exclusion certificate, there would be a risk of prejudice to national security if the information was disclosed or the witness called;
(b) whether such an order would have a substantial adverse effect on the defendant's right to receive a fair hearing, including in particular on the conduct of his or her defence; and(c) any other relevant matter.

Crucially, the Act provides that the court 'must give greatest weight' to national security considerations in making its decision, over and above considerations of fairness and justice.[68] Unlike the UK, security cleared counsel have not become a prominent feature of the Australian scheme. These 'special advocates' are able to see the information and test it in a closed hearing, though are unable to speak with the accused or take instructions regarding the closed material. These factors led one former special advocate to famously criticise the scheme as giving a 'fig leaf of respectability and legitimacy' to an 'odious' process.[69] That said, the Australian scheme operates in the absence of even this 'fig leaf'.[70]

The *NSI Act* was applied and subject to constitutional challenge in the course of Australia's first successful terrorism prosecution. In April 2004, Faheem Lodhi was arrested and charged with a number of preparatory offences under the *Criminal Code Act 1995* (Cth) ('*Criminal Code*') based on his association with French national Willie Brigitte and his alleged 'purchasing [of] maps of the electricity grid, making enquiries about the availability

[64] Ibid, 49.

[65] See also *Administrative Appeals Tribunal Act* 1975 (Cth), ss 35AA, 39B, which establish a similar scheme for hearings in the Security Division of the Administrative Appeals Tribunal. This scheme provided something of a template for the later *National Security Information (Criminal and Civil Proceedings) Act 2004* (Cth) and other like statutes.

[66] *National Security Information (Criminal and Civil Proceedings) Act 2004* (Cth), s 8.

[67] Ibid, s 31(7). The criteria in civil proceedings are much the same: s 38L(7).

[68] Ibid, s 31(8).

[69] UK Parliament Constitutional Affairs Committee, *Seventh Report 2004–05* (2005), [41].

[70] For comparison of the Australian and UK secret evidence schemes, see: T Tulich, A Lynch and R Welsh, 'Secrecy and Control Orders: The Role and Vulnerability of Constitutional Values in the United Kingdom and Australia' in D Cole, F Fabbrini and A Vedaschi (eds), *Secrecy, National Security and the Vindication of Constitutional Law* (Cheltenham, Edward Elgar, 2013), 154.

of chemicals, downloading aerial photographs of Victoria Barracks, Holsworthy Barracks and the HMAS Penguin and acquiring a large quantity of toilet paper', the last of which was allegedly for the production of nitrocellulose.[71] Lodhi was ultimately found guilty of possessing a thing in connection with a terrorist act, collecting a document in connection with a terrorist act, and doing an act in preparation for a terrorist act. He was sentenced to 10, 10 and 20 years imprisonment, respectively, for these offences.[72]

In the course of his trial Lodhi launched a Chapter III challenge to section 31(8) of the *NSI Act*. At issue was whether the law impermissibly enabled the executive to direct the federal judiciary as to how they should prioritise fair trial and national security considerations. Whealy J's decision to reject this challenge hinged on the preservation of the Court's inherent discretion and control of proceedings. He said:[73]

> Read fairly, it seems to me that the legislation does no more than to give the Court guidance as to the comparative weight it is to give one factor when considering it alongside a number of others. Yet the discretion remains intact and, particularly for the reasons I have outlined, it seems to me that there is no warrant for supposing other than that, in a proper case, the Court will order disclosure or a form of disclosure other than that preferred by the Attorney-General.

On appeal, the Court of Criminal Appeal endorsed these comments and confirmed that the 'tilted' balancing exercise in favour of national security did not amount to 'legislative usurpation of the judicial process'[74] and did not 'impinge upon the integrity of the process by which the judgment is formed. It may affect the outcome of the process but not in such a way as to affect its integrity'.[75] As these judgments reflect, a constitutional challenge grounded in the separation of powers will turn on the integrity of court processes, not on the fairness of the trial or on a notion of trial *rights*. In *Lodhi*, the preservation of inherent powers was held to overcome any threat to institutional integrity. This reasoning would be affirmed three years later when secret evidence provisions were again the subject of constitutional challenge.

In the years that followed the Lodhi trial, similar (though far less complex) schemes for secret evidence found their way into most Australian states and territories, most prominently incorporated within organised crime control order legislation.[76] These schemes concerned 'criminal intelligence' information, which the South Australian legislation defined as:

> [I]nformation relating to actual or suspected criminal activity … the disclosure of which could reasonably be expected to prejudice criminal investigations, to enable the discovery of the existence or identity of a confidential source of information relevant to law enforcement or to endanger a person's life or physical safety.[77]

[71] Phillip Boulten SC, 'Counter-Terrorism Laws in Practice' (Speech at the NSW Public Defenders Office Conference, Sydney, 4 October 2006) www.publicdefenders.nsw.gov.au/Documents/counterterrorismlaws.pdf 9.

[72] *R v Lodhi* (2006) 199 FLR 364, 383 [103]–[104] (Whealy J).

[73] *R v Lodhi* (2006) 163 A Crim R 448, 469 [108]. See also Whealy J's extrajudicial comments on this scheme: Justice Anthony Whealy, 'Terrorism and the Right to a Fair Trial: Can the Law Stop Terrorism? A Comparative Analysis' (Paper presented at the British Institute of International and Comparative Law, April 2010), www.biicl.org/files/5038_terrorism_and_the_right_to_a_fair_trial__2_.pdf 27.

[74] *Lodhi v R* (2007) 179 A Crim R 470, 489 [75] (Spigelman CJ, Barr and Price JJ concurring).

[75] Ibid, 488 [73]. Special leave to appeal this decision to the High Court was refused: *Lodhi v The Queen* [2008] HCA Trans 225.

[76] R Ananian-Welsh and G Williams, 'The New Terrorists: The Normalisation and Spread of Anti-Terror Laws in Australia' (2014) 38 *Melbourne University Law Review* 362, 380.

[77] *Serious and Organised Crime (Control) Act 2008* (SA), s 3.

Similar schemes in most Australian states and territories allowed for criminal intelligence information to be adduced and relied upon as secret evidence, subject to its classification by a Police Commissioner and a court determination (in a closed, ex parte hearing).[78]

State control order regimes were subject to a string of constitutional challenges on separation of powers grounds.[79] The High Court's decision upholding the secret evidence aspect of the Queensland scheme aligned with the NSW courts' earlier rulings in the *Lodhi* cases.[80] In *Assistant Commissioner Condon v Pompano Pty Ltd*,[81] the High Court held that the criminal intelligence provisions of the *Criminal Organisation Act 2009* (Qld) did not undermine judicial independence or institutional integrity as protected by Chapter III of the Constitution. French CJ opened his judgment with a strong acknowledgment that 'at the heart of the common law tradition' rests the fair trial, namely, a method that 'requires judges who are independent of government to preside over courts held in public in which each party has a full opportunity to present its own case and to meet the case against it'.[82] The Chief Justice identified secret evidence as '[a]ntithetical to that tradition';[83] nonetheless, the Court upheld the scheme on the basis that the state court was neither controlled nor conscripted by the executive government. Crucially, the state court maintained its usual inherent powers that could be employed to counteract any potential unfairness in the proceedings before it. For instance, their Honours reasoned that the court may attribute less, or even no, weight to the secret evidence, or order a stay of proceedings for want of fairness.[84]

First in *Lodhi* and then in *Pompano*, courts dismissed constitutional challenges to secret evidence by emphasising the maintenance of inherent discretions and control of proceedings, that is, the courts' inherent jurisdiction. The first judgment delivered in the Benbrika trial suggests how this discretion may be exercised, and further demonstrates the relative force with which the courts will protect their inherent jurisdiction.

The evidence against the 12 accused in the *Benbrika* trial included some 50 witnesses[85] and 482 intercepted conversations.[86] Predictably, national security information formed part of this body of evidence and the prosecution sought to rely on this information in the form of secret evidence. It did so by entering into agreements with the Attorney-General and the defendants concerning the disclosure, protection, storage, handling and destruction of the information.[87] Consent-based agreements of this nature are provided for by section 22

[78] Ibid, s 5A; *Criminal Code Act 1995* (Cth), ss 104.12A(3)(c)-(d); *Crimes (Criminal Organisations Control) Act 2009* (NSW), s 28; *Serious Crime Control Act 2009 (NT)*, s 73; *Criminal Organisation Act 2009* (Qld), pt 6; *Criminal Organisations Control Act 2012* (Vic), pt 4; *Criminal Organisations Control Act 2012* (WA), pt 5.

[79] Ananian-Welsh and Williams, 'The New Terrorists', 383–388; *South Australia v Totani* (2010) 242 CLR; *Wainohu v New South Wales* (2011) 243 CLR 181; *Assistant Commissioner Condon v Pompano Pty Ltd* (2013) 252 CLR 3.

[80] See also *Hogan v Hinch* (2011) 243 CLR 506, 532 [21] (French CJ), where the High Court cited the New South Wales Court of Criminal Appeal's decision in *Lodhi v R* (2007) 179 A Crim R 470 as an example of a case in which 'departure from the ordinary open justice principle [was] justified' by national security considerations.

[81] *Assistant Commissioner Condon v Pompano Pty Ltd* (2013) 252 CLR 38.

[82] Ibid 46 [1] (French CJ).

[83] Ibid.

[84] R Ananian-Welsh, 'Secrecy, Procedural Fairness and State Courts' in G Martin, R Scott Bray and M Kumar (eds), *Secrecy, Law and Society* (Abingdon, Routledge, 2015), 132. The court retaining power to stay proceedings was the only option under which the scheme was constitutional for Gageler J: *Assistant Commissioner Condon v Pompano Pty Ltd* (2013) 252 CLR 38, 289 [178].

[85] N McGarrity, '"Testing" Our Counter-Terrorism Laws: The Prosecution of Individuals for Terrorism Offences in Australia' (2010) 34 *Criminal Law Journal* 92, 108.

[86] *R v Benbrika* (2009) 222 FLR 433, 439 [21].

[87] See, eg, *R v Benbrika (Ruling No 1)* [2007] VSC 141 (21 March 2007) [19].

of the *NSI Act* – a provision that has allowed parties to strategically avoid much of the procedural complexity of the Act. Importantly, section 22(2) preserves the court's final say over the handling of national security information. Thorough analysis of this aspect of the *Benbrika* trial is not possible based on publicly available material. However, on 21 March 2007 the Court issued a ruling – its first published reasons in the pre-trial hearings – from which a number of points may be gleaned.

First, despite the consensual basis of the draft section 22 orders, the Court exercised its own review of their content. One set of draft orders 'were regarded by the Court as unsatisfactory in a number of respects' which are not specifically canvassed in the delivered judgment.[88] Revised orders requested in a subsequent application were made by the Court.[89] In issuing these orders, Bongiorno J relied on section 22(2) of the *NSI Act*, and observed that he might also have relied on sections 85B and 93.2 of the *Criminal Code*,[90] or the Court's inherent jurisdiction.[91]

Second, Bongiorno J emphasised that whatever the legal basis for this exercise of the Court's discretion,[92] his determination must turn upon 'the principle of open justice and the object of a fair trial for the accused', and effectively balance both security and fairness concerns in a manner that ensures that fair trial principles 'are faithfully adhered to'.[93] Thus the Court's discretion under section 22 was not impacted by the 'tilted' balancing exercise in section 31, but gave the usual emphasis to fair trial concerns and would be exercised in an identical manner to discretions under the *Criminal Code* and the inherent jurisdiction.

Finally, Bongiorno J's decision not only could have been grounded in an exercise of the Court's inherent jurisdiction, but it hinged on the preservation of that set of powers:[94]

> *Most importantly* all of these proposed orders are subject to variation, including revocation, at any time by the Court. Thus the whole process remains under the control of the Court at all times. This is probably the most important aspect of these orders as it makes clear that the Court can vary or even revoke the orders if they lead to unintended consequences which have an unacceptable effect on principles of a fair trial or open justice.

Thus, Bongiorno J's decision demonstrates some validity in the reasoning employed in the *Lodhi* and *Pompano* cases. In this case it appears that the inherent jurisdiction of the Court was deployed to control proceedings in the interests of fairness. The Court was prepared to withhold its discretion to make the orders pertaining to secret evidence as requested by the prosecution, even in circumstances where 12 defendants had consented to those orders. The two animating concerns of the Court in exercising its powers appear to be: first, preserving the fair trial and, second, preserving its ongoing capacity to ensure a fair trial and prevent abuse of process by operation of its inherent jurisdiction.

Here we see the Constitution and the inherent jurisdiction working in tandem to protect a fair trial. As I have argued elsewhere, Chapter III is an imperfect tool in the

[88] Ibid, [4].
[89] Ibid. See [19] for the full text of these orders, which extend to 45 paragraphs covering information storage, access, confidentiality, copying, transportation, declassification, destruction and more.
[90] Ibid, [14].
[91] Ibid, [16].
[92] Ibid, [15].
[93] Ibid, [16].
[94] Ibid, [7] (emphasis added). See also [15], in which his Honour emphasises the importance of a fair trial.

protection of fair trial *rights*.[95] Hopes that the High Court would achieve what Inglis Clark could not and find an implied due process clause in Chapter III have not been realised. Instead, the High Court has tended to uphold troubling schemes (including secret evidence provisions) provided they preserve the inherent powers and discretions of the court in question. Much, then, rests on judges exercising a strong and independent review of the secret evidence, and their discretion to refuse applications and even stay proceedings as appropriate.

V. Cells in the Dock: Courtroom Security

Where a person is standing trial for a serious offence, concerns around security within the courtroom during the trial may arise. These concerns are heightened in the highly politicised and publicised context of terrorism trials.

The Benbrika trial raised pointed concerns of courtroom security. These concerns were dealt with in ways that undermined the fair trial rights of the 12 accused, in particular, their right to the presumption of innocence and their capacity to defend the case against them. The almost inevitable classification of the accused as A1 prisoners appears to be the chief justification not only for their detention in a maximum security prison, but also for the creation of a novel structure *within* the courtroom.[96] In his Honour's twelfth published judgment during the pre-trial phase, Bongiorno J described this structure as follows:[97]

> [S]uperimposed on the dock is a Perspex structure which not only isolates the dock and its occupants from the body of the Court but also serves to create a number of small cells in the dock itself, each containing two seats bolted to the floor. Each cell is surrounded on three sides by the Perspex screen which sits on the floor and rises to a height of 1.8 metres. … [T]he position of the Perspex screen in front of each seat in the dock means that, for a person of average height or above, the occupant's knees are jammed hard against the Perspex necessitating frequent postural adjustment to achieve even a moderate degree of comfort.

In addition to this Perspex structure, computer screens were positioned in front of the accused which further obstructed sightlines between the accused and the rest of the court, including the judge, jury and witnesses.[98] Exceptional circumstances aside, it would seem that all persons charged with a terrorism offence could expect to be classified as A1 or equivalent prisoners and subject to similarly onerous conditions both within the courtroom and beyond.[99]

In the course of pre-trial hearings in 2007, the defendants lodged applications alleging procedural unfairness and seeking changes to the courtroom conditions outlined above.[100] The presiding judge retains control of courtroom security and so the application sought

[95] Ananian-Welsh, '*Kuczborki v Queensland*', (n 52) 69–70; R Welsh, 'A Path to Purposive Formalism: Interpreting Chapter III for Judicial Independence and Impartiality' (2013) 39 *Monash University Law Review* 66, 78–79.

[96] *R v Benbrika (Ruling No 12)* [2007] VSC 524 (12 December 2007) [17]-[19] (Bongiorno J).

[97] Ibid, [7].

[98] Ibid, [28]–[29].

[99] Before, that is, the judgments in this case were issued.

[100] *R v Benbrika (Ruling No 12)* [2007] VSC 524 (12 December 2007) [8].

to invoke the court's inherent powers in that respect. As Bongiorno J observed, the court's powers to control courtroom arrangements 'must always be exercised having regard to the paramount obligation on the Court to ensure, as far as possible, that the accused have a fair trial conducted according to law'.[101] Thus, in exercise of his Honour's powers to ensure security and a fair trial, Bongiorno J ordered the removal of the Perspex structure and repositioning of the computer screens.[102] Contrary to evidence asserting that 26 uniformed police officers would be required to ensure security in the absence of the Perspex screens, Bongiorno J also ordered that a maximum of 12 uniformed police officers be permitted in the court room at any one time.[103]

His Honour grounded these orders in fair trial considerations. He reasoned that the Perspex screens and computer monitors impacted the accuseds' presentation to the court room, 'in such a way as to render the accuseds' presence hardly more real than if they appeared by video link',[104] and 'materially diminish[ed] their right to the presumption of innocence – a right fundamental to the conduct of a fair trial and a right which is guaranteed to all persons on trial in this State'.[105] Moreover, the structure impeded the accuseds' communication with each other and access to their lawyers during the trial, thus undermining their right to adequately defend the case.[106] His Honour was not blind to, or dismissive of, the security concerns raised by the prosecution and its witnesses. Rather, Bongiorno J found that these were insufficiently supported to justify their serious incursion on the accuseds' fair trial rights. Here we see the classic balancing exercise, which the Court endeavoured to carry out in a reasoned, evidence-based way.

Bongiorno J concluded his judgment by issuing a warning that it in no way limited or precluded a future, contrary exercise of the inherent jurisdiction:

> [T]his ruling can be immediately revoked, modified … even to the extent, if necessary, of excluding the accused from the Court either temporarily or permanently. They should be under no misapprehension as to the power of the Court to ensure the orderly conduct of the trial and as to its willingness to use that power to the full should the need arise.[107]

Thus, just as in the secret evidence cases, the Court did not stop at invoking its inherent jurisdiction to preserve fairness, but strongly defended the jurisdiction itself from potential incursion.

VI. Strip-searched and Shackled: Prison Conditions

The court may have complete control over courtroom security, but its reach does not extend beyond those walls into prison management. In Bongiorno J's twentieth ruling in the course of the Benbrika trial, he dealt with an application by the accused for a stay of proceedings on grounds of unfairness. This unfairness was allegedly brought about by the conditions of the

[101] Ibid, [24]. See also [23].
[102] Ibid, [28]–[29].
[103] Ibid, [30].
[104] Ibid, [28].
[105] Ibid, [29].
[106] Ibid, [28].
[107] Ibid, [32].

accuseds' imprisonment and transfer to and from court. Bongiorno J's ruling on this issue was delivered on 20 March 2008, more than two years after the initial arrests and a month into the trial proper.[108]

Since their arrests, the accused had been held in Barwon maximum security prison under 'the most austere conditions in the Victorian prison system'.[109] When they were not in court, the men were mostly confined to their cells, sometimes for up to 23 hours a day. Their rights to associate with other prisoners, including each other, to have visitors and to access prison amenities were all restricted. Transfers both to and from the Supreme Court each day involved the defendants being strip-searched, handcuffed in cuffs attached to a waist belt, and shackled in leg chains. This process took around one hour for each prisoner.[110] At the time of the application, none of the men had ever been found to be in possession of prohibited items.[111] The drive between Barwon Prison and the Supreme Court then took between 65 and 80 minutes,[112] during which the defendants were held in 'small box-like steel compartments with padded seats'[113] in a prison van which had no natural light and which one expert described as '"very claustrophobic"'.[114] It is worth recalling that until December 2007, these conditions were compounded by the novel security arrangements inside the courtroom that were outlined above.

It was alleged, and ultimately held, that these conditions as a whole negatively impacted the fairness of the trial and, specifically, each defendant's physical health, mental health,[115] and fundamental right to attend his own trial 'and take an active part in defending the charges against him by instructing counsel'.[116]

The defendants lodged an application for a permanent stay of proceedings for want of fairness, invoking the Court's inherent jurisdiction. They also sought to rely on the right to a fair trial granted by the *Charter*. This second aspect of the application failed on two grounds. First, the conditions were imposed before the *Charter* commenced, so the transitional provisions of the *Charter* rendered it inapplicable.[117] Second, and ironically, compliance with the notice provisions of the *Charter* would risk significant delay and thus escalate the unfairness.[118] Bongiorno J commented that the mere fact that the accused had been in custody for two years or more was 'of itself unsatisfactory',[119] and he sounded a general warning that the notice provisions of the *Charter* might be 'used to delay or even disrupt the orderly conduct of criminal trials', effectively amounting to an abuse of process.[120]

It is unfortunate that the circumstances of this case prevented elucidation of how the *Charter* and the inherent jurisdiction might interact in the preservation of fair trial rights. The capacity of the *Charter* to protect prisoners' rights was demonstrated in *Castles v Secretary*

[108] *R v Benbrika (Ruling No 20)* (2008) 18 VR 410.
[109] Ibid, 418 [31].
[110] Ibid, 418–419 [33].
[111] M Groves, 'Editorial: Prison Conditions and the Right to a Fair Trial' (2008) 32 *Criminal Law Journal* 133, 133.
[112] *R v Benbrika (Ruling No 20)* (2008) 18 VR 410, 419 [34].
[113] Ibid, 419 [35].
[114] Ibid, 422 [54], quoting the evidence of Dr Amanda Silcock, occupational physician.
[115] Ibid, 427 [85].
[116] Ibid, 428 [88].
[117] Ibid, 415 [16], citing *Charter of Human Rights and Responsibilities Act 2006* (Vic), s 49(2).
[118] Ibid, 416 [17]–[19].
[119] Ibid, 417 [26].
[120] Ibid, 416 [18].

of Department of Justice.[121] In *Castles*, Emerton J applied the *Charter* to achieve a rights-compliant interpretation of the *Corrections Act 1986* (Vic) and allow a prisoner, Kimberly Castles, access to IVF treatment. However, unlike Bongiorno J, Emerton J stopped short of specifying further requirements such as prisoner transfer to facilitate the IVF procedures. Her Honour warned that courts should not 'enter into the process of fine-tuning arrangements' to accommodate the legislative, health and practical requirements in issue.[122] Julie Debeljak strongly criticised the *Charter*'s performance in the field of prisoners' rights, attributing this to judicial under-utilisation, reluctance to interfere in prison administration, and general uncertainty around the *Charter*'s enforcement mechanisms (amongst other factors).[123]

No such uncertainty impeded Bongiorno J in harnessing the inherent jurisdiction to address prison conditions in the Benbrika trial. His Honour considered the bases and nature of the Court's inherent jurisdiction to prevent unfairness and found that those inherent powers were sufficient in this case;[124] thus, the *Charter* was simply not required in order to assert the accuseds' fair trial rights. The reasoning process required in an exercise of the Court's inherent jurisdiction essentially involved a balancing exercise: 'balancing the interests of the community, represented by the Crown, against the interests of the accused'.[125] Beyond this vague notion of balance, Bongiorno J drew upon Deane J's candid observation in *Jago v District Court (NSW)*, noting that '[t]he identification of what constitutes unfairness and the steps which need to be taken to avoid it involve what his Honour described as an "… undesirably, but unavoidably, large content of essentially intuitive judgement"'.[126] Employing this intuitive balancing exercise, Bongiorno J concluded that:[127]

> [T]he evidence before the Court establishes that the accused in this case are currently being subjected to an unfair trial because of the whole of the circumstances in which they are being incarcerated at HM Prison Barwon and the circumstances in which they are being transported to and from court.

The inherent jurisdiction to preserve fairness may have supported his Honour's decision to stay the proceedings, but it did not permit the Court to dictate the conditions of the accuseds' imprisonment. Bongiorno J recognised this limitation under the separation of powers:[128]

> It is not for this Court … to order any specific alteration to the terms of the accuseds' detention. That is a matter for the Executive Government which must act, of course, according to law in the discharge of its obligations.

[121] *Castles v Secretary of Department of Justice* (2010) 28 VR 141. See also Matthew Groves' discussion of the case: M Groves, 'The Second Charters of Prisoners' Rights' in M Groves and C Campbell (eds), *Australian Charters of Rights a Decade On* (Annandale, The Federation Press, 2017).

[122] *Castles v Secretary of Department of Justice* (2010) 28 VR 141, 176 [145].

[123] J Debeljak, 'The Rights of Prisoners under the Victorian Charter: A Critical Analysis of the Jurisprudence on the Treatment of Prisoners and Conditions of Detention' (2015) 38 *University of New South Wales Law Journal* 1332, 1381–1385.

[124] *R v Benbrika (Ruling No 20)* (2008) 18 VR 410, 424–426 [71]–[86].

[125] Ibid, 425 [75], citing *Barton v R* (1980) 147 CLR 75.

[126] Ibid, 426 [79], citing *Jago v District Court (NSW)* (1989) 168 CLR 23, 57 (Deane J). *Jago* considered whether very lengthy delays in bringing a criminal prosecution gave rise to such unfairness that the prosecution amounted to an abuse of the court's processes, and thus enlivened the court's inherent jurisdiction to permanently stay the proceedings. The High Court accepted that the lower court had the inherent power to issue such a stay. However, it held that this power should not have been exercised in the case because the delay, while very significant, was not oppressive or clearly unfair.

[127] Ibid, 428 [91].

[128] Ibid, 429 [93].

Nonetheless, his Honour went on to list with great specificity the 'minimum alterations' necessary to remove the unfairness and therefore to avoid the granting of a stay. These included that the accused be moved to the Metropolitan Assessment Prison on Spencer Street in central Melbourne, that they be granted a minimum of 10 hours per day out of their cells (when not attending court), and that they no longer be subject to any restraining devices other than ordinary handcuffs not connected to a waist belt.[129] Matthew Groves has argued this decision therefore 'clearly amounted to an order for the specific alteration of the defendants' conditions, even though Bongiorno J had earlier asserted that it was not for the court to make such an order'.[130]

Bongiorno J's decision concerning the accuseds' conditions of imprisonment raises a host of complex questions concerning the extent to which judges can and should supervise prison management by operation of the inherent jurisdiction. The apparent extension of the court's reach into prisoner management raises separation of powers concerns. A tension certainly exists between a court respecting the separation of powers by leaving issues of prison management to the executive branch of government, and the imperative on courts to prevent administrative decisions and policies from grossly undermining the fairness (and thus integrity) of judicial proceedings. This decision also, as Groves argues, may provide prisoners (or even immigration detainees) with a more fruitful alternative to the rarely successful option of judicial review.[131] Debeljak's critique of *Charter* jurisprudence in the field of prisoners' rights suggests that the inherent jurisdiction may likewise present a more fruitful alternative than the *Charter* in this area. However, this 'intuitive', 'nebulous' and contextual set of powers is also unpredictable – Bongiorno J's decision may or may not signal an effective extension of judicial reach into the prison system by operation of the inherent jurisdiction.

VII. Inherent Jurisdiction and Fair Trial Rights

Threats to a fair trial can arise in countless ways, ranging from the predictable to the unforeseeable. In the context of terrorism trials, prosecutorial reliance on intelligence and national security information leads to applications for secret evidence under the *NSI Act*. Secret evidence undermines the public trial, equality of arms and defendants' capacity to properly understand and defend the case against them, including by adequately instructing counsel. Secret evidence also risks the perceived impartiality of the court. What is more, the nature of the evidence adduced in terrorism trials tends to prolong proceedings. *NSI Act* and public interest immunity applications – which may involve not only parties but media organisations – prolong the pre-trial period, and intelligence-based evidence such as telephone intercepts that may require translation, also take a considerable period of time to adduce in court.[132]

As the Benbrika trial demonstrated, the requirement of exceptional circumstances to support the granting of bail for those accused of terrorism offences means that defendants are highly likely to be incarcerated throughout the lengthy pre-trial and trial periods. Adding

[129] Ibid, 430–431 [100].
[130] Groves, 'Prison Conditions', (n 111), 134.
[131] Ibid, 137.
[132] See, eg, the comments of Bongiorno J in *R v Benbrika (Ruling No 20)* (2008) 18 VR 410, 413 [4], 417–418 [27].

to this, the operation of the law made the classification of Benbrika and his co-accused as A1 prisoners almost inevitable. That classification supported the imposition of some of the most severe conditions inside and outside the courtroom possible in Australia, undermining the accuseds' rights to, for example, the presumption of innocence, legitimate and proportionate punishment, and to adequately instruct counsel in their defence. The incredibly severe nature of these conditions was confirmed in the Court's repeated findings of unfairness. While Bongiorno J's rulings helped to shape future terrorism trials, it is clear that national security proceedings will continue to pose particular challenges to fair trial principles and this was neither the first nor last time that a court would be called upon to weigh fair trial principles against the public interest in national security.

Fair trial rights are subject to multiple layers of protection under Australian law. Writing in 2013, Scott Guy surmised that the Constitution 'now affords a substantial degree of protection for State Supreme Courts and their procedural processes'.[133] In the secret evidence cases, however, this protection was only borne out to the extent that courts must retain their inherent jurisdiction to preserve fairness and prevent unfairness and these cases provide little to suggest that the Constitution protects fair trial rights as such.[134] The High Court's robust protection of the inherent jurisdiction is reflected in Bongiorno J's decisions in the Benbrika trial. Not only did the inherent jurisdiction support his Honour's decisions regarding secret evidence, courtroom security and prison conditions, but in each of those rulings his Honour emphasised his continuing control of proceedings and undiminished capacity to exercise the inherent jurisdiction at any time.

The analysis of the Benbrika trial demonstrates some of the strengths of the inherent jurisdiction as a mechanism for the protection of fair trial rights. The great breadth of the inherent jurisdiction lends it flexibility, granting the court a wide variety of tools to achieve fairness and avoid unfairness as the specific case may require. The inherent jurisdiction is also a practical mechanism of rights protection, capable of satisfying the parties with a remedial outcome – as demonstrated in Bongiorno J's order for the removal of the Perspex screens, and in his Honour's threat to stay proceedings unless the accuseds' conditions of imprisonment were drastically improved. An exercise of inherent jurisdiction focuses on fairness in a broad and encompassing sense which invites judges to cut through statutory rules and to take into account changing circumstances and community expectations.[135] Thus, in invoking the inherent jurisdiction the court has a wide discretion to do what it considers necessary to remedy unfairness however it has arisen, and to stay proceedings if such a remedy is unavailable or beyond the court's power.

Despite the breadth of the inherent jurisdiction, it is a well-established and traditional – arguably the *original* – mechanism for protecting the fair trial in the common law system of justice. By contrast, current uncertainty and misunderstanding as to the nature, scope and operation of the *Charter* has complicated and deterred attempts to rely on its protections,[136] and constitutional fair trial principles are notoriously complex, dynamic and uncertain.[137]

[133] S Guy, 'The Constitutionality of the Queensland Criminal Organisation Act: *Kable*, Procedural Due Process and State Constitutionalism' (2013) 32 *University of Queensland Law Journal* 265, 285. For discussion of the constitutional protection of procedural fairness in federal courts see, eg, Bateman (n 10).

[134] Ananian-Welsh, '*Kuczborki v Queensland*', (n 52) 67. For more detailed discussion of the High Court's treatment of procedural fairness as an incident of Chapter III, see Williams and Hume (n 11) 375–379.

[135] *Dietrich v R* (1992) 177 CLR 292, 364 (Gaudron J); Spigelman, (n 20) 43.

[136] Debeljak (n 123).

[137] Williams and Hume (n 11) 325.

On a pragmatic, but not-unimportant, level the inherent jurisdiction may present a relatively cost and time efficient option for a party wishing to assert his or her fair trial rights. It can be invoked by simple application in the course of proceedings. No special notice or procedural requirements are involved and additional counsel or prolonged proceedings may not be required.

But the inherent jurisdiction also has its weaknesses. Its capacity to protect fair trial rights is limited to court proceedings. Its reach does not extend to administrative decisions, including for example adverse security assessments by ASIO which Ben Saul described as a 'legal black hole'.[138] A lesser concern is the shaky foundations of the inherent jurisdiction in the federal sphere. Having its roots in the unlimited jurisdiction of the common law courts of Westminster, courts of statute – including Australia's federal courts – cannot lay claim to inherent jurisdiction as such. Despite this, the High Court has employed constitutional and statutory interpretation to hold that Australia's federal and other statutory courts possess implied powers akin to inherent jurisdiction.[139] The High Court has reasoned that, as 'a matter of statutory construction', federal courts have all powers expressly or impliedly conferred by the statute that creates them and that proscribes their jurisdiction, as well as 'all such powers as are incidental and necessary to the exercise' of such.[140] Further, as courts exercising the judicial power of the Commonwealth, federal courts possess certain powers 'arising by necessary implication from Ch III'.[141] These implied powers include such classic incidents of inherent jurisdiction as 'the power to punish for contempt and the power to preserve the subject matter of a pending application for special leave to appeal'.[142] While in practice these implied powers serve much the same function as the inherent jurisdiction of courts of unlimited jurisdiction, unlike the inherent jurisdiction, these powers are clearly limited by the scope of the aforementioned Commonwealth statutes.[143]

The considerable breadth and flexibility of the inherent jurisdiction give it pragmatic and strategic efficacy, but also risk creating a well of loosely defined, unpredictable and relatively unconstrained power. The inherent jurisdiction has been described as amorphous, ubiquitous,[144] nebulous,[145] intuitive,[146] metaphysical,[147] and simply as including – although not being limited to – 'a general power, taking various specific forms, to prevent unfairness'.[148] It 'gives rise to a vast armoury of remedies',[149] several of which have been discussed in this chapter. This breadth and flexibility is a necessary aspect of the inherent jurisdiction. Its efficacy requires that it be sufficiently adaptable to equip the court to respond to 'the limitless ways in which the due administration of justice can be delayed,

[138] B Saul, 'Fair Shake of the Sauce Bottle' (2012) 37 *Alternative Law Journal* 221, 222.
[139] Lacey 'Inherent Jurisdiction', (n 52) 67–70.
[140] *DJL v Central Authority* (2000) 201 CLR 226, 241 [25] (Gleeson CJ, Gaudron, McHugh, Gummow and Hayne JJ), citing *Parsons v Martin* (1984) 5 FCR 235, 241 (Bowen CJ, Northrop and Toohey JJ).
[141] Ibid, 242 [27] (Gleeson CJ, Gaudron, McHugh, Gummow and Hayne JJ) [footnotes omitted].
[142] Ibid.
[143] Ibid.
[144] Jacobs, 'The Inherent Jurisdiction of the Court', 23.
[145] Groves, 'Prison Conditions', (n 111), 138.
[146] *Jago v District Court (NSW)* (1989) 168 CLR 23, 57 (Deane J); Groves, 'Prison Conditions', (n 111)138.
[147] Justice P de Jersey, 'The Inherent Jurisdiction of the Supreme Court' (1985) 15 *Queensland Law Society Journal* 325, 326; Mason (n 1) 459;
[148] *Connelly v Director of Public Prosecutions* [1964] AC 1254, 1347 (Lord Devlin).
[149] Mason (n 1) 449.

impeded or frustrated'.[150] However, when power is this broad and vaguely defined, it becomes unpredictable and may be insusceptible to the usual avenues of oversight, particularly appeal to a superior court. Likewise, the potential constitutional entrenchment of courts' inherent jurisdiction supports it as a robust protection for fair trial rights, but also hampers the prospect of oversight or constraint by the legislature.

An exercise of the inherent jurisdiction to protect a fair trial will involve balancing competing interests. In the cases considered in this chapter, these interests were in national security and fairness. Critiquing the High Court's decision in *Pompano*, Gabrielle Appleby observed that judges have failed to 'articulate the nature and mechanics of the balancing test to be undertaken'.[151] She argued that this:[152]

> [f]ailure to articulate the process of deliberation required within a balancing test reduces it to a rhetorical device that obscures, rather than clarifies, the judicial reasoning process. With no explicit process associated with "balancing", the weighing up is unpredictable and indefensible as a step within rational judicial decision-making.

Like Appleby, Denise Meyerson has also claimed that the absence of such guidance will cause judges to err on the side of restraint, even to the point of deference, at the cost of fairness.[153] Whilst there is little evidence of this kind of restraint in Bongiorno J's conduct of the Benbrika cases, these are valid concerns and have arguably played out in administrative law cases such as *Leghaei* and *Charter* cases such as *Castles*.[154] A solution posed by Meyerson, speaking to the *Charter* context, is judicial over-enforcement of rights, granting them greater weight in the rights-security balancing exercise.[155]

On the other hand, Bongiorno J's 'unprecedented'[156] decision concerning the accuseds' conditions of imprisonment sparked fears of judicial inconsistency and overreach. By venturing into prison management, Bongiorno J's decision 'sits awkwardly' alongside cases in which the High Court has been reluctant to enter disputes about the conditions of immigration detainees and against *Charter* cases concerning prison management.[157] The decision also risks undermining the separation of powers by encroaching on the domain of the executive government, and may ultimately be inappropriate for judges who are inexpert in issues of prison administration and management.[158] 'What would happen', Groves has asked, 'if a court were to order changes to prison conditions that prison officials could not satisfy'?[159]

Ultimately, one judge may be deferential, another might not be, and the concentration of relatively unrestrained power in the judiciary under the inherent jurisdiction means that '[f]aith is placed in the judgment of the individual judge in each instance'[160] as he or she

[150] Ibid, 449.
[151] Appleby, 'Protecting Procedural Fairness' (n 52) 91.
[152] Ibid, 92.
[153] Ibid, 93–94; Denise Meyerson, 'Why Courts Should not Balance Rights Against the Public Interest' (2007) 31 *Melbourne University Law Review* 873.
[154] For broader, pointed critique of the *Charter* cases concerning prisoners' rights, see Debeljak (n 123).
[155] Meyerson (n 153).
[156] B Carlton and J McCulloch, '*R v Benbrika and ors (Ruling No 20)*: The "War on Terror", Human Rights and the Pre-emptive Punishment of Terror Suspects in High-Security' (2008) 20 *Current Issues in Criminal Justice* 287, 288.
[157] Groves, 'Prison Conditions', (n 111) 138; Debeljak (n 123) 1339–1351.
[158] Groves, 'Prison Conditions', (n 111) 138.
[159] Ibid, 138.
[160] Appleby (n 52) 91.

undertakes an inherently 'intuitive' exercise.[161] Whilst some scholars have cogently argued for greater clarity around this balancing process, there is a risk that any such clarity might also constrain, and thereby undermine, the flexibility and efficacy of the inherent jurisdiction.

This examination of the inherent jurisdiction as a protection for fair trial rights highlights the crucial importance of judicial independence and impartiality in the trial context – including the hotly debated issues of judicial appointment practices, diversity and bias. The inherent jurisdiction is a well of undefined, highly discretionary power, concentrated in the hands of the judiciary for the purpose of administering justice. Whilst this kind of loosely controlled power ought to trouble anyone concerned with the rule of law, the fact remains that it has existed since the genesis of the common law and has, if anything, flown under the radar. History would suggest that this ancient and nebulous set of powers is a fundamental and useful mechanism for the protection of fair trial rights that enjoys a well-established and important place in preserving the rule of law within the common law constitutional framework.

VIII. Conclusion

Fair trial principles are central to our constitutional framework. Terrorism trials have challenged these principles in serious and sometimes severe ways. Perhaps schemes for secret evidence and requiring exceptional circumstances for the granting of bail, for instance, would not exist if Inglis Clark's due process clause had found a place in the federal Constitution, or perhaps they would. In the absence of a due process clause, fair trial rights have been left to a complex web of common law, statutory and constitutional protections. Analysis of but a few terrorism trials indicates that the inherent jurisdiction of courts has an important role to play in the patchwork of fair trial protections in Australia, and that its role should be considered in the future development of statutory and constitutional fair trial protections. Undoubtedly, however, the most important factor in the protection of fair trial rights is not the existence of legal protections but the individual presiding judge, specifically, how much weight he or she gives to fair trial concerns when they hang in the balance against national security.

[161] *Jago v District Court (NSW)* (1989) 168 CLR 23, 57 (Deane J). Similar concerns regarding a lack of transparency in decision-making and inconsistency between individual judges arise in relation to "intuitive sentencing", an approach under which judges determine sentences by the exercise of discretion alone, without apparent recourse to objective criteria: see, eg, A Lovegrove, 'Intuition, Structure and Sentencing: An Evaluation of Guideline Judgments' (2000) 14 *Current Issues in Criminal Justice* 182.

17

A Search for Rights: Judicial and Administrative Responses to Migration and Refugee Cases

EMMA DUNLOP, JANE McADAM AND GREG WEEKS*

I. Introduction

Migration and refugee cases occupy a unique place in Australia's administrative law jurisprudence. While it may be tempting to tie their significance to their 'explosion' in judicial review cases since the mid-1980s, or to their current and continuing ubiquity in the Federal Court and High Court,[1] they have a much longer historical importance. Indeed, the regulation of foreigners' movement into Australia has been particularly prominent in the imaginations of the judiciary, politicians and public since before Federation, and was a central influence in the framing of the Australian Constitution.

What has become increasingly notable about migration and refugee cases is the desire on the part of governments to dictate to courts what outcomes they should reach. This has manifested itself not only in legislative attempts to prevent judicial review through the use of privative clauses,[2] and to restrict judicial review on certain grounds, but also in political criticism of the judiciary by both Coalition[3] and Labor governments.[4]

Politicians' frustration at the perceived tendency of the judiciary to obstruct, or at least fail to comply with, the government's intentions with regard to migration and refugee matters raises fundamental questions about the role of the judiciary and the scope of judicial review. Many of the amendments made to the *Migration Act 1958* (Cth) ('Migration Act') over the past two decades can be traced directly to particular court decisions whose

* The authors thank Sophie Duxson for her research assistance. Emma Dunlop is grateful for the support of an Australian Government Research Training Programme scholarship (previously the Australian Postgraduate Awards).

[1] Stephen Gageler SC, 'Impact of Migration Law on the Development of Australian Administrative Law' (2010) 17 *Australian Journal of Administrative Law* 92, 92. The Federal Court's most recent annual report noted that in 2017–18, 80.7 per cent of all appellate proceedings concerned decisions under the *Migration Act 1958*: Federal Court of Australia, *Annual Report 2017–2018*, 32 www.fedcourt.gov.au/__data/assets/pdf_file/0003/52716/AR-2017-18.pdf, accessed 12 February 2019.

[2] See, eg, Mark Aronson, Matthew Groves and Greg Weeks, *Judicial Review of Administrative Action and Government Liability*, 6th edn (NSW, Thomson Reuters, 2017) ch 18.

[3] See, eg, the comments of Phillip Ruddock during his term as Minister for Immigration, which implicitly regarded judges who did not fulfil the expectations of the government as 'involv[ing] themselves in the political process': AAP, 'Ruddock Denies Accusation', *The Age* (3 June 2002) www.theage.com.au/articles/2002/06/03/1022982667563.html accessed 15 April 2018.

[4] See John McMillan, 'Federal Court v Minister for Immigration' (1999) 22 *AIAL Forum* 1, 1, fn 3.

effect the government sought to overturn.[5] While Parliament does not 'interfere with the judicial function or do anything that is in any sense constitutionally illegitimate' by 'amending a statute to avoid the consequences of a particular judicial interpretation',[6] this dynamic nonetheless raises important questions. Are judges obliged to facilitate the realisation of the legislatively-expressed wishes of elected representatives? To what extent can judges take account of Australia's obligations under international law in interpreting domestic statutes? Is it fair to say that judges cannot usurp the functions of the legislative and executive branches of government, and that judicial decision-making in migration and refugee matters inevitably occurs in a political setting to which judges, and particularly tribunal members, must be sensitive? Does it follow that, by taking a different view from the government as to the meaning or application of legal principles, a judge will have acted such that it would be 'more appropriate [for that judge] to resign from the bench and stand for parliament'?[7]

To investigate these issues, Part II of this chapter examines the human rights framework in Australia and principles of statutory interpretation. It notes that in the absence of a national human rights charter, there are few limits on Parliament's ability to enact legislation that is inconsistent with Australia's international legal obligations. The courts must give effect to such legislation if it is not ultra vires and the language of the statute is sufficiently clear. Part III charts the history of migration law in Australia, noting the enduring role of administrative discretion, the changing scope of judicial review, and the development of merits review. Part IV turns to the operation of merits review in migration matters. It examines changes to migration review procedures and the constraining role of policy on decision-making. Part V discusses judicial review, highlighting parliamentary efforts to limit judicial consideration of Australia's international obligations in the process of statutory interpretation, and to restrict judicial review. It examines the courts' responses to these developments, particularly with respect to incursions on core judicial functions.

II. An Introduction to Human Rights and the Courts

The structure of human rights in Australia remains 'haphazard and incomplete',[8] notwithstanding developments that have set it on a more stable footing.[9] Although Australia has ratified all the major international human rights treaties – evincing its commitment under international law to respect, promote and fulfil such rights – it lacks a national human rights charter giving effect to these obligations at the domestic level.[10] Australia's dualist approach to international law means that human rights obligations assumed by ratification

[5] Eg, the *Migration Reform Act 1992*, No 184 (Cth) inserted s 476 into the *Migration Act*, which sought to overturn the effect of *Kioa v West* (1985) 159 CLR 550. The insertion of s 197C through the *Migration and Maritime Powers Legislation Amendment (Resolving the Asylum Legacy Caseload) Act 2014* was intended to overturn the effect of the High Court in *Plaintiff M70/2011 v Minister for Immigration and Citizenship* (2011) 244 CLR 144 and the Full Federal Court in *Minister for Immigration and Citizenship v SZQRB* [2013] FCAFC 33.

[6] See Chief Justice Robert French, 'The Courts and the Parliament' (2013) 87 *Australian Law Journal* 820, 829.

[7] AAP (n 3).

[8] Hilary Charlesworth, 'The Australian Reluctance about Rights' (1993) 31 *Osgoode Hall Law Journal* 195, 196.

[9] Specifically, the minimum entrenched provision of judicial review (recognised in Commonwealth jurisdiction in a series of migration cases) and the revival of the principle of legality; see the essays in Dan Meagher and Matthew Groves (eds), *The Principle of Legality in Australia and New Zealand* (Annandale, Federation Press, 2017).

[10] On the two state/territory statutory charters of rights (*Human Rights Act 2004* (ACT) and *Charter of Human Rights and Responsibilities Act 2006* (Vic)), see generally Matthew Groves and Colin Campbell (eds), *Australian Charters of Rights a Decade On* (Annandale, Federation Press, 2017).

of international treaties are not directly enforceable in Australian courts unless they have also been incorporated into domestic law.[11] There are, of course, many federal statutes protecting aspects of human rights law.[12] However, as ordinary pieces of legislation they are subject to amendment or repeal by Parliament and they do not place any overarching limits on the kinds of laws that can or cannot be adopted. As a result, there are few limits on Parliament's ability to pass legislation that adopts a stretched interpretation of[13] – or is simply inconsistent with – Australia's international obligations. In the process of statutory interpretation, courts may nonetheless construe legislation in a manner that runs counter to the government's 'interpretation of its international obligations'.[14] However, as Byrnes notes, 'unless the courts have invoked a constitutional basis to declare a legislative measure invalid, a government can generally reinstate its preferred interpretation and policy through legislative amendment'.[15] Efforts to litigate 'what are essentially human rights claims' through the prism of administrative law[16] may therefore be constrained by Parliament, subject only to the constitutional protections which administrative law claims enjoy.[17]

Most common law countries have a domestic human rights framework in place that governs, or at the very least limits, Parliament's ability to pass laws contrary to accepted rights within that framework, and that provides remedies of varying strength and effectiveness[18] for individuals whose rights have been violated.[19] Australia is 'exceptional' in not having such a check on legislative power, nor such a vehicle for judicial review.[20] For instance, even though the UN Human Rights Committee has concluded that Australia's system of mandatory detention for non-citizens without a valid visa, as practised, is a violation of article 9 of the International Covenant on Civil and Political Rights (ICCPR),[21] there is currently no basis[22] on which the imposition or length of detention

[11] Australia remains responsible for any violations of its obligations as a matter of international law, and domestic law that purports to oust a treaty obligation has no effect as a matter of international law: Vienna Convention on the Law of Treaties (adopted 23 May 1969, entered into force 27 January 1980) 1155 UNTS 331 (VCLT) art 27.

[12] On which, see George Williams and David Hume, *Human Rights under the Australian Constitution*, 2nd edn (Australia and New Zealand, Oxford University Press, 2013) 14.

[13] See, eg, discussion of 'acceptability as a standard of interpretation' in Andrew Byrnes, 'The Meanings of International Law: Government Monopoly, Expert Precinct or Peoples' Law?' (2014) 32 *Australian Yearbook of International Law* 11, 15–17.

[14] Ibid, 17.

[15] Ibid.

[16] See Ben Saul, 'Australian Administrative Law: The Human Rights Dimension' in Matthew Groves and H.P. Lee (eds), *Australian Administrative Law: Fundamentals, Principles and Doctrines* (Port Melbourne, Cambridge University Press 2007) 50.

[17] See ch 1 of this volume at p 6.

[18] Eg, a declaration of incompatibility under the *Human Rights Act 1998* (UK) can only broadly be said to be an individual remedy, although it is a remedy that individuals do seek. The New Zealand Bill of Rights provides that no court shall 'hold any provision of [an] enactment to be impliedly repealed or revoked, or to be in any way invalid or ineffective', or decline to apply it, 'by reason only that the provision is inconsistent with any provision of this Bill of Rights': *Bill of Rights Act 1990* (NZ), art 4.

[19] See, eg, *Constitution Act*, 1982, Pt I, 'Canadian Charter of Rights and Freedoms'; *Human Rights Act* 1998, c. 42 (UK); *New Zealand Bill of Rights Act* 1990; *Constitution of the Republic of South Africa*, 1996, ch 2: Bill of Rights.

[20] See generally Michael Taggart, '"Australian Exceptionalism" in Judicial Review' (2008) 36 *Federal Law Review* 1.

[21] International Covenant on Civil and Political Rights (adopted 16 December 1966, entered into force 23 March 1976) 999 UNTS 171 (ICCPR). See, eg, *A v Australia*, UN Doc CCPR/C/59/D/560/1993 (30 April 1997) paras 9.3–9.5; *F.K.A.G et al v Australia*, UN Doc CCPR/C/108/D/2094/2011 (28 October 2013) paras 9.1–9.7; *M.M.M et al v Australia*, UN Doc CCPR/C/108/D/2136/2012 (28 October 2013) paras 10.4, 10.6. Compare discussion in *Al-Kateb v Godwin* (2004) 219 CLR 562, 642 (Hayne J).

[22] Subject to the observation in *Chu Kheng Lim v Minister for Immigration Local Government and Ethnic Affairs* (1992) 176 CLR 1, 36 (Brennan, Deane and Dawson JJ).

for a valid statutory purpose can be challenged in an Australian court,[23] regardless of the conditions of detention.[24]

In the absence of a federal bill of rights, the High Court has had the role of developing constitutional rights protections. Yet, the 'text and history of the Constitution have posed insurmountable obstacles' to the development of any 'rich, rights-protective constitutional jurisprudence'.[25] There has also been considerable resistance from some quarters to the idea that the judiciary[26] might seek to 'update the Constitution to reflect contemporary human rights norms'.[27]

The fact that Australia's binding international commitments are not directly enforceable in Australian courts in the absence of domestic legislation does not, however, mean they are irrelevant. In *Teoh*, Mason CJ and Deane J held that:

> ratification by Australia of an international convention is not to be dismissed as a merely platitudinous or ineffectual act, particularly when the instrument evidences internationally accepted standards to be applied by courts and administrative authorities in dealing with basic human rights affecting the family and children. Rather, ratification of a convention is a positive statement by the executive government of this country to the world and to the Australian people that the executive government and its agencies will act in accordance with the Convention.[28]

In *Teoh*, a majority of the High Court found that Australia's ratification of the Convention on the Rights of the Child (CRC)[29] gave rise to a legitimate expectation that, 'absent statutory or executive indications to the contrary … administrative decision-makers will act in conformity with the Convention and treat the best interests of the children as "a primary consideration"',[30] in accordance with article 3 of the CRC. The Full Federal Court has since clarified that *Teoh* 'does not state more than that, procedurally, the interests of the children are a primary consideration, not the only, or the only primary, consideration'.[31]

Since the decision of the High Court in *Lam*,[32] the Court has 'done about as much as judges can by way of *obiter dicta* in a case where the point was not argued to overrule' the legitimate expectation finding in *Teoh*.[33] Much of this has to do with the entire concept of legitimate expectations being rejected by the High Court in *Lam* and subsequent cases.[34]

[23] See *Al-Kateb* (n 21) 595 (McHugh J).

[24] See *Behrooz v Secretary, Department of Immigration and Multicultural and Indigenous Affairs* (2004) 219 CLR 486, 499 (Gleeson CJ); 507 (McHugh, Gummow and Heydon JJ).

[25] Williams and Hume (n 12) 2.

[26] We are generally invited to understand that any such decisions will be made by 'unelected judges', despite the fact that Australian jurisdictions boast no other kind of judge.

[27] Williams and Hume (n 12) 2.

[28] *Minister of State for Immigration and Ethnic Affairs v Teoh* (1995) 183 CLR 273, 291 (Mason CJ and Deane J) (footnotes omitted).

[29] Convention on the Rights of the Child (adopted 20 November 1989, entered into force 2 September 1990) 1577 UNTS 3.

[30] *Teoh* (n 28) 291 (Mason CJ and Deane J) (footnotes omitted). Toohey J (at 302) and Gaudron J (at 304–05) were the other judges who formed the majority; McHugh J dissented.

[31] *Nweke v Minister for Immigration, Multicultural Affairs and Citizenship* (2013) 136 ALD 235, [29] (Allsop CJ, Flick and Robertson JJ).

[32] *Re Minister for Immigration and Multicultural and Indigenous Affairs; ex parte Lam* (2003) 214 CLR 1.

[33] Taggart (n 20) 17.

[34] *Plaintiff S10/2011 v Minister for Immigration and Citizenship* (2012) 246 CLR 636; *Minister for Immigration and Border Protection v WZARH* (2015) 256 CLR 326. See Matthew Groves, 'Legitimate Expectations in Australia: Overtaken by Formalism and Pragmatism' in Matthew Groves and Greg Weeks (eds), *Legitimate Expectations in the Common Law World* (Oxford, Hart Publishing, 2017) 319.

However, the aspects of *Teoh* dealing with treaty interpretation remain good law and the case continues to be cited for these.[35] An additional basis for *Teoh*'s ongoing relevance[36] is arguably that obligations arising under a treaty may be the subject of procedural protections in courts' judicial review jurisdictions.[37]

Principles of statutory interpretation establish the extent to which international law is relevant to the interpretation of Australian law. Much depends on the nature of the domestic statute being interpreted. In *Applicant A*, Brennan CJ considered the applicable principles where Parliament has 'transpose[d] the text of a treaty or a provision of a treaty into the statute so as to enact it as part of domestic law'.[38] In such cases, 'the prima facie legislative intention is that the transposed text should bear the same meaning in the domestic statute as it bears in the treaty'.[39] Courts will seek to identify that meaning by applying the rules of treaty interpretation.[40] In the same case, McHugh J engaged in a detailed analysis of the key interpretative rule set out in the Vienna Convention on the Law of Treaties,[41] concluding that a 'holistic approach' was called for.[42] This requires Australian courts to 'examine both the "ordinary meaning" and the "context … object and purpose" of a treaty'.[43] McHugh J also noted the 'general principle that international instruments should be interpreted in a more liberal manner than would be adopted if the court was required to construe exclusively domestic legislation'.[44]

In *Teoh*, Mason CJ and Deane J considered the appropriate approach to construction if a statute is more 'ambiguous'.[45] In such cases:

> the courts should favour that construction which accords with Australia's obligations under a treaty or international convention to which Australia is a party, at least in those cases in which the legislation is enacted after, or in contemplation of, entry into, or ratification of, the relevant international instrument. … If the language of the legislation is susceptible of a construction which is consistent with the terms of the international instrument and the obligations which it imposes on Australia, then that construction should prevail.[46]

[35] Including in the High Court; see, eg, *CPCF* (n 5) 526–527 (French CJ); 557 (Hayne and Bell JJ); 627 (Gageler J); 644 and 650 (Keane J).

[36] See Matthew Groves, 'Treaties and Legitimate Expectations – The Rise and Fall of *Teoh* in Australia' (2010) 15 *Judicial Review* 323, 335–36.

[37] The NSW Court of Appeal has developed an extensive body of case law on articles of the CRC being mandatory relevant considerations in child protection cases: see Greg Weeks, *Soft Law and Public Authorities: Remedies and Reform* (Oxford, Hart Publishing, 2016) 134–36.

[38] *Applicant A v Minister for Immigration and Ethnic Affairs* (1997) 190 CLR 225, 230–31 (Brennan CJ).

[39] Ibid, 230–31 (Brennan CJ), citing his own judgment in *Koowarta v Bjelke-Petersen* (1982) 153 CLR 168, 265; see also *Applicant A* at 239–240 (Dawson J), 292 (Kirby J).

[40] See Jane McAdam, 'Interpretation of the 1951 Convention' in Andreas Zimmermann (ed), *The 1951 Convention Relating to the Status of Refugees and its 1967 Protocol: A Commentary* (Oxford, Oxford University Press, 2011) 81.

[41] VCLT, art 31.

[42] *Applicant A* (n 38) 254 (McHugh J); see McAdam (n 40) 84–85.

[43] *Applicant A* (n 38) 256 (McHugh J).

[44] *Applicant A* (n 38) 255 (McHugh J).

[45] This represents the approach taken when treaties are involved. There is no need to establish ambiguity where the principle of legality is invoked. See Dan Meagher, 'The Common Law Principle of Legality in the Age of Rights' (2011) 35 *Melbourne University Law Review* 449, 451.

[46] *Teoh* (n 28) 287 (Mason CJ and Deane J) (footnotes omitted), cited also in *Plaintiff S157/2002 v Commonwealth* (2003) 211 CLR 476, 492 (Gleeson CJ). See to similar effect *Chu Kheng Lim* (n 22) 38 (Brennan, Deane and Dawson JJ).

Generally, it is accepted that as a matter of statutory interpretation, domestic legislation should be construed 'as far as its language permits' in a manner that is consistent with international law.[47] Kiefel J applied this principle in the seminal case *Plaintiff M70/2011*,[48] which arose out of an asylum seeker transfer arrangement negotiated between Australia and Malaysia. The bilateral agreement provided that the next 800 asylum seekers to arrive unlawfully by boat in Australia would be sent to Malaysia, in exchange for which Australia would resettle 4,000 UNHCR-approved refugees from Malaysia. The Australian Immigration Minister was required by section 198A of the *Migration Act* to declare that Malaysia was a 'safe' country for the transfer of asylum seekers.[49] The High Court held that because Malaysia was not a party to the Refugee Convention and had no domestic legal regime for refugee protection, it failed to satisfy the relevant jurisdictional facts (of safety) in the Migration Act.[50] Kiefel J emphasised that the Court's construction of section 198A(3)(a) 'most closely accords with the fulfilment of Australia's Convention obligations and it is to be preferred to one which does not'.[51] The majority of the Court went on to spell out the content of those obligations,[52] showing the scope within Australian law 'for the limited recognition and application of international law, in particular through common law principles of statutory interpretation'.[53]

The interpretative principles set out above have their limits. A presumption of consistency with international law has no application if a contrary interpretation is expressly required by the language of a statute. The High Court has held that if there is a conflict between the terms of the Migration Act (or other relevant law) and the Refugee Convention, 'it is the words of the Act which govern'.[54] Thus, if the language of a statute is clear, then the court must give effect to it even if this places Australia in breach of its international legal obligations.[55] In such cases, statutory provisions 'must be applied and enforced even if they be in contravention of accepted principles of international law'.[56] In *Al-Kateb*, the High Court held (by a bare majority)[57] that indefinite mandatory detention was not

[47] *Teoh* (n 28) 287 (Mason CJ and Deane J); citing *Polites v The Commonwealth* (1945) 70 CLR 60, 68–69 (Latham CJ); 77 (Dixon J); 80–81 (Williams J). See also *Plaintiff M70/2011* (n 5) 234 (Kiefel J).

[48] *Plaintiff M70/2011* (n 5).

[49] Arrangement between the Government of Australia and the Government of Malaysia on Transfer and Resettlement (25 July 2011) www.loyarburok.com/wp-content/uploads/2011/08/Refugee-Swap-Agreement-Msia-Aust-250711.pdf accessed 15 April 2018.

[50] *Plaintiff M70/2011* (n 5) 182–83 (French CJ), 195–99 (Gummow, Hayne, Crennan and Bell JJ), 233–36 (Kiefel J). In response to *Plaintiff M70/2011*, Parliament amended s 198A, which now provides at s 198AB(2) that the 'only condition' for the Minister to designate a country as a 'regional processing country' is that 'the Minister thinks that it is in the national interest'.

[51] *Plaintiff M70/2011* (n 5) 234.

[52] Ibid, 196 (Gummow, Hayne, Crennan and Bell JJ). These included the principles of non-refoulement (art 33(1)), free access to courts of law (art 16(1)), non-discrimination (art 3), treatment as least as favourable as that accorded to its nationals with respect to employment (art 17(1)), elementary education (art 22(1)) and religious freedoms (art 4).

[53] Tamara Wood and Jane McAdam, 'Australian Asylum Policy All at Sea: An Analysis of *Plaintiff M70/2011 v Minister for Immigration and Citizenship* and the Australia–Malaysia Arrangement' (2012) 61 *International and Comparative Law Quarterly* 274, 288.

[54] *Minister for Immigration and Multicultural and Indigenous Affairs v QAAH of 2004* (2006) 231 CLR 1, 16 (Gummow ACJ, Callinan, Heydon and Crennan JJ). See also *Chu Kheng Lim* (n 22) 38 (Brennan, Deane and Dawson JJ); *Teoh* (n 28) 287 (Mason CJ and Deane J); *Plaintiff S157/2002* (n 46) 492 (Gleeson CJ).

[55] See, eg, *Kartinyeri v Commonwealth* (1998) 195 CLR 337, 384 (Gummow and Hayne JJ).

[56] *Koowarta* (n 39) 204 (Gibbs CJ).

[57] See AJ Brown, 'When Liberty Divides: Judicial Cleavages and their Consequences in *Al-Kateb v Godwin* (2004)' in Andrew Lynch (ed), *Great Australian Dissents* (Cambridge, Cambridge University Press, 2016) 311.

unconstitutional and was authorised by the clear language of section 198 of the *Migration Act*. McHugh J stated:

> It is not for courts, exercising federal jurisdiction, to determine whether the course taken by Parliament is unjust or contrary to basic human rights. The function of the courts in this context is simply to determine whether the law of the Parliament is within the powers conferred on it by the Constitution.[58]

The High Court reaffirmed this position in *CPCF*, in which the plaintiff argued that the Commonwealth's powers under the *Maritime Powers Act 2013* (Cth) to intercept, detain and remove asylum seekers at sea should be 'read down' to accord with Australia's international law obligations.[59] The Court reiterated that international law does not have direct effect in Australia,[60] and that statutory provisions must only be interpreted in accordance with international law if there is not statutory intention to the contrary.[61] Thus, 'Australian courts are bound to apply Australian statute law "even if that law should violate a rule of international law"'.[62]

There are nonetheless two safeguards that should, in principle, limit Parliament's capacity to legislate in a manner that is inconsistent with Australia's international human rights obligations. The first is the power of the electorate to dismiss a Parliament that has overstepped the bounds of public sentiment. This power may, however, have less force in cases where human rights restrictions are directed against people outside the voting polity (which is generally the case in migration matters). The second safeguard, introduced in 2011, is the requirement that any Member of Parliament who proposes to introduce a bill accompany that bill with a Statement of Compatibility detailing the extent to which it complies with Australia's obligations under the seven core international human rights treaties it has ratified.[63] A Parliamentary Joint Committee on Human Rights (PJCHR) was established to examine and report to Parliament on the compatibility of bills, legislative instruments and Acts with Australia's human rights obligations.[64] While the Statement of Compatibility process requires the member who introduces a bill to articulate his or her reasons for adopting a particular approach or interpretation, thus 'limit[ing] the capacity for uncontested interpretation by executive fiat',[65] the quality of analysis is often poor, and at times inaccurate.[66] Yet, even when the PJCHR, which takes the statements as the 'starting-point' for its own scrutiny,[67] has pointed out their inadequacies, it has rarely had a substantive impact on securing amendments to the provisions.[68] This is perhaps consistent with a statutory regime that states that a failure to comply with the obligation to prepare a Statement of

[58] *Al-Kateb* (n 21) 595 (McHugh J). See also at 581 (McHugh J); 642 (Hayne J); 661–62 (Callinan J).

[59] See 'Plaintiff's Submissions', 11 September 2014, www.hcourt.gov.au/assets/cases/s169-2014/CPCF_Plf.pdf, accessed 15 April 2018, para 65.

[60] *CPCF* (n 5) 650–51 (Keane J).

[61] Ibid, 526 (French CJ).

[62] Ibid, 643 (Keane J), citing, inter alia, *Polites* (n 47) 69 (Latham CJ).

[63] *Human Rights (Parliamentary Scrutiny) Act 2011* (Cth), s 8(1)–(3); s 3(1).

[64] Ibid, ss 4–7.

[65] Byrnes (n 13) 28.

[66] Writing in 2014, Byrnes noted that the Parliamentary Joint Committee on Human Rights (PJCHR) 'necessarily approaches [statements of compatibility] with a critical eye, as no statement of compatibility has yet suggested that any provision of a bill is incompatible with the relevant human rights': ibid 25.

[67] Ibid. Byrnes was the external legal adviser to the PJCHR from 2012–14.

[68] As Byrnes asked: 'If government does not modify its views or even accept that there may be other legitimate interpretations – whether "acceptable" or even preferable ones – what value does this process have, other than as another subject for academics to research?': ibid 27. See also George Williams and Lisa Burton, 'Australia's Exclusive Parliamentary Model of Rights Protection' (2013) 34 *Statute Law Review* 58, 86.

Compatibility does not, in the event of the bill becoming law, 'affect the validity, operation or enforcement of the Act or any other provision of a law of the Commonwealth'.[69]

III. A History of Judicial Review in Migration and Refugee Cases

The history of migration law in Australian courts is lengthy.[70] The development of laws regulating the entry of 'undesirable immigrants' began in the 1880s across the Americas, Australasia and southern Africa, building upon exclusionary rules already developed in the 1850s to regulate Chinese immigration and labourers,[71] and stem even further back to quarantine laws of the 1830s, which were 'effectively interchangeable' with immigration laws, 'enabling the deportation and return of people as well as their compulsory isolation, the latter almost universally including infectious disease as a reason to limit movement'.[72] As Crock and Berg have noted, Australia 'was self-consciously "created" out of a *selected* population'.[73] The development of the country's immigration law – and, indeed, the framing of the Constitution itself – was centred on racial, social and cultural identity. Although the drafters of the Constitution were not concerned with refugees, they were certainly concerned with immigration.[74] The idea that immigration should be *controlled*, and made subject to a considerable degree of executive discretion, has characterised the Australian experience.[75]

The *Immigration Restriction Act 1901* was among the first Acts passed by the new Commonwealth Parliament, indicating that the centrality of immigration to the political imagination is not a new phenomenon. That Act governed movement into Australia during the first half-century after Federation. Although it was 'the exemplary "raceless" act',[76] only 19 sections and five pages long, it was a model of brevity whose effect was to exclude non-white settlers and those who fell into undesirable categories for economic, physical, criminal or moral reasons.[77] The Act operated by vesting sweeping discretionary powers

[69] *Human Rights (Parliamentary Scrutiny) Act 2011* (Cth), s 8(5). A similar outcome is achieved under *Legislation Act 2003* (Cth), s 19.

[70] See Gageler (n 1).

[71] Chinese exclusion Acts were passed in every Australian colony between 1857 (Victoria, Act 80) and 1887 (Tasmania, Act 9). Bashford argues that the laws Acts were passed in every Australian colony between 1857 and 1887 which enforced 'strong disincentives' against Chinese immigrants, even if they did not 'exclude' them directly: Alison Bashford, 'Immigration Restriction: Rethinking Period and Place from Settler Colonies to Postcolonial Nations' (2014) 9 *Journal of Global History* 26, 30. In Queensland the regulation of Pacific Island workers commenced in 1868 with the passing of the first *Polynesian Labourers Act* (Act 17).

[72] Bashford (n 71) 35.

[73] Mary Crock and Laurie Berg, *Immigration, Refugees and Forced Migration: Law, Policy and Practice in Australia* (Annandale, Federation Press, 2011) 17.

[74] Klaus Neumann, *Across the Seas: Australia's Response to Refugees: A History* (Collingwood, Black Inc, 2015) 14. Prior to Federation, the Australian colonies admitted the occasional political exile. In the 1920s, although the federal government discouraged the arrival of Russian and Eastern European Jewish refugees, around 4,148 did come: Neumann, 22–27. Australia's first extensive experience with refugees came after the Second World War.

[75] Crock and Berg (n 73) 17.

[76] In that it 'replaced prior colonial laws that had specifically nominated Chinese or "coloured" exclusion or restriction': Bashford (n 71) 32.

[77] Bashford (n 71) 33; Alison Bashford and Catie Gilchrist, 'The Colonial History of the 1905 Aliens Act' (2012) 40 *The Journal of Imperial and Commonwealth History* 409, 414. The modern *Migration Act* was itself only 36 pages long when passed and only expanded to its current massive state after 1989.

directly in government officials (a construct that reappears in certain sections of the *Migration Act*). Its most notorious discretionary power was the ability of any Customs Officer to require 'any person … to write out at dictation and sign in the presence of the officer a passage of fifty words in length in an European language directed by the officer', or be declared a prohibited immigrant.[78] This was the central element of the 'White Australia Policy' which dominated the approach of the Commonwealth Government to immigration between Federation and the 1970s,[79] despite adjustments that allowed significant numbers of non-British migrants to settle in Australia after each of the world wars.[80]

The 'dictation test', drawn from Natal,[81] was highly malleable, particularly if the officer in charge of administering the test wished to exclude a person seeking to immigrate. Such was the case in *R v Wilson*,[82] in which the prominent left-wing journalist Egon Kisch, a Czechoslovakian employed by a German-language newspaper, was given the dictation test in Scottish Gaelic. In a challenge before the High Court, Kisch was successful in persuading a majority of the Court that Scottish Gaelic was an ancient form of speech and not a 'European language' within the meaning of the Act. Dixon J, with whom Rich, Evatt and McTiernan JJ agreed, was alive to doubts as to whether Scottish Gaelic was either a language (as opposed to a dialect) or European, when taking into account the objectives of the legislature in passing that section.[83] Nonetheless, Dixon J's uneasiness in reaching his conclusion was clear,[84] indicating the scope which existed as a matter of course for Customs Officers to abuse their broad statutory discretion.[85]

Discretion was, and remains, the hallmark of administrative decision-making.[86] This is generally considered a good thing: for example, Brennan J observed that some statutory discretions, such as that vested in the Immigration Minister under the *Migration Act* to deport certain individuals held not to be of good character, 'cannot be exercised according to broad and binding rules'.[87] In many ways, the broad discretionary powers under the *Immigration Restriction Act 1901* were unremarkable. However, it is noteworthy that, in migration cases in the early twentieth century, a person seeking to challenge an exercise of discretion had only judicial review as a potential mechanism for obtaining relief (in contrast to the tribunal system that emerged from the 1970s which enabled challenges to the merits of decisions as well).

[78] *Immigration Restriction Act 1901* (Cth), s 3(a). The dictation test was abolished with the passage of the *Migration Act*.

[79] However, some colonies had immigration laws that reflected the necessity of attracting migrants: see then Chief Justice Robert French, 'The Role of the Courts in Migration Law', Migration Review Tribunal and Refugee Review Tribunal Annual Members' Conference, 25 March 2011, www.hcourt.gov.au/assets/publications/speeches/current-justices/frenchcj/frenchcj25mar11.pdf, accessed 15 April 2018.

[80] John Vrachnas and others, *Migration and Refugee Law: Principles and Practice in Australia*, 3rd edn (Port Melbourne, Cambridge University Press, 2012) 10–12.

[81] Jeremy Martens, 'A transnational history of immigration restriction: Natal and New South Wales 1896–97' (2006) 34 *The Journal of Imperial and Commonwealth History* 323.

[82] *R v Wilson; ex parte Kisch* (1934) 52 CLR 234.

[83] Ibid, 244 (Dixon J); cf the certainty of Starke J in dissent (at 242).

[84] Ibid, 243.

[85] The High Court was not above approving racist decisions made impeccably in judicial review terms; see *Water Conservation and Irrigation Commission (NSW) v Browning* (1947) 74 CLR 492.

[86] Even developments which have limited that observation, such as the major reforms to the *Migration Act* between 1992 and 1994 which transformed it into a regime based on codified rights and protections, have tended to be both short-lived and the exception rather than the rule.

[87] *Re Drake and Minister for Immigration and Ethnic Affairs (No 2)* (1979) 2 ALD 634, 640.

The available grounds of judicial review, such as those argued in *R v Wilson*, were constrained. It was arguable that Kisch was given the dictation test for a purpose unauthorised by the Act,[88] either on the basis that it was intended to prevent him addressing the Congress against War and Fascism and other rallies or that it was administered by a particular police constable fluent in a specific language in order to circumvent Kisch's 'formidable skills as a linguist'.[89] However, the grounds of review mounted by Kisch did not go to these elements of the case.[90] Modern common law grounds of judicial review are more expansive (albeit their application has sometimes been reduced by statute in migration and refugee cases) and the High Court has stressed that further grounds may yet develop, since 'the metes and bounds of jurisdictional error' are not closed.[91]

The dismantling of the White Australia Policy during the 1960–70s[92] and the overhaul of administrative law in the 1970s[93] meant that greater opportunities developed to challenge decisions in migration and refugee cases. Because challenges to administrative decisions in these and other areas no longer depended on establishing legal or jurisdictional errors but could be made 'on the merits' of the case, the creation of tribunals opened up the prospect for higher quality administrative decision-making. However, while these goals were met in part, it must also be conceded that the quality of both merits-based and judicial decision-making in migration and refugee cases has become increasingly fraught since the 1970s. The next two sections consider, respectively, the availability of merits review for individuals who have either applied unsuccessfully for visas that would entitle them to remain in Australia or have had such visas revoked, and the prospects for judicial review of such decisions. It is implicit in Part IV that the broad political circumstances that have driven the development of migration policy over the course of several decades may carry weight in tribunal members' ultimate assessment of the 'correct or preferable' decision on the facts of each case.[94] Part V highlights legislative efforts to limit both the scope of judicial review and courts' recourse to international law in the process of statutory construction in migration and refugee matters.

IV. Developments in Merits Review and the Application of Policy

Since the introduction of tribunals into Commonwealth jurisdiction only a little more than 40 years ago, there has been a vast increase in the number of tribunals in Australia and their workload. Yet, the nature of tribunal justice remains misunderstood and, as will become

[88] The 'improper purpose' ground of judicial review covers this point. See generally Aronson, Groves, and Weeks (n 2) [5.510] and [6.290].

[89] Nicholas Hasluck, '*Kisch Case* (1934)' in Tony Blackshield, Michael Coper and George Williams (eds), *The Oxford Companion to the High Court of Australia* (South Melbourne, Oxford University Press, 2001) 396, 397.

[90] *R v Wilson; ex parte Kisch* (n 82) 236–7.

[91] *Kirk v Industrial Court of New South Wales* (2010) 239 CLR 531, 573 (French CJ, Gummow, Hayne, Crennan, Kiefel and Bell JJ).

[92] Although the policy was only formally abandoned by the Whitlam Government in 1973, significant steps had been taken to end it under Harold Holt several years earlier: John Vrachnas and others (n 80) 12–13.

[93] See, eg, *Administrative Appeals Tribunal Act 1975* (Cth); *Federal Court of Australia Act 1976* (Cth); *Ombudsman Act 1976* (Cth); *Administrative Decisions (Judicial Review) Act 1977* (Cth); and the *Freedom of Information Act 1982* (Cth).

[94] See *Drake v Minister for Immigration and Ethnic Affairs* (1979) 46 FLR 409, 419–20 (Bowen CJ and Deane J) (noting that while policy may be relevant, it should not be determinative). See also *Shi v Migration Agents Registration Authority* (2008) 235 CLR 286, 327 (Kiefel J).

evident, this is understandable in many respects. Tribunals conduct review of decisions 'on the merits' of the case before them.[95] Such hearings are generally, but not inevitably,[96] heard *de novo*. Although less formal, tribunals look in some respects like courts, but are essentially different since, to be able to affirm, vary or set aside the decision under appeal,[97] they must have been granted the statutory power to perform the same exercise of power as the original decision-maker. This makes them constitutionally distinct from Chapter III courts.[98] Much is made of this constitutional distinction; less is said about the fact that tribunals deal with the factual merits of cases because that is a task to which courts are generally unsuited. This is so because the accepted judicial method in Australia is for the court only to take account of the material put before it by the parties. When courts proceed in the more inquisitorial manner of tribunals,[99] confusion, unhappiness and appellate proceedings are the inevitable results.[100]

From its operation in 1976 until the establishment of two specialist tribunals – the Refugee Review Tribunal (RRT) in 1993 and the Migration Review Tribunal (MRT) in 1999 – the Administrative Appeals Tribunal (AAT) conducted merits review of migration and refugee decisions. It resumed such review in mid-2015 when the two specialist tribunals were merged with it. The RRT and the MRT operated differently from certain other tribunals in that, when the tribunal was not satisfied on the basis of an applicant's file that the challenged decision should be overturned, it invited the applicant to a hearing. Neither the Minister nor the Immigration Department was represented at such hearings, making them more intimate and accessible for the applicant. When the MRT and RRT, along with the Social Security Appeals Tribunal, were amalgamated into the AAT with effect from 1 July 2015, appeals previously heard by specialist tribunals were henceforth heard by a separate Division of the generalist AAT: the Migration and Refugee Division (MRD). While initially these matters were heard in much the same way as they had been in the MRT and RRT, many members are now assigned to more than one Division,[101] and all Divisions may yet adopt uniform procedures for consistency. The benefits to applicants of specialist tribunals might thus be lost.

A separate, 'fast-track' review system applies to asylum seekers who arrived in Australia by boat on or after 13 August 2012 and before 1 January 2014, were not transferred offshore, and have been granted the right to apply for a protection visa by the Minister.[102] This group

[95] The term 'on the merits' does not appear in the AAT Act but soon passed into general usage; see, eg, *Collector of Customs (NSW) v Brian Lawlor Automotive Pty Ltd* (1979) 41 FLR 338, 342 (Bowen CJ); 376 (Deane J).

[96] See, eg, *Shi* (n 94).

[97] *Administrative Appeals Tribunal Act 1975* (Cth), s 43(1).

[98] See *R v Kirby; ex parte Boilermakers' Society of Australia* (1956) 94 CLR 254.

[99] There is a spectrum between inquisitorial and wholly adversarial proceedings, and Australian tribunals are at neither end of that spectrum: Narelle Bedford and Robin Creyke, *Inquisitorial Processes in Australian Tribunals* (Australasian Institute of Judicial Administration, 2006).

[100] See *Kuek v Wade* [2017] VSCA 329.

[101] See President's Overview, in Administrative Appeals Tribunal, *Annual Report 2016–17*, 3 www.aat.gov.au/AAT/media/AAT/Files/Reports/AR201617/AAT-Annual-Report-2016-17.pdf accessed 15 April 2018; President's Overview, in Administrative Appeals Tribunal, *Annual Report 2017–18*, 4 www.aat.gov.au/AAT/media/AAT/Files/Reports/AR201718/AAT-Annual-Report-2017-18.pdf accessed 12 February 2019.

[102] See *Migration Act*, s 5(1) ('fast track applicant'); s 46A(1)–(2); Pt 7AA. Babies born in Australia between 6 November 2013 and 5 December 2014 to a parent who arrived on or after 19 July 2013 (by boat) and was taken to Nauru are also taken to be 'fast track applicants', along with their parents and siblings: *Specification of Class of Persons Defined as Fast Track Applicants* – IMMI 16/010 (Cth) F2016L00377 (18 March 2016) www.legislation.gov.au/Details/F2016L00377 accessed 12 February 2019. See also Linda Kirk, 'Accelerated Asylum Procedures in the United Kingdom and Australia: "Fast Track" to *Refoulement*?' in Maria O'Sullivan and Dallal Stevens (eds), *States, the Law and Access to Refugee Protection: Fortresses and Fairness* (Oxford, Hart Publishing, 2017) 258–268. On the operation of the regime, see *Plaintiff M174/2016 v Minister for Immigration and Border Protection* [2018] HCA 16.

is not entitled to access the MRD's general review process. If the Department refuses to grant a protection visa to an applicant in this group, a review is conducted by the Immigration Assessment Authority (IAA),[103] a 'separate office' within the MRD.[104] The IAA offers a significantly more limited form of review than that provided by the MRD.[105] Unlike the MRD, the IAA does not hold hearings and reviews are generally conducted 'on the papers'.[106] Under a Practice Direction issued by a former AAT President,[107] applicants can submit a document explaining why they disagree with the Department's decision.[108] The IAA must not consider any new information save in 'exceptional circumstances'.[109] If an applicant wishes to provide new information, he or she must submit an additional document explaining why 'the information could not have been given to the Department before the decision was made', or why 'the information is credible personal information which was not previously known and may have affected consideration of [the applicant's] claims, had it been known.'[110] Any such information must be provided within 21 days of the case's referral to the IAA.[111] Interviews may be held in 'very limited circumstances' and are 'generally … conducted by telephone'.[112] The IAA is not empowered to vary the decision under review – it may only affirm the decision or remit it for reconsideration.[113] If an applicant in this group is deemed an 'excluded fast track applicant', they are not entitled to a review by the IAA.[114]

Two seminal cases from the early years of the AAT – *Drake (No 2)*[115] and *Pochi*[116] – illustrate points of remaining relevance both to the migration and refugee jurisdictions and to tribunal review generally. Both were migration cases heard by Brennan J in his capacity as President of the AAT and both regarded deportation on character grounds due to alleged drug trafficking,[117] but with divergent results. While each case is now recalled for demonstrating a different proposition in administrative law, their relevance here is that they demonstrate that merits review can validly reach contrary results on very similar facts.

Mr Drake had been convicted in Darwin of possession of cannabis in 1978, 10 years after he had emigrated to Australia from the US. He had earlier been involved in growing

[103] Except in the case of 'excluded fast track review applicants', defined in *Migration Act*, s 5(1).
[104] See Administrative Appeals Tribunal Annual Report 2017–2018 (n 101) 66; *Migration Act*, s 473JA.
[105] In carrying out its functions, the IAA is to 'pursue the objective of providing a mechanism of *limited review* that is efficient, quick, free of bias and consistent with Division 3 (conduct of review)': *Migration Act*, s 473FA (emphasis added).
[106] See *Migration Act*, s 473DB; Administrative Appeals Tribunal Annual Report 2017–2018 (n 101) 66.
[107] In accordance with *Migration Act*, s 473FB.
[108] The applicant's document must be no longer than 5 pages in at least size 11 font: IAA, 'Practice Direction for Applicants, Representatives and Authorised Recipients' (Justice Duncan Kerr, President, 6 February 2017), paras 20–21 www.iaa.gov.au/IAA/media/IAA/Files/Practice%20Directions/Practice-Direction-1-Applicants-Representatives-and-Authorised-Recipients.pdf accessed 15 April 2018.
[109] *Migration Act*, s 473DD.
[110] IAA (n 108) para 24. These conditions reflect the requirements in s 473DD of the *Migration Act*.
[111] Ibid para 28.
[112] IAA (n 108) paras 35–36; see also *Migration Act*, s 473DF.
[113] *Migration Act*, s 473CC(2).
[114] *Migration Act*, s 5(1) ('excluded fast track review applicant'); s 473BA, though note s 473BC.
[115] *Re Drake and Minister for Immigration and Ethnic Affairs (No 2)* (n 87). The original decision of Davies J in the AAT had been overturned by the Full Federal Court in *Drake v Minister for Immigration and Ethnic Affairs* (n 94).
[116] *Re Pochi and Minister for Immigration and Ethnic Affairs* (1979) 36 FLR 482. The Minister was unsuccessful in a later appeal to the Full Federal Court (*Minister for Immigration and Ethnic Affairs v Pochi* (1980) 44 FLR 41) and had special leave to appeal to the High Court rescinded (*Minister for Immigration and Ethnic Affairs v Pochi* (1981) 149 CLR 139).
[117] The relevant provision in the *Migration Act 1958* was then s 12 and is now s 501.

cannabis in New South Wales. His conviction in the Northern Territory saw him sentenced to incarceration for a period of 12 months. Although he served only three months of that sentence, it nonetheless triggered the Minister's statutory power to deport Mr Drake. Through his delegate, he did so pursuant to a policy statement which provided in part that the deportation power would be exercised against persons 'who have revealed by their conduct that they represent a threat to [the Australian community] or that their continued presence is inimical to its existence or its welfare',[118] and in particular 'where sex offences against children or trafficking in or distribution of drugs [have] been involved …'.[119] The Minister was entitled to define a broad statutory power by issuing such a policy, particularly when it would in practice be exercised by a large number of delegates and in some cases reviewed and exercised afresh by tribunal members.[120] Brennan J upheld the decision to deport Mr Drake. *Drake (No 2)* remains well remembered and frequently cited for Brennan J's advice to tribunal members about how to deal with executive policies.

Mr Pochi, an immigrant from Calabria in Italy, had been arrested standing in a plantation of Indian hemp near Griffith and was sentenced to a period of imprisonment, of which he served one year. The drug trade in the Griffith area was notorious,[121] and there was some suspicion that Mr Pochi was more deeply involved in it than his conviction accounted for. Brennan J, in hearing Mr Pochi's appeal from a decision to deport him, needed to consider whether it was in Australia's interests to compound Mr Pochi's criminal punishment by deportation. One of the elements of Brennan J's decision was the fact that Mr Pochi's wife and children were Australian citizens and had every right to remain in the country.[122] Another was to determine whether Mr Pochi had an 'entrepreneurial' interest in the drug trade, rather than merely having been paid or rewarded for his labour. The evidence against Mr Pochi in this regard was considerable.[123] He had contributed over $117,000 in cash to a business venture in which Robert Trimbole, a leading local organised crime figure, was a partner. Mr Pochi was a tailor and did not have access to such a sum. His evidence listed a number of relatives who had made substantial gifts to him and related also a record of gambling wins that stretched Brennan J's credulity. Brennan J noted that it was doubtful that Mr Pochi would have committed to providing that sum of money prior to having secured it, as his account said that he had. Brennan J said of Mr Pochi's connection to the organised drug trade that the weight of suspicion against Mr Pochi was not determinative, since 'criminal conduct … should be proved, not merely suspected'.[124] Brennan J therefore recommended that the deportation order against Mr Pochi be revoked.

[118] *Re Drake and Minister for Immigration and Ethnic Affairs (No 2)* (n 87) 638.

[119] Ibid, 641–42.

[120] It is, however, an issue to know exactly where to strike the balance between consistency and flexibility in decision-making; see Weeks, *Soft Law and Public Authorities: Remedies and Reform* (n 37) 38–40.

[121] It was at about this time that Donald Mackay, an anti-drugs crusader from Griffith, disappeared and was presumed to have been assassinated. The Woodward Royal Commission into Drug Trafficking was explicit in naming the Calabrian mafia as being behind the Australian trade in cannabis, centred in and around Griffith.

[122] There was evidence to suggest that Mr Pochi would have become a naturalised citizen but for an administrative error for which he was not responsible: *Re Pochi and Minister for Immigration and Ethnic Affairs* (n 116) 485ff.

[123] A police officer attached to the Woodward Royal Commission sought to tender a substantial amount of evidence against Mr Pochi provided that the AAT was allowed to know its content but Mr Pochi was not. This kind of procedure is now familiar but Brennan J rejected it on the basis that not allowing such evidence to be refuted carried 'notorious risks': *Re Pochi and Minister for Immigration and Ethnic Affairs* (n 116) 512.

[124] *Re Pochi and Minister for Immigration and Ethnic Affairs* (n 116) 513.

Compared to Mr Drake, whose case was decided in the AAT by the same judge in the same year, Mr Pochi was extremely fortunate. The evidence against Mr Pochi was probably as strong as that against Mr Drake, and one gets the distinct impression that Brennan J did not doubt much of it. However, he was not 'reasonably satisfied' of the case against Mr Pochi as required by the *Briginshaw* principle.[125] Also, Brennan J's experience of criminal trials may have influenced him to set aside his personal reservations and demand that the case against Mr Pochi be made out to the appropriate standard. It was not. Mr Drake's conduct was neither more nor less grave, in the terms of the Minister's policy, but crucially left Brennan J with no doubt that he should be deported.

When so much of the law is discretionary and governed by policy, it is hard for tribunals to depart from that policy. Furthermore, refugee matters call for tribunals to inquire into matters that may not be capable of proof in the sense usually required.[126] For example, having won in the High Court on the issue of whether, as an asylum seeker, he should have relocated within his country of origin,[127] the appellant in *SZATV* had his case remitted to the RRT to be decided afresh. The tribunal member raised, for the first time, the question whether the applicant had been a journalist in the Ukraine, as he claimed. After the passage of almost 10 years, his movement to Australia and the fact that his records had been seized by the police, this was impossible to prove in the usual, legal sense (and through no fault of the applicant).[128] Tribunals are flexible, but even a model very loosely based on court procedure can mean that they do not always work well in migration and, especially, refugee matters. UNHCR's *Handbook and Guidelines on Procedures and Criteria for Determining Refugee Status* draws attention to the particular challenges that asylum seekers face, considering that the 'duty to ascertain and evaluate all the relevant facts is shared between the applicant and the examiner'.[129] It directs decision-makers to give applicants 'the benefit of the doubt', noting that 'it is hardly possible for a refugee to "prove" every part of his case and, indeed, if this were a requirement the majority of refugees would not be recognized.'[130]

Merits review can offer a flexible and responsive forum for migration and refugee cases. Arguably, a specialist tribunal is best suited to addressing the complex issues faced in matters that are often both personally fraught and politically charged. It remains to be seen whether the amalgamation of the MRT and RRT into the AAT will reduce the benefit to the applicant of the previous system. Certainly, the IAA offers a more restricted form of review that limits an applicant's ability to introduce new information after the initial application for protection. In addition to institutional and procedural factors, the constraining role of policy should also be considered. While a relevant policy relied on by the primary decision-maker will 'plainly

[125] This is a sliding scale which requires that, in civil matters, a greater cogency of evidence is required to prove matters of greater consequence: *Briginshaw v Briginshaw* (1938) 60 CLR 336.

[126] See UNHCR, *Handbook and Guidelines on Procedures and Criteria for Determining Refugee Status under the 1951 Convention and the 1967 Protocol Relating to the Status of Refugees*, HCR/1P/4/ENG/REV. 3 (1979, reissued 2011) (UNHCR *Handbook*), paras 196–97.

[127] *SZATV v Minister for Immigration and Citizenship* (2007) 233 CLR 18. See also *Appellant S395/2002 v Minister for Immigration and Multicultural Affairs* (2003) 216 CLR 473; *Minister for Immigration and Border Protection v SZSCA* (2014) 254 CLR 317.

[128] Ultimately, the tribunal member was satisfied once she reached a former colleague of the applicant by phone to confirm that he had been a journalist. We disclose that Greg Weeks represented the applicant in his RRT hearing and had been one of his solicitors in the previous High Court proceedings.

[129] UNHCR *Handbook* (n 126) para 196.

[130] Ibid, 203.

be a relevant factor' for a tribunal to consider, it is crucial that it does not 'abdicate its function of determining whether the decision made was, on the material before the Tribunal, the correct or preferable one in favour of a function of merely determining whether the decision made conformed with whatever the relevant general government policy might be'.[131]

V. Recent Legislative Developments: Government and the Courts in Conflict?

This part examines the role of judicial review by highlighting recent legislative changes that seek to restrict review and to ensure that courts apply the government's interpretation of Australia's international legal obligations, even if that interpretation is inconsistent with the obligation in question. The judiciary's response in key cases is also considered.

Successive governments have tightened the availability of judicial review under the Migration Act but their efforts have met with mixed levels of success. Legislative moves to restrict the available grounds of review have often provoked judicial ingenuity[132] or resistance.[133] Attempts to exclude review, or to impose severe restrictions on jurisdiction, have been held ineffective in both Commonwealth and state jurisdictions,[134] and a High Court bench not known for its strong interventionist streak made the decisions that had the effect of ending the processing of asylum seekers on Christmas Island[135] and invalidating the 'Malaysia Solution'.[136] Rather than fighting every battle, the High Court has shown a greater tendency to intervene when essential rule of law elements are threatened or to correct the precedential effect of common misapplications of law.[137]

However, a note of caution is necessary when emphasising judicial and parliamentary tensions in migration matters. The fault lines that the High Court's greater frequency of rulings on the Migration Act over the course of at least 40 years are alleged to have exposed have in fact featured in numerous matters. They include the involvement of Barwick CJ in the Constitutional crisis of 1975, during which he advised Governor-General Sir John Kerr that he had the power to dismiss the Whitlam Government; the attack on Kirby J under parliamentary privilege in the Australian Senate in 2002;[138] and, perhaps most notoriously, the reactions by politicians to the *Mabo* and *Wik* decisions about indigenous land rights.[139] Passionate reactions to judgments in migration and refugee matters are not

[131] *Drake v Minister for Immigration and Ethnic Affairs* (n 94) 420 (Bowen CJ and Deane J), adding the caveat that such abdication is impermissible 'in the absence of specific statutory provision' (such as one requiring the Tribunal to treat itself as bound by the policy in question).

[132] See, eg, *Minister for Immigration & Multicultural Affairs; ex parte Applicant S20/2002* (2003) 198 ALR 59, in which the High Court outflanked a statutory bar on using the *Wednesbury* ground of review.

[133] A reaction also often observed in the face of privative clauses; see Aronson, Groves and Weeks (n 2) [18.20].

[134] See ch 1 of this volume at […].

[135] *Plaintiff M61/2010E v Commonwealth of Australia* (2010) 243 CLR 319.

[136] *Plaintiff M70/2011* (n 5).

[137] See the cases cited at n 127 above.

[138] See Enid Campbell and Matthew Groves, 'Attacks on Judges Under Parliamentary Privilege: A Sorry Australian Episode' [2002] *Public Law* 626.

[139] *Mabo v The State of Queensland (No 2)* (1992) 175 CLR 1; *Wik Peoples v The State of Queensland* (1996) 187 CLR 1; see HP Lee and Enid Campbell, *The Australian Judiciary*, 2nd edn (Port Melbourne, Cambridge University Press, 2012) 71–74.

limited to conservative governments. The former Labor Prime Minister, Julia Gillard, and other Ministers reacted intemperately to the majority's decision on the 'Malaysia Solution' in *Plaintiff M70/2011*,[140] making negative personal comments about French CJ. As lamentable as some of the fissures between courts and politicians in migration and refugee matters have been, to some extent they simply reflect the modern political and legal importance of these policy areas. Similarly, to the extent that there have been other significant cases about migration or asylum matters,[141] this may in part be a function of the large number of *Migration Act* matters in federal courts, rather than evidence that the High Court is looking to make a point beyond the usual scope of judicial review.

When it comes to international law, Australian courts have long held that the validity of domestic legislation is not premised on its adherence to Australia's international obligations.[142] Recent amendments to Australia's migration laws have shown particular parliamentary disregard for such international obligations.[143] The Parliament has enacted legislation that is inconsistent with international treaties to which Australia is a party and taken steps that limit judicial recourse to international law in the process of statutory interpretation. The *Migration and Maritime Powers Legislation Amendment (Resolving the Asylum Legacy Caseload) Act 2014* ('*Legacy Caseload Act*') is an example of both actions. First, the Act amended the *Maritime Powers Act* to provide expressly that, inter alia, an authorised interception of asylum seekers at sea is not invalid under domestic law:

> (a) because of a failure to consider Australia's international obligations, or the international obligations or domestic law of any other country; or
> (b) because of a defective consideration of Australia's international obligations, or the international obligations or domestic law of any other country; or
> (c) because the exercise of the power is inconsistent with Australia's international obligations.[144]

A further change (that, to our knowledge, is unparalleled in the law of any other country) was the insertion of section 197C into the *Migration Act* which provides that Australia's *non-refoulement* obligations (obligations that prevent the removal of individuals to a risk of persecution or other serious harm) do not have to be considered prior to the removal of unlawful non-citizens under section 198. Sub-section 2 now provides:

> An officer's duty to remove as soon as reasonably practicable an unlawful non-citizen under section 198 arises irrespective of whether there has been an assessment, according to law, of Australia's non-refoulement obligations in respect of the non-citizen.

These amendments are inconsistent with Australia's obligations under international refugee law and human rights law to ensure that no individual is exposed to a well-founded fear of being persecuted or a real risk of being arbitrarily deprived of life or subjected to torture or cruel, inhuman or degrading treatment or punishment.[145]

[140] *Plaintiff M70/2011* (n 5).
[141] Eg, *Minister for Immigration and Citizenship v Li* (2013) 249 CLR 332.
[142] See discussion in Part II above.
[143] For analysis, see submissions by the Andrew & Renata Kaldor Centre for International Refugee Law on bills that were later enacted: www.kaldorcentre.unsw.edu.au/publications/131 accessed 2 May 2019.
[144] See *Maritime Powers Act*, ss 22A(1), 75A; see also s 75C.
[145] Australia's obligations derive from the Refugee Convention, art 33; Convention Against Torture, art 3; ICCPR, arts 6–7; and customary international law. See Guy S Goodwin-Gill and Jane McAdam, *The Refugee in International Law*, 3rd edn (Oxford, Oxford University Press, 2011) 285–86.

The *Legacy Caseload Act* also removed multiple references to the 1951 Refugee Convention from the *Migration Act*, notably in relation to the definition of 'refugee', which was previously drafted to conform with the Refugee Convention.[146] The amending Act instead introduced a 'new, independent and self-contained statutory framework which articulates *Australia's interpretation* of its protection obligations under the Refugees Convention'.[147] This was intended to ensure that the Australian Parliament would bear the responsibility for defining Australia's international obligations (rather, presumably, than the courts, having regard to international law). The Statement of Compatibility with Human Rights noted that a key concern was to establish:

> the Government's intended interpretation of a number of Refugees Convention-related concepts within domestic law when *more than one may be valid in international law, and where judicial interpretation of specific provisions has not been consistent with the Government's intended interpretations.*[148]

This is highly problematic in light of article 42 of the Refugee Convention, which prohibits any reservations to the refugee definition in article 1. Any backdoor attempt to codify the definition in a manner inconsistent with article 1 is contrary to international law.[149] Indeed, in contrast to the new Australian approach, Canada,[150] New Zealand[151] and the UK[152] all include specific references to the Convention definition of a refugee or transpose it directly in their relevant legislation.

These legislative actions have implications for the application of principles of statutory interpretation, discussed in Part II above. By insulating domestic law from Australia's treaty obligations and affirming that actions in violation of international law are nonetheless valid under Australian law, the amendments narrow the capacity of Australian courts to apply the interpretative presumption of consistency with international legal obligations. While at the domestic level, it is appropriate that courts give effect to clear statutory intention, this does not absolve Australia from violations of international law – including breaching its good faith obligations.[153]

Parliamentary efforts to quarantine domestic law from Australia's international obligations are also relevant to the global development of international refugee law. Common law appellate courts 'routinely engage in an ongoing and quite extraordinary transnational judicial conversation about the scope of the refugee definition, and have increasingly committed

[146] The previous provision read: 'a non-citizen in Australia in respect of whom the Minister is satisfied Australia has protection obligations under the Refugees Convention as amended by the Refugees Protocol': see former s 36(2)(a) in *Migration Act 1958*, Compilation No 118.

[147] 2013–2014, The Parliament of the Commonwealth of Australia, House of Representatives, 'Migration and Maritime Powers Legislation Amendment (Resolving the Asylum Legacy Caseload) Bill 2014: Explanatory Memorandum', 10 (emphasis added). See, eg, *Migration Act*, ss 5H, 5J, 5K, 5L, 36(2)(a).

[148] Explanatory Memorandum (n 147), Attachment A, 'Statement of Compatibility with Human Rights', 28 (emphasis added).

[149] VCLT, arts 26, 27, 31(1).

[150] *Immigration and Refugee Protection Act* (S.C. 2001, c. 27) (Canada) ss 95(1)(a), 96.

[151] *Immigration Act 2009* (NZ), s 129(1).

[152] *Immigration and Asylum Act 1999* (UK), ss 167(1), 82(1), 94(1).

[153] VCLT, arts 26, 46. Further, the conduct of a judicial organ is considered an act of state under international law: International Law Commission Articles on the Responsibility of States for Internationally Wrongful Acts, annexed to UNGA Resolution 56/83 (12 December 2001) art 4; James Crawford, *Brownlie's Principles of Public International Law*, 8th edn (Oxford, Oxford University Press 2012) 540, 548–49; *Jurisdictional Immunities of the State (Germany v Italy; Greece Intervening)*, Judgment, ICJ Rep [2012] 99, 154–155.

themselves to find common ground'.[154] In the absence of domestic precedent they often look to comparative jurisprudence for guidance,[155] and to the scholarship of leading academics in the field.[156] As Kirby J has observed, 'the search for a uniform and, if possible, consistent and international approach to the meaning of a part of the definition of "refugee" in the Convention is desirable'.[157] Moves to insulate Australia's domestic law from well-established interpretations of states' international legal obligations restricts courts' ability to partake in this conversation, denuding both Australian jurisprudence and the organic, transnational development of international refugee law as a whole.

Although avenues for considering international materials in the course of statutory interpretation have narrowed, some have argued that possibilities for the protection of rights remain inherent in the common law methods of statutory interpretation, citing, for example, the 'presumption against interference with fundamental rights' and the 'principle of legality'.[158] However, the protection afforded by these rights is weakened by Australia's lack of an enforceable bill or charter of rights. The principle of legality, for example, requires only that a legislature use express and clear words before it can validly infringe on a fundamental right.[159] It has been justified on the basis 'that Parliament must squarely confront what it is doing and accept the political cost' before infringing on fundamental common law rights.[160] The reality in Australia is that 'few principles or rights can claim to be so fundamental that it is unlikely that the legislature would want to change them'.[161] If it is within the legislative power of an Australian Parliament to infringe upon fundamental rights, the protection against it doing so is likely to be political rather than judicial. The High Court has preserved its authority to review administrative action under section 75(v) of the Constitution against attempted legislative encroachments, whether in the form of privative clauses,[162] procedural limitations that have the practical effect of impairing its review function,[163] or other attempts to 'deny[] to a court exercising jurisdiction under, or derived from, section 75(v) the ability to enforce the limits which Parliament has expressly or impliedly set on the decision-making power which Parliament has conferred on the officer'.[164] However, while

[154] James C Hathaway, *The Rights of Refugees under International Law* (Cambridge, Cambridge University Press, 2005) 1–2 (footnotes omitted).

[155] Ibid, 116.

[156] Hugo Storey, 'The Advanced Refugee Law Workshop Experience: An IARLJ Perspective' (2003) 15 *International Journal of Refugee Law* 422, 423.

[157] *Applicant A* (n 38) 296 (Kirby J, dissenting). See also his Honour's dissent in *QAAH* (n 54) 21; Guy S Goodwin-Gill, 'The Search for the One, True Meaning …' in Guy S Goodwin-Gill and Hélène Lambert (eds), *The Limits of Transnational Law: Refugee Law, Policy Harmonization and Judicial Dialogue in the European Union* (Cambridge University Press, Cambridge 2010).

[158] See Matthew Zagor, 'Adventures in the Grey Zone: Constitutionalism, Rights and the Review of Executive Power in the Migration Context' in John Bell and Marie-Luce Paris (eds), *Rights-Based Constitutional Review: Constitutional Courts in a Changing Landscape* (Cheltenham, Edward Elgar, 2016) 185.

[159] See, eg, *Potter v Minahan* (1908) 7 CLR 277, 304 (O'Connor J); *Coco v R* (1994) 179 CLR 427, 437 (Mason CJ, Brennan, Gaudron, McHugh JJ); *Saeed v Minister for Immigration and Citizenship* (2010) 241 CLR 252, 259 (French CJ, Gummow, Hayne, Crennan and Kiefel JJ). See also Matthew Groves, 'The Principle of Legality and Administrative Discretion: A New Name for an Old Approach?' in Matthew Groves and Dan Meagher (eds), *The Principle of Legality in Australia and New Zealand* (Annandale, Federation Press, 2016) 168.

[160] *R v Secretary of State for the Home Department; ex parte Simms* [2000] 2 AC 115, 131 (Lord Hoffmann).

[161] *Malika Holdings Pty Ltd v Stretton* (2001) 204 CLR 290, 298 (McHugh J).

[162] See *Plaintiff S157/2002* (n 46) 513–14 (Gaudron, McHugh, Gummow, Kirby and Hayne JJ).

[163] See *Bodruddaza v Minister for Immigration and Multicultural Affairs* (2007) 228 CLR 651, 671–72 (Gleeson CJ, Gummow, Kirby, Hayne, Heydon and Crennan JJ).

[164] See *Graham v Minister for Immigration and Border Protection* (2017) 91 ALJR 890, 902 (Kiefel CJ, Bell, Gageler, Keane, Nettle and Gordon JJ)).

the capacity for judicial review is safeguarded, the substance of that review may be limited where Parliament has expressed a clear intention to act in contravention of Australia's international obligations. As Burton Crawford has noted, 'the justice or otherwise of executive action ultimately depends in substantial part upon the laws that Parliament chooses to enact'.[165]

VI. Conclusion

The field of migration and refugee law seems destined to remain a political football in years to come, engaging significant public and parliamentary attention. This chapter has sought to chart the prospects for administrative and judicial review in this field under Australian domestic law. In the administrative sphere, the establishment of the IAA demonstrates an appetite to limit the opportunity for review afforded to a certain class of applicants. Those seeking judicial review of decisions in this field are also faced with the gulf that has emerged between the robust human rights obligations that bind Australia on the international level and its domestic legislation. The absence of a domestic human rights framework, coupled with a legislature eager to insulate Australia's domestic law from its international legal obligations, reduces courts' capacity to analyse and reflect Australia's international law obligations in the process of statutory construction. Greater consistency between Australia's domestic and international obligations may ultimately only be achieved through legislative amendment, led by changes in the inclinations both of politicians and the polity.

[165] Lisa Burton Crawford, 'Expanding the Entrenched Minimum Provision of Judicial Review? *Graham v Minister for Immigration and Border Protection*' (2017) 28 *Public Law Review* 282, 288.

18

Proportionality and the New Postwar Juridical Paradigm: A Challenge to Australian Exceptionalism?

SHIPRA CHORDIA

I. Introduction

Australian constitutional law is often described as exceptional. It is said to defy the trends and principles of other common law jurisdictions, and this is generally attributed to Australia's relatively unique constitutional framework. This chapter examines the ways in which Australian courts borrow from constitutional developments in overseas jurisdictions, as well as the structural and cultural limits on their ability to do so. It undertakes this analysis against the backdrop of the emergence of what has been described as a new 'postwar juridical paradigm' of human rights protection. The chapter examines recent cases engaging with what would be considered substantive 'rights' in other jurisdictions and considers the nature and degree of the High Court's engagement with the postwar juridical paradigm in these contexts. From there, it draws conclusions for the future of Australian exceptionalism and judicially-led constitutional rights protection.

II. Australian Exceptionalism

There are two discernible strands to the notion of 'Australian exceptionalism'. The first is doctrinal and static: it frames Australia's exceptional status as derived from the obvious fact that Australia does not have a judicially-enforceable, national bill of rights, and is therefore exceptional amongst English-speaking democracies.[1] As is well known, the writings of AV Dicey persuaded the framers of the Australian Constitution that their faith ought to be placed in parliamentary democracy and the ordinary common law as the primary protectors of individual rights. Any fettering of those powers by a bill of rights

[1] Brian Galligan and F.L. (Ted) Morton, 'Australian Exceptionalism: Rights Protection Without a Bill of Rights' in Tom Campbell, Jeffrey Goldsworthy and Adrienne Stone (eds), *Protecting rights without a Bill of Rights: Institutional performance and reform in Australia* (Aldershot, Ashgate, 2006) 17, 18.

would hand decision-making powers to unelected, and therefore unrepresentative and unaccountable, institutions, tempting the hand of tyranny. Under this influence, the overwhelming focus of the framers in drafting the Australian Constitution was to design a structure of government through which power might be distributed and exercised. To the extent that the framers were also influenced by federalist ideals emanating from the US, these did not manifest in any great desire to incorporate a bill of rights, albeit that there was some tortured debate regarding the inclusion of a due process clause equivalent to the Fourteenth Amendment which led to certain heavily diluted protections entering the draft. Overall, however, and in distinct contrast to most postwar constitutions, it has often been observed that the Australian Constitution is, as a consequence, 'a prosaic document expressed in lawyer's language'[2] and that it is devoid of 'grand declarations of national values or aspirations'.[3]

The obvious qualification to the observations just made is that the Australian Constitution does contain a small number of judicially-enforceable individual rights which operate as limits on government power, including in relation to religious freedom (section 116), a right to jury trial (section 80), freedom from discrimination based on state of origin (section 117) and the expropriation of property on just terms (section 51(xxxi)). These express rights have been supplemented by the product of the partial 'rights revolution'[4] that took place in the early 1990s, in the form of the judicial recognition of an implied freedom of political communication. Notwithstanding, most of the rights said to have some textual foundation in the Australian Constitution, including those that appear to be most analogous to civil rights found in other jurisdictions, such as sections 80 and 116, have been given a narrow interpretation by the High Court.[5] The overwhelming majority of constitutional cases decided in Australia deal not with matters directly related to civil and political rights but with structural limits on government power. While there may be secondary impacts on individual rights as a consequence of these decisions, and a general protective effect when structural limits are placed on exercises of power,[6] value considerations do not ordinarily play a leading role in the way in which cases are argued or decided.[7] It is generally not contested that the 'great rights victories' which have been achieved through judicial enforcement of entrenched constitutional rights in other jurisdictions have largely been achieved

[2] Sir Anthony Mason, 'The Australian Constitution in Retrospect and Prospect' in Robert French, Geoffrey Lindell and Cheryl Saunders (eds), *Reflections on the Australian Constitution* (Annandale, Federation Press, 2003) 8.

[3] Jeffrey Goldsworthy, 'Australian Exceptionalism' in Tom Campbell, Jeffrey Goldsworthy and Adrienne Stone (eds), *Protecting rights without a Bill of Rights: Institutional performance and reform in Australia* (Aldershot, Ashgate, 2006) 1.

[4] Brian Galligan and F L (Ted) Morton, 'Australian Exceptionalism: Rights Protection Without a Bill of Rights' in Tom Campbell, Jeffrey Goldsworthy and Adrienne Stone (eds), *Protecting rights without a Bill of Rights: Institutional performance and reform in Australia* (Aldershot, Ashgate, 2006) 17, 19.

[5] In relation to s 80, the High Court has held that its protection is not applicable in circumstances where it has been legislatively provided that an offence is to be tried summarily rather than on indictment: *R v Archdall & Roskruge* (1928) 41 CLR 128. With respect to s 116, it has been held that the provision does not limit the making of laws which would prohibit any hinderance with a war effort: *Adelaide Company of Jehovah's Witnesses Inc v Commonwealth* (1943) 67 CLR 116; nor does it limit the capacity of the federal government to fund religious schools: *Attorney-General (Vic); Ex rel Black v Commonwealth (DOGS case)* (1981) 146 CLR 559.

[6] Fiona Wheeler, 'Due Process, Chapter III and the New High Court' (2004) 32 *Federal Law Review* 205.

[7] Cheryl Saunders and Adrienne Stone, 'Reference to Foreign Precedents by the Australian High Court: A Matter of Method' in Tania Groppi and Marie-Claire Ponthoreau (eds), *The Use of Foreign Precedents by Constitutional Judges* (Oxford, Hart Publishing, 2013) 13, 14.

through political and democratic forces in Australia, particularly through legislative and administrative decision-making.[8]

The relative success of traditional Diceyan ideals in Australia, or perhaps just an 'excessive veneration of the Constitution's framers',[9] has meant that Australians have remained sceptical regarding the adoption of a bill of rights.[10] This in turn has given rise to the second strand of 'Australian exceptionalism': an ongoing cultural resistance to the adoption of a federal constitutional rights mechanism, including by means of novel judicial interpretation of the existing constitutional instrument. The spirit of restraint engendered in the structure and language of the Australian Constitution has passed into the wider legal discourse in the form of widespread acceptance of 'strict and complete legalism' and a broadly unsympathetic attitude towards claims that seek to expand recognition of individual rights beyond the strict textual confines of legal instruments. This strand of Australian exceptionalism is, in modern times, particularly notable as it persists despite international trends favouring strong judicial participation in the global project of human rights protection and increasing levels of transjudicial dialogue on matters concerning those rights.[11] It also has a dynamic quality to it, exhibiting not just in a straight judicial unwillingness to decide cases on rights grounds, but also in a more subtle 'reluctance to embrace foreign authority … despite what often appear to be similar human rights goals'.[12] Indeed, it is for this very reason that parts of the Australian judiciary have been criticised for rejecting the relevance of foreign precedents in human rights cases too readily.[13] On this score, Australian exceptionalism has something in common with the more prominent phenomenon of 'American exceptionalism'.[14] Both are said to take the form of an antagonism to foreign judgments as aids to construing the national constitution.[15]

In other ways, however, Australian exceptionalism is not nearly as extreme as its American counterpart. Indeed, although they have been reluctant, Australian courts – and particularly the High Court – have never been as dismissive of foreign sources as courts in the US, albeit that the degree of engagement and use to which those sources are put may vary considerably from judge to judge and case to case. It has been suggested that the use

[8] Brian Galligan and F.L. (Ted) Morton, 'Australian Exceptionalism: Rights Protection Without a Bill of Rights' in Tom Campbell, Jeffrey Goldsworthy and Adrienne Stone (eds), *Protecting rights without a Bill of Rights: Institutional performance and reform in Australia* (Aldershot, Ashgate, 2006) 17, 19.

[9] Bruce Stone and Nicholas Barry, 'Constitutional Design and Australian Exceptionalism in the Adoption of National Bill of Rights' (2014) 47 *Canadian Journal of Political Science* 767, 768.

[10] There is some suggestion that this scepticism may be more pronounced within the Australian political class than in the population as a whole: see Edward Santow, 'The Act that Dares Not to Speak its Name: The National Human Rights Consultation Report's Parallel Roads to Human Rights Reform' (2010) 33 *University of New South Wales Law Journal* 8, 8–9.

[11] Cheryl Saunders and Adrienne Stone, 'Reference to Foreign Precedents by the Australian High Court: A Matter of Method' in Tania Groppi and Marie-Claire Ponthoreau (eds), *The Use of Foreign Precedents by Constitutional Judges* (Oxford, Hart Publishing, 2013) 13.

[12] Ibid, 13, 38.

[13] Ibid, 13, 24.

[14] See, for example, Harold Hongju Koh, 'Foreward – On American Exceptionalism' (2003) 55 *Standford Law Review* 1479; Lorraine Weinrib, 'The postwar paradigm and American exceptionalism' in Sujit Choudhry, *The Migration of Constitutional Ideas* (Cambridge, Cambridge University Press, 2006) 84.

[15] Michael Kirby, 'Citation of Foreign Decisions in Constitutional Adjudication: The Relevance of the Democratic Deficit' (2009) 43 *Suffolk University Law Review* 117, 118.

of comparative analysis exists on a spectrum, ranging from 'soft' to 'hard' use.[16] At the 'soft use' end of the spectrum, Australian courts have referred to foreign sources in a variety of ways, including through passing reference and in empirically informing the development of otherwise purely domestic doctrine.[17] Somewhat more controversially, in what has been described as more of a 'hard' or direct use,[18] courts have referred to comparative constitutional law to highlight both similarities and differences with other systems and have incorporated these comparisons into their interpretation of the Australian Constitution.

At a general level, the greater the strength of the analogy between the textual foundation for a foreign law source and an equivalent Australian source, the greater the propensity of Australian courts to rely on foreign judgments directly as a source of guidance for interpretation. Thus, for example, in finding a basis for implying into the Australian Constitution a freedom of political communication, Mason CJ referred in *Australian Capital Television Pty Ltd v Commonwealth* to a similar jurisprudential turn taken by the Supreme Court of Canada in interpreting the *British North America Act 1867*.[19] While the existence of that Canadian precedent was not the only matter relied upon in reasoning towards the implication, it nonetheless provided some comfort in adopting such an approach in the Australian context.[20] On the other hand, when it came to deciding whether there was an analogy between US approaches to defamation on the basis of the First Amendment and Australian defamation laws in light of the implied freedom of political communication, the High Court was swift and unanimous in its dismissal of the relevance of American jurisprudence.[21] While the American version was a free-standing right recognised by the American Bill of Rights, the Australian freedom was characterised as merely a limitation on legislative and executive power.[22]

The strength of the perceived analogy between the just terms guarantee in section 51(xxxi) of the Australian Constitution and the 'taking' clause in the Constitution of the US has, likewise, been a relevant consideration in the High Court's determination of the appropriateness of drawing upon American jurisprudence. In *ICM Agriculture v Commonwealth*,[23] for example, French CJ, Gummow and Crennan JJ distinguished between the 'acquisition' of property on just terms under section 51(xxxi) from the US notion of a 'taking' of property on the basis that the latter could encompass the destruction of property while the former could not.[24] By contrast, Heydon J referred to the Fifth Amendment as having analogous operation to section 51(xxxi). His Honour offered a philosophically-grounded basis for the conclusion, suggesting that '[l]ike the Fifth Amendment to the *United States Constitution*, s 51(xxxi) has the effect of barring "Government from forcing

[16] Cheryl Saunders, 'Use and Misuse of Comparative Constitutional Law' (2006) 13 *Indiana Journal of Global Legal Studies* 37, 52.

[17] Ibid.

[18] Ibid.

[19] *Australian Capital Television Pty Limited v Commonwealth* (1992) 177 CLR 106, 140 (Mason CJ).

[20] *Australian Capital Television Pty Limited v Commonwealth* (1992) 177 CLR 106, 141 (Mason CJ). Ultimately, however, the Canadian implied freedom of speech was found to be 'more extensive as to subject matter' than the implied freedom identified in the Australian Constitution, which was limited to political communication rather than all speech.

[21] *Lange v Australian Broadcasting Corporation* (1997) 189 CLR 520, 560.

[22] Ibid, 563.

[23] (2009) 240 CLR 140.

[24] *ICM Agriculture v Commonwealth* (2009) 240 CLR 140, 179 [81].

some people alone to bear public burdens which, in all fairness and justice, should be borne by the public as a whole'".[25]

The role that analogous reasoning has played in setting comfort levels with respect to drawing constitutional comparisons with other jurisdictions has also spilled into the High Court's interpretive approach towards quasi-constitutional instruments, such as state-level charters of rights. In construing the Victorian Charter of Rights in *Momcilovic v the Queen*, for example, French CJ affirmed that the courts were free to refer to foreign judgments when interpreting domestic legislation only 'where they have logical or analogical relevance'.[26] Along those lines, Gummow J formed the view that limited reliance could be placed on the 'human rights systems' of the UK, Canada, South Africa, New Zealand and Hong Kong as they presented only 'imperfect analogues' to the Victorian Charter.[27]

III. The Postwar Juridical Paradigm of Human Rights Protection

How a particular constitutional right or freedom is treated by reference to the strength of the analogy with similar provisions in constitutions of other jurisdictions is, however, a rather blunt instrument for assessing the degree of judicial engagement in Australia with the global rights phenomenon, particularly when it comes to interaction with more subtle adjudicative trends. As Cheryl Saunders has observed, analysing the use of comparative constitutional sources in this way 'does not fully capture the complexity of the use of foreign experience by courts'.[28] Moreover, it fails to engage with the increasing sophistication of the postwar rights paradigm, which was in its early period shaped largely through the express words of constitutional rights instruments but has in the decades since gathered considerable nuance through layers of judicial interpretation and the application of interpretive methodology. Against this background, Lorraine Weinrib has described the emergence of a new paradigm in postwar constitutional law which extends beyond the hard text of constitutional instruments. Weinrib explains the paradigm as a shared constitutional conception which 'transcends the history, cultural heritage and social mores of any particular nation state', with the 'remedial purpose of building the primacy of equal citizenship and inherent human dignity into the basic structure of liberal democracy'.[29]

In the arena of judicial review, Weinrib considers that the paradigm proceeds in two stages of analysis. In the first, the onus falls on a person seeking to challenge a law to show that the law infringes a constitutionally protected right. At the second stage, the state is given the opportunity to show that even though a right has, prima facie, been infringed, the infringement is nonetheless justified.[30] The justification process, Weinrib argues, cannot be

[25] *ICM Agriculture v Commonwealth* (2009) 240 CLR 140, 209 [178].

[26] *Momcilovic v The Queen* (2011) 245 CLR 1, 36 [18].

[27] Ibid, 83–84 [146].

[28] Cheryl Saunders, 'Use and Misuse of Comparative Constitutional Law' (2006) 13 *Indiana Journal of Global Legal Studies* 37, 51.

[29] Lorraine Weinrib, 'The postwar paradigm and American exceptionalism' in Sujit Choudhry (ed), *The Migration of Constitutional Ideas* (Cambridge, Cambridge University Press, 2006) 84, 90.

[30] Ibid, 93.

satisfied through a bare assertion of political authority, fidelity to conservative social values or by pleading financial constraints. Rather, the justification process 'requires connection to the core constitutional principles through a sequence of analytic steps that maintain the primacy of the constitutional principles, even when particular crystallization of these principles must cede'.[31] The justification process proceeds through a staged analytical process now commonly known as 'structured proportionality'.

What is notable about the new postwar juridical paradigm is that it is not fixated on the promulgation of notions of substantive universality. Rather, the paradigm accepts that constitutional principles flourish in a diverse matrix of historical, social and cultural contexts and thus 'different legal systems will produce different results'.[32] The focus is instead on decision-making methods which promote judicial participation in a dynamic constitutional process of reasoning and justification. In this way, the postwar paradigm encourages a form of judicial dialogue with the other branches of government, coaxing constitutional courts to adjudge the legitimacy of exercises of power not merely at the level of bare authority but by the more sophisticated standard of the strength of the justification behind it. Although judicial review may continue to police the outer boundaries of legislative authority, within those boundaries the relationship of accountability between the legislature and the people is enhanced by the encouragement of explanation and rationalisation for exercises of power, described by some as a shift from a culture of authority to a culture of justification.[33] The nature and degree of engagement by Australian courts with this new postwar juridical paradigm, which is not attached to any particular form of rights expression, has the potential to tell us something deeper about the contemporary culture of exceptionalism in Australia.

IV. Freedom of Political Communication

The high level, two-staged justification process that makes up the postwar juridical paradigm is not unfamiliar to Australian lawyers in at least one area of constitutional law. The two stages Weinrib describes mirror precisely the two limbs of analysis that the High Court unanimously declared relevant in *Lange v Australian Broadcasting Corporation*[34] to deciding cases engaging the implied freedom of political communication.[35] The first limb is directed at the question of whether a law effectively burdens the implied freedom of political communication such as to engage the court's oversight jurisdiction. The second limb asks whether the law is justified, in the sense that it can be shown to be appropriate and adapted to serve a legitimate end the fulfilment of which is compatible with the maintenance of the constitutionally prescribed system of representative and responsible government found in the Australian Constitution.[36] It might be unsurprising, then, to observe that since the

[31] Ibid, 96.
[32] Ibid, 91.
[33] Etienne Mureinik, 'A Bridge to Where? Introducing the Interim Bill of Rights' (1994) 10 *South African Journal of Human Rights* 31, 32; David Dyzenhaus, 'Law as Justification: Etienne Mureinik's Conception of Legal Culture' (1998) 14 *South African Journal of Human Rights* 11.
[34] (1997) 189 CLR 520.
[35] *Lange v Australian Broadcasting Corporation* (1997) 189 CLR 520, 562 (Brennan CJ, Dawson, Toohey, Gaudron, McHugh, Gummow and Kirby JJ).
[36] *Lange v Australian Broadcasting Corporation* (1997) 189 CLR 520, 567. See also, *Coleman v Power* (2004) 220 CLR 1, 50 [93], 51 [95]–[96] (McHugh J); 78 [196] (Gummow and Hayne JJ).

earliest cases on the implied freedom, references have been made to a generalised notion of 'reasonable proportionality' as having relevance in this area,[37] and the Court in *Lange* itself acknowledged that its analytical method could be referred to as 'proportionality'.[38] What is more puzzling, however, is that the decision in *Lange* came about as a settlement of a disagreement within the High Court as to the best approach towards the newly implied freedom. In *Lange*, the High Court unanimously endorsed a narrow view of the implied freedom expressed by McHugh J in earlier cases[39] as being a freedom that could be derived strictly from the 'terms' of the Constitution only. Thus, while on one hand the Court had adopted one of the hallmark jurisprudential features of the postwar juridical paradigm, on the other hand it had also accepted that the text of the Australian Constitution would be paramount to limiting the scope of the freedom that was to be the subject of that analysis. It seems logical to conclude that this latter concession must have been made under the influence of the culture of exceptionalism, for the Australian Constitution is sparse in its indication of a textual foundation for the implied freedom. Its effect was to limit the use to which proportionality analysis was put, in any structured sense, in implied freedom cases that followed.[40]

More recent developments in this area have, to some degree, realigned the trajectory set by the decision in *Lange* while maintaining fidelity to the doctrinal framework the case established. In *Monis v The Queen*,[41] Hayne J made passing reference to the view that the second limb of *Lange* could be addressed by adopting tests of structured proportionality.[42] Similarly, Crennan, Kiefel and Bell JJ observed that the words 'reasonably appropriate and adapted' in the second limb of *Lange* were interchangeable with proportionality.[43] Their Honours developed the notion further by observing that *Lange* involved the application of 'a series of different inquiries'[44] involving both an assessment of a relationship of reasonable necessity between a law and the end it is seeking to pursue and an evaluation of the 'extent of the restriction imposed upon political communication'.[45] These inquiries, Crennan, Kiefel and Bell JJ declared, involved proportionality analysis.[46] In *Tajjour v New South Wales*,[47] the High Court was faced with submissions from the parties that the *Lange* test did not 'raise notions of suitability, necessity and strict proportionality as understood in other jurisdictions'[48] and that application of suitability and strict proportionality from 'European jurisprudence' would be 'problematic in Australia'.[49] Notwithstanding, Crennan,

[37] *Nationwide News Pty Ltd v Wills* (1992) 177 CLR 1, 30–31 (Mason CJ).

[38] *Lange v Australian Broadcasting Corporation* (1997) 189 CLR 520, 562 (Brennan CJ, Dawson, Toohey, Gaudron, McHugh, Gummow and Kirby JJ).

[39] In *McGinty v Western Australia* (1996) 186 CLR 140, for example, McHugh J had criticised the majority approach to the implied freedom which had been taken in *Theophanous v Herald & Weekly Times Ltd* (1994) 182 CLR 104 and *Stephens v West Australian Newspapers Ltd* (1994) 182 CLR 211 as leading to a situation in which 'the text and structure of the Constitution have receded into the background and it is the concept of representative democracy, not the text or structure of the Constitution, that governs the application of the Constitution in such cases': at 234.

[40] Leslie Zines, *The High Court and the Constitution*, 5th edn (Annandale, Federation Press, 2008) 61–62.

[41] (2013) 249 CLR 92.

[42] *Monis v The Queen* (2013) 249 CLR 92, 153 [144].

[43] Ibid, 193 [278] (Crennan, Kiefel and Bell JJ).

[44] Ibid, 193 [279] (Crennan, Kiefel and Bell JJ).

[45] Ibid, 194 [282] (Crennan, Kiefel and Bell JJ).

[46] Ibid, 193 [278] (Crennan, Kiefel and Bell JJ).

[47] *Tajjour v New South Wales* (2014) 254 CLR 508, 570–71 [110]–[116] (Crennan, Kiefel and Bell JJ).

[48] Ibid, 523 (Solicitor-General for the State of South Australia).

[49] Ibid, 528–29 (Solicitor-General for the State of Victoria).

Kiefel and Bell JJ described proportionality analysis as 'central to the second limb of the *Lange* test',[50] and applied the suitability and necessity tests.[51]

By 2015, momentum had built and in *McCloy v New South Wales*[52] a majority of the High Court, consisting of French CJ, Kiefel, Bell and Keane JJ, accepted that the second limb in *Lange* was answerable by the application of structured proportionality analysis.[53] *McCloy* concerned a challenge to New South Wales legislation – the *Election Funding, Expenditure and Disclosures Act 1981* (NSW) – which made it unlawful for prohibited donors, including property developers,[54] to make political donations.[55] The legislative amendments also placed a cap on donations[56] and restricted indirect campaign contributions.[57] The plaintiffs, most of whom were property developers within the meaning of the Act, argued in the High Court's original jurisdiction that the laws impermissibly burdened the implied freedom of political communication and were invalid. The Court disagreed, upholding the validity of the donation caps and restrictions on indirect campaign contributions unanimously and the validity of the prohibition on political donations from property developers by a 6-1 majority.

The majority judgment variously referred to the jurisprudence and commentary from Germany, Canada, the UK as well as international literature,[58] before settling on a version of proportionality which in its view was appropriately modified to suit Australian constitutional constraints. The approach can be contrasted with the altogether more cautious treatment given to foreign sources in the development of implied freedom jurisprudence in some earlier cases.[59] In applying the structured proportionality test, French CJ, Kiefel, Bell and Keane JJ adopted three stages of analysis broadly synonymous with the way structured proportionality is applied in most comparative jurisdictions.[60] Under the first stage of suitability testing, the Court inquired whether the impugned law had a rational connection with the purpose of the provision. Under the second stage of necessity testing, the Court asked whether there was an obvious and compelling, reasonably practicable alternative which could achieve the purpose of the impugned law with a less restrictive effect on the implied freedom. Finally, under the 'adequate in its balance test' – which is generally known in other jurisdictions as strict proportionality – the Court considered whether the importance of the purpose served by the impugned law was balanced when regard was had to the extent

[50] Ibid, 570 [110] (Crennan, Kiefel and Bell JJ).

[51] Ibid, 570–71 [110]–[116] (Crennan, Kiefel and Bell JJ).

[52] (2015) 257 CLR 178.

[53] *McCloy v New South Wales* (2015) 257 CLR 178, 194–5 [2] (French CJ, Kiefel, Bell and Keane JJ). The other part is 'compatibility testing', which is outside the scope of this chapter but which I have previously critiqued here: Shipra Chordia, 'Proportionality and McCloy v New South Wales: close but not quite?' on AUSPUBLAW (1 March 2016).

[54] As defined in s 96GB of the *Election Funding, Expenditure and Disclosures Act 1981* (NSW).

[55] *Election Funding, Expenditure and Disclosures Act 1981* (NSW), Pt 6, Div 4A.

[56] Ibid, Pt 6, Div 2A.

[57] Ibid, 96E.

[58] *McCloy v New South Wales* (2015) 257 CLR 178, 216–17 [74], [77]–[82] (French CJ, Kiefel, Bell and Keane JJ).

[59] *Theophanous v Herald & Weekly Times Limited* (1994) 182 CLR 104, 125.

[60] See, generally, Aharon Barak, *Proportionality: Constitutional Rights and their Limitations* (Cambridge, Cambridge University Press, 2012) 303–70; *Rowe v Electoral Commissioner* (2010) 243 CLR 1, 140 [460] (Kiefel J). Some jurisdictions also have a preliminary stage called 'proper purpose': 245–298. The functional purpose of this test is reflected in the High Court's 'compatibility testing': *McCloy v New South Wales* (2015) 257 CLR 178, 194 [2], [31]–[53] (French CJ, Kiefel, Bell and Keane JJ).

of the restriction imposed on the implied freedom.[61] Application of this last test explicitly required a value judgment, as acknowledged by the justices reasoning jointly in *McCloy*.[62]

On the surface, the majority's acceptance of structured proportionality appeared to signal the beginning of a new era of engagement with the postwar juridical paradigm in Australian constitutional law. Indeed, the justification given by the majority for adopting structured proportionality was in part an acceptance of the method's wider systemic influence in developing a culture of justification and increased 'dialogue' between branches of government. In this regard, French CJ, Kiefel, Bell and Keane J observed that the structured nature of proportionality analysis 'assists members of the legislature, those advising the legislature, and those drafting legislative materials, to understand how the sufficiency of the justification for a legislative restriction on freedom will be tested'.[63] The joint justices also openly acknowledged that the last stage of structured proportionality – strict proportionality – would require a balancing exercise, or value judgment, that would engage directly with the importance of the implied freedom and the reason for its existence.[64] Such an approach would, inevitably, involve deeper engagement with the philosophical foundations of Australia's constitutional system in a manner that would take the Court well beyond the bounds of the bare text of the instrument itself. If applied robustly, it would strike at the heart of much of the restraint that informs and sustains the culture of Australian exceptionalism. Nonetheless, it would be misleading not to observe the majority's extreme caution in developing the jurisprudence in the manner that they did in *McCloy*. The joint justices' hesitations were manifest in a number of areas of their reasoning. The first was in the majority's insistence that the development of the jurisprudence in this direction was nothing more than a derivation of the principles established in *Lange*.[65] It was not an explicit act of methodological 'borrowing' or an overt acceptance of the methodological approaches taken in other jurisdictions. The second was in applying a restrained standard in the application of the necessity test such that the Court would only examine alternatives that were 'obvious and compelling'. In the majority's view, the restraint was necessary to ensure that the courts did not 'exceed their constitutional competence by substituting their own legislative judgments for those of parliaments'.[66] The third was in declaring that, although they had accepted that strict proportionality as a part of the inquiries that make up proportionality, it would not 'assume particular significance' when applied by the High Court.[67] In effect, the majority were conceding that much of the benefit to be gained through an express adoption of structured proportionality was to be forfeited at the hands of an overriding need for judicial restraint.

In contrast to the majority's more subtle concessions, a strident reassertion of the culture of exceptionalism was palpable in some of the individual judgments. Justice Gordon, for example, explicitly rejected what she described as the majority's 'automatic adoption or application of forms of legal analysis made in overseas constitutional contexts'.[68] Her

[61] *McCloy v New South Wales* (2015) 257 CLR 178, 195 [2] (French CJ, Kiefel, Bell and Keane JJ).
[62] Ibid.
[63] *McCloy v New South Wales* (2015) 257 CLR 178, 216 [74] (French CJ, Kiefel, Bell and Keane JJ).
[64] *McCloy v New South Wales* (2015) 257 CLR 178, 219 [88] (French CJ, Kiefel, Bell and Keane JJ).
[65] Ibid, 196 [4], 214 [70] (French CJ, Kiefel, Bell and Keane JJ).
[66] Ibid, 211 [58] (French CJ, Kiefel, Bell and Keane JJ).
[67] Ibid, 219 [88] (French CJ, Kiefel, Bell and Keane JJ).
[68] Ibid, 288 [339] (Gordon J).

Honour's view was that the kind of analyses represented by the postwar paradigm, including proportionality, 'reflect the context in which they are made' and were therefore designed for different purposes to those underpinning the principles established by *Lange*.[69] In dismissing the relevance of proportionality, Gordon J cited the following passage from Gleeson CJ in *Roach v Electoral Commissioner*:[70]

> There is a danger that uncritical translation of the concept of proportionality from [other] legal context[s] … to the Australian context could lead to the application in this country of a constitutionally inappropriate standard of judicial review of legislative action. Human rights instruments which declare in general terms a right, such as a right to vote, and then permit legislation in derogation of that right, but only in the case of a legitimate objective pursued by means that are no more than necessary to accomplish that objective, and give a court the power to decide whether a certain derogation is permissible, confer a wider power of judicial review than that ordinarily applied under our Constitution. They create a relationship between legislative and judicial power significantly different from that reflected in the Australian Constitution.

Justice Gageler similarly cited passages of Gleeson CJ from *Mulholland v Australian Electoral Commission*,[71] where the Chief Justice had observed that, while the advantage of proportionality was that 'it is commonly used in other jurisdictions in similar fields of discourse', its disadvantage was that in the course of such use, it had 'taken on elaborations that vary in context and that may be imported sub silentio into a different context without explanation'.[72] In an apparent dig at the majority's approach, Gageler J dismissed the need to discuss the merits of the importation of a 'prescriptive form of proportionality analysis drawn from that which has come to be applied in relation to the *Canadian Charter of Rights and Freedoms* and the European Convention on Human Rights'.[73]

The concerns regarding the deployment of structured proportionality in a non-rights context continued in the next case in which the High Court was faced with a challenge to legislative action based on the implied freedom: *Brown v Tasmania*.[74] While, once again, a majority of the High Court accepted and applied structured proportionality in their reasoning, Gageler J declared that he did not find it 'to be a particularly useful tool'[75] and in support of that conclusion, made the observation that the structure of the analysis was not 'tailored to the constitutional freedom of political communication, which is not concerned with rights'.[76] A connection between constitutional rights jurisprudence and the appropriateness of structured proportionality analysis, particularly at the last strict balancing stage, was also made by Gordon J. Her Honour observed, that '[u]nlike other countries in which "balancing" has been used, Australia does not have a Bill of Rights. The implied freedom of political communication is not a personal right.'[77] The concerns expressed by these justices arguably overlook important aspects of the postwar juridical paradigm.

[69] Ibid.
[70] (2007) 233 CLR 162, 178–79 [17].
[71] (2004) 220 CLR 181.
[72] *McCloy v New South Wales* (2015) 257 CLR 178, 234 [139] (Gageler J), quoting *Mulholland v Australian Electoral Commission* (2004) 220 CLR 181, 197–8 (Gleeson CJ).
[73] *McCloy v New South Wales* (2015) 257 CLR 178, 234 [140] (Gageler J).
[74] (2017) 261 CLR 328.
[75] *Brown v Tasmania* (2017) 261 CLR 328, [159] (Gageler J).
[76] Ibid [160] (Gageler J).
[77] Ibid [433] (Gordon J).

First, structured proportionality has antecedents in a context where the analysis did not involve constitutionally-entrenched rights: the administrative law of Prussia in the late nineteenth century. Indeed, the tests that make up structured proportionality were first proposed as a method by which the judiciary could constrain the growing and increasingly powerful administrative state in the absence of a meaningful rights-based constitution. Although the form of proportionality analysis normally employed in that context was an abridged, proxy form where only the connection between means and ends was tested, this was reflective of the uncertain constitutional legitimacy of the courts conducting judicial review altogether. The full form of structured proportionality analysis, which also included an assessment of the importance of the ends as against the burden on a competing interest, had already been theorised, however, even if the courts lacked sufficient legitimacy to deploy it. This suggests that while structured proportionality might be helpful in modern constitutional rights adjudication, its application is not necessarily limited to that context.

Second, part of the concern expressed by Gageler J seems to proceed from the view that where there is a constitutional bill of rights, the 'text enshrining the right requires that a judgment be made and, by one means or another, that judgment must be made'.[78] That is, where a right is reduced down to constitutional text, courts have a licence to adjudicate upon it without needing to engage with the deeper constitutional principles which justified its recognition in the first place. By contrast, where a constitutional freedom is implied, as in the case of the implied freedom of political communication, the 'judgment to be made can never be divorced from the reasons why there is a judgment to be made'.[79] One might contend, however, that such a view fails to fully engage with one of the primary goals of the postwar juridical paradigm, which is to establish a structure of judicial review in which a constitutionally-protected interest, or right, can be engaged with at both the level of abstracted principle and the level of a concretised problem. This can be seen most particularly at the strict balancing stage, where a court is required to engage with the normative importance of a constitutionally-protected interest in order to ascertain whether an intrusion into it is justified. The capacity to engage with a constitutionally-protected interest at the level of 'reasons' for its existence sits at the heart of structured proportionality analysis.

The High Court's most recent engagement with the implied freedom of political communication, in *Unions NSW v New South Wales (No 2)*,[80] suggests that it is even further along in its path to retreating from an express acknowledgment of the value of structured proportionality analysis in this context. Across the five separate judgments, proportionality was mentioned in only the joint judgment, and that too, only once.[81] The case concerned the constitutional validity of a law enacted by the NSW legislature capping the lawful expenditure by third party campaigners to less than half of what it had been under the previous and now repealed law. The State of NSW argued that the new cap was aimed at the legitimate purpose of preventing the drowning out of voices in an election campaign other than those of third party campaigners. It further contended that the law was appropriate and adapted to that purpose.

[78] *McCloy v New South Wales* (2015) 257 CLR 178, 238 [149] (Gageler J).
[79] Ibid.
[80] [2019] HCA 1.
[81] *Unions NSW v New South Wales (No 2)* [2019] HCA 1, [42] (Kiefel, Bell and Keane JJ).

In their joint judgment, Kiefel, Bell and Keane JJ,[82] with whom Nettle J agreed,[83] considered that the new law was invalid as the State had not produced any evidence to support its view that a drastic cut to the expenditure caps was necessary to achieve its stated purpose. Justice Gageler considered that a 'compelling justification' was necessary to establish the validity of a law which restricted the implied freedom in the manner of the impugned law in light of the risk it posed to the maintenance of the system of representative and responsible government established by the Constitution.[84] His Honour went on to conclude that the law in question was not justified as it had not been shown to be 'reasonably necessary to achieve a level playing field for all participants'.[85] That is, it had not been demonstrated by NSW that the new cap would leave a third party campaigner with a reasonable opportunity to present its case.[86] Similar reasons were put forward by Gordon J,[87] while Edelman J formed the view that the laws were pursuing an illegitimate purpose of quietening voices of third-party campaigners.[88]

Despite the reticence to engage expressly, on one view, the judgments delivered in *Unions NSW (No 2)* applied an analytical lens entirely compatible with structured proportionality. Each of the four judgments aside from that of Edelman J could have reached a similar conclusion within the rubric of the suitability stage of structured proportionality. Each might have concluded, for similar reasons to those given, that the impugned law displayed no rational connection, grounded in evidence, with its purported purpose. While Edelman J, considered the case to turn on the 'compatibility' of the impugned law with the system of representative and responsible government – a precursor stage to structured proportionality under the approach set down in *McCloy*[89] – his Honour's analysis would not have been inconsistent with the application of structured proportionality had a different view been formed on the compatibility question. Accordingly, it is difficult to discern an explanation for the Court's rapid retreat from the language of the postwar juridical paradigm, despite its obvious analytical utility, other than the reassertion of Australian exceptionalism.

V. Voting Rights

Engagement with the postwar juridical paradigm has found even less of a toehold in areas of Australian constitutional law other than the implied freedom of political communication. One such context is in relation to the so-called 'implied right to vote'. In *Murphy v Electoral Commissioner*,[90] the plaintiffs sought a declaration that certain provisions of the *Commonwealth Electoral Act* 1918 (Cth) were invalid on the basis that they impermissibly infringed upon the electoral choice mandated by sections 7 and 24 of the Constitution. The provisions at issue prevented the Electoral Commissioner from adding names to the Electoral

[82] *Unions NSW v New South Wales (No 2)* [2019] HCA 1 [53] (Kiefel, Bell and Keane JJ).
[83] Ibid, [117]–[119] (Nettle J).
[84] Ibid, [53] (Kiefel, Bell and Keane JJ).
[85] Ibid, [101] (Gageler J) (emphasis added).
[86] Ibid.
[87] *Unions NSW v New South Wales (No 2)* [2019] HCA 1 [153]–[154] (Gordon J).
[88] Ibid, [222] (Edelman J).
[89] *McCloy v New South Wales* (2015) 257 CLR 178, 193–4 [2] (French CJ, Kiefel, Bell and Keane JJ).
[90] (2016) 261 CLR 28.

Roll between 8.00pm on the day of the closing of the Electoral Roll and the close of the poll for the election.[91] The period between the closing of the roll and election day is commonly referred to as the 'suspension period'. The Rolls were to be closed on the seventh day after the issue of the writ for the election.[92] The period between the issuing of the writ and the closing of the roll is commonly referred to as the 'grace period'. The impugned provisions also prevented consideration of a claim for transfer of enrolment[93] and the removal of a person's name from the Electoral Roll[94] until after the end of the suspension period. The first plaintiff contended that the impugned provisions were invalid for effectively disqualifying individuals from exercising the choice mandated by sections 7 and 24 of the Constitution in the absence of a 'substantial reason'.[95] The provisions would only be for a substantial reason if they were 'reasonably appropriate and adapted' to an end consistent and compatible with the maintenance of the constitutionally prescribed system of representative government.[96] The first plaintiff relied on *McCloy*-style structured proportionality in the presentation of his arguments.[97] In particular, he emphasised the necessity stage of such analysis, contending that the electoral systems in New South Wales and Victoria providing for enrolments up to and on polling day amounted to obvious and compelling, reasonably practicable alternatives to the Commonwealth 'suspension period'.[98]

The 'implied right to vote' or 'constitutional mandate' is an area of jurisprudence considered closely related to the implied freedom of political communication, since both are said to derive from the system of representative and responsible government established by the Constitution. Given that context, there was an expectation that the High Court would deal with the arguments raised by the parties by applying structured proportionality analysis. In the end, the Court unanimously dismissed the plaintiffs' case at the end of the second day of hearings.[99] In the reasons that followed, proportionality analysis was not relied upon by any of the Court with the exception of Kiefel J. French CJ and Bell J did not expressly exclude the possibility that structured proportionality might be relevant to a case concerning the constitutional mandate, but simply noted that such relevance would depend 'upon the character of the law said to diminish the extent of the realisation of that mandate'.[100] In the absence of a legislative burden in *Murphy*, consideration of policy alternatives under the necessity stage of structured proportionality would amount to the Court undertaking a 'hypothetical exercise of improved legislative design'.[101] Similarly, Keane J rejected the appropriateness of what he described as '*Lange*-style analysis' as recently applied in *McCloy* on the basis that the plaintiffs had failed to identify a burden.[102]

[91] *Commonwealth Electoral Act 1918* (Cth), ss 94A(4), 95(4), 96(4), 102(4) and 103B(5).
[92] Ibid, ss 152(1) and 155.
[93] Ibid, ss 102(4) and 103A(5).
[94] Ibid, s 118(5).
[95] Anthony John Murphy, 'Plaintiff's Annotated Submissions', Submission in *Murphy v Electoral Commissioner* [2016] HCA 36, No M247 of 2015, 11 April 2016, [23].
[96] *Roach v Electoral Commissioner* (2007) 233 CLR 162, 199 [85] (Gummow, Kirby and Crennen JJ).
[97] Anthony John Murphy, 'Plaintiff's Annotated Submissions', Submission in *Murphy v Electoral Commissioner* [2016] HCA 36, No M247 of 2015, 11 April 2016, [44]–[65].
[98] Ibid, [46]–[47].
[99] Transcript of Proceedings, *Murphy v Electoral Commissioner* [2016] HCATrans 111 (12 May 2016) 4455–4460.
[100] *Murphy v Electoral Commissioner* (2016) 261 CLR 28, 53 [38] (French CJ and Bell J).
[101] Ibid, 53 [39] (French CJ and Bell J).
[102] Ibid, 94 [202] (Keane J).

Other justices saw the case as an opportunity for a revival of some of the concerns they had raised in *McCloy*. Justice Gageler, for example, was critical of the plaintiffs' 'attempt to shoehorn their argument' within structured proportionality. His Honour considered the approach demonstrated that proportionality is 'at best an ill-fitted analytical tool' which had 'become the master' and 'taken on a life of its own'.[103] Justice Gordon also considered that there were questions about whether the rigid inquiry involved at the necessity stage of proportionality was 'appropriate at all in the Australian constitutional context'.[104] Nettle J, who had stayed somewhat neutral in *McCloy*, now observed that the validity of the features of the legislative scheme regulating elections ought not to 'depend on some finely calibrated weighing of detriment and benefit', or on the Court's view as to whether there existed 'another and apparently superior way of achieving the same objective'.[105] These comments appear to be unfavourable reflections on the balancing and necessity stages of proportionality, respectively.

VI. Freedom from Detention

A similar retreat from structured proportionality was evident in a recent case concerning Chapter III of the Australian Constitution: *Falzon v Minister for Immigration and Border Projection*.[106] Chapter III reserves the judicial power of the Commonwealth to federal courts and state courts exercising federal jurisdiction. Since *Chu Kheng Lim v Minister for Immigration, Local Government and Ethnic Affairs*,[107] it has been held that the power to adjudge and punish guilt for an offence against a law of the Commonwealth is exclusive to the Chapter III judiciary. Chapter III has been said to prevent the enactment of a law which vests any part of that judicial function in the Commonwealth executive. Accordingly, it has been held that an individual – whether a citizen or non-citizen – may only be subject to involuntary executive detention if that detention has not been imposed for a penal or punitive purpose.[108] Where the involuntary executive detention is found to have been imposed for a penal or punitive purpose it is considered a punishment and therefore a constitutionally impermissible attempt to exercise Commonwealth judicial power.

In recent cases, non-citizens facing deportation have sought to rely on the principles established in *Chu Kheng Lim* to argue that there exists a constitutional principle that prohibits detention of persons 'without just cause',[109] and that detention will be presumed

[103] *Murphy v Electoral Commissioner* (2016) 261 CLR 28, 72 [101] (Gageler J).

[104] Ibid, 123 [299] (Gordon J).

[105] Ibid, 107 [245] (Nettle J).

[106] (2018) 262 CLR 333.

[107] (1992) 176 CLR 1, 27.

[108] In *Chu Kheng Lim v Minister for Immigration* (1992) 176 CLR 1 at 27–8, Brennan, Deane and Dawson JJ identified some 'exceptional cases' which were said to fall outside this principle, including arrest on executive warrant pending trial, involuntary detention in cases of mental illness or infectious disease, parliamentary punishment for contempt, and the power of military tribunals to punish for breach of military discipline. Putting aside contempt of Parliament, which does not involve executive detention, it has been suggested that these 'exceptional cases' are in fact examples of executive detention for non-punitive purposes and therefore cases which fall within the rule rather than outside it: see Stephen McDonald, 'Involuntary Detention and Separation of Judicial Power' (2007) 35(1) *Federal Law Review* 25, 32–4.

[109] *Attorney-General (NT) v Emmerson* (2014) 253 CLR 393 at 429–30 [53].

to be penal or punitive 'unless justified as otherwise'.[110] The logical extension of these principles is that the legislature must justify its conferral of power on the executive to subject individuals to detention by providing reasons for that conferral. The existence of a free-standing constitutionally guaranteed freedom from executive detention has now been rejected by the High Court, as has the appropriateness of any application of proportionality analysis in this context.

In *Falzon v Minister for Immigration and Border Protection*,[111] the plaintiff argued that his involuntary immigration detention amounted to an exercise of judicial power by the executive. The plaintiff, a national of Malta, had been serving 11 years' imprisonment with a non-parole period of eight years for trafficking a large commercial quantity of cannabis. During his non-parole period, the plaintiff's Absorbed Person Visa, pursuant to section 34 of the *Migration Act 1958 (Cth)*, had been cancelled by a delegate of the Minister for Immigration acting under a power conferred by section 501(3A) of the Migration Act to cancel visas in circumstances where a person has a substantial criminal record and is serving a sentence of imprisonment. The effect of the cancellation was that the plaintiff's other visa – a Class BF Transitional (Permanent) Visa – was also taken to have been cancelled, and the plaintiff was transferred into immigration detention at the conclusion of his non-parole period.

In arguing that section 501(3A) involved a constitutionally impermissible conferral of executive power to detain, the plaintiff referred to a passage in *Chu Kheng Lim*, in which the joint judgment had addressed the issue of executive detention and observed that the authority conferred on the executive 'cannot properly be seen as an incident of the executive powers to exclude, admit and deport an alien. In that event they will be of a punitive nature and contravene Ch III's insistence that the judicial power of the Commonwealth be vested exclusively in the courts which it designates'.[112] The plaintiff further argued that in *Kruger v Commonwealth*,[113] Gummow J had referred to this passage from *Lim* and considered that whether or not the executive had exceeded its power would depend on whether the detention and custody enforced by the executive 'are reasonably capable of being seen as necessary for a legitimate non-punitive purpose'.[114] It was the plaintiff's contention that these observations, and particularly the reference to the words 'reasonably capable of being seen as necessary', which bear some similarity to the *Lange* test in the context of the implied freedom of political communication, involved the application of proportionality analysis.

In rejecting the plaintiff's contentions in their joint judgment, Kiefel CJ, Bell, Keane and Edelman JJ observed that proportionality analysis, at least as it is applied in the Australian constitutional context, is limited to circumstances where a legislative measure restricts a constitutionally guaranteed freedom. In such circumstances, the necessity stage of analysis is employed to ask whether the legislative measure is 'reasonably necessary to achieve the valid purpose of the statute in question'.[115] For the plurality, the limits on legislative and executive power deriving from Chapter III posed a different set of questions. In that context, there is an 'absolute prohibition on laws which involve the exercise of judicial power of the

[110] *Northern Australian Aboriginal Justice Agency Ltd v Northern Territory* (2015) 256 CLR 569 at 611–12 [98].
[111] *Falzon v Minister for Immigration and Border Protection* (2018) 262 CLR 333.
[112] (1992) 176 CLR 1, 33.
[113] (1997) 190 CLR 1.
[114] *Kruger v Commonwealth* (1997) 190 CLR 1, 162.
[115] *Falzon v Minister for Immigration and Border Protection* (2018) 262 CLR 333, [30].

Commonwealth'.[116] Accordingly, for the majority, the test in that context was whether the true purpose of the law was to authorise penal or punitive detention. The joint judgment expressed agreement with McHugh J's comments in a previous case that a 'law that confers judicial power on a person or body that is not authorised by or otherwise infringes Ch III cannot be saved by asserting that its operation is proportionate to an object that is compatible with Ch III'.[117] Although the inverse was being argued in *Falzon*, the plurality arguably shut down any potential revival in future cases of the arguments raised by the plaintiff by concluding that '[q]uestions of proportionality cannot arise under Ch III'.[118]

There are at least two observations that might be made of the plurality judgment in *Falzon*. First, the approach taken in the judgment flows directly from the plurality's own conclusion that Chapter III does not give rise to a free-standing freedom from executive detention. If such a freedom were recognised by the Court, then the onus would immediately shift to the legislature to justify its incursion into that freedom. In such circumstances, proportionality would, on the plurality's own admission, have a role to play in the analysis. The position of the plurality on this front is difficult to reconcile with the approach that has been taken in the context of the implied freedom of political communication. In that context, there is obviously no express mention of any such freedom in the Australian Constitution and even reference to the higher-order structural feature from which the freedom is said to derive is expressed in wafer thin terms. The Australian Constitution merely provides that the houses of Parliament must be 'directly chosen by the people'. While the implication was controversial at the time it was made, through the passage of time acceptance of a free-standing freedom of political communication has been universally accepted, paving the way for deeper engagement with values which underpin it and their interaction with exercises of legislative and executive power.

Second, the plurality's motivations in reaching the conclusions that it did in *Falzon* are unclear. On the one hand, it is correct to say that a test which is aimed at assessing the 'true purpose' of a law is directed at a different purpose to a test which is aimed at assessing whether a law has made an unjustifiable incursion into a constitutionally protected freedom. What is curious, however, is that although these tests might be directed at serving different analytical purposes, functionally they overlap. We might describe the first kind of test as a sort of 'smoking out' analysis, where a law's 'true purpose' is assessed by asking whether there are other ways to achieve the purpose that the legislature is seeking to achieve. If there are other ways, then this suggests (but does not definitively decide) that the law is aimed at achieving an illegitimate, or unconstitutional, purpose. At the necessity stage of proportionality analysis, a similar question is asked: was the stated purpose of the law capable of being achieved in a manner less intrusive on the protected freedom? If yes, then the law will be considered unconstitutional. The questions asked in both kinds of tests are extremely similar, with the only difference being that the question asked at the 'necessity' stage of proportionality analysis is expressed in a manner that directly takes into account a constitutionally protected interest, whereas 'smoking out' analysis leaves this consideration open-ended and unpegged to any particular interest, constitutional or otherwise.

[116] Ibid, [32].
[117] *Re Woolley* (2009) 225 CLR 1, 34 [80].
[118] *Falzon v Minister for Immigration and Border Protection* (2018) 262 CLR 333, [32].

Undertaking 'smoking out' analysis may have led the plurality to a deeper consideration of what the purpose of the detention might truly have been when effected in connection with deportation that only comes into force *after* a person has served their sentence and in circumstances where there is no requirement for the Minister to have regard to whether there is a protective benefit to the community of flowing from that deportation. Regard to the broader legislative scheme and the practical effect of that scheme, coupled with 'smoking out' analysis, may have moved the plurality further towards the conclusion that the true purpose of detention in this context was not the narrow purpose suggested by the Commonwealth of giving effect to immigration policy but rather the broader, and impermissible, purpose of punishing an individual for committing a serious crime.

In rejecting both proportionality and 'smoking out' analysis in circumstances where the latter might have been appropriate, the plurality decision in *Falzon* suggests that the motivation of the judges authoring that decision may not have been entirely fuelled by the aim of achieving methodological purity. Hints of support for that conclusion can be found in the plurality's willingness to distinguish between the manner in which the Constitution protects citizens and non-citizens. In this regard, the plurality said:

> The joint judgment in *Lim* did not suggest that the Constitution, and laws made under it, offer the same protection to an alien as they do to a citizen. The joint judgment pointed out that, whilst an alien present in this country enjoys the protection of our law, his or her status, rights and immunities under the law differ from those of an Australian citizen in a number of important respects. Relevantly, the most important difference lies in the vulnerability, arising under the common law and provisions of the Constitution, of an alien to exclusion or deportation. The effect is significantly to diminish the protection which Ch III provides a citizen against detention otherwise than pursuant to judicial power.[119]

The passage is instructive when it is considered that the Australian Constitution does not expressly refer to Australian citizenship, let alone distinguish between the rights that ought to be afforded to those citizens vis-à-vis citizens of other nations or dual citizens.[120] The passage is also instructive when contrasted against the facts of the case. The plaintiff arrived in Australia with his family when he was three years old. He had lived in Australia for 61 years. He had two sisters and four brothers, four adult children and 10 grandchildren in Australia, as well as other extended family. The Assistant Minister accepted that upon deportation to Malta the plaintiff was likely to suffer social isolation and emotional hardship. The plaintiff was, prior to his visa cancellation, eligible to become an Australian citizen. The only difference between the plaintiff and an Australian citizen, then, was an administrative process that might have acknowledged him as so being. Yet there is no constitutional protection for a person in the plaintiff's circumstances.[121]

[119] *Falzon v Minister for Immigration and Border Protection* (2018) 262 CLR 333, [39].

[120] The exception to this is s 44(i), which disqualifies citizens of a foreign power from being eligible to be chosen or to sit as a member of the federal Parliament. The provision has recently been the subject of a number of cases before the Court of Disputed Returns in which the constitutionality of the election of federal parliamentarians has been challenged: see *Re Canavan, Re Ludlum, Re Waters, Re Roberts (No 2), Re Joyce, Re Nash, Re Xenophon* (2017) 91 ALJR 209; *Re Gallagher* (2018) 92 ALJR 502. In perhaps a sign of its poor fit with the demographic composition of contemporary Australia, there have been calls for s 44(i) to be reformed: see, eg, Joint Standing Committee on Electoral Matters, 'Excluded: the impact of section 44 on Australian democracy' (May, 2018).

[121] Indeed, the deportation of long-term non-citizen residents of Australia has a long-established history: see Michelle Foster, '"An 'Alien' by the Barest of Threads" – the Legality of the Deportation of Long-Term Residents from Australia' (2009) 33 *Melbourne University Law Review* 483.

The plurality's decision in *Falzon* confirms that the High Court is maintaining its vigilance against allowing proportionality, and related forms of analysis, from becoming a backdoor mechanism of rights protection where this is seen as an undesirable outcome. Although the High Court did not expressly refer to analogous decisions in overseas jurisdictions in reaching its conclusion in *Falzon*, the conclusions reached in relation to its willingness to engage with the postwar juridical paradigm through the lens of proportionality analysis are broadly in line with sentiments expressed in earlier cases regarding the limited assistance that such foreign jurisprudence could offer.[122] In this sense, the result in *Falzon* is entirely in line with the culture of Australian exceptionalism and its desire to limit judicial interference with policies that have the imprimatur of democratically accountable institutions.

VII. Conclusion

Australian exceptionalism exhibits not just in an absence of a federal bill of rights, but also in a deeply-entrenched culture which shows a general reluctance to engage with the jurisprudence of foreign nations. In the most recent wave of international rights-based discourse, a new postwar juridical paradigm of human rights has emerged. Central to this paradigm is the adjudicative method of structured proportionality, which has been celebrated as a means by which constitutional courts might adjudicate upon rights in a manner that is both respectful of the historical, cultural and social context in which that process is taking place and, at the same time, enhances the relationship between structures of government and those being governed through promoting a culture of justification. While structured proportionality has, in a very limited way, entered Australian constitutional jurisprudence, the caution and resistance that has been exhibited towards it in the most recent cases suggests that the culture of Australian exceptionalism remains strong. While this may not have substantive implications in areas where constitutional freedoms are well-established, such as with respect to the implied freedom of political communication, it does suggest that the High Court will remain vigilant against structured proportionality becoming a medium of rights expansion in other, less-established areas. Against this background, any revival of the partial and judicially-led rights-revolution that took place in the early 1990s seems unlikely, and a meaningful and enduring shift away from Australian exceptionalism may only occur if led by a democratic mandate from the people of the Commonwealth.

[122] Eg, in *Forge v Australian Securities and Investments Commission* (2006) 228 CLR 45, Heydon J observed that 'Considerable reliance was placed upon cases on the European Convention for the Protection of Human Rights and Fundamental Freedoms, Art 6; the *Canadian Charter of Rights and Freedoms*, s11(d) and the Bill of Rights of the Constitution of the Republic of South Africa, s34. These documents all post-dated Ch III … Accordingly, no assistance is to be obtained from cases on these documents in construing Ch III and evaluating its impact on State laws.': at 139–140 [250].

19

A Common Law Bill of Rights

DAN MEAGHER*

I. Introduction

This chapter will outline the historical, political and jurisprudential developments in Australia which have led to the establishment of what has been called 'a common law bill of rights'.[1] In order to do so, Part II will interrogate and contextualise the foundational decision of the framers of the Australian Constitution to reject the need for and wisdom of a constitutional bill of rights. Part III will outline briefly those international and domestic developments (especially since World War II) which triggered the rise of fundamental rights as a core legal concern; and a series of (rights-hostile) legislative developments will be traced to explain how and why a new judicial rights consciousness has emerged in Australia. Part IV will then explain the manner in which a common law bill of rights has been judicially established. This will include an account of what rights, freedoms and principles fall within its purview and why; and how the courts seek to protect from them legislative encroachment. Then Part V will explore those controversies and questions which attend the establishment of the common law bill of rights in Australia. Finally, in Part VI, the manner in which its future development *might* proceed will be considered.

II. History

It is commonplace to state, often in pejorative terms, that Australia is the only Western liberal democracy without a constitutional or statutory bill of rights.[2] And in this regard Australia is often unfavourably compared to other Commonwealth nations such as Canada, New Zealand and the UK where formal rights guarantees now form an important part of their constitutional architecture.[3] Yet the framers of the Australian Constitution were well aware of the issue. The original 1891 draft Constitution, largely the work of the Tasmanian

* School of Law, Deakin University.

[1] James Spigelman, 'The Common Law Bill of Rights' in *Statutory Interpretation and Human Rights* (Brisbane, University of Queensland Press, 2008).

[2] See George Williams and Daniel Reynolds, *A Charter of Rights for Australia*, 4th edn (Sydney, UNSW Press, 2017) 17.

[3] Ibid, 18.

poet, philosopher, engineer, judge, politician and fierce republican Andrew Inglis Clark,[4] included the following formal rights guarantees:

> Clause 17: A State shall not make or enforce any law abridging any privilege or immunity of citizens of other States of the Commonwealth, nor shall a State deny to any person, within its jurisdiction, the equal protection of the laws. [At the 1897 and 1898 Conventions Clark sought (unsuccessfully) to delete clause 17 and replace it with a new clause 110 to read: The citizens of each state, and all other persons owing allegiance to the Queen and residing in any territory of the Commonwealth, shall be citizens of the Commonwealth, and shall be entitled to all privileges and immunities of citizens of the Commonwealth in the several states; and a state shall not make or enforce any law abridging any privilege or immunity of citizens of the Commonwealth, nor shall a state deprive any person of life, liberty, or property without due process of law, or deny to any person within its jurisdiction the equal protection of its laws.][5]
>
> Clause 46: The Federal Parliament shall not make any law for the establishment or support of any religion, or for the purpose of giving any preferential recognition to any religion, or for prohibiting the free exercise of any religion.
>
> Clause 65: The trial of all crimes cognizable by any Court established under the authority of this Act shall be by jury, and every such trial shall be held in the Province where the crime has been committed and when not committed within any Province the trial shall be held at such place or places as the Federal Parliament may by law direct.
>
> No Province shall make any law prohibiting the free exercise of any religion.

Clark was a firm believer in the importance of natural rights. This provided the normative justification for his unqualified support of an American-style bill of rights in the new Commonwealth of Australia. Yet his vision of entrenched rights did not survive the subsequent Constitutional Conventions. The framers consciously decided to renounce those provisions based on the American bill of rights and settled upon a final version of the Constitution that, in terms of rights, owed more to Albert Venn Dicey and his deep skepticism of formal rights guarantees.[6] In doing so, they strongly affirmed the quintessentially British faith in the rights protective capacity of the common law, representative democracy and responsible government.[7]

Yet these matters of high (English) constitutional principle and political theory were not the only reasons why the framers renounced formal rights guarantees. Clark, for example, clearly modelled the original clause 17 (and the amended clause 110) detailed above on the Fourteenth Amendment of the American Bill of Rights. But the rejection of a constitutional provision that would enshrine both due process of law and equal protection of the laws was motivated by considerations of 'race and discrimination'[8] not just a deep faith in the rights-protective capacity of the common law and parliamentary government. The framers were well aware that an Australian species of the Fourteenth Amendment would likely imperil the validity of existing colonial legislation that openly discriminated on the basis of race.

[4] See Richard Ely (ed) *A Living Force: Andrew Inglis Clark and the Ideal of the Commonwealth* (Centre for Tasmanian Historical Studies, 2001).

[5] See George Williams and David Hume, *Human Rights Under the Australian Constitution*, 2nd edn (Melbourne, Oxford University Press, 2013) 65–71.

[6] Albert Venn Dicey, *Introduction to the Study of the Law of the Constitution*, 10th edn (London, Macmillan, 1965) 206–207. See Eric Barendt, 'Dicey and Civil Liberties' [1985] *Public Law* 596.

[7] See Sir Owen Dixon, 'Two Constitutions Compared' in *Jesting Pilate and Other Papers and Addresses*, 2nd edn (US, William S Hein, 1997) 100, 102.

[8] John Williams, 'Race, Citizenship and the Formation of the Australian Constitution: Andrew Inglis Clark and the "14th Amendment"' (1996) 42 *Australian Journal of Politics and History* 10, 18.

This foundational decision on constitutional design has exerted an important and constraining influence on the manner in which Australian law provides for the protection of rights. Hilary Charlesworth has aptly characterised this as '[t]he Australian reluctance about rights'.[9] That reluctance is evidenced by the two, spectacularly unsuccessful, post-federation attempts to amend the Australian Constitution to incorporate formal rights guarantees.[10] And it has sunk even the more modest proposals to enact a statutory bill of rights which has been attempted on three occasions.[11] Consequently, for much of the twentieth century the constitutional vision of the framers to place no (fundamental rights) fetters upon legislative action[12] was realised.

However, a combination of legislative developments that began in the 1980s (and continues still) has led the courts to fill the formal rights lacuna in Australian to temper (if not on occasion) resist laws openly hostile to fundamental rights. They have done so by, amongst other things, developing a strong Australian species of clear statement rule for fundamental rights from an old common law interpretive presumption. It is to these developments that I now turn.

III. The Rise of (and Threat to) Fundamental Rights

There can be little doubt as to the significance of the rise of human rights as a core concern of the international legal order in the aftermath of World War II.[13] It led, swiftly, to the creation of the United Nations in 1945[14] and the promulgation of the Universal Declaration of Human Rights in 1948.[15] The international law of human rights was, then, firmly established when the International Covenant on Civil and Political Rights[16] and the International Covenant on Economic, Social and Cultural Rights[17] were adopted and opened for signature, ratification and accession by the General Assembly in December 1966. Australia ratified both treaties in 1980 and in so doing provided the courts with a rights touchstone and 'updated set of values'[18] from which to renovate common law rules and develop more rights-sensitive principles of statutory interpretation.[19]

[9] Hilary Charlesworth, 'The Australian Reluctance About Rights' (1993) 31 *Osgoode Hall Law Journal* 195.

[10] See Brian Galligan, 'Australia's Rejection of a Bill of Rights' (1990) 28 *Journal of Commonwealth and Comparative Politics* 344.

[11] See Peter Bailey, *The Human Rights Enterprise in Australia and Internationally* (Chatswood, LexisNexis, 2009) 144–152.

[12] See Dixon, above n 7, 102.

[13] See Conor Gearty, *Can Human Rights Survive?* (Cambridge, Cambridge University Press, 2006) 25–28.

[14] See Henry J Steiner, Philip Alston and Ryan Goodman, *International Human Rights in Context: Law, Politics and Morals*, 3rd edn (Oxford, Oxford University Press, 2008) 133–135.

[15] Universal Declaration on Human Rights, GA Res 217A(III), UN GAOR, 3rd sess, 183rd plen mtg, UN Doc A/810 (10 December 1948).

[16] International Covenant on Civil and Political Rights, opened for signature 16 December 1966, 999 UNTS 171 (entered into force 23 March 1976). On 25 September, 1991 Australia ratified the First Optional Protocol to the ICCPR which permits the United Nations Human Rights Committee to hear complaints from individuals who allege that the Australian Government has violated their rights under the ICCPR.

[17] International Covenant on Economic, Social and Cultural Rights, opened for signature 16 December 1966, 999 UNTS 3 (entered into force 3 January 1976).

[18] Claudia Geiringer, 'The Principle of Legality and the Bill of Rights Act: A Critical Examination of R v Hansen' (2008) 6 *New Zealand Journal of Public and International Law* 59, 89.

[19] See David Dyzenhaus, Murray Hunt and Michael Taggart, 'The Principle of Legality in Administrative Law: Internationalisation as Constitutionalisation' (2001) 1 *Oxford University Commonwealth Law Journal* 5, 32–33.

At around the same time after the 1983 federal election the newly elected Prime Minister Bob Hawke held a National Crimes Conference to consider and tackle the new challenges posed by organised and sophisticated forms of crime.[20] It led to the establishment of Australia's first standing crime commission in 1984 the National Crime Authority which was charged with the responsibility to investigate and gather intelligence on serious tax evasion and organised crime for prosecuting authorities.[21] There were similar (sometimes ad hoc) bodies established also in the states during this time.[22] In order to undertake their statutory functions these national and state crime commissions were given by statute extraordinary investigative powers including the power to compel persons to answer questions on oath on pain of penalty even when those answers might incriminate them.[23] As Justice Mark Weinberg has noted, '[t]hese powers greatly exceed[ed] those generally available to the police.'[24] Whilst this legislation and the powers they conferred was controversial, the absence of formally entrenched rights guarantees in the Australian Constitution made it unproblematic from a constitutional perspective.[25]

However in a trio of cases decided between 1987 and 1992 the timing of which was, arguably, far from coincidental the High Court began to react.[26] First, it revived the following interpretive presumption outlined in an early decision of the Court:

> It is in the last degree improbable that the legislature would overthrow fundamental principles, infringe rights, or depart from the general system of law, without expressing its intention with irresistible clearness; and to give any such effect to general words, simply because they have that meaning in their widest, or usual, or natural sense, would be to give them a meaning in which they were not really used.[27]

The Court then refashioned the content (and normative justification) for this fundamental rights presumption in its now seminal decision in *Coco*.[28] As the statement below details, the contemporary justification emphasises the salutary role the presumption can play when legislators are given clear and prior notice of the common law (rights) backdrop against which their legislation will be construed. This may improve the clarity and rights-sensitivity of legislation promoting democracy and rule of law values in the process.[29]

> The insistence on express authorization of an abrogation or curtailment of a fundamental right, freedom or immunity must be understood as a requirement for some manifestation or indication that the legislature has not only directed its attention to the question of the abrogation or

[20] See Stephen Donaghue, *Royal Commissions and Permanent Commissions of Inquiry* (Chatswood, Butterworths, 2001) 5–8.

[21] *National Crime Authority Act 1984* (Cth).

[22] See Justice Mark Weinberg, 'The Impact of Special Commissions of Inquiry/Crime Commissions on Criminal Trials' (Speech delivered at the Supreme Court of New South Wales Annual Conference, 1 August 2014) 2–6 http://assets.justice.vic.gov.au/supreme/resources/66d960d7-4dae-4b13-853c 71a94c97a424/the+impact+of+special+commissions+of+inquiry+weinberg+j+-+1+aug+2014.pdf.

[23] See Donaghue, above n 20, 59–72.

[24] Weinberg, above n 22, 2–3.

[25] *Balog v Independent Commission Against Corruption* (1990) 169 CLR 625.

[26] *Re Bolton; Ex parte Beane* (1987) 162 CLR 514 ('*Re Bolton*'); *Bropho v Western Australia* (1990) 171 CLR 1; *Coco v The Queen* (1994) 179 CLR 427 ('*Coco*').

[27] *Potter v Minihan* (1908) 7 CLR 277, 304 (O'Connor J) ('*Potter*') (footnotes omitted).

[28] *Coco* (1994) 179 CLR 427, 437 (Mason CJ, Brennan, Gaudron and McHugh JJ), 446 (Deane and Dawson JJ).

[29] See Brendan Lim, 'The Normativity of the Principle of Legality' (2013) 37 *Melbourne University Law Review* 372, 389–394.

> curtailment of such basic rights, freedoms or immunities but has also determined upon abrogation or curtailment of them. The courts should not impute to the legislature an intention to interfere with fundamental rights. Such an intention must be clearly manifested by unmistakable and unambiguous language. General words will rarely be sufficient for that purpose if they do not specifically deal with the question because, in the context in which they appear, they will often be ambiguous on the aspect of interference with fundamental rights.[30]

The contemporary manifestation of the presumption was, then, vigorously applied in the trio of cases to protect from legislative encroachment the fundamental common law rights to liberty[31] and property.[32]

Second, and even more significantly from a contemporary perspective, the Court began to expand the catalogue of rights and freedoms it would seek to protect through the application of the above principle beyond the common law's holy trinity of life, liberty and property to include, for example, religious equality[33] and freedom of speech.[34] In doing so, senior appellate judges in Australia were aligning themselves with important (common law) developments in the protection of rights occurring in the UK.[35]

Finally, since the early 1990s the High Court began to treat seriously the few express rights in the Australian Constitution.[36] It also implied from the text and structure of the Constitution rights to democratic participation, due process and court access.[37] These constitutional rights developments are not only significant in their own right, but they have buttressed and inspired the strengthening of the extant common law rights to fair trial, due process and access to the courts from legislative encroachment.[38]

In the absence of an entrenched bill of rights the Courts had recognised their capacity to protect fundamental rights so far as interpretively possible. This laid the normative and doctrinal foundation upon which they would establish a common law bill of rights.[39] It would do so in response (and if truth be told in resistance) to another tranche of federal legislation that seriously infringed fundamental rights. The methodological tool used was

[30] *Coco* (1994) 179 CLR 427, 437 (Mason CJ, Brennan, Gaudron and McHugh JJ) (footnote omitted), endorsed at 446 (Deane and Dawson JJ).

[31] *Re Bolton* (1987) 162 CLR 514.

[32] *Coco* (1994) 179 CLR 427.

[33] *Canterbury Municipal Council v Moslem Alawy Society Ltd* (1985) 1 NSWLR 525, 544 (McHugh JA); see Kevin Boreham, 'International Law as an influence on the development of the common law: Evans v New South Wales' (2008) 19 *Public Law Review* 271.

[34] *Nationwide News Pty Ltd v Wills* (1992) 177 CLR 1, 31 (Mason CJ) ('*Nationwide News*'); *Evans v New South Wales* (2008) 168 FCR 576 ('*Evans*').

[35] Lord Browne-Wilkinson, 'The Infiltration of a Bill of Rights' [1992] *Public Law* 397, 408–9.

[36] See Williams and Hume, above n 5, 107–110.

[37] See George Winterton, 'The Separation of Judicial Power as an Implied Bill of Rights' in Geoffrey Lindell (ed), *Future Directions in Australian Constitutional Law: Essays in Honour of Professor Leslie Zines* (Annandale, The Federation Press, 1994) 185–208; Graeme Orr & George Williams, 'The People's Choice: The Prisoner Franchise and the Constitutional Protection of Voting Rights in Australia' (2009) 8 *Election Law Journal* 123.

[38] See Chief Justice Robert French, 'The Common Law and the Protection of Human Rights' (Speech delivered to the Anglo Australasian Lawyers Society, Sydney, 4 September 2009) www.hcourt.gov.au/assets/publications/speeches/current-justices/frenchcj/frenchcj4sep09.pdf.

[39] See Spigelman, 'The Application of Quasi-Constitutional Laws', in *Statutory Interpretation and Human Rights*, above n 1, 86–97. It is fascinating to note, here, that in 1939 Professor Willis outlined strikingly similar interpretive (and constitutional) developments occurring in Canada where the courts, in the absence of a bill of rights or even a constitutional separation of powers, 'used their power of statutory interpretation and their control of the prerogative writs to establish a common-law Bill of Rights.' John Willis, 'Administrative Law and the British North America Act' (1939) 53 *Harvard Law Review* 251, 274.

the old common law presumption noted above now re-badged as the principle of legality[40] which would be developed into a strong Australian species of clear statement rule.

IV. A Common Law Bill of Rights

In Australia, since the early 2000s, migration policy has been characterised by the successive and ongoing legislative attempts of Australian governments to seriously limit and sometimes exclude the rights to liberty, natural justice and access to the courts of persons seeking asylum, especially those arriving by boat.[41] The policy now involves intercepting the boats at sea and taking those on board to offshore centres in small pacific nations such as Nauru and Papua New Guinea for processing.[42] The Australian Government has stated that no one seeking to migrate in this manner will be re-settled in Australia then sought to remove the ability of asylum seekers to challenge the legality of the relevant migration decisions made upon processing.[43]

This has triggered a steady flow of migration cases to the High Court and especially to the Federal Court of Australia.[44] The entrenched judicial review jurisdiction of the High Court provided by section 75(v) of the Constitution has loomed large in these cases. Section 75(v) provides that '[i]n all matters … in which a writ of mandamus or prohibition or an injunction is sought against an officer of the Commonwealth … the High Court shall have original jurisdiction.'[45] It has provided the legal avenue *to* the High Court (trumping federal statute that sought to exclude this access to asylum seekers wishing to challenge the migration decisions of the Australian Government[46]) and the constitutional vehicle used *by* the Court to develop the (entrenched) grounds upon which that review and relief is sought.[47]

In *Plaintiff S157* a 2003 case where the High Court read down a provision that sought to oust its review powers of migration decisions, Chief Justice Gleeson stated that section 75(v) 'secures a basic element of the rule of law. The jurisdiction of the Court to require officers of the Commonwealth to act within the law cannot be taken away by Parliament.'[48] Parliament may of course change the content of statute law subject to the Constitution. 'But the executive government must obey the law. That is what the rule of law means.'[49] And as to whether the relevant legislation authorised the Executive

[40] The terminology was first used in Australian law in *Electrolux Home Products Pty Ltd v Australian Workers' Union* (2004) 221 CLR 309, 329 (Gleeson CJ).

[41] See Jane McAdam and Fiona Chong, *Refugees: Why Seeking Asylum is Legal and Australia's Policies are Not* (Sydney, University of New South Wales Press, 2014).

[42] See Mary Crock and Daniel Ghezelbash, 'Due Process and Rule of Law as Human Rights: The High Court and the "Offshore" Processing of Asylum Seekers' (2011) 18 *Australian Journal of Administrative Law* 101–114.

[43] See Jane McAdam, 'Australia and Asylum Seekers' (2013) 25 *International Journal of Refugee Law* 435, 440.

[44] See Stephen Gageler SC, 'Impact of Migration Law on the Development of Australian Administrative Law' (2010) 17 *Australian Journal of Administrative Law* 92.

[45] Australian Constitution, s 75(v); see Mark Aronson and Matthew Groves, *Judicial Review of Administrative Action*, 5th edn (Rozelle DC, Thomson Reuters, 2013) 949–956.

[46] *Plaintiff S157/2002 v Commonwealth* (2003) 211 CLR 476 ('*Plaintiff S157*'); see Cheryl Saunders, 'Plaintiff S157/2002: A Case Study in Common Law Constitutionalism' (2005) 12 *Australian Journal of Administrative Law* 115.

[47] See Gageler, above n 44, 96–103; Will Bateman, 'The Constitution and the Substantive Principles of Judicial Review: The Full Scope of the Entrenched Minimum Provision of Judicial Review' (2011) 39 *Federal Law Review* 463.

[48] *Plaintiff S157* (2003) 211 CLR 476, 482 (Gleeson CJ).

[49] The Hon. Murray Gleeson, *The Rule of Law and the Constitution* (Sydney, ABC Books, 2000) 68; See Lisa Burton Crawford, *The Rule of Law and the Australian Constitution* (Annandale, The Federation Press, 2017) ch 7: 'The Rule of Law and Judicial Review of Executive Action'.

Government to make migration decisions without according natural justice to those persons affected, the Chief Justice was emphatic:

> [C]ourts do not impute to the legislature an intention to abrogate or curtail fundamental rights or freedoms unless such an intention is clearly manifested by unmistakable and unambiguous language. General words will rarely be sufficient for that purpose. What courts will look for is a clear indication that the legislature has directed its attention to the rights or freedoms in question, and has consciously decided upon abrogation or curtailment. As Lord Hoffmann recently pointed out in the United Kingdom, for Parliament squarely to confront such an issue may involve a political cost, but in the absence of express language or necessary implication, even the most general words are taken to be "subject to the basic rights of the individual".[50]

In the teeth of federal migration legislation, the ordinary meaning of which clearly and *intentionally* infringed upon rights, the High Court deployed the Constitution and the revitalised (old) common law presumption now called the principle of legality to protect the fundamental rights of asylum seekers to natural justice and access to the courts.[51] In 2004 these developments gathered apace. In another migration case, this time involving an ultimately unsuccessful challenge to compulsory and open-ended executive detention of asylum seekers, Chief Justice Gleeson, again, emphasised the link between the principle of legality and the rule of law:

> A statement concerning the improbability that Parliament would abrogate fundamental rights by the use of general or ambiguous words is not a factual prediction, capable of being verified or falsified by a survey of public opinion. In a free society, under the rule of law, it is an expression of a legal value, respected by the courts, and the acknowledged by the courts to be respected by Parliament.[52]

A year later Chief Justice Spigelman of the New South Wales Supreme Court published an important paper that expressly drew the link between the Australian common law (and constitutional) developments detailed above and American notions of clear statement.[53] Significantly, it was said the interpretive approach involved in the application of the principle of legality in Australia was more appropriately called 'the clear statement principle'.[54] It was so as it 'more accurately reflects the true judicial role'[55] when determining whether or not the principle of legality can be applied to the construction of a statute.

> If Parliament wishes to interfere where rights, liberties and expectations are affected, it must do so with clarity. The clear statement principle is the critical way that the law of statutory interpretation reflects and implements the principle of legality.[56]

[50] *Plaintiff S157* (2003) 211 CLR 476, 492 (Gleeson CJ).

[51] Ibid, 492 (Gleeson CJ), 505–519 (Gaudron, McHugh, Gummow, Kirby and Hayne JJ), 520 (Callinan J); see Gageler, above n 44, 101–103. Importantly, a majority of the High Court now considers that the intention of Parliament (subjective or objective) is irrelevant to the determination of a statute's legal meaning – see text accompanying notes 104–109 below.

[52] *Al-Kateb v Godwin* (2004) 219 CLR 577 (Gleeson CJ) ('*Al-Kateb*').

[53] The Hon. James J Spigelman AC, 'Principle of Legality and the Clear Statement Principle' (2005) 79 *Australian Law Journal* 769.

[54] Spigelman, 'The Application of Quasi-Constitutional Laws' in *Statutory Interpretation and Human Rights*, above n 1, 88.

[55] Ibid.

[56] Ibid.

Chief Justice Spigelman noted that in the US there has long been 'a clear interaction between constitutional and quasi-constitutional principles'[57] and that this was facilitated primarily through the collection of substantive interpretive canons known as clear statement rules.[58] In terms of their methodology, Professors Eskridge, Frickey and Garrett have explained their rule-like operation:

> If a presumption of statutory meaning is sufficiently powerful, it can rise to the level of a clear statement rule … In such instances, the Court is announcing a rule of law: in the absence of clear statutory text speaking to the precise issue, judges must interpret the statute a certain way. Sometimes the courts impose such a stringent requirement of statutory textual clarity as to require the legislature to draft statutes with highly targeted text containing what amounts to "magic language" if the legislature wishes to overcome the canon.[59]

In Australia, the contemporary jurisprudence of the High Court has demonstrated the parallel of the methodology of clear statement for the principle of legality.[60] Our judges proceed from the interpretive premise that a statute does not disturb or infringe the relevant set of rights and freedoms considered fundamental at common law. This first interpretive step is the critical one: the judicial identification of the right or freedom that is engaged upon an ordinary construction of the relevant statute. Once this is done and absent unmistakably clear statutory language to the contrary the principle of legality is applied and the legislation given a rights-protective construction. Relevantly, the High Court made clear in *Coco* that judges must construe legislation compatibly with fundamental rights unless the terms of the statute makes crystal clear 'that the legislature has not only directed its attention to the question of the abrogation or curtailment of such basic rights, freedoms or immunities but has also determined upon abrogation or curtailment of them.'[61]

Another migration case – *Saeed* – demonstrates how the principle of legality has hardened into a strong Australia species of clear statement rule and the significance of this development for the common law bill of rights. The right engaged on the ordinary meaning of the statute was the natural justice hearing rule.[62] The relevant provisions were 'an exhaustive statement of the requirements of the natural justice hearing in relation to the matters they deal with'[63] (which the Court said were onshore visa applicants). The common law right was abrogated for these visa applicants as the Minister for Immigration was not expressly required to give them an opportunity to deal with relevant adverse information, though she could, in her discretion, invite them to do so.[64] The applicant, however, was an offshore visa applicant. And though the relevant legislative history (explanatory memorandum and the

[57] Ibid, 89–90.

[58] See William N Eskridge Jr and Philip P Frickey, 'Quasi-Constitutional Law: Clear Statement Rules as Constitutional Lawmaking' (1992) 45 *Vanderbilt Law Review* 593.

[59] William N Eskridge Jr, Philip P Frickey and Elizabeth Garrett, *Legislation and Statutory Interpretation*, 2nd edn (Minnesota, Foundation Press, 2006) 354–355.

[60] *Lacey v Attorney-General (Qld)* (2011) 242 CLR 573 ('*Lacey*'); see Dan Meagher, 'The Principle of Legality as Clear Statement Rule' (2014) 36 *Sydney Law Review* 413, 424–429.

[61] *Coco* (1994) 179 CLR 427, 437 (Mason CJ, Brennan, Gaudron and McHugh JJ).

[62] *Saeed v Minister for Immigration and Citizenship* (2010) 241 CLR 252, 261 (French CJ, Gummow, Hayne, Crennan and Kiefel JJ) ('*Saeed*').

[63] *Migration Act 1958* (Cth), s 51A (1).

[64] Ibid, s 56.

Minister's second reading speech) made clear that the provisions *were* intended to cover all visa applicants the High Court held that these materials (and the subjective intentions of the Parliament) were not interpretively decisive:

> Statements as to legislative intention made in explanatory memoranda or by Ministers, however clear or emphatic, cannot overcome the need to carefully consider the words of the statute to ascertain its meaning.[65]

Consequently, the relevant provisions were interpreted in the following terms:

> Assuming, for present purposes, that s 51A as it applies to s 57, is valid and effective to exclude the natural justice hearing rule, it is excluded only so far as concerns onshore visa applicants … The position of offshore visas is not addressed … It follows that [upon the application of the principle of legality] the implication of the natural justice hearing rule with respect to offshore visa applicants was maintained. The Minister was obliged to provide the appellant with an opportunity to answer adverse material.[66]

This curial insistence that Parliament must consider and then decide whether its legislation is to infringe a fundamental right is the lynchpin of the principle of the legality. A proposition that was emphatically endorsed by Justice Gummow and Justice Bell in the High Court case of *Plaintiff M47* where they held that the *Migration Act 1958* (Cth) 'does not provide *in terms* that an unlawful non-citizen is to be kept in immigration detention permanently or indefinitely.'[67] In other words, Parliament had not 'squarely confronted' and then decided using clear statutory language to express that decision that the fundamental common law right to liberty of unlawful non-citizens (seeking asylum) was to be abrogated in this way.[68]

In this series of migration cases the principle of legality has operated as 'a kind of manner and form requirement imposed on Parliament'[69] requiring 'clear and unequivocal [statutory] language'[70] to interfere with fundamental rights. This suggests that in Australia as well the High Court has 'announc[ed] a rule of law: in the absence of clear statutory text speaking to the precise issue, judges must interpret the statute a certain way.'[71] It is in this sense that the principle of legality has developed into a strong Australian species of clear statement rule for fundamental rights. The significance is that the robust application of the principle has transcended an historically loose collection of rebuttable presumptions[72] with their origins as specific rules and immunities,[73] residual freedoms[74] and aspirational

65 *Saeed* (2010) 241 CLR 252, 264–265 (French CJ, Gummow, Hayne, Crennan and Kiefel JJ). See Matthew Groves, 'Exclusion of the Rules of Natural Justice' (2013) 39 *Monash University Law Review* 285, 290–291.

66 *Saeed* (2010) 241 CLR 252, 271 (French CJ, Gummow, Hayne, Crennan and Kiefel JJ).

67 *Plaintiff M47-2012 v Director General of Security* (2012) 292 ALR 243, 276 (Gummow J) (my emphasis), 377–380 (Bell J).

68 Ibid, 276 (Gummow J), 379 (Bell J).

69 Jeffrey Goldsworthy, *Parliamentary Sovereignty: Contemporary Debates* (Cambridge, Cambridge University Press, 2010) 311.

70 *Momcilovic v The Queen* (2011) 245 CLR 1, 46 (French CJ) ('*Momcilovic*').

71 Eskridge Jr, Frickey and Garrett, above n 59, 354.

72 See John J Doyle, 'Common Law Rights and Democratic Rights' in Paul D Finn (ed), *Essays on Law and Government: Volume 1 Principles and Values* (Pyrmont, Law Book Company, 1995) 144–167.

73 See W M C Gummow, 'The Constitution: Ultimate Foundation of Australian Law?' (2005) 79 *Australian Law Journal* 167, 176–177.

74 See Bailey, above n 11, 19.

judicial values[75] into a common law bill of rights that is strongly resistant to legislative encroachment, maybe defiantly so.[76]

It was no surprise, then, that in a series of lectures delivered by Chief Justice Spigelman in 2008 on the topic of statutory interpretation and human rights[77] the first was titled 'The Common Law Bill of Rights'.[78] In it he details how the progressive renovation of the old common law presumption into the principle of legality, using the methodology of clear statement, has given the bill of rights a quasi-constitutional strength.[79] The suite of rights, freedoms and immunities of which it comprises was said to include the following:[80]

(1) Non-retrospectivity.[81]
(2) Personal liberty.[82]
(3) Freedom of movement.[83]
(4) Freedom of speech.[84]
(5) Fair trial.[85]
(6) Access to the courts.[86]
(7) Open justice.[87]
(8) Lenity.[88]
(9) Natural justice and due process of law.[89]
(10) Property.[90]
(11) Freedom and equality of religion.[91]

[75] In 2004 Professor Paul Rishworth noted that '[i]t was not uncommon to have recourse to rights in legal argument, but they functioned more as broad aspirations … Common law rights were conceptions of generally desirable outcomes, not a tool for defining a baseline of acceptable law and conduct for government.' – 'Common Law Rights and Navigation Lights: Judicial Review and the New Zealand Bill of Rights' (2004) 15 *Public Law Review* 103, 106.

[76] Professor Goldsworthy has observed that, arguably, 'the courts have waged a stealthy, and ultimately successful, campaign to acquire – or usurp – authority to protect 'constitutional' values of their choice, by imposing a kind of manner and form requirement on Parliament … For example, in a jurisdiction lacking a statutory Bill of Rights, the courts might introduce one 'through the back door', by developing a common law bill of rights that protects the same rights as a statutory bill and provides the same level of protection.' – Goldsworthy, above n 69, 311 (citations omitted).

[77] These were the 2008 McPherson Lectures presented at the University of Queensland TC Bierne School of Law – see Spigelman, above n 1.

[78] Ibid, 1–50.

[79] Ibid, 86–97. See Williams and Hume, above n 5, 43–44.

[80] Ibid, 27–29; See D C Pearce and R S Geddes, *Statutory Interpretation in Australia*, 8th edn (London, LexisNexis Butterworths, 2014) 255–259.

[81] *Esber v Commonwealth* (1992) 174 CLR 430; *Rodway v The Queen* (1990) 169 CLR 515.

[82] *Re Bolton* (1987) 162 CLR 514.

[83] *Melbourne Corporation v Barry* (1922) 31 CLR 174; *Potter* (1908) 7 CLR 277.

[84] *Nationwide News* (1992) 177 CLR 1, 31 (Mason CJ) (Austl.); *Evans* (2008) 168 FCR 576, 594–596 (French, Branson and Stone JJ).

[85] *Malika Holdings Pty Ltd v Stretton* (2001) 204 CLR 290.

[86] *Plaintiff S157* (2003) 211 CLR 476.

[87] *Assistant Commissioner Condon v Pompano Pty Ltd* (2013) 252 CLR 38.

[88] *Krakouer v The Queen* (1998) 194 CLR 202.

[89] *Plaintiff M61/2010E v Commonwealth* (2010) 243 CLR 319.

[90] *Durham Holdings Pty Ltd v New South Wales* (2001) 205 CLR 399; *Clunies-Ross v Commonwealth* (1984) 155 CLR 193.

[91] *Evans* (2008) 168 FCR 576; *Canterbury Municipal Council v Moslem Alawy Society Ltd* (1985) 1 NSWLR 525.

The content of the common law bill of rights is now endorsed by senior appellate courts in Australia.[92] And its expansion, though slow and incremental in the common law way,[93] is being hastened by the influence of the Australian constitutional law principle as noted above.[94] Like the common law more generally, the bill of rights applies throughout the Australian federation notwithstanding that many of the key cases concerned federal legislation. Moreover, as then Chief Justice French observed extra-curially, 'the [principle of legality] can be regarded as "constitutional" in character even if the rights and freedoms which it protects are not.' To explain that 'constitutional' character he quoted with approval the following passage from Professor TRS Allan:

> The traditional civil and political liberties, like liberty of the person and freedom of speech, have independent and intrinsic weight: their importance justifies an interpretation of both common law and statute which serves to protect them from unwise and ill-considered interference or restriction. The common law, then, has its own set of constitutional rights, even if these are not formally entrenched against legislative repeal.[95]

In any event, the wave of legislation openly hostile to fundamental rights that began in 1980s and continues to this day[96] has awoken and inspired the rights consciousness of Australian judges. And in the absence of a constitutional bill of rights and a deeply entrenched political reluctance about formal rights, the High Court has filled this lacuna to temper (if not on occasion) resist these legislative developments. To do so the Court has turned to alternative legal sources – international law, common law and indigenous constitutional law – to develop a set of rules and principles to provide more robust protection of fundamental rights. And central to this judicial rights enterprise has been the development and application of a strong Australian species of clear statement rule for fundamental rights to establish a (quasi-constitutional) common law bill of rights that has proven strongly resistant to legislative encroachment.

These contemporary rights developments are significant but controversial as well. In Part V some of the controversies and questions which attend the establishment of a common law bill of rights in Australia will be explored.

V. Controversies and Questions

The original justification for what is now called the principle of legality was tied to authentic notions of legislative intent.[97] Yet as noted in Part III, the manner in which the principle of legality has been applied in contemporary Australian law to establish a common law bill of rights suggests that this justification no longer holds. Relevantly, Professor Jeffrey

[92] See *Momcilovic* (2011) 245 CLR 1, 177–178 (Heydon J) (Austl.); See Chief Justice French, 'Protecting Human Rights Without a Bill of Rights' (Speech delivered at the John Marshall Law School, Chicago, 26 January 2010) 3–4 www.hcourt.gov.au/assets/publications/speeches/current-justices/frenchcj/frenchcj26jan10.pdf.

[93] See The Hon Justice M H McHugh AC, 'Judicial Method' (1999) 73 *Australian Law Journal* 37.

[94] See French, 'Protecting Human Rights Without a Bill of Rights', above n 92.

[95] T.R.S. Allan, 'The Common Law as Constitution: Fundamental Rights and First Principles' in Cheryl Saunders (ed) *Courts of Final Jurisdiction: The Mason Court in Australia* (Annandale, The Federation Press, 1996) 146, 148 quoted in French, above n 92, 32.

[96] See Kieran Hardy, 'National Security Reforms and Freedom of the Press' (2015) 3 *Griffith Journal of Law and Human Dignity* 1.

[97] *See Potter* (1908) 7 CLR 277, 304 (O'Connor J).

Goldsworthy has rightly observed '[t]hat the presumptions are not really motivated by genuine uncertainty about Parliament's intentions; instead, they amount to quasi-constitutional 'manner and form' requirements, imposed by the judiciary, to enhance Parliament's accountability to the electorate.'[98] That proposition is, arguably, supported by the following observation made by then High Court Chief Justice Gleeson:

> A statement concerning the improbability that Parliament would abrogate fundamental rights by the use of general or ambiguous words is not a factual prediction, capable of being verified or falsified by a survey of public opinion. In a free society, under the rule of law, it is an expression of a legal value, respected by the courts, and the acknowledged by the courts to be respected by Parliament.[99]

But the principle of legality is not only 'an expression of a legal value, respected by the courts'. *It is an expression of a legal value that is made and enforced by the courts.* That is why Professors Dyzenhaus, Hunt and Taggart said the principle 'is controversial, at least in so far as it requires judges to construct common law values, and in respect of the material they can legitimately use in this building exercise'.[100] And those choices are especially controversial as the judicial assumption that certain fundamental rights are so deep-lying in the legal order that '[i]t is in the last degree improbable that the legislature would overthrow [them] … without expressing its intention with irresistible clearness'[101] is so interpretively significant: for the principle's application to protect the common law bill of rights may limit the otherwise clear meaning of legislation.[102] The potential for a strained (rights-compatible) meaning is increased further as statutory ambiguity is *not* required before the principle of legality can be applied in Australia.[103]

In any event, as the analysis in Part IV demonstrated the principle of legality is now applied to protect fundamental rights even in the teeth of legislation that aims to curtail or abrogate them. It is, then, difficult to square this with its original normative justification of vindicating authentic notions of legislative intent.[104] Even so, the principle is still one of *interpretation*. When it can be applied its role is to assist in working out the *meaning* of a statute. That is indeed mandated if federal judicial power is to be exercised compatibly with Chapter III of the Australian Constitution.[105] To this end as outlined in Part III, the High Court has reformed the normative justification for the principle of legality to now reflect and enhance core constitutional values such as the rule of law and representative democracy. As Gleeson CJ observed in *Electrolux Home Products Pty Ltd v Australian Workers Union*:

> The presumption is not merely a common sense guide to what a Parliament in a liberal democracy is likely to have intended; it is a working hypothesis, the existence of which is known both to Parliament and the courts, upon which statutory language will be interpreted. The hypothesis is an aspect of the rule of law.[106]

[98] Goldsworthy, above n 69, 308–309.
[99] *Al Kateb* (2004) 219 CLR 577 (Gleeson CJ).
[100] Dyzenhaus, Hunt and Taggart, above n 19, 6.
[101] *Potter* (1908) 7 CLR 277, 304 (O'Connor J).
[102] See Sir Philip Sales, 'A Comparison of the Principle of Legality and Section 3 of the Human Rights Act 1998' (2009) 125 *LQR* 598, 605.
[103] See *Daniels Corporation International Pty Ltd v Australian Competition and Consumer Commission* (2002) 213 CLR 543, 552–553 (Gleeson CJ, Gaudron, Gummow and Hayne JJ).
[104] See Lim, above n 29, 378–394.
[105] *Momcilovic* (2011) 245 CLR 1, 46. See Mark Aronson, 'Statutory Interpretation or Judicial Disobedience?', United Kingdom Constitutional Law Blog (1 June 2013) https://ukconstitutionallaw.org/2013/06/03/mark-aronson-statutory-interpretation-or-judicial-disobedience/.
[106] (2004) 221 CLR 309, 329.

This reformation of the principle's normative justification to provide it with a constitutional dimension reflects common law developments in statutory interpretation more generally. Relevantly, the High Court has recently stated in emphatic terms that 'legislative intention … is a fiction which serves no useful purpose.'[107] '[J]udicial findings as to legislative intention are an expression of the constitutional relationship between the arms of government with respect to the making, interpretation and applications of laws.'[108] Of which Richard Ekins and Jeffrey Goldsworthy have (critically) observed:

> This suggests that legislative intention is not something that exists before judicial interpretation, but instead, is a product or construct of interpretation; or in other words, that it is not the object that the process of statutory interpretation aims to discover, but rather is whatever that process produces.[109]

The High Court has in any event highlighted the centrality of the separation of powers to the interpretive role of Australian courts and firmly located that task within that *constitutional* framework. This underlines the recent extra-judicial observation of Basten J that '[i]f statutory interpretation is at the core of the judicial function, the Commonwealth Parliament must be constrained in its ability either to expand or diminish that function.'[110] It is in this regard that the common law rules of statutory interpretation of which the principle of legality is an important part now have a constitutional dimension.

This development is fascinating, controversial and question-begging. Yet it may be inevitable as well. For as Professor Ernest Young has noted in the context of American clear statement rules, if they are not applied in faithful service of congressional intent then judges 'must find some other source of legal justification for the normative values that the canons protect.'[111] He has suggested 'that that source is the Constitution itself.'[112] And arguably, that too is now the case for the principle of legality in Australia. To this end, the High Court has come to emphasise that the principle exists to protect 'rights, freedoms, immunities, principles and values that are important within our [constitutional] system of representative and responsible government under the rule of law'.[113]

Consequently, the contemporary (constitutionally-orientated) justification for the principle's application is to improve the clarity and rights-sensitivity of legislation promoting democracy and rule of law values in the process. It is these notions that lie at the heart of *Coco* and Lord Hoffman's famous passage in *Simms* that Parliament must 'squarely confront'[114] the rights issues in its legislation and consciously decide upon their abrogation or curtailment with unmistakably clear statutory language. Yet this brings to the surface an

[107] *Lacey* (2011) 242 CLR 573, 592 (French CJ, Gummow, Hayne, Crennan, Kiefel and Bell JJ). But see *Work Health Authority v Outback Ballooning Pty Ltd* [2019] HCA 2 at [74]–[77] (Gageler J).

[108] *Zheng v Cai* (2009) 239 CLR 446, 455–456 (French CJ, Gummow, Crennan, Kiefel and Bell JJ).

[109] Richard Ekins and Jeffrey Goldsworthy, 'The Reality and Indispensability of Legislative Intentions' (2014) 36 *Sydney Law Review* 39, 41. See also Stephen Gageler AC, 'Legislative Intention' (2015) 41 *Monash University Law Review* 1; Justice James Edelman, 'Constitutional Interpretation' (2018 George Winterton Memorial Lecture, Perth, Australia, 26 March 2018) 12–15.

[110] See Justice John Basten, 'Constitutional Dimensions of Statutory Interpretation' (Conference Paper, Constitutional Law Conference, Melbourne Law School, 24 July 2015).

[111] Ernest A Young, 'The Continuity of Statutory and Constitutional Interpretation: An Essay for Phil Frickey' (2010) 98 *California Law Review* 1371, 1380.

[112] Ibid.

[113] *Lee v New South Wales Crime Commission* (2013) 251 CLR 196, 310 (Gageler and Keane JJ) ('*Lee*').

[114] *R v Secretary of State for the Home Department; Ex parte Simms* [2000] 2 AC 115, 131 ('*Simms*').

issue and problem with the method of the principle of legality more generally. The essence of the principle's contemporary justification only holds if Parliament has clear and prior notice of the *content* of the common law bill of rights which it operates to protect. But that is not possible if the content of the relevant 'right' (ie what it requires or guarantees in a particular context) is highly contextual, indeterminate and contested.

This most clearly arises with rights such as freedom of speech, but the problem of indeterminacy, arguably, pertains to all fundamental rights, freedoms and principles at common law to some degree. Even long-established common law rights such as property, liberty and natural justice are highly contextual and subject to reasonable disagreement. For example, whilst the core of the right to natural justice comprises the hearing rule and the bias rule, what that right requires or guarantees turns on the relevant legislative context and the circumstances of the specific case in which it is said to arise. If so, then the content of the relevant 'right' in play must, necessarily, be determined by judges at the point of legislative application in order to resolve the case. The application of the principle of legality is not, then, asserting the relevant content of a *pre-existing* common law bill of rights, but enforcing a post-legislative judicial approximation of what that 'right' requires or guarantees in that specific context.

It may be that this methodological problem is intractable as it reflects the indeterminacy of rights, a common law manifestation of the controversy that has long attended the judicial role under statutory and constitutional bills of rights and the fact that in rights cases other competing rights and interests *always* come into play. Yet the principle can only operate coherently and in accordance with its contemporary justification if Parliament (and parliamentary counsel) has clear and prior notice as to the *content* of the common law bill of rights. Without this knowledge Parliament cannot 'squarely confront' the common law rights issues in its legislation and 'consciously decide' whether or not to curtail or abrogate the fundamental rights in legislative play. If the principle of legality operates to obscure from Parliament the common law (bill of rights) backdrop against which it legislates, the clarity or rights-sensitivity of that legislation cannot be improved. This undercuts the democratic and rule of law values that underpin the modern conception of the principle, its contemporary (constitutional) justification and the manner in which its application operates to protect a common law bill of rights.

VI. Future Development

In Parts III and IV it was suggested that a combination of the rise of human rights in global consciousness and a wave of rights-hostile legislation gave rise to a common law bill of rights in Australia. If anything, this dynamic has only intensified in more recent times. In terms of rights, the Australian Parliament has enacted the *Human Rights (Parliamentary Scrutiny) Act 2011* (Cth). This requires the Executive Government to affix to every bill and legislative instrument introduced into the Parliament a statement of its compatibility with the seven international human rights treaties to which Australia is a signatory.[115] And in the aftermath of 9/11, we have witnessed a new wave of rights-hostile (anti-terror) legislation[116]

[115] *Human Rights (Parliamentary Scrutiny) Act 2011* (Cth), ss 8, 9. See Crawford, ch 8 in this volume.

[116] See Kent Roach, *The 9/11 Effect: Comparative Counter-Terrorism* (Cambridge, Cambridge University Press, 2011) ch 6.

and the migration of these draconian legislative measures into the context of outlaw motorcycle gangs.[117] Moreover, in 2016 a landmark 600-page report of the Australian Law Reform Commission on *Traditional Rights and Freedoms – Encroachment by Laws* identified the serious and increasing legislative threat to fundamental rights.[118] Yet three years later, the Australian Government (which commissioned the report) is still yet to respond to it or its suite of recommendations. In the absence of a constitutional or statutory bill of rights, these contemporary developments may well see the content and scope of the common law bill of rights continue to develop by way of judicial response.

In terms of the content of the common law bill of rights, and its possible future development, Chief Justice French made the following extra-judicial observation:

> One area which awaits further exploration is the interface between human rights norms in Conventions to which Australia is a party or in customary international law and the presumption against statutory displacement of fundamental rights and freedoms of the common law. If the former can inform the latter through developmental processes of the kind mentioned in *Mabo* then the content of the so-called principle of legality may be deepened.[119]

Relevantly, Professors Dyzenhaus, Hunt and Taggart have said that it is legitimate and consistent with the common law's own methodology for it to draw on international human rights norms to update the 'set of values' that it protects through the application of the principle of legality. In doing so, they argue, it 'assists in combating eclecticism or subjectivity in the identification of fundamental rights [as] human rights treaties are an "ostensibly objective source", expressing the opinions, formed often over a considerable period of time, of many countries.'[120]

In *Kaba*,[121] a 2014 decision of the Supreme Court of Victoria Bell J endorsed a strong form of this argument when in detailed obiter comments he said that *all* the rights and freedoms in the International Covenant on Civil and Political Rights ('ICCPR') should now be treated as fundamental for the purposes of the principle. That is, the content of the common law bill of rights in Australia ought now to mirror the ICCPR. Significantly, the adoption of international human rights norms as the rights touchstone for the common law bill of rights necessitates the incorporation of its concomitant methodology – proportionality – into the framework of principle of legality. As Bell J observed 'most of the rights specified in the ICCPR are susceptible to limitation by a state provided that the standards of legality and proportionality (or necessity) are complied with.'[122] This related (common law) development was prudent in his Honour's view for 'Australian courts of high authority have, for some time, been applying a proportionality standard in the process of reading down legislation according [to] the principle of legality.'[123] But that important methodological claim

[117] See Rebecca Ananian-Walsh and George Williams, 'The New Terrorists: The Normalisation and Spread of Anti-Terror Laws in Australia' (2014) 38 *Melbourne University Law Review* 362.

[118] Australian Law Reform Commission, *Traditional Rights and Freedoms – Encroachment by Commonwealth Laws* (ALRC Report 129, 2015) https://www.alrc.gov.au/publications/freedoms-alrc129.

[119] Chief Justice Robert S French, 'Oil and Water? International Law and Domestic Law in Australia' (speech delivered at the Brennan Lecture, Bond University, 26 June 2009) 20 www.hcourt.gov.au/assets/publications/speeches/current-justices/frenchcj/frenchcj26June09.pdf.

[120] Dyzenhaus, Hunt and Taggart, above n 19, 33.

[121] *DPP v Kaba* (2014) 44 VR 526 ('*Kaba*').

[122] Ibid, 580.

[123] Ibid.

is not supported by the authorities cited by Bell J, in my view.[124] Indeed the language and method of proportionality was completely absent from the relevant cases of *Evans*, *Al Masri* and *Haneef*.[125] It would be surprising, then, if these judges were adopting and applying such a significant and controversial new development in common law method without expressly stating that this was, in fact, what was being done or at least contemplated.

In each of these cases the principle of legality was applied to determine the meaning of general statutory words or phrases where their ordinary and natural meaning engaged the common law bill of rights. That posed a particular challenge in a case like *Evans*.[126] The relevant provision was a broad law-making power conferred upon a local council to regulate a large religious event to be held on the streets of Sydney. It did not expressly authorise the abrogation or curtailment of fundamental rights (of persons wishing to protest at the event) but the very nature of the law-making power in this local government context appeared to authorise by *necessary implication* at least some interference. It was the *extent* of that interference that had to be judicially determined. The broad and general wording of the law-making power left open interpretive scope for the protection of the common law free speech rights of protesters. In the event, the Court's application of the principle gave effect to the object of the statute (the primary interpretive duty) in a manner that accommodated so far as possible the common law (free speech) rights of those affected in doing so (the important but secondary consideration). It was a classic example of 'where the text of a statute presents constructional choices, the principle of legality will favour that choice which least disturbs common law freedoms.'[127]

That process, I would argue, was still firmly within the realms of *interpretation*. It was done to ascertain the extent to which the law-making power authorised by necessary implication (by regulation or by-law) interference with the common law bill of rights in order to achieve its purpose. It was not undertaken to judicially evaluate whether the local council could *justify* the infringement of the common law free speech rights of protestors in pursuit of its legislative policy. That latter (justification) inquiry is the essence of proportionality, as I understand it. It is not a tool that assists in working out the *meaning* of legislation which is the object of judicial *interpretation* of which the principle of legality forms an important part. That is why, for example, the still unresolved controversy in Australian bills of rights jurisdictions as to the proper relationship between the interpretation and limitation provisions stems in part from the logical difficulty of seeking to incorporate proportionality which as Professor Paul Rishworth rightly notes 'is more a matter of *evaluation* than interpretation'[128] into the interpretive process itself.[129]

Proportionality does not, then, presently form part of the principle's methodology in my view, and nor should it on account of the fundamental distinction between interpretation and justification analysis just outlined. There are, moreover, legitimate separation of powers concerns that would attend its incorporation. The balancing of competing rights

[124] See Dan Meagher, 'The Principle of Legality and Proportionality' in Dan Meagher and Matthew Groves (eds), *The Principle of Legality in Australia and New Zealand* (Annandale, The Federation Press, 2017) 127–132.

[125] *Evans* (2008) 168 FCR 576; *Minister for Immigration and Multicultural and Indigenous Affairs v Al Masri* (2003) 126 FCR 54 ('*Al Masri*'); *Minister for Immigration and Citizenship v Haneef* (2007) 163 FCR 414 ('*Haneef*').

[126] *Evans* (2008) 168 FCR 576.

[127] Chief Justice Robert French AC, 'Bending Words: The Fine Art of Interpretation' (University of Western Australia, Faculty of Law, Guest Lecture Series, 20 March 2014, Perth) 7. www.hcourt.gov.au/assets/publications/speeches/current-justices/frenchcj/frenchcj20Mar14.pdf.

[128] Paul Rishworth et al, *The New Zealand Bill of Rights* (Oxford, Oxford University Press, 2003) 26.

[129] See *Momcilovic* (2011) 245 CLR 1, 40–44 (French CJ), 170–175 (Heydon J), 217–220 (Crennan and Kiefel JJ).

and interests, and striking a reasonable compromise of them in law, is a core function of the legislature. To the extent that proportionality requires this kind of analysis, there is a serious question as to whether judges have the time, expertise and resources to do so properly in the context of litigation. The very nature of the proportionality inquiry which involves evaluating whether the infringement of the common law bill of rights is justified in the pursuit of legislative policy also sits uncomfortably with the *interpretive* role of judges under the Australian Constitution and its strong separation of judicial power.[130] And there would, arguably, be significant doubt as to the compatibility of such a development with the contemporary justification for the principle detailed above. The courts require 'a clear indication that the legislature has directed its attention to the rights and freedoms in question, and has consciously decided upon abrogation or curtailment.'[131] But if the content of the common law bill of rights is qualified by a proportionality analysis that is, necessarily, context (and therefore case) specific, it is difficult to see how parliaments (and parliamentary counsel) can 'squarely confront' and 'consciously decide' common law rights issues in its legislation.

There is, however, an alternative legal source in Australia to which the High Court may well turn to inform the content and development of the common law bill of rights – the Constitution. And there is a separation of powers-based reason why the Court might choose to do so rather than look to international (human rights) law as suggested by Dyzenhaus, Hunt and Taggart. Australian judges appear keen to develop and apply the principle of legality but not the presumption of consistency with international law. The judicial ambivalence (and sometimes hostility) with the latter likely relates to the *source* of the rights that the presumption operates to protect. The rights protected by the presumption of consistency are derived from international law, so are necessarily derived from a source that is *external* to the Australian legal system. On the other hand, the rights protected by the principle of legality are derived from the common law, so in this sense are derived from an *internal* source. Australian judges may be concerned with the *legitimacy* of using an interpretive presumption to incorporate into the domestic legal system (through interpretation not legislation) norms derived from a source that is external to it. And this legitimacy concern is, arguably, prompted by the strong separation of judicial power established by the Constitution.

Moreover, the Constitution itself provides Australian courts with a potent internal and so quintessentially legitimate legal source from which to reason in order to protect and develop the common law bill of rights. This internal constitutional orientation is, arguably the focus of the passage from the judgment of Gageler and Keane JJ in *Lee* regarding the principle of legality outlined above.[132] It directs us to consider and identify those rights, freedoms and principles central to the proper functioning of *our* constitutional system of democratic government and the maintenance of the rule of law. Of course, the present content of the common law bill of rights already does so in important respects. Consider, for example, the common law rights to liberty, property, freedom of speech, natural justice, criminal due process, open justice and access to the courts. It is not too difficult to discern the important constitutional values that underpin these rights, freedoms and principles and which are, in turn, vindicated when the principle is applied to the construction of statutes. And there are certainly other constitutional principles that might inform further development of the common law bill of rights.

[130] Ibid, 44 (French CJ).

[131] *Coco* (1994) 179 CLR 427, 437 (Mason CJ, Brennan, Gaudron and McHugh JJ).

[132] See text accompanying n 113 above.

Australia's constitutional system of representative and responsible government might underpin and inform a range of fundamental political and democratic participation rights. For example, the rights to vote, associate, assemble and organise, communicate and access political information which the application of the principle to statutes would vindicate. This symbiotic relationship between the Constitution and statutory interpretation might inform also the recognition of freedom of religious belief and exercise as fundamental at common law;[133] and the right to non-discrimination as well, should there be successful reform of the Constitution to expunge its references to race and/or to recognise indigenous Australians and provide them with a constitutional voice to the parliament.[134]

It might be, however, that federalism is the (largely dormant) constitutional principle with the capacity to re-shape and expand the content of the common law bill of rights. In recent Commonwealth executive power cases, for example, the federal principle was central to the High Court's tightening of the constitutional limits on Commonwealth spending.[135] If so minded, could the High Court expand the scope of the principle to include a strong presumption that Commonwealth statutes do not encroach upon the core constitutional powers and functions of the states? The obvious constitutional obstacle is the *Engineers* decision and its 'explosion' of the reserved powers doctrine.[136] But, arguably, expanding the content of the principle along these lines is different. Its application would not limit the scope of Commonwealth legislative power and nor would that be its purpose. The plenary nature of Commonwealth legislative power remains intact but clarity and specificity in its exercise would be required when core state functions and areas of responsibility (eg education, health, public order and safety, intrastate commercial activity) were implicated. That is perfectly consistent with *how* the principle of legality operates with respect to the existing common law bill of rights. And in the *Melbourne Corporation* principle, the constitutional architecture exists already in Australia for such a development to occur at the common law interpretive level.[137] In this way, the federal principle would infuse both the construction and drafting of statutes. It may also bring greater clarity to the notoriously elusive *interpretive* task that bedevils the application of the constitutional inconsistency test under section 109.[138]

Finally, the Constitution might also inform the manner in which the principle of legality is applied to protect the common law bill of rights. For example, the constitutional separation of powers and the respective allocation of functions and responsibilities that it entails might point towards a more nuanced application of the principle depending on the nature and content of the relevant right, freedom or principle *and* the legislative context in which it has arisen. Yet the requirement of legality as detailed in *Coco* that only unmistakable and unambiguous statutory language operates to curtail or abrogate fundamental rights and freedoms applies (at least formally) to the entire common law bill of rights. But the rights, freedoms and principles of which it is comprised vary greatly in terms of the nature and

[133] See Boreham, above n 33.

[134] See Referendum Council, *Final Report of the Referendum Council* (30 June 2017) www.referendumcouncil.org.au/sites/default/files/report_attachments/Referendum_Council_Final_Report.pdf; Megan Davis, 'The Long Road to Uluru' (2018) 60 *Griffith Review* 13.

[135] *Williams v Commonwealth* (2012) 248 CLR 156; *Williams v Commonwealth* (2014) 252 CLR 416; see Stephen McLeish, 'Federal Implications Under the Australian Constitution' (2014) 25 *Public Law Review* 172.

[136] *Amalgamated Society of Engineers v Adelaide Steamship Co Ltd* (1920) 28 CLR 129 ('*Engineers*').

[137] *Melbourne Corporation v Commonwealth* (1947) 74 CLR 31 ('*Melbourne Corporation*').

[138] See Geoffrey Lindell, 'Grappling with Inconsistency between Commonwealth and State Legislation and the Link with Statutory Interpretation' (2005) 8(2) *Constitutional Law and Policy Review* 25.

specificity of their content; and this in turn conditions the ease (or difficulty) with which the courts can determine what a particular right or freedom might require in any given context.

There may be, then, a constitutional justification for the courts to apply the principle with a particular strictness to those fundamental rights such as liberty, property (including native title), natural justice, open justice, access to the courts and criminal due process that fall within the heartland (in terms of jurisdiction and expertise) of judicial power. On the other hand, when the content of the right, freedom or principle is 'highly contextual and contingent' and/or the primary responsibility for its vindication is allocated by the Constitution to the political arms of government such as freedom of speech then maybe the principle ought not to be applied with the same *Coco*-mandated strictness. I would add to this category religious liberty, federalism, non-discrimination and the suite of political and democratic participation rights outlined above, in the event they come to be recognised as fundamental at common law. In order to do so, the High Court could adopt a more flexible conception of 'necessary implication' than the one outlined in *Coco*. The nature of legislation that engages these sorts of highly contextual and contingent rights (such as freedom of speech) will, necessarily, be pursuing other important rights and interests (such as privacy, security, public order). In these contexts a more flexible conception might manifest as a judicial willingness to consider whether a statute necessarily implied *some* interference with fundamental rights without having to first meet *Coco's* high threshold requirement which is that an implication of this kind can be made only 'if it is necessary to prevent the statutory provisions from becoming inoperative or meaningless'.[139] A more flexible conception of 'necessary implication' already characterises some important legality cases in my view, especially those concerning the application of the principle to delegated law-making powers.[140] It is an interpretive approach, moreover, that sits easily within the directive of French CJ that 'where the text of a statute presents constructional choices, the principle of legality will favour that choice which least disturbs common law freedoms'.[141]

VII. Conclusion

In Australia, the High Court has transformed an old common law interpretive presumption into the principle of legality, a strong species of clear statement rule for fundamental rights. It has done so, arguably, to fill the lacuna in formal rights protection in Australia and to temper (if not on occasion resist) increasingly common legislative attempts to eradicate fundamental rights (especially of marginalised or despised minorities). The Court has, then, applied the principle of legality to establish (and protect from legislative encroachment) a common law bill of rights. As Sir Anthony Mason presciently observed in 1995, '[j]ust as the courts can protect common law rights by applying presumptive rules of construction, so they can protect fundamental rights, even in the absence of constitutional entrenchment and statutory backing'.[142] And so it has proven to be in Australia.

[139] *Coco* (1994) 179 CLR 427, 438 (Mason CJ, Brennan, Gaudron and McHugh JJ).

[140] See Dan Meagher and Matthew Groves, 'The Common Law Principle of Legality and Secondary Legislation' (2016) 39 *University of New South Wales Law Journal* 450, 469–477.

[141] See French, n 127 above, 7.

[142] See Sir Anthony Mason, 'Courts, Constitutions and Fundamental Rights' in Richard Rawlings (ed), *Law, Society and Economy: Centenary Essays for the London School of Economics and Political Science* (Oxford, Clarendon Press, 1997) 286.

20

Against a Constitutional Bill of Rights in Australia

JEFFREY GOLDSWORTHY

I. Introduction

In this chapter, I will argue against the constitutional entrenchment in Australia of an American-style Bill of Rights empowering the judiciary to invalidate legislation regarded as inconsistent with protected rights.[1] I will not argue against a statutory Bill of Rights that concerns only the interpretation of legislation; such statutes raise quite different issues that cannot be considered here.[2]

I acknowledge at the outset that the question is far from clear-cut. Strong arguments can be made both for and against constitutional entrenchment, because it would probably have both good and bad consequences. In the end, the question is whether the good is likely to outweigh the bad, which is hard to assess. The philosophical and practical issues I will discuss are complex, and subject to disagreement among well informed and reasonable minds. On the other hand, it is this very fact – the inevitability of reasonable disagreement – that underpins the case against constitutional entrenchment.

II. Historical Background

Australia is now the only major Anglophone country that has not adopted a national Bill or Charter of Rights of some kind. Since 1982, Canada, New Zealand, and the UK have all adopted either constitutional or statutory Bills of Rights. But for rights protection, Australia continues to rely mainly on the common law, a vigorous parliamentary democracy, statutes dealing with specific issues such as racial and sexual discrimination, and a generally tolerant and diverse culture.

Australia's national Constitution has been described as 'a prosaic document expressed in lawyer's language'.[3] It deals mainly with institutional, structural and procedural matters, and

[1] I am less opposed to the alternative Canadian model, which includes an "override clause": see Part V, below.

[2] For a critique of such statutes, see J D Heydon, 'Are Bills of Rights Necessary in Common Law Systems?' (2014) 130 *LQR* 392.

[3] Sir A Mason, in Robert French, Geoffrey Lindall and Cheryl Saunders (eds) *Reflections on the Australian Constitution* (Annandale, Federation Press, 2003) 8.

lacks grand declarations of national values or aspirations. Its framers borrowed heavily from the United States in designing the federal system, and included various provisions designed to suppress regional favouritism; for example, the states are not permitted to discriminate against the residents of other states.[4] But they included only a handful of scattered provisions that arguably protect individual rights.[5] Most of these bind the Commonwealth and not the states: for example, only the Commonwealth is prohibited from compulsorily acquiring property without just compensation, removing trial by jury for prosecutions on indictment, or violating freedom of religion.[6] These prohibitions arguably protect interests related to federalism rather than individual rights as such.[7] They have been described as 'a partial bill of rights'.[8] But the better view is that they 'cannot be compared to a Bill of Rights' because they 'do not hang together in a systematic way and vary in significance and potential', having 'produced a body of law of a technical and somewhat disparate character'.[9]

With respect to rights, the framers were influenced more by the British than the American constitutional tradition. The Australian federation resulted not from armed rebellion against perceived tyranny, but from calm, pragmatic reform by colonial politicians encouraged and assisted by the imperial government. Utilitarianism had replaced natural rights as the main currency of British political thought, and Australia has been described as a paradigmatically utilitarian society.[10] In general, the framers deemed it both unnecessary and unwise to fetter their parliaments. Given the progress of liberal ideas under British institutions, democratically elected parliaments seemed to them the best possible guardians of liberty. The harsh Australian environment was still being settled by Europeans, who wanted strong government to underwrite enterprise, provide necessary infrastructure, and enact social regulation. The framers feared that judicial interpretations of abstract rights could have unpredictable and undesirable consequences. For one thing, they did not want to be prevented from discriminating against people of other races in order to protect the racial and cultural homogeneity of their communities.[11] That is one reason why they

[4] Ibid; Australian Constitution, s 117. Other relevant provisions are ss 51(ii), 92 and 99. For many years, the High Court interpreted s 92, which guarantees freedom of interstate trade and commerce, as if it protected individual rights to engage in such trade and commerce free of unreasonable legal burdens; but that "laissez faire" interpretation was abandoned in *Cole v Whitfield* (1988) 165 CLR 360.

[5] Sections 41 (voting rights), 51(xxxi) ('just terms' for the acquisition of property), 80 (jury trial), 116 (religious freedom) and 117 (equal treatment of non-State residents). Section 51(xxiiiA), inserted by amendment in 1946, prohibits Commonwealth laws with respect to medical or dental services from authorising any form of civil conscription. See also ss 92 (freedom of movement between states) and 100 (right of state residents to use water from rivers). Sections 7 and 24 have recently been interpreted so as to protect voting rights, but that is almost certainly the result of modern conceptions rather than original design. Sections 41, 51(xxxi), 51(xxiiiA), 116, and 100 apply only to the Commonwealth.

[6] Australian Constitution, ss 51(xxxi), 80, and 116 respectively. Sections 41, 51(xxiiiA) and 100 also apply only to the Commonwealth.

[7] See Keven Booker and Arthur Glass, 'The Express Rights Provisions: Form and Substance (or Opportunities Taken and Not Taken?)' in HP Lee and Peter Gerangelos (eds), *Constitutional Advancement in a Frozen Continent: Essays in Honour of George Winterton* (Annandale, Federation Press, 2009) 155.

[8] Rosalind Dixon, 'An Australian (Partial) Bill of Rights' (2016) 14 *International Journal of Constitutional Law*, 80.

[9] Booker and Glass, above n 7, 172. The authors also dispute the common complaint that the High Court has adopted a pedantically narrow interpretation of these provisions.

[10] See, eg, Hugh Collins, 'Political Ideology in Australia: The Distinctiveness of a Benthamite Society' (1985) 144 (Winter) *Daedalus* 147.

[11] Jeffrey Goldsworthy, 'The Constitutional Protection of Rights in Australia', in Gregory Craven (ed) *Australian Federation Towards the Second Century* (Carlton, Melbourne University Press, 1992) 151, 152–4.

deliberately rejected proposals modelled on the Fourteenth Amendment to the United States Constitution, passed after the Civil War, which guarantees 'the equal protection of the laws'; the extraordinary circumstances that had led to this were said to be peculiar to the US.[12]

It was necessary to arm an independent federal judiciary with power to enforce the terms of the federal compact. But, with a few minor exceptions, the traditional British doctrine of parliamentary sovereignty was disturbed only to that extent. Provided that they were acting within their respective spheres of responsibility, and not violating either paramount Imperial laws or constitutional limits, Australian parliaments were deemed to exercise powers as plenary and ample – as sovereign – as that of the UK Parliament itself.[13]

The British Constitution, uncodified and fundamentally customary, had long rested on the principle of parliamentary sovereignty. After sometimes violent political conflicts, and for many reasons, by the end of the seventeenth century Parliament had come to be entrusted with ultimate responsibility for safeguarding the welfare of the community, including the rights and freedoms of the people. For centuries it was commonly said that only in Parliament could all the diverse and conflicting opinions and interests within the community be properly heard and brought to bear upon public decision-making. Starting in the early thirteenth century, it was often said that Parliament represented and spoke for 'the community of the kingdom' – 'the body of all the realm'.[14] It was described in the sixteenth century as 'the mouth of all England'.[15] This long-standing rationale for Parliament's sovereignty pre-dated, but was fortified by, the establishment of democracy in the modern sense in the nineteenth and early twentieth centuries. It was also frequently said to follow that Parliament embodied the combined wisdom of the community, which was necessarily superior to that of any other human authority. Parliament was the principal guardian of the liberties of the community – the 'storehouse of our liberties' and 'the bulwark' between rights and 'all designs of oppression'.[16]

Prominent Australians used to express a similar faith in this country's traditional reliance on parliamentary democracy and the common law to protect rights adequately, and to deny that there was any pressing need to adopt a Bill of Rights. In 1902, William Harrison Moore wrote that the 'great underlying principle' of the Australian Constitution was 'that the rights of individuals are sufficiently secured by ensuring, as far as possible, to each a share, and an equal share, in political power'.[17] In 1935, then Commonwealth Attorney-General Robert Menzies – a future Prime Minister – told a gathering of the Empire Parliamentary Association:

> We are told today that the parliamentary system is antiquated, that it is slow, inefficient, illogical, emotional. In the presence of each charge, it may admit to some degree of guilt. But with all its

[12] *Official Records of the Debates of the Australasian Federal Convention,* Melbourne, 8 February 1898, 668 (Isaacs); 672 (O'Connor); 673–4 (Barton); 685–6 (Cockburn); and 686 (Isaacs). For discussion see George Williams and David Hume, *Human Rights Under the Australian Constitution,* 2nd edn (Melbourne, Oxford University Press, 2014) 65–71.

[13] See John Quick and Robert Randolph Garran, *The Annotated Constitution of the Australian Commonwealth* (Angus & Robertson, 1901) 509–10; *D'Emden v Pedder* (1904) 1 CLR 91, 110 (Griffith CJ); *Nelungaloo v Cth* (1948) 75 CLR 495, 503–4 (Williams J).

[14] Jeffrey Goldsworthy, *The Sovereignty of Parliament: History and Philosophy* (Oxford, Clarendon Press, 1999), 30, quoting *The Statute of York 1322,* 17 Edw 2 and Chief Justice Thorpe in 1365.

[15] Peter Wentworth, quoted in ibid 68.

[16] Ibid, 106, quoting James Whitelocke and Bulstrode Whitelocke respectively.

[17] W Harrison Moore, *The Constitution of the Commonwealth of Australia* (John Murray, 1902) 329.

> faults, it retains a great virtue, alas! in these days, a rare virtue. Its virtue is that it is the one system yet devised which ensures the liberty of the subject by promoting the rule of law which subjects themselves make, and to which everyone, Prime Minister or tramp, must render allegiance.[18]

This sentiment was not confined to conservative Australian Anglophiles. Menzies' great opponent in the early 1950s, the Leader of the Labor Party Dr H V Evatt, said this in opposing the Communist Party Dissolution Bill that Menzies sponsored:

> I do not think that a bill of this character would receive a moment's consideration from the mother of parliaments, the British parliament, for in that parliament traditions of political liberty and established justice are always recognised and, are, indeed all powerful.[19]

Sir Owen Dixon, reputedly Australia's greatest judge, defended Australia's system of rights protection in a speech to the American Bar Association in 1944. He explained that although the founders of the Australian Constitution had borrowed heavily from the US model, particularly in relation to federalism, they had deliberately chosen not to include a Bill of Rights.

> In our steadfast faith in responsible government and in plenary legislative powers distributed, but not controlled, you as Americans may perceive nothing better than a wilful refusal to see the light and an obstinate adherence to heresies; but we remain impenitent.[20]

In a public lecture at the University of Virginia in 1967, Sir Robert Menzies, by then Australia's longest serving Prime Minister, reiterated the Australian orthodoxy. He explained that democratic responsible government, working together with the common law, was regarded by Australians as 'the ultimate guarantee of justice and individual rights'. 'I would say, without hesitation, that the rights of individuals in Australia are as adequately protected as they are in any other country in the world.'[21]

Menzies was a conservative, but at least until the 1970s, his counterparts on the left of the political spectrum agreed with him. The traditional attitude of the Australian Labor Party towards rights was eloquently expressed in 1955 by Gough Whitlam, who was to become its most erudite leader and in 1972, a Prime Minister:

> British history shows that Parliament has been our great liberating force. Parliament has conferred political freedom on those represented in it, first of all the barons and squires and then the merchants and now all adults. There is no freedom without equality. To redistribute and equalize liberty has been one of the principal functions of Parliament. Parliament alone can give equality of opportunity and thereby increase liberty for all. If we are to have economic equality of opportunity, which is the next stage in the advance of liberty, we must have effective parliamentary government and, accordingly, dispense with fetters on parliament rather than contrive them. For every person whose liberty has been prejudiced by government action, there are many whose liberty has been enhanced. The virtue of Parliament is that it provides publicity and works in the open. When Parliament is sitting, there are a great number of opportunities for calling as Government to account. The forum which Parliament provides is the best guardian of our liberties. As long as we have members on both sides of our Parliament who are able and willing to express

[18] *The Times*, 5 July 1935. I owe this quote to an unpublished paper by John Hirst, which I have on file.

[19] *Commonwealth Parliamentary Debates*, vols 213, 1951, 1213. I also owe this quote to the same paper by John Hirst.

[20] Sir Owen Dixon, *Jesting Pilate: and Other Papers and Addresses* (Law Book, 1965) 101–2.

[21] Robert Menzies, *Central Power in the Australian Commonwealth: An Examination of the Growth of Commonwealth Power in the Australian Federation* (Charlottesville, University Press of Virginia, 1967) 54.

> many and varied points of view, we have some liberty and can aspire to greater liberty. The price of liberty is eternal vigilance. Parliament has hitherto proved the best instrument for exercising that vigilance.[22]
>
> The High Court … is less representative of the Australian people than are their elected representatives. Judges are irresponsible in that they hold office for life, which is sometimes a very long life.[[23]] Some have used that asset for a political purpose. … We are constrained by our present Federal Constitution to leave the final disposition of many matters in the hands of lawyers. We are forbidden to do not so much what the Constitution forbids us to do but what the judges forbid us to do. If counsel has to advise whether a certain action is constitutional, he is less concerned with the Constitution than with the composition of the court. We thus run the risk that we shall be granted only such liberties as commend themselves to lawyers. Australians have developed a habit of asking the High Court to invalidate Acts of Parliament whenever they conceive their liberties have been infringed by those Acts. Advocacy has been so successful in recent years that the Court itself has developed an attitude of almost supercilious suspicion towards Acts of Parliament and actions of the administration. People who have successfully approached the Court in these matters are loud in their praise for the safeguard the Court affords. There are, however, hundreds and thousands of persons who have not a sufficient interest to be heard by the Court but who would have received benefits and enhanced liberties from the legislation in question. The Court, in other words, gives liberty to those who can establish a sufficient interest or a right of action and to them alone.[24]

Whitlam's views reflected Labor's long-standing distrust of judges – traditionally associated with 'the Establishment' – who had a track record of protecting rights to property and freedom of contract, by invalidating or restrictively interpreting legislation aimed at regulating business and advancing the interests of the working class.[25]

Of course, opinions evolved as times and intellectual fashions changed. In the 1960s, Australians were heavily influenced by social upheavals in the United States and elsewhere, including the civil rights campaign, the student protest movement, and the libertarian revolution. Justifiable concerns about capital punishment, censorship, the plight of indigenous peoples, discrimination against homosexuals, and the subordination of women undermined earlier confidence in Australia's track record in protecting rights. (Although it should be added that there is little reason to think that the judges of past eras would have done any better than our parliaments.) The policies of the Labor Party changed, and when in government in the early 1970s and 1980s, it made two unsuccessful attempts to adopt a Bill of Rights.

Although various public opinion polls indicate that most Australians favour enhanced protection of rights,[26] they have remained wary of doing so by constitutional entrenchment. In 1988, a modest proposal to amend the Constitution by extending to the states the existing guarantees of religious freedom, jury trial, and just terms for the expropriation of

22 E G Whitlam, in The Australian Institute of Political Science, *Liberty in Australia* (Angus and Robertson, 1955) 177–8.

23 Federal judges must now retire at the age of 70, due to a constitutional amendment in 1977.

24 Whitlam, The Australian Institute of Political Science, above n 22, 174.

25 Tom Campbell, *The Left and Rights: A Conceptual Analysis of the Idea of Socialist Rights* (London, Routledge & Kegan Paul, 1983); J A G Griffith, *The Politics of the Judiciary* (Manchester University Press, 1977); Lord Devlin, 'Judges and Lawmakers' (1976) 39 *Modern Law Review* 1, 13–14 observed that judges had often frustrated the democratic will of Parliament – by refusing to act on the ordinary meaning of statutory words – to protect a 'Victorian Bill of Rights' – individual liberty, property, freedom of contract and anti-taxation.

26 Summarised in Rosalind Dixon, 'An Australian (Partial) Bill of Rights', above n 8, 86–7.

property, suffered the worst defeat of any amendment ever proposed, being approved by less than 31 per cent of the electorate.[27] Of course, proposals for constitutional amendment fail at referendums for many reasons, including party politics.[28] Nevertheless, since then there has been no significant political impetus towards strengthening the protection of rights in the Constitution. As George Winterton observed, 'the prospects of securing referendum approval for the introduction of [an entrenched] bill of rights are minimal in view of the inevitable controversy it would generate.'[29] That is why an Expert Panel, appointed by the Gillard Labor Government to consider the desirability of constitutional recognition of indigenous Australians, advised against a general equality or non-discrimination clause; it emphasised that it was 'not advocating a bill or statement of rights'.[30]

On the other hand, with the tide of international opinion continuing to run strongly in favour of increased judicial participation in human rights protection, and Australians occasionally seeking redress from the United Nations Human Rights Committee, it is inevitable that demands for major statutory and perhaps even constitutional reform will grow over the coming years. Among younger generations of lawyers, older ideas of legislative supremacy are increasingly unfashionable, and Australian judges are more amenable to assuming the task of protecting rights.[31] As former High Court Justice Michael McHugh observed, during the 1980s and 1990s:

> [t]he thinking and many of the beliefs and values that permeated the Age of Menzies largely disappeared … Globalisation … opened up Australian society to new ideas, to a new way of seeing the world. And by the commencement of the period of the Mason Court [1987], human rights had become part of the political and social agenda, and international law and agreements were becoming a source of common law and domestic statute law …. It would be surprising if the judiciary had missed this message. Long ago, Judge Cardozo pointed out that judges cannot escape the currents of their times.[32]

III. The Global Expansion of the Subordination of Legislative Authority to Judicially Protected Rights

The principle of legislative supremacy was not unique to Britain. Until after the Second World War, judicial enforcement of written constitutions was relatively unknown across the globe. But we now live in a very different world in which, to quote an eminent constitutional comparativist, 'From France to South Africa to Israel, parliamentary sovereignty

[27] See Williams and Hume, above n 12, 73.

[28] See George Williams and David Hume, *People Power: The History and Future of the Referendum in Australia* (Sydney, UNSW Press, 2010), particularly 199–237.

[29] George Winterton, 'An Australian Rights Council' in Tom Campbell, Jeffrey Goldsworthy and Adrienne Stone (eds) *Protecting Rights Without a Bill of Rights: Institutional Performance and Reform in Australia* (Aldershot, Ashgate, 2006) 305, 306.

[30] Expert Panel on Constitutional Recognition of Indigenous Australians, Recognising Aboriginal and Torres Strait Islander Peoples in the Constitution: Report of the Expert Panel (2012) 169, 171, quoted in Rosalind Dixon, 'An Australian (Partial) Bill of Rights', above n 8, 97.

[31] Apart from extra-curial speeches, this is shown by the High Court's recognition of an implied right to freedom of political communication and to voting rights.

[32] Michael McHugh, 'The Constitutional Jurisprudence of the High Court: 1989–2004' (2008) 30 *Sydney Law Review* 5, 11–12.

has faded away.'[33] In 1939 only a handful of countries had judicial review under a written constitution; in 1951, 38 per cent had adopted it; by 2011 that number had grown to 83 per cent.[34] This extraordinary, widespread transformation of governance is now being studied by constitutional comparativists and political scientists. It is the subject of books with titles such as 'The Global Expansion of Judicial Power',[35] 'The Judicialization of Politics',[36] and 'Towards Juristocracy'.[37]

This phenomenon is often called the 'rights revolution'.[38] As one leading scholar puts it: 'In today's world, the ideology of rights has, arguably, achieved the status of a civic religion.'[39] The ancient idea that the legitimacy of government depends on conformity to a 'higher law' remains, but the law of nature or of God has been replaced by the law of human rights. Moreover, we are witnessing a global conversation about rights among judges of apex courts, who increasingly meet at conferences, share ideas, and cite and sometimes follow one another's judgments. Some scholars envisage the eventual emergence of a homogenised global constitutional law. It is also suggested that this is being propelled by a constant 'ratcheting up' process, in which courts outdo one another in discovering new rights and expanding existing ones.[40] One common method of 'upping the ante' in rights protection is to adopt the theory of interpretation commonly called 'living constitutionalism'. The most extreme version of this theory holds that judges are not limited to the original meaning of a constitutional provision, but can give it a new, more expansive meaning that they believe is more compatible with evolving social values.[41]

These developments amount to a constitutional experiment on a global scale. They raise the danger of democratic decision-making being subject to override not only by unelected judges, but by reference to a global judicial consensus about rights. But for many people, this is merely the next advance in the progressive evolution of constitutionalism – a term referring to the subjection of governmental power at the highest levels to the rule of law. On their view, just as democracy came to be widely adopted because it was an indisputable improvement on autocracy, so too has the judicial enforcement of constitutional rights spread because it is innately superior to unchecked majoritarian democracy, which threatens the rights of unpopular and vulnerable minorities.

[33] Tom Ginsburg, *Judicial Review in New Democracies: Constitutional Courts in Asian Cases* (US, Cambridge University Press, 2003) 3.

[34] Tom Ginsburg and Mila Versteeg, 'Why Do Countries Adopt Constitutional Review?' (2014) 30 *Journal of Law, Economics, and Organization* 587, 587.

[35] C Neal Tate and Torbjörn Vallinder (eds), *The Global Expansion of Judicial Power* (New York, New York University Press, 1995).

[36] Reginald S Sheehan, Rebecca D Gill, Kirk A Randazzo, *Judicialization of Politics: The Interplay of Institutional Structure, Legal Doctrine, and Politics on the High Court of Australia* (Carolina Academic Press, 2012); Martin Shapiro and Alec Stone Sweet, *On Law, Politics and Judicialization* (Oxford, Oxford University Press, 2002); Björn Dressel (ed), *The Judicialization of Politics in Asia* (London, Routledge, 2012).

[37] Ran Hirschl, *Towards Juristocracy: The Origins and Consequences of the New Constitutionalism* (Harvard University Press, 2004).

[38] Charles Epp, *The Rights Revolution: Lawyers, Activists, and Supreme Courts in Comparative Perspective* (Chicago, University of Chicago Press, 1998).

[39] Alec Stone Sweet, 'Constitutional Courts' in Michel Rosenfeld and András Sajó (eds), *The Oxford Handbook of Comparative Constitutional Law* (Oxford, Oxford University Press, 2012) 816, 829.

[40] See, eg, Mitchel de S-O-l'E Lasser, 'The Judicial Dynamics of the French and European Fundamental Rights Revolution' in Diana Kapiszewski, Gordon Silverstein and Robert A Kagan (eds), *Consequential Courts: Judicial Roles in Comparative Perspective* (Cambridge, Cambridge University Press, 2013) 289.

[41] For discussion see Grant Huscroft and Bradley W Miller (eds), *The Challenge of Originalism: Theories of Constitutional Interpretation* (Cambridge, Cambridge University Press, 2011).

As an empirical hypothesis, this idealistic explanation of the rights revolution is questionable. Social scientists who have examined the global expansion of judicial power have come to a less flattering conclusion: it has been driven much more by domestic political competition than by genuine idealism, when elites with waning influence vest power in independent courts in the hope of loading the dice to favour their policies over those of their rivals.[42]

Be that as it may, I accept that in most western democracies the increasing popularity of Bills of Rights has been motivated largely by a sincere commitment to protecting individual rights from violations resulting from majoritarian thoughtlessness, prejudice or hysteria. For example, there are genuine concerns about Australia's recent human rights performance, such as:

> the continuing relative deprivations of indigenous people and the lack of substantial recognition of their interests as the original inhabitants, oppressive laws against voluntary euthanasia, inadequate services for disabled people (particularly those suffering from mental illness), failure to protect children at risk, harsh treatment of asylum seekers, acquiescence in child poverty and gross economic inequality, readiness to introduce potentially oppressive anti-terrorist legislation, the use of mandatory sentencing for juvenile offenders (in Western Australia and the Northern Territory), and the Commonwealth Government's repeated and forceful rejection of quite reasonable criticism of these policies by the UN Committee on Human Rights.[43]

Respect for politicians and the business of politics seems to have declined. As a South African lawyer once said, 'the moral authority of the judiciary is expanding into the space vacated by the contraction of the moral authority of the executive and the legislature.'[44] The global rights revolution has had an enormous influence on lawyers in particular.

The elected branches of government are alleged to suffer from a variety of defects:

(1) Westminster Parliaments are widely regarded (rightly or wrongly) as too subservient to the executive governments that dominate their Lower Houses. Lord Hailsham's famous description of 'elective dictatorship' is still often quoted.[45]

(2) There are said to be 'agency problems': failures of elected representatives to faithfully advance the interests of their constituents. They are sometimes suspected of being unduly influenced by powerful interest groups, lobbying behind the scenes after purchasing privileged access to Ministers.

(3) Conversely, politicians are often criticised for being too subservient to public opinion. They are sometimes depicted as self-serving careerists and populists who put winning and retaining power before respect for human rights. In Australia, for example, very harsh treatment of asylum seekers who arrive, unauthorised, by boat – a paradigm case of a vulnerable and unpopular minority – is widely condemned as pandering to public hysteria.

[42] Ginsburg and Versteeg, above n 34.

[43] Tom Campbell, 'Human Rights Strategies: An Australian Alternative', in Campbell, Goldsworthy and Stone, above n 29, 319, 324.

[44] Etienne Mureinik, 'Administrative Law in South Africa' (1986) 103 *South African Law Journal* 615, 618.

[45] See, eg, Tom Bingham, *The Rule of Law* (London, Allen Lane, 2010) 26, 169. But cf, R Ekins and G Gee, 'Putting Judicial Power in its Place' ((2018) 36 *The University of Queensland Law Journal* 375, 391–92 nn 77–78 for arguments to the contrary.

My own impression is that in countries such as Britain, Canada, Australia, and New Zealand, a substantial proportion of the tertiary educated, professional class now has a much reduced faith in the ability of their fellow citizens to form opinions about public policy in a sufficiently intelligent, well-informed, dispassionate and carefully reasoned manner. Through the centuries, suspicion of majority rule has been rife among the better educated classes, who have feared the ignorance, stupidity and vulgarity of the masses.[46] The nineteenth century champion of civil liberties, John Stuart Mill, admitted that his commitment to democracy cooled in the 1840s because he 'dreaded the ignorance and especially the selfishness and brutality of the mass'; he proposed that the educated should have more votes, in proportion to the level of their education, than the bulk of the people, to ensure more enlightened and rational decision-making.[47] This idea has been taken up by recent proponents of 'epistocracy', which means rule by citizens with sufficient relevant knowledge to participate responsibly in public decision-making.[48] It appears that many modern civil libertarians want to entrust representative members of their own class (judges) – due to their educational attainments, intelligence, habits of thought, and professional ethos – with power to restrain popular passions and prejudices while 'educating' the community to embrace a 'rights culture'.

An obvious rejoinder is that the attraction of judicially enforceable rights is due much more to the procedures that judges follow than to their personal qualities. These procedures are said to promote more thorough, impartial and carefully reasoned enquiries into the actual impacts of laws on the individuals who come before the courts. In Alexander Bickel's words, judges deal with 'flesh and blood', whereas legislators typically tackle more 'abstract and dimly foreseen problems'.[49]

There is, of course, something to this rejoinder, but it is far from convincing. Courts do focus on the predicaments of the individuals appearing before them, but for that very reason, are less able to take into account relevant interests of other people or groups who may be affected, adversely or beneficially, by the laws in question. An aggrieved individual is usually just one of many who are affected by a law, and a particular case may be an atypical symptom of a widespread and intractable social problem that the courts cannot even fully grasp, let alone resolve.[50] To the extent that relevant considerations transcend the particulars of the individual parties before it, a court is arguably less competent than the other branches of government to assess them.

Furthermore, if the main problem were deficiencies in the deliberative procedures of elected legislatures, the most obvious remedy would be to improve those procedures to promote more careful and well-informed decision-making. Judicial enforcement of rights would then be a fall-back position, to be resorted to only if such reforms are unsuccessful.

[46] Anthony Arblaster, *Democracy* (Milton Keynes, Open University Press, 1987) especially 6, chs 3 and 4.
[47] Quoted in ibid, 48.
[48] Jason Brennan, *Against Democracy* (New Jersey, Princeton University Press, 2016). See also C.H. Achen and L.M. Bartels, *Democracy for Realists: Why Elections Do Not Produce Responsive Government* (Cambridge, Cambridge University Press, 2008).
[49] Alexander M Bickel, *The Least Dangerous Branch: The Supreme Court at the Bar of Politics* (Bobbs-Merill, 1962) 26.
[50] See Donald L Horowitz, *The Courts and Social Policy* (Brookings Institute, 1977).

IV. The Impact of the Judicial Protection of Constitutional Rights on Democracy

Judicial protection of constitutional rights may be highly desirable, or even essential, to preserve democracy, the rule of law, and human rights in many countries, in which corruption, populism, authoritarianism, or bitter religious, ethnic, or class conflicts are rife. But mature, stable and tolerant democracies do not have the same needs. The main argument against constitutional rights is based on the following premises.

First, any enumeration of rights must be couched in terms of abstract rights to free speech, due process of law, equality before the law, and so on. Secondly, no abstractly stated right can be absolute. Even the most fundamental right of all – the right to life – can be over-ridden, as in self-defence. It is possible to refer to the kinds of qualifications that experience has found to be most needed; for example, article 10 of the European Convention, after recognising the right to freedom of expression, states that the exercise of the right may be limited:

> as … necessary in a democratic society, in the interests of national security, territorial integrity or public safety, for the prevention of disorder or crime, for the protection of health or morals, for the protection of the reputation or rights of others, for preventing the disclosure of information received in confidence, or for maintaining the authority and impartiality of the judiciary.

But even then, judges are left with enormous discretion; they must decide whether or not the right, and one or more of these competing interests, are truly at stake, and if so whether, and to what extent, impingement on the former is 'necessary' for the protection of the latter. These are matters for discretion, because they require moral and political judgment. The grounds on which judges must decide these questions are identical to those which should guide legislatures. Appeals to policy, public welfare or the common good ought to be, and usually are, appeals to the rights of the countless diffuse individuals who may be affected.[51]

Thirdly, it is impossible to decide and make provision in advance for how, in particular cases, abstractly stated rights should be weighed against competing rights and interests. It follows that the power of judges to interpret and enforce these rights is the power to decide a vast number of controversial questions of public policy, and to substitute their decisions for those reached by lawmakers elected to represent the public. These questions include virtually all serious moral and political issues likely to arise in societies such as ours. Consider, for example, the following passage written by an American constitutional lawyer:

> Today federal courts control more important public decisions and institutions in more detail and for more extended periods than at any time in our history. Constitutional interpretations have important influence over a vast range of policies, including those relating to marriage, parent-child relations, abortion, zoning, public administration, police practices, aid to private education, commercial advertising, defamation, criminal penalties, aliens, women, jury selection, voting, affirmative action, and state taxation.[52]

[51] J M Finnis, 'A Bill of Rights For Britain?: the Moral of Contemporary Jurisprudence' (1985) LXXI *Proceedings of the British Academy* 303, 305, 307, 308–11, 315–29. This is demonstrated by Dworkin's own responses to objections to his thesis that courts do not and should not consider arguments of 'policy', but only those of 'principle': he shows that almost all alleged arguments of the former sort can be translated into arguments of the latter sort: see Ronald Dworkin, *Taking Rights Seriously* (Cambridge, Mass, Duckworth, 1977) 294–330.

[52] Robert F Nagel, *Constitutional Cultures: The Mentality and Consequences of Judicial Review* (Berkerley, University of California Press, 1989) 1–2.

All this leads to the main argument against a Bill of Rights, namely, that it is undemocratic for a small, undetected elite to have the power to override decisions made by the elected representatives of the people concerning such important questions of social policy. When a community must decide such questions – including questions involving rights – but its members are in disagreement, the fairest way of settling the disagreement is for unfettered debate in which every person's opinion can, in principle, have an equal influence on the final decision – which must therefore be made by majority vote. (Note that judges decide disagreements among themselves in the same way. Judicial review of legislation therefore does not overcome objections to majoritarianism: it merely substitutes decisions by a majority of a tiny group of unelected judges for decisions by a majority of a much larger group of elected legislators.) One of the most fundamental of all rights is therefore the right of ordinary people to participate, on equal terms, in the political decision-making that affects their lives as much as anyone else's. This right was hard won, through centuries of political struggle, and should not readily be surrendered.[53]

As Jeremy Waldron has argued, the large size of legislatures should enable all significant interests and opinions within the community to contribute to debate, ensuring that none are overlooked. All participants are treated with equal respect, rather than ignored or shouted down for being ignorant, prejudiced, or dishonest.[54] Decision-making by majority vote is the only way of giving every individual's view the greatest possible weight compatible with an equal weight being given to the views of everyone else.

Politicians, like the people they represent, are imperfect. They sometimes do the wrong thing, and enact clearly unjust, rights-violating laws. It can, quite understandably, seem desirable to give judges power to over-rule such laws. But the price that must be paid in order to give judges that power is that they must also be given power to override the democratic process in a much greater number of cases, where the requirements of justice and human rights are debatable, and legislative decisions are not clearly unjust. In a relatively tolerant democratic society such as Australia's, cases of clear injustice are relatively rare; in most cases, whether or not a law violates some basic right is open to reasonable arguments on both sides. But a Bill of Rights usually requires judges to review the validity of legislation in all cases, and not just those involving clear injustice.

One way to resolve this dilemma would be to provide that judges may invalidate statutes only in the comparatively few cases when rights have been *clearly* violated, and must defer to the legislature's judgments when there are reasonable arguments on both sides. But that is very difficult to do. There is a powerful temptation to reject as not only mistaken, but clearly mistaken and therefore unreasonable, value judgments that differ from one's own. This is especially so for judges who are, by virtue of their position, symbols of office and unchallenged authority, constantly exposed to 'the intoxicating notion that they may be wiser, more dispassionate and sure-footed than their fellow men'.[55] In one High Court case, for example, two judges held invalid a law based on a distinction they described as irrational; yet a third judge found the distinction to be not only rational, but necessary![56] Strong-minded judges with passionate moral and political convictions find it very difficult to stay

[53] This paragraph owes much to the writings of Jeremy Waldron, especially *Law and Disagreement* (Oxford, Clarendon Press, 1999).

[54] Ibid 111–12.

[55] Lord McCluskey, *Law, Justice and Democracy* (London, Sweet & Maxwell, 1987) 1.

[56] *Leeth v Commonwealth* (1992) 174 CLR 455, 479, 492.

their hand. Moreover, judges are constantly egged on by vocal interest groups demanding that their grievances be redressed, and by academic lawyers eager for their theories of rights to be implemented. Civil libertarians would condemn a policy of deference to the legislature as incompatible with the very purpose of a Bill of Rights. They often express the fear that judges, being on the whole politically conservative and professionally legalistic, would interpret such a bill timidly and restrictively, although many are confident that in the long run the judiciary would adopt the more self-confident, activist style of the US Supreme Court.[57] Notwithstanding their professionalism and independence, judges are inevitably susceptible to such cultural influences.

A policy of judicial deference would raise a further problem. The dismissal of a constitutional challenge to the validity of a law may tend to legitimise the law, as if the court had approved or endorsed it.[58] A court cannot refuse to determine a justiciable question properly brought before it; it cannot wash its hands of disputes involving constitutional rights and leave them to be resolved in the political arena. To dismiss an argument that a law violates a right the court must hold that it does *not* do so. The subtleties of judicial restraint are not easily understood, and the imprimatur of constitutionality may delegitimise the objections of those opposed to the law (with whom the judges might privately agree).[59] The possibility of this occurring must reinforce other pressures on judges to abandon a policy of restraint. American experience shows that patterns of judicial deference or activism can change dramatically in a short space of time, as the composition of the judiciary and the attitudes of elite sections of the legal profession change.

Moreover, just as the considered choice of a majority may be wrong or unjust, so too may the opinions of a minority. Even judges are imperfect; they also make mistakes. Indeed, as we have seen, it can be argued that with respect to rights, they are not as well placed as elected politicians to make wise decisions. Because rights are never absolute, and must be weighed against competing rights and interests, one person's complaint that his or her right has been violated usually raises questions about the interests of other members of the community. But those other members may not be represented in court, especially in Australia given its relatively strict standing requirements.[60] A Parliament is much more able to gather all the relevant facts, to consult widely with all affected parties, and arrive at an overall balance or compromise of the competing interests at stake. In addition, a particular case before a court might be atypical, leading to a judicial decision not well suited to the majority of situations that are likely to arise in the community at large.

By its very nature, adjudication under a Bill of Rights tends to over simplify and distort complicated political issues. Of the various competing interests, those expressly protected in a Bill of Rights are given a special priority which may not be warranted. Sometimes governments legislate to protect rights that cannot be included – for example, so-called 'positive' rights to education, social welfare, or employment at a fair wage. These are not usually

[57] See, eg, Michael Zander, *A Bill of Rights?* 3rd edn (London, Sweet & Maxwell, 1985) 57–64.

[58] Eg, after the US Supreme Court upheld the flag salute requirement challenged by the Jehovah's Witnesses in 1940, mobs attacked the sect's headquarters crying 'The Supreme Court is with us': Jesse H Choper, *Judicial Review and the National Political Process: A Functional Reconsideration of the Role of the Supreme Court* (Chicago, University of Chicago Press, 1980) 233.

[59] See Leonard Levy, 'Judicial Review, History and Democracy' in Leonard Levy (ed), *Judicial Review and the Supreme Court* (New York, Harper & Row, 1967) 1, 39–41.

[60] See Andrew Edgar, 'Standing to Maintain Public Law Proceedings', in Matthew Groves (ed) *Modern Administrative Law in Australia: Concepts and Context* (Cambridge, Cambridge University Press, 2014) 140.

included in a Bill of Rights because they are not generally regarded as judicially enforceable. But courts charged with enforcing certain rights, but not others, will tend to give priority to the former when they compete with the latter.

Furthermore, there are other legitimate community interests that may not be best conceptualised as rights at all, and these too can be given less weight than they deserve by judges who are required to enforce only a handful of privileged, enumerated rights. Many overseas observers were astonished when an American court held that Nazis were entitled to demonstrate in a Chicago suburb inhabited by many Jewish victims of the Holocaust. The Nazis' right to free speech, so provocatively and offensively asserted (after all, they could have demonstrated elsewhere) was held to outweigh all other considerations.[61] Perhaps judges in Australia would not apply a Bill of Rights in such an absolutist fashion. But when judges are required to protect rights that are enumerated in a constitution, rather than other rights or interests that are not, they give priority to the former over the latter.

Obviously, when a majority of legislators or electors disagrees with a minority, the majority is not necessarily wrong. In the absence of any independent, objective method of determining who is right, it is surely better that the majority should prevail. But at this point, an advocate of judicial supremacy might say: modern judges do have an independent, objective method of determining who is right – the method of proportionality analysis developed by rights-enforcing courts throughout the world.

To those who are unfamiliar with the term, proportionality analysis (ignoring different variants) involves: first, identifying both the right claimed to be infringed by some legislative or executive act, and the objective of that act (fostering some competing interest or right); and then determining whether or not the objective is legitimate, infringing the right was necessary to achieve it, and the benefits of doing so outweigh the losses.

This is typically how courts now decide disputes about rights. But rather than being an objective mode of analysis peculiar to dispassionate legal reasoning, proportionality analysis just formalises how any thoughtful person, including a politician, should think about such issues. Political judgment is all about trade-offs: whether some controversial measure adversely affecting one group of people is justified by the benefits it provides to other groups or the public as a whole. Balancing benefits and costs and deciding whether the benefits make the costs worthwhile is the very stuff of politics. Adding effects on individual rights to either or both sides of the scales does not change the subjective, value-laden nature of the choice that must be made.[62]

In addition to democracy respecting the right of ordinary people to participate in their own governance, it is also thought to have beneficial consequences. Since prejudice and intolerance tend to diminish when people engage in genuine dialogue with one another, democracy is thought to promote mutual respect, moderation, and compromise. Moreover, legislators must build coalitions to be effective: all majorities are groupings of minorities that have joined forces in a political party, a coalition, or a temporary alliance. Political power is impermanent, and opponents defeated today might turn the tables tomorrow.

[61] See Donald Alexander Downs, *Nazis in Skokie: Freedom, Community, and the First Amendment* (Notre Dame, University of Notre Dame Press, 1985).

[62] Francisco J Urbina, 'A Critique of Proportionality' (2012) 57 *American Journal of Jurisprudence* 49. See also Thomas Poole, 'Between the Devil and the Deep Blue Sea: Administrative Law in an Age of Rights' in Linda Pearson, Carol Harlow and Michael Taggart (eds), *Administrative Law in a Changing State: Essays in Honour of Mark Aronson* (Oxford, Hart Publishing, 2008) 34, 36.

The impetus towards moderation is propelled partly by the need to build the necessary coalitions, and the fear of backlash should defeated adversaries later gain the upper hand.

'Democratic debilitation' is a label used for ways that rights litigation may damage the health of representative democracy.[63] Some fear that legislators might devote less attention to the compatibility of proposed legislation with protected rights, if it is likely to be litigated in the courts. They might become reckless as to compatibility or, worse still, 'pass the buck' to the courts, and shirk responsibility for unpopular decisions. Frequent resort to litigation to advance rights claims might also divert vital funds and energies from grass-roots political mobilisation. In addition, if political debate is subsumed by legal debate, couched in legalistic jargon and formulae, the general public (including legislators) may feel excluded and become politically enervated and apathetic.[64]

On the other hand, active participants in political disputes who are defeated in the courtroom may become embittered or enraged. Two Canadian scholars have argued that:

> Rights-based judicial policymaking … [leads to] issues that should be subject to … ongoing … discussion [being] presented as beyond legitimate debate, with the [winners] claiming the right to permanent victory. As the moralism of rights displaces the morality of consent, the politics of coercion replaces the politics of persuasion. The result is to embitter politics and decrease the inclination of political opponents to treat each other as fellow citizens …[65]

Genuine and lasting respect for one another's rights cannot be imposed by judicial fiat, but it can emerge from the dialogue and compromise that characterise politics in a democracy.

The usual response to democratic objections to judicial enforcement of rights is to point out that democracy is imperfect. Not all laws that are passed enjoy the support of a majority of the people. At elections, voters must choose between a few party platforms, which they must accept or reject as a whole; they rarely agree with all the policies of the party they vote for. Moreover, legislation may be unduly influenced by powerful interest groups, by wheeling and dealing behind the scenes, or by unelected bureaucrats. Instead of frustrating public opinion, it is argued, judicial review can help to protect the public from unreliable or untrustworthy politicians.

But too much can be made of this response. Our system of government is democratic, even if only imperfectly. Governments must attract popular support, and not defy public opinion, if they wish to retain their power. The general public may be relatively passive between elections, but many representative organisations stimulate and contribute to public debate, and communicate the views of their constituencies to government. Moreover, no matter how imperfectly democratic our system of government may be, rule by judges would hardly be more democratic. If our existing system is imperfectly democratic, why not adopt reforms that would make it more, rather than even less, democratic?

It might be argued that some groups will never be adequately represented in politics because they lack the necessary numbers, resources or organisational ability. Indigenous peoples, the aged, the poor, the chronically ill, and some migrant groups are of concern.

[63] Mark V Tushnet, 'Policy Distortion and Democratic Debilitation: Comparative Illumination of the Counter-Majoritarian Difficulty' (1995) 94 *Michigan Law Review* 245.

[64] On the unfortunate effects of confining political debate to a procrustean bed of constitutional formulae, see Waldron, *Law and Disagreement*, above n 52, 220, 289–90.

[65] F L Morton and Rainer Knopff, *The Charter Revolution and the Court Party* (Peterborough, Broadview Press, 2000) 166.

Judicial review has been defended as a way of redressing their inability to get a 'fair go' in the political arena, by providing them with an alternative forum in which they must be heard and decisions are made that cannot be ignored. But these groups are typically not significantly assisted by judicial enforcement of constitutional rights: they usually need positive government assistance – land rights, education, employment, or financial or other forms of assistance – that courts cannot effectively provide. Enforceable 'positive' rights to government assistance or empowerment might require judicial power to amend the budget and possibly rates of taxation. Indeed, it is partly because of the need for the democratic process to provide such assistance or empowerment – and the danger of judicially enforceable negative rights being invoked to obstruct it – that judicial supremacy has often been most staunchly opposed by people to the left of politics.[66] And notably, the countries – which are mainly Scandanavian – that have best protected the welfare rights of the most vulnerable members of society, have historically not had constitutions protecting negative rights against the exercise of governmental power.

It is often argued that, at the very least, rights that are essential to the democratic process itself – such as the right to free speech, and to vote – must be given constitutional protection. But Jeremy Waldron has objected that:

> Democracy is in part *about* democracy: one of the first things on which the people demand a voice about, and concerning which they claim a competence, is the procedural character of their own political arrangements.[67]

He points out that there are reasonable disagreements about many aspects of democracy itself, including

> proportional representation, referendums, the frequency of elections, term limits, the basis of electoral districting, state-funded access to television airtime for candidates, and campaign finance generally ....[and] such topics as heckling, hate speech, ethnic representation, criminal defamation, and the concepts of sedition, insurrection, and subversion.[68]

I would add that even the right to vote itself can be the subject of reasonable disagreement, for example, concerning the minimum age at which citizens should be able to vote, or whether non-citizen residents should be able to do so. On Waldron's view these disagreements, too, are best settled by majority decision after deliberations in which everyone has had an equal right to participate. Should judges rather than the community's elected representatives be entrusted to decide whether 16-year-olds are to have a right to vote?

Other important objections to a Bill of Rights include the likely politicisation of the judiciary. Because the interpretation and application of constitutional rights is essentially a matter of political judgment, of striking a fair balance between competing rights and interests, prospective and serving judges would inevitably be evaluated partly according

[66] See, eg, Whitlam's views quoted at nn 22 and 24 above; J A G Griffith, *The Politics of the Judiciary*, 5th edn, (Harper Collins, 1997); Richard Bellamy, *Political Constitutionalism: A Republican Defence of the Constitutionality of Democracy* (Cambridge, Cambridge University Press, 2007); R Hirschl, *Towards Juristocracy; The Origins and Consequences of the New Constitutionalism* (Cambridge MA, Harvard University Press, 2004); Michael Mandel, 'A Brief History of the New Constitutionalism, or "How We Changed Everything So That Everything Would Remain the Same"' (1998) 32 *Israel Law Review* 250; Mark Tushnet, *Taking the Constitution Away from the Courts* (New Jersey, Princeton University Press, 1999).

[67] Waldron, *Law and Disagreement*, above n 53, 296.

[68] Ibid, 279.

to their political philosophies. The appointment of new judges by the government would depend on how congenial it found the candidates' political philosophies and anticipated decisions. Recent judicial appointments in Australia have occasionally been influenced by the suspected political attitudes of candidates,[69] but this would inevitably happen more frequently were judges to acquire power to enforce rights. If power to make essentially political decisions were transferred from elected representatives to judges, the former would naturally attempt to exert as much control over the judges' decisions as is legally permissible. And it would be hard to criticise taking into account the political philosophies of prospective judges. If an office requires the making of political judgments, then the ability to do so wisely must be a legitimate criterion for appointment, and in taking this into account, those making the appointment must rely on their own political philosophies. The end result may be undesirable – judges in the United States have been said to be 'more or less running for office', with 'political acceptability the name of the game'[70] – but it is a necessary consequence of the adoption of a Bill of Rights.

V. A Bill of Rights With an Override Clause

In a previous lengthy examination of arguments for and against a Bill of Rights in Australia, I concluded that:

> good arguments can be adduced on both sides. Rather than no bill of rights at all, or one which subordinates the democratic process to judicial policy-making, a compromise might better reflect the balance of these arguments.[71]

In referring to compromise, I had in mind Canada's famous over-ride clause, and other possibilities including a non-judicial council or committee charged with reviewing complaints that legislation violated rights and making recommendations to Parliament.[72] Section 33 of the Canadian Charter of Rights provides that Canadian legislation 'may expressly declare … that the Act or a provision thereof shall operate notwithstanding a provision included in section 2 or sections 7 to 15 of this Charter.' This 'notwithstanding' or 'override' clause permits legislatures to override those specified sections of the Charter, and the rights they protect, although only for renewable five-year periods.[73]

In a later publication, I again discussed the possibility that the Canadian model strikes 'an effective compromise' between the case for stronger rights protection and democratic objections to judicial review.[74] I argued that if judicial enforcement of entrenched rights is subject to legislative over-ride, then many of the usual democracy-based objections to judicial review are deflected. 'Judicial enforcement of the Charter can be argued to add a further

[69] See evidence in Rosalind Dixon and George Williams (eds), *The High Court, the Constitution and Australian Politics* (Cambridge, Cambridge University Press, 2015).

[70] Simon Lee, 'Bicentennial Bork, Tercentennial *Spycatcher*: Do the British Need a Bill of Rights?' (1988) 49 *University of Pittsburgh Law Review* 777, 796.

[71] Goldsworthy, 'The Constitutional Protection of Rights in Australia', above n 11, 176.

[72] Ibid, 173–75. On the latter idea, see Winterton, above n 29.

[73] It does not apply to other sections that protect democratic rights, mobility rights, and language rights.

[74] Jeffrey Goldsworthy, 'Judicial Review, Legislative Override, and Democracy' in Tom Campbell, Jeffrey Goldsworthy and Adrienne Stone (eds), *Protecting Human Rights, Instruments and Institutions* (Oxford, Oxford University Press, 2003) 263, 264 (republished in (2003) 38 *Wake Forest Law Journal* 451, 452).

check or balance to the political process without diminishing its fundamentally democratic character.'[75] However, this depends on the wording of the over-ride clause. I pointed out that the wording of the Canadian over-ride clause is objectionable, because it puts any legislature wishing to use it in an invidious position: it must misrepresent itself as deliberately overriding constitutional rights, rather than as overriding actual or potential judicial interpretations of rights that it sincerely and conscientiously disagrees with.[76]

To require a legislature to enact a 'notwithstanding clause' in order to overcome judicial interpretations of rights would be to insert into a Bill of Rights a kind of 'manner and form' requirement, which enables legislation to have a valid operation provided it uses a particular form of words to signify that the legislature has not acted inadvertently or carelessly. Such a requirement is somewhat similar to a requirement that some important prior law can only be amended or repealed expressly, and not by implication. Requirements like these can help to promote careful consideration and genuine deliberation of proposals within Parliament. Express repeal requirements, for example, can ensure that important constitutional principles are not amended or repealed inadvertently, without making it at all difficult for Parliament to amend or repeal them if after due deliberation it chooses to.

Thus, a strong constitutional protection of rights can in principle be achieved without violating the prerogative of the elected legislature to have the 'last word'. If the legislature chooses to exercise that right infrequently, because it fears a public backlash, then that is democracy in action. It does not follow that I am in favour of such strong protection of rights. It merely follows that, if judicial interpretations of rights are subject to legislative over-ride, they are less vulnerable to the objection that their enforcement is undemocratic.

VI. Conclusion

How have Australian parliaments discharged their historical responsibility to protect the rights and freedoms of the community? Their track record over the centuries is far from perfect. But judged by statutes passed over the last 50 years or so, they have done very well. Legislation has abolished the death penalty, greatly reduced censorship of literature and other forms of artistic expression, decriminalised homosexual conduct and legalised same-sex marriage, advanced the interests of women, outlawed many kinds of invidious discrimination, conferred land rights on indigenous people, legalised abortion within limits – the list could go on and on.

It is no coincidence that in rankings of nations according to the freedoms of their residents, Australia consistently falls within the top 10–20, and considering the company it is in, this is nothing to be worried about. Nor is its failure to rank higher due to its not having a constitutional Bill of Rights. For example, in a reputable index of World Freedom published by Canada's Fraser Institute in 2012, New Zealand ranked first out of 123 countries, despite having no written constitution and only a statutory Bill of Rights, and Australia ranked fourth, despite having no national Bill of Rights at all. The Netherlands ranked second, and

[75] Ibid.

[76] Jeremy Waldron agrees: see 'Some Models of Dialogue Between Judges and Legislators' in Grant Huscroft and Ian Brodie (eds), *Constitutionalism in the Charter Era* (London, LexisNexis Butterworths, 2004) 7, 34–9; 'The Core of the Case Against Judicial Review' (2006) 115 *Yale Law Journal* 1347, 1357 n 34.

as usual all Scandinavian countries also ranked highly, even though none of them has had a long attachment to rights-protection through judicial review. These are reasons not for complacency, but rather, for refusing to regard Australia's lack of a national Bill of Rights as perpetuating a long dark age in which rights have been widely suppressed.[77]

Robert Dahl, the pre-eminent modern theorist of democracy, once said: 'The democratic process is a gamble on the possibilities that a people, in acting autonomously, will learn how to act rightly.'[78] To authorise strong judicial enforcement of constitutional rights would amount to a verdict that the Australian people have failed to learn that lesson. It would indicate a lack of confidence in their ability to maintain a tolerant and fair society without the supervision of judicial chaperons, overseeing their decisions and correcting their mistakes. It would subject them to a kind of political guardianship. I do not believe that the history of Australian democracy warrants such pessimism. Indeed, despite many blemishes, I believe that its enviable record as a robust democracy in a generally tolerant multi-cultural community justifies the opposite conclusion.[79]

[77] Cf, Lord Neuberger, 'The Role of Judges in Human Rights Jurisprudence: A Comparison of the Australian and UK Experience' (Speech delivered at the Supreme Court of Victoria Conference, Victoria, 8 August 2014) 6 www.supremecourt.uk/docs/speech-140808.pdf.

[78] Robert A Dahl, *Democracy and Its Critics* (Yale University Press, 1989) 192.

[79] John Hirst, *Australia's Democracy: A Short History* (Sydney, Allen & Unwin, 2002).

21

Designing an Australian Bill of Rights: The Normative Trade-offs

SCOTT STEPHENSON

I. Introduction

If Australia were to introduce a bill of rights at the federal level, it is likely that the design and drafting process would devote a great deal of attention to the possible adoption of a 'dialogue' model.[1] Among the different constitutional approaches to rights protection, it has become the most popular in Australia and its closest constitutional relatives in recent decades. It is the model that was endorsed by the last federal inquiry into rights reform – the National Human Rights Consultation Committee – in 2009,[2] that formed the basis for the bills of rights enacted in the Australian Capital Territory in 2004,[3] in Victoria in 2006[4] and in Queensland in 2019,[5] and that is said to describe the bills of rights found in Canada, New Zealand and the UK.[6] The dialogue model has risen to prominence because it is often claimed to provide 'a better working coexistence of democratic self-governance and the constraints of constitutionalism, the twin concepts underlying constitutional democracy'.[7] It seeks to achieve this coexistence by simultaneously empowering courts to review executive and legislative acts for compatibility with rights while also preserving the centrality of legislatures in evaluating and resolving disagreements about the scope and limit of rights through the investiture of new responsibilities and powers before and after acts of judicial review.

[1] In previous scholarship, I have put forward several reasons for abandoning use of the term 'dialogue': Scott Stephenson, *From Dialogue to Disagreement in Comparative Rights Constitutionalism* (Annandale, Federation Press, 2016) 50–55. However, as it is the most common means of labelling the model in Australia and nothing in the present chapter turns on the term used, I will continue to refer to it as the 'dialogue' model.

[2] National Human Rights Consultation Committee, *Report* (2009) ('National Consultation Committee').

[3] *Human Rights Act 2004* (ACT). For the consultative committee report that endorsed the dialogue model, see Australian Capital Territory Bill of Rights Consultative Committee, *Towards an ACT Human Rights Act* (2003) ('ACT Consultation Committee').

[4] *Charter of Human Rights and Responsibilities Act 2006* (Vic). For the consultative committee report that endorsed the dialogue model, see Victorian Human Rights Consultation Committee, *Report: Rights, Responsibilities and Respect* (2006) ('Victorian Consultation Committee').

[5] *Human Rights Act 2019* (Qld). Section 3 of the Act states that '[t]he main objects of this Act are … (c) to help promote a dialogue about the nature, meaning and scope of human rights.' The Explanatory Notes to the Bill state that '[t]he Bill aims to promote a discussion or "dialogue" about human rights between the three arms of government (the judiciary, the legislature and the executive)': Explanatory Notes, Human Rights Bill 2018 (Qld) 6.

[6] See, eg, Mark Tushnet, 'Dialogic Judicial Review' (2009) 61 *Arkansas Law Review* 205.

[7] Stephen Gardbaum, *The New Commonwealth Model of Constitutionalism: Theory and Practice* (Cambridge, Cambridge University Press, 2013) 52.

This chapter highlights a set of considerations that should factor into the design and drafting process if a dialogue model were to be chosen. In particular, it argues that part of that process should focus on the normative trade-offs that arise with the model. A normative trade-off is a point of tension between two principles or features, each of which is capable of reasonable justification. The dialogue model gives rise to a number of points of tension with other aspects of Australia's constitutional system of government. For example, its system of legislative committee review, which facilitates legislative disagreement with the executive's positions on rights issues, is in tension with Australia's existing system of responsible government, which operates to minimise disagreement between the executive and legislature. If these points of tension are not addressed prior to the enactment of a bill of rights, it will fall to institutional actors (ie members of the executive, legislature and judiciary) to resolve them after enactment. If this occurs, the risk is that these actors will prioritise the existing features of the constitutional system because they are well-established and well-known, which would undermine the dialogue model's ability to function in practice and thus achieve the working coexistence mentioned above.

This chapter puts forward three, related suggestions about the way in which the design and drafting process should proceed in order to identify, analyse and, as far as is reasonably possible, resolve the normative trade-offs before the enactment of a bill of rights. First, the process must go beyond the four walls of the bill of rights to include potential reforms to other aspects of Australia's existing constitutional system of government. Reform of the system of responsible government, for example, should be one potential option for resolving the point of tension between it and legislative committee review. Second, the process should include, and indeed prioritise, the possibility of implementing a dialogue bill of rights by means of a constitutional rather than statutory instrument. In the event of a point of tension between a statutory instrument (the dialogue bill of rights) and a feature of the existing constitutional system, the latter will almost invariably prevail due to the priority that is accorded to constitutional law. For any of these normative trade-offs to be resolved in a manner that favours the operation of the dialogue bill of rights, it must have the same status in the hierarchy of laws as the competing principle or feature. Third, the enactment process must be inclusive and popular rather than exclusive and elite. Not only will this give any proposed constitutional reforms a greater likelihood of success at the required referendum, it also counters the perception from scholars evaluating the advent of bills of rights in similarly-situated countries that they are the product of inter-party competition and elite self-interest rather than a broad-based, popularly-supported movement.

Part II of the chapter provides a brief overview of the dialogue model's components and objective. Part III sets out three illustrative normative trade-offs that arise between the dialogue model and Australia's existing constitutional system of government. Part IV details the three suggestions for how the drafting and design process should proceed to identify, analyse and resolve these normative trade-offs.

II. What is a Dialogue Bill of Rights?

Before it is possible to evaluate the points of tension between a dialogue bill of rights and Australia's existing constitutional system of government, it is necessary to understand what a dialogue bill of rights is. There are problems with speaking of a 'dialogue model' because each bill of rights that has attracted the label does not have the exact same set of features. Furthermore, scholars disagree as to the objective that these features seek to achieve. While these differences are important and would have to factor into the drafting and design process of a dialogue bill of rights, they do not detract from this chapter's principal argument – that the design and drafting process should be designed in a way that takes account of the normative trade-offs that arise with the adoption of a dialogue model – and do not prevent a broad overview of its features and objective from taking place. The differences do, however, affect the precise normative trade-offs that arise, a point that will be discussed below in Part III.

A. Features

While each instantiation of the dialogue model is different, the most comprehensive versions to date contain four stages of rights review. First, the executive is required to review proposed laws for their compatibility with rights prior to their introduction into the legislature. The product of that review is the statement of compatibility. When a proposed law is introduced into the legislature, the executive is required to issue an accompanying statement of compatibility that sets out the reasons why the law, if enacted, will or will not be compatible with rights.

Second, a legislative committee is empowered to review proposed laws for compatibility with rights. After a proposed law is introduced into the legislature, the committee reviews the law, including the executive's statement of compatibility, and issues a report that sets out whether it considers the law to be compatible with rights and, if not, possible amendments to the proposed law that would rectify the incompatibilities with rights it has identified.

Third, courts are empowered to undertake rights-based judicial review of executive and legislative acts.[8] A wide range of judicial powers are compatible with the dialogue model. Courts can be given, for example, the power to invalidate statutes that are found to be incompatible with rights, as in Canada, the power to interpret statutes compatibly with rights, as in New Zealand, or the power to interpret statutes compatibly with rights and, where that it not possible, the power to issue a declaration of incompatibility that alerts the executive and legislature to its finding, but does not affect the validity or operation of the statute, as in the ACT, Queensland, the UK and Victoria.

Fourth, legislatures are empowered to override judicial decisions on rights using the ordinary lawmaking process. The precise power that needs to be given to the legislature will depend on the powers given to the courts and whether or not the bill of rights is constitutionally entrenched. A constitutionally entrenched bill of rights that empowers courts to invalidate statutes will require an explicit legislative override power. An unentrenched, statutory bill of rights that empowers courts to interpret statutes compatibly with rights and issue declarations of incompatibility does not require an explicit legislative override power because judicial interpretations of statutes can be overridden using the power to amend statutes and no positive step is required to override declarations of incompatibility because they have no legal effect.

[8] For a discussion of the impact of a dialogue model on judicial review of executive action, see ch 11 in this volume.

B. Objective

The objective of the dialogue model is, I have argued in a previous scholarship,[9] to facilitate disagreement on rights issues between the three arms of government. The four stages of rights review provide each arm of government with the opportunity to evaluate and, where appropriate, challenge determinations about the scope and limit of rights made by the other arms of government. Legislative committee review allows the legislature to review and, where appropriate, disagree with the executive's determinations on rights by recommending amendments to the executive's proposed law. Rights-based judicial review allows the courts to review and, where appropriate, disagree with the legislature's determinations on rights by finding a law to be incompatible with rights. Legislative override allows the legislature to review and, where appropriate, disagree with the judiciary's determinations on rights by exercising its override power.

The cumulative effect of the four stages further facilitates disagreement. As the judiciary does not bear the moral and political weight of having the 'final word' on contested rights issues, the need, as a matter of practice and principle, for it to defer to the legislature is diminished (as compared to a system of constitutional or judicial supremacy where courts do have the 'final word'). In other words, the presence of stage four (legislative override) facilitates disagreement at stage three (rights-based judicial review). Furthermore, as the legislature has reached an independent and considered view on a proposed law's compatibility with rights prior to enactment, it has stronger grounds for challenging a judicial decision finding a law to be incompatible with rights. It can point to the legislative committee's report to help substantiate the claim that its disagreement with the judiciary is the product of a good faith, reasonable difference of opinion about the scope or limit of a right rather than an adverse reaction to having lost a court case. In other words, the presence of stage two (legislative committee review) facilitates disagreement at stage four (legislative override).

The dialogue model thus aims to structure the constitutional system of government to use the interactions between the three arms of government as a mechanism for expressing and resolving the reasonable, good faith disagreements about the scope and limit of rights that exist in society. Each arm of government is apt to bring a different perspective to bear on rights issues and to allow the public to participate in different ways. The executive brings the high-level, political perspective of the governing political party (or parties) that is informed by the work of the public service and that allows participation by the public writ large through, for example, bureaucratic data collection and opinion surveys. The legislature brings the mid-level, political perspective of legislators, including non-governing political parties (and individual legislators), that allows the public to participate through, for example, interest group lobbying and submissions to the committee. The judiciary brings the case-specific, legal perspective of judges that allows members of the public directly affected by a particular executive or legislative act to participate through the initiation of, or intervention in, court cases.

[9] Stephenson, above n 1, ch 6.

III. The Normative Trade-offs

A constitutional system of government never pursues a single objective. Constitutional drafters (before enactment) and institutional actors (after enactment) often have to strike a balance between different objectives, and their concomitant features, that are in tension with each other.[10] The attainment of an efficient form of government may create points of tension with, for instance, the attainment of a federal form of government because federalism invariably creates points of overlap and duplication. The attainment of a responsive form of government may create points of tension with, for instance, the separation of powers because separation slows down the ability of government to take particular types of action (eg the requirement for imprisonment only to occur after a finding of criminal guilt by a court[11] slows down the ability of the government to remove a dangerous person from the community). Importantly, each competing objective is capable of justification (ie a normative trade-off arises). It is not a case of a valuable constitutional aim being impeded by a practical inconvenience (ie a practical trade-off). The pursuit of efficient and responsive government are valuable constitutional objectives, as are the pursuit of federalism and the separation of powers.

A constitution's system of rights protection is no exception. Every approach to rights protection creates normative trade-offs that must be resolved. Legislative supremacy (ie a constitutional system without a bill of rights) pursues the objective of legislative primacy in relation to rights (ie the legislature is the institution responsible for evaluating and resolving rights issues). However, that may be in tension with the principle of legislative legitimacy (ie the legislature enjoys its position of primacy in the lawmaking process because it is the electorally accountable arm of government). The reason is that the legislature's primacy allows it to alter those rights that form the basis for its legitimacy. For example, in a system of legislative supremacy, the legislature has the power to abrogate the right to vote even though that would undermine its legitimacy because the legislature's legitimacy relies on the people voting for its members.

Australian constitutional lawyers are all too familiar with this normative trade-off. With its system of legislative supremacy at the federal level, the difficult task of resolving the tension between legislative primacy and legislative legitimacy has come before the High Court in recent decades. The Court has held that limits must be placed on the legislature's ability to curtail the right to vote[12] and freedom of political communication.[13] These are implications that preserve the legislature's legitimacy – its place of primacy rests on the maintenance of representative and responsible government. However, these implications sit at odds with the principle of legislative primacy, which is also at the heart of Australia's

[10] For a more comprehensive, comparative-oriented discussion of normative trade-offs, see Stephenson, above n 1, ch 7.

[11] There are, of course, some limited exceptions where detention without a finding of criminal guilt is permitted. In Australia, see, eg, *Chu Kheng Lim v Minister for Immigration Local Government and Ethnic Affairs* (1992) 176 CLR 1.

[12] *Roach v Electoral Commissioner* (2007) 233 CLR 162; *Rowe v Electoral Commissioner* (2010) 243 CLR 1.

[13] *Nationwide News v Wills* (1992) 177 CLR 1; *Australian Capital Television v Commonwealth* (1992) 177 CLR 106.

constitutional system of government – as the Constitution does not have a bill of rights, it assigns responsibility for resolving rights issues to the legislature, not the judiciary. To minimise this tension, the Court has attempted to tie these implications as closely as possible to the constitutional text and, in general, adopted narrow interpretations of their scope.[14] Thus, it has sought to reconcile the normative trade-off by recognising and preserving the principle of legislative legitimacy without encroaching on the principle of legislative primacy to a significant extent.

Tensions also arise in systems of judicial or constitutional supremacy (ie a constitutionally entrenched bill of rights where the judiciary has the 'final word' on rights issues). This approach to rights protection pursues the objective of judicial primacy in relation to rights (ie the judiciary is the institution ultimately responsible for evaluating and resolving rights issues). However, that may be in tension with the principle of judicial independence (ie the judiciary should be free from interference by the executive and legislature). All public officials, including judges, are expected to be accountable for their exercises of public power. The pressure for judicial accountability is particularly acute in systems of judicial supremacy because judges have the 'final word' on significant moral and political issues over which there is good faith, reasonable disagreement within society. However, many mechanisms for ensuring accountability may give rise to points of tension with the principle of judicial independence. Holding judges to account through, for instance, the appointments process may undermine the perception that judges are independent from the other arms of government. This tension is manifest in systems of judicial supremacy such as India and the US where the non-judicial arms of government have sought to render the judiciary accountable for its decisions on rights through the appointments process, which has threatened the appearance of independence.[15]

The dialogue model of rights protection also requires a set of normative trade-offs to be made, all of which follow a similar pattern. In short, the dialogue model's facilitation of disagreement between the three arms of government is in tension with other aspects of the constitutional system of government that seek to minimise or suppress disagreement between the three arms of governments. Three illustrative examples of the types of normative trade-offs that may arise in the Australian context are discussed below.

A. Responsible Government

The dialogue model is in tension with Australia's system of responsible government because the former seeks to facilitate disagreement between the executive and legislature while the latter operates to minimise disagreement between them. Responsible government minimises disagreement by forging a close link between the two arms of government. In particular, it provides that the executive 'is chosen by, is answerable to, and may be removed by' the

[14] See, eg, the reformulation of the implied freedom of political communication doctrine, purporting to tie it closer to the text of the Constitution, in *Lange v Australian Broadcasting Corporation* (1997) 189 CLR 520.

[15] For the US, see, eg, Michael J Gerhardt, *The Federal Appointments Process: A Constitutional and Historical Analysis* (Chicago, University of Chicago Press, 2001) 313; Christopher L Eisgruber, *The Next Justice: Repairing the Supreme Court Appointments Process* (New Jersey, Princeton University Press, 2007) 145, 158–59, 189–90. For India, see, eg, Anashri Pillay, 'Protecting Judicial Independence through Appointments Processes: A Review of the Indian and South African Experiences' (2017) 1 *Indian Law Review* 283.

legislature.[16] In the contemporary era of relatively well-disciplined political parties, responsible government operates to ensure that the executive enjoys a large degree of control over the legislature.[17] The senior members of the political party (ie the executive) can be confident that the other members of the political party will support them in the legislature in most circumstances.[18]

This point of tension manifests at stage two (legislative committee review) of the dialogue model. The executive can use its power in the legislature to frustrate the operation of legislative committee review, suppressing it as a mechanism for the legislature to express disagreement with the executive on rights issues. This suppression can occur in a number of ways. The executive might be able to pack the legislative committee with members from its own political party, helping to ensure that the committee rarely issues reports critical of the executive's positions on rights.[19] The executive might be able to use its control of the legislature's timetable to prevent the committee from having sufficient time to conduct a thorough investigation of the rights issues raised by a proposed law. The executive might be able to use its majority in the legislature to ensure that the legislative committee's report has no effect on the final form of, or even the deliberation on, the proposed law.

This point of tension gives rise to a normative trade-off because reasonable justifications can be put forward for each principle. Executive-legislative disagreement on rights issues is justifiable on the basis of the reasons set out above in Part II(B). Responsible government is justifiable on the basis that it creates an effective, efficient form of government with clear lines of political accountability. Minimising disagreement between the executive and legislature more readily allows the state to respond to pressing social issues – it reduces the space for executive-legislative disagreement to prevent the state from taking action – and offers greater clarity about who is responsible for those actions – there is less room for the executive and legislature to 'pass the buck' by blaming each other for a problematic act.

Australians are all too familiar with this species of tension and the problems that can arise from its unresolved dimensions. The 1975 constitutional crisis was, at base, a dramatic manifestation of the tension between the Constitution's elements that facilitate disagreement between the executive and legislature and the elements that minimise disagreement between them. On the one hand was the principle of responsible government, which operates to minimise the possibility of disagreement between the executive and legislature by ensuring that the executive retains the confidence of the House of Representatives at all times. On the other hand was the principle of bicameralism, which operates to create opportunities for

[16] David Hamer, *Can Responsible Government Survive in Australia?* (Department of the Senate, 2004) xvii.

[17] See John Uhr, 'Parliament and the Executive' (2004) 25 *Adelaide Law Review* 51.

[18] As Stephen Gardbaum notes, '[t]he party [has] replace[d] parliament as the central non-executive political institution and locus of power, so that a prime minister is more likely to lose office by being replaced as leader of the party than by being defeated in parliament on a vote of confidence': 'Separation of Powers and the Growth of Judicial Review in Established Democracies (or Why Has the Model of Legislative Supremacy Mostly Been Withdrawn From Sale?)' (2014) 62 *American Journal of Comparative Law* 613, 634. The replacement four sitting Prime Ministers in recent years (Kevin Rudd in 2010, Julia Gillard in 2013, Tony Abbott in 2015 and Malcolm Turnbull in 2018) appears to confirm that observation in the Australian context.

[19] After the Liberal-National Party Coalition acquired a majority of seats in the House of Representatives and Senate in 2005, it used its majority to undermine the effectiveness of the existing legislative committee system by, for example, 'chang[ing] the structure of the Senate committee system to give itself the majority and the chairs of all of the legislative and general purpose standing committees, which are the main inquiry vehicles for the chamber': Harry Evans, 'The Senate, Accountability and Government Control', *Papers on Parliament No 48* (January 2008), available at www.aph.gov.au/senate/~/~/link.aspx?_id=17EF4947DD5D4214BC6C1162200D893E&_z.

disagreement between the executive and legislature in the form of an upper chamber with almost co-equal powers to the lower chamber that is not necessarily, or even generally,[20] controlled by the same political party that has the confidence of the House of Representatives. Responsible government supported the position of the Whitlam Government while bicameralism supported the position of the Fraser opposition. The events of 1975 left this tension unresolved, leaving open the question of which should prevail when they come into direct conflict.[21]

The tension highlighted by the 1975 constitutional crisis has relevance for the present discussion of the dialogue model. While the principle of responsible government can frustrate the operation of legislative committee review, other features of Australia's constitutional system of government can work to assist its operation by facilitating disagreement between the executive and legislature. And bicameralism is a cogent example. An upper legislative chamber can strengthen legislative committee review if it is structured and empowered in a way that limits the executive's ability to control or ignore it. If half (or more) of the committee's members come from the upper legislative chamber, its electoral system will assume particular significance. An electoral system that generally precludes the same political party from winning a majority of seats in both legislative chambers will reduce the executive's ability to influence the composition of the committee. The upper legislative chamber's powers to affect the passage of proposed laws will also assume considerable importance. The power to block proposed laws, for instance, will give the legislative committee a part of the legislature to which it can appeal to ensure the consideration of its recommendations (ie the upper legislative chamber can ensure that proposed laws are not passed until the legislative committee's report is given careful consideration).

Other aspects of the constitutional system can also affect the patterns of interaction between the executive and legislature. The electoral system for the lower legislative chamber is an obvious example. The likelihood of executive-legislative disagreement is increased under a system where a single political party is unlikely to win a majority of seats at an election (eg a system of proportional voting). The reason is that, if the executive is a coalition of political parties, there is a greater likelihood of disagreements within the executive, some of which may manifest in the legislature (eg one member of the coalition may express its disagreement by speaking out, or even voting, against a proposed law supported by the other members of the coalition).[22]

The normative trade-off to be made is, therefore, a complex one. It not only involves evaluating the respective merits of legislative committee review and responsible government.

[20] 'Since 1949 there have been only four relatively short periods (1951–56, 1959–62, 1976–81, 2005–07) in which a ministry has had a majority in the Senate': Harry Evans (Rosemary Laing (ed)), *Odgers' Australian Senate Practice*, 14th edn (Department of the Senate, 2016) 13.

[21] For a discussion of the unresolved constitutional dimensions of the events of 1975, see Brendan Lim, *Australia's Constitution after Whitlam* (Cambridge, Cambridge University Press, 2017).

[22] For an evaluation of the precise extent to which this has occurred in New Zealand since the introduction of a new electoral system that tends not to give a single political party a majority of seats, see, eg, Ryan Malone, 'Who's the Boss?: Executive-Legislature Relations in New Zealand under MMP' (2009) 7 *New Zealand Journal of Public and International Law* 1; Jonathan Boston and David Bullock, 'Experiments in Executive Government under MMP in New Zealand: Contrasting Approaches to Multi-Party Governance' (2009) 7 *New Zealand Journal of Public and International Law* 39; Nicholas Aroney and Steve Thomas, 'A House Divided: Does MMP Make an Upper House Unnecessary for New Zealand?' (2012) 3 *New Zealand Law Review* 403.

It also involves evaluating other features of a constitutional system of government that alter the patterns of agreement and disagreement between the executive and legislature.

B. Separation of Powers

The dialogue model is in tension with the separation of powers because the former often seeks to invest courts with novel powers while the latter, in Australia, seeks to confine the powers courts may exercise. One of the dialogue model's principal innovations is the development of a suite of new powers that courts can exercise when a statute is found to be incompatible with rights. As mentioned in Part II(A), courts no longer need to be given the power to invalidate statutes. In addition to, or as a substitute for, the traditional power of invalidation, they can be given the power to rewrite a statute to remove the incompatibility with rights and/or they can be given the power to issue declarations of incompatibility, which have no effect on the validity or operation of the statute, but serve as a public statement alerting the executive and legislature to the court's findings.

As Australian constitutional lawyers know all too well, the High Court has interpreted the Constitution, and Chapter III in particular, as requiring a separation of judicial powers that prevents courts exercising federal jurisdiction from being vested with non-judicial power. The Court has never defined the concept of judicial power with complete precision because it generally considers the concept incapable of an exhaustive definition.[23] Nevertheless, it has tended to construe judicial power in a narrow manner, confining it to the issuance of binding and authoritative decisions resolving disputes about the existing rights and obligations of the parties.[24] This conception of judicial power is at odds with the power to rewrite statutes because that power goes beyond the resolution of the dispute between the parties and is at odds with the power to issue declarations of incompatibility because they are not binding.

Indeed, the Court has said as much, holding that these two powers would be incompatible with the exercise of judicial power in *Momcilovic v The Queen*.[25] In that case, the Court was asked to determine the scope of the interpretive power in Victoria's bill of rights (section 32(1) of the *Charter of Human Rights and Responsibilities Act 2006* (Vic)). The provision states that, '[s]o far as it is possible to do so consistently with their purpose, all statutory provisions must be interpreted in a way that is compatible with human rights.' French CJ,[26] Gummow,[27] Hayne,[28] Crennan and Kiefel,[29] and Bell JJ[30] held, with Heydon J dissenting,[31] that the provision does not grant courts the power to rewrite statutes. As a result, it does not confer a non-judicial power on courts and is, therefore, compatible with the separation of judicial powers doctrine. As Gummow J said, 'the provision does not confer upon the courts a function of a law-making character which for that reason is repugnant to

[23] See, eg, *Precision Data Holdings Ltd v Wills* (1991) 173 CLR 167, 188–89.
[24] See, eg, *Huddart, Parker & Co Pty Ltd v Moorehead* (1908) 8 CLR 330, 367 (Griffith CJ).
[25] (2011) 245 CLR 1.
[26] Ibid, 50 [51].
[27] Ibid, 92–93 [171].
[28] Ibid, 123 [280].
[29] Ibid, 210 [545].
[30] Ibid, 241 [661].
[31] Ibid, 181–82 [450].

the exercise of judicial power. Section 32(1) is not invalid.'[32] If the provision were construed to permit courts to rewrite statutes, it was clear that it would have been declared invalid for violating the separation of judicial powers doctrine.[33] This restriction is a well-established aspect of the separation of judicial powers doctrine. In 1948, Latham CJ stated that '[t]he Court cannot re-write a statute and so assume the functions of the legislature.'[34]

In *Momcilovic*, the Court was also asked to determine whether the power to issue declarations in incompatibility (section 36(2) of the Act)[35] was an exercise of judicial power. The Court unanimously answered no.[36] As French CJ said:[37]

> a declaration of inconsistent interpretation made under s 36 does not involve the exercise of a judicial function. … The declaration sets down no guidance for the disposition of future cases involving similar principles of law. It has no legal effect upon the validity of the statutory provision which is its subject. … The declaration of inconsistent interpretation cannot be regarded as analogous to the judicial function nor to any functions historically exercised by courts and which, for that reason, have been regarded as judicial.

Gummow J observed that the issuance of a declaration was, in effect, the provision of formal advice to the executive about the Court's view on a statute's compatibility with rights,[38] which is foreign to the conception of judicial power in Australia:[39]

> It is no part of the judicial power, in exercise of a function sought to be conferred on the courts by statute, formally to set in train a process whereby the executive branch of government may or may not decide to engage legislative processes to change existing legislation.

In sum, the Court held that both the power to rewrite statutes and the power to issue declarations of incompatibility are not judicial in character.

The most important point for the purposes of the present discussion is that a normative trade-off must be made because a tension exists between the creative forms of judicial power in the dialogue model and the narrow conception of judicial power in the Australian Constitution, and each principle is capable of reasonable justification. On the one hand, the creative forms of judicial power offer courts greater flexibility to tailor the remedy they issue to the circumstances of the case. Declarations of incompatibility, for instance, may prove to be a useful mechanism for a court to state to the public and the other arms of government that it has found a statute to be incompatible with rights in circumstances where invalidation of the statute might cause considerable problems and generate few, if any, benefits (eg where invalidation would cause significant disruption to the way private persons order

[32] Ibid, 92–93 [171]. See also Heydon J: 158 [398].

[33] See, eg, ibid, 208 [537] (Crennan and Kiefel JJ).

[34] *Bank of New South Wales v Commonwealth* (1948) 76 CLR 1, 164, cited by Heydon J in *Momcilovic*: ibid 159 [399].

[35] The provision calls it's a 'declaration of inconsistent interpretation' rather than a 'declaration of incompatibilty'.

[36] (2011) 245 CLR 1, 44 [37] (French CJ), 97 [188] (Gummow J), 123 [280] (Hayne J), 185 [457] (Heydon J), 222 [584] (Crennan and Kiefel JJ), 241 [661] (Bell J). A majority of the Court (Gummow, Hayne and Heydon JJ dissenting) held that s 36(2) did not violate the separation of judicial powers doctrine. For the purposes of the present discussion, it is unnecessary to consider those reasons in detail. In short, while the doctrine prevents the Commonwealth Parliament from conferring non-judicial power on courts, it does not prevent state Parliaments from conferring non-judicial power on courts unless that power is incompatible with the exercise of institutional integrity of state courts: see, eg, *Kable v Director of Public Prosecutions (NSW)* (1996) 189 CLR 51.

[37] (2011) 245 CLR 1, 65 [89].

[38] Ibid, 95 [181].

[39] Ibid, 96 [184]. Cf Crennan and Kiefel JJ: 222 [584].

their affairs, and the executive and legislature are already in the process of considering reforms to the statute to redress the incompatibility with rights). Furthermore, the creative forms of judicial power may help to reduce the democratic concerns associated with rights-based judicial review. As declarations of incompatibility do not affect the validity or operation of a statute, they do not encroach on the legislature's ability to determine the state of the law as much as invalidations of a statute.[40]

On the other hand, the narrow conception of judicial power arguably restricts courts to the issuance of remedies best tailored to their expertise and resources. The power to rewrite statutes, for example, requires courts to engage with the complexities of statutory lawmaking without the expertise and resources that are available to members of the legislature (eg drafts from parliamentary counsel and review by specialist committees). Furthermore, the narrow conception of judicial power may reduce the potential for injustice for successful rights claimants. A wide range of remedies provides potential rights claimants with less certainty about the type of relief they can reasonably expect if they are successful in their claim. More specifically, declarations of incompatibility have the potential to cause injustice because they leave successful rights claimants without a remedy even though a court has found that one of their fundamental rights has been unjustifiably infringed.

The purpose of this part of the chapter is not to resolve this normative trade-off one way or the other. Instead, it is to emphasise that each principle is capable of reasonable justification and that, therefore, the narrow conception of judicial power is not merely an inconvenient feature of a constitutional system of government that should, to the best of one's ability, be avoided or circumvented. There is a normative trade-off. And the fact that one exists should have implications for the design and drafting process of a dialogue bill of rights, as will be discussed below in Part IV.

C. The Rule of Law

The dialogue model is in tension with the rule of law because the former empowers the political arms of government to avoid the legal effects of judicial decisions on rights while the latter suggests that no one, including the political arms of government, is above the law. The dialogue model's most well-known innovation is the legislative override mechanism.[41] Having the ability to empower legislatures to override judicial decisions on rights through the ordinary lawmaking process constitutes a significant departure from the traditional conception of a bill of rights whereby courts issue judgments that are not easily reversible by the political arms of government.[42]

[40] A declaration of incompatibility may still place some burden on the legislature to determine the state of the law. It would be possible to draft a bill of rights that requires the legislature to consider each declaration of incompatibility issued by the judiciary. The ACT, Queensland and Victorian bills of rights, for example, impose a similar obligation on the executive: *Human Rights Act 2004* (ACT), s 33; *Human Rights Act* (Qld), s 56; *Charter of Human Rights and Responsibilities Act 2006* (Vic), s 37.

[41] See, eg, Tushnet, 'Dialogic Judicial Review', above n 5, 205.

[42] Functional equivalents to the legislative override mechanism do, however, exist. A well-known example is the power to amend constitutions, which serves as a functional equivalent to legislative override in jurisdictions where constitutional amendment is not an onerous task: see Rosalind Dixon & Adrienne Stone, 'Constitutional Amendment & Political Constitutionalism: A Philosophical & Comparative Reflection' in David Dyzenhaus and Malcolm Thorburn (eds), *Philosophical Foundations of Constitutional Law* (Oxford, Oxford University Press, 2016) 95.

The rule of law is a complex, contested concept that is capable of multiple, divergent definitions.[43] However, one well-established feature of the rule of law that is at the core of the concept is the proposition that no one is above the law. Tom Bingham described it in the following terms:[44]

> … all persons and authorities within the state, whether public or private, should be bound by and entitled to the benefit of laws publicly made, taking effect (generally) in the future and publicly administered in the courts.

In 2015, Lord Neuberger of the UK Supreme Court expressed it even more directly:

> … one of the "fundamental components of the rule of law … is … that a decision of a court is binding as between the parties, and cannot be ignored or set aside by anyone, including (indeed it may fairly be said, least of all) the executive."[45]

The dialogue model's legislative override mechanism does not directly violate this aspect of the rule of law. It does not allow a government official, state authority or the executive to avoid compliance with a judicial decision. Only the legislature has the power to override a judicial decision under the dialogue model. And there is nothing inherently or necessarily offensive to the rule of law with the legislature overriding a judicial decision. It occurs all the time when legislatures enact statutes to override aspects of the common law and amend statutes to override judicial decisions interpreting that statute in a particular way. Indeed, part of a legislature's constitutional responsibility in a democracy is to update the law in response to changing circumstances and community requirements. This task requires the legislature to make changes that will affect the continued applicability of common law decisions and judicial interpretations of statutes.

Although the dialogue model does not directly violate the rule of law, the two concepts are nevertheless in tension with each other for the following reason. There is a risk that legislative override will, in effect, operate as a form of executive override. As mentioned above in Part III(A), the executive typically exerts a large degree of control over the legislature in a system of responsible government. In particular, it generally has the ability to introduce proposed laws into the legislature, use its control over the legislative timetable to ensure proposed laws are debated according to its preferred schedule, and secure the passage of proposed laws through the lower legislative chamber. As discussed above, other features of the constitutional system of government will alter the precise degree of control the executive exercises over the legislature. The presence of an upper legislative chamber dilutes the executive's control to the extent that the chamber is not controlled by the executive and is able to block the passage of the executive's proposed laws. However, an upper legislative chamber tempers rather than eliminates the executive's position of superiority in the legislature. Even if the executive does not hold a majority of seats in the upper legislative chamber, it is generally in a strong position to negotiate with other members and parties to secure

[43] For an overview of the debate about its meaning and utility, see, eg, Joseph Raz, *The Authority of Law: Essays on Law and Morality* (Oxford, Oxford University Press, 1979) ch 11; Judith Shklar, 'Political Theory and the Rule of Law' in Allan C Hutchinson & Patrick J Monahan (eds), *The Rule of Law: Ideal or Ideology* (Carswell, 1987) 1; Richard H Fallon Jr, '"The Rule of Law" as a Concept in Constitutional Discourse' (1997) 97 *Columbia Law Review* 1; Brian Z Tamanaha, *On the Rule of Law* (Cambridge, Cambridge University Press, 2004).

[44] Tom Bingham, *The Rule of Law* (London, Allen Lane, 2010) 8.

[45] *Evans v Attorney General* [2015] 1 AC 1787, 1818 [51]–[52].

their support (eg it can agree to take action on a separate issue in exchange for the member or party's support for the proposed law).

The greater the degree of control the executive exercises over the legislative process, the more that legislative override will operate, and appear to operate, as executive override. When legislative override is, in effect, executive override, the risk is that invocations of the override mechanism will constitute attempts by the executive to avoid unfavourable judicial decisions on rights, which would offend the rule-of-law notion that no one is above the law, rather than constitute attempts by the legislature to express reasonable, good faith disagreement with the judiciary about the scope and limit of rights, which is the purpose of the override mechanism.

The issue of executive dominance of the legislature in parliamentary systems is a potential concern that affects the resolution of all issues, not just rights. Whenever the executive exerts a large degree of control over the legislature, there is a risk that this control will be used to avoid unfavourable judicial decisions (ie to put the executive above the law). There is, in short, a general point of tension between the rule of law and executive-dominated legislatures. However, the tension is particularly acute in the context of rights issues and thus particularly relevant to discussions about the dialogue model.

The executive is rarely, if ever, the plaintiff and typically, if not always,[46] the defendant in human rights cases. As a result, it seldom has anything to gain, in a direct and immediate sense,[47] from human rights litigation and frequently has much to lose in the form of adverse verdicts preventing it from taking particular actions and requiring it to pay damages to successful claimants. Thus, the issue of rights is an area where the executive is likely to be strongly tempted to use its control of the legislature to avoid the effects of judicial decisions because they generally hinder and rarely help it.

Furthermore, judicial decisions on rights often concern the most fundamental interests of the most vulnerable persons in society. A racial or religious minority seeking to be treated in a non-discriminatory manner, a prisoner seeking not to be subject to cruel or unusual punishment, and a group of indigent persons seeking access to healthcare or shelter are paradigmatic instances of the types of cases that arise in the rights context. If the executive should comply with any category of unfavourable judicial decisions, it is arguably those that touch on these types of interests and protect these types of persons in society.

This point of tension may manifest in practice in one of two ways. It may lead to the overuse and abuse of the override power. In this scenario, the executive uses its control of the legislature to invoke the override mechanism on a regular basis whenever it receives an unfavourable judicial decision. Or it may lead to the atrophy of the override power.[48] In this scenario, the executive refuses to exercise the override power even when it has a reasonable, good faith disagreement with the judiciary because its control of the legislature makes any invocation of the override mechanism appear to be a violation of the rule of law. Put alternatively, the executive's control of the legislature makes any use of the override mechanism appear to be the pursuit of executive self-interest. It is also possible for both scenarios

[46] The executive will not always be the defendant where the bill of rights has horizontal effect. On the concept of horizontal effect of rights, see Stephen Gardbaum, 'The "Horizontal Effect" of Constitutional Rights' (2003) 102 *Michigan Law Review* 387.

[47] There the executive does, of course, gain in a less direct and immediate sense through the creation of a society where human rights are respected.

[48] On the concept of atrophy, see Adrian Vermeule, 'The Atrophy of Constitutional Powers' (2012) 32 *OJLS* 421.

to occur at the same time. The executive may refuse to exercise the override power even when it has reasonable, good faith disagreements with the judiciary except for in relation to discrete policy areas where it is determined to avoid any unfavourable judicial decision (eg a policy area where the executive obtains electoral advantages by disagreeing with the judiciary even if it has no justifiable reason for doing so).

IV. Implications for the Design and Drafting Process

In light of the foregoing discussion highlighting that a dialogue model will give rise to a number of normative trade-offs, this Part makes three suggestions for the design and drafting process of a bill of rights to ensure that they are identified, analysed and, as far as is reasonably possible, resolved prior to enactment.

A. Beyond the Bill of Rights

The normative trade-offs indicate that the design and drafting process must extend beyond the four walls of the bill of rights. In previous processes relating to dialogue bills of rights in Australia, the focus of discussion and debate has typically been on the terms of the legal instruments – the rights to be included, and the powers and responsibilities that will be conferred on each arm of government. Committees of inquiry have directed their work to answering questions such as whether the bill of rights should include economic, social and cultural rights,[49] which public entities should be subject to the bill of rights,[50] whether courts should have the power to award damages for violations of rights,[51] and whether the executive and legislature should be placed under an obligation to respond to judicial declarations of incompatibility.[52]

The surrounding constitutional environment factors into discussion, but only as a relevant piece of contextual information. It informs, for example, which jurisdictions are chosen to guide the design and drafting of the legal instrument. The ACT Consultation Committee, for example, analysed the bills of rights in Canada, New Zealand, South Africa, the UK and the US on the basis that they were 'countries with similar legal systems to Australia's.'[53] For those discussions that are centred on statutory instruments, the surrounding constitutional environment is also considered to the extent that it may pose a potential obstacle to reform. The National Consultation Committee, for example, considered whether the judicial power to issue declarations of incompatibility would be compatible with the Constitution's separation of judicial powers doctrine.[54]

[49] ACT Consultation Committee, above n 3, ch 5; Victorian Consultation Committee, above n 4, ch 2; National Consultation Committee, above n 2, [14.5].
[50] ACT Consultation Committee, above n 3, [4.53]–[4.54]; Victorian Consultation Committee, above n 4, ch 3; National Consultation Committee, above n 2, [14.3].
[51] ACT Consultation Committee, above n 3, [4.72]–[4.78]; Victorian Consultation Committee, above n 4, ch 6; National Consultation Committee, above n 2, [14.11].
[52] ACT Consultation Committee, above n 3, [4.36]; National Consultation Committee, above n 2, 329–30.
[53] ACT Consultation Committee, above n 3, [3.1].
[54] National Consultation Committee, above n 2, 327–29.

Importantly, however, in these discussions the surrounding constitutional environment was taken as a given. There was no consideration of the possibility that the introduction of a dialogue bill of rights might require reforms to other aspects of Australia's constitutional system of government. The foregoing discussion of normative trade-offs indicates that this omission is a serious mistake. As the dialogue model may give rise to points of tension with a number of features of the surrounding constitutional environment such as responsible government, the separation of powers and the rule of law, the design and drafting process must address the following three questions.

First, what are the pertinent points of tension between the dialogue model and the surrounding constitutional environment? While Part III of this chapter and other works have identified some of the most salient points of tension that are likely to arise,[55] there may, of course, be more. Furthermore, the points of tension will differ depending on the version of the dialogue model under consideration. For example, only the versions that incorporate the novel judicial remedies create a point of tension with the separation of powers.

Second, what are the respective merits of each principle? As mentioned in Part III, it is possible to advance reasonable justifications for both the dialogue model and for each competing principle. This step thus requires careful consideration of these justifications. For instance, what is the value of, on the one hand, facilitating disagreement between the executive and legislature on rights issues (ie the objective of the dialogue model's system of legislative committee review) and, on the other hand, minimising disagreement between the executive and legislature on rights (and other) issues (ie the objective of responsible government)?

Third, how should each normative trade-off be resolved? This step involves identifying the different ways in which the points of tension can be reconciled and selecting the option that most closely accords with the answer obtained to the previous question. If, for example, responsible government was considered to be a principle of fundamental importance and great value, one might decide to remove legislative committee review from the dialogue model so as not to risk facilitating any disagreement between the executive and legislature on rights issues. If, by contrast, legislative committee review was considered to be of fundamental importance and great value, one might decide to undertake sweeping reforms to the system of responsible government, even going so far as to move away from a parliamentary system (eg to a semi-presidential system) to ensure legislative disagreement with the executive on rights (and other) issues. If, however, both principles were considered to be of some merit, one might decide to undertake reforms that would adjust the balance between the two without eliminating either. For example, one could alter the upper legislative chamber's structure and powers to ensure it had sufficient incentive and capacity to draw on the legislative committee's findings to challenge the executive's positions on rights without abolishing the system of responsible government.

The important point is that resolution of these normative trade-offs requires reform of the surrounding constitutional environment to be put on the table. It requires Australia's conceptions of, inter alia, responsible government, the separation of powers and the rule of

[55] See, eg, Will Bateman & James Stellios, 'Chapter III of the Constitution, Federal Jurisdiction and Dialogue Charters of Human Rights' (2012) 36 *Melbourne University Law Review* 1; Janet L Hiebert & James B Kelly, *Parliamentary Bills of Rights: The Experiences of New Zealand and the United Kingdom* (Cambridge, Cambridge University Press, 2015); Stephenson, above n 1, ch 7.

law to be carefully scrutinised and, depending on the answers reached to the second and third questions, open to modification. While putting such well-established principles on the table for discussion may appear to be a large, daunting step, it is no less significant than seeking to introduce a bill of rights into a constitutional system that has, since its founding, not had one. Broadening the inquiry to include these matters is not akin to undertaking a wholesale revision of the constitutional system of government. A dialogue model does not create normative trade-offs with every aspect of the system. However, as it does interact closely with some features of the surrounding constitutional environment, those features must also form part of the conversation about reform.

B. Constitutional vs Statutory Reform

Given the constitutional dimensions of many normative trade-offs, the design and drafting process should include, and indeed prioritise, the possibility of introducing a bill of rights by means of constitutional, as opposed to statutory, reform. The risk with a statutory bill of rights is that all the normative trade-offs will be resolved in favour of the competing constitutional principles or features, leading the dialogue model to fail to achieve its stated objectives. Put alternatively, the features of Australia's constitutional system of government that operate to interfere with, and even suppress, aspects of the dialogue model will take precedence, causing the bill of rights to founder.

It is important to note that the points of tension mentioned in Part III are not directly embedded in the text of the Australian Constitution. The system of responsible government is principally a product of constitutional convention (eg the convention that the executive is formed by the political party (or coalition of parties) that holds a majority of seats in the House of Representatives) and statute (eg the *Commonwealth Electoral Act 1918* (Cth) establishes the voting system that generally results in one or two parties gaining a majority of seats in the House of Representatives). The narrow conception of judicial power embedded in the separation of powers doctrine is a product of judicial interpretation.[56] The notion that no one is above the law is a product of political norms (ie a member of the executive would face censure in the legislature if they sought to ignore a judicial decision) reinforced by judicial statements[57] and scholarly writings.[58]

As a result, it is theoretically possible to resolve these normative trade-offs in favour of the dialogue model with a statutory instrument. The introduction of a statutory bill of rights *could* prompt the legislature to challenge the executive's positions on rights on a regular basis in a robust manner and *could* prompt the judiciary to revisit its definition of judicial power. However, it is unlikely to occur for two reasons. First, the relevant institutional actors have incorporated the existing state of affairs into their conception of the constitutional system of government and thus understand a constitutional amendment to be the sole method of altering it. For example, the High Court understands the narrow definition of judicial power to form part of the separation of powers created by

[56] See above n 20.

[57] Courts are not able to enforce their judgments directly because, in the well-known words of Alexander Hamilton in *The Federalist No 78*, they have 'no influence over either the sword or the purse': 'The Judiciary Department', *The Federalist Papers* (McLean's edn, 1810), available at http://avalon.law.yale.edu/18th_century/fed78.asp.

[58] See above n 39.

the Constitution, as evidenced by the fact that it is willing to invalidate statutes that do not comply with it. As it is a well-established element of its case law, it is unlikely to alter this definition unless prompted to do so by an amendment to the Constitution.[59] Second, some of the options for altering the existing state of affairs will require constitutional amendment. For example, one method of facilitating legislative disagreement with the executive is, as mentioned above, to alter the structure and powers of the upper legislative chamber. As some aspects of the Senate's structure (eg the ability of Ministers to be selected from the Senate[60]) and powers (eg the Senate's power to block proposed laws[61]) are set out in the Constitution, they can only be changed via the formal amendment procedure.

From a design and drafting standpoint, therefore, constitutional reform should be put on the table. Furthermore, it should not be considered a subsidiary or second-best option. If anything, it should be prioritised over statutory reform because only constitutional reform allows the full range of reform options to be open for discussion.

C. Elite vs Popular Reform

Given the foregoing preference for a constitutional rather than statutory instrument, the design and drafting process will need to be inclusive and popular rather than exclusive and elite.[62] The principal reason is that an exclusive, elite reform process would generate the narrative for the proposed instrument's defeat at the referendum – that the bill of rights is an attempt to take power away from the people's representatives and place it in the hands of elite judges. While this observation may appear to be a straightforward one, to follow it would require a complete rethink about the process of rights reform that has developed in Australia over the last two decades.

Since the failed attempt to amend the Constitution to broaden its protection for rights in 1988,[63] reform efforts have focused on options that do not require popular ratification. First, energy shifted from the federal to the state and territory level where their traditions of uncodified constitutions, similar to that of the UK, impelled them towards the pursuit of bills of rights introduced by means of an ordinary Act of Parliament. In addition to the three jurisdictions (the ACT, Queensland and Victoria) that enacted statutory instruments, reports have also been produced in Tasmania and Western Australia recommending the

[59] There are, of course, no guarantees in constitutional design. Even a clear constitutional amendment purporting to alter the definition of judicial power could be ignored by the Court. On the potential for this issue to arise in the rights context in Australia, see Rosalind Dixon, 'An Australian (Partial) Bill of Rights' (2016) 14 *International Journal of Constitutional Law* 80.

[60] Australian Constitution 1901, s 64.

[61] Ibid, s 53.

[62] While it is beyond the scope of this chapter to provide a detailed account of what an inclusive and popular design and drafting process might look like, there are no shortage of examples of such processes, including the First Nation Regional Dialogues on the constitutional recognition of Indigenous Australians (Referendum Council, *Final Report* (2017)) and the constitutional conventions in Ireland (Scott Stephenson, 'Reforming Constitutional Reform' in Ron Levy et al (eds), *New Directions for Law in Australia: Essays in Contemporary Law Reform* (Canberra, ANU Press, 2017) 369).

[63] Brian Galligan, 'The 1988 Referendums and Australia's Record on Constitutional Change' (1990) 43 *Parliamentary Affairs* 497.

introduction of reforms along similar lines.[64] Second, when energy did shift back to the federal level in the late 2000s, constitutional reform was taken off the table. The National Human Rights Consultation Committee was directed by the government not to recommend a constitutionally entrenched bill of rights.[65]

This preference for statutory reform prioritised achievability at the cost of ambition and acceptance. While it maximised the likelihood of securing the enactment of a bill of rights (though even the attempt to introduce a statutory instrument at the federal level failed), it precluded the more comprehensive and far-reaching types of reforms mentioned above and meant that the public's direct approval did not need to be sought. As a result, the Australian experience to date is at risk of aligning with two hypotheses put forward by political scientists about the origins of bills of rights in other liberal democracies, neither of which should be a cause for celebration.

David Erdos has argued that inter-party competition lies behind the adoption of the bills of rights in Canada, New Zealand and the UK.[66] In each country, one of the main political parties shifted its stance from opposing to supporting the introduction of a bill of rights while in opposition during a period in which the governing political party was perceived to have abused its power. It thus used its support for a bill of rights as a policy position to defeat the governing political party at the next election by claiming it would stop future abuses of power. When that party next formed government, it followed through on its commitment and led the enactment of a bill of rights.

Ran Hirschl has argued that elite self-interest lies behind the adoption of the bills of rights in Canada, Israel, New Zealand and South Africa.[67] In each country, political, economic and judicial elites worked together to enact a bill of rights not out of a genuine commitment to human rights, but instead as a mechanism for preserving their interests by transferring power from legislatures, where their hegemony was under threat, to courts, where their interests would be protected from the vicissitudes of democratic politics.

In Australia, the pursuit of statutory reform has allowed one main political party to pursue the enactment of a bill of rights over the opposition of the other main political party,[68] aligning with Erdos' thesis about inter-party competition, and has allowed the pursuit of rights reform to be portrayed as a project principally to benefit lawyers (irrespective of the actual design of the bill of rights),[69] aligning with Hirschl's thesis about elite self-interest. By contrast, the pursuit of constitutional reform would force advocates to seek, as far as is reasonably possible, cross-party support for the proposal and inclusion of the public at

[64] Tasmania Law Reform Institute, *A Charter of Rights for Tasmania* (Report No 10, 2007); Western Australian Consultation Committee for a Proposed WA Human Rights Act, *A WA Human Rights Act* (2007). Developments continue to occur at the state and territory level: see Legal Affairs and Community Safety Committee (Queensland), *Inquiry into a Possible Human Rights Act for Queensland* (Report No 30, 55th Parliament, 2016).

[65] National Consultation Committee, above n 2, 383.

[66] David Erdos, *Delegating Rights Protection: The Rise of Bills of Rights in the Westminster World* (Oxford, Oxford University Press, 2010).

[67] Ran Hirschl, *Towards Juristocracy: The Origins and Consequences of the New Constitutionalism* (Cambridge, Mass, Harvard University Press, 2007).

[68] In Victoria, for example, the opposition, the Liberal Party, voted against the bill establishing Victoria's bill of rights and, when elected to office in 2010, made public statements indicating a desire to repeal the law, though never followed through on them: Alexander Williams & George Williams, 'The British Bill of Rights Debate: Lessons from Australia' [2016] *Public Law* 471, 475–76.

[69] See, eg, Susan Harris Rimmer, 'Some Lawyers Take Cheap Shots, Some Even Work Pro Bono', *Analysis & Policy Observatory*, 27 January 2009, available at http://apo.org.au/node/6318.

the drafting and design stages to increase its chances for success at the referendum. As a result, a dialogue bill of rights implemented by means of a constitutional instrument not only increases its likelihood of success in practice, but also enhances its normative appeal by reducing the risk that it can be criticised on the basis that it is the product of inter-party competition and/or elite self-interest.

V. Conclusion

One might assume that the advent of the dialogue model created a more straightforward and easier path to the achievement of a bill of rights in Australia. With its legislative override mechanism, one might assume that it cleared away the largest normative impediment to rights reform – the democratic concerns that surround the exercise of rights-based judicial review. And with its ability to be implemented by means of a statute, one might assume that it cleared away the largest practical impediment to rights reform – meeting the requirements of section 128 of the Australian Constitution. This chapter challenges these assumptions.

While the dialogue model has a number of significant advantages over the traditional constitutional approaches to rights protection,[70] its numerous stages of rights review require a sophisticated and meticulous design and drafting process. That process must be one capable of undertaking a number of normative inquiries (ie identifying, analysing and resolving the various normative trade-offs) and, as a consequence, must keep the option of constitutional reform on the table despite its practical difficulties. While that may be unwelcome news for advocates of rights reform, it will help ensure that any bill of rights that does result is the product of an inclusive, popular process, a cause for celebration.

[70] Stephenson, above n 1, ch 6.

INDEX

Note: Alphabetical arrangement is word-by-word, where a group of letters followed by a space is filed before the same group of letters followed by a letter, eg 'legal value' will appear before 'legalism'. In determining alphabetical arrangement, initial articles and prepositions are ignored.

Page numbers followed by the letter 'n' refer to footnotes on the quoted pages.